PEARSON CUSTOM
Education

TED 550

Travis Plowman

College of St. Rose

PEARSON

Custom
Publishing

Sponsoring Editor: Natalie Danner
Development Editor: Abbey Briggs
Editorial Assistant: Jill Johnson
Marketing Manager: Amy Dyer
Operations Manager: Eric M. Kenney
Production Manager: Jennifer M. Berry
Rights Editor: Francesca Marcantonio
Art Director: Renée Sartell
Cover Designers: Kristen Kiley

Cover Art: "Textbooks and apple" used by permission of istock; "Teacher and students" used by permission of istock; "Classroom, globe on desk, US flag hanging from blackboard" Copyright © 1999-2008 Getty Images, Inc. All rights reserved.

Please visit our websites at *www.pearsoncustom.com* and *www.customliterature.com.*
Attention bookstores: For permission to return any unsold stock, contact us at *pe-uscustomreturns@pearsoncustom.com.*

ISBN-13: 978-0-558-14349-7
ISBN-10: 0-558-14349-0

Package ISBN-13: N/A
Package ISBN-10: N/A

PEARSON CUSTOM PUBLISHING
501 Boylston Street, Suite 900, Boston, MA 02116
A Pearson Education Company

Contents

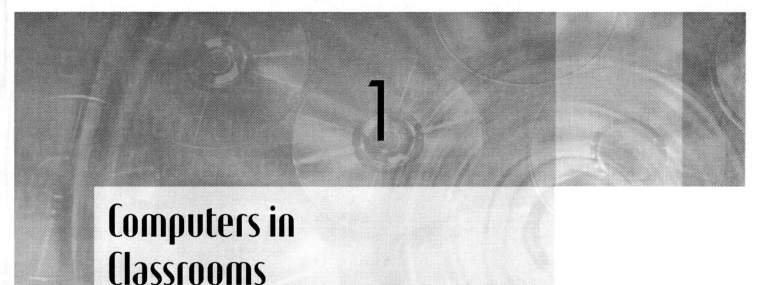

Computers in Classrooms

Education is undergoing dramatic changes. Left behind is the world in which a teacher had considerable latitude with the curriculum. Pre-service teachers are entering a profession that is focused on standards and reform. States increasingly set standards and define curricula for districts and competencies for students. Then districts build on state mandates and add their own local standards and requirements. When all of the standards, mandates, and curricula finally reach thirty students and one teacher in a classroom, the success enjoyed by the students, apart from their own diligence, rests largely on the ability of the teacher to present information well and interact skillfully with students. Where does educational technology fit in this demanding setting?

> Standards and reform

The premise of this book is that educational technology provides a sophisticated set of both production and cognitive tools that help learners acquire facts as well as provide a fertile and challenging environment for problem solving and critical thinking. Key to this premise is the notion that educational technology is adaptable to the information and problems posed by the standards, curriculum, and competencies required by school districts and states.

APPLICATION SOFTWARE: YOUR TOOLS

The information in this book focuses almost completely on the use of **tool software:** Internet, presentation/visualization, word processing, database, and spreadsheet software. Unlike instructional software that is built to teach specific content, tool software

> **TOOL SOFTWARE**
> Software that has no content of its own. Also called *application* software.

1

COGNITIVE TOOL
A structure or process that helps students analyze and retain information.

is structured to assist a user who wants to create content. Each tool can be used to find, analyze, and/or present many different kinds of information. Used by a skillful teacher, these tools support content and many teaching methods that districts and states require of their teachers. Educators who read this book should come to it with a fundamental set of computer tool skills or should plan to learn them as they read about the instructional models applicable to each tool. The introduction to each tool will provide you with a list of basic tool skills that you need to know or look up and learn.

The information in this book is not directed toward either Mac or Windows users. The screen shots are taken from a Windows operating system, but all concepts apply to the Mac as well. Tool software transcends these environments. You may use Word Perfect or Word as your word processor, Excel or Lotus as your spreadsheet, and PowerPoint or Hyperstudio as your presentation software. The same flexibility is true of your web browser (Netscape or Explorer) and database (Access and Filemaker Pro). You may be using another tool not named above, such as Works. You can apply the principles you will learn in the following chapters to any brand of application software. This ability to design lessons based on tools rather than a specific brand name of software should help you when you go to a classroom that may not use the same kind of software that you are using in your training.

PURPOSE OF COMPUTING IN K-12 CLASSROOMS

This book is full of narrative examples of classroom life. You will be an invisible observer that can get into both students' and teachers' heads as we go on virtual field trips to see how teachers integrate technology into the teaching/learning process. The primary goal is to demonstrate good strategies for using technology to support teaching, but another goal is to expose the misconceptions that lead to the failure of computer-supported teaching and learning. Some common attitudes and misunderstandings account for how both children and teachers react to computers.

Observing your own learning

When you are working on activities suggested in this book (called "Checking Your Understanding"), be sure to note where you have problems with either your computer skills or your conceptualization of the instructional problem on which you are working. If you have difficulty, you can be sure that some of your future students will have a similar experience. One of the very best qualities of a computer-using teacher is to have experienced repeated attempts and even failure to solve problems with a computer. This preparation will help you anticipate your own students' experiences.

The computer as a cognitive tool

Using a computer in your teaching should promote improved analytical thinking and information management skills among your students. The point is not to teach them computer skills, though sometimes this is necessary. Rather, the point is to teach them to better acquire, process, and present information using the computer as a tool. It is important to recognize that although computers are wonderful machines capable of motivating and challenging students with the **cognitive tools** they provide, they are only one tool among many. Other cognitive tools include outlines, flowcharts, and Venn diagrams. Used systematically, databases, spreadsheets, and presentation software also are cognitive tools. Although computers can help students learn facts as well as improve their problem-solving strategies and critical thinking skills (Schacter, 1999), so can books, field trips, discussions, and other tools teachers use. Consequently, another goal of this book is to help you know what computers do best and when their use is appropriate.

WHAT MUST I KNOW TO TEACH WITH COMPUTERS EFFECTIVELY?

There are some basic computer skills and tools that you need to have or acquire as you read this book. Although several organizations (The Milkin Exchange and CEO Forum, for example) promote the use of computers in the K–12 classroom, ISTE (International Society for Technology in Education) is one of the largest and perhaps the most influential concerning technology standards for both teachers and students. Six foundational areas of competence are recommended for teachers by ISTE (2004):

> The field of educational technology

- ■ Technology operations and concepts
- ■ Planning and designing learning environments and experiences
- ■ Teaching, learning, and the curriculum
- ■ Assessment and evaluation
- ■ Productivity and professional practice
- ■ Social, ethical, legal, and human issues

As you can see, teachers must have a big picture that includes hardware, software, the instructional process, their own administrative work, and the larger nontechnical or instructional issues that arise from the culture in which we live. As you begin your study of computers in the teaching/learning process, you must always be alert to these issues. In the following sections of this chapter, we explore these themes as a foundation for the technology integration process.

Technology Operations and Concepts

In spite of teachers' best efforts, some students will always know more about how to operate computers and the software that is on them. However, there are some basic standards for students in which teachers themselves should be competent. An excellent definition of these standards is found in ISTE's National Educational Technology Standards for Students (ISTE, 2004). Although teachers may not have explored every function on every menu of every computer tool, they should know most of the functions on each menu and be able to work through online or printed Help manuals to solve a problem if necessary. Probably everyone has heard a story about how "the children know more than the teacher about computers and isn't it wonderful that Johnny can show the teacher how." It is wonderful, to a point. Although the role of the teacher is changing from lecturer to guide or even co-learner, it is necessary for teachers to have the same basic skills as students. It is *not* wonderful to watch a second-grade student show the teacher how to cut and paste.

> Teacher skills

Furthermore, teachers should endeavor to acquire some basic hardware trouble-shooting knowledge. Schools do not generally have the technical support they need, and when something goes wrong the teacher should (a) know some basic diagnostic strategies, and (b) know enough terminology to be able to talk to a technical support person over the telephone and explain a problem. Most of all, the teacher should display a can-do, positive, troubleshooting attitude in front of students when things go wrong. This model will help students develop a positive approach that will be useful throughout their lives.

Learning Environments

Using technology effectively in the classroom requires more than basic computer skills because computers should fit into a larger context: the learning environment. The learning environment is determined by the kinds of tasks students complete, the way teachers and students interact, and how students are exposed to information. The challenge to construct an effective lesson that is well received by students requires much planning and knowledge on the part of the teacher.

One kind of learning environment in which computers fit well is based on the constructivist theory of learning. Although constructivism does not describe just one school of thought, there are some common elements of a constructivist perspective (Woolfolk, 2000). These include:

Constructivism

- ▨ Complex, challenging learning environments and authentic tasks
- ▨ Social negotiation and shared responsibility as a part of learning
- ▨ Multiple representations of content
- ▨ Understanding that knowledge is constructed (Woolfolk, p. 334)

Reiser and Dempsey (2002) further state that in a constructivist learning environment learners "engage in activities authentic to the discipline in which they are learning" (p. 68). In this context, technology is especially appropriate. For example, students can work with real data in spreadsheets and databases as they study the sciences and social sciences. In the arts and in language arts, students use the tools that professionals use to display information (audio, video, text, graphics, and animation).

This philosophy of education requires students to be active participants in the learning process while the teacher is an instructional designer. To help you gain further insight into learning environments in which computers are effective, we will be even more specific and talk about problem/project-based learning.

Problem-based learning

Problem-based learning is one concrete expression of how constructivist theory may be implemented at a practical level. In later chapters, much of what you will learn about designing instruction that includes computers is based on the understanding that students are solving problems. Problem-based learning "is a teaching and learning model that focuses on the central concepts and principles of a discipline, involves students in problem-solving and other meaningful tasks, allows students to work autonomously to construct their own learning, and culminates in realistic, student-generated products" (Thomas, Mergandoller, & Michaelson, 1999, p. 1). The key words in this definition are:

- ■ Central concepts of a discipline
- ■ Problem solving
- ■ Meaningful tasks
- ■ Construct their own learning
- ■ Student-generated products

Problem-based learning takes place in many formats. Within a single project, students may work alone, in pairs, in small or mid-size groups, and in large groups as well. Each configuration has its advantages for different learning tasks (Thomas et al., 1999). Observe the examples in Table 1.1. Listed there are some typical classroom activities as well as some computer activities. Although you may not yet understand what the computer activities might be or how they would work, it is important to know that you do not always have to have a computer for each student. Some computer activities are more helpful when several students are working at the same computer. In later chapters, you will learn which computer tools are appropriate for group work and which are more appropriate for individual work.

Teaching based on constructivist theory and problem/project-based learning should not only provide for the acquisition of facts but also stimulate **higher-order thinking skills** among students. Both facts and higher-order thinking skills are acquired when students process information. Computers allow students to process a great deal of information in complex ways that were not available to them before the advent of computing. Learning these different approaches to information processing is the focus of this book. This takes us to a discussion of "Teaching, Learning, and the Curriculum." Constructivism and problem-based learning provide a framework for instruction, but what goes into this framework?

Teaching, Learning, and the Curriculum

As you learn more about integrating computers into the teaching/learning process in later chapters, you will find that a teacher is a mentor and instructional designer who helps students focus on problem-solving activities. A teacher works with children who have many different learning styles and backgrounds and who bring to class many different levels of skill and knowledge. To use computers to help students solve problems that will lead them to construct their own knowledge about a content area, you need

HIGHER-ORDER THINKING SKILLS Activities in which students predict outcomes, judge between or among alternatives, or analyze problems or situations.

TABLE 1.1	Examples of Problem-Based Learning
Grouping Strategy	**Activities**
Individual	Conducting library research; word processing
Pairs	Peer critiques; working with a database or spreadsheet to enter information, solve a problem, or answer a question
Small groups	Designing questions for a database; preparing presentations
Large groups	Learning how to use a computer tool; observing presentation

to know exactly how to design instruction that guides them through this process. To design effective instruction, you need to know some teaching models.

While you are learning to be a teacher, you learn many different kinds of instructional models. Models of teaching that are most useful for planning computer-supported instruction are in the information processing family (Joyce, Weil, & Calhoun, 2000; Woolfolk, 2000; Bransford, Brown, & Cocking, 1999). As you continue to read this text, you will recognize that all the models for computer-supported lessons fit into larger, common models of teaching that most teachers learn and use throughout their careers.

Models of teaching

What Is an Instructional Model?

An **instructional model** is based on research that has been done on how people best learn certain kinds of information. The model is a series of steps or techniques for presenting information in a way that helps learners remember and use it. Although there are many models, we will look at just one example, the inductive-thinking model. It consists of three strategies with nine steps and is used to teach concepts. In a practical sense, concepts are ideas and their associated examples. Examples of concept lessons include the parts of speech and classification (of rocks, plants, animals, kinds of governments, kinds of literature, etc.). The bulleted items below list the steps for using the inductive-thinking model to teach a concept lesson.

Inductive-thinking model

> **Strategy One: Concept Formation**
> ▓ Phase One: Enumerating and Listing Examples
> ▓ Phase Two: Grouping Examples
> ▓ Phase Three: Labeling, Categorizing Examples (Classification)
> **Strategy Two: Interpreting Data**
> ▓ Phase Four: Identifying Critical Relationships
> ▓ Phase Five: Exploring Relationships
> ▓ Phase Six: Making Inferences
> **Strategy Three: Applying Principles**
> ▓ Phase Seven: Predicting Consequences, Explaining Unfamiliar Phenomena, Hypothesizing
> ▓ Phase Eight: Explaining and/or Supporting the Predictions and Hypotheses
> ▓ Phase Nine: Verifying the Prediction (Joyce et al., 2000, p. 140)

When executed well, this teaching model helps students learn concepts efficiently and thoroughly. Your question might be, "What do computers have to do with this teaching model?" The answer is that computers provide tools that enhance many steps in the inductive-thinking process. They either provide or process information in such a way that students gain a deeper understanding of the concepts they are studying. Table 1.2 revisits the steps of the inductive-thinking model. Note the computer tools associated with each phase of the model.

Using computer tools to support teaching models

Later chapters in this book answer questions such as, How would I use the Internet to help students enumerate and list concepts? How would I use visualization software to help students identify critical relationships? How would I use spreadsheets

INSTRUCTIONAL MODEL
A series of steps or techniques for presenting information in a way that helps learners remember and use it effectively.

TABLE 1.2 Using Computers with the Inductive-Thinking Model

Inductive-Thinking Model	Computer Tool
Strategy 1	
Concept formation	
Phase One: Enumerating and listing	Internet for research; word processor
Phase Two: Grouping examples	Visualization tools (Inspiration, presentation software)
Phase Three: Labeling, categorizing examples (classification)	Visualization tools (Inspiration, presentation software)
Strategy 2	
Interpreting data	
Phase Four: Identifying critical relationships	Visualization tools (Inspiration, presentation software)
Phase Five: Exploring relationships	Database; spreadsheet
Phase Six: Making inferences	Database, spreadsheet
Strategy 3	
Applying principles	
Phase Seven: Predicting consequences, explaining unfamiliar phenomena, hypothesizing	
Phase Eight: Explaining and/or supporting the predictions and hypotheses	Presentation software; word processor
Phase Nine: Verifying the prediction	Internet for research

or databases to help students explore relationships? How would I use presentation software to help students explain and/or support their predictions and hypotheses? The inductive-thinking model is just one of many teaching models. As you learn more about computer tools and how to use them, you will begin to anticipate when they are useful. The models you will learn about in this book span the K–12 grade levels and apply to all content areas.

Assessment and Evaluation

Assessment and evaluation are significant elements of the instructional planning process. In fact, when teachers design instruction, one of the first questions they ask is, "What should my students know and be able to do when they have finished this lesson?" Fortunately, just as there are models for teaching effective lessons, there are also models for evaluating them. One very common lesson evaluation model is called Bloom's taxonomy. Originally discovered and articulated by Benjamin Bloom in 1956, Bloom's taxonomy was revised by Anderson et al. (2007), and will provide a guide for computer use throughout the book. The taxonomy will help us understand the role of the computer in the learning process. First we will look at the taxonomy itself, then look at the relationship of different kinds of software to the learning categories presented in the taxonomy.

First look at Table 1.3. In the first column you will see listed four kinds of knowledge, each with a short, footnoted explanation. Read these carefully. Now look at the second row of the table beginning with the column "remember, understand, etc." You may think of these columns as the depth or complexity of thinking students achieve as they work with each kind of knowledge. As they study a unit of knowledge, "remember," which means "recognizing" or "recalling," is usually the first and most fundamental type of knowledge students engage in as they learn. For example, it would be impossible to classify plant species without being able to recognize and name differently shaped leaves and the way they are arranged on stems. After students acquire a basic vocabulary, then they can engage in the activities in the third column of Table 1.3. That is, they can use facts to interpret, classify, infer, compare, and so forth. If they were learning to identify plants, for example, they would perhaps see specimens, use a key, and attempt to name each specimen. Notice as we move from top to bottom down the table, beginning at "remember" and ending at "create," each set of activities builds on the previous activity and is more complex than the previous activity.

TABLE 1.3 Bloom's Taxonomy Revised

The Cognitive Process Dimension	The Knowledge Dimension			
	Factual[1]	Conceptual[2]	Procedural[3]	Meta-Cognitive[4]
Remember	recognizing; recalling	recognizing; recalling	recognizing; recalling	recognizing; recalling
Understand	interpreting, exemplifying, classifying, summarizing, inferring, comparing, explaining	interpreting, exemplifying, classifying, summarizing, inferring, comparing, explaining	interpreting, exemplifying, classifying, summarizing, inferring, comparing, explaining	interpreting, exemplifying, classifying, summarizing, inferring, comparing, explaining
Apply	executing, implementing	executing, implementing	executing, implementing	executing, implementing
Analyze	differentiating, organizing, attributing	differentiating, organizing, attributing	differentiating, organizing, attributing	differentiating, organizing, attributing
Evaluate	checking, critiquing	checking, critiquing	checking, critiquing	checking, critiquing
Create	generating, planning, producing	generating, planning, producing	generating, planning, producing	generating, planning, producing

[1]Fundamental terminology and details that students must know to understand a body of knowledge; knowing the difference between rational numbers, integers, and whole numbers is an example.

[2]Knowledge of the relationships among elements of a larger idea—ecosystem is a concept.

[3]How to do something or use the tools of a domain—sounding out a word and long division are procedures.

[4]Knowing how to think and knowing what you know—knowing that different domains have tools that provide a framework for solving problems.

Source: Anderson, L., Krathwohl, D., Airasian, P., Cruikshand, K., Mayer, R., Pintrich, P., Raths, J., & Wittrock, M. (2001). *A taxonomy for learning, teaching, and assessing.* New York: Longman.

Using Table 1.3 to classify the different skills that computer tools support will simplify the task of planning learning strategies that involve the computer. To quickly pinpoint which computer tool would be most useful to help a student learn to a specific Cognitive Process Dimension (column 1) in a Knowledge Dimension (row 2), the procedure would look like this.

1. Decide on the body of information to be learned.
2. Look at the second row of Table 1.3 and identify the kind of knowledge to be learned.
3. Next, decide how much skill the students should acquire with that knowledge by looking down the first column beginning with "remember"—do they only need to recognize or remember it, or do they need to use it in some way?
4. Once you have determined the knowledge dimension (row 2) and the knowledge process (column 1), look at Table 1.2 to discover which computer tools are appropriate.

Computer tools work differently with column 5 than with the rest of the columns. The meta-cognitive knowledge in the final column consists of knowing that there are computer tools that help people solve problems as well as create and pass on information: word processors, databases, spreadsheets, and presentation software, to name the major, mainstream tools. This meta-cognitive knowledge also includes knowing which tool(s) work best for which problems.

For the remainder of the book, one chapter devoted to each tool will provide a table like Table 1.2 devoted completely to that tool. If you forget what the Knowledge Dimension or Knowledge Process entails, remember to refer to Table 1.3 in this chapter.

Your goal for any lesson or unit that you teach will be to help your students attain thinking levels as high on Bloom's taxonomy as they are capable of achieving. Later chapters reference Bloom's taxonomy as a way of creating a perspective and context for the use of computers in the teaching and learning process. For now, don't worry that you don't know everything about all of the computer tools listed in Table 1.2. The table is another way to demonstrate how and where computers fit into the teaching/learning process. Details will come later on.

Productivity and Professional Practice

The computers in your school will influence how you do your administrative work. You may be required to maintain a web site for your class where you update assignment information and report to parents. You will be asked to communicate more with parents because there are electronic tools available for communication, such as e-mail. It is likely that you will use electronic attendance reporting systems. In addition, you may have to learn how to use an Integrated Learning System (ILS). These systems contain libraries of software that tutor and drill students in basic language arts and mathematics skills. They track student progress and provide a variety of reports.

Another administrative use teachers may now find invaluable is the growing number of standardized test scores stored electronically. Student test scores (e.g., Iowa Test

QUERY
A way of asking a database or spreadsheet for specific information or patterns of information.

of Basic Skills) in many districts are reported and maintained as electronic databases. This format gives teachers the ability to do more than just look up how a single student scored on math computation, for example. If teachers know how to use a database or spreadsheet, they can perform **queries** to answer questions such as:

▩ Is there a group of students in my class that performs poorly on capitalization?
▩ Does my class really need to review punctuation before we learn how to write paragraphs?
▩ Which math concepts do I need to review with my class before I start on first-degree equations?
▩ Which students scored below the fortieth percentile in both spelling and punctuation?

Data-driven
decision making

Using data that school districts routinely collect in this manner is called *data-driven decision making*. In the past, although school districts collected reams of data about their students, it was impossible to do much more with it than give students and their parents test scores and compare district scores to national scores. Now, with electronic databases, teachers and administrators can use the data to make instructional decisions in single classrooms, buildings, and entire districts. In a later chapter you will learn how to teach with spreadsheets and databases. In the process of learning that, you will learn how to use them well enough to help you make instructional decisions for your classroom.

Distance education

Another way computers are helping teachers is in distance education. Over the course of your career, your state will ask you to take classes to stay current in your field. At some time in your life, it is likely that you will take a class taught entirely over the Internet, television, or a combination of delivery technologies. You may also teach one yourself or monitor students who are taking one. Some people are reluctant to try such courses in spite of the fact that "distance courses" allow them to make their own schedule and save the time that it takes to drive to and from a class. Research demonstrates that distance classes can be as effective as traditional classes. Roblyer and Edwards (2000) say that many studies done over a forty-year period indicate there is no significant difference in instruction using distance technologies and traditional instruction. They further indicate that research has shown that the delivery system isn't the determining factor in the success of a course, but rather it is the quality of the course materials that determines its success (p. 197). We will go into more detail about distance classes when you study the Internet in a later chapter. For the time being, however, be aware that distance education is a growing and thriving area in the field of educational technology.

Social, Ethical, Legal, and Human Issues

Finally, as important as knowing which keys to press to get a spreadsheet to work, how to fix a jammed printer, or how to construct an effective technology-supported lesson, you will become a role model for your students about the human side of technology. You will have to make sure that all of your students have equal access to the computers in your room or laboratory, that the aggressive and/or skilled ones do not monopolize them while others who have fewer skills are intimidated. Furthermore, because

Using expensive computer
resources effectively

computers are still not as common as pencils, you will do the educational triage that funnels scarce computing resources to the students who need them the most. It will be your responsibility to ensure that those from diverse backgrounds will get the same chance to learn and use the premier tool of the information age.

It is possible that the child who will **hack** your school network—or the Pentagon, for that matter—is sitting at a desk in your classroom. To do this the *hacker* uses special programs to figure out passwords that ordinarily protect the computer from such intrusions. Some hackers are not malicious; they do it for the same reason other people climb mountains—because the challenge is there. Nevertheless, the activity is illegal and wrong. Other hackers break into computers to get information or to disrupt e-mail or other organizational functions. It is important for students to understand that electronic crimes are as punishable as physical crimes, and that people who are caught are punished. It could be your model and your teaching that changes adventurous students before they go too far.

You can almost be sure that at least one of your students will send an inappropriate e-mail to someone. Your school may have guidelines for computer usage that students (and, often, their parents) will have to read and sign, but you will have front-line responsibility for seeing that the guidelines are followed. Again, your reaction to situations and the guidance you give will help students understand that there is right and wrong in the electronic world, and that wrongdoers are accountable.

You will want to research and discuss copyright issues with your students. Because electronic plagiarism is so easy, you will want to design tasks for your students that will minimize the possibility of their using information, graphics, video, and audio without both transforming it and giving appropriate credit to the owner of the material. This is so important that we will spend some time on copyright issues as we study the Internet and its uses.

> **HACK**
> Break into a computer or network without permission.

> Copyrights

Preparing Students for the World of Work

Another perspective on using computers in school classrooms involves our need to prepare students for the world of work. The tools that they use to analyze information in schools are the tools they will use when they enter the job market. Bill Gates, in *Business @ the Speed of Light* (1999), lists the characteristics of successful business in the information age. In the following list are those items related directly to the technology tools students should know how to use. The associated tools for each item are listed in side notes.

- ▨ Insist that communication flow through the organization using e-mail so that you can act on new information with reflex-like speed.
- ▨ Study sales data online and find patterns and share insights easily. Understand overall trends and personalize service for individual customers.
- ▨ Use digital tools to create cross-departmental virtual teams that can share knowledge and build on each other's ideas in real time, worldwide. Use digital systems to capture corporate history for use by anyone.
- ▨ Convert every paper process to a digital process, eliminating administrative bottlenecks and freeing knowledge workers for more important tasks.

> E-mail

> Spreadsheet; databases

> The Internet; e-mail

> All of the tools

All of the tools

All of the tools

- ▦ Create a digital feedback loop to improve the efficiency of physical processes and improve the quality of the products and services created. Every employee should be able to easily track all the key metrics.
- ▦ Use digital tools to help customers solve problems for themselves, and reserve personal contact to respond to complex, high-value customer needs.

THREE KINDS OF COMPUTER USE

This book is primarily about using computer tools to support the teaching/learning process. Nevertheless, it is important that we touch briefly upon all of the possibilities for helping your students learn with computers. There are three major possibilities:

- ▦ Teaching your students about computers
- ▦ Using a computer as a teacher
- ▦ Using computer tools to assist your students to acquire and learn information and to develop higher-order thinking skills

Because of the nature of computing in K–12 schools, you will probably be involved in teaching at least *some* children *some* computer skills for reasons you will learn in a few paragraphs. In addition, with the right software and the right population of students, you will also use the computer as a teacher. These activities are relatively easy for a teacher to think through and do successfully. For this reason, we will touch on them only briefly. The challenge comes in designing lessons that use computer tools effectively. This topic will be the focus of the remaining chapters in this book.

Teaching about Computers: Computer Literacy

As more children grow up with computers in their homes, teachers will spend less time teaching students about computers. For the time being, however, many students still come to school without basic computer skills.

Basic skills for computer use

There are certain things that students need to know about computers, both as a life skill and before they can use them as a cognitive tool. They need to know the names for different parts of a computer so they can discuss computer problems with other people. They also need to know some basic troubleshooting techniques to try when a computer or one of its **peripherals** will not work. In addition, they need to understand how to save and retrieve files successfully. Finally, they need to know the fundamentals of the tool software they use, such as cutting and pasting, working with images, writing formulas in spreadsheets, sending and receiving e-mail and attachments, and doing sorts and queries in databases. Your students will have acquired some of their skills from other teachers, but unless your school has a district-wide scope and sequence for teaching skills to students, it is unlikely that your class will be uniformly computer literate.

Those who do not come to school with basic computer skills are probably victims of the *digital divide* (U.S. Department of Commerce, 2000). The digital divide is a popular term for the cultural barrier that faces people who do not have access to tech-

PERIPHERAL
Printers, scanners, probes, zip drives, cameras, and other devices that provide input to or output from a computer.

nology and the Internet—or the ability to use them effectively if they are available. According to the U.S. Department of Commerce, the digital divide exists because of one or more factors, including geography, ethnicity, education, and economics. Statistics from this report indicate that although many of your students will be acquainted with computers, you will still have a significant number of students who are not. Some of the most dramatic statistics in the report indicate that household income is the most important indicator of whether there are computers in your students' homes (Newberger, 2000). As you look at Table 1.4, think of the implications for your approach to your students. Sixty-eight percent of your students will have used a computer before they get to you. They will probably know how to find and save a file, do simple word processing, and work with photographs they have taken with their digital cameras. Then think of the thirty-two percent that will not have those skills. How will you work with the two groups of students in your classroom? How will you teach basic computer skills to students who have picked them up hit-and-miss with no place to practice? How will you keep the more advanced students engaged while you work with skills and build confidence in students who do not have access to computers at home? Also, notice the difference income has on those who have access and those who do not. This difference is significant. If students in low income homes are to have an opportunity to move to a different income level in their adult lives, we must help them overcome their lack of access to computers.

Computer literacy, though certainly not as important as reading, can be viewed in a similar fashion. Other learning is based on it. In order for students to learn history, mathematics, science, or language arts, they need to be able to read. In order for students to use the cognitive tools that computers provide to facilitate learning in history,

Digital divide

TABLE 1.4 U.S. Census Bureau 2007 Statistical Abstract Reflecting 2004 Computer Availability in Homes

User Characteristic	Number of Children (1,000)	Percent Using Computers at School	Percent Using Computers at Home	Home Use Activity (Percent)				
				Word Processing	Connect to the Internet	E-mail	Complete School Assignments	Play Games
Total	**53,561**	**84.5**	**68.6**	**33.4**	**46.6**	**32.9**	**49.2**	**56.9**
Age: 5 to 7 years old	11,785	72.2	59.3	9.6	23.3	7.7	16.6	51.7
8 to 10 years old	11,849	86.3	66.1	23.5	38.2	19.5	42.7	58.0
11 to 14 years old	17,173	89.0	72.0	42.7	54.8	40.9	61.8	61.0
15 to 17 years old	12,753	87.9	75.0	51.9	64.7	57.7	68.1	55.4
Sex: Male	27,422	84.2	68.0	31.2	45.5	30.2	47.5	57.8
Female	26,139	84.7	69.3	35.6	47.7	35.7	50.9	56.0
Family income:								
Under $20,000	16,459	81.3	51.7	23.1	30.7	21.7	36.2	41.2
20,000 to 34,999	8,615	81.9	55.7	22.9	33.3	23.2	38.2	45.4
35,000 to 49,999	6,993	85.9	72.2	33.2	46.7	32.3	50.5	60.5
50,000 to 74,999	9,053	86.0	80.5	38.6	56.7	39.2	57.6	67.1
75,000 or more	12,441	88.5	89.3	50.5	69.3	50.1	67.0	76.4

mathematics, science, or language arts, they must have some rudimentary computer skills. Alert and skillful teachers will discover which students are not computer literate and will assist them in learning the necessary skills to use the tool.

For this reason, if you are just becoming literate in some or all of the computer tools this book presents, it is important that you do two things:

1. Be reflective as you learn new computer skills during this course. Ask yourself what was not clear to you. Note any tricks or tips that you discover during the learning process so you can share them with other beginners.

2. Watch how the person who is teaching you computer skills demonstrates and explains each concept. Be aware of your own reactions, as well as the reactions of other students in your class. If you have an opportunity, watch someone else teach computer skills to children at the grade level you intend to teach.

Be a reflective learner

How people react to learning new skills varies with their learning style and degree of intimidation. Remember that people learn by doing. When you are showing others how to use a computer, let *them* have the mouse in their hand and their fingers on the keyboard. Talk them through processes, explaining as you go.

It is important to teach students to operate the software they will be using, even though doing this takes valuable class time. Computer skills are **prerequisite knowledge** that will help students learn faster and better using your technology-supported lessons. Do not overload students with computer skills they do not know as you teach them new content. Just as it is impossible to learn to do long division before learning how to add and subtract, if students do not know the key presses they need to complete a complex, computer-supported lesson, you will be wasting their time.

How to teach computer skills

The **cognitive load** involved in learning new computer skills and new content at the same time makes it impossible for students to learn either very well. In a classic study, G. A. Miller (1956) determined that our working memory (where information resides before it goes to long-term memory) only allows us to hold "7 ± 2" chunks of information in our minds at one time. According to Gagne, Yekovich, & Yekovich (1993), "Because of the limited capacity of WM [working memory], it is difficult to perform several mental tasks at once. . . . Usually people are comfortable doing only one cognitively demanding task at a time."

The first time you make an assignment that uses a computer tool, use an LCD projector to demonstrate to the whole class the computer skills they will need by modeling a simple activity for them. Then give students some computer time and some practice activities to help them learn or remember. As the school year progresses, you will have to do this less and less.

PREREQUISITE KNOWLEDGE
Knowledge that students must have in order to assimilate and learn new information.

COGNITIVE LOAD
How many chunks of information a person can think about at one time.

Using the Computer as a Teacher for Your Students

Introduction   Instructional software was education's first genuine attempt to put computers to work in classrooms. The idea that the computer is a teacher grew out of Skinnerian research that suggests immediate feedback, along with rewards, motivates learners and improves knowledge retention. During the 1960s and 1970s, educators and software developers worked very hard to make computers into teachers. This effort resulted in large collections of instructional software that ran on mainframes, such as Control Data's PLATO system, developed by William Norris. Norris believed that computers could replace teachers for the delivery of instruction (Roblyer & Edwards, 2000). This genre of software has shown some success in specific areas of education (which we will discuss shortly), but it has not lived up to its early promise. Instructional software that is effective usually is quite expensive and/or very narrow in scope. In other words, educators do not need to fear that a computer will replace them. However, educators do need to know how to judge whether instructional software is effective or not and when its use is appropriate.

Kinds of Instructional Software Titles   There are three kinds of instructional software. They are usually identified as tutorials, drill and practice, and simulations.

Tutorials.   Tutorials cover a specific topic. They explain a subject. Often they contain elements that allow students to explore information, practice using the information they have explored, and take a test when they have finished exploring and practicing. One derogatory name for poor tutorial software is "electronic page turner." Page upon page of text interspersed with graphics and a question every page or so is the worst kind of tutorial software. It offers hardly more for a learner than a book (if anything) and is not nearly as portable. Better tutorials are written in a nonlinear fashion using **hypertext** and **hypermedia** so that learners may follow themes or strands of thought. Well-written tutorials, as well as drill-and-practice programs, are especially useful with exceptional students. "For students who require small steps and many repetitions to learn a new concept, computers are the perfect, patient tutors, repeating steps and lessons as many times as necessary" (Woolfolk, 2000).

Drill-and-Practice.   Before students use this software they should have already had some related instruction. Drill-and-practice software contains questions or problems that students answer and on which they receive feedback. This kind of software can be quite helpful for specific learning problems. It is helpful when students need to learn basic facts or skills before they can move on to higher-order conceptual thinking. In a typical drill-and-practice session, the computer gives the student a problem, the student suggests a solution, and the computer indicates whether the suggested solution is correct. Sometimes, better drill-and-practice software allows students to ask for hints or gives an explanation with the solution. Some software titles allow students to challenge themselves with a timer. Drills on math facts, as well as spelling and other skills associated with language arts, are examples of typical content that drill-and-practice programs address. The main idea for teachers to remember is that drill-and-practice software is not written to introduce concepts. *Teachers* introduce new concepts and assign activities to reinforce what has been taught. After an adequate introduction, drill-and-practice software is *one* useful way to help students interact with content.

Simulations and Modeling.   Simulations and models, if they are well written and really do represent the real world, are the most complex and helpful of the three kinds of instructional software. Because of the computer's ability to do complex calculations quickly, programmers can build models of reality. Sometimes these models contain

History of computer-based instruction (CBI)

Tutorials vary widely in quality

Drill and practice helps students with factual knowledge

HYPERTEXT
New windows of text that expand on a topic when the user clicks a "hotlink" word or icon.

HYPERMEDIA
New windows that show related graphics, sound, or video when the user clicks a "hotlink" word or icon.

Simulations stimulate higher-order thinking

graphics that help students visualize what is being simulated. Others are purely numerical. "Some scholars assert that simulations and computer-based models are the most powerful resources for the advancement and application of mathematics and science since the origins of mathematical modeling during the Renaissance" (Bransford et al., 2000, p. 201). Examples of simulation software include SimCity (and the rest of the Sim series), Oregon Trail, and Geometer's Sketchpad.

Simulations provide "what if" sessions for students. In Oregon Trail, for example, students can ask "what if" questions such as:

- What if I spend all of my money on food at the beginning of the trip?
- What if I save my money and depend on hunting?
- Should I cross the river or get to my destination by going the long way?

Simulations reflect the real world

Models are different from simulations because students build them with real-world data. Models are built with computer-based visualization and analysis tools into which students may import real-world information. Once students have imported real-world information, they may then ask "what if" questions or view alternative representations of the data. Examples of concepts students have studied successfully with modeling tools include acceleration, light, sound, climate, population, ecology, history, genetics, Newtonian mechanics, velocity, and water quality (Bransford et al., 2000, p. 204).

The complexity of a simulation or model has to do with the number of parameters or variables that a student can set. The likeness to reality that the simulation produces has to do with the accuracy of the mathematical formulas behind the **user interface.** Oregon Trail, used mostly in upper elementary grades, has only a few parameters for users to set. Geometer's Sketch Pad, on the other hand, has many more. Simulations are different from tutorials and drill-and-practice software in two major ways:

- Simulations require higher-order thinking skills: analysis, judgment, and synthesis.
- Good simulations are rare. Teachers can't say, "I think I will go to a software catalog and pick out a simulation on this week's social studies (or science, or language arts) unit," and expect to find a good one that applies to their grade level and specific curriculum. After careful research you may find one or a few (depending on the content area) simulations that will help you during a school year.

To see how simulations work, you can explore some that exist on the Internet. One site supported by the Shodor Education Foundation (1996) contains tools for both modeling and simulation on astronomy, environmental issues, fractals, mathematics, and biomedical problems. You will find the address of this site in the Annotated Resources section at the end of this chapter.

USER INTERFACE
How the screen displays information and provides opportunities for the user to navigate through the program to find more information to modify or display.

The Computer as a Teacher Computers can be used to deliver lessons if they are used wisely. First, the software must match the curricular goal. This restricts the number of titles available for many topics, especially beyond the elementary grades. While there are many programs that teach early math and reading concepts, an English teacher might have a hard time finding a piece of software related to a particular short story or novel. A social science teacher may likewise find nothing on the colonial period in America that a book cannot do just as well. Teachers of mathematics have a larger choice of drill-and-practice programs on topics ranging through calculus. Science teachers will find some isolated software on topics that match their curriculum, but still cannot depend on software to teach more than perhaps 10 percent of their science curriculum. Students with cognitive disabilities historically have benefited the most from instructional software because of the nature of the computer itself: patient repetition of facts.

> Instructional software covers a limited amount of information

Second, the software must be used appropriately. Drill-and-practice and simulation software provide practice with facts and ideas after a teacher has presented them. Tutorials provide a backup or review for a teacher presentation but are rarely good enough to teach a concept without a teacher's help. However, if an existing book, classroom activity, or worksheet can do the job as well as a software title, then it is more cost effective to use what is available.

> Instructional software must be used appropriately

Using a Computer as a Cognitive Tool

This third use of computers in the teaching/learning process is full of even more possibilities for teaching and learning. Computers provide new and effective ways for students to gather, analyze, and present information. The computer tools provide motivation, incentive, and even feedback to students doing tasks that lie at all levels of Bloom's taxonomy (Jonassen, 2000). Computer tools support three components of the information processing tasks that students use to acquire facts and skills: gather, analyze, and display/present information.

> Data analysis tools

Gathering Information   Achieving information literacy is key to the economic well-being of our students. As our school system developed, it was based on what nineteenth-century students in industrial America needed: skills in reading, writing, and arithmetic. The information age has not so much changed the need for those basic skills, but has added another: information literacy. "Learning how to learn is fundamental to economic and personal success" (Carr, 1998, p. 1).

> Information literacy is a key to success in the twenty-first century

The Internet is the premier tool of our era for gathering information. Internet browsers (e.g., Explorer, Netscape), associated search engines (e.g., Google, Lycos), and e-mail clients (e.g., Hotmail, Eudora, Outlook) are all specialized tools for finding information or communicating on the Internet. Gathering information on the Internet includes knowing how to find, retrieve, and use text, audio, and video files as well as how to communicate with others.

> Gathering information reflectively

However, there is much more to the information-collection process than just using the tools. In addition to knowing how to get information, students need to know what to do with it once they have it. Figure 1.1 is a first step. They need the skills to decide whether it is fact or opinion. If the information is fact, they need to know how to determine whether the facts are accurate. They also need to know how to cite information and understand copyright issues.

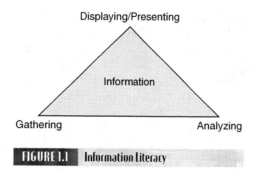

FIGURE 1.1 Information Literacy

Presentation software helps students understand relationships among ideas

Displaying and Presenting Information When people think of using computers to present information, what often comes to mind is the PowerPoint presentation. A finished PowerPoint presentation is the proverbial tip of the iceberg in terms of student learning. The power of presentation software for students lies in the planning process they must use to make the presentation. The act of using presentation software teaches students concepts and processes as they visualize the relationships among ideas.

In order to do a presentation, students first write an outline, then create a **concept map** (see Figure 1.2). Drawing a concept map, either on paper or in a computer application such as Inspiration, helps students acquire facts and also helps them see relationships that exist among the facts.

Next, students write a **storyboard**. In this phase of the preparation, they think about how to display the information from their concept maps effectively. They decide which ideas should be emphasized, and how. They decide where to make hyperlinks between screens to reflect the structure of the information they are presenting. Only after they have written the storyboard do they begin to create the actual presentation.

The nonlinear nature of online presentations is one of the reasons student authors learn so much as they develop a presentation. In an electronic report, students can make hyperlinks from page to page. They do not have to think "from first to last," as they would in writing a traditional report; instead they think about the logical connections among ideas. Rather than being simply a fun way to prepare a speech, presentation software provides effective and meaningful tasks to help students learn facts (at the lower end of Bloom's taxonomy) and relationships (at the higher end of the taxonomy).

CONCEPT MAP
Sketch of the relationship (possibly hierarchical) among concepts or topics.

STORYBOARD
Author's tool for planning screen elements, possible user interactions, and the sequence and flow between screens.

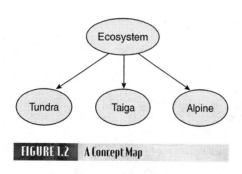

FIGURE 1.2 A Concept Map

Word processing is another way of presenting information. The word processor is a powerful tool because it:

Word processing software expands each student's collection of writing and editing tools

- Provides high-quality output for children with coordination problems (e.g., those who cannot write well with a pen)
- Permits students to edit their work and change it without having to recopy a whole paper or report
- Provides students another way to check their spelling, punctuation, and grammar
- Has reading index indicators to help students judge the level of their writing
- Provides students with the ability to create tables easily and quickly
- Allows students to import graphics, charts, and graphs to illustrate and amplify their writing

Looking at the list above, it is clear that the word processor makes the act of writing easier, makes the result look better, provides some feedback to the student that only a teacher could otherwise give, and adds variety to the ways that students can present information in a report.

Analyzing Information   Tools for analyzing information include databases and spreadsheets. In the past, when students gathered information, they often collected it from textbooks, encyclopedias, and magazines. The facts that they gathered had been pre-analyzed for them, and their job was to learn the facts and memorize the conclusions of the author who provided the information. When students wrote reports, they would sometimes read several authors, who might have interpreted the facts differently. In this case, the students then were asked to weigh the merits of the arguments and judge which arguments seemed to make the most sense. Rarely, however, did students start with just the facts, analyze them, make their own judgments, and then go to the experts for information. Databases and spreadsheets make this process possible for academic topics.

Data analysis tools

Computer tools allow students to make their own judgments

Databases and spreadsheets allow students to input raw data and find patterns in it from which they can make predictions, draw inferences, and describe unknowns. Databases and spreadsheets are alike in two ways. First, they both provide **sorts** and queries. For example, a user could perform a sort to find the tallest animal and a query to find all animals that are carnivorous and nocturnal. A second similarity between databases and spreadsheets is that users can do calculations using both. However, databases are built to analyze text and spreadsheets are most useful for numbers. You will learn much more about the different strengths of databases and spreadsheets in later chapters. The key point to remember now is that students are working with raw data when they use databases and spreadsheets to analyze information. They are not working with someone else's analysis of the raw data. In this sense and in line with the constructivist perspective on education, students first construct their own knowledge. Then, with that background, they consult experts so they can make their own judgments about the topic at hand. The ability to analyze data is another element of information literacy.

SORTS
Sorts put information in order (a to z or 0 to 100, for example).

TABLE 1.5 Technology in the Teaching and Learning Process

Topic	Example
Technology operations and concepts	• Knowing the basics of computer operation and maintenance • Knowing how to use the Internet, word processor, database, spreadsheet, and presentation software
Planning and designing learning environments and experiences	• Constructivist learning environment • Problem-based learning
Teaching, learning, and the curriculum	• Models of teaching that nurture and use information processing skills such as problem-based learning and constructivism
Assessment and evaluation	• Develop goals and objectives based on a learning taxonomy like Benjamin Bloom's
Productivity and professional practice	• Increase communication with parents • Distance learning • Use of integrated learning systems to track student performance
Social, ethical, legal, and human issues	• Understanding the ethical use of computers • Being careful to recognize the effects of the digital divide

■ SUMMARY

Educational technology is a broad field, with potential for high impact on teaching and learning. It is more than computers, more than computer tutorials, drill-and-practice, simulations, or tools. Proper use of educational technology requires an understanding of the computer and its associated software and peripherals and how they all support the teaching and learning process. That support of the teaching and learning process is manifest in several ways, which are summarized in Table 1.5 (ISTE 2001).

The focus of this book will be to demonstrate instructional models for tool software that is found on most computers. Tool software is effective for two reasons. First, it provides learners practice with information across the levels of Bloom's taxonomy. Second, it is the software of the "real world." As students learn to use tool software to solve problems, they are learning not only the information and the skills they need in their classroom, but also skills that will serve them well when they reach the world of work.

■ REFERENCES

Anderson, L., Krathwohl, D., Airasian, P., Cruikshand, K., Mayer, R., Pintrich, P., Raths, J., & Wittrock, M. (2001). *A taxonomy for learning, teaching, and assessing.* New York: Longman.

Bransford, J. D., Brown, A. L., & Cocking, R. R. (Eds.). (1999). *How people learn: Brain, mind, experience, and school.* Washington, DC: National Academy Press.

Carr, J. A. (1998). Information literacy and teacher education. ERIC (ED4242331). Retrieved from www.ed.gov/databases/ERIC_Digests/ed424321.html.

Gagne, E., Yekovich, C., & Yekovich, F. (1993). *The cognitive psychology of school learning.* New York: HarperCollins.

Gates, B. (1999). *Business @ the speed of thought.* Malden, MA: Blackwell Publishing.

International Society for Technology in Education (ISTE), NETS Project. (2004). National educational technology standards for students (2nd ed.). Eugene, OR: Author. Retrieved from www.ISTE.org.

Jonassen, D. (2000). *Computers as mindtools for schools.* Upper Saddle River, NJ: Merrill.

Joyce, B., Weil, M., & Calhoun, E. (2000). *Models of teaching.* Boston: Allyn & Bacon.

Markham, T., Larmer, J., & Ravitz, J. (2003). *Project-based learning: A guide to standards-focused project-based learning.* Novato, CA: Buck Institute for Education.

Miller, G. A. (1956). The magical number seven, plus or minus two: Some limits on our capacity for processing information. *Psychological Review.* 63, 81–97.

Reiser, R., & Dempsey, J. (2002). *Instructional design and technology.* Upper Saddle River, NJ: Prentice-Hall.

Roblyer, M. D., & Edwards, J. (2000). *Integrating educational technology into teaching.* Upper Saddle River, NJ: Prentice-Hall.

Schacter, J. (1999). The impact of education technology on student achievement: What the most current research has to say. Santa Monica, CA: Milken Exchange on Education Technology. The Milkin Family Foundation. www.mff.org/publications/publications.taf?page=161. Retrieved February 19, 2007.

Shodor Education Foundation. (1996). Master tools. www.shodor.org/master. Retrieved February 19, 2007.

Thomas, J., Mergendoller, J., & Michaelson, A. (1999). *Project-based learning handbook.* Novato, CA: Buck Institute for Education.

U.S. Census Bureau. (2007). The 2007 statistical abstract. www.census.gov/compendia/statab. Retrieved February 16, 2007.

U.S. Department of Commerce. (2000). Falling through the Net: Defining the digital divide. Washington, DC: Author. Retrieved from www.ntia.doc.gov/ntiahome/fttn99/contents.html.

Woolfolk, A. (2000). *Educational psychology* (8th ed.). Boston: Allyn & Bacon.

▓ ANNOTATED RESOURCES ▓

Bain, C., Rice, M. (2006). The influence of gender on attitudes, perceptions, and uses of technology. *Journal of Research on Technology in Education.* 39(2), 119–132.

> This article addresses one postulated digital divide—the difference between how different genders view computer use. Fifty-nine sixth graders participated in the study. While the study showed no difference between the genders on attitudes, perceptions, and uses of computers, males did view themselves as more skilled with computers than did their female counterparts.

Barnes, P. (2007). Is technology the solution? *Teaching Pre K–8.* 37(5).

This is a short article by a classroom teacher on practices he has developed to make computer technology useful. He stresses using the tech people that schools keep on staff, keeping things structured, and making the most of at-home opportunities.

Barron, A., Kemker, K., Harmes, C., & Kalaydjian, K. (2003). Large-scale research study on technology in K–12 Schools: Technology integration as it relates to the national technology standards.

This study gives the reader insight into how computer technology is being implemented in public schools. It gives information on 156 of the largest districts in the country, focusing on technology integration and how teachers do it. It also provides data on numbers of classrooms that have different available technologies such as computers and the Internet, and tracks changes in availablity over time.

www.digitaldividenetwork.org

This site contains a wealth of information, articles, and discussion on the digital divide. On this site you will learn more about what the digital divide is as well as learn more about who is doing what to work toward solutions to the problem. Although some of this information is somewhat dated, the issues have not changed.

www.iste.org

On this site, you will find ISTE standards for both students and teachers. In addition, you will find a rich library of lesson plans, books about specific areas of educational technology, news of events, and professional conferences for K–12 teachers.

Labbo, L. (2006). Do computers belong in the world of young children? *Journal of Reading Education.* 31(2).

This article outlines uses for computers and conditions for computer use in early childhood education. The author indicates that computer use should be functional and gives examples of functional uses for young children. She continues by saying that a successful experience with computers for young children depends on a supportive social environment and then defines that environment.

McGrain, E. (2007). Laptop technology and pedagogy in the English language arts classroom. *Journal of Technology and Teacher Education.* 15(1).

The research noted negative outcomes such as isolation, off-task behavior, and limited communication with teacher or peers when students used laptops in the language arts classroom. Causes of these negative outcomes included: limited space, cumbersome furniture, poor infrastructure, and a mechanical use of the computers such that teachers used the computer as a substitute for pencil and paper rather than planning computer uses suited to its role in the language arts classroom. This is a good article for teachers of any content area who wish to acquaint themselves with common pitfalls and solutions.

The science of learning. *Educational Leadership.* November 2000.

> This edition is devoted to the science of learning. Two articles especially describe the application of constructivist principles to the classroom: "The Brain-Compatible Curriculum" and "Brain-Based Instruction in Action." These articles are well written and very readable.

www.shodor.org/master

> This web site is a fascinating place to visit, with many working simulations that are appropriate for middle school through grade 12. Names of the simulations at this site include GalaxSee, SimSurface, Environmental Models, Fractal Modeling Tools, GnuPlot, BioMedical Modeling, and The Pit and the Pendulum. On this page there are further links to "Models in Medicine and the BioSciences" and an "Environmental Sciences" page. Each of these pages has additional interactive modeling and simulation problems.

Taylor, J. A. (2006). Teaching social studies with technology: New research on collaborative approaches. *The History Teacher.* 40(1), 9–25.

> Although the title indicates that the article is about history teaching, many of the ideas are true of using technology with any curriculum. This is a quick read, with ideas for using different computer tools to teach with as well as a listing of common implementation pitfalls.

Companion Web Site   www.ablongman.com/thorsen3e

1. Go to the TechTactics web site for Chapter 1 and click on the ISTE (International Society for Technology in Education) link. Go to the NETS (National Educational Technology Standards). Write a short paper on NETS. What is it? As a teacher, which standards will challenge you the most? Which standards do you feel are most important for children to master, and why?

2. Go to the TechTactics web site for Chapter 1 and click on the Digital Divide link. Browse the content of the site. Then write a reflective paper on how the digital divide affects your community. Are there socioeconomic or ethnic factors, or locations that impact access and use of technology? Are there solutions? If so, what are they?

3. Go to the TechTactics web site for Chapter 1 and click on the Shodor web site. In the "Curriculum Areas" tab you will find some fascinating simulations and other interactive software. Browse the many different applications and find two that you think would be especially motivating for students. What characteristics of these applications make them good learning materials?

An Introduction to Computers for Teaching

OBJECTIVES

- Give examples of how computer tools are integrated into the teaching/learning process.
- Analyze an example of computer tools integrated into the teaching/learning process using a general instructional model.
- Name content areas for which each of the tools is most useful.
- Name commonly taught cognitive processes or skills associated with each tool.

Role of the teacher

Good teachers know how to design lessons that help students remember what they learn. Teachers in a learner-centered classroom are not primarily lecturers and presenters, but rather knowledge engineers. They design presentation strategies that play to the strengths of how their students learn best. The purpose of computers for educators has not been primarily for computation, but for the presentation of information to students.

Throughout this book, we will take virtual field trips. We will visit classrooms in which teachers and students are using computer tools, and after the field trip, you will read observations on the lesson that you observed. You will learn the strategies that the teacher used to set up the lesson and why they were used. Before we start talking about "a general teaching model," we will take our first two field trips.

FIELD TRIP
2.1

Teaching in a mainstreamed classroom

Text-reading software

A Technology-Supported High School Classroom

This mainstreamed classroom provides instruction to children of many abilities, some who cannot read the text and understand what they have read, and others who read very well and score high on standardized tests. Ms. Anthony has struggled with the problem every year for the eight years that she has taught. In the beginning, she taught to the readers and let the nonreaders drift, so long as they did not disrupt the rest of the class. Then, feeling guilty, she taught to the nonreaders and let the readers drift, which didn't work either. Readers can be just as disruptive as nonreaders when they are not challenged.

Ms. Anthony learned about text-reading software in a summer workshop and decided to try to solve the reading problem that kept her and her students from the content that she loved and wanted to teach. After two or three tries, she figured out how to use technology effectively to involve all of her students in learning and doing science.

Her fourth and most successful technology-supported unit was the astronomy chapter in the science book. In this unit, like the others she taught, she provided the students with several activities. One activity required the students to read the textbook for information that she wanted them to know. If they chose, students could scan the text of the assignment into the computer, transfer it to text-reading software, sit, and listen while the computer displayed the text on the screen as it read that same text back to the students. She gave all of her students training in this process and then allowed them to either use the process or read to themselves silently. Along with the reading assignment, Ms. Anthony gave students an assignment involving an electronic database. While she was preparing for this unit, she found a NASA database of objects in and near our solar system. The database provided her with the name, mass, density, atmosphere (if any), distance from the center of the Milky Way, and several other fields of information for the students to peruse. Before she provided her students with the electronic database, she removed the name of each object and substituted a letter.

| Electronic database |

She then set up a problem for them. Working in teams, the students became NASA scientists who had successfully launched a probe that had sent the information contained in the database back to Mission Control on Earth. Using sort and query functions, the students worked with the database to name as many objects as they could, given information from their assigned reading and other information they could glean from the library and the Internet. Their goal was to draw a map of the part of the galaxy represented by the database and to write a report describing the objects on the map. Ms. Anthony hoped the students would recognize their solar system and the Earth.

| Developing an assignment |

She was pleased with the results. Her assignment had something for everyone. Because of the text-reading software, the nonreaders had an opportunity to get the information they so often missed because they could not read. Those students who enjoyed problem solving had an opportunity not only to solve problems with the database but also unobtrusively model the process for their less skillful teammates. Students who were more graphically inclined were able to model their graphical skills by making maps, while other students who enjoyed writing used the word processor to model their writing skills. Everyone was involved. No one missed information because of a skill deficiency.

Our second field trip in this chapter will take us to an elementary language arts classroom where students are learning how to organize sentences into paragraphs and paragraphs into compositions.

| Teaching writing |

A Technology-Supported Elementary Classroom

FIELD TRIP
2.2

Mr. Robbins has found the concept of organization to be one of the most difficult language arts topics that he teaches. During the first ten years that he taught, he showed children how to outline. Although this technique works for some children, many others believe that outlining is busywork and do not see the connection between outlining and a finished composition. Still others simply never understand the hierarchy of importance that topics take on in an outline.

| Concept mapping |

After attending a workshop on concept mapping, Mr. Robbins began teaching children how to map concepts in preparation for writing a composition. In the workshop he learned how to use a piece of software called Inspiration to actually do the mapping. The great feature of the software is that it not only allows students to make concept maps, it converts concept maps to outlines and outlines to concept maps. The children then cut and paste the final outline into a word processor, where they fill in the outline they create.

Concept maps are graphical outlines. In the workshop that Mr. Robbins' school district provided for him, he learned to capitalize on having students do both an outline and concept map. Because the outlining and concept mapping were done on a computer and could be viewed quickly and easily (as either an outline or a map–the software made the change), students could look at their topics in several different ways before they actually began writing. They could write an outline first and turn it into a concept map by just clicking on a menu item. Alternatively, they could start with a concept map and then turn it into an outline, again by simply clicking on a menu item. From there, they could cut and paste their outline into a word processor and begin fleshing it out. While they were working with the concept map and outline in Inspiration, they began to see that when they did their concept maps they would often think of many different and sometimes unrelated ideas.

| Seeing relationships |

When they turned these concept maps into outlines, they could tell that some ideas just did not fit or that they were in the wrong place. They could easily fix their errors in logic by cutting and pasting. When they clicked back from their outlines to their concept maps, they found that they could generate more ideas and rearrange them quickly. They began seeing the outline and concept map as tools to help them think, not as wasted effort that they would have to repeat once they began writing with a word processor.

| Using computers to enhance learning requires thought and planning |

You can see that using computers in a classroom is a complex process that requires some training as well as much thought and planning. The first few times you use a computer to support a topic that you teach, it will be more work, not less. It will not be anything like having students sit in front of a computer and absorb knowledge from software that someone else wrote.

| How computers help students |

With respect to student learning, you can draw two conclusions. First, in some cases computer tools help students with skills they lack, such as reading and/or computational skills. When they use computer tools this way, they are not held back in a content area because of their lack of skill with reading, writing, or numbers. Second, students using computers are able to think at a higher level on Bloom's taxonomy than they would without the computer. The computer does the low-level tasks, giving students the mental space to analyze and synthesize information.

| Teaching methods and computers |

With respect to teaching, you can also draw some conclusions. Students and teachers must have a goal with an interesting problem or several problems to solve. The solution to the problem may require more than one kind of computer tool. And, finally, computer skills are not taught for their own sake, but as a means to an end. Curricular objectives are always the goal. Computers support those objectives.

Table 2.1 lists the most useful and available software commonly used for solving problems or completing projects at different grade levels and in different content areas. Each type of software will be discussed in more detail later in this book. For now, just familiarize yourself with this table. As you read this book, you will learn more about each item as you acquire more understanding about the tools themselves and the instructional situations in which they are used.

Most tool software is applicable at most grade levels and for content areas. There is a notable exception. Notice that instructional software heads the list of useful software for grades K–3. Instructional software is especially useful for students who are learning the facts that they need to help them reason and think at higher levels. Drill-and-practice software for vocabulary and spelling are good examples. Software titles that teach such items as making change or doing fractions are two other examples.

TABLE 2.1 Useful Tools

Useful Tools: Grades K–3	Useful Tools: Grades 4–12	
For English Instructional software Word processor for young children Hypermedia/presentation software Internet	**For English** Word processor Database Presentation software Internet Instructional software	Common uses of software by grade level
For Science Instructional software Internet Databases Hypermedia/presentation software Word processor	**For Science** Spreadsheet Internet Database Presentation software Instructional software Word processor	
For Social Studies Instructional software Databases Presentation software Internet Word processor	**For Social Studies** Spreadsheet Internet Databases Presentation software Instructional software	
For Mathematics Instructional software Calculator Word processor Internet	**For Mathematics** Word processor Spreadsheet Calculator Instructional software Internet	
For Foreign Language Internet Instructional software Presentation software	**For Foreign Language** Internet Instructional software Presentation software	
Music Notation software The MIDI	**Music** Database Presentation software Notation software The MIDI	

INSTRUCTIONAL MODELS AND COMPUTERS

When a teacher is new to integrating computers into the teaching/learning process, it is difficult to know which elements of instruction the technology improves on, which it neither helps nor hinders, and which it actually impedes. Instructional time is such a precious commodity and computers are so scarce and expensive that the first thing a teacher should try to understand is what they are good for. A case in point is drill-and-practice software. A computer is an expensive set of flash cards when it is used merely to generate spelling or multiplication problems and give quick feedback. Cards can do this function as well. Similarly, computer tutorials that are simply electronic page turners are an extravagance for students who can read and turn their own pages in a textbook.

On the other hand, for students using a large electronic database to investigate the relationships among creatures in a biome, the computer is unmatched in its ability to elicit analytical and synthetic thinking on the part of the user (Bransford, Brown, & Cocking, 1999, p. 203). Similarly, editing on a computer is faster, easier, and suits the attention span and physical writing skills of children better than a pencil (Roblyer & Edwards, 2000, p. 117). Tables 2.2 and 2.3 list many of the learning activities or models for which each tool is best suited. These learning activities are models because they are shells into which teachers of any grade level or content area can fit their own curriculum. They are models because they describe an instructional process.

What Does the Research Say about Using Computers in Classrooms?

Policy makers, teachers, and parents often ask whether research supports the use of computers in classrooms. Although no one, definitive study says that students who have access to computers learn faster and better than students without them, evidence of more specific successes has begun to accumulate. It is impossible to generalize about research that demonstrates the general effectiveness of computers in classrooms, but it is not nearly so difficult to find examples of research that define situations and methods especially suited for computers and students.

Teachers can look at three different kinds of resources for gathering information about improving their practice in the area of educational technology: empirical

TABLE 2.2 Lesson Construction Models for Software Tools	
Tool	**Learning Activities (Models)**
Word processor	The newspaper
	The research report
	Rewriting (style, content)
	Revision editing
	Journaling; lab reports; notetaking; group investigations
	Composition
	Creative writing
	Substitution exercises [supply the missing (words, sentences, paragraphs); remove the extra (words, sentences, paragraphs)]
	Ordering; sorting
	Outlining; logical sequencing
	Grammar; thesaurus; spell checker
	Following directions; writing directions

TABLE 2.3 More Tools and Their Uses	
Tool	**Uses**
Databases	Describe an unknown
	Make a prediction
	Make a decision
Spreadsheets	Solve story problems
	Teach what-if thinking
	Teach estimation
	Show relationships
Presentation software	Classify and describe knowledge
	Illustrate steps in procedures or processes
	Expose students to information in many different contexts (text, video, graphics, animation, and audio)
	Provide students an opportunity to construct knowledge in unique ways and different contexts
Internet & e-mail	Talk to the expert; data collection; newspaper; simulation; role playing; electronic debate; classroom discussion; research; communication; presentations

research published in professional journals, theory-building articles, and essays and reports by practicing teachers.

Empirical Research Published in Professional Journals   To find examples of research based on statistical evaluation, the journal *Educational Technology: Research and Development* is an excellent resource. Other excellent resources are the *British Journal of Educational Technology* and the *International Journal of Educational Technology*. The articles in these journals are written at a very high level, including descriptions of the statistical basis the authors used to make their conclusion. Consequently, they may be difficult to read for those who are not used to the format. However, these articles are very precise. They clearly indicate what works and what doesn't work, and how the teaching method was implemented. The K–12 educator must sift through the articles, because some are not relevant to K–12 education. Examples of titles of articles in these journals include: "Teacher Ratings of Student Engagement with Educational Software" (Bangert-Drowns & Pyke, 2002) and "When Each One Has One: The Influences on Teaching Strategies and Achievement Using Laptops in the Classroom" (Tzeng & Schwen, 2003). Large numbers of studies that focus on K–12 classrooms do not yet exist. Finding such studies is a matter of being watchful and periodically reviewing the table of contents of these journals as they are published.

Theory-Building Articles   Some researchers who have taught, done empirical research, and read much research have ideas about how educational technology works best in classrooms. By building on the research of others, citing their work and then drawing conclusions, they give us insight into new and what they hope are better and more effective ways to use educational technology. These kinds of articles appear on the web and in the journal *Educational Technology* as well as the publication *Leading and Learning with Technology*. The reader of theory-building articles will want to accept the conclusions of these authors thoughtfully. They have been peer reviewed by other experts, so they are not "opinion" pieces. On the other hand, the methods themselves have not withstood the careful scrutiny of a scientific study.

Essays and Reports by Practicing Teachers   By far the largest amount of information on the use of educational technology is authored by teachers themselves. These articles report on specific activities in specific content areas. They have been published because the teacher who developed the idea believes that it works well and because other, similarly skilled professionals who have read the article believe that it works as well. Currently, the most prolific printed source of this kind of information is *Leading and Learning with Technology*, published by the International Society for Technology in Education, which is published September through May. Additionally, the web is also a source for many of these kinds of reports. One outstanding example is the George Lucas Educational Foundation web site (www.glef.org). Not only is information on the web site peer reviewed, it contains large amounts of excellent video that demonstrates the projects with real teachers in real classrooms.

If you choose to look beyond the sources suggested here, try to find articles that have been submitted through some kind of peer-reviewed process. It is easy to become enamored of a technique or method that has worked once in one class and think that it will work again anywhere.

Approach your own implementation of a new idea slowly and thoughtfully. One thing that those of us in the behavioral sciences (education, psychology, sociology) learn early is that when we are working with people, we are working with an enormous number of variables that we can neither control nor sometimes even account for. Some slight variation in circumstance can dramatically alter the effects of what seemed like a good idea.

Constructing Technology-Supported Lessons

When we think about constructing a technology-supported lesson, we want to think about the kind of teaching model we are using. In your teaching methods classes you will learn about many different kinds of teaching models. Teaching models are the framework on which lessons are built. For example, role playing, lecturing, and problem-based learning are all models. One that you have read about already is the inductive model introduced in Chapter 1. All of these models require that students have foundational knowledge of a topic, such as knowing definitions. They also require students to think at higher levels of Bloom's taxonomy, to analyze, synthesize, and judge. The kinds of computer-supported tasks that facilitate student learning across the taxonomy are listed in Tables 2.2 and 2.3. Teachers often choose a model or a combination of models and then develop a set of learning activities that will help them implement the model.

One example of a teaching model that computers support very well is project-based learning. Briefly, building a project-based lesson includes developing a driving question that is tied to a real-world problem, often in the students' immediate community. Children investigate the problems by gathering many different kinds of data, such as interviews, surveys, chemical analyses, analyses of public records and historical documents, and video recordings (Markum, Larmer, & Ravitz, 2003). Students often use computers to analyze these data. This means that they input the data into spreadsheets and databases and then use the tools these applications provide to see patterns that answer their questions. Finally, they use computer tools to summarize and report the conclusions they have reached.

CHECKING YOUR UNDERSTANDING

2.1 Analyze the ways Mr. Robbins and Ms. Anthony used the computers in their classrooms. To do this, use Tables 2.2 and 2.3. Identify the tools that these teachers used and the instructional model or models the teachers used with each tool.

2.2 Analyze the learning outcomes of Mr. Robbins's and Ms. Anthony's students with Bloom's taxonomy, Table 1.3. Find each learning outcome or product that resulted from the lesson and place it at one of the levels of the table.

2.3 Below you will find an outline to use as a guide for planning a computer-supported lesson. Pick a topic that you know very well and design a lesson for students at a level you think you might teach.

I. Name the unit for which you want to use computer support.

    A. State your goals for this unit.

    B. Name all of the tools that could be used (Table 2.1) for this unit.

II. Add detail to your *first* goal:

    A. Concepts students are to learn.

    B. Problem they will solve.

    C. Computer tools (Table 2.1) and associated models (Tables 2.2 and 2.3) your students will use.

    D. Possible ways to use the tool to teach the content or solve the problem described in II.A.

    E. What products do you want your students to produce or skills they should demonstrate as they work on this goal? Use Bloom's table to classify your student's products or skills.

III. Add detail to your *second* goal: Repeat steps in section II until you have described your approach to accomplishing your goals.

2.4 Go to the following web site http://edtech.boisestate.edu/fipse and learn more about the project–based teaching model. Then look at Tables 2.2 and 2.3 for examples of activities for which computers are especially helpful. In a short paper, describe a potential project-based learning activity related to your community. Which computer tools would you use to support the project to gather data and to report results?

■ SUMMARY

Using computers to teach involves looking at content first and identifying computer tools whose function facilitates student interaction with the material. In our field trips we learned that computer tools have a wide range of applicability—from helping students read, to helping them reason. Although understanding how computer tools apply to teaching content seems complicated, it can be approached in an organized and ultimately intuitive fashion.

In the remainder of this book we will explore this organization (the models of Tables 2.2 and 2.3). First you will learn how to match models to information that you must teach. Then you will learn that each model associated with each tool is composed of a series of steps. You will learn to apply these steps to build lessons for your students. In addition, you will learn some ways to determine if you achieved your goal—a satisfactory learning outcome for your students.

■ REFERENCES

Bangert-Drowns, R. L., & Pyke, C. (2002). Teacher ratings of student engagement with educational software: An exploratory study. *Educational Technology: Research and Development.* 50(2), 23–38.

Bransford, J. D., Brown, A. L., & Cocking, R. R. (Eds.). (1999). *How people learn: Brain, mind, experience, and school.* Washington, DC: National Academy Press.

Markum, T., Larmer, J., & Ravitz, J. (2003). *Project based learning: A guide to standards-focused project based learning.* Novato, CA: Buck Institute for Education.

Roblyer, M. D., & Edwards, J. (2000). *Integrating educational technology into teaching.* Upper Saddle River, NJ: Prentice-Hall.

Tzeng, J., & Schwen, J. T. (2003). When each one has one: The influences on teaching strategies and student achievement of using laptops in the classroom. *Educational Technology: Research and Development.* 4(3), 5–22.

■ ANNOTATED RESOURCES

The titles of the following references are self-explanatory. Although this is by no means an exhaustive listing of research done in educational technology over the past five years, it does represent many of the articles available to one with access to an average university library. Many, although not all, are available in online databases as full-text articles if your library subscribes to an education index.

The number of focused, relevant articles using experimental or quasi-experimental methods is a very large improvement over the listing in the previous edition of this book. In fact, it is a complete revision, because research in the area has improved both in quality and quantity. However, there is much left to do. Lynne Schrum (2005), editor of the *Journal for Research in Educational Technology,* planned a special issue to focus on "research about the uses of technology for teaching and learning in K–12 classrooms or with K–12 learners." When it came time to publish the issue she remarked in an editorial "it has been surprising how few studies were submitted, reviewed, and accepted that meet the focus of the issue" (p. 113). As you read through the list of articles you will see that some areas have more articles listed than others. These numbers represent (approximately) the ratio of research that I found in the fields listed overall. It was far easier to find research on teaching science with technology than pre-school, for example. In the area of Special Education there is much research on technology that is assistive. However, since this book does not include assistive technology I did not include those references.

Early Childhood/Elementary

Plowman, L., and Stephen, C. (2005). Children, play, and computers in pre-school education. *British Journal of Educational Technology*. 36(2), 145–157.

English, Reading, Language Arts

Jones, J., Staats, W., Bowling, N., Bickel, R., Cunningham, M., & Cadle, C. (2004). An evaluation of the merit reading software program in the Calhoun County (WV) middle/high school. *Journal of Research on Technology in Education*. 37(2), 177–195.

Martindale, T. (2005). Effects of an online instructional application on reading and mathematics standardized test scores. *Journal of Research on Technology in Education*. 37(4), 349–360.

McNabb, M. (2005). Raising the bar on technology research in the language arts. *Journal of Research on Technology in Education*. 38(1), 113–119.

Putman, S. M. Computer-based reading technology in the classroom: The affective influence of performance contingent point accumulation on 4th grade students. *Reading Research and Instruction*. 45(1), 19–38.

Vogel, J., Greenwood-Ericksen, A., Cannon-Bowers, J., & Bowers, C. (2006). Using virtual reality with and without gaming attributes for academic achievement. *Journal of Research on Technology in Education*. 39(1), 105–118.

General

Barron, A., Kemker, K., Harmes, C., & Kalaydjian, K. (2003). Large scale study on technology in K–12 schools: Technology integration as it relates to the national technology standards. *Journal of Research on Technology in Education*. 35(4), 489–507.

Debevic, K., Shih, M.-Y., & Kashyap, V. (2006). Learning strategies and performance in a technology integrated classroom. *Journal of Research on Technology in Education*. 38(3), 293–307.

Gholson, B., et al. (2006). Promoting constructive activities that support vicarious learning during computer-based instruction. *Educational Psychology Review*. 18(2), 119–39.

Kadakia, M. (2005). Increasing student engagement by using "Morrowind" to analyze choices and consequences. *TechTrends*. 49(5), 29–32.

Pollard, C., & Pollard, R. (2005). Research priorities in educational technology: A delphi study. *Journal of Research on Technology in Education*. 37(2), 145–60.

Wijekumar, Meyer, B., Wagoner, D., & Ferguson, L. (2006). Technology affordances: The 'real story' in research with K–12 and undergraduate learners. *British Journal of Educational Technology.* 37(2), 191–209.

Wong, A., Quek, C., Divaharan, S., Liu, W., Peer, J., & Williams, M. (2006). Perceptions of computer-supported project work classroom learning environments. *Journal of Research on Technology in Education.* 38(4), 449–479.

Math

Ganesh, T. G. (2006). Challenges in linguistically and culturally diverse elementary settings with ath instruction using learning technologies. *The Urban Review.* 38(2), 101–43.

Martindale, T. (2005). Effects of an online instructional application on reading and mathematics standardized test scores. *Journal of Research on Technology in Education.* 37(4), 349–360.

Papanastasiou, E. C., et al. (2006). Computer use and mathematical literacy: An analysis of existing and potential relationships. *The Journal of Computers in Mathematics and Science Teaching.* 25(4), 361–71.

Vogel, J., Greenwood-Ericksen, A., Cannon-Bowers, J., & Bowers, C. (2006). Using virtual reality with and without gaming attributes for academic achievement. *Journal of Research on Technology in Education.* 39(1), 105–118.

Science

Guan, Y., Tsai, C., & Hwang, F. (2006). Content analysis of online discussion on a senior-high-school discussion forum of a virtual physics laboratory. *Instructional Science.* 34(4), 279–311.

Hsu, Y. (2006). "Lesson rainbow": The use of multiple representations in an Internet-based discipline-integrated science lesson. *British Journal of Educational Technology.* 37(4), 539–557.

Jimoyiannis, A., & Komis, V. (2001). Computer simulations in physics teaching and learning: A case study on students' understanding of trajectory motion. *Computers & Education.* 36, 183–204.

Wang, S., & Reeves, T. (2006). The effects of a web-based learning environment on student motivation in a high school earth science course. *Educational Technology Research and Development.* 54(6), 597–621.

Wekesa, E. (2006). Improving students' understanding and perception of cell theory in school biology: Using a computer-based instruction simulation program. *Journal of Educational Multimedia and Hypermedia.* 15(4), 397–410.

Zydney, J. M. (2005). Eighth grade students defining complex problems: The effectiveness of scaffolding in multimedia program. *Journal of Educational Multimedia and Hypermedia.* 14(1), 61–90.

Social Sciences

Saye, J. W., & Brush, T. (2006). Comparing teachers' strategies for supporting student inquiry in a problem-based multimedia-enhanced history unit. *Theory and Research in Social Education.* 34(2), 183–212.

Tally, B., & Goldenberg, L. (2005). Fostering historical thinking with digitized primary sources. *Journal of Research on Technology in Education.* 38(1), 1–21.

Taylor, J. A., & Duran, M. (2006). Teaching social studies with technology: New research on collaborative approaches. *The History Teacher.* (Long Beach, CA) 40(1), 9–25.

Special Education

Beacham, N. A., & Alty, J. L. (2006). An investigation into the effects that digital media can have on the learning outcomes of individuals who have dyslexia. *Computers & Education.* 47(1), 74–93.

Ely, R., Emerson, R., & Maggiore, T. (2006). Increased content knowledge of students with visual impairments as a result of extended descriptions. *Journal of Special Education Technology.* 21(3), 31–43.

Companion Web Site www.ablongman.com/thorsen3e

1. Go to the TechTactics web site for Chapter 2 and click on the Project-Based Learning web site. There you will find examples of many projects along with instructions for implementing project-based learning. After you have familiarized yourself with the basics of project-based learning, explain how computer technology facilitates this method of teaching. Use examples from the video and text on this web site to support your arguments.

2. Go to the TechTactics web site for Chapter 2 and click on the Environmental Models (Simulations) web site. Although you may not understand the science behind all of these, you can, however, experiment with how they work. Explain, using examples from the Environmental Models web site, how simulations work.

3

Information Retrieval

OBJECTIVES

- Describe the history of the Internet.
- Use a research model and the Internet to write a report.
- Know how to judge the quality of information on the Internet.
- Know rules of copyright for Internet materials.
- Know two ways courses are delivered at a distance.
- Judge the quality of distance courses.

To use the Internet effectively, you (and your students) will need to be able to do the following:

- Find the address bar in a browser, enter an address, and go to a site
- Download text, graphics, and plug-ins from an Internet site
- Bookmark Internet sites for later reference
- Navigate through Internet sites
- Use the Refresh button
- Download and save text, graphics, audio, and video files
- Display downloaded files in appropriate applications

A SHORT HISTORY OF THE INTERNET

The vision for describing the Internet was articulated long before we had the technology to implement it. The first public description of the Internet is credited to Vannevar Bush, a U.S. government employee, in an article in the *Atlantic Monthly* in 1945. He said:

> Consider a future device for individual use, which is a sort of mechanized private file and library. It needs a name, and to coin one at random, "memex" will do. A memex is a device in which an individual stores all his books, records, and communications, and

36

which is mechanized so that it may be consulted with exceeding speed and flexibility. It is an enlarged intimate supplement to his memory.

It consists of a desk, and while it can presumably be operated from a distance, it is primarily the piece of furniture at which he works. On the top are slanting translucent screens, on which material can be projected for convenient reading. There is a keyboard, and sets of buttons and levers. Otherwise, it looks like an ordinary desk.

Bush implemented his vision during the waning years of World War II. Others who followed him, notably J. C. R. Lickleider (1960) and later Tim Berners-Lee, honed it to what we know as the Internet today. It is literally a web of millions of computers connected worldwide. From its humble beginnings as a tool to send a text message from one research university to another, computer scientists have developed hardware and software that allow us to find and use text, audio, video, and graphics in a virtual library larger than humankind has ever known. Computer scientists have built *spiders* that roam the web seeking and indexing new information constantly.

THE MODERN INTERNET

First – a Caution: Viruses, Worms, and Trojan Horses

In an environment such as a school, you will almost certainly be challenged by a piece of malicious computer code written by a malicious person meant to disrupt the computers that you use. This type of computer code, categorized as a virus, worm, or Trojan horse, does one or more of the following:

■ Slows down a computer
■ Makes a computer unreliable by disabling software on the computer
■ Slows down the Internet
■ Deletes files on computers
■ Slows down or halts a network disrupting e-mail and the storage and retrieval of files
■ Engages in identity theft

Viruses are spread by users—often inadvertently. Viruses spread on disks carried from one machine to another or on files shared across the network. They travel in files made by Word and Excel, for example, and are released when an infected file is opened. At that point they can delete other files on the computer, cause the computer to operate erratically, slow it down, or cause it to become unusable. Interestingly enough, data files (such as MP3 files, PDF files, and MOV files) do not carry viruses. They simply contain data and there would be no way for a virus to execute.

Worms, unlike viruses, do not require a user in order to spread. They operate and replicate independently on networks. They travel from **node** to node, replicating in an attempt to acquire more and more **bandwidth,** eventually stopping traffic that is attempting to enter or leave a node, or performing other actions that interfere with the operation of a server.

NODE
A computer that stores or sends information it receives until a user on a personal computer can retrieve the information. E-mail travels to its address through many nodes on the Internet.

BANDWIDTH
The amount of information that can pass through the cable that carries Internet information to a computer. Text does not take much bandwidth; graphics, audio, and video do. Bandwidth in schools is often a problem. As students download graphics, audio, or video, access slows for everyone on the system.

Trojan horses travel inside seemingly legitimate programs like games, utilities, clocks, or weather reporting systems. Once the program is activated, the malicious code is released to do whatever its creator intended—delete files, disable software, and so on.

Viruses, worms, and Trojan horses can be detected and removed—most of the time. Norton Antivirus and McAfee Antivirus software are two leading antivirus programs. These programs should detect Trojan horses as well. Every personal computer should have antivirus software installed and activated. Additionally, network administrators protect servers with antivirus software and software that protects against worms. In spite of your best efforts and the efforts of your network administrator, new viruses appear, or one careless user can unleash an old virus into a network.

One thing a user can do is to never open a spreadsheet, document, or executable file such as a game or utility that does not come from a trusted source. For example, if you receive an e-mail attachment from someone you do not know and it is a word processed document or a spreadsheet, don't open it. This will not entirely protect you. For example, suppose a colleague unknowingly gets an infected word processed document from a student and thinks it is so good she wants you to see it too. She has failed to update the virus detection on her machine; she sends the document to you. For some reason when you were clicking around the other day you inadvertently de-activated your own virus protection. You open the document. By the end of the day your computer seems sluggish, so you think you will reboot. You reboot and the machine takes ten minutes to settle down. You click to start your e-mail program and nothing happens. You have a virus. The very worst part of this scenario is that at the beginning both you and your colleague may have had active antivirus software running but the virus was too new to be detected, or perhaps your antivirus software hadn't been updated for a week or two. Protecting yourself against malicious code is 99 percent vigilance. But even with your best efforts you may fail if the virus is new. Be prepared by backing up all of your important files on a CD, the network server, or a thumb drive.

Getting Started with the Internet in Your Classroom

GRAPHICALLY BASED
The modern browser supports pictures as well as text. This has not always been true. Older machines in some schools do not handle some graphics well. If Internet pages in your school display slowly, consider switching off the display of graphics.

The modern Internet is far different from the text-based Internet that people used until the early 1990s. The "toolbox" that holds the many tools the Internet provides is the web browser, the two most popular being Explorer and Netscape and, increasingly, Firefox by Mozilla. The browsers are **graphically based,** but as the Internet matures and **bandwidth** increases, the information that we receive over the Internet will gradually include more video and audio as well.

To use a browser, type in the Internet address of the site of interest, press Enter, and if all goes well, within a few seconds (or a minute if your bandwidth is low and the page to which you are going has many graphics) you will see the page to which you have pointed your browser. From there, you may choose to go to other pages at the site by clicking on buttons or highlighted text. If you do not already know how to execute this process, you should find out from a reference book or your instructor.

All browsers do the same things. They allow you to go to different Internet sites, search for, view, and download information. Although browsers do the same things, there are subtle differences between them that cause them to run better at some sites than others. When this is the case, the site will often tell you by saying something like "Before you click on this button, you should know that this link will run better in Netscape, Explorer, or Mozilla." Since you know that this will happen if you spend much time browsing the Internet, it is a good practice to make sure that at least these three browsers are available on your machine and the computers in your classroom or lab to begin with. Nothing is more frustrating than to go to a great site and learn that your browser will not handle it. To get to your great site you will have to spend a half-hour downloading and installing new browser software or, worse, wait for your school's technology coordinator or a technician to come and install it for you.

Attached to the code that runs in browsers are "plug-ins." Plug-ins are small programs that help a browser do something such as play a video or audio segment, display a graphic, or display text in some special way. Your browser will come with a set of basic plug-ins that will do all of this for you. As new technologies develop or old ones improve, new plug-ins appear with them. Consequently, when you go to a site and want to see or do something special, your computer may ask you if you want to download a special plug-in that will make something at that site work. Usually plug-ins are self-extracting and installing, and you don't have to do much to make them work. There is always the exception, however. Then you have to delete and start over. Sometimes they never work, and you do not get to see or do the special activity for which the plug-in was written. Examples of plug-ins are QuickTime, RealPlayer, Flash, LiveAudio, and Video for Windows.

While browsers display information on your computer, using your browser's "save" or "save as" function on the File menu allows you to download almost anything that you can see for future reference. This is where students genuinely need guidance from teachers. Questions that should come up include:

▓ Is this information or graphic worth downloading?
▓ Once it is downloaded, how should it be used?
▓ What copyright issues should be addressed?
▓ How should this information be referenced?

We will answer these questions in the next section of this chapter.

◉ USING THE INTERNET FOR RESEARCH

As a student, you are familiar with doing research and writing reports or presenting the results of your research. Chances are, you have been doing research since the third

| The web browser |

| Issues in Internet research |

| How the Internet complicates the information-gathering process |

or fourth grade. Although having access to the Internet does not change the basic research model, it does complicate the process for three reasons:

- The quality of the information on the Internet is highly variable.
- The information is not limited to text and pictures/charts as printed in books. It is also formatted as animation, audio, and video.
- Most textual information can be copied directly from the Internet into a word processor.

A research model

Defining a research process with clear rules and expectations will help students be aware of some of the challenges of Internet-based research. There are many research models and some are more appropriate to certain content areas than others, but for the purposes of our discussion we will use the NetSavvy Skills Framework (Jukes et al., 2000). The five steps in this model include: ask, access, analyze, apply, and assess.

Asking Questions

Begin with a problem

Asking a question and/or defining a problem is the key to a successful research project. No amount of technology can take the place of this first critical step. The assignment must be meaningful and its scope appropriate. A good research assignment will provide an opportunity for students to gather facts, look at them critically, analyze them, and make judgments about how those facts relate to each other and to the world that they know and live in. A good research assignment starts with a clearly stated question or problem.

There is a great deal to be gained by starting students with a good question. A well-structured question serves as a guide as well as a motivational tool. Consider the following example.

Poor:
What would happen if we dropped an atomic bomb during a war?

Better:
Would we be justified in dropping an atomic bomb on a hostile country?

Best:
What would justify dropping an atomic bomb on an enemy, and how would it affect our country, the other country, and the rest of the world?

The poor question gives a student virtually no guidance, whereas the best question gives the student many hints about where to start the research process. Given the poor question, the only thing for the student to do would be to look up atomic bombs and find out what they do. On the other hand, the student who received the best question would have a variety of research hints and starters. Given the best question, an enterprising student might be motivated to say, "Hm, we dropped an atomic bomb on an enemy once before. What reasons did we have then? What are the effects of an atomic bomb? What has it been like for the post-bomb Japanese? What do doctors say about the effects of radiation on people? Where is the hostile country? Where would the wind carry the fallout?"

Provocative driving questions are described (Markum, 2003) as being

- Provocative
- Open-ended
- Going to the heart of a discipline or topic
- Challenging
- Arising from a real-world dilemma
- Consistent with curricular standards and frameworks

Some projects take advantage of Internet-based resources better than others do. To really use the resources of the Internet to motivate your students as well as give them a starting point for their project, you should focus the project on some initial piece of information. From that point, your students can use other sites to interpret the initial information or problem. For example, you could use a web site such as

> Examples of kinds of Internet sites that help articulate a problem

- A virtual museum
- A social issue discussed in an online newspaper
- An online magazine or journal
- An online science project or experiment
- A data collection project that you will learn more about in Chapter 5

From that initial scrap of information, you may develop the question and help your students understand the scope of the project. For example, you could send your students to an online art museum to begin a research project on how art reflects the prevailing philosophy of a historical period.

One reason that it is so important for students to begin with a question is the ease with which they get off task. There are many interesting topics on the Internet, and it is easy to click on one hyperlink after another. Because real learning requires an effort to relate new knowledge to old knowledge, learners who browse the Internet do not often learn the information they are passing through (Jonassen, 2000).

> Real learning comes from processing information, not just viewing it

Accessing Information

Search Engines   Knowing that information on any topic you can think of is probably somewhere on the Internet is one thing. Knowing how to find it is another entirely. To find information on the Internet, you use a search engine. You access Internet search engines from your browser by typing in an address. There are many different search engines to choose from. Each has its strengths and weaknesses. Examples of search engines are found in Table 3.1.

> Search engines usually do not index the whole Internet

An example of strengths and weaknesses of search engines was documented by Grimes and Brand (2000) when they compared Fast Search to Google. According to the authors, Google seems to find the most relevant links and Fast Search uncovers links that other engines overlook. If you do not find what you want with one search engine, use another search engine. There is a special site, a kind of search engine review page, at http://searchenginewatch.com/reports/index.html. Here you can find a list of commonly used search engines, their sizes, and other pertinent information. You may

> Search engine review page

TABLE 3.1	Search Engines		
For Adults		**Suitable for Children**	
Google	www.google.com	Ask Jeeves for Kids	www.ajkids.com
Yahoo	www.yahoo.com	KidsClick	www.kidsclick.org
Ask Jeeves	www.askjeeves.com	Looksmart's Kids Directory	http://search.netnanny
AllTheWeb	www.alltheweb.com		.com/?pi=nnh3&ch=kids
HotBot	www.hotbot.com	Yahooligans	www.yahooligans.com
Teoma	www.teoma.com		

Source: Search Engine Watch (2007).

wonder what "size" means. Search engines do not always search the whole web. The owner of the search engine may index only a quarter or a half of the Internet. That is why using more than one search engine is helpful if you do not find the information you need on the first try.

Fortunately, there are resources on the Internet that address even this issue. These resources are called "meta search engines." When they receive your request for information, they invoke several other search engines. For example, the meta search engine Dogpile invokes Google, Yahoo, LookSmart, Teoma, and MSN Search. Some meta search engines include:

- Dogpile, http://dogpile.com
- SurfWax, www.surfwax.com
- Copernic Agent, www.copernicagent.com

Using search engines with children is different than using search engines yourself. Search engines for adults do not discriminate among the links they deliver. If children are doing searches on their own and your school has no filtering process (no proxy server), they should use search engines made for young people. These search engines generally will return only selected information that is appropriate for children. Table 3.1 clearly differentiates search engines that are appropriate for children.

Children should use age-appropriate search engines

Searching and the time your students spend on it is a process you must plan. You want your children to learn search skills, and your students must gather information to complete their reports, presentations, database, or spreadsheet assignments; however, computer resources are often an issue. There are usually not enough computers in a classroom or in the library to provide students an ideal amount of time to conduct a full search on a topic, download the information they find, and convert it to the format they need. A successful search with limited resources can be conducted at least two different ways.

To be effective, you should plan the search process carefully

First, you can divide the research topic into subcategories and assign those categories to groups of students who work together to compose their searches (which you will learn about in the next section). For example, if you have five computers in your classroom, you can divide your class into five groups and your research project into five subtopics. Each group can work together to conduct searches, choose and download relevant information, and label it in a common folder that all students in the class can

Divide a topic into subtopics and assign each topic to a subgroup

43

see and access. If you have one computer in your classroom, you can still divide your class into groups to do the research and make your computer one center among several others. Then, as the children rotate through the centers, they will get the research done. Using this model, children use a common body of information from which to write their research project or presentation, so you will not be evaluating them on the quality of their research but rather the skill with which they use the information they have.

A second method for using Internet searches to gather information requires the teacher to do part of the research and the students to individualize or customize with their own research. The teacher finds sites ahead of time, bookmarks them in the browser on the computers to which the class has access, and then gives the students time to go to the bookmarked pages and gather information. Then, in any remaining time, students may do their own searches. As you bookmark sites for your students, consider the following questions:

> Find some sites ahead of time and let the children customize the search in the remaining time

▓ Are there "biases, error, or misleading omissions in the document" (Branch, Kim, & Koenecke, 1999)?
▓ Is there advertising that is not appropriate for students?
▓ Is the information dated?
▓ Is the reading level appropriate?
▓ Is there unsuitable vocabulary or ethnic or gender stereotyping?
▓ Is the information clearly presented with appropriate headings and subheadings (Branch et al., 1999)?

If you decide that you will bookmark sites for students, you can still include sites that you consider poor because of biases, errors, or misleading omissions, and challenge your students to find the information that they should not use. This is one good step to prepare them for when they do their own searches on the open Internet.

Conducting Effective Searches   Searching is a skill for which there are helpful rules and tips. Not all search engines use exactly the same rules, but if the rules vary much from the rules in Table 3.2, there are usually instructions. Many children's search engines format these rules as menus, so that children do not have to remember the symbols. Ivy's Search Engine Resources for Kids, for example, not only provides menus that allow for menu-based searching, but also allows students to select the grade level of the text of articles in the list it returns.

> Search rules

Older students should learn more about effective search strategies. One good article on advanced search strategies can be found at www.searchenginewatch.com/facts/article.php/2156031. This article provides advanced search strategies and examples beyond those presented in Table 3.2. Strategies in Table 3.2 do not work for every engine. You must investigate strategies suitable for each search engine you use.

Analyzing

Information Literacy   Although we all try to teach children to be critical of the information that they gather, no matter where they get it, it is becoming increasingly important to teach them how to be critical readers because of the huge variation in the

TABLE 3.2 Conducting Effective Searches	
Symbol	**Example**
+ (plus sign) This sign marks search terms that must appear on each web page. When a term is not preceded by a plus sign, the engine considers it a request, not a requirement.	+ "Civil War" + "revolutionary war" + "War of 1812" The search above will return a list of pages on which all three of these wars are mentioned. The quotation marks tell the search engine to treat what is inside of them as a single search term.
– (minus sign) This sign marks words that you *do not* want to be present on any of the pages that the search returns.	+ reptiles + amphibians – arachnids This search limits sites to pages about reptiles and amphibians but not arachnids.
AND Using AND between two search terms prompts the engine to return a list of web pages that contain both terms.	"short story writers" AND playwrights
OR OR between two or more search terms returns a list of pages that contains at least one of the search terms.	llamas OR alpacas The search engine will produce a list of pages containing one of the other terms but not both.

quality of information they will find on the Internet. In the days when print was king, most (not all) widely circulated texts had some claim to legitimacy because a panel of editors or scholars had reviewed it. Now, any individual may post an opinion for all six billion people in the world to see, without consulting anyone. Consequently, one step in the research model is to authenticate and evaluate information.

When we assign a research project involving the Internet we are responsible for much more than reviewing students' work for accuracy. We must approach these projects from a meta-cognitive level (see Bloom's taxonomy, Table 3.4, to review "meta-cognitive level"). "The diverse perspectives within Internet-based environments provide opportunities for learners to develop evaluative standards to judge the merits of information and knowledge, thus exploring some epistemological issues" (Tsai, 2004, p. 537). These "opportunities" for students are challenges for teachers.

These challenges involve providing **scaffolding** for students to help them find answers for the following issues:

▥ Which information is more important than other information?
▥ Which information or knowledge items are more reliable and valid than others?
▥ What counts for "knowledge"?
▥ What is the nature of their knowledge (and learning)?
▥ How to resolve the conflicts between various perspectives of knowledge?
▥ How to effectively integrate all sorts of knowledge into a coherent or viable framework? (Tsai, 2004, p. 538)

SCAFFOLDING
The teaching of foundational ideas.

First, scaffolding will involve helping students with search strategies for information. Where are the best places to look? What are reliable sources in the content area? Who are recognized experts in the content area? What is a search term? What are relevant search terms for this project? Are there creative ways to use search terms to get more information? Next, scaffolding will help students identify useful and relevant information. In any given Internet search a student will receive thousands of links that might be helpful. How and why should the student distinguish between the relevant and the interesting? How is relevance determined (for example, does the information fit into an outline or concept map the student as created as a guide)? Finally, scaffolding will help students determine the correctness of the information they have found. Determining correctness, or authenticating information, is probably the most important task the student does. Without correctness, neither finding sources nor determining their relevance matters.

Authentication is the process of deciding whether the information is accurate. To do this, the student must answer some questions, such as:

Authenticating information

- ▓ Who wrote this? Is this person an expert or a lay person?
- ▓ Is the information based on facts, or is it an opinion?
- ▓ Is this person trying to convince readers about an ethical or moral issue?
- ▓ Is this person trying to sell something?
- ▓ Can I find two other corroborating articles or pieces of information?

One striking example of the need to teach children critical thinking skills is described by Alan November (1998) in *High School Principal* magazine. It is a true story of a 14-year-old student whose task was to research a unique topic. Zack, the 14-year-old, was doing research on the Holocaust. Based on an article that he found on the Internet, he told his teacher that he was working on a paper "about how the Holocaust never happened."

Zack found a paper on the Internet authored by Arthur R. Butz of Northwestern University that explains very logically how and why the Holocaust is a myth. The home page and the web site still exist. November goes on to quote the following material from the article, which you can read yourself if you go to http://pubweb.acns.nwu.edu/%7eabutz/di/intro.html:

> I see three principal reasons for the widespread but erroneous belief in the legend of millions of Jews killed by the Germans during World War II: US and British troops found horrible piles of corpses in the west German camps they captured in 1945 (e.g. Dachau and Belsen), there are no longer large communities of Jews in Poland, and historians generally support the legend.
>
> During both world wars Germany was forced to fight typhus, carried by lice in the constant traffic with the east. That is why all accounts of entry into the German concentration camps speak of shaving of hair and showering and other delousing procedures, such as treatment of quarters with the pesticide Zyklon. That was also the main reason for a high death rate in the camps, and the crematoria that existed in all.
>
> When Germany collapsed in chaos then of course all such defenses ceased, and typhus and other diseases became rampant in the camps, which quartered mainly

political prisoners, ordinary criminals, homosexuals, conscientious objectors, and Jews conscripted for labor. Hence the horrible scenes, which however had nothing to do with "extermination" or any deliberate policy. Moreover the west German camps involved were not the alleged "extermination camps," which were all in Poland (e.g. Auschwitz and Treblinka) and which were all evacuated or shut down before capture by the Soviets, who found no such scenes.

November points out that to a 14-year-old, this information might seem believable. It was, after all, written by a university professor.

November proceeds to point out that had Zack applied those bulleted principles discussed above, he might have discovered that the information in the article is not what it seems to be, nor is Professor Butz what he seems to be.

How would Zack have done this? Two key techniques that November cites and illustrates include:

- ▦ Doing a search on the author's name
- ▦ Looking at meta web information on the site

If Zack had done a web search on "Arthur Butz," he would have found this web page: www.williscarto.com/butz.html. On it he would have learned that Arthur Butz is Associate Professor of Electrical Engineering at Northwestern, not a history professor. Knowing that, he could have concluded that Arthur Butz has no special credibility in the field of history.

Second, if Zack had looked at some meta web information, he would have discovered that he was looking at a personal home page. He could have known this by looking at the web address of the site: http://pubweb.acns.nwu.edu/%7eabutz/di/intro.html. The letters "eabutz" are the clue that we are looking at someone's personal home page. A second kind of meta web information Zack could have gathered was information about what others think about Butz's site. He could have done this by using the Link command. Going to a search engine such as Google or Altavista, Zack could have typed in: link:http://pubweb.acns.nwu.edu/%7eabutz (note that there is no space on either side of the colon in the link command, and the the last element of the address indicates a directory and not a web page). When it is executed, this command searches the web for all links to Butz's web site. Some titles of sites linked to Butz's site include:

- ▦ *Northwestern on the Holocaust* Northwestern University's Response to Charges of Management Failure Relating to the Use of Its WWW Server for Publishing Holocaust-Revisionist Propaganda.
- ▦ *White Supremacists, Neo-Nazis, Holocaust Revisionists* Hate on the Internet. This page is dedicated to: White Supremacists, Neo-Nazis, Holocaust Revisionists, Racist Skinheads, The Klan
- ▦ *Holocaust Denial* Holocaust Denial Pathfinder. This guide is designed for anyone who is looking for information on the Holocaust denial movement.

This article points out how important it is that we teach students how to think about the information they find in the Internet. They must scrutinize their sources carefully, and they have some tools to help them do it.

This process is called triangulation (see Figure 3.1). Students should be careful about this step. If the original information came from the president of the Society for the Preservation of White Pine Trees, and the two corroborating pieces of information came from the vice president and secretary of the same organization, then the triangulation is a failure.

This step is quite time consuming but also key to teaching children how to negotiate the real-world questions that living in an information-based society poses for them. Remember that students may use other sources of information—books, encyclopedias, people—in conjunction with their Internet searches.

Applying   Once students have acquired information, they can analyze it and make judgments about it. The analysis and judgments usually are presented in a product: a report, presentation, chart, or graph. As you proceed through this book, you will find that there are intermediate steps between acquiring information and presenting the final product. You will learn that students may find information on the Internet and use a database, a spreadsheet, or presentation software to do the actual analysis.

> By applying information to solve a problem and draw a conclusion, children connect it to what they already know and consequently learn it

Assessing   After students have completed a research project and have had the opportunity to have their product evaluated either by peers or by their teacher, they should reflect on the research process itself. During this part of the project, they define what they have learned, how they learned it, and how the process they used could be modified (Jukes et al., 2000). This part of the process may be part of a class discussion or a journal entry. In an information-based society, knowing how we learn is nearly as important as what we learn.

> Reflection

The WebQuest

The WebQuest is a slightly different way of approaching Internet research than the research model we have just explored. It is an "inquiry-oriented activity in which some or all of the information that learners interact with comes from resources on the Internet, optionally supplemented with **videoconferencing**" (Dodge, 1998). In the case of a WebQuest, the videoconference could be between the class doing the WebQuest and an expert, or with another class on a similar quest. Dodge was one of the first to define and formally use the WebQuest. He indicates that there are two kinds of WebQuests,

> **VIDEOCONFERENCING**
> Participants use the Internet to send audio and video of themselves to other people.

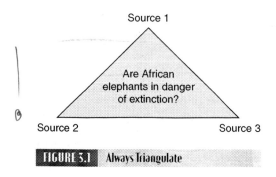

FIGURE 3.1   Always Triangulate

48

short-term and long-term. The goal of a WebQuest is to challenge students to use higher-order thinking skills (analysis, synthesis, and evaluation) as they interact with information. Before you read further, you should look at a sample WebQuest on the Internet to see how they are constructed. Just do an Internet search for WebQuest to find one. Also, you can check the Annotated Resources section of this chapter, where you will see references to more WebQuests in different content areas, if you would like to look at other examples.

Now that you have worked with a real WebQuest, we will spend some time thinking about the theoretical underpinnings of WebQuests and learning the steps teachers use to build them—that is, the *model*. WebQuests fit under the umbrella of constructivism because they include the following elements of the constructivist perspective:

- ▨ Multiple representations of content
- ▨ Student construction of content
- ▨ Complex learning environment
- ▨ Social negotiation and shared responsibility as a part of learning (WebQuests are often done as group projects.)

In other words, the question posed to the students cannot be answered simply by collecting and spitting back information. A WebQuest requires students to "transform information into something else. . . ." (March, 1998). Furthermore, WebQuests are an example of problem-based learning because they are "inquiry-oriented" and based on a "do-able, engaging task" (Dodge, 1998).

The steps for building a WebQuest include the following (Dodge, 1998):

- ▨ Introduction
- ▨ Task
- ▨ Process for completing the task
- ▨ Evaluation
- ▨ Conclusion

The list of steps for developing a WebQuest breaks down into some specific tasks for the teacher (Peterson & Koeck, 2002). During the *introduction* to the task, the teacher defines the problem and develops a set of open-ended questions for students to answer. To support the *process for completing the task,* the instructor searches for and evaluates resources on the web. In addition, the instructor builds a web site to display both instructions and links to resources. To *evaluate* student work, the instructor builds a rubric to guide students as they work through the WebQuest. Finally, the instructor *concludes* the project by synthesizing and discussing the students' work with them and possibly giving them ideas for new places to look for information. Peterson and Koeck suggest that once students have done a few WebQuests so that they understand the process, an even more challenging exercise is to have the students develop a WebQuest themselves. Peterson and Koeck (p. 12) provide a comparison (see Table 3.3) of the kinds of cognitive skills students use when they develop a WebQuest rather than just do one. To solidify your knowledge about WebQuests, you can go to http://

TABLE 3.3 Doing and Developing a Web Quest

Tasks for Developing a WebQuest	Tasks for Doing a WebQuest
Define a problem	Respond to a problem
Develop questions	Respond to questions
Search for and evaluate resources	Evaluate information within preselected resources
Design a site with an audience in mind	Navigate within a site
Work on a team for project creation	Work on a team for problem solution
Synthesize information	Synthesize information
Apply logical thinking	Apply logical thinking
Consider and accept multiple possible solutions	Arrive at a possible solution to the problem

webquest.sdsu.edu/webquestwebquest.html and try a WebQuest called "A WebQuest about WebQuests" (Dodge, 2003).

Using the online WebQuest(s) you reviewed as your model, think about your options for completing each step in the process of WebQuest creation. Thinking about the introduction and the task, you should remember, first of all, that the WebQuest you write should be carefully connected to the rest of your curriculum (March, 1998). It should build on what your students know and should include information and skills that are included in competencies required by your district or state. Once you are sure that your quest is connected to the curriculum, then you can design a problem. Examples of some classes of problems include:

■ Contemporary problems (human rights, ecology, politics)
■ Evaluating history (wars, tragedies, discoveries, exploration, the development of great ideas)
■ Understanding common activities (finding a job, taking a trip)
■ Using the imagination (journeys to distant places and times, including places where people can't go physically like inside of the human body or into space) (Yoder, 1999)

Note that WebQuest problems are written like a story, not an assignment. The teacher who authors a WebQuest should write to make the problem interesting with much descriptive detail. Typically the problems are fuzzy, meaning that there is not one correct answer.

Once the students understand the problem, they usually require help completing the associated tasks to solve the problem. Timelines help because they benchmark the activities and products that the WebQuest requires. It is also helpful to give students the **scoring rubric** that will be used to grade their work on the WebQuest. To see a sample scoring rubric for a WebQuest, go to http://edweb.sdsu.edu/webquest/webquestrubric.html.

Another important part of the teacher's work is to provide students with relevant resources. These may be found on the web, in print, or they may be people with whom

SCORING RUBRIC
Tool for grading assignments that do not end in an answer that is either right or wrong, used to help students understand how to complete the process properly and provide standards by which they can judge a finished product.

students correspond, have a videoconference, or meet in person. If you author your WebQuest on the web itself, you may include the resources as hyperlinks on your site. This is very efficient for students, who then do not have to type addresses to get to the information that they need. If you cannot put your quest on the web, then a list of links on paper will work. Be sure to include sources that do not always agree with each other or do not give the students a complete answer to the problem in one reading. The goal of the WebQuest, aside from providing an opportunity for students to learn many facts, is to give them an opportunity to analyze, synthesize, and evaluate multiple, incomplete, and conflicting sources of information.

In order to evaluate students' work with the WebQuest, they must produce some kind of product. Examples of kinds of products include:

- ▦ A searchable database in which the categories in each field were created by the learners
- ▦ A microworld that represents a physical space through which users can navigate
- ▦ An interactive story or case study created by learners
- ▦ A document that describes an analysis of a controversial situation, takes a stand, and invites users to add to or disagree with that stand
- ▦ A simulated person who can be interviewed. The questions and answers will be generated by learners who have deeply studied the person being simulated. (Dodge, 1997)

You can see that the WebQuest is a very structured Internet-supported research project. There are many WebQuests already written by teachers and available on the Internet. Before you write one of your own, you might consider using one that has already been written and tested, if you can find one that fits your curriculum. The first time you try the WebQuest with your students, you might also consider doing a short one more focused on facts, just to help both you and your students learn the process.

Copyright Issues and the Internet

Recognizing copyright issues should be a part of the curriculum that students learn by doing. In the course of any research project, students will use other authors' work. Students should use this information according to copyright guidelines and should cite authors, artists, musicians, and videographers appropriately. Knowing the rules is a matter of referring to guidelines, and proper citation is a matter of looking at templates for each kind of citation.

The TEACH (Technology, Education, and Copyright Harmonication) Act of 2002 When teachers use media they have not created themselves, there are some legal issues of which they should be aware. Copyright law, last updated in 1976, is the basis on which we treat information created by others in this society. However, educational institutions are special entities. The law recognizes that the foundation of a free society rests on the education of its people and that educational institutions must have access to information. At this point, the government attempted to amplify copyright law and develop a set of Fair Use Guidelines to provide educational institutions and their instructors the ability to use copyrighted information for free and without author permission for teaching purposes. Although the very large committee whose task it was to develop these Fair Use Guidelines could not come to a consensus about the guidelines, they nevertheless published them as their best effort, and they are endorsed by the U.S. Copyright Office.

However, the Fair Use Guidelines are not the end of the story. The landscape of education and the delivery of information to students have changed dramatically even since the Fair Use Guidelines were written. Consequently, Congress wrote the TEACH Act (107th Congress, 1st Session, 2002). Fundamental to the TEACH Act are the following guidelines:

1. Previous to the TEACH Act, many dramatic works as well as audiovisual materials and sound recordings could not be displayed electronically. Now they can. Works that can be displayed electronically include:
   ▨ Performances of nondramatic literary works
   ▨ Performances of nondramatic musical works
   ▨ Performances of any other work, including dramatic works and audiovisual works, but only in "reasonable and limited portions"
   ▨ Displays of any work "in an amount comparable to that which is typically displayed in the course of a live classroom session." (American Library Association, 2004)
2. Works specifically excluded are materials created for instruction on digital networks. This means that you cannot, for example, take the materials from a CD accompanying an examination copy of a text and use them with your students. You buy the books in order to use them.
3. Instructors should accompany the digital materials that they use with instruction. It must be evident that they are related to material in your class.
4. If you digitize analog works (convert a videotape to a digital format, for example), you should only convert the amount of material that conforms to the law, and you should only digitize works that have not already been digitized.
5. All copies of material distributed electronically should be made from legal sources.

There is one more question to consider: "How much information should a teacher use, and what can be done with it?" The answer must be general, because institutions may create their own guidelines. A good set of guidelines can be found at www.halldavidson.net/copyright_chart.pdf (Davidson, 2002). Check the "Resources" section at the end of this chapter to find the web addresses of all of these documents.

Understanding Plagiarism and Copyright Infringement   Because electronic information is so easy to acquire and use, teachers often find themselves confronting students who have either plagiarized or infringed on a copyright. The difference between copyright infringement and plagiarism is a fine one, and neither is ethical. Copyright infringement occurs when someone other than the copyright holder reproduces a work without permission. Music sharing is an example of copyright infringement. Digitizing a short story and e-mailing it to students or printing it out for all of them to read is another example of copyright infringement. Plagiarism, on the other hand, occurs when people present someone else's work and pass it off as their own.

Given the plethora of term papers and other information online, it is easy for students simply to cut and paste. Teachers can combat this when they suspect it. One easy way is to cut and paste a sample of the suspicious writing into a search engine such as Google. There are also sites that specialize in helping teachers find plagiarized information. TurnItIn.com is one of the best.

Proper Citation of Multimedia Materials   Teaching students to cite their sources is important. Ethics entailed in fair use guidelines require it, and by engaging in the process your students will acquire a skill they will use for a lifetime. Following is a general citation model (Grabe & Grabe, 2000):

Author/editor. (Year). Title (edition) [Type of medium]. Producer (optional). Available: Protocol (e.g., ftp, http): Site/Path//file. [Access date].

An example of this format looks like the reference below:

Ekham, L. (1999). Tips for promoting collaboration and interactivity in online distance learning. State College of Education, University of West Georgia, USA. Available: http://computed.coe.wayne.edu/Vol5/Ekhaml.html. [Retrieved from the World Wide Web on 8/28/00].

The reason the access date is included is because of the transient nature of information on the Internet. Date of access gives a reader some idea of how efficient it might be to try to find a piece of information. The older the retrieval date, the less likely the information still resides at the quoted Internet address.

Bloom's Taxonomy and Internet Research

Student research on the Internet is a complex process that promotes thinking at many levels of the taxonomy. In a sense, the unreliability of the accuracy of information on the Internet is helpful. Students no longer can copy information as they once did from encyclopedias and hand it in either untransformed or only modestly modified or paraphrased. In addition, strict adherence to copyright laws also prevents students from using just one author to provide them with information. Although teachers must always be alert to the students who cut and paste information from sites they find on the Internet, students who follow the rules work at almost all levels of the taxonomy (Table 3.4).

⬤ LISTSERVS

Listservs are like mailing lists

Being on a computer listserv is like being on a mailing list. Listservs are focused discussions on a specific topic. When a member of a list e-mails information on the topic at hand, the rest of the members of the list receive that e-mail and may respond to it if they have something pertinent to say.

Mailing lists are not all the same size. Some lists have hundreds of members who have communicated for several years, whereas other lists are for small, local discus-

TABLE 3.4 Bloom's Taxonomy Revised

The Cognitive Process Dimension	The Knowledge Dimension			
	Factual	**Conceptual**	**Procedural***	**Meta-Cognitive**
Remember	Use Internet searches to acquire facts	Use the Internet to determine the properties associated with concepts	–	–
Understand	Understand relationships among facts	Use the multiple sources of information about a concept to construct a schema (give meaning to an abstract idea)	–	What counts as knowledge
Apply	Use facts to solve a problem/answer a question	Relate the new concepts to other concepts	–	Knowing which items are more reliable or valid than others
Analyze	Use triangulation to analyze facts	Classify new instances of a concept—use information on the Internet to find new instances and check their classification	–	How to resolve conflicts among various pieces of information
Evaluate	Based on triangulation, decide which information is accurate	Based on triangulation—multiple sources of information about the same concept—judge, criticize, or otherwise come to conclusions about ideas that the learning of new concepts generate	–	Knowing which information is more important than other information
Create	Synthesize the acquired facts into a product	Create a web site, concept map, paper, speech, poster, PowerPoint or other presentation that explains the concept(s) being studied	–	How to integrate all kinds of knowledge into a coherent whole

*Many of the items listed for concept knowledge apply somewhat to procedural knowledge. However, procedural knowledge is a different kind of knowledge not usually associated with the fact gathering we do on the Internet.

sions devoted to a topic that lasts only a few months. Since the software and computing resources for managing a list are neither complex nor expensive, school districts or universities may maintain such lists for instructors who want the advantages of the mailing list format for class discussion.

Large, public mailing lists are another source of information available on the Internet, especially if you or your students have a question for which you cannot find an answer. As a user, you may subscribe to a list and unsubscribe from a list as well. The only software you need for using a list is your e-mail software. However, there are some conventions and procedures you should be aware of if you decide you want to subscribe to a mailing list.

Each list has two different addresses, an administrative address and a submission address. If you want to join a list, remove yourself from a list, or suspend receipt of mail from the list while you are on vacation, you send messages to the administrative address of the list. If you want to submit e-mail related to the discussion at hand, you send your messages to the submission address.

To join a list you should create a message addressed to the administrative address of the list, leave the subject line blank, and in the body of the messages type: subscribe listname (your) firstname lastname. If I were to join the Community Learning Network (CLN) list (a list of educational lists), I would send an e-mail to the administrative address of the list with a blank subject head and the following message: subscribe CLN_UPDate Carolyn Thorsen. Once I have done this, I will begin receiving all of the e-mail that the members of the list send. I will also receive a list of instructions from the administrator of the list that will tell me how to suspend receipt of e-mail while I am gone, and other options. It is important to keep this information. To remove my name from a list, I have to create an e-mail addressed to the administrative address saying: unsubscribe listname.

There are many lists for educators. There are indexes of listservs to help you find a listserv you need. A good example of a list of listservs is the Community Learning Network, maintained by a Canadian educational organization. To give you an idea of the variety of lists available that are of interest to educators, the mailing lists posted by this organization beginning with the letter "e" are in Table 3.5.

The CLN is an especially good location for finding educational listservs. The lists themselves are reviewed for content. In addition, if you subscribe to the CLN list itself, the organization sends weekly bulletins detailing new lists that appear on the Internet. Because lists are public, anyone can submit a comment. Unless you are sure of the contributors to a list, it is wise to subscribe to a list and monitor it for a while before you allow your students access to the list. Another way of working with a list in a K–12 classroom is to subscribe to the list yourself and e-mail appropriate entries to your students by using your e-mail client to forward them.

CHECKING YOUR UNDERSTANDING

3.1

Problem 1
To become a good searcher you must know a little about your tools—search engines, for example. For this exercise, search "Information Literacy" in each of the search engines listed in Table 3.1. Answer the following questions:

■ Which search engine gives you the *most* hits?
■ Which search engine gives you the most *relevant* hits?
■ Which search engine gave you the *best* hit?

Now repeat the previous exercise using "Plagiarism" and "WebQuest" as your search terms and answer the three questions above about each term. Choose and read what you believe are the best articles. List the criteria you used to determine which articles are best.

Problem 2
Develop a topic for a research project for a class that you teach or will teach someday. Using Table 3.2, construct a list of at least twenty search terms that you would use to gather information on this topic. A search term or key word is a combination of words and symbols found in Table 3.2. Write down the search terms and conduct the search for each term using one of the search engines listed for adults in Table 3.1. Record how many hits you get for each search term. Record how much usable information you obtain from each search. Now repeat your search using one of the children's search

engines. Again, record the number of hits and the quality of information that you receive. Write a short paper on your experience with searching using the two different kinds of search engines.

DISTANCE LEARNING

Distance learning is a rapidly growing area in education that serves students who cannot attend school in a traditional manner. Most distance courses are delivered using one of two delivery technologies: interactive television (IT) and the Internet. These technologies allow students dispersed over a wide geographic area to get instruction. There are a number of reasons for using one or the other of these technologies. Small, rural districts find them useful because they provide courses that students would otherwise be unable to take, such as AP (advanced placement) classes and foreign language classes. They are also useful for students who cannot be in a traditional classroom because of job or family responsibilities. These two technologies are alike in that they serve populations that are not served by the traditional classroom. They are different because students in an interactive television class must "attend" at a specified time, whereas Internet-based coursework can be completed by a student working alone, at any time of the day (or night).

Interactive Television

Interactive television is delivered using a variety of technologies—microwave, satellite, fiber optic cable, cable, and digital telephone lines. The instructor and even part of the class may be in one location while the rest of the class is in several different locations. Each location can see the other location, though few systems allow participants to see all locations at once. In a typical configuration, the instructor talks to a class, which meets simultaneously in several different geographic locations. The instructor can

TABLE 3.5 Educationally Appropriate Mailing Lists Beginning with the Letter "E"

earth	euthanasia	Egypt	England	equity
earthquakes	evangelism	elections	English	ergonomics
eating	events	electrical	enlightenment	estates
ecology	evolution	electromagnetics	entertainerment	ethics
economics	exercise	electronics	entertaining	Ethiopia
economy	exhibitors	email	entertainment	ethnicity
ecosystems	existentialism	emergencies	entomology	ethnography
editing	exobiology	emergency	entrepreneur	ethnology
editorials	expatriates	emigrants	environment	Eritrea
editors	exploration	employees	environmental	eugenics
export	extraterrestrial	employment	epilepsy	Eurasia
ezines	engineering	energy	epson	Europe

Source: Community Learning Network, www.cln.org/lists/home.html.

see one other location on a monitor but hear comments from all of the locations. To display information to the class, instructors have various display devices that make their job easier. For example, they can switch the video output, allowing students to see the instructor's computer screen rather than the instructor. Students can still hear the instructor explain what is on the computer screen. When student attention needs to be focused on notes being written on a large pad of paper, the instructor clicks another button to switch to a camera positioned over the pad. These cameras are called document cameras. Sometimes the instructor can split the video so that both the pad of paper and the instructor appear on the screen for the students. This allows students to both see the pad of paper being used as a chalkboard and to see their instructor at the same time. Instructors also may use video output to a VCR, allowing their students to view a video as well.

> **Teaching techniques**

You may one day teach using such an arrangement. A well-designed instructor station that provides the tools described in the last paragraph is not difficult to learn to use. It is disconcerting at first not to have face-to-face contact with all of your students. You must make a conscious effort to include everyone—to keep switching the video that you see to different sites so that all of your students feel they are a part of the class. Getting students from different sites to interact with each other and with the rest of the class takes an extra awareness and special planning on the part of the instructor. Increasingly, school districts have this technology available, and knowing how to use this kind of classroom is an advantage when you seek employment.

The Internet and Distance Education

The Internet is a rapidly evolving component of K–12 education. Chances are, in your professional lifetime you will teach or take a class delivered over the Internet. Distance-based programs are accredited by many agencies. The Commission on Trans-Regional Accreditation (CITA) is one notable example of such an organization. It accredits more than 30,000 public and private institutions in 100 countries serving more than 10 million students (CITA, 2007). If you were to look at the CITA's distance accreditation standards, you would not see anything that looks very different than accreditation standards for a physical school.

Distance education takes many forms. It may be a simple correspondence course conducted on paper. It may be conducted with interactive television, or it may be delivered using the Internet. It is on this third method of delivering distance instruction that we will concentrate.

If you have never taken a class delivered on the Internet, you may wonder how this instruction takes place. You may have questions like the following:

▦ How are complex concepts explained in online classes? Isn't learning over the Internet like a correspondence course?
▦ Do teachers who teach using the Internet need special skills?
▦ Is there special software or equipment that is useful in online courses?
▦ Can the depth of student/teacher dialogue found in a site-based class take place in a course delivered on the Internet?

How are complex concepts explained over the Internet? Unlike the Internet of even five years ago, which was, for instructional purposes, mostly text based with a few graphics for support, today's Internet provides many methods for delivering information. Complex concepts often need to be delivered to learners in many different formats: text, audio, video, animation. Additionally, these formats should include some interactivity with either the information (such as interactive software) or with the teacher.

The question arises, "Do students learn as much when they take a class on the Internet as they do when they are physically present in a classroom? Current studies support the conclusion that there is no difference between what students learn online and what they learn in a traditional classroom (Cavenaugh et al., 2004).

Do teachers who teach on the Internet need special skills? Teachers who teach this way must bring not only their traditional skill set to their teaching but also some additional skills. They must understand the fundamentals of instructional design and the presentation of information. Paying attention to information presented in Educational Psychology classes and in introductory computer classes is of great importance. Teachers should have a deep and thorough knowledge of computer tools—word processors, presentation software, graphics programs, course management tools (sometimes called Virtual Learning Environments, VLEs), **chat rooms,** and e-mail programs—and know how to create and upload both audio and video files. Knowing how to arrange information on a screen (Chapter 6 in this book) is also very important.

Teaching online

Is there special software or equipment that is useful in online courses? VLEs provide teachers and students a framework that allows the ordinary functions of classroom activities to take place. A current search for VLEs yielded thirty-two different systems. Among the largest and most well known are Blackboard, Web CT, Breeze, Illuminate, and Moodle. The first four cost the sponsoring institution much money, in the tens of thousands of dollars, and need their own server. Moodle, a very popular VLE with online instructors and useful from grades 7–20 is open source (anyone may see and change the code that supports it) and free.

VLEs organize a distance course and allow for the methods and procedures that we follow in classrooms that provide a motivating and helpful learning experience. Following is a list of functions that VLEs often often provide.

■ Information to be learned—usually a place where links to instructor-made files (text, audio, and video) are available
■ Assignments
■ Turning in assignments
■ Grade book visible to students where individual students see only their own grade
■ Grade book where instructors enter student grades. Depending on the grade book, most will allow different point assignments as well as averages.
■ Testing and survey creation. Many VLEs allow for the creation of several different kinds of tests: multiple choice (and within the multiple choice category, tests that allow either one or several answers per question), surveys, essay tests, and matching.
■ Announcements
■ Chat rooms and e-mail

CHAT ROOM
A computer site where two or more participants conduct a conversation with text messages in "real time."

Not every VLE has every capability, and sometimes instructors use two VLEs. For example, an instructor may use Moodle to support text/graphic based instruction, e-mail, and online chats, and Breeze to support video and audio conferencing with students. Breeze capabilities include both 1-to-1 conversations as well as group and whole class meetings.

Figures 3.2 and 3.3 are examples from a real-life implementation of Moodle. They are from the same screen, with Figure 3.3 being the second half of the screen. Notice the different kinds of presentations, resources, and help that are available to students. Not everything is based in Moodle. There are links to other software with different capabilities.

Can the depth of student/teacher dialogue found in a site-based class take place in a course delivered on the Internet?   Five or ten years ago this was a valid question, when the only way that students could communicate with each other and with the instructor was with e-mail. However, the emergence of new Internet tools has made it possible for instructors to meet with students individually using chat, audio, and video. In addition, instructors can meet with groups of students or a whole class simultaneously.

Breeze, an Adobe product, allows an instructor to meet simultaneously with a group of students, some of whom might have high-speed Internet connections that support video while others might have Internet connections that support only audio. During that meeting, students see video of the instructor. The instructor can yield control to students who are, for example, giving a presentation to the class or small group. The person giving the presentation can display a file that supports the presentation, such as a graph, chart, or PowerPoint. Students can take notes that are saved as text files to their accounts, and page other students or the instructor for a private or public conversation (if, for example, they have a question).

Instructors can take polls during the class. For example, if there is uncertainty about whether students know the difference between when to use *like* and when to use *as* before a lesson on writing, the instructor quickly types in a sentence that uses *as* incorrectly and then asks the students to click on either Correct or Incorrect in a dialogue box on their screens. Results of this informal poll are displayed immediately and the instructor learns that only 30 percent of the class answered correctly, so some scaffolding is necessary before the main lesson starts.

Teaching and learning on the Internet are exciting and promising frontiers in education that have a place in the lives of many different kinds of students: nontraditional students (those who must work or travel, for example), those who are ill, and those who wish to take classes not offered at their current location. Some students and parents simply prefer this kind of learning. It is cost effective because there are no physical facilities required other than a server and supporting software.

Recap of Key Elements of Distance Instruction

Whether you are using interactive television or computer-mediated instruction as a teacher, student, or as a counselor to students who are taking a distance course, there are some critical elements for success. Garrels (1997) describes four critical elements for successful teaching and learning at a distance:

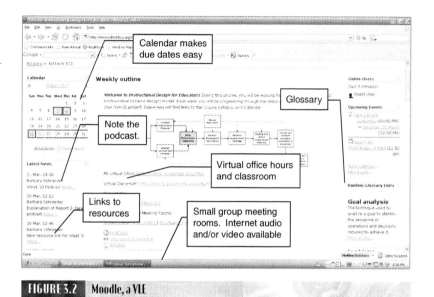

FIGURE 3.2 Moodle, a VLE

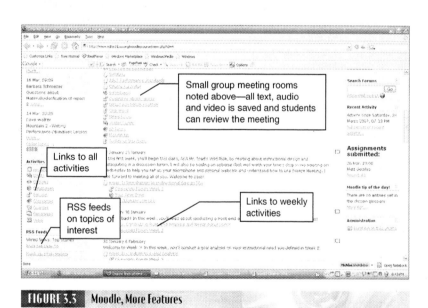

FIGURE 3.3 Moodle, More Features

- ▦ Instructor enthusiasm. This requires animation and comfort in front of the cameras, or with the technology utilized. Faculty support and interest are critical to the success of distance learning endeavors.
- ▦ Organization. Teaching materials must be prepared in advance; timing, variation, and smooth transitions must be planned. Instructors should allocate from three to five hours of preparation for each hour of distance instruction. Great attention to detail is required long before the actual classroom activity occurs.

■ Strong commitment to student interaction. Whatever the modality used to teach at a distance, the instructor must encourage and facilitate ongoing communication between the students and the instructor.

■ Familiarity with the technology used in the class format.

■ SUMMARY

The Internet is a vast repository of information that varies in quality. The U.S. government funded its development to provide for rapid and reliable communications and data transfer among scientists and the military. Today's Internet has become a powerful teaching tool because of the amount and variety of information that resides there and because it provides for the rapid exchange of information. In order to find this information, students must learn to use search engines and search strategies. The one important caveat for all to remember is that the variation in the quality of information places the burden on the student to be information literate—to know which information is the most usable and to use triangulation to test the accuracy of information.

The Internet has also opened up a new format for learning called the virtual classroom. Students who cannot attend class because they are ill, have family responsibilities, or live in rural or remote areas now have the opportunity to take courses and in some cases earn certificates or degrees over the Internet. Being a teacher or student in a distance class requires a new set of skills and a different mindset. Students must be motivated self-starters. Students taking computer-mediated distance instruction must have a basic set of computer competencies as well as the ability to learn with less visual and kinesthetic input than they receive in a traditional classroom.

CHECKING YOUR UNDERSTANDING

3.2 In the Annotated Resources sections of this book, you will find web addresses for the references you will need for the following activities. Read the following scenarios and describe how you would handle the copyright and fair use issues associated with each.

a. You have created an electronic presentation for your class and want to use several graphics from Intel's web site, The Journey Inside (www.intel.com/education/journey/index.htm). Do you need to cite these graphics in your presentation? Where do you place the citation? What would the citation look like?

b. Several of your students have digitized several short scenes from *Hamlet* to illustrate Hamlet's difficulty making a decision about revenge. They display these scenes on a web site along with explanation. Is it legal for your students to make the conversion? Is it legal for them to display the conversion on the Internet? How long should the scenes be? Do they have to cite the scenes? Where should they place the citation? What should the citation look like?

c. You have found an article in *Time* magazine that you would like your students to read, so you digitize it and give them access to it using your school's server. Is this legal?

▓ REFERENCES ▓

American Library Association. (2004). New copyright law for distance education: The meaning and importance of the TEACH Act. *Distance education and the teach act.* www.ala.org/Template.cfm?Section=Distance_Education_and_the_TEACH_Act&Template=/ContentManagement/ContentDisplay.cfm&ContentID=25939#context. Retrieved August 16, 2004.

Anderson, L., Krathwohl, D., Airasian, P., Cruikshand, K., Mayer, R., Pintrich, P., Raths, J., & Wittrock, M. (2001). *A taxonomy for learning, teaching, and assessing.* New York: Longman.

Branch, R. M., Kim, D., & Koenecke, L. (1999). Evaluating online educational materials for use in instruction. ERIC ED430564.

Bush, V. (1945). As We May Think. *Atlantic Monthly.* July 1945.

Cavanaugh, C., Gillan, K., Kromrey, J., Hess, M., & Blomeyer, B. (2004). The Effects of Distance Education on K–12 Student Outcomes: A Meta-Analysis. Naperville, IL: Learning Point Associates. www.ncrel.org/tech/distance/index.html. Retrieved April 1, 2007.

CITA. (2007). www.citaschools.org. Retrieved March 22, 2007.

Davidson, H. (2002, October). Copyright and fair use guidelines for teachers. *Tech-Learning.* www.halldavidson.net/copyright_chart.pdf. Retrieved August 16, 2004.

Dodge, B. (1997). "Some thoughts about WebQuests." http://edweb.sdsu.edu/courses/edtec596/about_webquests.html. Retrieved April 2, 2001.

Dodge, B. (1998). Webquests: A strategy for scaffolding higher level learning. Presented at the National Educational Computing Conference, San Diego. http://edweb.sdsu.edu/webquest/necc98.htm. Retrieved August 13, 2004.

Dodge, B. (2003, February). *A web quest about web quests,* http://webquest.sdsu.edu/webquestwebquest.html. Retrieved August 13, 2004.

Garrels, M. (1997). Dynamic relationships: Five critical elements for teaching at a distance. Faculty development papers. Indiana Higher Education Telecommunication System. www.ihets.org/distance-ed/fpapers/1997/garrels.html. Retrieved September 15, 2001.

Grabe, M., & Grabe, C. (2000). *Integrating the Internet for meaningful learning.* Boston: Houghton Mifflin.

Grimes, B. (2000, August). The best of the web. *PC World.* p. 108.

Jonassen, D. (2000). *Computers as mindtools for schools: Engaging critical thinking.* Upper Saddle River, NJ: Prentice-Hall.

Jukes, I., Dosaj, A., & McCain, I. (2000). It's not the Internet, it's the information: Net savvy for the information highway (presentation handout). Thornburg Center for Professional Development, www.thecommittedsardine.net/handouts/in.tiiti.pdf. Retrieved October 1, 2000.

Leiner, B., Cerf, V., Clark, D., Kahn, R., Kleinrock, L., Lynch, J., Roberts, L., & Wolff, S. (2000). A brief history of the Internet by the men who built it. www.isoc.org/internet/history/brief.shtml. Retrieved February 12, 2001.

Licklider, J. C. R. (1960, March). Man-computer symbiosis. *IRE* (now IEEE) *Transactions on Human Factors in Electronics.* HFE-1, 4–11.

March, T. (1998). Why Webquests? An introduction. http://ozline.com/webquests/intro.html. Retrieved April 5, 2001.

Markham, T., Larmer, J., & Ravitz, J. (2003). Project Based Learning. Novato, CA: Buck Institute for Education.

November, A. A. (1998, September). *The web—Teaching Zack to think.* http://anovember.com/articles/zack.html. Retrieved August 11, 2004.

Peterson, C. L., & Koeck, D. (2002). When students create their own WebQuests. *Leading and Learning with Technology.* 29(1), 10–15.

Tsai, C. (2004). Beyond cognitive and metacognitive tools: The use of the Internet as an 'epistemological' tool for instruction. *British Journal of Educational Technology.* 35(5), 525–536.

Yoder, M. (1999). The student WebQuest. *Leading and Learning with Technology.* 26(7), 6–9.

■ ANNOTATED RESOURCES

www.big6.com (Retrieved April 2, 2007)

The "Big 6 Research Model" has six steps: task definition, information-seeking strategies, location and access, use of information, synthesis, and evaluation. The site provides detailed information on how to implement this model in a classroom. K–3 teachers, look for the link "the super three" under resources for an age-appropriate model.

Bolkan, J. (2006). Avoiding the plague: Tips and tricks for preventing and detecting plagiarism. *Learning and Leading with Technology.* March.

You are not completely helpless against students who plagiarize. This article by practicing teachers provides techniques to help you find the cheaters.

Chen, D., Wong, A., Hsu, J. (2003). Internet-based instructional activities: Not everything should be on the Internet. *Journal of Research on Technology in Education.* 36(1), 50–59.

This article helps achieve a balanced perspective on using the Internet in the classroom.

www.cln.org/lists/home.html

Community Learning Network. This site is a list of lists. It is especially helpful because it is edited for educational content. As a teacher I would be reluctant to recommend that students themselves join a list, because lists are open to the public and the quality of discussion varies. On the other hand, as a teacher I would join a list myself to learn about the latest issues, arguments, and information on a topic of interest.

Etter, S., Cramer, J., & Finn, S. (2006). Origins of academic dishonesty: Ethical orientations and personality factors associated with attitudes about cheating with information technology. *Journal of Research on Technology in Education.* 39(2), 133–155.

Find out more about the kind of people who cheat with information technology. If you understand the underlying mindset you may be able to talk to your students about these underlying attitudes and provide some scaffolding for your discussions of plagiarism. The students studied in this article are college age, but the information about them can be generalized.

Feyton, M., Ducher, Y., Park, C., & Meros, J. (2002). *Teaching ESL/EFL with the Internet: Catching the wave.* Upper Saddle River, NJ: Merrill/Prentice Hall.

This is a practical approach full of daily lesson plans and activities for the ESL/EFL teacher. ISBN-13-088540-1.

Keating, M., Wiles, J., & Piazza, M. (2002). *LearningWebs: Curriculum journeys on the Internet.* Upper Saddle River, NJ: Merrill/Prentice Hall.

This book has many ideas for using the Internet, as well as a comprehensive listing of sites with information from "Aardvark" to "Zebras." To give you a flavor for some of the topics in between, topics include weather, rainforests, world literature, wedding customs, subtraction, and Vikings.

Leiner, B., Cerf, V., Clark, D., Kahn, R., Kleinrock, L., Lynch, J., Roberts, L., & Wolff, S. (2003). A brief history of the Internet. www.isoc.org/internet/history/brief.shtml. Retrieved April 4, 2007.

Previous editions of this book had a discussion of how the Internet evolved, a fascinating topic. Not unlike other technologies (nuclear power for example), it came about because of the need for rapid communication among scientists during the development of the atomic bomb. Many of the authors of this article were participants in the development of the early Internet. This is a fascinating read and not so dense that it is difficult. The authors talk about the future of the Internet, as well.

www.lib.berkeley.edu/TeachingLib/Guides/Internet/MetaSearch.html (June 2006)

Written in 2006, this short piece provides more information on meta-search engines along with some cautions about using them.

Lim, B. (2004). Challenges and issues in designing inquiry on the Web. *British Journal of Educational Technology.* 35(5), 627–643.

This article presents a thorough discussion of 6 issues involved in the design of instruction in which students use the Internet to seek information.

www.searchenginewatch.com/facts/article.hph/2156031 (Retrieved April 2, 2007)

This article provides advanced search strategies and examples beyond those presented in this chapter.

BOX 3.2 ADDITIONAL INTERNET SOURCES

The following Internet addresses and articles will provide you with more information about copyright guidelines, the TEACH Act, and fair use policies.

Educational Multimedia Fair Use Guidelines Development Committee. Fair Use Guidelines for educational multimedia.

Johnson, D., & Simpson, C. (2005). Are you the copy cop? *Learning and Leading with Technology.* 32(7), 14–20. www.utsystem.edu/ogc/intellectualproperty/ccmcguid.htm. Retrieved April 2, 2007.

107th Congress, 1st Session. (2002, November). *S. 487 An Act.* http://frwebgate.access.gpo.gov/cgi-bin/getdoc.cgi?dbname=107_cong_bills&docid=f:s487es.txt.pdf. Retrieved April 2, 2007.

Langran, E., & Langran, R. (2005). Copyright law and technology. *Learning and Leading with Technology.* 32(7), 24–26.

No Author. (2005). Copyright resources. *Learning and Leading with Technology.* 32(7), 22–23.

Thompson, K. (2005). Copyright 101. *Learning and Leading with Technology.* 32(7), 10–12.

Scheidet, R. (2003). Improving student achievement by infusing a web-based curriculum into global history. *Journal of Research on Technology in Education.* 36(1), 77–94.

Key concepts covered in this article include multimedia learning, web-based curriculum, and self-directed learning activities. The article discusses how teachers use the web to promote all three.

Tallent-Runnels, M. K., et al. (2006). Teaching courses online: A review of the research. *Review of Educational Research.* 76(1), 93–135.

This is an in-depth and more technical discussion of teaching online. It covers the effects of demographics of the online population in detail.

Tan, S. C., Yeo, J., and Lim, Y. (2005). Changing epistemology of science learning through Inquiry with computer-supported collaborative learning. *The Journal of Computers in Mathematics and Science Teaching.* 24(4), 367–86.

This is a discussion of teaching students how to be scientists using the Internet. It is a study of 13 secondary school students who participated in a research project. The research question was whether their inquiry skills improved as they completed and Internet-based research project.

Tsai, C. (2004). Beyond cognitive and metacognitive tools: The use of the Internet as an 'epistemological' tool for instruction. *British Journal of Educational Technology.* 35(5), 525–536.

This article is an excellent tie-in to the metacognitive level of Bloom's taxonomy. It talks about evaluating the information and knowledge found on the Internet and also shows how the ability to evaluate information makes people more effective users of the Internet.

Watkins, R., & Corry, M. (2004). *E-Learning Companion.* Boston: Houghton Mifflin.

This book and its associated web site are helpful introductions for student who need to know more about taking a class online. It is written simply, for students who do not have a great deal of technical background. It addresses such topics as maximizing your potential for success, planning, time management, e-learning vocabulary, technical tips, developing online relationships, study tips, and motivation.

Companion Web Site   www.ablongman.com/thorsen3e

1. Go to the TechTactics web site for Chapter 3 and click on the link called Information for Student Research in the Content Areas: KidsConnect. Use the content and grades that you teach, or plan to teach, as a basis for your thought process. Design an introductory lesson for your class based on the research process listed in this web site.

2. Go to the TechTactics web site for Chapter 3 and click on the link called The WebQuest with Examples: WebQuests—A Strategy for Scaffolding Higher Level Learning. Using one of the WebQuests at the bottom right as a basis for your work, explain how this WebQuest satisfies each of the categories listed in the other boxes (Definitions, Parts, Underpinnings, etc.).

4

Web Tools

OBJECTIVES

- Describe the elements of e-mail software using appropriate terminology.
- Describe basic models for teaching e-mail–supported lessons.
- Judge the quality of student work based on e-mail–supported lesson models.
- Describe the elements of Internet conferencing.
- Provide models of teaching for Internet conferencing-supported lessons.
- Judge the quality of student work based on Internet conferencing-supported lessons.
- Describe uses for, as well as tools and skills for, creating web pages.

This chapter is about teaching models that use e-mail. This seemingly simple technology, which many of us take for granted, has much potential for improving student communication and writing skills (Russell, 2001). Effective use of e-mail technology depends on the teacher's skill in applying an appropriate teaching model and using the intrinsic motivation that writing for an audience supplies for students. To get the most out of reading this chapter you should be able to:

- Address and send an e-mail
- Add entries to an address book
- Find entries in an address book
- Make a distribution list (nicknames) and save it
- Use a distribution list (nicknames) to send the same e-mail to several different people
- Make folders (mailboxes) for filing the e-mail messages you receive
- Make rules (filters) for screening or directing your e-mail to special folders
- Add an attachment to an e-mail message
- Open an attachment (text or graphic) to an e-mail message
- Save an attachment to an e-mail message in a file on your hard drive or other media
- Know how to forward a message

E-MAIL

E-mail software (called *clients*) allows users to communicate with each other **asynchronously.** If you want your students to communicate with students in another school, district, state, or country, e-mail is an ideal medium for two reasons. First, because it is asynchronous, e-mail enables you to avoid scheduling conflicts caused by different daily schedules, school vacation schedules, and time zones—problems that are inherent in some other technologies such as telephone conferencing. A second important advantage of e-mail is motivation. Students write better when they know they are writing for an audience (Gordon, 1999; Harrington, Holik, & Hurt, 1998; Lambert, 1999; Stoicheva, 2000). If the students are not initially motivated, they become motivated. The scenario in the next few paragraphs is real writing from real seventh-grade students.

Scenario

Seventh-grade students are engaged in an electronic debate (e-mail is the tool). School 1 is debating School 2 on the topic of whether people are responsible for their actions if they are under the influence of drugs or alcohol. The two classes have just read a novel in which the main character had to make this decision. The "Barbarians" is the name of one group of four students involved in the debate. The "Piranhas" is the name of the other group of four students.

School 1

"Dear Barbarians,

We desagree. For the first time the punishment should have got and 2 week in community service. The fine was to expensive since she returned the bracelet and worked most of it the fine should only be $200."

School 2

"Dear Piranhas,

Again, we disagree completely. And for one, Kit didn't return the bracelet; she got caught. Also, her community services were fine because she needed to learn. She should have been given the full time because if they let her off easy this time, she might think she could get off the hook again. Also, in the end the community services helped her figure her problem out.

P.S.

Your writing was confusing and difficult to understand. We usually check our work before we send it."

E-MAIL SOFTWARE
A program such as Eudora, Pegasus, or Microsoft Outlook, used for writing and sending messages.

ASYNCHRONOUS COMMUNICATION
The parties involved are not all present at the same time. Messages sent are not received or acted upon until later; examples are U.S. mail and e-mail. In contrast, a phone conversation is synchronous.

After that postscript, the Piranhas did check their writing before they sent it. They were embarrassed. The Barbarians learned the effect of sloppiness as well. When they sent their admonition back to the Piranhas, they checked it many times so they would not leave an opening for their opponents to level a similar accusation.

The question now is, "How does one set up an effective lesson that uses e-mail, a listserv, or a discussion board?" To begin to answer that question we will take our next field trip. Be aware that during our field trips, events do not always occur the way the teacher expects them to. Unexpected circumstances pop up when you are using computers in the teaching process. It is as important to know what to do when things go wrong as it is to know the correct way to lay out a technology-supported lesson. With that introduction, let us begin with our next field trip.

Solving a Problem

FIELD TRIP
4.1

Ms. Anderson's fifth-grade social studies class was buzzing with excitement. Ms. Anderson had recently begun a unit on the geography of their state, and the students had a problem to solve. When they began the unit, Ms. Anderson had told them that when they finished the unit they would know how to read maps, know about other communities in their state, and know how to write to people they did not know. Although there was some mild interest in map reading and distant children, Ms. Anderson's objectives were not what caused the excitement among the students. It was the problem. Ms. Anderson presented the problem to her students this way.

"We are going to learn about another community in our state by talking with children in that community in a class just like this one. To talk to these children we are going to use e-mail. Here is the problem: I am not going to tell you the name of these students' community, and their teacher is not going to tell them the name of our community. Instead, you are going to have to ask them questions about where they live and what they do; they are going to ask you questions as well, because they have the same problem to solve that you do. You can ask them questions about what the land looks like, the population of the community, recreation opportunities—anything that you can think of to give you clues about where they might be. When you get answers back, you will want to get a map out as well as your textbook on state geography and history, and compare those answers to the information in your books and maps.

| Setting up a problem |

"You are going to work in groups of four. Every other day your group will write five questions for the children at the mystery school. They will also work in groups of four to write questions for you. Each day that we send questions, a different person in your group will e-mail the questions your group has to the group you are working with at the mystery school—but first, another person in your group will proofread the questions. So, Susan, John, Sam, and Maria, you are in the "Orange" group. Adam, Yolanda, Ed, and Holly, you are. . . . Now, just to get ourselves started, this first day let's write our five questions as a whole class. Then each group can go to the computers and send the questions together. One person can type them in while the others watch and check for typos. Also, remember what you have learned about netiquette (Figure 4.1). You will want to make a good impression on the students in the mystery community. If you have forgotten how to send e-mail, take a notebook with you and write down notes about the key presses that you have forgotten, so you will be able to send the questions when it is your turn. Before we begin writing questions together, let's look at the big map of our state on the wall and think about the possibilities."

| Explaining the process |

At this point, Ms. Anderson began teaching the content that she needs to teach about her state's geography and history. She made sure her students knew where their own community is on the map, pronounced the names of other communities, and asked students to talk about communities they have visited. She reviewed the features of a topographic map that indicate elevation, longitude, and latitude. Using an LCD projector (a device that projects a computer image to a screen; see Figure 4.2) attached to her computer, she even took the students on a virtual airplane trip around their own community using encyclopedia software provided by her school district. Students were able to compare the topography of the paper map to the more dynamic topography of the virtual airplane

Writing effective e-mail is not like writing an effective letter. There are issues and concerns that apply to electronic communication that have not arisen during the history of paper communication. Following a few simple guidelines will save you both wasted time, embarrassment, and even grief. To be electronically literate, your students should absorb these same guidelines whether you teach them in a lesson, provide them with a set of printed guidelines, or work with them individually as they send and receive e-mail. Many of these guidelines are common sense, and most seem intuitive after you have read through them. There are many places on the Internet where you can find the guidelines. The guidelines below are brief and you can find further, detailed explanation by consulting either www .emailreplies.com (2006) or Miller (2003).

1. Write simply and concisely.
2. There is no need for a salutation like "Dear xxxx." You can simply begin with the person's name or just begin with no name.
3. Answer all of the questions that the sender of the email asks. Both you and your reader are less likely to be confused if you cut and paste the questions the reader asked into your reply and separate or mark them by space or some other device like symbols (for example, ******).
4. Always use your best spelling and grammar. Use your e-mail editor's spell checker.
5. Do not indent your paragraphs; separate them with double spaces.
6. Acknowledge e-mails that you have received if they are too long or too difficult to answer immediately. Tell the sender you will reply when you are able to. Make a goal of getting back to the sender within 24 hours.
7. Only send attachments that are absolutely necessary.
8. Sign your message with your name and e-mail address.
9. Be sure to check your attachments for viruses before you send them.
10. Use short sentences and short paragraphs. It is more difficult to read from a screen than from a paper, so help your reader in as many ways as you can. When you have a list of items, write them as a list using numbers or bullets. Do not actually use bullets (for example the kind of bullets that Word supplies) because some e-mails cannot read the code that they are written in. Instead use an asterisk or a hyphen, for example.
11. When you are sending e-mails to multiple recipients who do not know each other, use the BCC field for addresses. By doing this you will not disclose the names and addresses of everyone on your list to all recipients. If you fill in the "To" field with your own email address, your recipients will not get the sense that they are being spammed.
12. Do not reply to spam.
13. If you send someone a link, make it clickable.
14. Do not copy a message or an attachment that another user has sent you unless you ask for their permission.
15. Be careful of what you send. Do not send an e-mail that you would not want the world to see.
16. Try to use a "subject" entry that encapsulates the contents of your e-mail.
17. Never use all capitals. It is the equivalent of shouting.
18. Always re-read your e-mail before you send it.

FIGURE 4.1 Suggestions for Making Your E-Mail Effective

trip. Then she began soliciting questions from the students and writing them on the board. As students suggested questions, she modeled the writing and thinking process by helping them pick just the right words, adding commas where they were needed and explaining why, and making sure that each question had a question mark at the end. She mentioned several times that when people com-

A key piece of equipment to know how to use is a computer display device. Currently, there are two popular devices for classroom use: the large television monitor and the LCD projector. A large television monitor with computer-to-video conversion hardware and software is most affordable. Most schools have televisions, on carts for their classrooms. Cable runs from the computer to the television, and special software is installed on the computer to adapt the video signal that it produces to a video signal the television can understand. The advantage of the television/computer display is the price. Most conversion software and hardware costs less than $150. The disadvantage is the readability of the screen. Letters are ragged, and the last rows of students in a thirty-person class cannot see the screen well. LCD projectors attach directly to the computer and need no special software to make them work. The better projectors are light, portable, and project well enough to be used in an undarkened room. They often come with built-in speakers as well, supporting audio as well as video. The disadvantage is their cost, which is significantly more that the cost of the computer-to-video conversion kits for televisions.

FIGURE 4.2 **Computer Projection Devices**

municate with someone that they cannot see and do not know, the only impression the other person gets is based on how expressive and how correct the writing is. When she finished the discussion, tours, and admonitions, students divided into their groups, went to their computers, typed in their questions, and sent them, knowing that the day after that they would get their first communication from the unknown school.

Ms. Anderson had carefully thought through the organization of the activity. Students spent fifteen minutes in their groups every other day analyzing the previous set of responses and using those responses to generate more questions. At the beginning of each day, she had a student volunteer print the responses from the other school so they would be ready for the class at the appropriate time. She typically does this because any number of things can go wrong if she waits until the actual lesson time to print responses to questions. Whenever anything goes wrong, it takes time away from instruction that she cannot afford to lose.

What can go wrong? The printer may run out of paper or it may jam. The network may be down so that the printer will not work. The other school may not have sent answers to the questions for one reason or another. If her student volunteer works on the printouts first thing in the morning, then if there is a problem she will be able to adjust and not lose that precious fifteen minutes of lesson time tinkering with the printer or making something up to fill in the gap. If all goes well, she collects the printouts for each group, previews them for appropriateness, and sets them in her "out" basket where they will be ready when she needs them.

How does she solve the problems? The first two, running out of paper and printer jams, are simple. They just take time, which she has if she tackles the job first thing in the morning. If the network is down, she e-mails, calls, or visits the network administrator to find out the seriousness of the problem and then either makes other plans or has the volunteer print out later. If responses from the other school have not shown up, she checks her e-mail because the teacher in the remote community is usually careful to inform her about glitches that happen occasionally. It is usual for either class to have an assembly or a fire drill at least once during the three weeks they have planned for the cooperative project. If the exchanges take place every other day, it is more likely that these occasional interruptions will not disturb the flow of work, since there are two chances for a class to get its responses back. There are, however, days when no responses arrive. (Teachers can plan for different spring breaks, but snow days and flu epidemics just happen). Communication between the two cooperating teachers is essential in this case.

| Solving problems |

Nothing kills a project like this faster than not keeping the schedule that the two of you have planned and then not communicating about it.

A more difficult problem than not having all of the responses show up is having just some of the responses show up, such as four groups get their responses but the fifth does not. This can happen because the child at the other end thinks he or she has sent the response and has not. On an every-other-day schedule, there is usually time to inform the other teacher of the missed responses. If, however, it appears that the responses are not going to arrive in time for the lesson, the teacher should write the responses so that her students can get on with the business of learning.

In the end, when the two schools finally guessed each other's locations, students in each pair of groups introduced themselves to each other and sent pictures. Ms. Anderson's students, who each had a copy of all the questions and answers that they received from the mystery school, wrote a report about that region of the state. They included not only the information that they received from the other school, but information from their books, maps, and encyclopedias as well.

Student products

Because we are looking at e-mail as a tool that challenges students to work at all intellectual levels, we will now look at Ms. Anderson's assignment using Bloom's taxonomy as a backdrop (Table 4.1). You can see that in this example, no level of the taxonomy was neglected, although this will not always be true for every tool and every lesson. It is most important that you are aware of the levels of learning that your lesson does cover. Then, if some levels of the taxonomy are excluded because you have used an electronic tool for its ability to work at other levels of the taxonomy effectively, you must design other worksheets or exercises to fill the gaps.

Not all assignments cover all levels of the taxonomy

DISCUSSION BOARDS

Our next look at asynchronous communication is the **discussion board,** which provides more structure for students than e-mail does. If your school has a server set up to manage discussion boards, you can engage your class in an electronic discussion. All the students will be able to see each other's questions and responses.

To help you understand the kind of interface students are working with in the next field trip, look at Figures 4.3 and 4.4. These two screen shots are from a discussion board built with a Microsoft FrontPage **wizard.** The wizard used to build this discussion board consisted of eight dialogue boxes. The teacher creating it was prompted to enter a name for the discussion, to define "categories" for the students' responses, and to select and arrange the items. The discussion board took the teacher less than fifteen minutes to create.

The welcome screen states the topic of the discussion and gives students directions on how to proceed. Students post a new article to the board by choosing a subject, indicating their identity, choosing a category, and making their comments, as illustrated in Figure 4.4. Figure 4.5 shows the expanded category box. By setting up categories, the teacher gives students cues that will guide the discussion.

Let us take Field Trip 4.2, to see how a discussion board can support a role-playing assignment.

DISCUSSION BOARD
Electronic forum where people can write ("post") comments and read other people's responses. Sometimes access is limited by user names and passwords.

WIZARD
Software feature that prompts users through the steps of a task so they need not know all the technical details.

TABLE 4.1	Bloom's Taxonomy for Geography Lesson			
The Cognitive Process Dimension	**The Knowledge Dimension**			
	Factual	**Conceptual**	**Procedural**	**Meta-Cognitive**
Remember	Students locate geographic features and towns on a map.	–	Students learn how to find locations on maps.	–
Understand	Students summarize the information they have received from another school to help them write a report.	Students understand the meaning of distances and scales on maps.	–	–
Apply	Using information students receive from another school, they find a place on the map.	Students learn to apply concepts of longitude and latitude.	–	–
Analyze	Students compare information that they have received from the mystery school to information they have collected.	–	–	–
Evaluate	When information they have received from the mystery class conflicts with their own research from other sources, students must judge which information is correct.	–	–	Students see their town and its place in the world in comparison to other places and people.
Create	From information received from the mystery school along with information from their research they create a verbal and physical picture of the mystery school.	–	Given any mystery location a student should know the process for finding out where it is.	–

Role Playing

FIELD TRIP
4.2

John Sanders's junior literature class was nearing the end of its first semester. The students had studied the early Puritan writers, the writers of the American Revolution, the early Romantic poets, and the short story writers and novelists of the mid-1800s. To any given ethical or moral question, all of these writers bring the habits of mind and philosophies of the era in which they lived. Mr. Sanders knew it was time to summarize and teach students the difference between the Puritan, Colonial, and Romantic periods in American writing and wanted to do more than just give a lecture and have students write a comparison/contrast paper. He does this every year, and every year it is the same. One or two gifted students come up with something original, almost everyone else hands in nothing more than slightly embellished lists that are really converted lecture notes, and a few just don't get the point and hand in disorganized papers that don't answer the question.

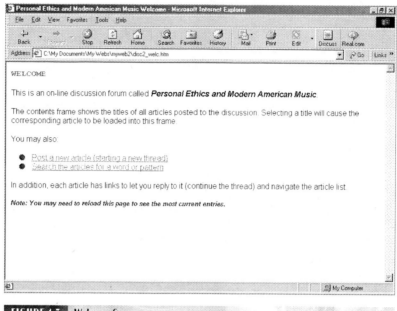

FIGURE 4.3   Welcome Screen

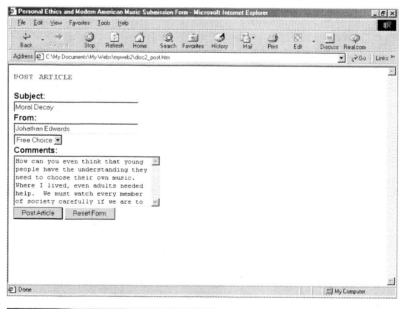

FIGURE 4.4   Posting a New Article

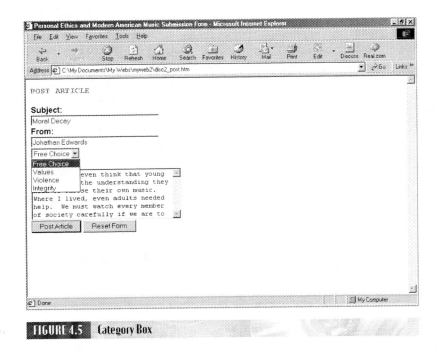

This year, Mr. Sanders is approaching this assignment differently. Instead of assigning the comparison/contrast paper "cold," with only his lecture for preparation, he has provided an electronic role-playing assignment he believes will give his students enough writing and thinking practice to improve the quality of their comparison/contrast papers. He believes this "hook" will capture his students' attention, for this role-playing assignment will be an interesting problem. The logistics of the assignment are not trivial. It is a lot of work to think things through. First, he defines his instructional objective: All students will be able write a reflective paper comparing and contrasting themes in early American literature.

The content and instructional problem

Next Mr. Sanders writes the problem. It reads like this:

Due to a science experiment involving a time machine gone awry, the authors Jonathan Edwards, James Fenimore Cooper, and Mark Twain are transported to a research laboratory somewhere in North America. Although somewhat confused at first, all of them are adjusting to their new lives and have decided to accept the inevitable. Researchers are slowly acclimating them to modern society. They all live in a small dormitory at the lab, where they share a kitchen and living room. One night, while flipping through the channels on their big-screen TV, Jim Cooper discovers MTV and stays, fascinated by the costumes, music, and violence. Jonathan Edwards, horrified, insists that the machine be turned off. When Cooper refuses, Edwards threatens to smash the television and Twain intervenes. Cooper turns the volume to mute, and a lively debate about violence, bad words, modesty, and other pertinent topics ensues.

The problem for the students

After Mr. Sanders has defined his instructional objective and written the problem, he began thinking about how he would organize this lesson. At first glance, the project seemed like a huge organizational nightmare. He planned to have each student secretly play the part of one of the time-shocked authors. Having secret identities would let students avoid the stereotypes about themselves and their abilities that inevitably build over the course of the semester. But *he* still wanted to know who sent each message, in case someone tried to use anonymity as a license to behave badly. He also wanted to make sure that the discussion was organized, so the students would be sure to cover the most important themes. He

Organizing the lesson

Deciding on the tool

planned to check out the LCD projector one day and review the highlights and best exchanges in all of the discussions with the whole class before they write their papers.

After all of this, Mr. Sanders finally got around to thinking about which electronic tool would help him the most. First, he considered e-mail. In one way, e-mail would be easiest. He and his students are e-mail aces. They had exchanged e-mail with another class in an electronic debate and talked with an expert on Mark Twain using e-mail and did not have too many problems. However, Mr. Sanders just could not figure out how to work out two items: anonymity and keeping all the threads of the discussion straight. When a person uses e-mail, the address is obvious, especially the addresses at his school. Also, it would be almost impossible to keep all of the threads of the discussion straight. The students would not able to consistently make up the name of a theme and type it into the "subject" area of the e-mail. Taking a big leap, he decided that the tool to use was the web-based discussion board that he had taken an in-service on just the previous month.

Presenting the problem to students

Having made up his mind about the goal of the assignment, the structure of the assignment, and the tool he would use, Mr. Sanders spoke to his class like this:

"Your goal as you execute this assignment is to take the role that has been assigned to you and become that person in the discussion. Take the position on the issue that you think your historical counterpart would take. If you are Jonathan Edwards, you will begin the debate. If you are James Fenimore Cooper, you will speak second, and if you are Mark Twain, you will speak third.

Explaining the process

"Remember that these were all passionate people who had strong beliefs about right and wrong and the world in which they lived. If you can, try to use the language they would use and the arguments that you think they might have used. Do not hesitate to be creative and to extrapolate (use things you know about them to say things you think they might say). Once you have written your first exchange, then you must add to the discussion every other day. Reply to the points the other members of your group make as well as make points of your own. Remember that you must not reveal your identity to anyone in the class. The only way others will be able to communicate with you is through your writing, so you will have to make an extra effort to make your work readable. Choose your words carefully. If something in one of your opponents' replies is unclear to you, say so. You can't argue with a statement that you don't understand. I will monitor your discussions so that I can understand your thinking. If your group starts spinning its wheels or there is a problem, I will help. Before we start, let's go to the lab—I have reserved it for this hour to show you how a discussion board works. After that, we will rotate through the computers in our classroom. Starting tomorrow for the next two weeks, you will get an opportunity to read your groups' messages and send one yourself every other day."

Now let us apply Bloom's taxonomy to Mr. Sanders' assignments (See Table 4.2). What range of intellectual skills did the students use as they argued with each other about ethics as they played their roles as early American writers? You can see from the table that one level of thought was not addressed, but that students did activities associated with both the upper and lower levels of the taxonomy.

TECHTIP 4.1 | *Streaming Video and Internet Chat*

Video over the Internet is a powerful teaching tool that is improving as tools for its creation and dissemination improve. Streaming video is one efficient way of transporting video from its origin on a server to an end user's desktop. Because raw video is resource intensive, it must be compressed before it is transmitted and uncompressed when it reaches its destination—the user's desk. Streaming video

TABLE 4.2	Bloom's Taxonomy and an Electronic Discussion Board Assignment			
The Cognitive Process Dimension	**The Knowledge Dimension**			
	Factual	**Conceptual**	**Procedural**	**Meta-Cognitive**
Remember	In order to argue effectively, students must look up facts about the writers or find them in the author's works.	In order to write effectively students come to understand the meaning of "style" and how it affects an author's writing.	–	–
Understand	Students must summarize author's views for the different categories of the discussion board.	Students learn that there are categories of thought and within a category there can be many different opinions.	Students learn to attack an argument by segmenting it into categories.	Students learn that answers to big questions do not have rigid boundaries–that there are many shades of gray to "truth."
Apply	Students apply their writing skills to write convincing arguments.	–	–	–
Analyze	Students compare the view points of different writers.	–	–	–
Evaluate	Using viewpoints other than their own personal point of view, students judge the validity of another's arguments.	–	Students learn to "walk in another person's shoes."	Students see their town and its place in the world in comparison to other places and people.
Create	–	–	–	–

may be either live or originate from a file of video that has been previously shot. The file is sent in small packages so that the user does not have to wait for the whole file to arrive before it begins to play on the user's machine.

Another promising Internet technology is chat. Opening an Internet chat session with a number of people is easy and free. Windows Messenger is an example of a chat tool that will allow two or more people to conduct a synchronous text conversation over the Internet. Students, most commonly, can connect with a distant expert and ask questions or exchange information. In the past, the better approach to this kind of interaction was the telephone.

New tools have been developed that will allow the contents of a text-based chat session to be saved and placed in a searchable online database. Using this database the chat remains available for students to search and review as they are doing reports and other summary activities. These kinds of tools are available on course management systems like Blackboard. There is at least one stand-alone version available commercially, called LogLibrary (www.loglibrary.com), which charges a nominal fee (less than $10 a month). This is an excellent tool that allows the kind of privacy needed when students are involved.

A MORE ELABORATE USE OF E-MAIL

Ms. Anderson's fifth graders' use of e-mail for their geography project, the Mystery School, was simple group-to-group communication. In the next field trip we will look at a more complex use of e-mail in which individual students will work in groups to solve a problem.

**FIELD TRIP
4.3**

The instructional shortcoming

Getting ready to begin the exercise

Using E-Mail for a Math Project

Mr. Grant, a high school math teacher, knows that the National Council of Teachers of Mathematics (NCTM) has suggested that students improve their problem-solving skills. He has tried to incorporate more problem solving into his classes, but sooner or later, the whole process bogs down. At first students work well in groups, but as the year wears on, it seems that it is always the same students who contribute the most, while others hang back and let the aggressive students talk. By the time the first semester ends and the second semester begins, the aggressive, talkative students are solving the problems. The listeners might as well be listening to them stand up and lecture at the whiteboard for the amount of effort they are putting into their problem-solving sessions. Last year's test scores reflected this dichotomy, and Mr. Grant wants to do something about it. He has devised an electronic problem-solving activity using e-mail to stimulate participation by each member of a problem-solving group.

Mr. Grant prepared his students for their next problem-solving exercise by explaining that they will do it electronically, still in groups, but using e-mail as the vehicle for communication. He presented the change in format positively, not mentioning that it was an effort to get those who will not participate in oral discussions to participate in written discussions. Instead, Mr. Grant explained that it is important for everyone in class to become comfortable with the language of problem solving, and be able to articulate in writing the process and procedures that they are applying.

Mr. Grant has five computers in his classroom and twenty-eight algebra students. He shuffled a deck of three-by-five-inch cards with students' names written on each and made five piles of cards: three piles with six cards and two piles with five cards. Then he read aloud the names of the members of each group as the students wrote down the names of the people in their groups. The groups then huddled for ten minutes and exchanged e-mail addresses. This first day of the assignment, Mr. Grant did not present the problem. Instead, he taught their first lesson on linear equations.

Following general instructions he gave them, in the part of the class period that is set aside for doing end-of-section problems, each member of each group took a turn at his or her assigned computer. The students had been told to type a **distribution list** using the e-mail addresses they had collected earlier during the class period and including Mr. Grant's address. After creating a distribution list, each student sent one test message using the list. Next, each student created a folder ("mailbox") called "Chocolate Problem" to hold all of the e-mail exchanges that would occur during this assignment. Finally, each student made a **rule (filter)** to route any incoming e-mail message with "Chocolate Problem" in the subject line to that folder.

The next day students again went to their assigned computer to see if they had received the test e-mail messages from the other members of their group and if the e-mail messages had gone to their Chocolate Problems folder.

This did not go smoothly. Mr. Grant had hoped to introduce the actual problem during that class period, but instead he spent his entire time during the period helping students fix incorrect e-mail addresses, incomplete distribution lists, and rules that did not work. Tired and a little frustrated, he reflected that in ten years he would not have to do this. These skills will be so much a part of the culture it will not be an issue anymore. For the time being, however, if he wants to attempt an assignment like this, he knows he will spend some time teaching technology skills.

DISTRIBUTION LIST
E-mail function that allows users to send out the same message to a group of people rather than sending it out to one person at a time. Some e-mail software calls this function "nicknames."

RULE OR FILTER
Instructions to categorize incoming and outgoing e-mail.

On Thursday, three days after Mr. Grant told the class about the new way of approaching their bi-weekly problem, the class was ready. Every member of every group received messages from every other member of the group, and they all went directly to each students' Chocolate Problem folders. This was a problem-solving experience in itself! And now the problem:

Setting up the problem

Mr. Grant began, "If you will focus on the overhead now, I am going to give you your problem. You don't have to write it down because I have e-mailed it to each of you. Here it is:

> Augustus is trying to make chocolate milk. So far he has made a 10 percent chocolate milk solution (this means that the solution is 10 percent chocolate and 90 percent milk). He has also made a 25 percent chocolate milk solution. Unfortunately, the 10 percent solution is too weak, and the 25 percent solution is way too chocolaty. He has a whole lot of the 10 percent solution, but he only has thirty gallons of the 25 percent solution. How many gallons of 20 percent solution should he add to the 25 percent solution to make a mixture that is 15 percent chocolate (which Augustus is sure will be absolutely perfect)?" (Herr & Johnson, 1994)

Mr. Grant continued, "Since we haven't tried solving a problem like this before, I want to give you some rules.

- First, as you might have guessed, I don't want you to discuss this out loud. If you get an idea, you should write it down for the rest of your group.
- Second, the same rule applies about this problem as for the others: If your group solves the problem, do not tell others your solution. You may be cutting off discussion that will show us a different way to solve the problem.

The process

- Third, and most important: You must contribute one comment (no more) to the discussion every day. Your comment may be either a relevant question or a relevant answer. Here is an example of a relevant question: Why did you decide to use the guess-and-check method instead of looking for a pattern? A relevant answer does not have to be a correct answer, just something that moves the discussion forward and adds a new perspective to the problem.
- Finally, you will get a grade for this assignment. As you remember, I am on your distribution list, so every assignment that you send to the other members of the group will come to me as well. This is how I will grade your work." Mr. Grant displayed a table on his overhead (Table 4.3).
- You will schedule your contributions so that one day you will go to the computer, read, and print out your e-mail. You will spend a day reflecting on the contributions of the other members of your group. The next day you will provide either a question or a comment."

So that is how Mr. Grant began his assignment. The problem itself was complex because it involved two problem-solving strategies: guess-and-check and subproblems (Herr & Johnson, 1994, p. 361). Every day he skimmed his students' work. He kept students' scores in a spreadsheet and at the end of the week cut and pasted the students' scores into e-mail so they could get a feel for the quality of their contributions.

He was generous for this first electronic assignment because neither he nor his students knew what to expect. He used the scoring rubric he had handed out the first day. He had planned to extract some of the best questions and responses each day to show the class examples of good work. However, he decided that would give students too many answers and compromise the effectiveness of the assignment. Instead, at the end of the assignment, when the problem had been solved, he printed out especially good comments, questions, diagrams, and exchanges, and transferred the printout to an overhead so he could show his students what they did right. It would have been much easier if he had a computer projector for his room. As it was, he would have had to check out a projector and move one of the student computers or his computer to hook up to the projector. When he looked at the trade-off in time, he decided printing out and making transparencies backed up by e-mail to individual students was a more efficient use of his time. Checking out the LCD projector and setting it up would be using technology for the sake of technology, something he did not have time for.

End-of-lesson summary

Using technology is not always appropriate

TABLE 4.3 Scoring Rubric for Problem-Solving Assignment	
	Point value
Questions	
Question is directly related to the information in another person's comments.	15
Question uncovers a logic flaw in someone else's question or answer.	25
Comments	
Comment restates what the group already knows.	10
Comment restates what the group already knows in a unique way.	15
Comment restates what you know and adds information.	25
Charts	
Improves a diagram or chart that someone else has already submitted.	15
Provides a diagram or chart that helps explain the problem.	25
The Solution	
Solves the problem	25 points for the person who solves the problem 20 points for each member of the group who has contributed at least one 25-point question, comment, or diagram to the discussion.

Now that you have had an opportunity to observe a sophisticated use of e-mail in a classroom—one that uses the functions available with most e-mail software—we will again analyze the lesson with Bloom's taxonomy (Table 4.4). Note that students do not deal with the first level of the taxonomy at all, but are quite engaged in the higher levels of the taxonomy.

CHECKING YOUR UNDERSTANDING

4.1 Having now read three examples of e-mail–supported instruction, it is time for you to think of a lesson of your own. Do not worry about technical details. Concentrate on the design of the lesson. As with any technology-supported assignment, your concerns are what students need to know and finding a technology that will help them learn faster or better. Write it in the form of a story, much like the field trips you have read. Make sure that your story touches on the following:

- The reason for the technology-supported lesson
- ■ Student objectives
- ■ The information you want your students to learn

TABLE 4.4 Bloom's Taxonomy and a Problem-Solving Lesson				
The Cognitive Process Dimension	**The Knowledge Dimension**			
	Factual	**Conceptual**	**Procedural**	**Meta-Cognitive**
Remember	–	–	Student learns a process.	–
Understand	–	The student is given points for restating concepts the group already knows.	–	–
Apply	–	Student solves the problem.	–	–
Analyze	–	Student tests other students' solutions.	–	–
Evaluate	–	Students judge the adequacy of others' solutions.	–	–
Create	Students create a chart or diagram.	–	–	–

- The problem you will ask them to solve
- Problems that you anticipate as you execute the lesson
- The technology that will be available to you
- Management of your classroom (Will you use groups? If you do, how will they work?)
- Amount of time the lesson/unit will take
- How you will evaluate your students' performance

After you write your lesson, make a table with the levels of Bloom's taxonomy like the tables in this chapter. Place the activities in your lesson in the appropriate cells of your new table.

ASYNCHRONOUS COMMUNICATION: TOOLS AND METHODS

You have just explored three different ways of using e-mail in three different content areas for three different student grade levels. You should look beyond the content and grade level presented in each of the field trips to the pedagogy. In the upcoming discussion, we will explore some of the technical details of these assignments, but you should have some instructional content and problems of your own to think about as you read. Also as you read, keep your response to "Checking Your Understanding 4.1" in the back of your mind. Knowing more about technical details may require you to change your response.

E-mail

Since the first e-mail message was sent in 1972, the complexity of e-mail software has increased. The very first e-mail software allowed the user to type in an e-mail address

Common e-mail features

and send a message. Now e-mail software includes many features, including address books, distribution lists, folders (mailboxes), rules (filters), and attachments. We are going to cover all these as we go into some detail that explains how Ms. Anderson, Mr. Sanders, and Mr. Grant managed their lessons.

Free e-mail software

There are at least two good e-mail programs that you can download for free from the Internet: Eudora and Pegasus. Both are quite functional, and you can find both download sites by doing an Internet search on their names. Although your school provides you with e-mail software at work, you may want to use one of these at home, or you may want to recommend these to your students for their use at home. Besides using e-mail software that resides locally on your computer, you can also use web mail that is supported by your Internet service provider or provided free on the net along with an account. To use free web mail, you must be willing to put up with advertisements. People access web mail software by typing an Internet address into their Internet browser, pressing Enter, and going to the web mail site the address points to. One popular example of web mail is Microsoft's Hotmail. This service is accessible from the Microsoft home page.

Address books

Address books do not have direct instructional use, but an address book would certainly have helped Mr. Grant set up his project much faster. Do you remember how he asked his students to huddle for ten minutes and exchange e-mail addresses? Some students wrote the addresses incorrectly and others typed them incorrectly. It took Mr. Grant two days to fix all of the problems. If, on the other hand, Mr. Grant had created a class address book and copied it to the e-mail directories of the computers in his classroom, things would have gone much more smoothly. Then, as his students were making their distribution lists, they could type in the names of the classmates in their groups and the correct e-mail addresses would have been inserted automatically.

Common problems with one-on-one e-mail exchanges

Individual versus Group E-Mail Projects   When teachers began using e-mail in their classrooms, one common strategy was to pair students in their class with students in another, remote class and promote pen pal exchanges. The activity seems simple enough, but it is time consuming and filled with many possibilities for failure. Children in their first blush of excitement would write the introductory message and then run out of things to say. That in itself is disconcerting if you have planned on a year's worth of highly motivated exchanges between your seventh graders and their pen pals in the Ukraine. The solution is to carefully monitor every set of exchanges and to assign a topic for the exchange. This takes time, and whether you will achieve your instructional objective as the result of the exchanges is uncertain. And then, how do you deal with your student who sends the barest minimum on each exchange to Alexy on the other side of the world, who writes volumes and is terribly interested? If you have only one such student in your class you might be able to fill the gap, but if you have six or seven, something or someone will go by the wayside.

Absences are another difficult problem with one-on-one exchanges. Recall that Ms. Anderson checked every day that all of the groups in the other school had responded. She only had five groups. What if she were worried about twenty or thirty individuals instead? What if a child in the Ukraine were to come down with the flu and be out of school for two weeks? Or what if the same were to happen to one of your students? The task of "ghost writing" messages for twenty children is a chore, even once a week. In other words, if you decide you are going to undertake a project involving one-on-one exchanges, you should have a well-defined instructional objective, a limited scope of exchanges, standards that your students understand ahead of time, and backup plans—along with the extra time that it takes to execute them. For more information on one-on-one exchanges and some references to successful exchanges, see Harris (1998a), "Curriculum-Based Telecollaboration."

Web Boards

If your school supports one, web-based discussion boards are wonderful alternatives to e-mail. They are not difficult to set up and maintain and are much easier to use for discussions. You may remember that Mr. Sanders used a web discussion board format for the review in his American literature class. There are several products on the market that perform this function. Two that have been very stable over the last several years are WebBoard and Microsoft FrontPage.

| Web conferencing software |

Most web discussion boards are very similar. Notice in Figure 4.6 that the contents column allows the user to access any previous message (the titles of which are underlined, followed by the authors' names and the posting date. From this screen,

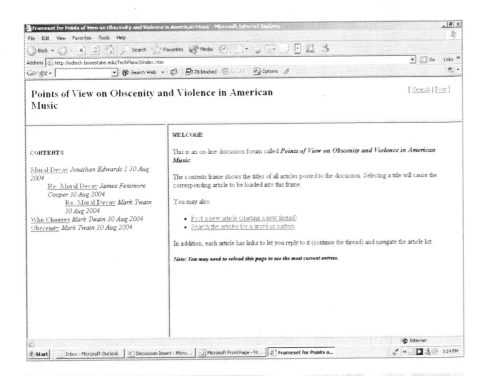

FIGURE 4.6 Introductory Screen After Several Exchanges

students can do three things: read previously posted messages, search for text in any of the previously posted messages, and post a new message. Because the students in Mr. Sanders' class each had an alias, we see the names of the authors they played rather than the students. Only Mr. Sanders knew who the authors really were. In order to set the discussion up like this, Mr. Sanders had to ask the network administrator to provide sign-ons and passwords for each student. He also asked the network administrator to set up a separate discussion space for each group of students, so that the whole class would not be contributing to the same discussion board. This means that each group went to a different Internet address to activate its discussion space.

> Setting up a discussion

Keeping Track in a Discussion: Three Ways

First let us look at the process of posting a new message. Figure 4.7 illustrates the screen just before Jonathan Edwards hits the Post Article button. As with e-mail, the message has a subject line, but notice the untitled box below the "From" entry. In order to guide learners' discussion, the teacher may set up categories, called *strands,* ahead of time. The strands here encompass the themes Mr. Sanders expects students to address from their character's historical and cultural perspective: values, violence, free choice, and obscenity. Here we see that "Mark Twain" has posted a comment that he classifies as being in the category of free choice. In Figures 4.8 and 4.9, both Cooper and Twain reply.

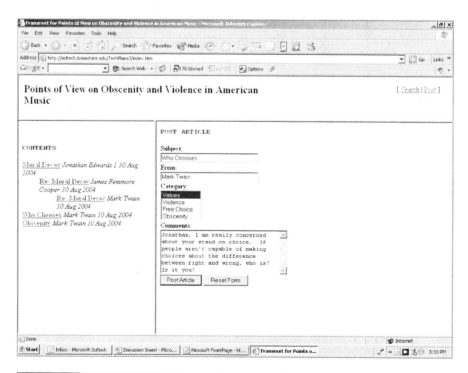

FIGURE 4.7 Mark Twain Chooses His Category and Writes His Message

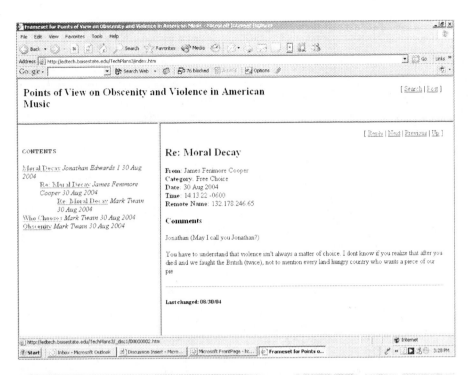

FIGURE 4.8 James Fenimore Cooper Responds to Jonathan Edwards

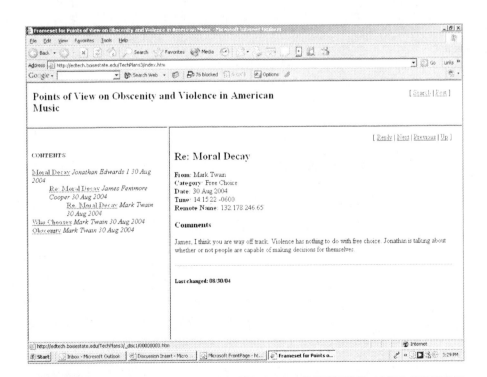

FIGURE 4.9 First Part of Mark Twain's First Response Window

83

Keeping track of messages

Notice that on the left side of the screen, students can keep track of replies because they are indented under the message that prompted them. If you compare this capability of a web discussion board to having to sort through messages all dumped into the same folder during an e-mail discussion, you can see the advantages. The web board gives members of a discussion group two ways to keep track of and categorize messages: using categories and separating messages into a lead message and its replies.

Web board software gives users a third method of categorizing messages. If a group member wants to start a discussion on a new topic, then rather than reply to a previously posted message, the participant may choose to start a new strand. This is what Mark Twain does when he starts worrying about who gets to set the standards in Figure 4.10. When Edwards replies to this challenge, his reply will be indented just like the replies in the strands in Figures 4.8 and 4.9.

New strands

Search Function

One final, useful feature of web discussion software is the search function. If a discussion is active and continues for two or three weeks, a large number of messages will accumulate. Again, emphasizing that the software (discussion board) and the method (a discussion) are not the objective of the lesson, but rather some final, thoughtful project such as a paper, speech, or speech accompanied with a computer presenta-

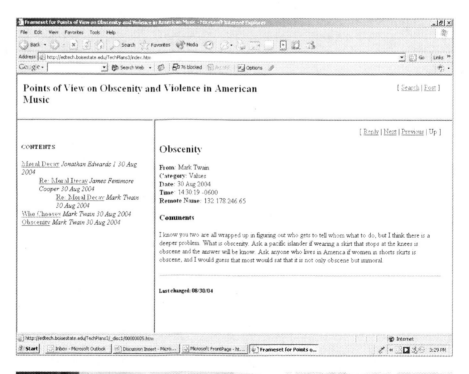

FIGURE 4.10 Mark Twain Has Begun Another Strand

tion, it is helpful for the participants of a web board discussion group to have access to the messages that have been sent. It is even more helpful if the hundred or so messages are organized and searchable. If, for example, the student who played the role of Mark Twain were trying to get her thoughts together on everyone's comments about "choice," she could go to the search screen (Figure 4.11) and set up a search. The particular discussion board she is using lists the results of her search in Figure 4.12. The items are listed by name, are clickable, dated, and each is given a score that provides some indication of relevance to the topic. This student can now follow this theme through the messages and synthesize the information and make judgments about it. She is working at a very high level on Bloom's taxonomy. Contrast this to the alternative: listening to Mr. Sanders lecture for an hour, discussing a few questions here and there, and doing a five- or ten-minute role play involving three students with five minutes at the end of the lecture for students to ask questions.

Discussion Monitoring

Web discussion software provides Mr. Sanders one further, behind-the-scenes opportunity that we have not yet discussed. Aware that there are pranksters in his class who would love to use their anonymity to add some spice to the discussion, Mr. Sanders read all of the new entries to the discussion every day. And sure enough, the very

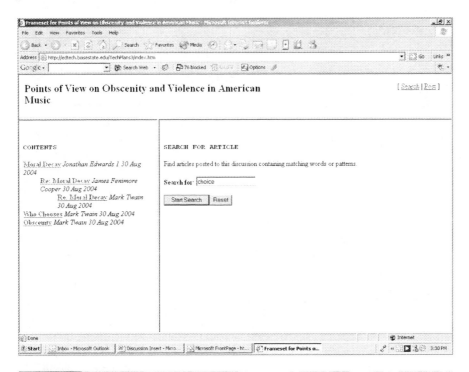

FIGURE 4.11 Setting Up a Search

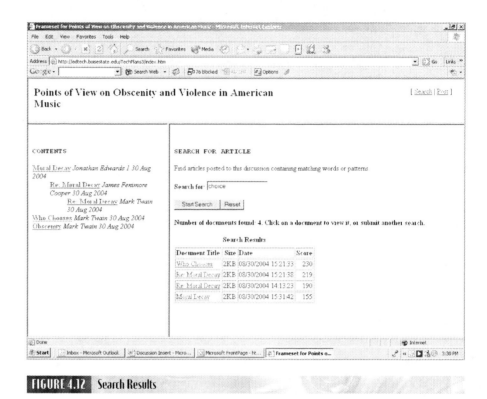

FIGURE 4.12 Search Results

first week, one student chose to test the rules on obscenity. Mr. Sanders simply left the message headers in the discussion so that he would not disable all of the existing links and replaced the offending messages with "This message has been removed." He reminded the student about rules and etiquette. Remember that Mr. Sanders warned his students ahead of time that he would be reading their e-mail. The warning, though not absolutely necessary in a legal sense, is courteous and shows respect for students (Harris, 1999). There were no more problems. Mr. Sanders continued to read the messages and assisted students when their discussions stalled. Sometimes he would go to a member of a discussion group that seemed to have run out of words and plant a suggestion that got the group going again. He felt free to do this since he wasn't grading the students.

Planning and Evaluating Asynchronous Communication Projects

Although we have not taken a field trip to classrooms doing activities based on each of the models in Table 4.5, we have talked about the major planning strategies as well as possibilities for failure involved in using e-mail and discussion boards. Almost all of the activities in Table 4.5 are possible, using either of the two technologies that we have discussed, either simple e-mail or a discussion board.

TABLE 4.5 Uses of E-Mail and Web Conferencing

Name of Activity	Description of Activity	Advantages = "+" Disadvantages = "−"
Student-to-student communication in different parts of the world	Students studying geography, culture, or science "journal" for or otherwise communicate with a student from a different culture in a distant location.	+ Some individual students learn a great deal from the exchanges. − Hard to keep going; difficult to match to the curriculum.
Classroom-to-classroom exchanges	These kinds of activities often center on collecting and sharing data. Classes along the same river may collect water samples, for example.	+ Easier to organize and manage than one-to-one exchanges. − The teacher(s) of the other class(es) must be committed to the project.
Peer tutoring	Older or more experienced students work with younger or struggling students.	+ One more way to get help (if it works) to students who need it. − Difficult to find an older student with the time and interest in a long-term tutoring relationship; students who are struggling often have difficulty reading and writing well enough to make e-mail work for them to participate in this activity.
Exchanging e-mail with an expert	Teachers may seek out and find an expert in a topic their class is studying: a writer, scientist, or professional, for example. The class works together to formulate questions that the expert answers. This may be a one-time exchange, or several exchanges may take place.	+ Easy to organize; class is highly motivated if the expert is famous. − The expert may have trouble speaking in a language your kids understand. You may have trouble finding an expert with enough time to help you.
Group investigation and brainstorming	Students are placed in groups and asked to solve a problem.	+ Students not only help each other learn content but also model their problem-solving skills for each other; students must write well to communicate well. − The groups' e-mails must be read and monitored on a daily basis for two reasons: to provide help when students run out of words and ideas and to check for offensive postings.
Simulations	Discoveries, voyages, expeditions, and battles can be simulated, e.g., the Oregon Trail, the Battle of Gettysburg.	+ Very motivational for students; students learn a great deal of content doing research so that they can respond appropriately to the events that the simulation requires them to respond to. − Preparation for simulations is extensive. The timing and amount of student response to the simulation must be carefully choreographed. Students must have reference materials and some background. There must be a goal or product to measure student performance.
Role playing	Any modern or historical situation in which there is a clash of culture, ideas, or philosophy provides a topic for role-playing activities.	+ Easy to set up. Students are motivated and like the activity. May be used as preparation for papers or tests. − If each student in the group doesn't take his or her role seriously, the rest of the students in the group miss a point of view; postings should be checked daily.

TABLE 4.6 General Scoring Rubric for Student Messages		
1	**2**	**3**
Evaluation of the Entire Discussion		
Contributes three messages.	Contributes five messages.	Contributes seven messages.
Some messages have spelling and grammar errors.	All messages have been spell checked.	All messages are grammatical; all messages have been spell checked.
Individual Messages		
Comments unrelated to discussion topic or repeat previous messages.	Comments related to discussion; repeats another student's message but with different words.	Comment adds at least one new perspective.
Student neither finds a logical flaw nor adds perspective; does not address the issue.	Student finds a logical flaw in another student's message but offers no alternative.	Student response correctly argues another student's message.

Although we have touched on evaluation (Table 4.4), it is time to say more. The kinds of activities that we have been exploring are not ends in themselves, but rather a means to help students acquire information and achieve curricular objectives. It seems odd to evaluate this learning process. An analogy might be watching a child's eyes as she or he reads paragraphs in a book while preparing for a test. The real evaluation of a communication-supported activity is the end product (test, paper, presentation), not the method of acquiring information. However, there are times when a teacher needs or wants to evaluate students' activities. For this situation, Table 4.6 is a general rubric that is applicable to most Internet communication supported activities. If you compare Table 4.6 to Table 4.4, you can see that Mr. Grant modified it to suit the needs of his content area. He really did not care as much about spelling and grammar as he did about the problem-solving process and getting everyone to participate. Table 4.6 gives you some general ideas that you will almost certainly have to modify depending on your objectives.

As you decide how asynchronous computer communication may help you achieve your instructional objectives, you will begin to recognize some tasks that you must complete whether you decide to conduct a role-playing activity, a simulation, or use e-mail to connect your students to an expert. Box 4.3 has some steps you should always think through before you start.

CHECKING YOUR UNDERSTANDING

 4.2   **1.** Look in the "Annotated Resources" section of this chapter for Internet sites with e-mail– or discussion board–supported lessons other teachers have created. Find a lesson plan that addresses the content area and grade level in which you teach or wish to teach. Compare this lesson plan to the steps listed above. If the lesson plan does not address one of the steps above, decide how you would execute that step.

2. Prepare and teach a lesson to a group of your peers on how to use an e-mail client or web board. Because your peers probably have these skills already, they should role-play students at the age that you specify. The purpose of this activity is for you to get used to teaching technology skills to other people. As you complete this activity, you will find that you take for granted many steps that must be explained and demonstrated to naive users.

3. Using the steps outlined in Box 4.1, plan a complete activity for a grade level and topic of your choice. Evaluate your activity against Bloom's taxonomy.

INSTANT MESSAGING

With the cell phone, Instant Messenger (Windows), and Google Talk (to name a few messaging mechanisms), students and teachers have increased opportunities for learning and for problems. Instant messaging provides students and teachers with three different forms of communication:

■ Asking and answering questions
■ Expressing opinions or feelings
■ Show-casing projects or links (Huffaker, 2004)

BOX 4.1 STEPS FOR PREPARING ASYNCHRONOUS COMMUNICATION–SUPPORTED INSTRUCTION

1. Decide on your instructional objective.
2. Decide on and construct your evaluation for the activity.
3. Decide whether the students will work alone, in groups, or as a class.
4. Decide how long you want to spend on the lesson.
5. Choose a model (Table 4.5).
6. Choose a tool (e-mail/discussion board).
7. Think through all of the technical features of the tool.
   a. If you are using e-mail, how will you give students e-mail addresses?
      i. Plan to create distribution lists, if necessary.
   b. If you are using web conferencing, how will you set up your discussions—one discussion group or multiple?
      i. Provide student sign-ons to the web discussion group.
      ii. Create appropriate strands (categories) for your discussion group.
8. Write a compelling, challenging problem for students with appealing context (write a story).
9. Locate/write and assemble supporting materials for students.
10. If students haven't been trained in the use of the technology you will use, train them.
11. On the first day of the unit or lesson, explain the objectives and tell students how they will be evaluated. If possible, show students examples of previously executed projects so that they will know what is expected. At this point in the history of the use of computers in classrooms, students often have no models on which to base their performance.

Instant messaging can be one-to-one, or many-to-many. Unlike older versions of instant messaging programs, newer software allows the user to archive conversations, which is especially valuable when the student is getting information about links or about answers to questions. It is an easy way to talk to a distant expert for both individuals or for an entire class if the teacher has a projection device attached to the computer on which instant messaging is taking place.

Seen in this light, instant messaging is benign. However, there are pitfalls. Whether teachers shows students how to do instant messaging or not, students will do it if they have access to the technology. Consequently, teachers must be literate about the dangers of instant messaging. First, instant messaging can be used to bully people. Secondly, it can transmit viruses and worms to unprotected computers. And finally, it allows unscrupulous people—predators—contact with students who are naive and trusting. There are some basic rules that everyone should follow when they use instant messaging (Wolfsberg, 2006). For bullying:

- Don't respond to someone who "flames" (insults, ridicules, is angry). If you feel you must respond for some practical reason, do not respond in kind. Simply state the business you need to respond to and let the rest go.
- Print objectionable e-mail messages so that you will have paper proof of the objectionable writing.
- If you don't know who is harassing you, change your screen name and tell the new name only to your friends.
- Try to identify the person harassing you by getting their e-mail address. Then inform your service provider.

For other, more general situations, students should be aware of the following guidelines:

- Never meet with an unknown person. That means a person that you didn't know before you began instant messaging with that person.
- If you met the person you are sending an instant message to in a chat room, remain anonymous. Never give out personal information.
- Never say something you wouldn't want your mother to hear.
- After an instant messaging session, log off. This will close ports on your computer that allow unwanted intruders to invade your machine.

These rules are really common sense. Teachers have so many tools available, it is important to ask oneself if instant messaging for a particular lesson is really critical. It is a Pandora's box of possible complications that should be treated with respect.

WEB AUTHORING – ANOTHER IMPORTANT TOOL

Web authoring is a tool that is important for teachers because the percentage of home computers connected to the Internet is so high. The information that a teacher posts to a web site opens up new ways of communicating with parents and students. Examples of items that can be posted on web sites include:

■ Homework assignments
■ Any electronic document that the teacher has created (for example, PowerPoint presentations)
■ Electronic documents that students have created (for example, class projects, student presentations)
■ Messages to parents (for example, announcements, summaries of work the class is doing in a content area)
■ Calendars and schedules
■ Announcements
■ Links and reference information

A web site opens up possibilities for communication with both students and parents that teachers never had time for before.

There are many different tools for building web sites. Some are more time intesive than others. Generally speaking, there are three approaches for web site building:

■ Using a free online web site building tool for educators
■ Using an Internet development tool like FrontPage (SharePoint)
■ Learning to write HTML (XHTML)

These approaches all have advantages and disadvantages mostly relating to time, money, and the permanence of the site. An ideal situation would be to use a combination of these methods. Most teachers are too busy to build an entire web site using HTML code. However, web sites can be created using Internet development tools and fine-tuned if the author knows HTML. Some free or fee-based Internet sites provide online web site building tools that do allow authors with a knowledge of HTML to modify the web sites they have built.

Online Web Site Building Tools

Online web site builders range from providing very simple functions to very complex ones. Sometimes they are free and sometimes these sites charge a nominal fee for space. For example, one free site called Filamentality (AT&T Knowledge Ventures, 2007) provides menu-driven pages that allow the user to:

■ Add links
■ Edit links
■ Build a scrapbook
■ Build a Web Quest
■ Hotlist (another place to add links)
■ Hunt (designed to build factual knowledge)
■ Sampler (a page for links)

Teacher Web (TeacherWeb, 2007), on the other hand, allows the user many different functions from listing homework, giving quizzes, putting up calendars, schedules, and lesson plans as well as providing for e-mail. The example currently on the web for one teacher's site currently lists twenty-one different kinds of pages. The price per teacher is $27 per year. Neither site allows teachers to see and modify the code with which the pages are built. Teacher Web, especially, allows the teacher to customize pages with colors and graphics.

Since these sites go in and out of existence and evolve over time, there would be no purpose in recommending a best site. In a search for sites of this nature there were many that someone had recommended that no longer existed or that were in the process of phasing out. This is one disadvantage of free or low-cost, menu-driven sites. A teacher may have put many hours into building the perfect site for a class only to have the site close down. In the case of a menu-driven site there is no way for a teacher to recover the code of the web pages and re-post the site elsewhere—the work is lost. If, however, you are looking for these kinds of sites, search terms that yield results include: "free site builders," "web site creation for teachers," "web site creation resources," and "web sites for schools." Such a site can certainly work as a short-term stop gap measure or a limited-use site for posting homework and announcements.

One makeshift way of having a web site is to develop a blog. Blogs accept both text and graphics and, though not as flexible as sites designed for education, they nevertheless can be adapted to post assignments, announcements, and calendars.

Internet Development Tools

Internet development tools like FrontPage and DreamWeaver offer a middle ground. Such tools offer templates for special kinds of pages though they are more oriented toward business than education. A user can put a web page together using a menu-only approach, code-only approach, or a combination. Although the menu-driven approach sounds easy, there is a learning curve and unless the user is conversant with web technology, it is usually necessary to take a short class or buy a book and spend some hours learning about how it all works. Then your school needs to provide space on a server for the web site that you create. If your school does not provide space for teacher web sites, you will need to pay for one; the cost ranges from $30 to $100 per year, depending on the features that you select. Furthermore, Internet development tools cost money. Teachers may buy them at a reduced price—an "Education" version. Nevertheless, either the teacher or the school district can expect to spend between $150 and $300 on good Internet development software. The two biggest advantages of web development tools are the speed of menu-driven programming and the access to the code so that it can be saved and posted on any web site the author chooses.

Writing XHTML Code

The least expensive and most work-intensive way to make a web page is to write code. XHTML is a simple computer language that allows its users to display information on a screen. It does not allow for interactivity, simply display. It can be written in any text editor, appended with a .htm or .html extension, and uploaded to a web server. The vocabulary of the language is not large. There are tags for setting fonts and colors, making lists, and manipulating how the text appears on the page (line breaks and paragraphs, for example). Tables are used to structure pages, and the language allows the user to display graphics as well. Again, using XHTML requires an investment in time, and either a class for those who have only basic knowledge of computers and how web technology works, or a good instruction book for those who are more advanced. On the other hand, authors always have the code they have written, and if a web server ceases functioning, the code may simply be moved to another server.

▨ SUMMARY

In this chapter we have been looking into classrooms to see some of the more common uses of e-mail and e-mail–based discussion. We have looked at their advantages and disadvantages and seen some success and a little failure too. The field trips that we took describe only a few of the possibilities.

▨ REFERENCES

AT&T Knowledge Ventures L.P. (2006). "Filimentality." www.kn.att.com/wired/fil/index.html. Retrieved May 24, 2007.

EmailReplies.Com (2006). Email etiquette. www.emailreplies.com/index.html. Retrieved April 17, 2007.

Gordon, C. (1999). Students as authentic researchers: A new prescription for the high school research assignment. ERIC EJ603683.

Harrington, M., Holik, M., & Hurt, P. (1998). Improving writing through the use of varied strategies. ERIC ED420874.

Harris, J. (1998a). Curriculum-based telecollaboration: Using activity structures to design student projects. *Learning and Leading with Technology.* 26(1), 7–15.

Harris, J. (1998b). *Virtual architecture: Designing and directing curriculum-based tele-computing.* Eugene, OR: International Society of Technology in Education.

Harris, J., & Jones, G. (1999). A descriptive study of telementoring among students, subject matter experts, and teachers: Message flow and function patterns. *Journal of Research on Computing in Education.* 32(1), 36–51.

Herr, T., & Johnson, K. (1994). *Problem solving strategies: Crossing the river with dogs.* Emeryville, CA: Key Curriculum Press.

Huffaker, D. (2004). Spinning yarns around the digital fire. *Information Technology in Childhood Education Annual.* 63–74.

Lambert, G. (1999). Helping twelfth grade honors English students improve writing skills through conferencing. ERIC ED427344.

Miller, D. (2003). How to keep out of trouble with your email. www.penmachine.com/techie/emailtrouble_2003–07.html#top. Retrieved April 17, 2007.

Russell, M. (2001). The Secretary's Conference on Educational Technology: Measuring impacts and shaping the future. www.ed.gov/Technology/techconf/2000/report .html. Retrieved February 1, 2001.

Stoicheva, M. (2000). The digital divide and its implications for language arts. ERIC ED442138.

TeacherWeb (2007). Teacher Web. www.teacherweb.com. Retrieved May 24, 2007.

Wolfsberg, Jeffrey S. (2006). Student safety from cyberbullies, in chat rooms, and in instant messaging. *Education Digest.* 72(2), 33–37.

■ ANNOTATED RESOURCES

Flanagan, B., & Calandra, B. (2005). Podcasting in the classroom. *Learning and Leading with Technology.* September 2005.

Podcasting is another way of reaching students. It may not yet be a mainstream tool for all students because of the technology needed by the student. To use podcasting in a computer laboratory, the student would need head phones. Nevertheless, if a teacher is trying to teach a particularly difficult concept that an oral explanation would illuminate, a podcast might be appropriate. Like web authoring, podcasting requires some expertise on the part of the teacher to create.

Naik, D., & Teelock, V. (2006). Enhancing the teaching and learning of history and geography through information and communications technology: A Mauritian experience. *Educational Technology Research and Development.* 54(4), 422–34.

This is a good reading for K–6 teachers looking for methodologies for using communications technology to teach history.

Telecollaborators wanted. (2001). *Leading and Learning with Technology.* 28(8), 46.

This article describes a clearinghouse where you can find teachers who are interested in participating in telecollaborative projects.

Structuring Internet-enriched learning spaces for understanding and action. (2000). *Leading and Learning with Technology.* 28(4), 24–31.

This article will help you focus on lesson design using the kinds of Internet-based communication discussed in this chapter. There is an excellent chart listing activities, their structures, and the kinds of learning they support. In addition, there are links to sites that support many of the listed activities.

U.S. Department of Education (2004). How the Internet, the law, and today's students are revolutionizing expectations. *National Education Technology Plan.*

This is a discussion of the implications of the virtual classroom.

1. Go to the TechTactics web site for Chapter 4 and click on and study the links about E-Mail Etiquette. What breaches of etiquette can you find in this e-mail? After you have found them, rewrite the e-mail so that it communicates what needs to be said correctly. Hints: (1) your new e-mail will be shorter. (2) Look for the legitimate points the writer makes and restate them acceptably.

    To: Mira Franks

    Subject: Stuff

    Hi,

    Just wanted to touch bases with you on Jason S. who is in your Language Arts class. I don't know about you, but he is driving me crazy. He just don't seem to be able finish anything – just sits and stares and plays with his hare. When I talk to him about his work habits he just nods and agrees and doesn't change anything. I am wondering if you have any clues. COULD HE JUST BE DUMB? In my professional opinion I think we need to speak with the special ed folks and have him tested.

    Otherwise the school year is going pretty well. I get a little tired of the principal harping on integrating content areas, but I guess that is just part of the game we play. Maybe we could think of something that integrates Language Arts and Science and get that requirement out of the way. Let me know if you have some time after school some afternoon this week to talk about it.

    Tanner

2. Write a short description of the ideal class you expect to teach some day, including: grade, subject, location (rural, urban, etc.), and demographics of your students. Now go to the TechTactics web site for Chapter 4 and click on the Teacher web link. Click on the "Teachers" tab and then click on the "Features" tab to see an example of a web site. Once you have browsed this area, sign up to create a site of your own including all of the elements you think would be necessary to help you manage your class.

5

Presentation Software

- Describe a lesson that uses presentation software.
- List the steps for preparing a presentation.
- Name software used for creating presentations.
- State the reasons why presentation software helps students learn.
- List five ways information may be represented with presentation software.
- Match the steps for creating a presentation to levels of Bloom's taxonomy.

OFFICE SUITES AND TEACHERS: HOW DO THEY APPLY TO CLASSROOMS?

Capabilities of Office Suites

The most common software found on school computers is an office suite that contains a word processor, database, spreadsheet, presentation software, and maybe authoring software for Internet presentations as well. Additionally, drawing programs are often embedded in word processors. These drawing programs allow authors to include a number of different kinds of graphics, including shapes (ovals, rectangles, etc.), flow charts, callouts, arrows, lines, connectors, special fonts, shadowing, and three-dimensional representations of the objects they draw. The reason these software packages are called "suites" is that the individual programs in them work together seamlessly.

Office Suites and Projects

One teaching method that teachers use often is project-based learning (Markum et al., 2003). Although this technique is too complex to describe in the scope of this book, understanding how project-based learning works helps to understand how much help an office suite can be. When teachers deliver a unit of study based on student projects, they develop a driving question. They base this driving question on some problem that is relevant for students. The problem may be environmental, societal, related to health, economics, writing—virtually any topic students study. Students solve the problem by gathering information from their community, talking to experts, doing surveys, conducting tests of their environment, or analyzing data that they gather from reference resources. Then they think and talk about the information they have gathered and suggest solutions for the problem in papers, video presentations, and speeches. An office suite supports every phase of this process, and the information that they gather or record with one electronic tool during one part of the process is easily transferred to other tools in the office suite in other parts of the process.

One example is student papers. The work students do on word processors often does not stand in isolation. To come to the conclusions that they are writing about, they might have created a table in a spreadsheet to analyze data they have collected and then turned that data into a chart. They can then easily transfer the table and the chart to their word processor. When they are explaining their table, they can use the embedded graphics program to draw arrows and diagrams to illustrate and further define the conclusions they have written about.

Another example is an activity in which students use mail surveys on some topic of their research. Using a database, they can create a mailing list. Using a word processor, they can create their survey, and using the Mail Merge menu item in the word processor, import the inside addresses of all of the people to whom they intend to send the survey for the letter of introduction to the survey. When they receive the results of their survey, they can enter them into their database, analyze the data, and then cut and paste results to a word processor or even a spreadsheet for further analysis.

Learning about multimedia is much like using multimedia. It is not a linear process. Sometimes it is important to understand a little about the middle and the end of a process before the beginning makes sense. You will want to skim this chapter and the next two before you read them all in detail. In skimming these chapters, your goal will be to get a sense of the focus and elements of multimedia projects.

You can read far enough into Chapters 5 and 7 to learn the basics of presentation software assignments, and then go to Chapter 6 to read about screen design techniques that will help you develop your own skills as you practice with presentation software. Then, when you start thinking about how to implement a presentation software-based assignment in your classroom, you can go back and read about idea mapping and storyboarding in Chapter 7, to learn how to maximize student learning. If you would like to know more about concept mapping, see Appendix D. After you glean what you can on first reading, practice a while and read these chapters again. You will understand more the second time and will be able to hone your skills for using presentation software to improve the teaching/learning process in your classroom. Skills that are needed for using presentation software are listed below.

▓ Make a button and link to another page.
▓ Make a hot word and link to another page.
▓ Make a text box.
▓ Change fonts in a text box.

- Change levels in a list.
- Change foreground and background colors.
- Scale graphic objects.
- Digitize graphics, sound, and video.
- Scan documents and images.
- Capture computer screens.
- Import a graphic.
- Import or insert an object (image, sound, etc.).
- Use a paint program to create graphics composed of lines, rectangles, ovals, and so on.
- Use a graphics program to enhance scanned images.
- Understand the advantages and disadvantages of different file graphics formats.
- Insert a new slide (card, page).

We start this chapter with a field trip. Probably the first thing you want to know about presentation software is what a classroom looks like when it is getting ready to start a hypermedia project. You will read about Jeff, who has learned the skills for making presentations with computers but has never been asked to use the software to complete an assignment.

Although this example involves a tenth-grade biology class, those who teach in the early grades can benefit from this snapshot of a classroom as much as middle or high school teachers. Younger students work with less information, but the methods for working with information and presentation software are similar. The same is true of content areas. If you are an English, language arts, or social studies teacher, you should think about topics that you teach and draw some conclusions about how an assignment like this would look with your content and your students. Here are some questions the field trip should help you to answer:

Useful for all grade levels, content	

- What does an assignment that uses presentation software look like?
- How would you introduce such a unit to students?

Jeff's biology class is just starting a new unit on plant and animal cells. The teacher, Mrs. Hansen, told the students they will have a test over the new unit in three weeks. Then she told them about the activities that will help them prepare for the test.

FIELD TRIP 5.1

Learning about Cells

Explaining the activities

Jeff, who is wincing at the thought of writing definitions in his lab notebook and answering end-of-chapter questions, imagines himself using a ruler to measure the stack of worksheets for the unit. He hopes the class will at least get to use the microscopes to see some cells. That would make the thought of all of the other work nearly bearable. Instead, the teacher surprises him. She says, "No definitions this time, no end-of-chapter questions, and no worksheets." Jeff, suddenly interested, wonders cynically if she has something even worse in store.

She says, "We are going to use the computers a new way for this unit. You will write an electronic report called *A Hypermedia Guide to Cells.* We will divide our time among talks and demonstrations by me, reading the text, doing and documenting microscope work, writing idea maps and storyboards for your presentations, getting graphics and animations from the Internet, and actually writing your presentation on the computer. We will have to plan our activities carefully so that everyone will have enough time at the computer and the microscopes to get the work done. To help you understand how you will be graded on your project, I will hand out a scoring rubric after you understand a little more about the project."

Jeff, astounded and interested, listens carefully to the specifics of the computer assignment. His teacher says, "I want you to include these topics in your computer project: parts of the cell, cell functions for both animals and plants, and a step-by-step explanation of meiosis and mitosis.

"I want you to include a picture that shows an example of each major idea, like the parts of a cell. And I want you to show mitosis and meiosis graphically, either with an animation, video, or a series of graphics. I will give you some ideas about where you can find this information on the Internet. I also want you to write and record a short audio piece—about one minute—to include in your presentation, on how cells differentiate to perform different tasks.

| Defining a product |

"Your finished presentation should have between fifteen and twenty-five screens and should start with a title page followed by a menu page. Your program should allow a user to get to any piece of information with three clicks of the mouse. Every word in your report that is not common knowledge should have some kind of hyperlink to an explanation that could be text, a graphic, an audio, or a video clip. Only half of your hyperlinks can point to text. The rest should point to audio, graphic, video, or animation. You will also want to document all of your sources by providing a page called "References" at the end of your presentation. We will talk about copyright rules and how to set that page up tomorrow, because you will want to document information as you get it.

| Working with information |

"Spend the next fifteen minutes just browsing through the chapter in your book on cells and think about how you might organize the information you need for the hypermedia presentation you are going to write. Then, I will give you some ideas about how to start." Jeff looks at his textbook and begins thumbing through the chapter and starts thinking about how he will organize his hypermedia guide to plant and animal cells.

Now that you have read a little about what happens in a classroom before students start a hypermedia project, we will look at some of the reasons why Jeff's teacher thinks that this assignment using presentation software will replace learning activities she has used in the past.

PRESENTATION SOFTWARE

Presentation software is a unique blend of formats for displaying information. It has three names—presentation, multimedia, and hypermedia software—but software with any of those names usually will do about the same thing. In this book we generally use the term *presentation software*. Its power lies in its ability to display information in many different formats arranged in a variety of helpful combinations. Presentation software enables people to do the following:

| Methods of displaying information |

■ Display information in five different formats: text, video, audio, graphic, and animation
■ Present information in a hypertext (nonlinear) format, allowing the user to jump from one related idea to another

Beyond these two fundamental functions found in all presentation software, the user must supply everything else, including organization and content, thereby setting up an excellent opportunity for learning. Names of different presentation software include PowerPoint, HyperStudio, and, oddly enough, Internet authoring software. For younger children, teachers use KidPix and KidWorks. Prices range from free (for Internet software if you already have it) to around $100 per copy for the other kinds of software.

Names of software

This genre of software is menu driven and allows authors to easily import graphics, animations, audio, and video to pages, cards, or screens. It allows authors to draw geometric figures such as squares, rectangles, lines, and circles using color, as well as to display text in many fonts, sizes, colors, and styles. Finally, it allows authors to link information any way that they deem appropriate. Presentation software is simple to learn, and is quite intuitive after some instruction and a little practice.

Characteristics of presentation software

Some presentation software allows skilled users to write "script" (computer programs) that actually get input from the end user. This capability allows authors to create exercises and tests within their finished product and generally provides for more forms of interactivity. Scripting is beyond the scope of this book.

How can students learn better when they create presentations? Presentation software helps them see relationships among facts, which is helpful for two reasons: When students organize isolated facts into a presentation, they remember the facts better (Plotnick, 1997; Pohl, 1998); when students see relationships among facts, they often generalize and come to understand some problem or process more deeply (Merrill & Tennyson, 1987; Spoehr, 1995; Lehrer & Romberg, 1996).

Presentation software and learning

Now, do you remember the assignments Jeff has to complete for his hypermedia project? He has to do an outline and an idea map. He also has to do a storyboard, which may be new to you. A storyboard helps people translate the ideas in their outlines and idea maps into a blueprint that guides them as they work on their presentation at the computer. Looking at Table 5.1, you can see that a hypermedia assignment, if designed properly, challenges students at all levels of the taxonomy. Consider how important it is to teach students to think critically and how difficult it is to design lessons that encourage this. You can see from the table that hypermedia-supported lessons provide many opportunities for students to think at the highest levels of the taxonomy. Any successful work that they do above the "knowledge" level of Bloom's taxonomy involves critical thinking.

Before we continue with Jeff, Mrs. Hansen, and the assignment, you need to understand a few more basics about how and why hypermedia is so powerful. Knowing how and why will help you decide which kinds of content you teach are best suited for hypermedia-supported lessons. Presentation software does not help teach all content most efficiently.

Displaying Information: Key to Creating Understanding

Researchers tell us that some people learn better when they read information, others when they hear it, others when they see it presented graphically, and still others when

TABLE 5.1 Bloom's Taxonomy and Hypermedia Lessons			
The Cognitive Process Dimension	**The Knowledge Dimension**		
	Factual	**Conceptual**	**Procedural**
Remember	Gathering facts for the presentation	–	Making a flowchart and concept map; making graphics, sound, and video; using a multimedia creation tool
Understand	Reformatting information for a multimedia format	Sorting out relationships among facts in order to organize the presentation	Making a flowchart and concept map; making graphics, sound, and video; using a multimedia creation tool
Apply	Using technology skills to create multimedia	Flowcharting and concept mapping before building the presentation	Making a flowchart and concept map; making graphics, sound, and video; using a multimedia creation tool
Analyze	Comparing facts students have gathered for conflicts and differences	Storyboarding from the flowcharts and/or concepts maps students have built	Working with other students to solve technical problems
Evaluate	–	Observing other students' projects	Observing other students' presentations
Create	Creating an accurate representation of the facts students gathered	Creating a finished presentation that is logical and appealing	Creating a finished presentation that works

they interact with it in some physical way (Gay, 2000). Computers accommodate all of these learning styles because the machines can present information in five different formats:

> Presentation software and Bloom's taxonomy

- ▓ Graphics
- ▓ Text
- ▓ Audio
- ▓ Audio and video
- ▓ Animations

> Building context with varied formats

Also, computers encourage complex interactions with content. The act of organizing information helps people learn. The richer the information they organize, the richer their learning will be. Student or teacher presentations with presentation software are *not* the reason for using computers to teach. The value of presentation software does not lie so much in the finished product as in the process of creating it.

> Process is as important as product

The Role of Interactivity

For many years, the primary way people learned to organize their writing was the outline. Organizing ideas with presentation software is like outlining in three dimensions. To prepare a hypermedia assignment, a student does a traditional outline, an idea map (an outline of relationships), and a storyboard. The storyboard translates the facts and relationships derived from the idea map and outline into a blueprint for the computer. For a student author this task is complex enough that it can supplant many traditional activities such as doing worksheets, answering questions at the end of the chapter, and writing definitions.

> Supplants many traditional activities

Conveying information with hypermedia is different than conveying it in print. Hypermedia adds a third dimension to the formatting of information. Print media runs front to back, beginning to end. It operates in a single dimension. With print-based information delivery, students are taught how to think about a beginning, middle, and an end for the story, report, or paragraph. Then they chunk the information they want to convey into paragraphs, decide on an order for the paragraphs (or at least they are told to think about an order), and finally write their piece.

> Allows students to think nonlinearly

Knowledge itself does not naturally fall into paragraphs that start at one place and end at another. If you were writing a report on geographic regions of the United States, you might divide the country into six regions: Northwest, Southwest, Northeast, Southeast, Midwest, and the Plains. In your written report, you would have to talk about each of these areas in some order. Although there is no reason that Northwest should be first and Southwest should be second, given the limitations of print you will have to talk about some region first, another next, and another last.

From another perspective, if people do not understand a word in your report, they might need to go to the glossary or a dictionary to look it up. Most likely, they will try to guess from the context and move forward. Hypermedia allows us to transcend these limitations of print if it is designed properly. It is in the act of designing the product that students learn from the information that they are trying to organize.

Think about Jeff and the hypermedia report he was just assigned to do. Knowledge about cells does not start at one place and end at another. A cell performs both mitosis and meiosis. But what about cell function and structure? You have to know something about cell function and structure to understand mitosis and meiosis. You also have to know something about structure to understand function, and vice versa. Furthermore, you have to think about cells in order to make the decision to describe cells based on their function and structure.

> Author must always think about relationships

If you think about the possibilities for creating hypermedia reports, you can see that the nonlinear environment provided by presentation software nudges its users into thinking clearly and logically. The writer must spend time working out relationships in ways that transcend the traditional paper outline to make a coherent, understandable, and informative hypermedia presentation.

The life cycle of a hypermedia-supported assignment is straightforward. Let's look in on Jeff's classroom to see how he and his classmates are doing with their new project, *A Hypermedia Guide to Cells*.

**FIELD TRIP
5.2**

Cells Project Continues

Jeff and his classmates began their work in earnest. After they spent a few minutes getting an overview of the information from their textbooks, Jeff's teacher explained their assignment. She gave them a partially completed idea map about cell function and structure to start their thinking. She also gave them a list of graphics to find on the Internet. Mrs. Hansen gave the class the names of some pictures she wanted them to find. She said, "I know you will need at least these graphics (vacuole, mitochondria, and nucleus), so you can get started. As you work on your presentation you will learn which others you will need to find or prepare for your project." Finally, she gave them a template to help them build their storyboards. Jeff's head was spinning. This was all so new!

Because this was the first time Jeff and his classmates had studied a unit using hypermedia, they had to learn a few things. They had all done regular outlines half-heartedly in their English classes, but they had never tried *idea mapping.* Therefore, their teacher had to show them how to do it. At first Jeff thought idea maps were going to be easy. All he would have to do was draw some boxes with lines between them, stick some relevant-sounding words in the boxes, and that part of the assignment would be done.

> Organizing information

Jeff discovered that idea mapping is quite a challenge. When the teacher asked, "OK, now what are some of the things that all plant and animal cells, have in common?" Jeff could not figure out why she thought "structure" was a better answer than "nuclei." Then, after a lot of practice with the teacher and the rest of the students, Jeff learned how to look for relationships among things and ideas.

By the time Jeff was done with the outline and the idea map, he had come into contact with quite a few facts. To fully understand how knowledge about cells is organized, a person has to know and understand some detail.

As Jeff's idea-mapping efforts progressed, his teacher helped him understand that most of the key ideas in his concept map could be shown in ways other than with words. He spent his computer time consulting his idea map as he hunted for information from the Internet, scanned pictures, and made audio recordings to put in his presentation.

As the pieces of information about cells began making sense, Jeff started his storyboard. To make a storyboard, he drew each screen of the presentation on a piece of paper. He wrote down information about fonts and colors, as well as "hot words" (words users can click on for information or navigation). He recorded the instructions for linking each page to the others in his flowchart. He made notations of the names of graphics files and their locations. He wrote headings and paragraphs about cells, what they do, and their composition. In addition, he created definitions and added pictures along with some audio clips to further explain the ideas he was working with.

> Preparing to display information

As his storyboard began taking shape, Jeff used his computer time to create the actual product with PowerPoint (other software would have served as well). Because of his preparation, Jeff was able to use his limited time at the computer efficiently. He had done all of the organization. He could finally pay attention to the mechanics of creating a hypermedia presentation—thinking about which key to press, experimenting with special effects, and just making it look good.

> Creating the project

At the end of three weeks, the unit was finished. Mrs. Hanson narrowly averted three classroom management disasters. She underestimated the amount of computer time the students would need. Fortunately, she was able to send some students to the computer lab on certain days and others to the library computers. In a classroom with five computers and thirty students who were only in the room fifty minutes a day, the maximum amount of time a student could get was two hours over three weeks. Next time she would provide the students with a small library of graphics (the best of this year's efforts) rather than ask the students to do the Internet search themselves. This time she quickly provided some modest graphics when she realized they would not have enough time to find them individually. She also overestimated what the students would remember about running presentation software from last year's computer applications class. Next year she vowed she would spend a day reacquainting students with the skills they would need to use it. And then there was that one day when almost everyone was confused about the idea map—more on that later.

> Error #1: Underestimating time and resources needed

> Error #2: Overestimating students' recall of skills

> Error #3: Failing to teach idea maps before assigning them

She asked the students to hand in their idea map, outline, and storyboard. Students gave a short, five-minute demonstration of their presentation for the whole class. Then she divided the class into four groups. Group members individually gave in-depth displays of their presentations to the other members of their group. The group then chose one of the presentations to display on the Internet and save as an

> Presenting the product

example for next year's class. She gave the class a thirty-question multiple-choice test followed by an essay question to evaluate what they had learned about cells. As she corrected the tests, it was clear that the test was easy for Jeff and most of the others—quite a change from last year.

Evaluating the product

As she looked over the students' products, she realized that she had more information than she needed for grading the unit. Rather than grade each piece of work, she quickly scanned each storyboard and idea map and placed a check by the student's name if the work was acceptable. She then wrote a short, one-sentence, "What you did right" comment on each paper. She could see that the students would need more practice with idea mapping and storyboarding, but this was a good first step. She graded the students' tests, listened, and watched as they gave their presentations. Their next hypermedia presentation, *Organ Systems in Mammals,* would be a little easier.

EXECUTING A HYPERMEDIA-SUPPORTED LESSON PLAN

Browse Table 5.2 for a list of the activities in a typical hypermedia-supported unit. The elements are the same whether the learner is in kindergarten or twelfth grade. The difference lies in how much help the teacher provides and how much information the student is required to process. Bear in mind that students will do other things, too, such as read their text, take tests, and participate in class discussion. They will do fewer worksheets, answer fewer questions, and memorize fewer lists and definitions.

The information students process varies by grade

It is important to match the computer portion of the assignment with the students' abilities. Table 5.3 will help you understand what this means. It is divided into three different segments: beginning, intermediate, and advanced. As a teacher, you know that these divisions do not necessarily refer to grade levels. I would, and have, given the assignment for beginners described in Table 5.3 to adults. I have seen students in upper elementary grades and middle school who are easily capable of doing the advanced assignment. The goal is to move everyone forward as much as possible toward the advanced level. Why? Because the advanced level gives students practice

TABLE 5.2 Activity, Materials, and Products		
Activity	**Materials**	**Product for Evaluation**
Outline	Pencil/paper or computer	Written outline
Idea maps	Pencil/paper or computer	Hand-drawn or written idea map
Storyboard	Pencil/paper or computer	The completed storyboard
Flowchart	Pencil/paper or computer	The completed storyboard
The software	Computer	CD or Internet display is graded on: • Following directions • Completeness • Design of the information (presented logically) • Screen design

doing high-level analytical thinking tasks and provides opportunities that create context for the information that they are learning. This context will help them remember the information better for a longer period of time (Woolfolk, 2000).

You probably recognize that the advanced lesson plan does require some creative thinking. However, you might ask, "Why are the beginning and intermediate plans any better than a worksheet?" The answer is that the plans provide opportunities to learn from text, graphics, audio, animation, and video while the student is physically interacting with the machine that delivers the information. Those five information delivery modes play to a variety of learning styles. Again, you are providing opportunities for students to put the content that they are learning into a context so that they can understand and remember it better.

TABLE 5.3 Assignments Using Presentation Software	
Level of Learner	**Kinds of Assignment**
Beginner	
The learner does not have presentation software skills.	Create the outline and idea map together as a class. Provide the storyboard. Provide all of the graphics on the network or disk so students do not have to look for them.
The learner is young (grades K–4).	
The content is very difficult or foreign to the learner.	
The learner has never created a concept map before.	The number of links between pages depends on the age and cognitive abilities of the child. A kindergartner might be required to make two or three pages while a twelfth grader might have to manage 10–15 pages on his or her first attempt.
The learner has had difficulty reading and mastering idea mapping and storyboarding.	
Intermediate	
The learner is aquainted with presentation software.	Give the list of concepts you want them to know and ask them to write them in outline form.
The learner has the cognitive ability of an average middle school student.	Give them a half-finished idea map.
The learner knows how to create concept maps.	Give them a template for a storyboard and work through the title screen, main menu, and two or three screens with them.
The learner has access to the Internet and knows how to look for graphics and text information.	
Advanced	
Learners are familiar with presentation software, file formats, and downloading information from the Internet.	Give students a list of topics they should cover. The topics Jeff's teacher gave the class are plant and animal cells, what they are made of, what they do, and how they reproduce. Students should use this list as the basis for the outline, idea map, and storyboard.
They have had practice creating concept maps.	
The learners know and understand how concepts can share properties or characteristics.	

■ SUMMARY

Planning a lesson that uses the full capabilities of presentation software involves more than having students go to the computer and construct a series of slides inhabited by some text and graphics. Using presentation software to maximize learning involves planning the lesson in such a way that students are required to organize and connect the information that they are learning. There is a process for developing a presentation that provides opportunities for students to interact with the same information in several different contexts: the outline, concept map, and storyboard.

Furthermore, students should consciously search for different representations of the information they are organizing so that they have two or three different opportunities for making links in their memories to what they are learning. If they are learning the definition of the word "urban" they will want to write about urban (text), show pictures representing an urban setting (graphics), and find or create either a video or animation that also represents some element of "urban." Furthermore, they will probably want to think about consequences or implications of "urban" and represent these topics in multiple formats as well.

■ REFERENCES

Gay, G. (2000). *Thinking and learning skills.* Center for Adaptive Technology, University of Toronto. http://snow.utoronto.ca/Learn2/mod3/mistyles.html.

Lehrer, R., & Romberg, T. (1996) Exploring children's data modeling. *Cognition and Instruction.* 14(1), 69–108.

Markum, T., Larmer, J., & Ravitz, J. (2003). *Project based learning: A guide to standards-focused project based learning.* Novato, CA: Buck Institute for Education.

Merrill, D., & Tennyson, R. (1987). *Teaching concepts: An instructional design guide.* Englewood Cliffs, NJ: Educational Technology Publications.

Plotnick, E. (1997). Concept mapping: A graphical system for understanding the relationships between concepts. ERIC ED407938.

Pohl, M. (1998). Hypermedia as a cognitive tool. ED-MEDIA/ED-TELECOM 98 World Conference on Educational Multimedia and Hypermedia & World Conference on Educational Telecommunications. Proceedings (Tenth, Freiburg, Germany).

Spoehr, K. T. (1995). Enhancing the acquisition of conceptual structures through hypermedia. In K. McGilly (Ed.). *Classroom lessons: Integrating cognitive theory and classroom practice.* Cambridge, MA: Bradford Books.

Woolfolk, A. (2000). *Educational psychology.* Boston: Allyn and Bacon, p. 283.

■ ANNOTATED RESOURCES

Hsu, Y. (2006). 'Lesson rainbow': The use of multiple representations in an Internet-based discipline-integrated science lesson. *British Journal of Educational Technology.* 37(4), 539–557.

Hsu's research explores the relationship between student acquisition of knowledge and the use of multimedia. The delivery tool for the multimedia in this case is the Internet, but the principles are the same. Hsu measures both increases in students' conceptual knowledge and student attitude toward learning.

Ray, L. (1999). Multimedia authoring tools: Challenges to effective use. *Computers in Schools.* 15(1), 79–87.

Using multimedia authoring tools is not always easy. This article examines the challenges of the appropriate use of multimedia authoring for students. Ray focuses especially on literacy development.

Reed, W., & Wells, J. (1997). Merging the Internet and hypermedia in the English language arts. *Computers in Schools.* 13(3/4), 75–102.

This article provides some detail on merging the Internet and Hypercard for students studying *Hamlet.* Whether your class is studying *Hamlet* and using Hypercard does not matter. You will read about some interesting strategies and methods for using the Internet and hypermedia in language arts.

Srinivasan, S. (2005). Multimedia in a science learning environment. *Journal of Educational Multimedia and Hypermedia.* 14(2), 151–167.

Although this article does not address the activity of student construction of multimedia projects, it does address the effectiveness of multimedia for learning. The important information to be gained from this article is a review of the principles of good multimedia construction and how they work.

Companion Web Site   www.ablongman.com/thorsen3e

1. Go to Chapters 5–8 of the TechTactics web site. Click on the Inspiration web site with concept mapping tutorials and examples in most content areas—download a free copy of Inspiration software and install it. Now choose a topic that you might assign to a class that you teach, or might teach, and do a concept map for that topic.

2. Using the Inspiration software that you downloaded in Question 1 and the two links on the web site pertaining to the creation of an effective web page or web site, make a concept map that illustrates the major components of the planning involved in building an interactive presentation (either a web site or a presentation built with presentation software).

Graphic and Interface Design Principles

OBJECTIVES

- Appreciate the value of planning and designing effective screens.
- Design screens that present information effectively.

As students prepare their presentations, they must also think about how to make the presentation convey information well. We have established that clarity of thought is an important element in the preparation of a presentation. It is not comforting to know, however, that bad graphic design can destroy all of the hard work involved. The task of building a good presentation is not over when all of the outlining, idea mapping, and storyboarding are finished. Unless your students use some basic principles of graphic design as they build their screens, their work may not communicate well and may reflect poorly on both them and you.

Simplicity and consistency are *the* principles of graphic design for computers. Understanding graphic design is a matter of your own practice and your observations of screens that other people make. Expecting good graphic design techniques of yourself as well as your students is as important as expecting students to use good spoken and written grammar. The reason people use grammar at all is to make their communication more clear and precise. Graphic and **interface** design are the grammar of the eye.

As you teach interface design, consider the age and ability of your students. Work on a few rules at a time. There are some rules that very young students cannot understand—see a rule about type justification, for example. Not much is gained by teaching kindergartners about type justification unless a student accidentally stumbles on the control in the software and wants to know what it is for.

Whole books have been written on the topic of good graphic design for computers. I have listed three of the best in the references at the end of this chapter. The guidelines I provide below do not cover technical details such as kerning and anti-

> **Simplicity and consistency are the basis of graphic design**

INTERFACE
The consistent color, font style, and placement of informational and navigational elements of a program or an operating system. A good interface is essential.

aliasing, among others. The guidelines I have chosen are fundamental ones that novice designers often violate, making a presentation difficult to view and understand. Using presentation software to convey information is a strange, new world for many people. They must understand the basics first. We will approach the topic as a series of rules with examples.

> Graphic design is a large field—teach students the basics.

Rule 1: Use General Design Principles

Use general design principles based on research. Richard Mayer, in *Multimedia Learning* (2001), discusses seven general design principles based on empirical research that he has conducted over several years. For each of these principles he provides two pieces of empirical evidence: a retention effect and a transfer effect. A *retention effect* is a measure of how well students remember information, and a *transfer effect* is a measure of how well students can transfer what they have learned from one problem to a new problem. Mayer explains these principles as follows.

- ▩ *Multimedia principle:* Students learn better from words and pictures than from words alone.
- ▩ *Spatial contiguity principle:* Students learn better when corresponding words and pictures are presented near rather than far from each other on the page or screen.
- ▩ *Temporal contiguity principle:* Students learn better when corresponding words and pictures are presented simultaneously rather than successively.
- ▩ *Coherence principle:* Students learn better when extraneous words, pictures, and sounds are excluded rather than included.
- ▩ *Modality principle:* Students learn better from animation and narration than from animation and on-screen text.
- ▩ *Redundancy principle:* Students learn better from animation and narration than from animation, narration, and on-screen text.
- ▩ *Individual differences principle:* Design effects are stronger for low-knowledge learners than for high-knowledge learners and for high-spatial learners than for low-spatial learners.

Rule 2: Orient Users

Provide information on each screen that tells users where they are in the presentation. Use headings and captions as organizers. Headings and captions should reflect the way students organize content in the outline and idea map. Level-one items often serve as screen headings. Menus are level-two items, and level-three items serve as individual facts that students display in text boxes, audio and video clips, animations, and sound files. At this point it is easy to see why so much planning is important. Without it, the students' products are only a collection of disorganized facts and pictures.

Though the colors cannot be seen in Figure 6.1, the layout that Jeff developed uses both color and screen location to help users assimilate and understand content

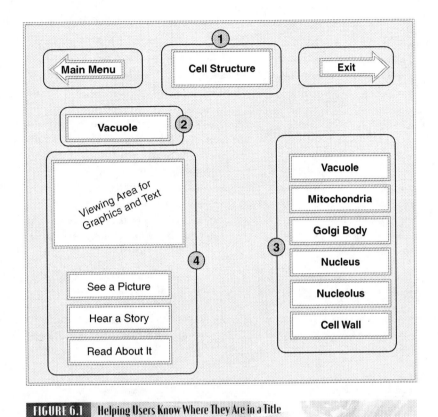

FIGURE 6.1 Helping Users Know Where They Are in a Title

as well as navigate the program. The list below describes the parts of the screen that are indicated on the figure.

1. Area 1 is the title of this topic—one of three main topics in Jeff's presentation. The other main topics are Cell Function and Cell Reproduction. Jeff decided to use gray as the background color for this section. This topic title is in a dark blue-green box, similar to the other colors on this screen but different enough to stand out. For the Cell Function topic, Jeff used a green background, and for Cell Reproduction he used purple. In other words, the background color of the screen, along with a title at the top, cues Jeff's user to a change in topic.

2. This box contains the title of the subtopic that the user has chosen from the bank of buttons at the right (in area 3). The subtopic title box is blue and matches the color of the subtopic buttons in area 3. Jeff wanted his users to mentally connect the subtopic title box with the related buttons.

3. These six buttons represent the subtopics a viewer can choose. When a user clicks on one of these, the new subtopic title appears in area 2.

4. This is the display area with three selection buttons below it. This is where information on a subtopic is presented. In this example with Vacuole chosen as the subtopic, when the user clicks on See a Picture, a picture of a vacuole appears

in the display area. When the user clicks on Read About It, text about vacuoles appears. When Hear a Story is selected, there is no change to the display but the user hears an audio segment about vacuoles that Jeff has recorded. These three buttons are a different color from the six subtopic buttons, because they perform a different set of functions.

Not numbered in Figure 6.1 are the two primary navigation buttons. The Main Menu button takes a user back to the menu that lists this and the two other main topics in Jeff's presentation. The Exit button takes a user out of the presentation. These buttons occupy the same positions on all the screens in Jeff's presentation.

To see how a presentation author can achieve consistency from screen to screen, now look at Jeff's screen for Cell Reproduction (Figure 6.2) The background color has changed, but the topic title is still at the top of the screen. All navigation buttons are in the same place, along with the viewing area for content. This is the kind of consistency that good planning yields.

Rule 3: Justify Text Appropriately

Everything should be left justified except for numbers in a table, which should be right justified. Numbers should be right justified so that they line up correctly as the number of digits to the left increases. However, if the numbers include decimals, then they

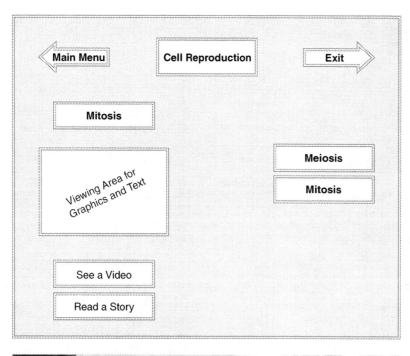

FIGURE 6.2 Mockup of Cell Reproduction Presentation

TABLE 6.1 Numbers and Justification		
Left Justified	**Decimal Justified**	**Right Justified**
1	1.0	1
12	12.0	12
123	1.23	123

should be aligned on the decimal point, if the software being used has that capability (and most software does). Table 6.1 shows left-, decimal-, and right-justified text. Figure 6.3 shows a different type of justification, in which both left and right margins are straight because extra spaces have been inserted (by the software) between words. Although traditional books use justified margins, justified text on a screen can be hard to read.

Rule 4: Limit Type Styles

Do not use more than three type styles per screen. You may use one style for headings, one for text, and one for navigation buttons and controls, although even this much diversity is not necessary. These text styles should remain consistent throughout a short hypermedia product and at least within sections of longer products. Navigation text (button and menu text), especially, should remain consistent through a presentation. Different font styles beyond this minimum should have a real reason. For example, you may import a graphic or graphics with different text styles than the ones you are using. Don't worry about it. Do not follow the rule if there is a good reason not to. On the other hand, if you adhere to the rule you are less at risk of producing "busy" screens.

Difficult to Read
Although it seems like a good idea, justified text is hard to read. The variable spacing and the monotony of the margins make it difficult to read quickly. Just like everything else on a computer screen, spacing means something.

Easier to read
Although it seems like a good idea, justified text is hard to read. The variable spacing and the monotony of the margins make it difficult to read quickly. Just like everything else on a computer screen, spacing means something.

FIGURE 6.3 Justification Examples

Rule 5: Limit Colors

Do not use more than three or four colors per screen. Colors should stay consistent for the entire product if it is short, or could change somewhat to accommodate different topics (consisting of several screens) within a presentation. Colors in imported graphics do not count toward the three- or four-color specification. Have a good reason for using color. Reasons for using color include:

▓ To attract, hold, or direct attention; in that sense, color could be a navigation tool
▓ To show relationships
▓ To provide data (example: a blue line changing to red implies cold to hot)

Rule 6: Standardize Use of Colors

Set up a color scheme and use it consistently. Some colors work very well for certain tasks. Blue, for example, is a great color to use for a background rather than a foreground because the human retina has fewer blue-sensitive cells than sensors for any other color. Additional colors for backgrounds are black, white, and yellow, but consider two things—contrast and expense in printing. Too much contrast between type and background is hard to read for some people. And be considerate if you think your audience might appreciate your presentation enough to want to print a personal copy; solid black or dark-colored backgrounds consume a lot of expensive printer ink. Consider using red and green in locations where you intend the viewer to focus. Otherwise, the viewer is likely to miss them. When choosing colors for text and its accompanying background, do not use low-contrast colors (for example, orange on yellow, green on blue, or white on beige). Also, avoid the following color combinations: red on green, green on blue, and red on blue. They are hard to read and create after-images (Marcus, 1991).

Rule 7: Enhance Text with Graphics and Interactivity

Do not allow students to hand in screens that are only text. Text-heavy documents are perceived as difficult to read (or worse, boring), whether on screen or on paper. Text-heavy presentations also do not take advantage of the computer's power to organize information. Text should be accompanied by charts, illustrations, diagrams, boxes, and—above all—*interactivity* (menus, hot words), because these elements make documents visually appealing, which is important if you want people to read what you have researched, written, and produced.

Rule 8: Eliminate Superfluous Items

Every object on the screen should have meaning. Decoration for the sake of decoration is superfluous. Examples of superfluous designs are elaborate borders that do not contribute information to the presentation, and clip art that has only a vague relationship to the objective of the screen.

Rule 9: Use Upper- and Lowercase

Don't use all caps.   Instead of using all capital letters, use both upper- and lowercase type (Figure 6.4), because it is easier to read.

Rule 10: Keep Text Lines Short

Keep line lengths between eight and ten words.   Short sentences and paragraphs are more visually appealing and are more likely to be read.

Rule 11: Use Single Spacing

Double space between paragraphs rather than indent.

Rule 12: Simplify the Structure

Make it is as easy as possible for a user to find information in the program.   People using hypermedia products prefer consistency in the structure of screens. It is difficult to know how to get around when the structure changes frequently. Remind students that a hypermedia product should not be a hide-and-seek game (the author hides the information and the user looks for it). The student's goal should be to structure information so it is easy for someone to access and understand.

Rule 13: Limit the Focus

Feature one idea per screen.   A good rule of thumb is to have only one main topic per screen, but this main topic may have several subtopics. The best guideline for

---

ALL-UPPERCASE TEXT IS REALLY DIFFICULT TO READ BECAUSE OF THE LACK OF CONTRAST. USERS MISS WORDS AND PUNCTUATION, AND READING SLOWS DOWN SIGNIFICANTLY. PEOPLE GENERALLY SCAN COMPUTER SCREENS RATHER THAN READ THEM CAREFULLY, SO CLARITY IS ESPECIALLY IMPORTANT.

All-uppercase text is really difficult to read because of the lack of contrast. Users miss words and punctuation, and reading slows down significantly. People generally scan computer screens rather than read them carefully, so clarity is especially important.

FIGURE 6.4 Upper- and Lowercase Text

grouping subtopics on a screen is "Miller's 7 ± 2" rule (Gagne, Yekovich, & Yekovich, 1993). This means that the reader of the screen can most easily handle between five and nine ideas at one time. Fewer than five ideas do not give the user enough information on which to generalize, and more than nine ideas is confusing. This is especially true of concepts. Notice in Figure 6.1 that there were six different topics from which to choose. Jeff could have added three more without making the screen too confusing.

Rule 14: Provide Emphasis

Use bold, italics, or underlining to emphasize ideas.

Rule 15: Know Your Audience

Decide ahead of time on the purpose and audience for the product. If the student will present the product to the whole class, certain elements, particularly the type size, will be much different than if the product is meant for the use of one person at a time. In *Illustrating Computer Documentation* (1991), William Horton cites a study by Kantowitz and Sorken on recommended sizes of type for different distances from the monitor (Figure 6.5). Although font size may seem like a minor consideration, it is another way of getting students to reflect on the purpose for their work and to think about the audience for whom they are writing. Also, because computer screens have lower resolution than the printed page, **sans serif** fonts are recommended, especially for small type, as in **body text.** (In traditional printed media, serif fonts were considered to be more legible.) Arial and Helvetica are two common sans serif fonts.

SANS SERIF
Lettering styles with lines and curves of uniform thickness (usually), and no decorative "feet," "tails," or other flourishes—all of which were descended from hand lettering.

BODY TEXT
Text that comprises the main part ("body") of written communication. Contrast this with *titles,* which are "display" text.

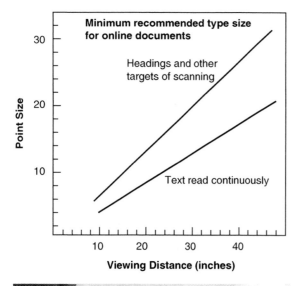

FIGURE 6.5 Using the Right Font Size

Rule 16: Do Not Flash

Do not use flashing text to get the attention of the users. It irritates rather than interests them. Flashing text makes it hard for the user to focus on anything else. Use color and location to call attention to information.

Rule 17: Use Lists

Lists are especially helpful on computer screens. They help people find information quickly. There are several ways to delineate lists: numbers, bullets, and check boxes are the most common.

Rule 18: Navigate Consistently

Keep navigation buttons in the same position from one screen to the next. Jeff did this, as you saw already (Figure 6.1).

Rule 19: Do Not Stack Text

Stacked (vertical) text is hard to read. See Figure 6.6. The label for the figure on the left is hard to notice and read.

Rule 20: Include Multiple Graphic Types

Remember that pictures are only one kind of graphic element. Other kinds of graphics include charts, maps, tables, lists, diagrams, photographs, and clip art.

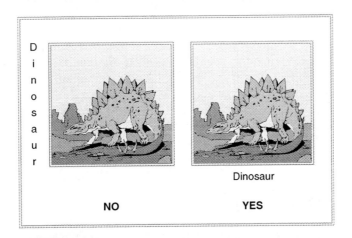

FIGURE 6.6 Stacked and Unstacked Text

The images used herein were obtained from IMSI's MasterClips©, Master Photos©, Clipart&More© or Animations&More© Collection, 100 Rowland Way, Novato, CA 94945, USA.

Rule 21: Organize the Screen

Group objects for meaning and better visual clarity.   Use borders, lines, white space, or color backgrounds to group objects with similar functions and make them stand out.

Rule 22: Size Matters

Realize that the relative size of an object on a screen determines its importance to the reader.   Examples of this principle are illustrated in Figures 6.7 and 6.8. A menu for the life cycle of a monarch butterfly that is arranged like the one in Figure 6.7 emphasizes the adult stage in the cycle. The user of this software will most likely see, remember, and click on the adult. However, if the viewers of this presentation must know about each stage of the monarch's life cycle, they are at a disadvantage—and a very quiet, sneaky disadvantage, at that. In fact, this is a very good point to make to your students, who must not only make presentations but also view the presentations of others. Someone may be trying to manipulate their perception of reality by the way graphics are displayed on a screen. Figure 6.7 implies that the adult monarch is most important without using a single element of text to do it, whereas Figure 6.8 implies that all stages in the life cycle of a monarch are important, again using no text.

Rule 23: Placement Matters

The location of items on the screen determines their importance.   Items at the top of the screen appear to the viewer to be more important than items at the bottom of the screen. If, for example, you were displaying a picture of your class on the computer screen with individual portraits of the class officers, the pictures of the class officers would be placed above the portrait of the class. If you were graphically representing the wars in which the United States has participated, the most important (whatever your criteria for importance is) should be at the top of the screen and the least important at the bottom. If a student were doing a presentation on major and minor romantic poets of the early 1800s, pictures of the major poets would belong at the top of the screen, with minor poets below them. This is a simple principle, but again, a principle that the informational literate student should understand. Newspaper design is a good example of hierarchy in design: The more important the story, the bigger and higher the headline is placed on the page.

CHECKING YOUR UNDERSTANDING

6.1 Following is a list of web sites. Some are good and some are bad examples of design techniques that you have read about in this chapter. Visit each site and decide whether it is an example of good or bad design and cite at least two rules that were either followed or broken.

▓ www.roman-britain.org
▓ www.state.nj.us

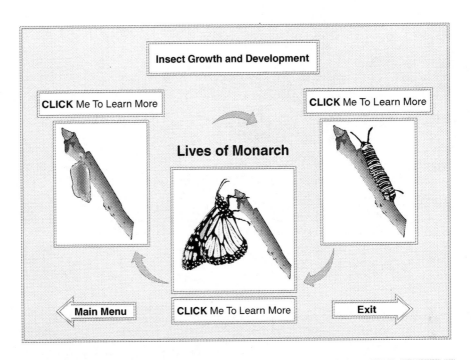

FIGURE 6.7 Size Matters – Undue Emphasis on the Adult

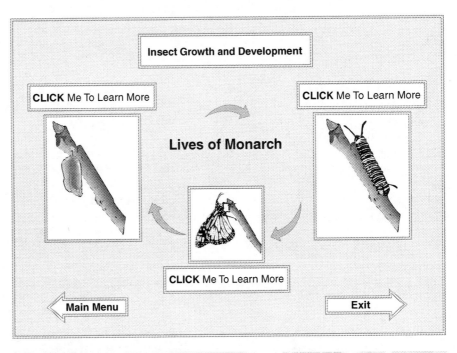

FIGURE 6.8 Size Matters – Correct Proportions

The images used herein were obtained from IMSI's MasterClips©, Master Photos©, Clipart&More© or Animations&More© Collection, 100 Rowland Way, Novato, CA 94945, USA.

118

121

▓ www.f1jordan.com
▓ www.nationalenquirer.com
▓ www.environment.ky.gov
▓ www.eternalegypt.org/EternalEgyptWebsiteWeb/HomeServlet
▓ http://mintmuseum.org/penland
▓ www.hawking.org.uk/home/hindex.html

 6.2 Visit the two sites listed below and learn all you can about good and bad web site design. View the examples listed by each web site. Based on your viewing, cite the best web site and the worst web site that you can find, and explain why the sites you have chosen are the best or the worst.

▓ www.webpagesthatsuck.com
▓ www.lynda.com/resources/inspiration/index.html

▓ SUMMARY

Teaching fundamental graphic design principles to students is neither time consuming nor superfluous. Graphic design is an emerging literacy that many students will use often in their academic and professional lives. In addition, thinking about design often involves thinking about the content that has generated the design problem, which provides students with another way to interact with what they are learning.

Design problems for computers involve both page layout and interface design. While solving page layout problems, students grapple with who their audience will be, the relative importance and relationships among chunks of information, and how their audience can easily read and understand the information being displayed. Interface considerations require students to think about how information is linked. In the process of thinking about links among chunks of information, students must come to understand the structure of the knowledge itself. If they do not, the presentation that they build will appear disorganized and hard to move through. Graphic design, then, is not just one more topic for teachers to present, but rather one more tool to help them build a deep understanding of the information their students learn.

▓ REFERENCES

Gagne, E. D., Yekovich, C. W., & Yekovich, F. R. (1993). *The cognitive psychology of school learning.* Boston: Little, Brown.

Marcus, A. (1991). *Graphic design for electronic documents and user interfaces.* New York: ACM Press.

Horton, W. (1991). *Illustrating computer documentation.* New York: Wiley.

Mayer, R. E. (2001). *Multimedia learning.* Cambridge: Cambridge University Press.

▓ ANNOTATED RESOURCES

The following web sites will provide help with several challenges for teachers putting together units that require design skills and graphics:

Advanced Design Topics

Fleming, M., & Levie, W. (1993). *Instructional message design: principles from the behavioral and cognitive sciences* (2nd ed.). Englewood Cliffs, NJ: Educational Technology Publications.

This book provides a thorough coverage of design principles and the theories behind them. The book discusses and gives examples for principles in the following areas: motivation, perception, psychomotor, learning, concept-learning, problem solving, and attitude change.

Design

www.webstyleguide.com/index.html?/contents.html (last updated 2005)
www.colin.mackenzie.org/webdesign (last updated 2007)

Graphics

www.freefoto.com/index.jsp (last updated 2007)
www.animationfactory.com (last updated 2007)
www.webdeveloper.com/animations (last updated 2007)
www.awesomeclipartforeducators.com (last updated 2007)

Companion Web Site   www.ablongman.com/thorsen3e

1. Go to Chapters 5–8 of the TechTactics web site. Click on the Inspiration web site with concept mapping tutorials and examples in most content areas—download a free copy of Inspiration software and install it. Now choose a topic that you might assign to a class that you teach or might teach and do a concept map for that topic.

2. Using the Inspiration software that you downloaded in Question 1 and the two links on the web site pertaining to the creation of an effective web page or web site, make a concept map that illustrates the major components of the planning involved in building an interactive presentation (either a web site or a presentation built with presentation software).

7

Outlines, Idea Maps, and Storyboards

OBJECTIVES

- Apply your knowledge of outlining to the design of a presentation.
- Convert an outline into an idea map.
- Design and develop idea maps for concepts and processes.
- Convert an idea map to a storyboard.
- Provide several examples of how students benefit from making idea maps.
- Know how to convert a storyboard to a finished presentation.

After looking in on Jeff's class, we learned that a hypermedia-supported lesson plan must be thought through carefully before it is executed. Almost any hypermedia assignment can be broken down into the components listed below:

Step 1: Outline
Step 2: Idea map(s)
Step 3: Storyboard
Step 4: Flow chart
Step 5: Development of software product
Step 6: Presentation of the final product (explaining it to a group, burning it to a CD, putting it on the Internet)

> Steps in a presentation assignment; each results in a product

Ideally, the student must complete each step in the planning process to make a product. Each product may be graded, although they all do not have to be. The organization and sophistication of the final product is a reflection of the planning that goes into it. Consequently, if a student does not do an adequate outline and idea map, the resulting storyboard and software product probably will be poor as well. Let's look a little deeper into how each of these steps fits together.

OUTLINES

If we were to look at Jeff's outline on plant cells, we would see something like the outline in Figure 7.1. Jeff has done nothing more than a traditional outline. But doing

121

Levels of information in electronic documents

- I. Function of Cells
    - A. Plant Cells
    - B. Animal Cells
- II. Structure of Cells
    - A. Vacuole
    - B. Nucleus
        - 1. Nucleolus
        - 2. Chromatin
    - C. Mitochondria
- III. Cell Reproduction
    - A. Meiosis
        - 1. Interphase
        - 2. Prophase
        - 3. Metaphase
        - 4. Anaphase
        - 5. Telophase
    - B. Mitosis
        - 1. Interphase
        - 2. Prophase
        - 3. Metaphase
        - 4. Anaphase
        - 5. Telophase

FIGURE 7.1 Jeff's Outline

it has caused him to start thinking about the topic. It is an easy, comfortable skill that he already knows, and his teacher is taking advantage of that by using it as the springboard for the assignment.

Notice that the three-level outline is not complicated. One way to relate an outline to a finished hypermedia presentation is to think of moving between levels of the outline by way of mouse clicks. For example, a user of the finished presentation who wants to learn about chromatin will need three clicks: one click to choose one of the main topics, Structure of Cells; a second click to go to the submenu Nucleus; and a third click to go to Chromatin.

Planning a presentation is iterative

The idea mapping and storyboarding phases will flesh out these topics so that the students study them from many different perspectives. Planning is not entirely a step-by-step process. A student may start a storyboard after finishing an idea map and realize that the idea map is wrong and needs to be redone. Or a student may do an idea map and find out that the outline is wrong. A student may be working on a computer product and find out that the storyboard could have been done better a different way. When this happens, students go back to the part of the process where they went wrong and correct their mistakes.

Outlines need three layers—at most

Generally speaking, for most information displays, a person should be able to get anywhere in the content in three clicks (Lopuck, 1998). Consequently, the outline may be simple. This rule helps students use the outline as a tool. The outline will seem less like busywork to students when they see its relationship to the software that they will build. Younger students may build two-level outlines, and advanced students studying complex topics may add another level or two to the outline. Idea mapping and storyboarding will tease out the details, revealing additional relationships that simple outlines miss.

In the old days, the organizational part of writing a paper or report required an outline. In one sense, computer technology has not changed the need for outlining, but it has certainly changed the purpose of an outline and the amount of outlining that must be done. My favorite metaphor for organizing hypermedia products is "outlining in 3-D." Writing a traditional outline as a guide produces only a traditional report displayed on a screen instead of a piece of paper. Though writing an outline is part of the process, an outline alone does not take advantage of the power of the computer, the software, or, most important, a student's mind. There are other organizational techniques such as idea mapping that teachers can use to provide context and interaction with content for students.

IDEA MAPS

When I ask students to interact with content, I try to eliminate any opportunity for them to copy information and hand it in "untransformed." Many times the student paraphrases an encyclopedia article or other nonfiction, or even worse, chooses a few words to change and leaves the rest intact. Current practices encourage this kind of laziness. The wide availability of information on the web and the ease of cutting and pasting facilitates the act of copying information without thought. It is difficult to copy others' writing and put it into a hypermedia report, however. The delivery mechanisms are so different that information transferred directly from long text passages looks silly and is virtually useless when a student pastes it directly into a presentation.

> Presentation software makes copying more difficult

Using presentation software to organize and explain information requires thinking through ideas and breaking them into smaller chunks of information that can be displayed on a monitor and linked together logically. It is the difference between approaching every topic with the mindset of "What comes first, second, and last?" compared to "How are these ideas related to each other?" This is the point at which idea or concept mapping becomes a valuable tool. Pohl's (1998) observations indicate, "The efficacy of concept mapping as a methodology of learning is to a certain extent supported by empirical evidence." In a 2002 study, Marra and Jonassen found that students who first constructed concept maps built more complex expert systems than those who did not.

> Presentation software encourages students to think about relationships

Although idea mapping may be done by hand, computer tools make the process faster and easier for students. Two important tools are Inspiration and Visio. A version of Inspiration for younger students is Kidspiration.

We will leave Jeff to his own devices for a while and look in on a fifth-grade class studying world history and culture. As a part of this study, the students are working on a year-long project to develop a multimedia presentation on the exploration of this planet and beyond. Their teacher, Mr. Hess, hopes that this presentation will provide some context for the dates and names that his students must inevitably memorize during the course of the year.

FIELD TRIP
7.1

Explorations

Motivating and preparing
the class

Mr. Hess shows the class a presentation on the Internet made by a student from last year's class, the *History of Inventions* (the theme that year). He told his class that they would put their presentations on the Internet as well, so that anyone who has a computer and a connection to the Internet would be able to see their work. Jamie, a student, is excited that she will get to use a computer to draw pictures other people will see, though she is not particularly interested in exploration, this year's theme.

Outlining

The teacher divides the class into groups and asks them to begin working on the presentation by outlining what they think a presentation on exploration might look like. After the students have spent about twenty minutes in their groups, he asks each group to write its outline on the blackboard for the other students to see. Their assignment for tomorrow is to think about what they have seen and talked about and be ready to make suggestions on the construction of a perfect outline for the topic.

Tomorrow comes, and the teacher hands out copies of all of the groups' outlines from yesterday. The class again discusses how a topic such as exploration should be organized. Some think it should be organized by the name of the explorer, others by the name of the country explored. To solve the dilemma, Mr. Hess tells the students to use a tree map to describe how the presentation should be organized. He gives the students fifteen minutes to draw their maps.

Idea mapping

Jamie is confused. She thinks the easiest way would be just to list the explorer and what he or she explored, but she cannot make her tree map work. There is no way to put branches on it. As she tries to visualize the piece of software that she will create, all she can see is one page after another listing explorers and their biographies. That isn't how the *Inventions* project created by last year's students looks. It is cool: you can see categories of inventions depending on your interest. So, Jamie thought, "How would this map look if I did it by areas of the world? Let's see. I know America was discovered and explored. So were the North and South poles."

Using an idea map

Jamie makes a tree map representing her current knowledge of exploration. "America" is one branch of the tree, "Poles" the other branch of the tree, and "North" and "South" were branches from Poles. Her fifteen minutes were up and she found that others in the class had come to similar conclusions. Among all of them, they came up with six areas of the world where exploration had occurred: the Americas, Asia, the Pacific, the Poles, Africa, and Space. Mr. Hess again had the students work in groups to flesh out this general tree map into a more specific map. He asked them to use their textbooks and other reference materials to define more clearly the areas where exploration had occurred. Their ideas were starting to take shape.

Finding the properties
of exploration

The next day Mr. Hess asked the students to put their tree maps on their desks in front of them and "put on their thinking caps." Mr. Hess said, "We have decided where exploration happened, but we want to put more in our presentation than just a place. Is there something more to exploration than just the place? We all know about Columbus exploring the Americas. And we just read the story in our reading books about Marco Polo in China. Using Columbus and Marco Polo as examples, let's think of some other things that are important for exploration. For the next five minutes, talk with the person next to you about possible topics related to exploration. Use a web map to help you plan."

Martin, Jamie's partner, immediately said, "Well, you always hear that the Queen of Spain was the person who gave Columbus the money to go on his trip. Maybe the country the explorer came from or worked for is important." So Jamie began a web. In the first circle she wrote, Exploration. In another circle she wrote Home Country, and connected it with a line to the first circle. The planning went on for several minutes until Mr. Hess called the class to order again. He began methodically combining the children's suggestions on the blackboard by making a web of five different ideas, all connected to the central circle, Exploration. The lesson was over for the day.

Making a storyboard

The next day, as the project resumed, one of the more vocal students commented, "I hope you aren't going to make us PLAN any more. When do we get to use the computers?" Mr. Hess laughed and said, "This is a good news/bad news situation. Making a presentation takes a lot of computer time, so each of us has to plan very carefully. You must make every minute that you spend at the computer count. But the good news is that you have done the hardest part of the planning and now you get to dream about what your presentation is going to look like. Today I am going to show you how you can use your tree map and your web map to design the first four screens of your presentation. After that you can begin your storyboard. Once you have the first page of your storyboard, you can begin working on your presentations at the computer. You will rotate. While some people work at the computer, others will begin their next set of storyboards. Some of you can go to the library to use the computers to get materials, such as pictures and videos from the Internet, for your presentation. Tomorrow I am going to teach you a little bit about how to do good Internet searches and give you the addresses of some sites to get you started."

> Using the Internet for research

Jamie was elated. She was finally going to get to draw and collect pictures and organize them all into something that other people would see.

The fundamental rule for using computers to display information is to use the organization of the content to guide the organization of the hypermedia presentation (Pohl, 1998). If you look in Appendix D, you can see some examples of templates for idea maps. Notice that they all have names. This is because knowledge has some basic "shapes." All knowledge can be classified in one of three categories: conceptual, procedural, and conditional knowledge. Concepts have properties and examples, procedures have steps, while conditional knowledge is the meta-knowledge of when and why to apply conceptual and procedural knowledge (Woolfolk, 2000). Once your students understand the significance of these categories and begin to see information as belonging to one of them, they will have a better idea of how that information is organized and, consequently, will organize it correctly for their presentations. A good analogy for this understanding of concepts and procedures is knowing how to solve word problems in arithmetic or algebra. Once you learn a pattern, you can solve a variety of problems—whether it is two boats meeting mid-stream, two trains meeting between points A and B, or two cars meeting on a drive between Leadville and Coppertown. Understanding concepts and events gives students a formula to apply to the organizing process for their presentations.

> Information is conceptual, procedural, or conditional

Concepts: Examples and Properties

Concepts are facts or ideas. They usually belong to a family of related facts or ideas. They appear in the curriculum as themes that children study: exploration, English literary periods, inventions, the westward migration, biomes, and the short story. Concepts have two characteristics that are helpful for learners. They have examples and they have properties (Gagne, Yekovich, & Yekovich, 1993).

Examples   First, let us discuss examples. Tundra is an example of a biome; the Renaissance is an example of a period in English history; the jet engine is an example of an invention; and Cortez in Mexico is an example of exploration. Many times examples can be classified into categories and subcategories. Consider Exploration, which could fall into categories including (from a European point of view) the exploration of Asia, the Americas, Africa, the Pacific, the North and South Poles, and Space.

> Examples have categories and hierarchies

These categories could be further broken down into more categories with examples for each. To represent Exploration visually, students might use a tree map or a brace map because these maps graphically demonstrate the hierarchy of categories that they are studying. A student should be able to use either a brace or a tree map to divide a concept into categories. Figure 7.2 shows the categories of Exploration with a brace map, and Figure 7.3 shows the categories of Exploration with a tree map. Neither is superior to the other. One represents ideas horizontally and the other vertically. (Their contents do not match exactly because they were generated by different student groups.)

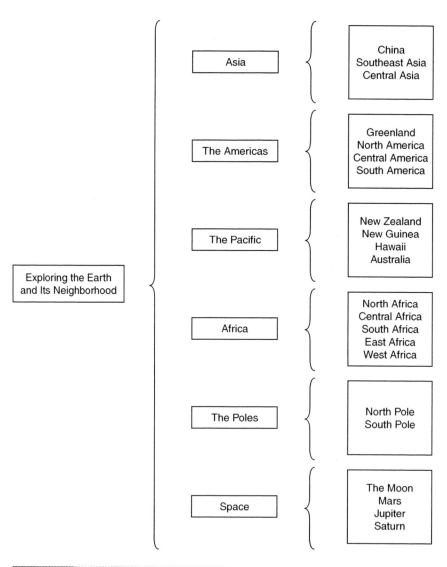

FIGURE 7.2 Brace Map of the Categories of Exploration

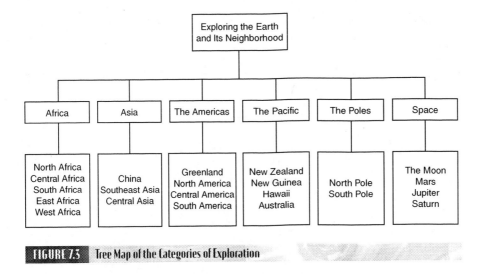

FIGURE 7.3 Tree Map of the Categories of Exploration

Properties However, really understanding a concept means more than just being able to categorize it and provide examples. Concepts also have properties. Think of properties as the defining characteristics of a concept. The properties of concepts are often those items related to a concept that you want the children to learn. Table 7.1 shows examples of some concepts accompanied by a few of their properties. One example from this table, Exploration, is further represented as an idea map (called a "web map" in the story about Mr. Hess's class) in Figure 7.4. Notice that a properties map is not hierarchical. It is descriptive, and all properties have the same weight.

> Properties are not hierarchical

When students structure a concept with tree and properties maps, they are taking their first step toward visualizing the navigational system and screen design of the presentation they will write. The center or hub of their properties map, or the main concept heading of their tree or brace map, will be the title screen. The brace or tree map will define one set of menus and the properties map will define another set of menus or hot words. The properties map provides the organization for information about the topics on the final level of the brace map. You may observe in Figures 7.5 through 7.8 mockups of the screens derived from the idea maps in Figures 7.2 through 7.4.

> Relating idea maps to the design of the presentation

As you can see, it is three clicks of the mouse (after the title screen) to the most detailed information in the presentation. All of the screens are consistent, and at worst, it would be hard for a user to get lost. At best, a user of such a software title would be learning from the structure of the software as well as from the information on the screens. How much more would the *designer* of the software (your student) learn?

Questions and Answers about Idea Mapping

We have spent many pages on a subject that does not appear to have much to do with presentation software. Although the connection should be clearer now, you may still have questions about using idea mapping to support your use of presentation

TABLE 7.1	Sample Concepts and Their Properties
Concept	**Properties**
Explorations	Name of explorer
	Country explored
	Native country of explorer
	Time period when exploration took place
	Was the exploration a success or failure?
English Literary Periods	Major discoveries
	Artistic styles
	Musical styles
	Literary styles
	Historical events
Inventions	Name of the invention
	Time of the invention
	Importance of the invention
	Country where the invention happened
	People involved with the invention
	Names
	Number
	Knowledge needed to make the invention
	Materials necessary for the invention
The Westward Migration	Reasons people moved west
	When they moved west
	How they moved west
	Changes they made to the west
Ecosystems	Name
	Kinds of animals
	Kinds of plants
	Climate
	Soil
	Topography
Short Story	Theme
	Plot
	Character
	Setting
	Mood

software. Following is a question-and-answer session that should help clarify a few ideas that still might be a little fuzzy to you.

How extensive should an idea map be? Remember the three-click rule? Don't forget that an outline only needs to be three levels deep. The same is true for an idea map. The maps do not need to be extensive. Detailed explanations can be written later and assembled as resources for the presentation. The purpose of the idea map is to tease

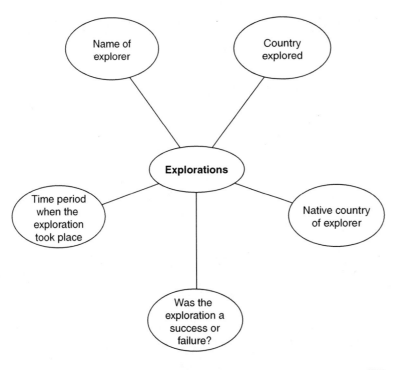

FIGURE 7.4 Concept Map of Properties of Exploration

out the organization of the content for students, and to create a template with cubby-holes where students can tuck away the facts.

How should I grade idea maps?   The grade on the idea map should not be a large proportion for the grade on the multimedia project. If you use a rubric to grade presentations, you might consider having one row in the rubric for the outline and one row for the idea map. The work done with the idea map will influence the student's success on

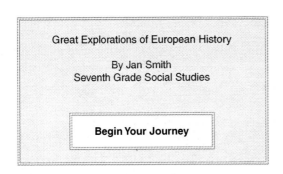

FIGURE 7.5 Title Screen of Exploration Presentation

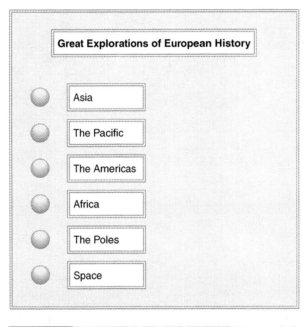

FIGURE 7.6 First Menu Level of Exploration Presentation

the project as a whole. Idea mapping can be treated like practice problems. The teacher challenges the students to create an accurate idea map and then immediately provides an example for them to see. Students can do this alone or in groups. Groups should review idea maps created by single students, or the class should review maps created by groups. Ultimately, the teacher, when he or she is sure that the students have a clear picture of how the elements of their multimedia project are connected, may decide not to require each student to hand in a correct idea map as a part of the assignment.

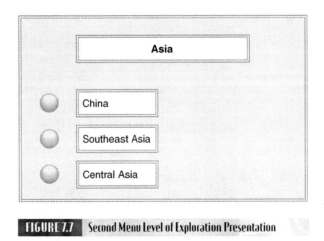

FIGURE 7.7 Second Menu Level of Exploration Presentation

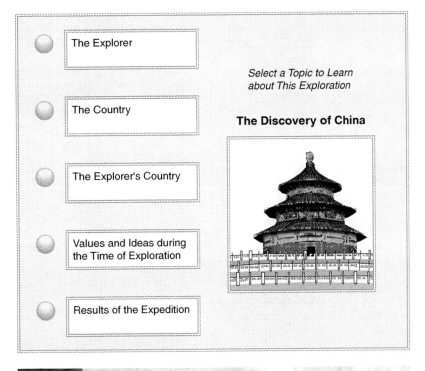

The Explorer

The Country

The Explorer's Country

Values and Ideas during the Time of Exploration

Results of the Expedition

Select a Topic to Learn about This Exploration

The Discovery of China

FIGURE 7.8 **Final Menu Level of Exploration Presentation**

The images used herein were obtained from IMSI's MasterClips©, MasterPhotos©, Clipart& More© or Animations&More© Collection, 100 Rowland Way, Novato, CA 94945, USA.

How do I teach idea maps? Most students do not learn how to do idea mapping without some trial and error. Since idea mapping is not consistently taught in our educational system, teachers should plan to spend some time training students in this process. In fact, it is better to teach students the skills for completing a multimedia assignment (outline, idea map, storyboard, presentation software) separately rather than overwhelming them with four new activities at the same time.

You can begin teaching idea mapping by supplying your students with completed idea maps and discussing them. Next, ask students to fill in blank maps that you have created. Do it as an assignment in class and immediately show students the correct entries. Another way of teaching the skill is to give them an outline and ask them to turn it into an idea map. Finally, name the content that you want your students to map and then ask them to do it.

What did Jeff's idea map look like? Jeff's final map is shown in Figure 7.9. It is about "average" in regard to the detail and accuracy asked for by his teacher. (Some of the information in the map in this figure is truncated because of space, but you can get the idea.) Some students drew more detailed maps; some students drew maps where the information was incorrectly placed. Jeff's teacher encourages the students to turn in

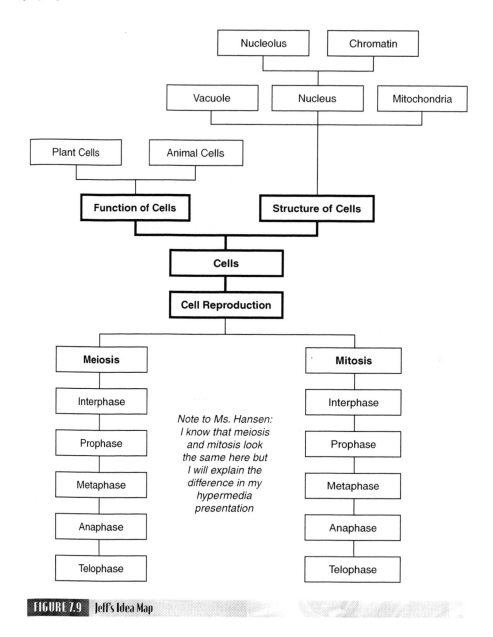

FIGURE 7.9 Jeff's Idea Map

legible, readable idea maps. Usually students draw several maps during the course of the assignment. Jeff's first map was his best initial guess at what a map should look like. He made his second map with the rest of the class during an interactive discussion with the teacher. Jeff drew the map that he finally handed in using his first two attempts as a guide. He used a ruler and compass to make straight lines, square boxes, and round circles, and he printed information carefully and legibly. These maps can be done more quickly and neatly online if your students have access to Inspiration, Visio, or Kidspiration.

Looking at Jeff's map in Figure 7.9, you can see some of the patterns that we have just studied. The topics connected with the thick, black lines came from a concept map of properties. Cell Function and Cell Structure are tree maps arranged upward (truncated here because of space). Reproduction, the third characteristic or property of cells, is really two processes that look alike but unfold differently. They are represented as chain maps. Students often must tape several pages together to complete their idea maps.

What did Jeff's menu screens look like?   This is the best question of all. To answer it you will have to look at another illustration. Figure 7.10 has two examples of Jeff's menus. In the first menu, if the user clicks on the button next to Anatomy of a Cell the computer presents the next menu shown there.

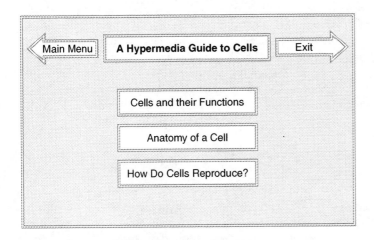

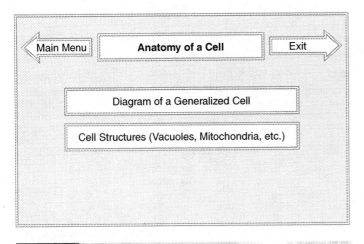

FIGURE 7.10 Screens Jeff Built Based on His Outline and Idea Maps

How might I justify the use of idea mapping to my students?   Here are some advantages of using idea maps:

▦ Students will not waste time on the computer with many false starts. False starts are costly. Without careful planning, students may spend a great deal of time working before they realize their plan is awkward, uninformative, or unworkable.

▦ Students will be searching for information with a purpose. Instead of memorizing lists and definitions, they will uncover patterns and form links that will help them remember.

▦ Outlines and idea maps are "low-overhead" activities. They require only a pencil and paper and may be as formal or informal as a teacher wishes to make them. They allow students to make the best use of precious time at the computer.

Is there idea-mapping software and how useful is it?   Yes, there are two affordable titles available for idea-mapping software. Inspiration Software, Inc., has two titles—one for very young students called Kidspiration and one for older students called Inspiration. Both are intuitive and easy to learn, and both run on Mac and PC platforms. One of the nicest features of the product is the ability to convert outlines to concept maps and concept maps to outlines. This makes the planning process much faster by providing students instant visual feedback. Microsoft also has a very usable product called Visio.

⬤ STORYBOARDS

The storyboarding process

The storyboard is started after the idea mapping process is well along. The students must have identified all of the concepts and processes in the content they are preparing. After the students know how a topic is structured, they can start building menu screens and designating screen areas for graphics, text, video, audio, and navigation. They can decide on color and font size and record all of their information on cards or paper, one card or sheet per screen. They can start gathering resources, the text, audio, video, graphic, and animation files they will use to build their presentations. And finally, they must decide how all of these screens will fit together. Idea mapping provides only the main branches of the software. As students begin to gather and format resources for their project, they will add more screens.

Young students, or students who are just beginning to learn how to write hypermedia presentations, will not be able to respond to every design principle that you reviewed in the previous chapter. For a kindergarten child who is new to the process, one to three connected screens with a background color, a few graphics, and few words or letters should be acceptable. On the other hand, an advanced student who knows the mechanics of creating hypermedia presentations very well could be responsible for every specification in the storyboard template and every design principle that you learned in Chapter 6.

Teach your students how to storyboard

Because you are the first generation of teachers to use this medium, you will work harder preparing both materials and your students for the first few hypermedia-supported projects that they do. Some of your students may have created idea maps before, but at this point there will be very few who know how to storyboard. You will have to lead most of them, step by step, through the creation of their storyboards. You may also have to teach many of your students how to use presentation software.

In fact, you should consider discussing storyboard format with other teachers who teach in the grades above and below you. If your school were to develop a scope and sequence for storyboarding, ultimately you would spend only a small amount of time teaching storyboarding instead of the content that you must teach. Storyboarding, once students know how to do it, will enhance the amount of information that they retain because storyboards are another type of organizational device, like idea maps and outlines.

Looking at an idea map is like looking at a molecule represented as a flat object, such as the one in box A of Figure 7.11. An idea map gives us a general understanding of how ideas are connected. A storyboard is much like the 3-D molecule in box B of that figure. It defines the actual method of displaying the information, the links between hot words and their explanations, the links between menus and pages, and choices of fonts and colors that all add meaning to the ideas the student is organizing.

BRANCHING

During the storyboarding process, students decide on branches. *Branching* is a term used in computer programming to indicate the action of moving from one part of a program to another. As indicated previously, branches are the embedded concepts or events that students must understand in order to really know whatever it is they are studying. Branching in a presentation may take several forms. Students can use hot words, hot graphics, menus, or icons to allow their users to initiate the branching process.

A

B

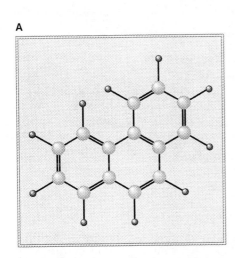
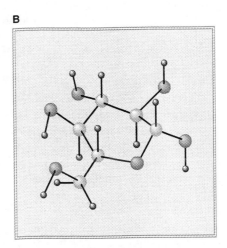

FIGURE 7.11 Flat and 3D Representations

The images used herein were obtained from IMSI's MasterClips©, MasterPhotos©, Clipart&More© or Animations&More© Collection, 100 Rowland Way, Novato, CA 94945, USA.

Hot Words

Hot words are perhaps the simplest method of initiating a branch. Branches that result from these hot words should be very simple. A hot word, which is a word in the text of a presentation that indicates that the user may click on it for more information, should go to a short pop-up definition or graphic. Ideally, the user should never leave the original screen. If the user does leave the original screen, a Back button should be clearly visible and easily accessible, with no other branches available. Use other methods for initiating branches for more complex ideas. Hot words are indicated several different ways. The way that your students will indicate hot words will, no doubt, depend on the software that you are using. Authors indicate hot words to users by applying a different color to them, underlining them, or by having the cursor icon change shape when the mouse is dragged over them. The cursor icon is the symbol that tells you the location of the cursor and what it can do at the moment. For example, an hourglass cursor icon tells you the computer is working and that you should wait until the cursor changes back to the shape of an arrow. When the cursor turns into the shape of a hand, you can move the object or click on it. In the presentation software that you use, you will see a menu item called either "Create Hot Word," or "Create Link." Either of these will serve your purpose.

Hot Graphics

When your students are working with an idea that may be visualized and placed on the computer screen as a graphic, they may make portions of this graphic "hot," allowing their readers to click on this hot area for more information. There is no reason why a whole presentation may not be organized around a hot graphic. Such a graphic might be a main menu screen and the basis for all branches in the program. For example, your students could use their idea maps or modifications of them as the basis for their main menu screens and even some of the branches. Such an approach will give your students added incentive for taking their idea maps seriously.

Another approach to using hot graphics as the basis for menu screens is for your students to find a metaphor into which their approach to their topic will fit. Web site designers and software developers successfully use these metaphors to organize software on a regular basis. One example of this technique is organizing a menu page like a floor map of a school with several classrooms, each indicating different topics or pieces of the presentation, a library where users can go to find definitions or other information, and a student recreation area where students can go to see graphics, videos, or animations about the topic they are working on.

Icons

The Back arrows in the figures to which you just referred are called *icons*. They are a special kind of graphics file, often followed by an extension ".ico." You may buy libraries of these icons with many different kinds of pictures on them, or your students may make their own icons using a drawing program. Icons are very simple diagrams that capture the meaning of a more complex idea. For example, a trashcan on your computer's desktop screen symbolizes the process that you use to delete a file. If, for example, your students were working on the Evaporation Cycle, they might do a simple

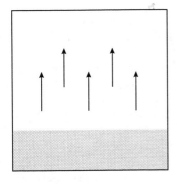

FIGURE 7.12 Icon for Evaporation

text menu (e.g., Figures D.9 and D.10, p. 307). However, they could turn the buttons to the left of the text into icons that describe each step of the process symbolically. Figure 7.12 is an example of an icon a student might make to describe evaporation. This icon is very simple, but it requires a conceptual understanding of the elements of evaporation. Making or choosing an icon makes the students translate content into a simple, summarized format that requires a significant cognitive effort.

Menus

Menus are the most typical navigational devices used to organize presentations. These may be as simple as a button followed by a line of descriptive text. (The menus in Figures D.9 and D.10 are examples of this approach.) They are helpful for users of the software because they always keep the organization of the topic clear.

Branches That Help Users Get around in the Software

There is another kind of branch that has nothing to do with content and everything to do with the usability of a presentation. These are the branches that get users back to where they came from, as well as entirely out of the program. Your students should be very careful to provide these options for their users. (Figures D.9 and D.10 illustrate this technique very simply.) Notice two characteristics of the Back and Forward branches: They are illustrated with an arrow that is always the same, and these two icons are always in the same place on the screen. This is a fundamental presentation skill with which students should become familiar early in their use of presentation software.

Consistency is the key to navigational branches

Return to the Biology Class Example

FIELD TRIP
7.2

Now we'll look in on Jeff again.

Jeff, almost finished with his idea map (he has the rough draft done), began his storyboard. He was waiting to do his final draft of the idea map until he had mostly finished the storyboard. Mrs. Hansen previously told the class that storyboards sometimes bring out ideas that are overlooked in the idea-mapping process.

He had a rough idea of the kinds of pictures she had found for the class and placed in a library on the server. Mrs. Hansen decided that there was not enough time for every student to search for every picture. She downloaded the graphics from the Internet, gave each file a descriptive name, and printed the directory listing for the class. Now students will only need to look for enough additional graphics, audio, or video to customize their work.

Mrs. Hansen said that she wanted the class to make the storyboards with a pencil, ruler, and compass, and to use the template (Figure 7.13) as a guide for the information to put into the storyboards. She told the class that the first page of the storyboard had to be a title page. Items on that page would include the following:

■ Title of the hypermedia report
■ Name of the author
■ Date
■ Two navigation buttons (next, exit)
■ A relevant graphic

To help her students, she filled in some of the blanks in the first column of the table. Since this was their first storyboard, she gave the class many clues. In later assignments, she would coach them by talking to them about what should go in the blanks. Mrs Hansen had a stack of blank template forms for the students to use—one template form for each screen of their presentations. So Jeff filled in the blanks and wrote a description of what could happen on each screen.

While working on his main menu screen, Jeff raised his hand, suddenly unsure of himself. It had occurred to him that if he started out wrong and did very much, he would waste a lot of time. Putting together a computer screen is a lot of work. And then there are the links. Undoing and redoing links between pages is confusing and really easy to do wrong. Worse yet, because each student's computer time was so limited, he didn't have time to make a mistake.

"How should this work?" he asked himself. "I have one concept (cells) and two processes (mitosis and meiosis). So should my main menu (Figure 7.14) look like box A? Or like box B, or C, or D?"

His teacher arrived and looked at his four attempts. She complimented Jeff for trying several ideas and said, "Look back at your idea map (Figure 7.9). Usually the name of the idea map is the title of the menu page. Notice the names of the boxes at the ends of the spokes (structure, function, and reproduction). Those names will be the labels for buttons on your main menu page. If you click on structure, then where will you go, Jeff?" she asked.

With his eyes, Jeff followed the line from "structure" to the next level of detail on the idea map. He guessed that he would set up a page to show the names of the cell parts as well as the text, pictures, video, or sound resources that he has made or collected from the Internet.

Jeff answered Mrs. Hansen and could now see which experimental screen in Figure 7.13 is the best menu screen: screen B. As he used his idea map to guide him, he realized that following a line and going from one box to the next represents one click of the mouse. Each box usually represents a screen. Jeff easily visualized the next set of screens. Figure 7.15 is one of Jeff's finished storyboard pages.

The area at the top is where the student draws and labels the features of the screen. Below the proposed screen are the specifications for all of the objects on that screen. In the case of buttons and hot words, the page to which those objects are linked is listed. Sometimes the actual page number is not known until the storyboard for that page has been made. The storyboard template even gives students a little help, allowing spaces for links to no more than nine different topics (e.g., mitochondria, vacuole, etc.) according to Miller's "7 ± 2" rule.

Blank screen

Rough draft of screen design goes here. Student draws it with a pencil.

Object	Color/Font	Branch/Link
Page or Screen Number		
Background		
Foreground		
Controls		
Button: Next		
Button: Back		
Button: Home		
Button: _____		
Button: _____		
Button: _____		
Selection Area		
Background		
Foreground		
Item 1: Caption		
Item 2: Caption		
Item 3: Caption		
Item 4: Caption		
Item 5: Caption		
Item 6: Caption		
Item 7: Caption		
Item 8: Caption		
Item 9: Caption		
Text Display Area		
Background		
Foreground		
Video Display Area		
Background		
Foreground		

FIGURE 7.15 A Storyboard Template

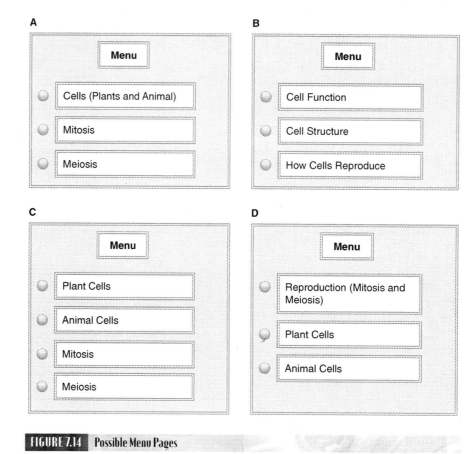

FIGURE 7.14 Possible Menu Pages

CHECKING YOUR UNDERSTANDING

7.1 Use Jeff's idea map (Figure 7.9) and storyboard (Figure 7.15) to help you draw the storyboard screen for mitochondria. Assume that Jeff has a graphic showing mitochondria and has recorded a short audio segment to supplement the graphic. You might even consider designing this storyboard on your computer with whatever presentation software you use. After you have finished drawing your picture, look at Figure 7.16 and compare your work to the figure. Answer the following questions.

1. Did I indicate bold for the hot word that is selected so that the user will know where he or she is?
2. Did I eliminate the video controls?
3. Did I change the name in the title of the screen?

Are the text, media, and navigation areas consistent with Jeff's storyboard? (You may wonder why your text, media, and navigation areas must be consistent with Jeff's, because you have some good ideas of your own. The answer is because within a presentation they must be the same. Consistency is the rule.)

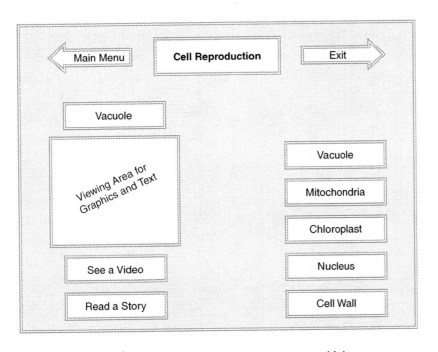

Object	Color/Font	Link
Page		
Background	Blue	None
Text	Yellow/Times 12/Button	None
Controls		
Button: See a Video	Grey/Times 12/Button	None
Button: Read a Story	Grey/Times 12/Button	Link to audio file selected in "Click on a…"
Button: Main Menu	Grey/Times 12/Button	Link to Main Menu
Button: Exit	Grey/Times 12/Button	End Presentation
Selection Area	Beige/inset	None
Click a Topic	Gray/Times 12/Inset box/	Each hot word links to an identical page with the information about that hot word on it.
Vacuole/hot word	Black/Times/12	To Storyboard 12
Mitochondria/hot word	Black/Times/12	To Storyboard 13
Chloroplast/hot word	Black/Times/12	To Storyboard 14
Nucleus/hot word	Black/Times/12	To Storyboard 15
Cell Wall/hot word	Black/Times/12	To Storyboard 16
Text Display Area	Beige background/black text/box	None
Video Display Area	Light Blue background/box	None

FIGURE 7.15 One of Jeff's Storyboards

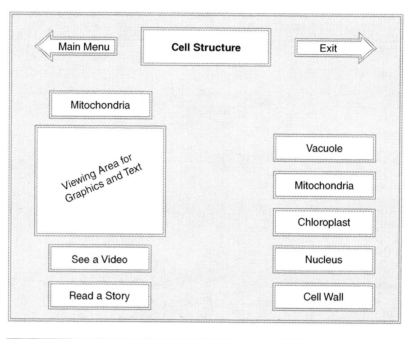

FIGURE 7.16 The First Page of Your Storyboard

■ SUMMARY

It is clear that presentation software is more than a motivational device. Used well, presentation software adds significantly to the number and quality of interactions students have with the content that they are studying. We know that repetition is one way to learn facts. When students use the complete process for preparing a presentation, they work with the facts that they are learning at least four times—in the outline, concept map, storyboard, and the presentation itself. Within each step (for example, the concept map) they may work with a fact or idea several more times—arranging it and rearranging it within the structure of the topic they are studying.

Another way students learn is by developing an understanding of the organization of a topic when they work to put the facts into their hypertext context. Students must understand the organization of a topic to do a presentation "in 3-D." To design a menu screen and use links that take viewers three mouse clicks into a topic requires an active organization effort on the part of the student.

Finally, students see content represented in many different formats: audio, video, text, graphics, and animation. These different representations of information provide avenues for students with different styles of learning. They also increase the richness of the context of the information, thus increasing the likelihood that the students will retain the knowledge with which they are working.

CHECKING YOUR UNDERSTANDING

7.2 Below is a list of web sites. Web site authors use many of the same kinds of techniques that presentation authors use; in fact, web site authoring software can be used to create presentations. Although the "look" of a web site and a presentation are different, the principles are the same. Someday you may have to create a web page for your class. When you do, you will use the same graphic and navigation design principles that you use for presentations.

In the following list are some good and some bad examples of design techniques that you have read about in this chapter. Visit each site and decide whether it is an example of good or bad design and cite at least two rules that were either followed or broken.

- ▨ www.roman-britain.org
- ▨ www.state.nj.us
- ▨ www.f1jordan.com
- ▨ www.nationalenquirer.com
- ▨ www.environment.ky.gov
- ▨ www.eternalegypt.org/EternalEgyptWebsiteWeb/HomeServlet
- ▨ mintmuseum.org/penland
- ▨ www.hawking.org.uk/home/hindex.html

7.3 Visit the two sites listed below and learn all you can about good and bad web site design. View the examples listed in each web site. Based on your viewing, cite the best web site and the worst web site that you can find and explain why the sites you have chosen are the best or the worst.

- ▨ www.webpagesthatsuck.com
- ▨ www.lynda.com/resources/inspiration/index.html

▨ REFERENCES

Gagne, E. D., Yekovich, C. W., & Yekovich, F. R. (1993). *The cognitive psychology of school learning*. Boston: Little, Brown.

Marra, R. M., & Jonassen, D. H. (2002). Transfer effects of semantic networks on expert systems: Mind tools at work. *Journal of Educational Computing Research*. 26(1), 1–23.

Lopuck, L. (1998). *Designing multimedia: A visual guide to multimedia and online graphic design*. Berkeley, CA: PeachPit Press.

Pohl, M. (1998). Hypermedia as a cognitive tool. ED-MEDIA/ED-TELECOM 98 World Conference on Educational Multimedia and Hypermedia & World Conference on Educational Telecommunications. Proceedings (Tenth, Freiburg, Germany).

Woolfolk, A. (2000). *Educational psychology*. Boston: Allyn and Bacon.

▨ ANNOTATED RESOURCES

Boon, R., Burke M., Fore, C., Spencer, V. (2006). The impact of cognitive organizers and technology-based practices on student success in secondary social studies classrooms. *Journal of Special Education Technology*. 21(1), 5–15.

In this study the authors compared student learning based on their use of cognitive organizers (concept maps) or textbooks. Students were learning facts (declarative knowledge). Students who used cognitive organizers significantly out-performed students who used textbooks. This article is interesting reading because it describes the methods teachers used as they implemented cognitive organizers with special education students.

Dimitriadi, Y. (2001). Evaluating the use of multimedia authoring with dyslexic learners: A case study. *British Journal of Educational Technology.* 32(3), 265–275.

Practical wisdom indicates that children with learning disabilities and attention deficit disorders find learning with multimedia motivational. This is a case study involving two children with learning difficulties. These children, with the author of the study, developed a multimedia presentation and in the process learned authoring, composition, revision, proofreading, and presentation skills. The author believes that this experience was both positive and motivating for the children.

Fortner, R. (2005). A long walk to the water's edge. *Science Activities.* 42(2), 30–35.

In this lesson plan, middle school science students study climate change data with concept maps. The activity is outlined in detail, with Internet site references where students can gather data, objectives, materials, and the procedure for implementing the lesson. It is a classic use of concept mapping.

Gallenstein, N. (2005). Never too young for a concept map. *Science and Children.* 43(1), 44–47.

This is an excellent article for pre-2 teachers. The author, in easy-to-read language, provides an example science lesson plan using an ingenious and home-made concept mapping device and then ties the plan to science standards. All of those who teach K–6 and special education should read this article.

Harrington, M., Holik, M., & Hurt, P. (1998). Improving writing through the use of varied strategies. M. A. Action Research Project, Saint Xavier University.

This article describes an action research project that investigates the use of graphic organizers (concept maps) and other strategies to improve student writing. The project is focused on upper elementary children. A summary may be found in ERIC (ED-420874). The project itself is 67 pages long and includes examples of graphic organizers.

Khentout, C., Harous, S., Douidi, L., Djoudi, M. (2006). Learning and navigation assistance in hypermedia. *International Journal of Instructional Media.* 33(3), 265–276.

Although this does not specifically address concept mapping, it is a thorough and fascinating discussion of the learning psychology of online navigation. It is a view of the other side of the navigation coin. That is, How does the process of navigation affect learning?

Wet, C. (2006). Beyond presentations: Using PowerPoint as an effective instructional tool. *Gifted Child Today.* 29(4), 29–39.

This article is a comprehensive look at PowerPoint use in the classroom. It identifies benefits and possible pitfalls and gives many practical suggestions. It has an excellent reference list on the topic of multimedia and concept maps in the classroom.

If you would like more examples and information about concept maps, see Appendix D.

Companion Web Site www.ablongman.com/thorsen3e

1. Go to Chapters 5–8 of the TechTactics web site. Click on the Inspiration web site with concept mapping tutorials and examples in most content areas—download a free copy of Inspiration software and install it. Now choose a topic that you might assign to a class that you teach, or might teach, and do a concept map for that topic.

2. Using the Inspiration software that you downloaded in Question 1 and the two links on the web site pertaining to the creation of an effective web page or web site, make a concept map that illustrates the major components of the planning involved in building an interactive presentation (either a web site or a presentation built with presentation software).

Evaluating Student Presentations

OBJECTIVES

- Describe the criteria relevant to your content area that you could use to evaluate student presentations.
- Adapt or build a scoring rubric based on criteria for evaluating student presentations.

RUBRICS

Rubrics are good for evaluating presentations

Evaluation of multimedia projects, though time consuming, can be fair and consistent. In order for presentations to be evaluated fairly, students should be given evaluation criteria before they start the project. Rubrics are a great strategy for grading presentations. Creating a clear, well-organized rubric for students and explaining it carefully at the beginning of the project will save both students and teacher some grief when evaluation time comes. Construction of your rubric depends on the age and sophistication of your students, their experience using presentation software, and the content for which you are holding them responsible. In the following outline are some suggestions for elements that you might include in a rubric.

I. Writing
   A. Structure
      1. Grammar
      2. Sentence mechanics
      3. Vocabulary and writing level
   B. Content
      1. Coverage of topic
      2. Organization of information
II. Navigation
   A. Branches and links

1. Branches and links work
2. Branches and links are logical
  B. Necessary branches always present (e.g., Menu, Exit)
III. Screen design
  A. Rules for color
  B. Rules for fonts
  C. Rules for displaying text
  D. Rules for consistency
  E. Rules for displaying information
IV. Development of presentation
  A. Outline
  B. Idea map
  C. Storyboard
  D. Completed presentation

The preceding outline listed suggestions for topics that you might include in a rubric. But what would a real rubric look like?

Creating Standards for Your Students

If you look on the web or in educational journals for assessment ideas, you will see many sample rubrics (Barnett, 2000; Taricani & Clariana, 2006; Besterfield-Scare, Gerchak, Shuman, & Wolfe, 2004). You can gain much insight into how to design a rubric by reading those created by others. It is rare, however, that you can simply lift a rubric from some source and use it unmodified. In my own practice, I have never used the same rubric for the same content two years in a row, because classes and areas of focus are different. Tables 8.1 through 8.4 are examples of rubrics that cover elementary through high school multimedia projects. Although these sample rubrics are based on specific assignments ("The Four Seasons" for the elementary rubrics and "Poetic Devices" for middle/high school) they are worded in such a way that they could be modified to suit any topic. The three elementary examples on the four seasons illustrate three approaches to designing a rubric:

> Grading rubrics should be based on the assignment

▓ Students who are just learning how to use presentation software or are very young (Table 8.1).
▓ Students who have completed one or two assignments with presentation software and are acquainted with the process as well as the basic mechanics of using presentation software (Table 8.2).
▓ Students who understand the development process well, the mechanics of using the software, and for whom the creation of graphics, audio, and video is easy (Table 8.3).

An average kindergartner may never get beyond the Acceptable level in Table 8.1, whereas a precocious fifth grader may be able to score often in the Excellent column in Table 8.4 that we have not yet mentioned. Consequently, if you were constructing

> Consider your students' skills as you construct a rubric

TABLE 8.1 Rubric for Elementary Beginning Users of Presentation Software

Topic: The Four Seasons

	Excellent (3)	Acceptable (2)	Needs Improvement (1)
Development of presentation	The student has developed an idea map that represents both main ideas for the menu screen and detail for information screens.	The student has developed an idea map that reflects the menu screen.	The student's idea map is not developed or it is wrong.
Writing	The student is writing to the standard of the grade level. (This will vary by grade level and teacher.)	The student is generally writing at grade level, but the writing has some spelling or grammar errors.	The student is not writing at grade level or the errors interfere with the reader's understanding or appreciation of the presentation.
Navigation	The student has a main menu from which the user chooses the season to display. The seasons on the main menu are in order.	The user navigates through the program linearly, i.e., first a title page, next the first season, then the second season, etc.	There is only one page in the presentation, with all seasons on the page, or the links between pages don't work.
Content	All content is covered and is illustrated with two or more of the following ways of representing information: text, graphics, video, audio, or animation.	All content is covered.	Not all content is covered.
Screen design	The student has followed the rules of screen design that the teacher has chosen for emphasis in this presentation. (At this level the teacher might emphasize three or four.)	The student has followed half of the rules of screen design that the teacher has chosen for emphasis in this presentation.	The presentation exhibits serious screen design problems.

a rubric for your kindergarten class you might use something like the "Acceptable" standards in Table 8.1 as your standard for "Excellent." On the other hand, if you are constructing a rubric for experienced, second-semester first graders, the "Acceptable" column in Table 8.2 could be the "Excellent" column in your rubric. It is so relative that the example rubrics are meant only to help you in a general way. Your curriculum and your class will determine the specifics.

Table 8.4 provides a rubric for an assignment based on the assumption that students are older, more cognitively developed, and more experienced users of presentation software. I did not develop rubrics for beginning and intermediate users at this age level. If you read Tables 8.1 through 8.3, you can see how you might make the rubric easier for beginners and intermediates. The same principles that worked in these tables will also work for Table 8.4. For inexperienced users, decrease the number of organizational tasks (omit an outline or idea map), decrease the difficulty of building the navigational structure (let them do a linear presentation the first time), and do not add any extra writing tasks, such as requiring specific sentence constructions or vocabulary. For the second presentation assignment, add a few more requirements, for the third assignment add a few more, and finally require something on the scale of the rubric in Table 8.4.

TABLE 8.2 Rubric for Elementary Intermediate Users of Presentation Software

Topic: The Four Seasons

	Excellent (3)	Acceptable (2)	Needs Improvement (1)
Writing	All spelling is correct.	Spelling is mostly correct.	Spelling errors interfere with the user's ability to use or appreciate the presentation.
Content	Each season is described by three sentences. Each sentence is accompanied by one descriptive graphic.	Each season is described by two sentences. Each sentence is accompanied by one descriptive graphic.	One or more seasons aren't described by a sentence. There are no descriptive graphics or the graphics do not reflect the meaning of the sentences.
Navigation	A menu follows the title page. The seasons are listed on the main menu in order. From the menu a user can choose any of the seasons.	The presentation starts with a title screen. From there the presentation goes from one season to the next in order. Each season is described on one page of the presentation. The pages are linked and go from one season to the next.	One or more links don't work. Seasons aren't listed in order either in a menu or in a linear presentation.
Screen design	The student has followed the screen design guidelines the teacher requested. (At this level, four to six guidelines are appropriate.)	The student has followed most of the screen design guidelines that the teacher requested.	The student has not followed the guidelines. The screens are hard to read and disorganized.
Development of the presentation	The student has developed an idea map and the main ideas on the idea map match the main navigational options. The student has written a storyboard that is consistent with the idea map and also consistent with the finished presentation. The student did both the idea map and storyboard before keying in the presentation.	The student has developed an idea map and there are major similarities between the idea map and the navigational structure of the presentation. The student has developed a storyboard that resembles the finished presentation. Both the idea map and storyboard were developed before the presentation was keyed in.	The idea map is missing or does not resemble the presentation, or The storyboard is missing or does not resemble the presentation, or The idea map and storyboard were developed after the presentation.

Some Notes on the Components of the Rubrics

As you develop the rubric, remember that you may add required components in the "Writing" section that are completely unrelated to doing presentations but do support good writing skills. As teachers in the content areas are pressed to teach "writing across the curriculum," these presentations act as a display opportunity for the writing skills students study. Be careful when you add these extra requirements. Make sure that your students are not struggling with the mechanics of using presentation software. They

> Make sure students aren't trying to learn too much at once

TABLE 8.3	Rubric for Elementary Advanced Users of Presentation Software

Topic: The Four Seasons

	Excellent (3)	Acceptable (2)	Needs Improvement (1)
Writing	All spelling and grammar are correct. Student uses constructions (such as compound sentences) on which the teacher has asked him or her to focus.	Grammar and spelling are mostly correct. Student attempts to use constructions on which the teacher has asked him/her to focus; they are mostly correct.	Spelling errors interfere with the user's ability to use or appreciate the presentation.
Content	Each season is described by a paragraph. Each paragraph is accompanied by another way of presenting information than text (graphic, video, audio, animation). Alternate forms of presenting information may not all be graphics.	Each season is described by a paragraph. Each paragraph is accompanied by a graphic.	One or more seasons aren't described by a sentence. There are no descriptive graphics or the graphics do not reflect the meaning of the sentences.
Navigation	A menu follows the title page. The seasons are listed on the main menu in order. Each season is described on two screens. From the menu a user can choose any of the seasons. The user can get back to the main menu from any screen.	A menu follows the title page. The seasons are listed on the main menu in order. Each season is described on one screen. From the menu a user can choose any of the seasons. The user can get back to the main menu from any screen.	One or more links don't work. Seasons aren't listed in order either in a menu or in a linear presentation.
Screen design	The student has followed the screen design guidelines the teacher requested. At this level, seven to ten guidelines are appropriate.	The student has followed most of the screen design guidelines that the teacher requested.	The student has not followed the guidelines. The screens are hard to read and disorganized.
Development of the presentation	The student has developed an outline. The student has developed an idea map and the main ideas on the idea map match the main navigational options. The student has written a storyboard that is consistent with the idea map and also consistent with the finished presentation. The student did both the idea map and storyboard before keying in the presentation.	The student has developed an idea map and there are major similarities between the idea map and the navigational structure of the presentation. The student has developed a storyboard that resembles the finished presentation. Both the idea map and storyboard were developed before the presentation was keyed in.	The idea map is missing or does not resemble the presentation, or The storyboard is missing or does not resemble the presentation, or The idea map and storyboard were developed after the presentation.

will be frustrated because they are trying to learn too many things at once. Once you are sure that they are confident users of the software, understand the development process, and possess some basic screen design knowledge, then you can begin adding challenges that will improve their writing.

TABLE 8.4 Rubric for Middle School/High School Users of Presentation Software

Topic: Poetic Device

	Excellent (3)	Acceptable (2)	Needs Improvement (1)
Writing	All spelling and grammar are correct. Student uses constructions (such as compound sentences) on which the teacher has asked him or her to focus.	Grammar and spelling are mostly correct. Student attempts to use constructions on which the teacher has asked him or her to focus; they are mostly correct.	Spelling errors interfere with the user's ability to use or appreciate the presentation.
Content	Each kind of imagery is accompanied by an example from a poem the class has studied. Three different forms of explanation (text, graphic, video, audio, animation) accompany each example. Explanations are clear, accurate, and complete.	Each kind of imagery is accompanied by an example from a poem the class has studied. Two different forms of explanation (text, graphic, video, audio, animation) accompany each example. The student does not always use a graphic and text to provide the explanations. Explanations are clear, accurate, and complete.	One or more poetic devices are missing. Examples are incorrect. The student explains a device(s) with only text or a graphic.
Navigation	A menu follows the title page. The major sections of the presentation appear on the menu page. Those devices with subcategories (alliteration: consonance, assonance) allow navigation to a separate page for each. The user can get back to the main menu from any screen.	A menu with the names of all of the poetic devices for the lesson follows the title page. Each device and its subcategories is described on one screen. The user can get back to the main menu from any screen.	One or more links don't work.
Screen design	The student has followed all screen design guidelines listed by the teacher on a style guide.	The student has followed most of the screen design guidelines listed on a style sheet.	The student has not followed the guidelines. The screens are hard to read and disorganized.
Development of the presentation	The student has developed an outline. The outline and idea map are similar. The student has developed an idea map and the main ideas on the idea map match the main navigational options. The student has written a storyboard that is consistent with the idea map and also consistent with the finished presentation. The student did both the idea map and storyboard before keying in the presentation.	The student has developed an outline. The outline and idea map are similar. The student has developed an idea map and there are major similarities between the idea map and the navigational structure of the presentation. The student has developed a storyboard that resembles the finished presentation. Both the idea map and storyboard were developed before the presentation was keyed in.	The outline is missing or does not resemble the idea map. The idea map is missing or does not resemble the presentation, or The storyboard is missing or does not resemble the presentation, or The idea map and storyboard were developed after the presentation.

Help students understand
the level of detail
you expect

When you see sample rubrics you will often see "number of screens" or "number of cards" specified. I am reluctant to make this specification because it makes the development process more difficult for students. If they do their idea maps and flow charts correctly, they will plan and produce the correct number of screens. It is not a bad idea to give them a range, such as between five and eight screens or between twenty and twenty-five screens, just to help them understand the scope of the assignment. However, in specifying the number of screen/storyboards for them to do, you are trying to make sure that they cover the content. You can really judge this outcome more effectively by telling them whether they did or did not provide the correct coverage in the "Content" section of the rubric. Furthermore, it is better to look at their idea maps and storyboards and say, "Don't you think you should include something about this?" Alternatively, "You know, maybe you should narrow this down and leave this section or screen out." Your students will learn more if their goal is to deal with the content they need to know rather than produce a specific number of screens or storyboards.

Give students specific
screen design guidelines

Table 8.5 is a list of fundamental screen design guidelines that we spoke about earlier, which have been summarized in a format that students can use to check their own presentation or a peer's presentation. As noted in the rubrics, however, the first time, second time, or even third time that students build a presentation is not the time to ask for compliance with every standard. Pick a few standards and teach them; review them at the beginning of the next assignment, and then add some more. If a student violates one of the guidelines to good effect, be flexible and figure out why the violation works and show it to the rest of the class. That is one way to foster creativity without grading it.

Students peer edit
using a rubric

One suggestion that helps students apply these guidelines and saves you time is to have students check each other's work against the guidelines and perhaps even the grading rubric before the work is handed in. This may not work for very young children, because they cannot read well enough to interpret the rubric and apply it. For children who can, however, it is the analog to peer editing in a writing class. Not only will peer editors learn more about the presentation design process, they will also cover the content one more time in a different context.

Creativity is difficult to
grade and to justify

One difficult issue that arises is that some rubrics include a row for creativity. Most descriptions are too vague to be helpful in scoring the presentation. For example:

> Good original artwork is included. Clip art, photos, and so on are used in creative ways. Color carries the theme and sets the tone for the stack. Animation is used very effectively to illustrate a concept. (Barnett, 2000, p. 31)

First, requiring students who have no native drawing ability but who are toiling toward some kind of grade in science (social studies, language arts) to produce good original artwork isn't fair. That they can't draw good pictures doesn't mean they aren't creative; it means they can't draw. Second, could the originator really define to an angry parent or a hurt child the standards for the sentence, "Clip art . . . (is) used in creative ways." The sentence is so broad as to be meaningless. The author of this rubric probably means that the students should follow the rules of good screen design for displaying graphics. This holds true for the last two sentences of this rubric

TABLE 8.5 Sample Screen Design Style Evaluation Sheet

Guideline	Yes	No
1. Windows provide regions for different kinds of content.		
2. Window for each kind of content appears in the same place on every page.		
3. Text is left justified. Numbers in tables are right or decimal justified.		
4. Navigational buttons for the same function appear in the same place consistently.		
5. Larger items are more significant, smaller items less significant.		
6. Items at the top of the screen are more important than the items below them.		
7. The background does not interfere with the delivery of information—it is an integral part of the presentation.		
8. Buttons reveal their purpose immediately.		
9. The size and location of the control buttons are proportional to the purpose they serve.		
10. If the presentation uses transition effects, the effects are consistent.		
11. Audio is clear and easily understood.		
12. Video is short and to the point.		
13. Text is easy to read against its background.		
14. Different kinds of graphics are used (scanned images, clip art, screen dumps, charts, diagrams, lists, maps, tables, and student-drawn graphics).		
15. Each screen has at least one relevant graphic.		
16. Users always know where they are in the presentation.		
17. There are three or fewer text styles per screen.		
18. Each screen has four or fewer colors (excluding imported graphics).		
19. Every object on the screen is meaningful.		
20. All text is in caps and lower case.		
21. The font is readable for its intended purpose.		
22. Each screen should have one idea or purpose.		
23. No flashing text is used.		
24. Vertically stacked text is not used.		
25. Lists are used where appropriate.		

as well. Because the student used color and animation doesn't mean that the student is especially creative. It means that the student followed screen design rules for color, thought carefully about the concept, and decided that animation would represent the concept well.

David Jonassen (2000) suggests a different way of approaching creativity. He lists the different parts of developing a presentation and then defines specific creative thinking skills associated with those parts of the presentation. Table 8.6 summarizes Jonassen's approach. If you were to attach a row of cells labeled "creativity" to one of the rubrics mentioned previously, Table 8.7 would give you an example of what this row might look like. Remember that this is aimed neither at the highest nor the lowest grades, nor at any particular content area. If you were to use this creativity block as part of your rubric, you would have to modify it to suit your needs. Notice that the row "Synthesizing" in Jonassen's table is not included in Table 8.7. That is because we have covered that topic quite thoroughly in the previous evaluation rubric.

TABLE 8.6 Creative Thinking Skills Described by Jonassen

	Researching Information	Organizing and Designing Presentation	Managing Project
Elaborating			
Expanding	X	X	
Modifying	X	X	
Extending		X	
Shifting	X	X	
Categories			
Concretizing		X	
Synthesizing			
Analogical thinking			
Summarizing	X	X	
Hypothesizing			
Planning			X
Imagining			
Fluency		X	
Predicting		X	X
Speculating		X	
Visualizing		X	
Intuition		X	

Source: D. Jonassen (2000). *Computers as mindtools for schools.* Upper Saddle River, NJ: Merrill Prentice Hall, p. 224.

TABLE 8.7 Rubric for Judging Creativity in a Presentation

Excellent	Acceptable	Needs Improvement
Research for the project included expanding on what was found. The student modified what he or she found to fit the context of the project. Some categories of information were used to explain and amplify the meaning of other categories of information.	There is no evidence of cutting and pasting re-searched information from sources into the project. All information the student obtained was paraphrased and reordered.	Evidence of cutting and pasting exists. Information appears to have been obtained from only one or two sources and slightly modified.
The student used the information that he or she found to provide original conclusions. The forms that these conclusions can take include: predictions not made by the authors of the research the student has gathered but based on that information, speculations and hunches that could be wrong but show that the student has done much "What if" thinking, and/or visualizations, i.e., original visual interpretations (graphics, diagrams, tables, charts) of textual material.	The student does provide predictions, speculations, or visualizing, but relies on other authors to provide those insights. The student has not engaged in original "What if" thinking.	The student simply reports information.

159

I am inclined not to attempt to judge other forms of creativity or the lack of it, because it is difficult to score and even more difficult to defend. You and others will recognize special creativity when you see it, but you cannot teach it in such a way that you can grade it. Some students follow every rule of screen design, every writing and content specification, and use appropriate grammar and spelling—producing a good presentation but not a creative one. Other students will do the same and produce a spectacular presentation. Those students who produce the creative presentations will receive the intrinsic rewards of creativity—appreciation from you and their class-mates. This is probably enough. The primary goal, remember, is for the student who produces the presentation, either spectacular or average, to learn the content in a way that is motivating and which adds rich connections to the knowledge the student already has.

> Creativity is difficult to teach

CHECKING YOUR UNDERSTANDING

8.1 Many school sites on the Internet provide examples of student-created presentations. It is likely that the schools in your town have such a site. Choose a site that has examples of student presentations at the grade level that you teach or intend to teach. Choose a set of student presentations. With a group of students in your class, decide what the assignment must have been for that group of presentations. Then, as a group, develop a rubric to judge the presentations. Grade each presentation yourself and then compare your grades and your justification for them with your colleagues. You might even take this exercise one step further. Have one of your peers choose a presentation that did not receive an "A." Role play the situation between the parent of the student and the teacher, or role play the teacher explaining to that student why he or she did not receive an "A."

QUESTIONS AND ANSWERS ABOUT USING MULTIMEDIA PRESENTATIONS

Do students always do their projects alone?   Not at all—students often work in teams to complete projects. In another year or two, when Jeff's teacher gets more confident with presentations, she will have the entire class cooperate on a presentation called "The Physiology of Mammals." Then the class will divide into groups and take sections of the topic to outline, to map, storyboard, and write presentation software. Groups could organize themselves in several ways. They could assign themselves roles such as editor, researcher, story boarder, software writer, etc., and do the project jointly. Or, each could take a topic, develop it alone, and then figure out how to merge everyone's individual project into a unified presentation. The way the teacher actually manages the assignment depends on the personality and skills of the class.

When is it appropriate to make hypermedia-based assignments?   Not every kind of content should be the basis for a hypermedia assignment. Sometimes it is more effi-cient to use a spreadsheet, database, or word processor, or even to say, "Memorize this." For example, there are more efficient ways to teach students how to bisect an angle or factor an equation than to have them make a hypermedia presentation on the topic. A spreadsheet might be a better way to learn about the lever, and using a database might be a better way to study presidents of the United States.

Presentations are good for summaries, for taking the large view, and for helping students tie together ideas whose relationships get lost over weeks and months. You may spend six weeks on a literature or reading unit. Rather than having students do several small hypermedia assignments, it may be better to have them do one project for the unit that ties together themes, character types, or whatever you must emphasize.

Is it ever appropriate for a teacher to be the author and presenter of a hypermedia title? Yes, there are times when it is appropriate for you to be the author of a presentation. Most teachers do not have extra time to really do a presentation correctly very often, i.e., do an idea map, storyboard, and finally the presentation with appropriate graphics, audio, and video. If your goal is to put an outline in front of your class as you speak, and you have to check out an LCD projector and set up a computer with all of the attendant hassles, your time is better spent in other ways. Over time, you may develop a set of very nice presentations that introduce units or help you teach particularly difficult topics. These are the kinds of presentations that you want to spend your time on. You should put your best efforts on CDs for your class and allow them to check the disks out for review. They will be good models for students.

Should students add videos to their presentations? Student videos should be very short. A one-minute video on most topics will be sufficient. Realistically speaking, if every student in the class does several one-minute videos, your class will use considerable space on the school's server or on your local classroom machines. Use this space limitation to your advantage. Require your students to make every word count and to structure and practice their oral presentation carefully. Your students can record these videos as .avi files using one of the ubiquitous "quickcams," which are made by many different companies and which come with many different features. These cameras are easy to install and many cost less than $100. One or two cameras for the entire class will be enough.

■ SUMMARY

Teachers should approach the assessment of hypermedia presentations thoughtfully. Giving the student one grade for the whole presentation with a comment is not adequate feedback. As teachers plan a presentation assignment, they should include an assessment rubric that students are aware of at the beginning of the assignment. The rubric should cover both the process of developing the presentation as well as the finished product. The rubric should assess the quality of the presentation, the quality of the writing, and the quality of the coverage of the content. The teacher should weight each according to its importance.

For students who are new to developing presentations, scoring rubrics and expectations should be simple. It is important to avoid teaching students too many skills at the same time. For beginning users you may want to use it as a tool for reviewing information that you have already covered. If, on the other hand, your students are skilled users of presentation software and understand how to capture and process digital audio and video, you can use presentation software to explore a new topic.

▓ REFERENCES

Barnett, H. (2000). Assessing the effects of technology in a standards-driven world. *Leading and Learning with Technology.* 27(7), 31.

Besterfield-Scare, M., Gerchak, J., Shuman, L. J., & Wolfe, H. (2004). Scoring concept maps: An integrated rubric for assessing engineering education. *Journal of Engineering Education.* 93(2), 105–115.

Jonassen, D. H. (2000). *MindTools: Computers in the classroom.* Englewood Cliffs, NJ: Merrill Prentice Hall.

Taricani, E., & Clariana, R. (2006). A Technique for automatically scoring open-ended concept maps. *Educational Technology Research and Development.* 54(1), 65–82.

Companion Web Site   www.ablongman.com/thorsen3e

1. Go to Chapters 5–8 of the TechTactics web site. Click on Inspiration web site with concept mapping tutorials and examples in most content areas and download a free copy of Inspiration software and install it. Now choose a topic that you might assign to a class that you teach, or might teach, and do a concept map for that topic.

2. Using the Inspiration software that you downloaded in Question 1 and the two links on the web site pertaining to the creation of an effective web page or web site, make a concept map that illustrates the major components of the planning involved in building an interactive presentation (either a web site or a presentation built with presentation software).

9

Educational Applications of Word Processing

OBJECTIVES

- Understand classroom management issues related to word processors.
- Know which lower-level learning activities the word processor supports.
- Know which higher-level learning activities the word processor supports.
- Use tables and the word processor.
- Use the word processor to organize Internet links for your class.
- Direct your students in the effective use of a spell checker.
- Use readability statistics to sharpen your students' writing skills.
- Know how to use text-reading software to help poor readers acquire information.

To complete this chapter successfully, you should be able to perform the following tasks:

- Cut and paste
- Make a table
- Create or remove borders
- Create an outline using the outline function
- Scan text and use OCR to transform it
- Import graphics into a word processor
- Use the graphics program associated with your word processor
- Create bulleted and numbered lists
- Import information from spreadsheets
- Set up and use a spell checker, thesaurus, and grammar checker

This chapter is really a follow-up to Chapter 5, "Presentation Software." In that chapter, you learned much about the organizational process, the precursor to actually keying in the screens for the presentation itself. All of the information you learned about outlining and idea mapping applies to word processing as well. As with creating a presentation, writing with a word processor is a solitary activity. Yes, you can have steps in the process that are not solitary, such as group brainstorming and peer editing. However, the final act of writing becomes the interaction between the writer and the

| Same principles as in creating presentations |

158

machine—one person to one computer. You will learn later that almost the opposite is true of spreadsheets and databases: A group of children, even an entire class, may profitably use a database or spreadsheet simultaneously. That is not the case with word processing.

Since people learned to write, they have sought ways to make the physical process more efficient. The word processor is a great improvement over typewriters, which represented the same scale of improvement over pens and pencils. Word processing has made composition possible for people who could not write before, such as young children and people with learning and coordination disorders (MacArthur, 1996; Hetzroni & Schreiber, 2004). For those who become somewhat adept with a keyboard, good writing is attainable and with work, improvement is steady. The challenge for educators is to structure the limited access that students have to word processors in a way that is most beneficial.

> Help people think about larger ideas, much as calculators do in math

MANAGEMENT ISSUES: HOW MANY COMPUTERS DO YOU HAVE?

One-Computer Classroom

Word processing in a one-computer classroom helps teachers with administrative chores. However, it is difficult to rely heavily on a word processor in a one-computer classroom and still give students a meaningful learning experience. In a typical class during the school year, the maximum time a student would have to do word processing assignments might be seven hours if the computer were used for other center activities involving the rest of the tools on an equal basis. In this case, you cannot count on the word processor to significantly improve the writing of your students. In a one-computer classroom, the computer is largely a tool for the teacher.

> One computer mostly a teacher's tool

Five-Computer Classroom: "Jigsaw Model"

The five-computer classroom provides students with a more realistic amount of time to complete assignments on a regular basis. In a well-managed, five-computer classroom, a student can expect to have access to a computer for writing at least an hour a week. An ideal situation for using these five computers is to train students to use a word processor in two or three one-hour sessions in a laboratory first. However, if a laboratory is not available, students can still learn word processing skills using a "jigsaw" model. Students start with a home group. Then each person in the home group goes to a different expert group to learn a skill or a set of skills. Forming the expert groups is as easy as having each student in the home group count off. Then all "ones" go to Group One, "twos" to Group Two, and so forth. Once in their expert groups, students investigate a set of word processing skills defined for them by the teacher. They learn these skills by using the Help menu and by completing, as a group, an exercise designed by the teacher. Group One may learn page-formatting skills, such as fonts, spacing, portrait/landscape orientations, and justification. Group Two

> "Jigsaw" model for word processing skills

	See		22
	How		44
	The		56
	Colors		22
	Change	Sum of Column 5 =	144

FIGURE 9.1 Table Exercise

may learn about importing and formatting graphics; Group Three importing spread-sheets, charts, and graphs; Group Four creating and formatting tables and columns (see an example of a "table exercise" in Figure 9.1); and Group Five, headers, footers, footnotes, selecting, cutting, and pasting. The students return to their home groups to teach what they have learned and to learn what the others in the group have to teach. After this initial activity in which students learn or refresh their word processing skills, they can rotate through the computers to complete selected writing assignments.

Laboratories helpful for teaching skills

Laboratory

A laboratory is the best place to teach students how to use word processors. Several long or many closely spaced shorter blocks of time help students learn how to use a word processor quickly. It is important that students get to use their new skills early in the learning process in several closely spaced assignments. Students should learn the same topics that are suggested in the section on the five-computer classroom. The best way to do this is to provide an activity for each skill. Then assign a project that involves content requiring the use of most or all of the skills they have learned.

Another effective way to use a laboratory for writing is in conjunction with a five-computer classroom. If students have to write a report or do a research project, they can do the first draft with a pencil and paper. Entering this first draft on the computer takes some time, and if possible, the school laboratory should be reserved for this assignment. Once the first draft has been entered and printed out, then students edit their own papers as well as submit them to others for peer editing and review. In a five-computer classroom, there is time for students to do revisions.

THE MODELS: USING THE WORD PROCESSOR TO TEACH CONTENT AND SKILLS

Now that you have looked at some general management and skill issues, it is time to turn to content, the real reason you have computers with word processors in your classroom. Review the models for word processing in Table 9.1. Most of these uses are self-explanatory, and most of these activities may be done with pencil and paper. The

Word processors speed student work

TABLE 9.1 Models for Word Processing	
Targeted Learning Problems	**High-Level Analysis**

1. Ordering/Classification
  a. Sorting
  b. Outlines
	1. Rewrite (style, content)
	  a. Revision
	  b. Editing

2. Substitution Exercises
  a. Supply the missing
    (words, sentences, paragraphs, pictures)
  b. Remove the extra
    (words, sentences, paragraphs, pictures)
	2. Information analysis
	  a. Research report
	  b. Journaling
	  c. Lab reports
	  d. Note taking

3. Grammar
  a. Thesaurus
  b. Spell checker
	3. Newspaper

	4. Brochure

4. Logical sequencing
  a. Follow directions
  b. Writing directions
	5. Group investigations/
	  brainstorming

	6. Composition
	  a. Creative writing
	  b. Letters
	  c. Writing roulette

benefit of using a word processor is the speed with which children can manipulate information. Take outlines, for example. Children have been outlining with pencil and paper for a very long time. However, think about the outlining process. People outline when they are just beginning to think about a topic—when their thoughts may not be entirely clear. Sometimes the entire outline must be rewritten because the writer has more or different ideas. Changing an outline with a word processor is only a matter of cutting and pasting or pressing the Enter key to make a new line.

It is important to notice that a student product is implicit in each model in Table 9.1. Furthermore, the process that is used to create the product for the "High-Level Analysis and Skills" models may require the use of additional tool software. On the other hand, the "Targeted Learning Problems" models require students to manipulate smaller chunks of information often represented as text, a function that is facilitated by a word processor.

High-Level Analysis and Skills

"The Newspaper," the "Research Report," creative writing, and writing roulette are activities that you no doubt have models for already. Using a word processor doesn't change the activity much. It does provide for a better-looking product from the students, and it allows them to add graphics that they might not ordinarily use.

Students experiment with different formatting

Journaling, lab reports, and note-taking activities may be improved with computers if students know how to keyboard. However, using computers for these activities is questionable considering the other functions computers do that students cannot do with pencil and paper (databases and spreadsheets). In a science class, precious computer time might be better spent with probes and spreadsheets than with entering lab reports or note taking.

Let us look at an example of how a teacher might execute a high-level activity using a word processor. Producing a newspaper requires a different set of skills than producing a research report. Students use a different writing style as well as more and different formatting techniques. To get the flavor of how a newspaper assignment can be used as a tool for learning, let us visit Mr. Harrison's fifth-grade social studies class. They are studying medieval Europe.

**FIELD TRIP
9.1**

Creating a Newspaper

Adam, an avid fan of both Mr. Harrison and sixth-grade social studies, was excited to begin the new unit on medieval Europe. In preparation for the unit he had spent the previous evening slaying dragons in the backyard with his wooden sword. Today was the day they would actually start reading and learning about knights, castles, and the misty world of the Middle Ages.

Mr. Harrison began the unit by asking students what they knew about the world a thousand years ago. He had a computer and projector and was using a word processor to list the students' contributions.

Setting up a problem

Before class he had made a table with headings to help students remember what they knew about the period. Headings at the top of his table included: government, military, daily life, religion, language, common people, aristocracy, pastimes, important events, medicine, and law. As students begin trying to fill in cells in the table, they discuss their contributions and decide that there are some things that they do not know. In fact, there are quite a few things they do not know. Mr. Harrison said, "Adam, if you were to wake up tomorrow morning and the date were March 1, 1066, what would your day be like? What would the headlines in the newspaper that day be?" Adam was smart enough to know that there would be no newspaper and said so, which made everyone laugh. But he had to admit that he didn't know much more than that.

Mr. Harrison used the laughter and Adam's answer to propose to the class the method they would use to learn about medieval Europe. He said, "Newspapers reflect the daily life of the people who write them." Quickly he double clicked an icon at the bottom of the computer screen that opened to some excerpts titled "100 Years Ago Today" he had scanned from his local paper. He read them to the class. After the class listened to and reflected on the newspaper examples, Mr. Harrison suggested to the class that they write a newspaper that would reflect daily life in England on October 15, 1066. The class was delighted, and full of energy they began collecting information from their textbooks, the library, and a

Providing tools to help students solve the problem

selected list of Internet sites that Mr. Harrison had prepared for them. Each student could pick six topics from the table that Mr. Harrison and the class had brainstormed. In fact, Mr. Harrison printed the table and duplicated it so that each student would have a copy. On the days students were doing their research, Mr. Harrison also led class discussions on newspapers and how they are written and formatted. Mr. Harrison gave the class some guidelines for their articles.

Analyzing and judging information

After each student had researched and written on six topics, the class then used a word processor to format and publish individual newspapers. When all of the newspapers were finished, each student printed a copy and the students read and critiqued each other's work. In cases where students disagreed about the facts, Mr. Harrison arbitrated the discussions and helped students make accurate conclusions. After students made corrections, Mr. Harrison then put all of the newspapers on the class web site for students' parents, relatives, and friends to see.

Adam was excited about his project and handed in this newspaper as a first draft:

King Harold Defeated!

King Harold was defeated yesterday at Hastings. Surviving soldier stated that they creamed us. It was a sad ending For King Harold who so boldly defeated King Harold of Norway. Duke Williams army was an army looking for plunder and conquest. They were not fighting for any humane reason. Men of education suspect that this invasion will have an effect on the English language. Orevua!!

An Explanation

Duke Williams raided England because he wanted every body to be Roman catholics. Normandy had been getting stronger and stronger Because of all the strong lords they had been having. Harold promised the Throne to William but Harold refused to give up the throne. So that is Why Wiliam invaded, out of greed.

An Effect

An effect will be the change in our language. There will be a lot of French words introduced To our language.Dumb, huh!

We the media suspect that Normandy England will be more powerful than before.

Dear Lord Abby, I am a poor bloke Who can barely survive. I don't have any money because I spent it on the paper to write this letter. How can I get some money? Sighned poor Man.

Dear Poor man, get a life!

Second letter.

Dear lord Abby, I own a business and it isn't going to well my business is farming. What can I do? Dear Farmer, Your business Is not my business.

Sports

Yesterday's Joust was very exciting, the lists were filled the fans were chearing, Blake had just finished with Nare and was chooseing an opponent. He chose Drake The only one who hadn't he hadn't won. (Blake was getting a lot of armor and horses). They both mounted Their horses, and charged. Strangely they both Knocked each other off their horses, but Drake fell harder. Blake Quickly got up and hammerd him With his mace. Blake had almost torn of Sir Drake's helmut when Drake swung his sword up and hit Blakes hand broad side. Blakes hand was paralyzed for the moment. Drake saw his chance and quickly tore off Blakes helmet, there by Having to challenge and fight all the other men Blake had beaten.

Obituary

This morning Cathy Robin died this morning of unknown cause.
Blake III Died of pox, at age 40.
Trank Blabber died of Apoplexy at age 19.
Araph Linger died of a club at age 15.
Fander Fish died of Apoplexy, age 10.
Lady Crane died of a curse, kitchen maid suspected.

Editorial

Topic: chamber pots
I think that people should find a better way to empty their chamber pots. There are problems with just dumping it out a window. For instance, people could get waste on them if they happened to walk by when somebody was emptying their chamber pot. Here is another reason why people should find another way, if someone dumped the contence of a chamber pot into a stream The fish might die from the foulness of the waste, and that wouldn't be good for the fishermen. Here is my solution, you build a system of gutters (something you'll hafto invent) that all lead to a pit just outside of the village. You dump the waste into these gutters and the waste will flow into the pit.

Advertisements and Announcements

Cany Flounder is sick and will probably die on Tuesday. Flan's Fats is having a sale on fat. Remember Flan's Fats don't taste like rats. Lord Lutany has Bought a fresh shipment of fish from Ireland, you can to at a very low price (price will be yelled at town auction). Dave Thatcher will thatch your roof for only two hundred poinds. The fishing fleet will be back the fourth. Most of the men will be back from the trip, I don't think anyone has drown. Sowrenson's Swords is having a sale on German and French Imports. Lady Becket is turning to a rip old age of forty.
Lorsa Cling died of Child birth.

Table Tips

Remember to have a blessing, don't belch, don't touch your ears or your nose, be sure to have a toothpick, and don't forget to keep your elbows on the table, clean your nails and hands.

The draft shown here is an actual rough draft submitted by Adam, a sixth-grade student (Thorsen, 1990). You can see that the process of writing the newspaper has connected the student with many facts about daily life in the Middle Ages. Furthermore, the student has not simply memorized these facts but put them into a larger context. He tried to think about them as though he were there when they happened. The word processor helped him express his thoughts in a way that other people could read them because Adam had never been able to print or write legibly. You can also see that Adam has some editorial work to do. Mr. Harrison has teamed with the language arts teacher so that the editing will take place in her class.

CHECKING YOUR UNDERSTANDING

9.1

1. Since this is the first draft of this student's work, explain how you would manage your classroom as you helped this student and the rest of the class work on spelling and sentence mechanics. Since you will post these on the web, you will want students to hand in final copies that are very clean. Assume that you have a five-computer classroom.

2. Since you will ultimately want to assess your students' knowledge of the Middle Ages with a test of some kind, use this student's paper to develop one essay question and five multiple-choice questions that you could use on an assessment. Remember, one activity in this unit is for all of the students to read each others' newspapers. An example of one multiple-choice question is:

   1. Probably the most common reason that women often died young during the Middle Ages was

      a. Childbirth problems
      b. Household accidents
      c. Jousting injuries
      d. Travel dangers

TECHTIP 9.1 *Technology Hardware*

As a teacher, you may be asked to serve on your building or district technology committee. Or, as a classroom teacher you may be asked to vote or give opinions on technology issues that directly affect your classroom. If you are new at this, these kinds of issues can seem intimidating at first. There are some things that you can do to help yourself be more informed about the issues of the replacement of old technology and understanding the specifications of new equipment.

How computers work—foundational information. Intel has an excellent web site at www97.intel.com/scripts-tji/index.asp to help you (and your students, if you choose) understand how computers work. Reviewing this site will give you the terminology that you need when you want to think about old and new technology. To learn more about the PC, go to http://computer.howstuffworks.com/pc.htm. Here you will find all of the terms that you might have heard but still wonder about, for example, firewire, USB (universal serial bus), serial port, hard disk, parallel port, DSL (digital subscriber line). Taking the terms above and putting them into a classroom context, you will probably download the digital pictures that your students take with a digital camera using a *firewire.* Most external devices such as color printers now attach to your computer with a *USB,* while most laser printers, though not all, require a *parallel port.* Your computer may be slow because you are low on *hard disk* space. You may want to check into a *DSL* at home so that you will have fast Internet access. You might have a problem with a new mouse because your school's computers are old and do not have *USBs* and you have bought a *USB* mouse instead of a *serial* mouse.

Once you have the foundational vocabulary and understanding of how computers work, you should start looking at the configuration of the computers in your environment. Although in the Mac and PC environments the keystrokes are different, you can easily find out the speed of your microprocessor (this tells you how fast your machine is) and the size of your hard drive (this tells you how much information you can store). You can look for the firewire on your machine as well as its USB. You will want to locate your parallel and serial ports, as well.

Targeted Learning Problems

Like the models for "High-Level Analysis and Skills" and "Targeted Learning Problems," models may be used with either group or individual learning activities. In most content area topics, students need a basic level of knowledge or skill in order to progress further. A word processor can provide a different context and medium for student interaction with these problem areas.

"Removing or supplying text" requires students to work with the language of a discipline and hone their vocabulary skills. Ordering steps in procedures is another way of practicing a skill in the early stages of learning it. Teachers can build sorting exercises for word processors quite easily. Figure 9.2 is an example of a sorting exercise for geometric shapes. Using a computer, children either cut and paste or drag the labels to the appropriate graphics. They do similar exercises with pencil and paper by drawing lines, or cutting and pasting—for "real," this time. If you have computer resources, you can create these kinds of activities for your children. If your resources are marginal, have your students use the computers for something they can't do as well or as fast with pencil and paper.

Build traditional worksheets

WORD PROCESSING TIPS

Bullets and Numbered Lists

A numbered list indicates steps in an event or a prioritized list. Bullets indicate that there is no special sequence of events or order of importance. Students should learn to do each type of list using automatic numbering and bulleting features of the word

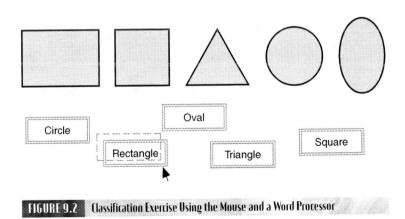

FIGURE 9.2 Classification Exercise Using the Mouse and a Word Processor

processing software. Encourage more adept students to explore the different styles of numbers and bullets that can be used.

Using Tables to Organize Information

Teach your students to use tables to help them organize word-processed documents. When students include graphics in their documents, sometimes they appear cluttered and disorganized. Using a table as an organizational tool helps students keep their thinking straight and their presentation of information clear. Looking at the table in Figure 9.3, do you recognize some organizational tips that you learned in Chapter 7?

> Tables help students organize and format information

The page is organized around the concept "regions of the Western hemisphere." The properties of the regions are native food and animal supplies. Examples of the properties are listed in the left-hand column. Note how the student has arranged the graphics with the northernmost landmasses first and the southernmost last. Furthermore, notice how easy it is for the reader to scan up and down the column of example foods and animals and observe how few foods and no animals moved north or south. The arrangement of the items in the table reflects what the words in the first cell of the table say. The student started with a table like the one in Figure 9.4.

Making Links to the Internet

Although students cannot use word processing software to present information non-linearly as with presentation software, they can link to articles or other information on the Internet. Here is one scenario in which that capability is useful. Remember when we talked about "information literacy" in Chapter 3? We learned that students must learn to be able to judge the quality of information that they get from the Internet because so many different kinds of authors post their work there. Imagine that your students are working on a research project on the pros and cons of genetic engineering. Also, imagine that as a part of this research assignment you are trying to teach them the difference between reliable and unreliable information. Your assignment to them is this:

- ▨ Find three good Internet sources of information in favor of genetic engineering for food crops.
- ▨ Find three good Internet sources of information against genetic engineering for food crops.
- ▨ Find three good Internet sources of information in favor of genetic engineering for humans.
- ▨ Find three good Internet sources of information against genetic engineering for humans.

In this assignment, you are teaching them two things about information literacy: triangulation and judging the quality of sources. Now comes the hard part. How will you look at and grade or give them feedback on their sources? You have three alternatives:

1. Have them write down the address of the Internet site when they find it so that you can type it in and check it out.

Prehistory of the Americas

The Americas consist of three different regions—North America, Central America, and South America. Because of their arrangement (north/south), crops and livestock that thrive in one part of the Americas do not necessarily thrive in other parts of the landmass. Furthermore, because of impenetrable jungle and hostile conditions, crops and livestock from South America (the Andes) that might have thrived in North America because of a similar climate, never moved north or south (Diamond, 1999).

Food crops:

Maygrass, little barley, knotweed, goosefoot, Jerusalem artichoke, squash

Domesticated animals:

None

North America

Food crops:

Corn, common bean, tepary bean, scarlet runner bean, cotton, yucca, agave, jicama, squash

Domesticated animals:

None

Central America

Food crops:

Quinoa, corn, lima bean, common bean, peanut, cotton, manioc, sweet potato, potato, oca

Domesticated animals:

Llama and alpaca

South America

FIGURE 9.3 Using a Table to Format Information

FIGURE 9.4 Students' Starting Point for Figure 9.3

2. Have them print out the Internet site.
3. Have them cut and paste the Internet site into a word-processed document and give you an electronic copy. When you are ready to look at their searches you will load their document into a word processor on a computer connected to the Internet, and click on the addresses they have cut and pasted. You will then review the documents they have chosen and type feedback or grades directly into the document they gave you, save it, and give it back to them.

You can tell right now that choice 1 will be quite ineffective. Students will write down some addresses incorrectly, and you will type some incorrectly. After you get the addresses right (if you ever do), you will have to create a new document and save it under their name. Choice 2 is wasteful but possible. You could have the students underline portions of the printed pages and underline words or phrases that reveal biased opinions. Choice 3 is a winner: It is quick and easy. If you wanted to do something similar to underlining words and phrases that reveal biases, students could simply cut and paste them into their documents.

Importing Information from Other Applications

Although we have not yet discussed spreadsheets, you should encourage students to import supporting work that they have done with spreadsheets into documents they make with a word processor. Reports no longer have to be all words. Students can include tables, charts, and graphs that they make with other electronic tools. When you read Chapters 10 through 12 you will learn that working with a database or a spreadsheet is usually never an end in itself. There is usually a requirement for some kind of product—a presentation, speech, or written report. Figure 9.5 includes an example of an imported spreadsheet and its accompanying chart.

> Display information from other applications

When students use a word processor, they can include many different kinds of information. Besides graphs, charts, and tables from a spreadsheet, they can import

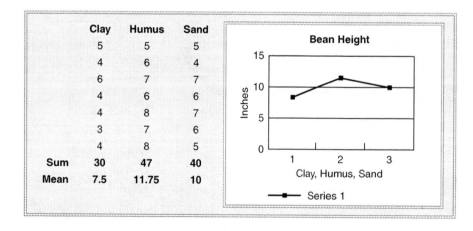

FIGURE 9.5 Spreadsheet and Chart Inserted into a Word Processed Document

graphics. Students have some choices about how to display graphics. They can learn to wrap text around a graphic, or lay the graphic over the text or under the text. Figure 9.6 is an example of using word wrap around a graphic. Although the instructional utility of having this skill is marginal, learning how to format graphics and text on the same page is a minor part of basic computer skills for the information age.

Spelling and Spell Checkers

Be careful about spell checker settings

There has been a lively debate among English teachers about whether children should use spell checkers. A study done recently by Cope (2000) adds some perspective to this debate. He used two groups of high school English students in grades 9–12 and administered the California Test of Basic Skills (CTBS) for spelling as a pretest. He disabled the spell checker on the computers used by the experimental group ($n = 42$). The control group of students ($n = 64$) continued to use their spell checkers with the auto-correct feature. This feature changes errors it recognizes as the writer types without notifying the writer, who may never know about the errors. This treatment continued for a semester. At the end of the semester, Cope tested the students again using a different form of the CTBS test. Students in the control group (students using automatic spelling correction) scored significantly lower (p .05) than students in the experimental group who did not have access to spell checkers. Conclusions that Cope drew from this experiment are that spell checking with auto correct does not help students. You may want to make sure that this feature is turned off in your classroom.

Jupiter is the largest planet in the solar system. It has more mass than any object

in the solar system other than the sun. It is the sixth planet from the sun, and it is a very cold place at the top of its clouds and a very hot place below their surface. Its atmosphere is unbreathable for human beings. Composed of hydrogen, helium, ammonia, and methane, Jupiter is called a "gas giant" because it is mostly gas and liquid with a small rock core. Jupiter has 16 moons. Galileo saw them first.

Just what would it be like to be a human on Jupiter? You would need a special space. . . .

FIGURE 9.6 Importing a Graphic and Placing Text around It

In another study, we get more clues about how word processors work in classrooms (Figueredo & Varnhegen, 2006). The question is, do spell checkers and grammar checkers influence the way that people revise their work? Although this study was done using freshman and graduate college students, the results seem relevant to K–12 teaching as well. The authors of this study found that the checkers did help students fix surface problems but did not affect their revision of content. The key point is that spell checkers and grammar checkers should be turned off while students are composing and then turned and used once the composition process has been completed.

TECHTIP 9.2 *Hardware—How Old Is Too Old?*

Acquiring and replacing hardware in schools is a difficult issue. There is not a black-and-white answer for knowing when to replace a computer. If you have a computer that you think needs replacing, here are some questions to ask:

- ▓ Is the latest operating system that it will support one or two generations behind the current operating system?
- ▓ Is it difficult and bulky with peripherals even after you have tried to download appropriate new drivers (your new digital camera, your printer)?
- ▓ Does it crash frequently, even after you have reformatted the hard drive and reinstalled the operating system and other software you use?

If you are planning on a large scale, a general estimate of the useful life of a computer is about three years. However, there are exceptions. You might not be able to do current multimedia kinds of tasks on a three-year-old computer, but it would still be fine for word processing, spreadsheets, and databases. It is better to think about how well the computer runs and what it is used for than its age.

Readability Statistics and Grammar Checkers

Most word processors provide a simple utility that displays readability statistics for a selection or for a whole file. This allows students to measure themselves on a variety of different items (Figure 9.7). The "Flesch Reading Ease" is a scale from 1 to 100. The higher the number, the easier a selection is to read. Microsoft documentation (2003) indicates that for general readability at the adult level, writers should achieve scores in the 60s or 70s. "Flesch-Kincaid grade level" is tied to the United States school system indications of grade level. On this scale, a level between 7.0 and 8.0 indicates general readability. Younger children, of course, would use different standards. Teachers at different grade levels can create standards for their students by scanning in items of work that they have judged to be outstanding at the grade level or performance level that they teach and recording the readability indicators and other statistics. These, then, could be given to students as one standard by which to judge their writing. Although mechanics can never substitute for content, it rarely hurts to give a student at least one concrete goal for which to aim.

Readability statistics give
students one baseline

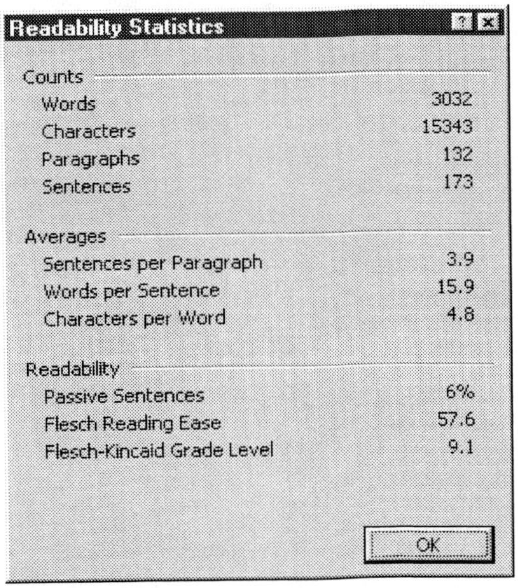

Readability Statistics

Counts
Words 3032
Characters 15343
Paragraphs 132
Sentences 173

Averages
Sentences per Paragraph 3.9
Words per Sentence 15.9
Characters per Word 4.8

Readability
Passive Sentences 6%
Flesch Reading Ease 57.6
Flesch-Kincaid Grade Level 9.1

OK

FIGURE 9.7 Readability Statistics

Another way to use readability statistics is to have students accumulate them in a spreadsheet during the year. Once they do this, they can graph or chart each statistic and look at their progress over the year. You may, for example, be teaching them to write complex sentences. This goal would translate into more words per sentence. Although the readability statistics don't tell you if the sentence is well constructed or meaningful, it can still be one piece of the puzzle that helps students measure their progress. You will be the one who gives them a grade on how meaningful their work is, and that grade can be entered into the spreadsheet along with the readability statistics. If grades are going up on how meaningful sentences are and numbers of words per sentence is going up as well, then the student is probably writing more good, complex sentences.

Grammar checkers can
find some mistakes but . . .

The grammar checker on word processors is a valuable tool for students who are trying to learn the mechanics of writing. It is important to recognize that a grammar checker cannot check grammar as well as a teacher can. A grammar checker cannot help students with the logical connection they must make between paragraphs, for example. A grammar checker cannot check to see that every paragraph has a topic sentence and a summary sentence. A grammar checker can, however, alert students to purely mechanical problems with their writing, and there is a long list of those. See Figure 9.8 for a complete listing of mechanics checked by Microsoft Word.

Furthermore, you may use grammar checks in various combinations. Word provides for four basic styles: casual, standard, formal, and technical. This option allows writing teachers to help students understand the differences among writing styles. This option box is displayed in Figure 9.9. In addition, the software provides a "custom" setting that allows you to put checks in the boxes that you choose, enabling you to closely define the problems that you want your students to focus on.

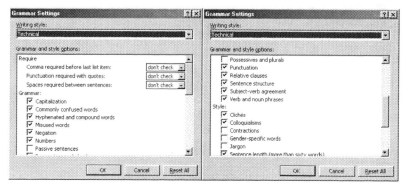

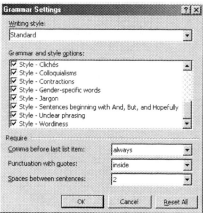

FIGURE 9.8 Settings for Checking Grammar (Examples of Features)

TEXT-READING SOFTWARE

> Text-reading software
> helps students who can
> learn but not read

Text-reading software, although not really a word processor in the traditional sense, can be used in conjunction with word processors to help with not only the reading process but also the writing process. When people with reading and writing disabilities are mainstreamed, they sit alongside those who can be told, "Read in your social studies book pages 52 through 57." If students cannot read but can learn social studies, understand and enjoy stories and literature, learn science and learn mathematics, there is an alternative to failure based on their inability to read. Using text-reader software, a computer will read a story or a textbook to a student while the student follows along. Students may change the font, size, or color of the text to accommodate individual differences. The computer will also read students' stories or reports back to them. Such a text reader will read information continually or read it one word at a time, at the student's request. Students can select the volume, pitch, and speed of the computer's voice as well. While the computer is reading, the student may also take notes in a special notes pane. Upon request, the computer will read the notes back

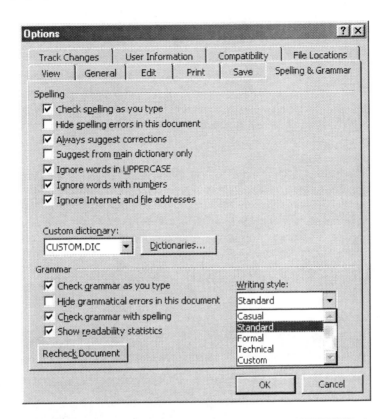

FIGURE 9.9 Choose Your Writing Style

to the student. CAST AspireReader is such a product, with information at www.cast .org/products/ereader/index.html.

How do students put text into a text reader? Some is available on the Internet at "e-text" sites. Houghton Mifflin provides a disk with the text of its social studies books, for example. If both of those options fail, students scan in text with scanners equipped for OCR (optical character recognition).

Text readers are not especially new, but are underutilized in classrooms. The software itself is relatively inexpensive—$40 for a single copy and less for multiple copies. A classroom would need a scanner, though not an expensive one. West (1998) lists six different activities for which she uses text-reading software in her elementary school classroom, including:

- On-screen note taking
- Modified reading activities
- On-screen talking worksheets
- Creative writing activity
- Sight/articulation word practice
- A talking word processor

West has successfully used text-reading software to work with mainstreamed children with learning disabilities. She reports that "of the thirty-one students in my fifth-grade classroom, nine tested at a second- or third-grade reading level and qualified for special education help. Three of these students had poor motor skills which made writing a long, difficult task. Attention Deficit Disorder and a lack of motivation were also challenges." Though her students were not measured against a control group, they were pre- and posttested. She reports that for the nine students, "year-end test results showed increased fluency, decoding, and vocabulary skills."

There is also some evidence that this use of computers helps at least some children to *learn* to read. Richard Sirase (1997) completed a small study with thirteen children and concluded that scanned text read by a computer does benefit elementary children with "global" reading delay. He could find no evidence that scanned text is helpful for children with specific reading problems. This is only a preliminary study, and much work needs to be done in this area. Enough evidence exists to suggest that if you have children in your class who have reading problems for whom proven methods fail and you have the resources, a scanner and text-reading software might help.

TECHTIP 9.3   *Computer Maintenance*

What maintenance should I perform on my computer to keep it running well? You can do a few things to keep your computer running well. They are simple and do not require the services of an expert.

- ▓ Keep your hard disk clean. Remove files that you do not use. Store your pictures on a CD.
- ▓ Uninstall software that you do not use. It will free space on the hard drive.
- ▓ Disable cookies and pop-up windows. Run a program that will clean your computer of software that has been automatically downloaded from the Internet without your knowledge
- ▓ Install a virus checker on your computer, and run and update it regularly.
- ▓ Check to see whether your hard drive needs to be defragmented and do it when necessary. You can find out how to do this if you go to your operating system's Help page.

CHECKING YOUR UNDERSTANDING

9.2

1. Write a 500-word paper on using the word processor to improve student vocabulary and writing skills, in a content area of your choice. Your paper should be written with the "casual" style chosen in the grammar-checker dialogue box. Grade level should be 5–6.

   - ▓ Check your paper with the "standard" style chosen in the grammar-checker dialogue box. Rewrite to accommodate the two following restrictions: grade level should be 8–9; passive sentences should be below 10 percent.
   - ▓ Check your paper with the "technical" style chosen in the grammar-checker dialogue box. Rewrite so the grade level is 7–8.
   - ▓ Check your paper with the "formal" style chosen in the grammar-checker dialogue box. Rewrite so the grade level is 7–8.

2. Write a brochure describing the features of word processors and Internet communications activities that help students write better. Design your layout with a bi-fold (three-panel) landscape orientation, using a table to help you place your text and graphics. The audience for your brochure is your students' parents.

▦ SUMMARY

This is a short chapter, but not because word processing is unimportant. It is short because, of all the computer-based instruction tools, many teachers are already most familiar with using the word processor to teach writing and have methods for teaching with it. Word processors make writing faster, easier to edit, and easier to read. For students who do not write well with pencils, word processing software removes the barrier that prevents people from reading and understanding their work. For students who do not *read* well, a word processor is an integral tool in the text-reading process. Word processors also perform many of the same functions as presentation software. Given an assignment that requires students to summarize and organize information (writing a brochure, outline, or newspaper), the word processor provides a medium that allows students to focus on constructing products that convey information effectively. Table 9.2 summarizes the instructional applications for the spreadsheet. The challenge is having sufficient computer resources to use these methods effectively.

TABLE 9.2   Bloom's Taxonomy and the Word Processor

The Cognitive Process Dimension	The Knowledge Dimension			
	Factual	**Conceptual**	**Procedural**	**Meta-Cognitive**
Remember	Spell checking	–	–	–
Understand	Sorting; supply the missing words, paragraphs, pictures; remove the extra words, sentences, paragraphs, pictures	–	–	–
Apply	Grammar checker	–	Outlining; using a word processor	Knowing how to put together a document
Analyze	Thesaurus	Following directions; research report; journaling; lab notes	–	–
Evaluate	Proofreading for grammar/ punctuation	Proofreading for flow of ideas	–	–
Create	–	Writing directions; newspaper; brochure; creative writing	Same as above	–

▩ REFERENCES

Cope, D. (2000). The effect of a spell checker on the spelling ability of high school students. Unpublished master's thesis, Boise State University, Boise, ID.

Diamond, J. (1999). *Guns, germs, and steel.* New York: Norton.

Figueredo, L., & Varnhagen, C. (2006). Spelling and grammar checkers: Are they intrusive? *British Journal of Educational Technology.* 37(5), 721–732.

Hetzroni, O. E., & Schreiber, B. (2004). Word processing as an assistive technology tool for enhancing academic outcomes of students with writing. *Journal of Learning Disabilities.* 37(2), 143–154.

MacArthur, C. A. (1996). Using technology to enhance the writing process of students with learning disabilities. *Journal of Learning Disabilities.* 29(4), 344–354.

Microsoft. (2003). Word documentation for grammar checker. Accessed online February 2005.

Sirase, R. (1997, October). Using scanners linked to talking computers as tools for teaching children to read. *British Journal of Educational Technology.* 28(4), 308–310.

Thorsen, A. (1990). *The Middle Ages.* Unpublished report.

West, P. (1998). Integration of text reading software in an elementary school setting. Unpublished master's thesis, Boise State University, Boise, ID.

▩ ANNOTATED RESOURCES

Cavanaugh, T. (2004). *Word processing software revisited, some tips for making better use of a basic software application.* Jacksonville, FL: Terrance W. Cavanaugh. Retrieved June 8, 2007, from www.unf.edu/-tcavanau/publications/tesol/tesoli.htm.

This short document is a an informal discussion of miscellaneous ways a teacher uses a word processor to advantage.

Dowling, C. (1999). *Writing and learning with computers.* Acer Press, available from Stylus Publishing at www.styluspub.com.

Although the book is not just about word processors, three of the eight chapters are devoted to writing and word processors, including discussions of the writing process and classroom activities using the word processor. The remaining chapters focus on writing and the Internet, and writing and multimedia.

Kennedy, K. (2006). Write on time. *Technology & Learning.* 27(4), 12, 14, 16.

Some software allows students to do not only word processing but also provides feedback and tutorials. The article lists and discusses three such programs.

McDonald, L., & Caverly, D. C. (2006). Techtalk: Word processing from adoption to innovation. *Journal of Developmental Education.* 30(2), 36–37.

This short article outlines word processor use for writing, reading, mathematics, and study strategies.

McPherson, K. (2006). Wikis and student writing. *Teacher Librarian.* 34(2), 70–72.

The author of this article, a librarian, reluctantly suggests that though he may be contributing to the "demise of the written word," nevertheless teachers should consider going beyond the word processor to online writing to expand and improve student writing skills. The article is reflective, informative, and interesting reading. He suggests using "wiki's" and provides suggestions for student writing projects for primary and secondary school students.

Mongomery, D. J., & Marks, L. J. (2006). Using technology to build independence in writing for students with disabilities. *Preventing School Failure.* 50(3), 33–38.

Word processing and organization software are beneficial for students with disabilities. The author discusses techniques for using the following: word prediction, voice output, spell checker, thesaurus, and grammar checker.

Pedler, J. (2001, January). Computer spell checkers and dyslexics. *British Journal of Educational Technology.* 32(1), 23–37.

Although the focus of this study is on improving spell checkers for use by students with dyslexia, the article could be read to obtain a methodology for analyzing typical errors. As a result, teachers could help students analyze their errors with the use of the spell checker.

Companion Web Site   www.ablongman.com/thorsen3e

1. Go to Chapter 9 of the TechTactics web site. Click on the link Using Technology to Enhance the Writing Processes of Students with Learning Disabilities. This article is especially important for any teacher who has students that are otherwise motivated and able to learn, but have difficulty with reading. Synthetic voice reading software has changed and improved since this article was written. Do a search for the most current synthetic voice reading software. Make a table in your word processing software which includes headings for the name of the software you have found, price, and features.

2. Go to Chapter 9 of the TechTactics web site. Click on the link Align Student Documents with Rubric Indicators and read the page. Write a 300-word paper on important uses of the word processor for your grade level and content area. You should state the use and then describe the implementation of that use briefly. Your paper will be graded on mechanics, spelling, and content. Highlight each topic sentence in yellow. Highlight each active verb in blue. Underline each major use that you suggest.

Databases: What They Are and How They Work

OBJECTIVES

- Describe the functional difference between a list (table) view and a form view in a database.
- Predict how an ascending or descending sort on a given database will look.
- Describe the pattern of information that a query will yield.
- Know when to use a sort and when to use a query.
- Explain the difference in the kind of information in rows and columns of a table.
- Explain why an electronic database with a database engine is more than a collection of facts.

The following are skills you should know and practice before you read Chapters 9, 10, 11, and 12.

- Set up a table
- Do simple and complex queries
- Build a report
- Distinguish between design view and data sheet view
- Explain and identify fields and records in list or table view
- Do ascending and descending sorts
- Build a form
- Format fields (text, date, numeric, etc.)
- Understand how to use Boolean terms to write queries

Many people understand that databases are collections of facts, and that is true. However, electronic databases are *more* than just collections of facts. They provide tools for a skilled user to detect patterns among the facts from which they are built. The next question is, "What kind of patterns would people want to detect?" To begin to answer this question and to help you make the connection between databases and their practical applications, we will begin with three brief narratives describing how people use databases outside schools.

> More than a
> collection of facts

SOLVING PROBLEMS OUTSIDE THE CLASSROOM: THREE STORIES

A Business Problem

Cornell Andrews is a buyer for a department store chain. He has worked hard, made good choices, and received promotions. He graduated from college twenty years ago—

179

Projecting trends and
making predictions

before electronic databases were such a key to being successful in his job. In the old days he would buy "by the seat of his pants." He had a sixth sense about what would be popular and when. After fifteen years he was handling accounts worth millions of dollars a year.

Then his lead began to erode. Younger buyers' sales volume moved closer and closer to his. Soon he was just an average buyer, and finally he began to fall behind. What was the problem? He went to Ann, one of the most successful buyers in his area, and asked her how she could be so right so often. Ann showed Cornell her database. By keeping a record of all the items she buys and how soon the items are sold, with the electronic database she was able to construct seasonal profiles of the best sellers as well as predict color and fabric combinations that would be successful.

A Scientific Problem

Describing unknowns

Susan Pacheco is an astronomer. She works for NASA and is the lead scientist analyzing information that is being returned to her computer from a deep-space probe. The probe was launched ten years ago to study the furthermost reaches of the solar system. Information on Uranus has been coming in for more than a year now. She gets information on temperature, amounts of certain gasses at specific locations in space, and readings that indicate the location of solid bodies in space.

She puts all of this information into a database and then goes to work on her hunches. She relentlessly asks questions of the database, reformulating and refining her ideas. At last, with all the data gathered and all the questions asked, Susan realizes that she and her team have discovered a new moon circling Uranus.

An Ethical and Sociological Problem

Gary Johnson is an insurance company employee. He is working feverishly on a key project for the company. The state legislature is debating changing the speed limit from 65 miles an hour to 75 miles per hour. Opponents say that more people will be killed and insurance rates will go up if the speed limit is raised. Those in favor of the bill say that people will just get places faster. Gary's insurance company needs to know how they should approach this issue.

Analyzing problems

One way Gary decides he can find out is to build a database defining characteristics of past accidents. Then, by asking questions of the database, Gary hopes to find some patterns, such as the conditions under which crashing at 75 miles per hour are most and least deadly, and how such crashes compare to fatal accidents in which the speed is less. Millions of dollars are at stake for both his company and consumers.

Databases Help People Think about Difficult Problems

People use databases widely in business, the professions, and science to enable them to sort through and analyze immense amounts of information. When people hear the term *database,* they most commonly think of a place to find a specific fact or answer to a question. An almanac, for example, is a database. When people use an almanac in its print form, they look up facts such as the population of a country, its major products, or statistics about crime or education.

But what happens when a print database, such as an almanac, is placed inside a database engine (such as Microsoft Works, or Claris Works, or Microsoft Access) on a computer? Then people can use databases to sift through the raw material to help them analyze complex problems. Why? Because a computer can reconfigure large amounts of information into many different patterns far more quickly than humans can with their minds, a pencil, and a piece of paper.

If all of the information in a print almanac were placed in an electronic database, then the almanac would become a much more potent tool. The difference to the user would be something like using a table saw rather than a handsaw. A table saw makes faster, more precise cuts, just as an electronic database finds information faster and more precisely than people do when they use a print-based database. Used skillfully, databases provide the bridge between individual, seemingly unrelated facts and the synthesis that allows a user to describe unknowns, make predictions, and render judgments.

Databases supply relationships

DATABASES IN THE CLASSROOM

An eleventh-grade U.S. history class is studying Native American culture and history. Students have learned about Native Americans in different regions of the country and are nearly finished studying the major tribes of each region. Over the course of the unit they have built a database of Native American tribes, their main foods, clothing, and environmental challenges. The students are now ready for their major synthesis activity for Native American cultures.

Databases and Native Americans

FIELD TRIP 10.1

The teacher poses this problem for the class:

"As we have learned, Native American cultures weren't all the same. Cultures varied across the country, depending on the local resources and on the history of each tribe. If you were a Native American back then, depending on the culture and the region in which you lived, your answer to each of the following questions would be different: What would you eat? Where would you sleep? How would you stay warm? How would you get clothing? What would you do for fun? How long would you live? What would happen to you when you became ill?

"Pretend, for this exercise, that you have come to America on a boat with the Pilgrims, and have decided that Pilgrim life is not for you. You strike out into the forest on your own, looking for a culture and lifestyle that suits you better. Which Native American tribe would you fit into best?"

The teacher poses a problem

After the teacher posed the problem, the students went to the computers in groups of five to do preliminary planning. Together they agreed on a lifestyle for the sake of exploring the problem together. Later each student used a similar process to do the exercise alone.

Students in one group decided that they would be most interested in being the member of a tribe that travels extensively, uses horses, lives in a warm climate, has plenty to eat, and has a long life expectancy. Together the students formulated the questions that would yield the name of the perfect tribe from the database. As they worked, they discovered that they had to make some compromises because they found that no tribe was able to live in such continual prosperity. Then they began debating what

Students see the solution more realistically

to give up: Perhaps it should be the horses (if you are full and warm it might be better than having a horse and being cold or hungry).

After some practice together, students distributed themselves through the four centers in the classroom and began their individual database assignments. Students began by formulating questions. Then, as computers become available, they tested their questions, recorded the answers, and returned to their seats to rewrite and summarize the information they received from the database, as well as write more questions. When the computers were not available, students did assigned reading, worksheets, and worked on maps of sixteenth-century America. The teacher moved through the classroom, tutoring and asking questions. Occasionally she noticed that several students were having trouble with the same question and gave short mini-lectures to the whole class, giving them information about content or how to formulate better questions for the database.

After students had asked the questions of the database that enabled them to analyze the information and draw conclusions, they created a hypermedia presentation describing the Native American tribe they wanted to join and why they wanted to join it. Because there are only five computers in the classroom, they began this report with a hand-written storyboard. Then, over the course of two weeks, they rotated through the computer centers to get computer time to finish their work. They presented their work to the class and compared what they learned and inferred from the database to information they gleaned from encyclopedia articles and other reference works.

| Working with a database is iterative |

| Using database info to construct a presentation |

How Do Databases Support Student Learning?

Students, like their counterparts in the work world, process large amounts of information. When people use electronic databases, they not only access large amounts of information but also use that information to reason and draw conclusions if they know how to ask the right questions of the database. When students cover information, they usually memorize definitions, do worksheets, read books, listen to the teacher talk about the subject, and participate in discussions with their classmates. The database builds the bridges among rote memory work, reading, classroom discussions, and reports. In between learning facts and making judgments about what the facts mean, the students derive opportunities from the database to make some sense of the facts—to analyze them.

There has not been much empirical research on the effects of database use in classrooms. Some studies show positive effects of database use relating to student skills in question asking (Ennals, 1995), classification (Underwood, 1987), and learning in science (Hecht et al., 1993). Both Jonassen (2000) and Grabe and Grabe (1996) build a case for the use of databases despite the lack of much research at this point. Their reasoning is based on students' use of higher-order thinking skills to complete database assignments. Based on that, we can reasonably assume that databases improve student learning. The challenge for the future is to further investigate this hypothesis and to define exactly how, what, and why students learn with databases.

Also, databases are not equally effective across all content areas and grade levels. There are some uses for databases in a mathematics class. There are relatively more uses for databases in social science classes (such as history, government, economics, and psychology), in language arts and literature, and in the sciences—especially the sciences in which classification is key, such as biology and geology. Students' ability to use a database differs by grade level and cognitive ability, as well.

| The value of databases lies in the higher-order thinking skills they promote |

| Databases are useful in most content areas |

Field experience has proven that third graders can understand the concept of a database when the teacher guides the class through an exploration of a topic. Some time during the fourth or fifth grade, students can begin to use small, premade, or teacher-made databases effectively. By the time children reach middle school, their cognitive abilities are such that they can both create databases themselves and use large premade databases.

> Less useful in the primary grades

Databases have been used effectively with at-risk students, also. In a year-long study in a government class at an alternative school in Idaho, at-risk students used databases to predict the next president of the United States. They also completed a project that included choosing the worst war in which the United States has been involved (Fisher, 1996). Students and the teacher were trained to use the database software, but the project started slowly because the students could not see the point in what they were doing.

> At-risk students use databases successfully

Once the students began the actual assignments, their skills improved and they used the database to guide them as they completed their projects. By the end of the project, the students worked with the database and stayed on task as they began to understand how to ask meaningful questions of the database. When they understood that the skills they were learning would transfer to the work world, they expressed even more interest in learning how to use databases effectively.

What Do Students and Teachers Need to Know?

Everyone needs three different types of skills to use databases successfully. First, students *and* teachers need the nuts-and-bolts skills to build a database and navigate an existing one. Second, they need conceptual understanding that will enable them to perform sorts and queries (use filters). Third, they need analytical skills to interpret the resulting information and make inferences. Before we look at how a teacher builds a database lesson like the one on Native Americans, consider some basic terminology and concepts.

> Fundamental skills

GETTING STARTED: TEACHING THE TOOL

No matter what kind of computer or database software you use, you will find that databases from different software manufacturers have many common features. After all, they perform the same functions. They help us manipulate words and numbers to make predictions, describe unknown places, people, ideas, objects, or animals, and make decisions or analyze information. A person needs to understand the following concepts (listed in the order which they are explained):

- ▦ Form view
- ▦ Field
- ▦ Record
- ▦ Table view (list view)
- ▦ Sort
- ▦ Query (find, filter)

Students must know how to use the tool before you give them a complex assignment

Students need to know these terms well enough so that a teacher can give instructions such as:

▪ "Do a descending sort on the *weight* field."
▪ "Find the *record* for 'black bears.'"
▪ "Do a query to find all of the records of presidents who went to college and were married."

As your students get better at using databases, they should be able to generate these kinds of tasks for themselves. For example, a student might write a position paper defending the 75-mile-an-hour speed limit on freeways. As the student searches for facts to support the argument, she or he might say, "I want to find out how many people were killed last year in traffic accidents in the states that have speed limits of 75 mph and in states that have speed limits of 65 mph. So, I will go to the database, and I will perform a query on 'speed limit equals 75 and deaths greater than some number per thousand.' Then I will do the same thing for states with speed limits of 65 miles per hour."

Most students will not reach this degree of sophistication quickly. It will take two or three database projects in several subjects, and some students will never make such a sophisticated connection. Nevertheless, any student may someday become an anthropologist who uses databases to make inferences about ancient cultures, or a worker in the parts department of an auto supply store who uses a database to find the right part for your car. The tool can help students think about the information they must learn in school and provide them with skills they can use when they enter the work world.

Form View

People who use databases usually work with them in two different formats. The format in Figure 10.1 is called *form view* because it represents a paper form that once would have been filled in with pencil or pen. The white rectangles on the form (which once were blank) are called *fields.* The information that is typed into each field is the field's *value* or *property.* For example, the field named Tribe has the property "Tlingt." When you design the record structure for a database, it is helpful to students if the first field in the record reflects the main idea of the database. In this example, the database is about tribes, so Tribe is the name of the first field on the record form.

The nine fields on this form comprise one *record.* As you can imagine, there are multiple records in this database—one record for each tribe. No two records have exactly the same field properties—unless there are duplicate records.

Someone who is putting new information into this database would start with a blank record and use the Tab key to move from field to field, typing information in each field.

Table View or List View

(Some database software calls the second viewing format *table view,* and some software calls it *list view.* In this book we will use both names.) Information that has been put into the database using the form view that we just explored can also be viewed

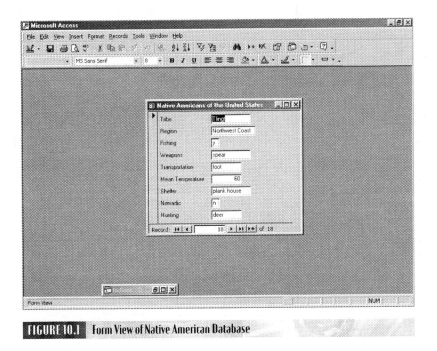

FIGURE 10.1 Form View of Native American Database

(or—for that matter—*entered*) in tabular format. Figure 10.2 shows eighteen records, each in a row of nine cells that represent the nine fields of the form view. Read across a single row to see all the properties of an individual tribe. Read down a single column to see the different values for each tribe in the field that column represents.

Someone putting information in the database using this format would also use the Tab key to move from field to field (or, with some software, the direction keys on the numeric key pad). Working in table or list view can be a faster way to enter data than the form view, but beginning users may find the form view more intuitive.

CHECKING YOUR UNDERSTANDING

10.1 You may be wondering about topics in your content area and how they might be used to generate a database. Some topics are good for databases and others are not. In order to learn which kinds of topics are most suitable for databases, try the exercise below. Get a piece of scratch paper or index card and cover the answers to the list of possible topics for a database listed below. As you look at each topic, write down whether you think it could be the foundation for a database-supported lesson. Write "yes" if it could be used for a database or "no" if it could not. If your answer is "yes," then write down five related ideas that could serve as fields in your database. Then uncover the answer and explanation below the question.

Question 1: Short Stories

Yes, a database could support a lesson on short stories. Such a database would include the following kinds of information if a class were studying theme, character, and setting. If you are an English

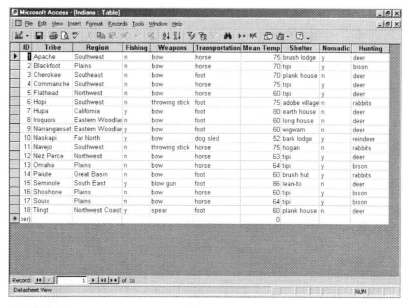

	ID	Tribe	Region	Fishing	Weapons	Transportation	Mean Temp	Shelter	Nomadic	Hunting
	1	Apache	Southwest	n	bow	horse	75	brush lodge	y	deer
	2	Blackfoot	Plains	n	bow	horse	70	tipi	y	bison
	3	Cherokee	Southeast	n	bow	foot	70	plank house	n	deer
	4	Commanche	Southwest	n	bow	horse	75	tipi	y	deer
	5	Flathead	Northwest	n	bow	horse	60	tipi	y	deer
	6	Hopi	Southwest	n	throwing stick	foot	75	adobe village	n	rabbits
	7	Hupa	California	y	bow	foot	80	earth house	n	deer
	8	Iroquois	Eastern Woodlar	n	bow	foot	60	long house	n	deer
	9	Narranganset	Eastern Woodlar	y	bow	foot	60	wigwam	n	deer
	10	Naskapi	Far North	y	bow	dog sled	52	bark lodge	y	reindeer
	11	Navejo	Southwest	n	throwing stick	horse	75	hogan	n	rabbits
	12	Nez Perce	Northwest	n	bow	horse	63	tipi	y	deer
	13	Omaha	Plains	n	bow	horse	64	tipi	y	bison
	14	Paiute	Great Basin	n	bow	foot	60	brush hut	y	rabbits
	15	Seminole	South East	y	blow gun	foot	86	lean-to	n	deer
	16	Shoshone	Plains	n	bow	horse	60	tipi	y	bison
	17	Souix	Plains	n	bow	horse	64	tipi	y	bison
	18	Tlingt	Northwest Coast	y	spear	foot	60	plank house	n	deer

FIGURE 10.2 Table or List View of Native American Database

teacher, you might be able to think of other fields that could be included in the database. The kinds of information include:

- The socioeconomic status of the female and male characters
- Time period in which the story was written
- Occupations of the characters
- Time of year when the story takes place
- Theme (man against man/man against nature/man against himself/man against God)
- Philosophy (romantic, existential, etc.)

Question 2: Socialist Governments

"Socialist governments" would be another good candidate for a database. Some of the fields that could be included in the database are listed below:

- Names of countries with socialist government
- Time periods when the socialist government ruled the country
- Attitudes toward women
- Attitudes toward private property
- Productivity
- An environmental consciousness rating
- Gross national product
- Size of the military
- Length of time the government has been or was in existence

Question 3: Diagramming a Sentence

No, diagramming a sentence would not be a good topic for a database. Diagramming sentences is something that children *do.* An English teacher might use a database to teach parts of speech, but diagramming sentences is an event with steps.

Question 4: Biomes

"Biomes" is another example of a unit that could be enriched with a database. Examples of biomes are tundra, grasslands, northern coniferous forests, deciduous forests, deserts, and tropical rain forests. Some fields related to biomes are:

- Annual precipitation
- Plant life
- Animal life
- Temperature

Here is another question for you. Would the *examples of biomes* listed above (tundra, grasslands, etc.) be listed in a database as fields? Yes, they would. Examples of biomes are like the names of Native American tribes in the Native American database in Figures 10.1 and 10.2. They are what the database is about, but they are a field, like any other field.

Question 5: Writing a Paragraph

Writing a paragraph is another poor candidate for a database. Again, writing a paragraph is something people *do,* not a group of related facts.

Question 6: How the Heart Works

How the heart works is not a good candidate for a database. Organ systems of the human body, on the other hand, would be a good topic for a database-supported lesson.

Question 7: Governments of the World

Yes, governments of the world would make an excellent foundation for a database-supported lesson. Examples of fields that would make up the database include:

- Kind of government (socialist, capitalist, etc.)
- Size of country
- Number of violent revolutions in last two hundred years
- Do women have the vote?
- Population of country

As you can see, one key to the successful use of databases to support student learning is choosing the right topic. As you think about databases and the information that you teach, remember that databases are mostly about facts and their relationships. A database, in the language of Chapters 6 through 8, is a concept. Its columns are properties of the concept, and the rows are examples of the concept. A database can help people see the relationships between many seemingly unrelated facts. See Table 10.1.

10.2 Now it is time to create a database on a computer. Choose one of the topics from "Checking Your Understanding 10.1" that is appropriate for a database.

TABLE 10.1 A Simple Database on Native Americans

Name	Food	Travel	Housing	Tools
Nez Perce	Deer	Horse	Pole covered with hides	Bow
Example	Value	Value	Value	Value
Example	Value	Value	Value	Value

1. Using your database software, set up the database. Create five fields and complete five records.
2. Print out one record in form view, and label your paper "Form View."
3. Print out the whole database in table or list view and label your paper accordingly.
4. On the printout of the entire database, write the name of the main idea that you are describing.

SORTS AND QUERIES

Database engines

Now that you know how information in a database is arranged in records and fields, your next task is to learn how to make the database work for you. The key to tapping into the incredible, analytic power that lies dormant in a database is in the user's ability to formulate good questions.

One difference between a print database and electronic database is the *database engine*. The "engine" for a print database is the user thumbing through the index, table of contents, and any other features that arrange information in the book for easy access. An electronic database offers more sophisticated techniques for extracting information. These techniques are called *sorts* and *queries*. *Filter* and *find* are synonymous for *query* in some brands of database software. A sort puts information in order, and a query extracts specific information or combinations of information from the database.

The Sort: Putting Information in Order

Sorts

Of the two major tools that a database provides, sort is the easier to understand and to work with. There are only four possibilities for a sort. They are displayed and defined in Table 10.2. Computers really only work with numbers, but programmers make it seem as if the machine understands letters, too. Every letter and many symbols and sounds (such as the beeps that you hear when your computer is booting up) have a number associated with them called an ASCII code. When you tell the computer to do an "alpha" sort, it is really translating the letters on the screen to numbers and going from highest to lowest or lowest to highest. The result, however, is transparent to the user.

If you tell the computer to do a descending sort of the Tribe field in the Native American database, it will look at the first letter of every value in the Tribe column.

TABLE 10.2 Kinds of Sorts

Direction of Sort	Description of Sort
A–Z	Ascending alpha sort
Z–A	Descending alpha sort
1–100	Ascending numeric sort
100–1	Descending numeric sort

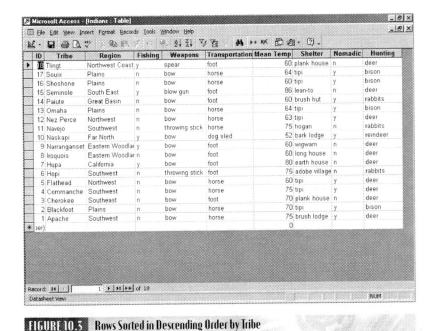

ID	Tribe	Region	Fishing	Weapons	Transportation	Mean Temp	Shelter	Nomadic	Hunting
18	Tlingt	Northwest Coast	y	spear	foot	60	plank house	n	deer
17	Souix	Plains	n	bow	horse	64	tipi	y	bison
16	Shoshone	Plains	n	bow	horse	60	tipi	y	bison
15	Seminole	South East	y	blow gun	foot	86	lean-to	n	deer
14	Paiute	Great Basin	n	bow	foot	60	brush hut	y	rabbits
13	Omaha	Plains	n	bow	horse	64	tipi	y	bison
12	Nez Perce	Northwest	n	bow	horse	63	tipi	y	deer
11	Navejo	Southwest	n	throwing stick	horse	75	hogan	n	rabbits
10	Naskapi	Far North	y	bow	dog sled	52	bark lodge	y	reindeer
9	Narranganset	Eastern Woodland	y	bow	foot	60	wigwam	n	deer
8	Iroquois	Eastern Woodland	n	bow	foot	60	long house	n	deer
7	Hupa	California	y	bow	foot	80	earth house	n	deer
6	Hopi	Southwest	n	throwing stick	foot	75	adobe village	n	rabbits
5	Flathead	Northwest	n	bow	horse	60	tipi	y	deer
4	Commanche	Southwest	n	bow	horse	75	tipi	y	deer
3	Cherokee	Southeast	n	bow	foot	70	plank house	n	deer
2	Blackfoot	Plains	n	bow	horse	70	tipi	y	bison
1	Apache	Southwest	n	bow	horse	75	brush lodge	y	deer
						0			

FIGURE 10.3 Rows Sorted in Descending Order by Tribe

Then it will rearrange the records in the database in reverse alphabetical order based on tribe names. Each row of the database, representing one record, is moved up or down in the table based on the alphabetical order of the value in the Tribe field. In the sort performed on the Native American database in Figure 10.3, all of the cells in the Tlingt record have moved to their new place in the database.

At first glance, the computer's ability to do a sort does not seem like much. Nevertheless, the utility of knowing how to do either a simple sort or a multiple-level sort can help people pluck information from large amounts of data. Put yourself in the place of the student in the U.S. history class that is studying Native Americans and read the problem in Field Trip 10.2.

FIELD TRIP 10.2

A Student's Point of View

We rejoin the eleventh-grade U.S. history class working on their Native American database project. As one student worked on the assignment to find the tribe that would be most suitable for her, she thought temperature would be a primary consideration. (She lives in the South and would like to go somewhere where it is a little cooler.) So she looked at her database and decided that even though "mean temperature" doesn't tell her everything, she can get a good idea of where the cool places are by doing an ascending sort on "Mean Temp."

Figure 10.4 is the result of her sort. She got closer to her goal as she glanced at the names of the ten tribes that seemed to live in cooler climates. Some of them seemed a little too cool, but she wasn't going to worry about that now. The next problem was to figure out which of them had horses, one of her other criteria.

Asking questions
of the database

195

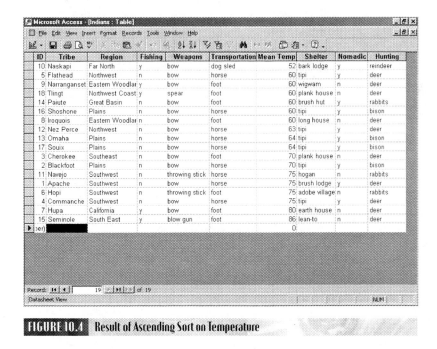

FIGURE 10.4 Result of Ascending Sort on Temperature

In the case of the American Indian database, it would not be too difficult for the student to look for and write down names of tribes who lived in lower temperatures, along with the values of the rest of the fields in those records, requiring perhaps five or ten minutes. The database accomplished the same function in less than a second. The student can do many sorts on an electronic database in the same amount of time that it takes to do only one manual sort. Consider also the possibility of the student making clerical errors or dealing with a database consisting of fifty, a hundred, or even a thousand records. The power of the database to do a tedious job quickly and precisely is evident. Sorts combined with queries make an even more powerful tool. A query will help our student decide how to satisfy her next criterion. She wants to live with a tribe that has horses.

> Databases speed
> information analysis

CHECKING YOUR UNDERSTANDING

10.3 Before you start on queries, make sure that you understand the mechanics of how a database works. Try the problem below. Cover up the answer in italics while you write your answer.

Problem

If you did a descending sort of the Mean Temp field, what information would be found in the first row of the database represented in table or list view? Write the values and check them against the answer below.

Seminole, South East, y, blow gun, foot, 86, lean-to, n, deer

The Query: Classifying Information

People classify information on a daily basis. Grocery stores, for example, are giant physical databases. When you walk into the store you look for cereal, then corn flakes, and finally a particular brand of corn flakes. Or, you go to the produce area of the store, look for apples, and then choose a Braeburn or Jonathan. The store is the database and you are the search engine. You know from experience that a good store is organized to help you find what you want quickly. The Yellow Pages of the telephone book is another example of a database. The difference between these two databases and an electronic database is the amount of time that it takes to find an item of information, especially if you don't know exactly what you are looking for.

Information in databases is even easier to find than products in stores if you know how. The tool that databases provide for finding information is called the *query* (synonyms are *filter* or *find*). To employ the query function, the user must have a small vocabulary of special words called comparison operators and logical operators. *Comparison operators* include the following symbols:

> Queries reveal patterns

- ▨ is equal to ($=$)
- ▨ is less than ($<$)
- ▨ is greater than ($>$)
- ▨ is less than or equal to ($<=$)
- ▨ is greater than or equal to ($>=$)

Logical operators are the following words:

- ▨ and
- ▨ or
- ▨ not

To form queries, combine comparison operators, logical operators, and the names of the ideas, places, or things. Thinking back to the student in the class who wants to find the Native American tribe to which she could adapt most easily, let's look at how the student might approach the problem with queries. Remember the student looking for a cooler climate whose sort resulted in Figure 10.4? Now she wants to find a cool-climate tribe that used horses, because they would be an advantage in both war and hunting.

In this situation, a sort is not really a possibility. Sorts order information, but they do not find specific pieces of information. Therefore, the student attacks the problem with a query. First she states the question in ordinary human language:

> Asking questions of a database

"Database, tell me the names of all the tribes that use horses for transportation."

Then she goes to the database and translates the question into language that it will understand by pressing the keys or using menus that are appropriate for whatever brand of database software is available in the classroom.

The procedure typically consists of several steps that are listed below.

1. Choose the field for comparison, in this case "Transportation."
2. Choose the criterion for comparison. In this case the student wants to find all entries in the field that are equal to ($=$) "horse."
3. Execute the search by choosing the appropriate function provided by the software.

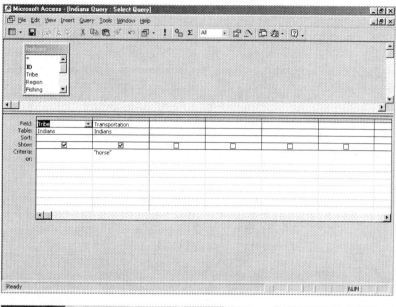

FIGURE 10.5 Query for All Tribes Using Horses for Transportation

The student's translation to the language of the database is made easy with the user interface shown in Figure 10.5. What you see there is the screen the student created just before pressing the "Apply Query" button. The database's response to the student's query is a list of every record in which horse is listed as transportation. Figure 10.6 shows the computer's response.

This database is small enough that the student could have simply looked at the "Mean Temperature" column and the "Transportation" column of Figure 10.4 and decided that she would like to live with the Blackfoot, Nez Perce, Omaha, or Sioux. However, a student who is dealing with a larger database with hundreds of records would need to do a query using conjunctions (the logical operators *and, or,* and *not*). If a student did such a query, the setup would look something like Figure 10.7. The results of this query would give the student a list at only the records of interest. The results for the query in Figure 10.7 are shown in Figure 10.8.

When teaching novice users, it is important to show them that after they have performed a query, the other records have not disappeared. They are only hidden and can be seen again when the user tells the computer to show all of the records.

Grade-Level Suggestions

The query in Figure 10.7 is quite complex. For a child to think independently of such a query and to enter it into a computer successfully requires cognitive abilities that not all children possess. An average fifth grader would not be able to do such an operation. Many seventh graders would also have difficulty, both with the skills for entering the query and the ability to think of such a complex query. If we were to analyze the task, we would find that the student would have to know or be able to do all of the following:

> Adjusting database skills to grade level

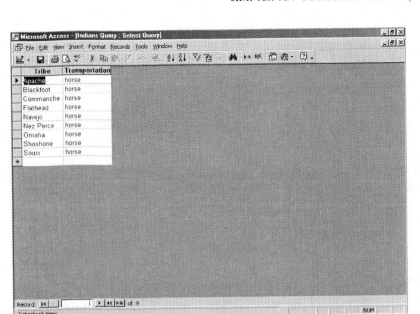

FIGURE 10.6 Results of Query for All Tribes Using Horses for Transportation

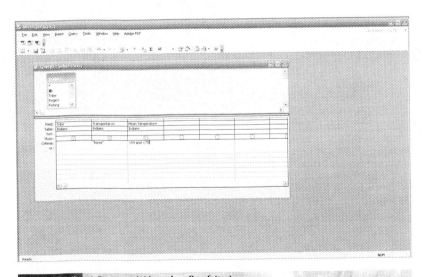

FIGURE 10.7 A Query with More than One Criterion

▦ Know why the student is asking the question
▦ Understand how to phrase the question in ordinary language so that it is easy to translate into a language that a computer understands
▦ Understand that a query is needed and not a sort
▦ Understand which areas on the menu to click in order to get this query screen (Figure 10.7) to appear

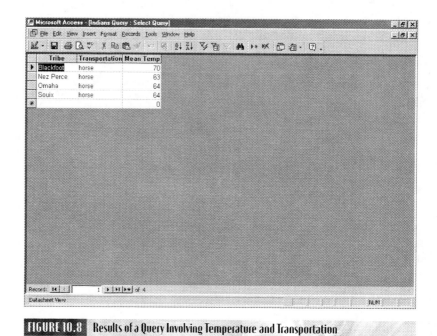

FIGURE 10.8 Results of a Query Involving Temperature and Transportation

▓ Understand inequalities, and be able to select appropriate delimiters
▓ Know how to use conjunctions
▓ Know how to interpret the results of the query and draw a conclusion (Figure 10.8)
▓ Know how to use the results of the question to generate more questions

This list of skills associated with queries shows that students are juggling eight different plates at the same time. Younger students or novice database users will have difficulty with this procedure, while older or more experienced students should be expected to perform this routinely. There are ways of lightening the cognitive load on younger or less able students or those students who are just learning how to use databases, no matter what their academic ability. In Table 10.3 are some suggestions for grade-level abilities and parts of the process with which teachers can assist students.

The assumption behind Table 10.3 is that students have had actual training in the use of database software. They would know which keys to press to go to form view or table view and how to do a simple sort or query. Table 10.4 is a list of suggestions for the grade levels and database skill introduction.

How to Provide Student Assistance

Table 10.3 has many cells indicating that students need assistance. As you know, a teacher's time is at a premium. Considering everything that must be taught, we have little time to move around the classroom telling students which keys to press and individually guiding students from thought to thought as they attempt to use a database to do their

TABLE 10.3 Task Analysis for Database Assignments and Recommendations for Teacher Assistance

Student Task	Upper Elementary or Beginning Database User	Middle School (if student has used databases previously)	High School (if student has used databases previously)
Know why student is asking the question.	Needs assistance	Needs assistance	Student is independent
Understand how to phrase the question in ordinary language so that it is easy to translate to language a computer understands.	Needs assistance	Student is independent	Student is independent
Understand that a query is needed and not a sort.	Needs assistance	Student is independent	Student is independent
Understand which areas on the menu to click in order to get this menu screen to appear.	Student is independent	Student is independent	Student is independent
Know that a string (series of letters) needs quotes in order for the computer to interpret it correctly. This is not true of all software. Each database has its quirks, and this item is representative of the kinds of special action students need to take to make a database work.	Student is independent	Student is independent	Student is independent
Understand inequalities.	Needs assistance	Student is independent	Student is independent
Know how to use conjunctions.	Needs assistance or not applicable	Student is independent	Student is independent
Know how to interpret the results of a sort or query.	Needs assistance	Needs an introduction and practice, then can work independently	Student is independent
Know how to use the results of the sort or query to generate more sorts and queries.	Needs assistance	Needs an introduction and practice, then can work independently	Student is independent

thinking about a particular problem. The solution to this dilemma lies in three different methods: teacher modeling, group work, and lesson templates.

Teacher modeling is important. The first time that you use a database to solve a problem with your class (whether they are third graders or twelfth graders new to databases), you will want to show the database on a computer projection device to the whole class. You will also want to choose a student who already knows how to use databases, or you should train one to operate the computer for you while you talk to the class.

Your best approach will be to downplay the mechanics (e.g., what keys to press to do a sort) and concentrate on the kinds of problems that the database can help your class solve. With a third-grade class you might have a database of dinosaurs and help them learn how to ask questions such as

> Teach the value of asking questions before the mechanics of sorts and queries

■ "Which dinosaurs ate plants?"

TABLE 10.4 Database Skill Introduction in Grades K-12

Grade	Skill
3	Teacher demonstrates use of database in classroom projects
4	Use a teacher-made database to enhance learning in a lesson
	Enter data into a form and use sorts and queries to manipulate the data
5–6	Enter data into an existing database
	Recognize fields, records, files, and entries
	Compare paper and computer databases
	Move cursor around the database
	Use a database to make simple inferences
7	Use basic functions of a database (report generation and creation of address books)
	Enter data into a previously prepared template
	Make increasingly complex inferences by using the sort and query function of the database
8	Give examples of appropriate database use
	Plan and create a database
	Reinforce sort and query skills
	Use a database to explore content
	Generate reports
	Integrate database research into a word-processed report
9	Have the following skills automated: sort, query
	Be fluent with the following terms: list view, form view, search criteria, conjunctions
	Use databases on a regular basis to solve problems and analyze information in science, social studies, and English
10–12	Create a form
	Add and delete fields in an existing database
	Add and delete records in an existing database
	Create reports from a database
	Arrange information using sorts and queries
	Query a database for specific information
	Edit, move, and change field properties and sizes
	Manipulate numeric fields–calculations
	Import and export database information to spreadsheets and documents
	Use software-specific help
	Use logical operators when querying a database
	Create macros to present database information
	Create links within a relation database
	Draw conclusions from a database query or report
	Use databases on a regular basis to solve problems and analyze information in science, social studies, and English

- ■ "Which dinosaurs ate animals?"
- ■ "Were dinosaurs that ate animals generally bigger or smaller than dinosaurs that ate plants?"

As you work with students, gradually move from being the only source of questions to guiding the class as they ask questions of the database. At the end of a class database activity, you will want to require some kind of product of the students, such as a short paragraph or story that summarizes the information, and inferences that they have made from both their questions and yours.

Be sure their questions lead to a conclusion

Small-group work is also important. Once students understand what databases do and have a *general* idea of the meaning of the terms record, field, table view, form view, sort, and query, the next step is to teach them the specific meanings of those terms. This can be done in a five-computer classroom with small groups. A fun activity to help students learn the mechanics of how to use a database is a database of the class itself.

Group database work uses high-level skills

For this project the students decide what they want to know about the class members. Together with the teacher, the students brainstorm field headings such as favorite food, favorite book, age, height, gender, favorite subject, favorite musical group, and so on.

Students set up a database

The teacher has to help students understand that information must be entered consistently in order for the database to be usable. For example, the class has to decide whether Gender will be entered as boy/girl or as m/f. Numbers also must be consistent. When students talk about the Height field, they need to decide whether the measurement will be metric or English. If they decide on the English system of measurement, for example, they need to decide which would be more useful, feet and inches or just inches. These kinds of questions all help students think more carefully and develop foresight and planning skills.

Once the teacher and students have selected and defined the fields, each student writes the name of each field and his or her own information on a three-by-five-inch card. Depending on the age of the students, either the students themselves enter the information or the teacher or an aide enters the information into a class database.

If students enter the information themselves, they get many good lessons in the importance of spelling and accuracy. One good strategy is to have the students enter information and not caution them ahead of time about the importance of accuracy. Then, as the class tries to do sorts and queries that are either inaccurate or do not work at all, the teacher can point out the reason why. For this strategy to be successful, the teacher needs to have entered all of the information accurately ahead of time and have disks ready to hand out or the correct database accessible on the network once students see how and why they have failed. Then the lesson can move forward. The process creates some confusion and consternation, but students are generally more careful about their spelling when they use databases after such an experience.

One variation on this exercise is to have the students not write their name, but rather give each student a secret letter or number as an identifier. One of the activities for the class can then be to guess the name of the person represented by each letter in the database. One fifth-grade teacher uses this activity as an icebreaker at the beginning of the year. Over the summer she sends a survey to her new students requesting all of the information she needs and enters the information into the database herself so that it is ready for the first week of class.

The culmination of the lesson after students have an accurate class database in front of them is a series of sorts and queries. The teacher provides the questions and the students work in groups to provide the answers. Students rotate so that each one gets to press keys at the keyboard, but the student at the keyboard may only strike a key when told which key to strike by the rest of the group. This activity may be performed as a class under the direct supervision of the teacher, or it may be performed from a worksheet as a center with students writing their responses.

Not all students will be able to work on a database independently after this exercise. However, all will have a better grasp of the skills necessary to operate a database. Students working in groups will have enough skill to do a database assignment in a content area after this exercise if the assignment is well planned and written.

PLANNING YOUR DATABASE

| Planning a database is a high-level thinking activity |

Planning the database is a key element in making any database assignment work. If you are building the database yourself, then it should work flawlessly for your students. If it doesn't, they will be confused and the value of the lesson could be lost in the resulting chaos. Planning databases that students will create themselves is an excellent way for them to work with content. They have to think carefully about the content of the database and how they will use it. As students plan the fields of the database, they will discover two important pieces of information about the topic they are studying:

1. First, they will have to decide on field names for the topic.
2. Next, they will have to decide on a consistent method for expressing the contents of each field.

| Data should be formatted carefully |

Numbers present a challenge for students. For example, students will have to determine how to represent temperature in the Native American database. Will they use sixty degrees, 60°, or 60°F, or just 60? Whatever they decide should make sorts and queries easy. When they understand how a sort works, they will learn to put measurement data in the column heading (insert it as part of the field name) and have numbers as the only entry in the field. They will also learn that there are special formats for date and time as well as currency and that being careful about these formats makes a great deal of difference in the usability of the database.

Text also presents a challenge for the novice database user. If some of the entries in the transportation field are spelled "horse" and some are spelled "horses," the database will not give an accurate response to student's queries about which tribes used horses for transportation.

Another pitfall students often overlook is putting a space before an entry, whether it is text or numeric. The computer sees the space as a character and will sort the contents of the field according to the ASCII code assigned to the space, not the first letter of the word or the first numeral in the number. These errors are particularly problematic because the space is invisible. When you are working on your own database or with students as they create their databases, this is a common error that is difficult to spot if it is not in a checklist of "debugging" strategies in your head.

CHECKING YOUR UNDERSTANDING

10.4 Now that you have focused on what databases can do, it is time for you to try your skills. Below is a set of eight questions about a database of mammals. Fields in this database include: height, color, nocturnal/diurnal, herbivore/carnivore, life span, habitat, length of reproductive cycle, and number of young per birth. Put a card or piece of paper over the answer to each question. Then answer the following question: Would you *sort* the "Animals" database or *query* the "Animals" database to get the data that you need?

Question 1: What is the tallest animal?

(Sort)

Question 2: What are the names of all nocturnal carnivores?

(Query)

Question 3: Which animal has the most young per birth?

(Sort)

Question 4: Which animals have a reproductive cycle greater than 60 days and less than 100 days?

(Query)

Question 5: Which animals are herbivores and live more than 10 years?

(Query)

Question 6: Which animal has the longest reproductive cycle?

(Sort)

Question 7: Are there any animals that are nocturnal and white?

(Query)

Question 8: Which animal has the shortest reproductive cycle?

(Sort)

Question 9: Are there any animals that live on the tundra and are black?

(Query)

10.5 Here is another set of questions for you. Below is the name of each field in the "Animals" database. While you cover the answer, decide how each field should be formatted so that the database will yield accurate search results. Below, in italics, is a suggested answer.

Height

(Inches or centimeters)

Color

(A text string chosen from a list of colors—avoid using many different colors unless the distinction is important)

Time When Most Active

(Nocturnal/Diurnal)

Food Preference

(Herbivore/Carnivore)

Life Span

(Days)

Habitat

(Name of a biome [tundra, deciduous forest, etc.])

Length of Reproductive Cycle

(Days)

Number of Young Per Birth

(A number [3, 5, 8, etc.])

■ SUMMARY

Databases are powerful tools used by many different kinds of organizations to help them access information efficiently. A database is as useful to an automotive parts store sales associate as to a NASA scientist.

Basic skills for using databases include understanding how information is formatted and set up in tables and analyzed using sorts and queries. It is important that teachers ensure that their students understand these basic skills before they ask them to work independently with databases. Students are motivated to learn these skills when you demonstrate the power of the database by showing them how to ask questions and solve problems with the information they receive.

It is often better to encourage groups to manipulate databases together rather than assign students to work on projects alone. When students in groups brainstorm questions and how to format them so the computer can understand them together, they are often more successful than when they work alone.

■ REFERENCES

Ennals, R. (1995). Micro-prolog and classroom historical research. In I. Reid and J. Rushton (Eds.). *Teachers, computers, and the classroom.* Manchester, England: Manchester University Press.

Fisher, T. S. (1996). Integrating computer database applications into the social studies curriculum. Master's thesis, Boise State University, Boise, ID.

Grabe, M., & Grabe, C. (1996). *Integrating technology for meaningful learning.* Geneva, IL: Houghton Mifflin.

Hecht, J. B., Dwyer, D. J., Roberts, N. K., Schoon, P. L., Kelly, J., Parsons, J., Nietzke, T., & Virlee, M. (1993). *Project homeroom second year experiences: A final report on the project in the Maine East High School, New Trier High School, Amos Alonzo Stagg High School.* Illinois State University. ERIC ED366638.

Jonassen, D. (2000). *Computers as mindtools for schools.* Upper Saddle River, NJ: Merrill.

Underwood, J. D. M. (1987). Chapter in I. Reid and J. Rushton (Eds.). *Teachers, computers, and the classroom.* Manchester, England: Manchester University Press.

Companion Web Site www.ablongman.com/thorsen3e

1. Go to Chapters 10–12 of the TechTactics web site. You will see links to many databases. Some of these links provide numbers only, which you must import into a database like Access or a spreadsheet like Excel. Others store their data in an online database, which allows you to do queries online without having to import data into Access or Excel. Two such databases on the web site are Valley of the Shadow 1 and 2 and County and City Data Books.

   ▨ Browse each database to find out what it is like and how it works.

   ▨ Write a question that you would like to answer using each database.

   ▨ Enter your queries and draw your conclusions. List your queries and in a short paragraph explain your conclusions.

   ▨ Write a short essay (less than 200 words) comparing and contrasting the operation of the two databases.

2. Go to Chapters 10–12 of the TechTactics web site. Go to any of the links that provide data as numbers that must be imported into a database for the creation of queries and sorts (NASA and the U.S. Census Bureau are two examples).

   ▨ Successfully import the data into the database that you are using.

   ▨ Write three questions you would like to answer with the data.

   ▨ Do the appropriate sorts and write related queries. Note these on the paper that you turn in to your instructor.

   ▨ Write a short essay (less than 200 words) on the conclusions that you drew from your sorts and queries.

11

Building a Database-Supported Lesson

OBJECTIVES

- Describe three kinds of problems to which databases apply.
- Know the steps and products in a database assignment.
- Write an appropriate problem.
- Develop database-supported lessons for three kinds of problems.

TEMPLATES FOR BUILDING DATABASE-SUPPORTED LESSONS

Teacher-made lesson templates provide students with a great deal of guidance and provide the bridge between directed and independent activity. Building a lesson template takes some time and thought, but the result is a product that will substitute for and improve on a number of traditional activities. Some traditional activities that can be replaced when an appropriate database is available include answering end-of-chapter questions, writing and memorizing definitions, and doing worksheets.

Database lessons can be divided into three categories: describing an unknown, making a prediction, or making a decision. The process a teacher uses to create a template for each category is very similar. Once a teacher knows how to define a problem or set up a case, creating the rest of the lesson falls into place. Table 11.1 lists some examples of databases that we have talked about already, as well as some new examples of topics for databases. These topics are classified according to one of the categories of problems (describe an unknown, etc.) listed above.

This chapter will be devoted to teaching you how to create templates for students to explore these different kinds of problems. The activities in these templates promote those higher-order thinking skills that help students understand and make judgments about the content they are learning.

CHECKING YOUR UNDERSTANDING

 At this point, these kinds of lessons are not generally packaged commercially with textbooks. Teachers must make their own lessons, and students sometimes must build their own databases.

202

TABLE 11.1 Topics for Databases		
Describe an Unknown	**Make a Decision or Analyze a Problem**	**Make a Prediction**
Find a city, country, culture, county, or state different from yours in specific ways and describe it.	Trace the changing role of women/men during historical (literary) time periods.	Describe the kind of person the next president (governor of your state) will be.
Describe a planet, moon, or star that contrasts sharply with our own.	What was the worst war in the history of the world?	Predict the country in which the next major war will occur.
Find and describe an animal (plant, rock, celestial object, culture, time period) with certain characteristics.	Make a list of the five best occupations suited to your skills and personality.	Predict the next five animals that will become extinct.

Building a database is not especially exciting, but neither is answering questions at the end of a chapter or doing worksheets. The added value for a student building a database is that once students have entered the facts into the database, they may manipulate them for analysis. This is not possible for students who have finished a worksheet or answered end-of-chapter questions except through class discussion.

Look back at the three introductory vignettes at the beginning of Chapter 10 and answer the following questions. The answers are listed at the end of this exercise.

Questions

1. In which vignette is an unknown described?
2. In which vignette is someone trying to make a prediction?
3. In which vignette is someone making a decision?
4. Reread the database lesson on Native Americans. Was the assignment to describe an unknown, make a prediction, or make a decision?

Answers

1. The astronomy vignette
2. The marketing vignette
3. The insurance vignette
4. Make a prediction (Which culture would be best for me to live with?)

LEARNING WITH A DATABASE: DESCRIBING AN UNKNOWN

One useful purpose of databases is to help people get a picture of a location or thing that they have never seen and know nothing about. When NASA scientists send probes to distant reaches of the solar system, the information that comes back is not formatted in well-written paragraphs. Rather, it consists of numbers and other descriptors that can be formatted into tables something like the table (list) view of a database.

After scientists have put this information into table format, they use it to describe objects that they have never actually seen. They do this by asking questions of the database and making inferences.

Applying databases to classroom problems

Astronomy is not the only topic that requires people to understand a thing, location, or idea that they cannot see. Social scientists also use similar data to describe cultures, populations, or locations. Our next field trip, Field Trip 11.1, is a database exercise for a unit in U.S. geography. Read through it carefully. Even though you might not ever teach this unit because you are a science teacher or English/language arts teacher, you can learn a great deal about how to create a database-supported lesson for the content that you teach. For example, if you are a science teacher, substitute the "Periodic Table of Elements" for the states. Bear in mind that the language and difficulty of the lesson always must be adjusted to the grade level that you teach.

FIELD TRIP 11.1

Solving a Mystery with a Database: The Mystery State

Mrs. Whiting began, "We learn about the world we live in many different ways. Sometimes we can see, hear, or feel what we need to know. Other times we must depend on 'educated guesses' to know what is going on in the world around us.

"One way to make an educated guess is to compare what you know to what you don't know to find and describe the difference. This is what you are going to do in this lesson. You are going to choose the state that you think is different in as many ways as possible from the state in which you live.

Setting up the problem

"To do this you will be provided with a database of states, but the states, other than your own, will not be named. Your electronic database will look much like the example in Table 11.2. You will have to rely entirely on your skill in asking your database good questions and interpreting the answers that the database gives you. When you have asked the database all of the questions below in addition to more that you will compose, you will write a travel brochure for people living in your state who might want to take a trip to the Mystery State. Your goal is to write an article about the state that you pick. This article should be as accurate as an encyclopedia article and as interesting as a travel brochure."

Step 1

"The first thing you should do is get to know your database and think about how you might use it. Take a few moments to study the names of the fields below and think about the kind of information they provide for you. All of these fields are in your electronic database.

1. Mortality rate
2. Percent Hispanic, Caucasian, Black, etc.
3. Annual precipitation

TABLE 11.2 List or Table View of States' Database

State	Highest Point (ft)	Lowest Point (ft)	Mortality (per 1,000)	Population
A	5,000	0	5	10,000,000
B	12,600	565	12	6,000,000
C	8,320	30	8	25,000,000
D	12,000	265	4	1,500,000

4. Number of square miles
5. Population
6. Gross state product
7. Highest point
8. Lowest point
9. Highest temperature
10. Lowest temperature
11. Mean temperature
12. Number of sunny days
13. Percent of gross state product from agriculture
14. Percent of gross state product from mining
15. Percent of gross state product from fishing
16. Percent of gross state product from tourism
17. Major agricultural product
18. Number of lakes
19. Crime rate
20. Births per 1,000 people per year
21. Mean age
22. Number of people in the largest city
23. Number of towns above 50,000 people
24. Gross state product from manufacturing

"When you use a database to help you learn about something, you must ask questions. Usually, the more clever you can be about asking questions, the more information you can get from a database. For example, knowing the population of a state doesn't tell you much if you want to live there. You really don't want to know the population size so much as understand how the population will affect your quality of life. It is more important to know how crowded the state is than to know how many people live in the state. To find out how crowded a place is you must think about both the population and the amount of space in which people are living. Let's answer the questions on Worksheet 1 together."

> Learning to ask questions

Worksheet 1

1. **If you wanted to find out how crowded a state is, what fields would you use and what would you do with them?**
   a. **What fields would you consider?**
      i. *Population*
      ii. *Number of square miles*
   b. **What facts would you gather?**
      i. *Fact: Descending sort on the states by population and find the state with the highest population.*
      ii. *Fact: Ascending sort on the states by population and find the state with the lowest population.*
      iii. *Fact: Descending sort on the states by land area and find the state with the largest land area.*
      iv. *Fact: Ascending sort on the states by land area and find the state with the smallest land area.*
      v. *Fact: Find the record for my state and record the population and land area.*
   c. **What conclusions could you draw from the facts that you gathered?**
      i. *I will divide the population into land area for each state to figure out number of persons per square mile. The state that is most different from mine in population per square mile will be the answer to one question.*

> Teaching students to ask questions

> Using the answers to come to a conclusion

2. **The farmers in your state can't raise warm-weather crops and irrigate because there isn't enough rain. You want to find out what states can grow warm-weather crops without irrigation, which seems to you like a very different kind of agriculture.**
   a. **What fields would you consider?**
      i. *Percent of gross state product (GSP) from agriculture*
      ii. *Mean temperature*
      iii. *Precipitation*
   b. **What facts would you gather?**
      i. *Fact: I want to find names of states where agriculture is possible. States g, h, m, o, l, x, gg, and aa have the largest agricultural GSP.*
      ii. *Fact: States g, o, gg, and aa have the highest mean temperature*
      iii. *Fact: States g, o, gg, and aa have the amount of precipitation per year that warm-weather crops need.*
   c. **What conclusions could you draw from the facts that you gathered?**
      i. *Warm-weather agriculture is most feasible in state g, o, gg, or aa.*

   "Below you will find more questions that will lead you to conclusions that you wouldn't come to if you just looked at the fields and records of your database individually. To answer these questions, you will have to use two functions of your database: sorts and queries. Sometimes you will have to sort on two or three fields at the same time. Sometimes you will have to use conjunctions like *and/or* in your queries to get the answer you want. The questions below are a 'dry run' for you. They will help you understand how to write your own questions and analyze the information the database yields to you."

3. **If you wanted to find a state that had a lot of young people in it:**
   a. **What fields would you consider?**
      i. _____
      ii. _____
      iii. _____
   b. **What facts would you gather?**
      i. _____
      ii. _____
      iii. _____
   c. **What conclusions could you draw from the facts that you gathered?**
      _____
      _____

4. **If you wanted to find a state that had excellent ski resorts:**
   a. **What fields would you consider?**
      i. _____
      ii. _____
      iii. _____
      iv. _____
      v. _____
   b. **What facts would you gather?**
      i. _____
      ii. _____
      iii. _____
      iv. _____
      v. _____
   c. **What conclusions could you draw from the facts that you gathered?**
      _____
      _____

5. **If you wanted to find a state with many cultural attractions and activities like concerts and professional sports events:**
   a. **What fields would you consider?**
      i. _____
      ii. _____
      iii. _____
      iv. _____
      v. _____
   b. **What facts would you gather?**
      i. _____
      ii. _____
      iii. _____
      iv. _____
      v. _____
   c. **What conclusions could you draw from the facts that you gathered?**
      _____
      _____

Step 2

Mrs. Whiting continued, "Before you actually start asking your own questions of the database, you must decide which features of a state make it quite different from the one you live in. On Worksheet 2 below write down a list of items that you think would make a state very different than the one that you live in now.

"Do not be concerned about the items in your list having the same names as the field headings listed above. As you have seen, you can sometimes get information from databases by working with several fields at the same time, as you did when you figured out how to get data about crowding."

Worksheet 2

1. _____
2. _____
3. _____
4. _____
5. _____
6. _____
7. _____
8. _____
9. _____
10. _____

Step 3

"Now that you have decided what would make a state very different from the state that you live in, it is time to use that information to build questions for the database on your computer.

"Some questions you ask will be very straightforward, such as 'What is the most important agricultural product?' Other questions will have to be more clever, like the example questions in Worksheet 1. Try to think about your questions like you thought about the questions above. **Ask a question, decide what fields are relevant, gather some facts, and make a conclusion.**

"Your work should look like the sample worksheet except for the number of facts that you gather. Sometimes you will gather only one or two facts and be able to make a conclusion. Other times you may need to find five or six facts before you can make a conclusion. Three facts are not the magic number.

'Fact' is listed three times to help you remember that many times it will take more than one fact for you to reach a conclusion."

Step 4

"Now that you have spent some time gathering information and thinking about your Mystery State, it is time to describe it. Your goal is to write a report that is factually accurate as well as appealing. You want to convince your reader that this state would be a good place to vacation or even move to. If you do your report electronically, be sure that you include pictures of the Mystery State that look like the facts you have gathered. Be prepared to present your report to the class."

Step 5

Make a guess about the actual name of your mystery state and write it in the blank below.

_____

Mrs. Whiting finally provided the information that students had been anticipating. She said, "Now I will tell you the actual name of your Mystery State. Go to the encyclopedia or other reference work, look up, and read the information about your Mystery State. Answer the questions below."

Worksheet 3

What facts or observations did you include in your brochure that were not included by the encyclopedia?

1. _____
2. _____
3. _____
4. _____

What facts or observations in your brochure were different from those in the encyclopedia article?

1. _____
2. _____
3. _____
4. _____
5. _____

Go to another source and resolve the discrepancies you found above. Write the resolution in the spaces below.

1. _____
2. _____
3. _____
4. _____

Conclusion

Mrs. Whiting concluded by helping students step back and take a larger view of their work. "As you have worked with this exercise, you have thought about states many different ways. The database helped you process and analyze information very quickly and accurately. You could have done all of the research 'by hand,' but it would have taken you much longer because you would have had to look up answers for every state each time you asked a question. The database did that work for you. Databases are useful tools that help you organize and think about large quantities of information. Databases are good for studying other geographic topics besides states. Think about other geographic ideas a database might help you study and list them below. I will give you two hints. See if you can supply more."

1. Other economic systems
2. Other cultures
3. _____
4. _____
5. _____
6. _____
7. _____
8. _____
9. _____
10. _____

ANALYZING A LESSON PLAN

Below you will see a modified version of the "States Database Activity Plan." All of the blanks and some of the questions have been left out. You may need to look back to refresh your memory if you get lost. Using the steps described below, you can create a database lesson for any appropriate topic.

A Lesson in U.S. Geography: Describing an Unknown

**FIELD TRIP
11.2**

You learn about the world we live in many different ways. Sometimes you can see, hear, or feel what you need to know. Other times you must depend on "educated guesses" to know what is going on in the world around you.

Step 1

One way to make an educated guess is to compare what you know to what you don't know to find and describe the difference. This is what you are going to do in this lesson. You are going to choose the state that you think is different in as many ways as possible from the state in which you live. To do this, you will be provided with a database of states, but the states, other than your own, will not be named. Your electronic database will look much like the example below.

    You will have to rely entirely on your skill in asking your database good questions and interpreting the answers that the database gives you. When you have asked the database all of the questions below in addition to more that you will compose, you will write a travel brochure for people living in your state who might want to take a trip to the Mystery State. Your goal is to write an article about the state that you pick that is as accurate as an encyclopedia article and as interesting as a travel brochure.

Set up the problem

Step 2

The first thing you should do is get to know your database and think about how you might use it. Take a few moments to study the fields below and think about the kind of information they provide for you. When you use a database to help you learn about something, you must ask questions. Usually, the more clever you can be about asking questions, the more information you can get from a database. It is one thing to state the population of a state and another thing to know what the population means to the quality of life of a person living in a particular location. Knowing the population of a state doesn't tell you much if you want to live there. What is more important to know is how crowded the state is. Whether

Teach students to write questions

or not a place is crowded is the result of the interaction between population and the amount of space in which people live. Knowing that, how would you answer the questions below?

Below you will find more questions that will lead you to conclusions that you wouldn't come to if you just looked at the fields and records of your database individually. To answer these questions you will have to use two functions of your database: sorts and queries. Sometimes you will have to sort on two or three fields at the same time. Sometimes you will have to use conjunctions such as *and/or* in your queries to get the answer you want. Try answering the questions below with your states' database.

Step 3

Before you actually start asking questions of the database you must decide what characteristics of a state make it quite different from the one you live in. In the space below, write down a list of items that you think would make a state very different from the one that you live in now. Don't be concerned about the items in your list having the same names as the field headings listed above. As you have seen, you can sometimes get information from databases by working with several fields at the same time, as you did when you decided how to get data about crowding.

Step 4

Now that you have decided what would make a state very different from the one that you live in, it is time to use that information to build questions for the database on your computer. Some questions you ask will be very straightforward, such as "What is the size of the gross state product?" Other questions will have to be more clever, such as the example questions in Step 2. Using the list that you developed above to guide you, write your questions in the blanks below.

Step 5

Now that you have spent some time gathering information and thinking about your Mystery State, it is time to describe it. Your goal is to write a report that is factually accurate as well as appealing. You want to convince your reader that this state would be a good place to vacation or even live. If you do your report electronically, be sure that you include pictures that look like the facts you have gathered.

Step 6

I will tell you the actual name of your Mystery State. Go to the encyclopedia or other reference work, look up, and read the information about your Mystery State. Answer the questions below.

1. What facts or observations did you include that were not included by the encyclopedia?
2. What facts or observations in your article were different from those in the encyclopedia article?
3. Go to another source and resolve the discrepancies you found above. Write the resolution in the spaces below.

Step 7

As you have worked with this exercise, you have thought about states in many different ways. The database helped you process and analyze information very quickly and accurately. You could have done all of the research "by hand," but it would have taken you much longer because you would have had to look up answers for every state each time you asked a question. The database did that work for you.

Databases are useful tools that help you organize and think about large quantities of information. Databases are good for studying other geographic topics besides states. Think about other geographic topics a database might help you study and list them below. I will give you two hints. See if you can supply more.

Encourage students to focus on a specific area to explore

Teach students how to ask questions

Require a product of the student

Encourage students to resolve discrepancies

Encourage students to think about how to apply the process to other projects

UNDERSTANDING THE STEPS

The lesson plan just described applies not only to states and geography, but also to topics in the sciences, other social sciences, and language arts. A similar exercise could be constructed for mammals, short stories, or time periods in history. This model also applies to decisions and predictions as well. Whatever the topic, there is an underlying sequence of steps for building a lesson plan that uses databases efficiently. You will proceed a little differently for each step, depending on whether a prediction, decision, or analysis is your goal, but the steps themselves are the same.

Problems for content areas

Set Up the Problem

Setting up the problem is a key part of the process. It provides both motivation and structure for the student. The sample lesson, "Mystery State," was an exercise in describing an unknown. Other examples of exercises in which students might describe an unknown object or idea by comparing it to a known could be constructed of a database of animals, rocks, plants, cities, counties, countries, bodies of water, dinosaurs (for young students), or planets.

Doing an analysis or making a decision is very similar. You and your students could build a database of time periods in history and include fields ranging from number of wars to the rights of women, to literacy rates. From such a database, students could extract a large number of ideas for writing and debate. The same kind of assignment would be appropriate in a literature class. This database might consist of literary periods, short stories, or some other genre. In the short story database, the class could explore everything from the changing role of women to the evolution of a theme from one literary period to another. On a more practical level, for a class of students marginally interested in school, let alone databases, making a decision about which car to buy is a good topic for a database lesson.

Other examples of the kinds of topics that would be appropriate for using a database to make a decision would include the speed limit example discussed previously. In the case of the last two examples (the speed limit and buying a car), the decision is a practical one that directly affects the lives of students. However, other scenarios can be set up that use making a decision as a focus. Picking a Native American tribe to live with is an example of this kind of decision. Picking a time to live in history is another example of interacting with content in an academic area to focus on making a decision.

Setting up problems requiring students to make a prediction is a very similar process. Other problems students could study that result in predictions include:

▪ Predicting the next president, senator in your state, mayor in your city, etc.
▪ Predicting the characteristics of the next downturn or upturn in business cycle
▪ Predicting the country or part of the world where the next war will take place
▪ Predicting which occupation will provide the best jobs in the year that your students will graduate from college

As you conceptualize a problem that you want your students to solve, you will no doubt be concerned with more than just using a database. You will probably be worrying about exposing them to the information that they will need to pass an assessment that you have not created, such as an achievement test. You will be thinking about the actual resources available to your students to gather information to complete their assignment. You will also be trying to develop a problem to which your students can respond. Below are some guidelines and suggestions for writing problems:

1. Write your problem in the form of a story. Students and people in general respond positively to stories. If you write a story, your students will be able to visualize the characters and conflicts. They will automatically add detail from their own experiences and the problem will become more meaningful to them (Shank & Cleary, 1995).

Set your problems up
as a story

2. Define the problem clearly. If you do not define the question that you want your students to think about, they could select a different question and study a different set of information. If you need to have them assimilate certain information to prepare them for achievement tests, make sure that you define the problem they are to solve clearly enough to cause them to interact with the information that they need to know.

3. If the students must design and enter the data into the database themselves, be sure that you embed clues in your problem that will lead them to include fields that will contain the information you want them to study. Before your write your problem, decide if you want students to work alone or in groups.

CHECKING YOUR UNDERSTANDING

11.2 Below you will find three short examples of problems. They have been written to give you examples of problems and to demonstrate the principles above. To help yourself identify some of the features listed above, answer the questions provided after each problem. Answers to each problem are listed after the questions.

Problem A: Building a Power Plant

You are a biologist working for a company that would like to build a coal-fired power plant somewhere in the world. Your company president is quite environmentally conscious and wants to build it in a biome where it will have the least impact. The company has located coal reserves in the tundra, northern coniferous forests, a deciduous forest, grasslands, several deserts, and a tropical rain forest.

Your job is to help her predict the impact of such a power plant on the plant and animal life in each biome. You have a database of biomes, their vital statistics (temperature range, precipitation, etc.) and common plant and animal life. You will need to find some information about the effects of coal-fired power plants on the environment. Use the sample environmental impact statement attached to this assignment to format your report.

Questions for Problem A: Building a Power Plant

1. Does this problem ask students to
   a. Analyze a problem?
   b. Make a prediction?
   c. Make a decision?
2. Underline all of the embedded suggestions for field names in this problem.

3. Who are the characters in the story?
4. How could you help your students personalize this story?
5. What mechanism does the teacher use to make sure that the students interact with the information she wants them to learn?
6. Right now, this problem is written for an individual. How could the teacher turn this problem into a group assignment?

Answers for Problem A: Building a Power Plant

1. The students analyze a problem. They do not make a decision; the company president does that. They do not make a prediction either. They simply present the facts.
2. Italicized below are words that will give the students hints about the fields they should include in their database.

   You are a biologist working for a company that would like to build a coal-fired power plant somewhere in the world. Your company president is quite environmentally conscious and wants to build it in a biome where it will have the least amount of impact. The company has located coal reserves in the *tundra, northern coniferous forests,* a *deciduous forest, grasslands,* several *deserts,* and a *tropical rain forest.*
   Your job is to help her predict the impact of such a power plant on the *plant* and *animal* life in each biome. You have a database of biomes, their vital statistics (*temperature range, precipitation,* etc.) and common plant and animal life. You will need to find some information about the effects of coal-fired power plants on the environment. Use the sample environmental impact statement attached to this assignment to format your report.

3. The characters in this story are the biologist (with whom the student should identify) and the company president.
4. To personalize this story, students use the biome in which they live. They should also learn about the effects of coal-fired plants and consider how they would feel about living close to one. If they already live close to such a plant, how do they feel about living near it?
5. She makes sure that they interact with the proper information by requiring their report be framed as an environmental impact statement. Older students may actually fill out parts of a real environmental impact statement, whereas younger students would be given an outline appropriate to their grade level.
6. This problem could be a debate between an energy production company and an environmentalist group.

Problem B: Buying a Car

You have been working as a grocery store bagger and dreaming about having wheels for two years now. You have saved faithfully and have $3,500 for a down payment on a used car. Fortunately, you have a database listing every major make and model of car along with standard features such as gas mileage, standard accessories, and manufacturer's price from 1985–2005. You are interested in making a good buy because you have worked so hard and waited for so long. You decide you are not going to make this decision on the spur of the moment. After you have made a list of features that you really want and calculated how much you can afford to pay each month, you sit down with the database and go to work. You know you must go to the loan company with your parents to justify your decision in order to get a loan for the remainder of the purchase price.

Questions for Problem B: Buying a Car

1. What does this problem ask students to do?
   a. Analyze a problem
   b. Make a prediction
   c. Make a decision

2. Underline all of the embedded suggestions for field names in this problem.

3. Who are the characters in the story?

4. How could you help your students personalize this story?

5. What mechanism does the teacher use to make sure that the students interact with the information she wants them to learn?

6. Right now, this problem is written for an individual. How could the teacher turn this problem into a group assignment?

Answers: Problem B: Buying a Car

1. The students *make a decision.*

2. Italicized below are words that will give the students hints about the fields they should include in their database.

> You have been working as a grocery store bagger, dreaming about having wheels for two years now. You have saved faithfully and have $3,500 for a down payment on a car. Fortunately, you have a database available listing every *major make and model* of car along with standard features such as *gas mileage, standard accessories,* and *price* for cars manufactured from *1985–2005.* You are interested in making a good buy because you have worked so hard and waited for so long. You decide you are not going to make this decision on the spur of the moment. After you have made a list of features that you really want and have calculated how much you can afford to *pay each month,* you sit down with the database and go to work. You know you must go to the loan company with your parents to justify your decision in order to get a loan for the remainder of the purchase price.

3. There is just one main character in this story, the student. However, the student is given some context and character.

4. You could personalize this story by changing the job to fit each student in your class. You could make the effort to find out what they do to make money and write a vignette for each one of them or have them fill in a blank with the name of their part-time job.

5. The student must go to the loan company to ask for a loan. This part of the assignment could be completed in class as role playing, a speech, or as a written report.

6. Problem B might be an assignment to a team working for a simulated company to buy the best vehicle for a certain function.

Problem C: What Will the Next President Be Like?

> You are in high school and you know that the person who is elected to be the next president will affect the quality of your life in many ways, such as the wages that you earn (or even if you have a job), whether you will be called to fight in a war, and the amount of taxes you pay. The two candidates running for office are very different. One is moderately liberal and the other is a hard-line conservative; one was a soldier in Vietnam, the other was never in the military; one is married and the other isn't; one has concerns about businesses using up the environment, while the other says there are plenty of natural resources; one graduated from college, and the other didn't. The list of possible differences includes: voting records for civil rights, abortion, and the death penalty. You decide to look at a database of presidents to find out which of these two people is most likely to be elected based on the characteristics of past presidents. Once you decide who will win, you will write a letter to the editor of your local newspaper supporting the person whom you think should win.

Questions for Problem C: What Will the Next President Be Like?

1. What does this problem ask students to do?

    a. Analyze a problem

      b. Make a prediction

      c. Make a decision

2. Underline all of the embedded suggestions for field names in this problem.
3. Who are the characters in the story?
4. How could you help your students personalize this story?
5. What mechanism does the teacher use to make sure that the students interact with the information she wants them to learn?
6. Right now, this problem is written for an individual. How could the teacher turn this problem into a group assignment?

Answers: Problem C: What Will the Next President Be Like?

1. The students make a *prediction.*
2. Italicized below are words that will give the student hints about the fields they should include in their database.

You are in high school and you know that the person who is elected to be the next president will affect the quality of your life in many ways: the *wages* that you earn, or *even if you have a job, whether you will be called to fight in a war, the amount of taxes you pay.* The two candidates running for office are very different. One is moderately liberal and the other is a hard-line conservative; *one was a soldier in Vietnam, the other was never in the military;* one is married and the other isn't; one has concerns about businesses using up the *environment,* while the other says there are plenty of *natural resources; one graduated from college, and the other didn't.* The list of possibilities for differences is long: *voting records for civil rights, abortion,* and the *death penalty.* You decide to look at a database of presidents to find out which of these two people is most likely to be elected based on the characteristics of past presidents. Once you decide who will win, you will write a letter to the editor of your local newspaper supporting the person whom you think should win.

3. There is just one main character in this story, the student. However, the student has real motivation to find out who might win the election. All of the italicized topics affect a person's daily life.
4. You could personalize this story by pointing out that if the next president provokes or enters a large war, young people are ultimately drafted. Or, if the economy gets bad because of poor decisions, the young who have the least skills and experience are often the first to go without jobs.
5. The student must write a letter to the editor on a specific topic.
6. This problem could be altered to become a debate on the worthiness of a candidate based on historical similarities to other good or bad presidents.

Teach the Nature of the Questioning Process

Until students have worked extensively with a database, they will not understand how to ask good questions. Most students only know how to ask a single-level question that yields a fact, for example, "What is the population of Ohio?" or "How tall are grizzly bears?"

The challenge is teaching students to ask questions that will yield facts from which they can draw conclusions. If they ask questions that lead to conclusions, not only will they be thinking analytically, they will also be adding to the catalogue of facts they must learn anyway.

Take the question in the Mystery State exercise about crowding, for example. As you thought about the factors involved in crowding, you also practiced several different skills that are important for any literate person. You worked with the following facts and processes:

- Learning specific state populations
- Learning specific state land areas
- Practicing the mathematical problem-solving skills found in a story problem by generating the story problem yourself
- Practicing arithmetic skills as you did the division problem required to get the answer

When you finally extracted all of the facts you needed, you had to do three different division problems to form a basis for comparison. Although the division problems did not take place in the real world, it was nevertheless more meaningful for you than doing division problems 5, 6, and 7 at the end of a chapter in an arithmetic book. Furthermore, it was important to you for your calculations to be correct in order for you to draw a correct conclusion. To use a database effectively, students should learn that conclusions and reasoning are built on facts. This is the reason for the explicit requirement that students format their questions for databases as sequences of question/hypothesis or fact, fact, fact/conclusion sequences.

Classroom management is important in this phase of the process. To help students learn how to ask and answer more complex questions or for students just learning how to use databases, the activity designed to teach questioning should be done in pairs, in small groups, or as a class. Pairs and small groups should work at the computer. A teacher who decides to work with the whole class should use a computer projection device and ask a student to key in sorts and queries. The point of the exercise is not computer skills but rather problem-solving skills. If the students work in groups, one student can sit at the computer and type in the sorts or queries after the group has formulated a series of questions.

If students are still novice database users, the student who types in the problem can wait for explicit instructions for each keystroke from the group. In this way, students who do not know how to do sorts or queries see each step in the process. Also, the keyboarder can change for each series of questions. It does not take long for every member of the group to have an opportunity to participate at the keyboard.

Focus and Explore

In the case of the Mystery State project, students need to decide which qualities about a state make it different from their own. To do this they might look at the database's field headings for hints as well as brainstorm with each other. The teacher should encourage students to help each other think broadly, because they are not in competition. The emphasis should be on ideas and a thorough coverage of the topic.

While working on the Mystery State project, students had to decide what would make a state most different (setting up a contrast). Furthermore, they grow to understand that to different people, "most different" means different things. To a sports enthusiast, a state without skiing or professional sports might be very different, while to a rural person, a state with large population centers might be very different. In the case of the Biome project, the students will ultimately have to come to the conclusion that the problem is "How can I help my boss decide where a coal-fired plant will do the least damage?" Then students will have to ask questions such as, "What is damage—losing an endangered plant in one location or an endangered animal in another?" "Do such energy-producing plants destroy whole ecosystems?" "Which ecosystems are most fragile?" "What makes an ecosystem fragile?" Students will be able to use the database to answer some of the questions and will use other resources to answer others.

For the students who have to make a decision about a car, the question will be "What will serve my needs, be economical, and last until I can buy a different car?" Once students can focus on a problem (bearing in mind that all students may not choose to solve the same problem unless told to do so), then they are ready to ask questions.

Students Write Their Own Questions

Young or inexperienced students should write questions with each other. Experienced students may work alone at a location away from the computer in order to preserve computer time for those who have thought through problems and have written their questions down. The questioning process is iterative. Students can write a few questions, go to the computer, enter them, take their answers back to their work area, and work on their product for a while, or think of new questions. To help students write good questions and minimize time at the computer, the teacher should ask them to underline conjunctions and logical operators, mark field headings so they stand out, and indicate whether the question will be a sort or a query before they go to the computer.

One way to assist students who are learning to ask questions is to help them with steps of the process. Helping them involves giving them some of the answers to begin with and then withdrawing that support as students become more experienced. Students in grades 3 through 6 will always need prompts that older students do not need. Students who are learning content with a database for the first time will need more prompts than students who have studied several database-supported topics.

> Scaffolded learning experiences help students ask questions

Box 11.1 has an example of how a teacher might structure the Mystery State investigation for young or novice database users. We will assume that you teach in Florida and you decide that focusing on finding out which states might have ski resorts would be a good problem for your students. Notice that your students do a series of queries and come to a conclusion. You could have asked them to provide the names of relevant fields. Or, you could have asked them to establish the parameters for where skiing is possible using the database itself rather than outside sources.

To provide such parameters they could have looked at highest points and decided how many feet above sea level a mountain should be in order to be both high enough and remain cold enough for skiing. To establish whether a place is cold enough, students could have looked at the lowest temperatures and the mean temperatures and picked the lowest third or fourth of the states as possible places for skiing.

If the Mystery State project were the second or third database project your students had done, the worksheet that the teacher hands out might look like the next one in Box 11.2. Note that the thinking represented in this example does not often happen the

BOX 11.1 EXAMPLE 1: MYSTERY STATE INVESTIGATION

No one skis in Florida, so a state in which people can ski would be very different. Fields that will help you figure out where people might ski include highest point, low temperature, and annual precipitation. Next, you must decide how the information in these fields can help you make a comparison. To help yourself work this problem through, think of a place where you know that people ski. Go to the almanac and find the highest point, low temperature, and annual precipitation of that place.

Name of the place you selected _____

Your approach:

Find the identifying letters of all of the states in your database that have low temperatures equal to or less than the place you selected, annual precipitation greater than the place you selected, and highest points within 2,000 feet of the place you selected. What should you have the computer do?

(Answer: Query all of the states for low temperature close to or less than the place you selected.)

Fact: _____

Question: Which states have mountains high enough for skiing? What should you have the computer do?

(Answer: Query all of the states for mountains that have mountains nearly as high, as high as, or higher than the place you selected.)

Fact: _____

Question: Where is there enough moisture to make snow? What should you have the computer do?

(Answer: Query all of the states for precipitation with nearly as much as, equal to, or more than the place you selected.)

Fact: _____

Now make a list of the states that satisfy all three of your requirements for low temperature, highest point, and precipitation.

Conclusion (names of states):

_____
_____
_____
_____

first or second time that students use a database to solve a problem. Young students may never achieve the ability to work as independently on assignments such this one. On the other hand, beginning in grade 7 or 8, some students are capable of this kind of independence, and by grade 12, most students should be able to engage in this kind of thinking with no prompts if they have had consistent exposure to lessons of this nature.

You will have to model these kinds of investigations to the whole class often, and perhaps start every database activity with some questions of your own to demonstrate and clarify important topics and trains of thought. Furthermore, many students may

BOX 11.2   EXAMPLE 2: MYSTERY STATE INVESTIGATION

Being able to go to a ski resort would make a state very different from ours. You must decide which available fields will give you information about this problem. What are they? _____

Describe how numbers in the fields that you chose will show you that a state could support skiing
_____

Gather the facts you need from each field:

Fact: _____

Fact: _____

Fact: _____

Now that you have some actual ideas about states where people could ski, which ones do you think are most likely to have skiing?

Conclusion: _____

need to work in groups or with a peer in order to think through problems. It is safe to say that having students work in groups to formulate and enter questions for databases is always appropriate.

Another point to consider is that a complete database project will consist of many problems like the one in Examples 1 and 2. The number of problems that result in a product will depend on the size of the database (number of records *and* number of fields), the complexity of the product, and the age of the students. Table 11.3 lists very general guidelines by grade level for students who have been introduced to databases and use them regularly as a tool.

When the students have a list of well thought out questions, it is time for them to go to the computer. Again, this does not have to be a solitary activity. Two students can pool their questions and work together. Sometimes getting a query to work requires some thinking and discussion, which necessitates several trips to the computer. This is one reason your students should have cooperative learning experiences before

> Grade level appropriately assigned

TABLE 11.3   Breadth of Assignments by Grade Level

Grade Level	Number of Problems or Questions	Size of Database	Size of Product
4–5	4–6	20–30 records 6–10 fields	3–6 paragraphs 3–6-page electronic report
6–7	7–15	50–75 records 10–15 fields	5–10 paragraphs 6–15-page electronic report
8–12	Number required to support a well-informed product	75+ records 10+ fields	The range of product size can vary from a simple five-paragraph position paper to a research report or electronic presentation.

you try database-supported lessons. It is hard enough to learn how to participate in a cooperative learning group. Adding the computer and databases to the mix can be overwhelming. Learning how to think with databases is a skill that improves with practice.

Require a Product

| A conclusion or recommendation is the goal of a database assignment |

Throughout the life of a database-supported unit, teachers should emphasize that the database is only a tool and that the goal of the project is a product. These products can take many forms. They can be in a traditional report format, an electronic report done with presentation/hypermedia software, a speech with or without presentation software, a debate, or even a picture. If the object of the assignment is to describe an unknown, pictures and graphics may be very helpful, especially with younger children and those who do not write well.

| Evaluating student products |

Evaluation of the product is a key element of the database-supported lesson. The usual items (spelling, grammar, and organization) can be evaluated along with how well the student used the database information to shape the final product. If the students hand in all of the questions that they prepared for the database, the teacher can compare the questions to the product and make suggestions about how to improve database use.

Also, comparing the questions to the product will help prevent copying and pasting text from an electronic encyclopedia, throwing in a few pictures and calling the result a product. For example, the Mystery State project requires an accurate travel brochure. The Biome project requires a report based on the format ecologists use when they do an environmental impact statement. The car-buying project might require a sales speech in which the students try to sell the car that they have chosen to the class. The project described at the beginning of the previous chapter in which the student had to choose a Native American tribe to live with might be a journal, "A Day in the Life of a Nez Perce Boy," accompanied by a picture of a tribal village. One of the most important benefits of a good database-supported assignment is the original thinking students do.

Have Students Make Comparisons

| Students should compare their findings to those of experts |

Although having real-world materials that enable students to corroborate their conclusions is not always possible, it is helpful when they are available. It should be a goal for teachers to create or obtain source materials so students can use them for comparing their analysis, description, or prediction to a similar case. This will help students remember the facts they have worked with as well as help them generalize about the ideas they have studied.

In the case of the Mystery State project, the teacher tells students the name of the state they have been working on and students go to encyclopedias and compare their article with the encyclopedia article. In the Biome project, the teacher could have some case studies of the effects of coal-fired power plants on the environment for students to work with. Students who were "buying" a car could go to a car dealership and talk to a car dealer, read newspaper advertisements, or talk to another adult about the purchase.

Encourage Students to Resolve Discrepancies

Students should, again, create some kind of product that is a result of the comparison of their work to the work of others, even if it is only a brief paragraph, a two-minute presentation to the class, or a short discussion in a group. This activity provides closure to the unit and gives students a last chance to solidify the knowledge and relationships that they have come to understand.

> Students should learn to use a database

Encourage Students to Think about Using Databases to Solve Other Problems

This part of the lesson can also be very brief. It is the segment of the lesson that will help your students become life-long learners. No tool is useful to a person who does not know when it should be used. This piece of the lesson may be written down as a part of a worksheet as it was in the Mystery State project, or it may be the topic of a short, teacher-led presentation. The point for students is to generalize what they have learned so they can be proactive about their own learning in the future. Beyond the learning of a specific topic, a teacher's goal is to someday hear a student say, "I'll bet if I had that information in a database I could find the answer to that problem."

SUMMATIVE EVALUATION OF A DATABASE PROJECT

Evaluating a student's work with a database from beginning to the end of the project is a complex task. It is tempting to want to grade only the final product, with the justification that if the groundwork that the student has done is good, then the final product will be good. This reasoning is faulty, however. Grading math papers is analogous to grading database assignments. Math teachers learned some time ago that just grading the final answer to a complex math problem does not give the teacher or the student accurate insight into the student's mastery of the information under study. In a database assignment, there are a number of visible products of student thinking that teachers can evaluate.

Each step that you complete in teaching the assignment has a student outcome. Table 11.4 lists each step and its associated student outcome. As students complete each of those steps, their work may be scored using a scoring rubric so that the whole grade for the assignment is not based on just the final product.

> Grade based on all work, not just project

Tables 11.5, 11.6, and 11.7 are simple rubrics adaptable to any grade level for scoring student work. Each column lists only a heading with the number of points available for that segment of the assignment. You will want to adjust these values to your scoring system. Notice that there is a column that allows for no points even though the student hands in something. Note that you will use the rubric in Table 11.5 only if you are having your students build their own database. You should also note that Table 11.7 does not include suggestions for scoring the format of the products. There could be cells in this table where you provide students with standards for grammar, sentence mechanics, spelling, organization, and content.

TABLE 11.4	Steps in Database Lessons and Student Outcomes
Step	**Student Outcome**
1. Provide the students with a story or scenario that sets up the problem.	Students must formulate or restate the problem and break it into its components.
2. Teach students to write questions.	Students use the database to answer questions.
3. Have students focus on areas to explore.	Students decide on questions that will lead them to the answers they want.
4. Students write questions (Fact-Fact-Fact-Conclusion) for the database.	Students see beyond individual facts to logical sequences of ideas.
5. Require a product.	Students produce a written product, speech, or other summary and analysis of their findings.
6. Resolve discrepancies.	Students compare and contrast their conclusions with the conclusions of experts.
7. Generate new problems.	Students apply what they know about finding the answer to one question to finding the answers to other questions.

TABLE 11.5	Scoring Rubric for Student-Planned Database (Design)		
Criterion	**2 Points**	**1 Point**	**0 Points**
Design of fields	The database contains all of the fields that the students will need to help them answer the question posed by the scenario.	The database is missing one or two key fields, but all fields are relevant.	The database is missing more than two key fields and has included irrelevant fields.
Ease of use	Students assigned an appropriate common metric for each field.	There is evidence that students have thought about a common appropriate metric for each field, but some metrics that they have used aren't appropriate (i.e., 5'6" to measure height).	Students show no evidence of having planned how to express entries in appropriate common units.
Mechanics	All entries are spelled correctly.	Depending on the size of the database, there are a few spelling errors.	The number of spelling errors significantly affects the usability of the database.

TABLE 11.6 Scoring Rubric for Student-Planned Database (Use of a Database)

Step	2 Points	1 Point	0 Points
1. Learning to write questions.	Can translate a teacher- or class-generated question into a database sort or query.	Knows whether a sort or query is needed, but lacks the skills to make the computer execute the sort or query.	Does not understand sorts and queries and cannot execute them on the computer.
2. Student focuses on the question and areas of exploration.	Translates the scenario into a question that can be explored with the database. Approach to the problem will be fruitful.	Translation of the scenario into a question that is too broad or too narrow.	Student does not attempt to translate the scenario into a question or reformulate it into a problem.
3. Students write questions to ask the database.	Writes questions that produce facts that lead to a conclusion (writes Fact-Fact-Fact-Conclusion questions).	Writes questions that yield mostly unrelated facts. Produces only one or two Fact-Fact-Fact-Conclusion questions.	Writes questions that aren't related to the problem. Writes few or no questions.

TABLE 11.7 Scoring Rubric for Student-Planned Database (Product)

Product	2 Points	1 Point	0 Points
Report, speech, discussion	Demonstrates both analytical and synthetical thinking; has broken the problem into several parts; has generalized series of Fact-Fact-Fact-Conclusion questions to reach conclusions.	Has applied the facts from the database to formulate new ideas; has explained the relationships implied in Fact-Fact-Fact-Conclusion sequences.	Has recited a series of unrelated facts.
Resolving discrepancies	Finds more than one source for each piece of the problem and produces a logical discussion of differences and similarities.	Finds only one source for comparison, or Misses comparisons for pieces of the problem, or Comparison of differences and similarities is not logical.	Finds only one source for comparison, and Misses comparisons for pieces of the problem, and Comparison of differences and similarities is not logical.
Generating new problems	Can generate more than one new associated problem that could be solved with database research.	Can generate one new, associated problem that could be solved with database research.	Cannot think of a related problem that could be solved using a database.

CHECKING YOUR UNDERSTANDING

11.3 Use one of the vignettes or ideas presented earlier in this chapter to build a database lesson. Make your lesson similar to the Mystery State project. Be sure that you explain and include each step. Remember what you learned about writing a scenario and be sure that you include complete instructions and examples for your students. Assume that your students know how to use a database, but this is the first time that they will actually do a complete lesson using a database to help them understand a topic. Include a cover page for your project that specifies the grade level for which you are writing the lesson and the kind of lesson it is (prediction, describing an unknown, or analysis/decision). After you have finished your lesson, include a one-page vignette at the end of your project modeled on the vignette based on the Native American project that describes the actual "look of the classroom" while the project is in progress. Also, include a scoring rubric that you would use to score the work students would produce as a result of this lesson.

Topics of the vignettes are
- Buying and selling merchandise
- Choosing the next president
- Advisability of the 75-mile-an-hour speed limit
- Learning about another culture
- Biomes
- Studying novels, short stories, or poetry

Table 11.8 is a summary of activities associated with databases and their relationships to Bloom's taxonomy. Notice that when students design, build, and use the database that every level of the taxonomy is represented. As you look at Table 11.8, try to match the "Database Activity" in the third column with the step for constructing a database-supported lesson that you learned earlier in this chapter.

▥ SUMMARY

Using a database to teach literature and language arts, social science, and science can be an extremely valuable and rewarding experience for both teachers and students. The current situation in classrooms is such that teachers will not be able to do this instantly. There are several hurdles to overcome.

1. Teachers must be sure that their students have the prerequisite skills to operate databases until that skill becomes a general part of the curriculum.
2. Databases and lessons using them have to be created by students and teachers.
3. Students and teachers need to work in a cooperative learning environment. If they don't have those skills already, then they must learn them before they tackle databases.

Once students and teachers have the resources and expertise to use databases to study topics, using databases becomes an extremely valuable teaching tool (see Box 11.3).

TABLE 11.8 Bloom's Taxonomy and Databases				
The Cognitive Process Dimension	The Knowledge Dimension			
	Factual	Conceptual	Procedural	Meta-Cognitive
Remember	Gathering facts for the database	–	Learning how to enter data into the database	–
Understand	Entering facts into the database consistently	Deciding on the names of columns in the database	Understanding how rows and columns interact	–
Apply	Applying knowledge of databases to create a working database	–	Creating and writing queries for a database	–
Analyze	Assigning facts into categories	Writing queries for the database	Analyzing failures of the database	Troubleshooting technical problems
Evaluate	Testing the database for accuracy	Interpreting the results of the questions	–	Looking at conclusions for logic and believability
Create	–	Creating new knowledge based on the results of queries	Writing a query	Planning, generating, and producing a database

1. Databases assist student acquisition of facts and definitions.
2. When students use databases to think through a problem, they build relationships among related ideas.
3. Databases are "idea generators" when students use sorts and queries creatively.
4. After they have created their product, students compare what they have learned to what other people have said and thought about the same topic.
5. When they have compared their conclusion to the conclusions of others, students judge the accuracy of their own work.

BOX 11.3 STEPS FOR CREATING A DATABASE LESSON

1. Set up the problem.
2. Teach the nature of the questioning process.
3. Encourage students to focus on a problem.
4. Have the students work with the database and get answers to the questions. Support young or inexperienced students by providing parts of the questioning process. As students become more adept, remove support gradually until they can work through the questioning process without guidance.
5. Require a product of the students.
6. Have the students compare their conclusions to the conclusions of other authors.
7. Ask the students to resolve any discrepancies between their work and the work of other authors.
8. Ask the students to think of other ways that a database could help them think about a problem in the content area.

6. In the questioning process, students start with an idea or theme (the problem) and build on it with increasingly complex concepts.

7. When students are questioning a database, they receive immediate feedback about two items:

   ▨ Facts
   ▨ Accuracy (logic) of the questions they are asking.

8. Database software (the tool itself) is widely available and inexpensive. It runs on any kind or vintage of machine. Most machines that are sold to educational institutions have a "suite" of tool products including a database.

▨ REFERENCES

Jonassen, D. (2006). *Modeling with technology: Mindtools for conceptual change.* Upper Saddle River, NJ: Pearson Merrill Prentice Hall, 91–100.

Shank, R. C., & Cleary, C. (1995). *Engines for education.* Hillsdale, NJ: Lawrence Erlbaum Associates.

▨ ANNOTATED RESOURCES

Everhart, N., & Harris, F. (2002). Using primary sources and creative writing to teach middle school history. *Knowledge Quest.* 31(2), 52–54.

   Not every database unit needs to be based on a student-built database. This discussion is based on students gathering knowledge from primary sources (databases) and then basing their stories on that information. This is a must-read for English, language arts, and history teachers.

Hillis, P. (2003). Multi-media and databases for historical enquiry: A report from the trenches. *Journal of Educational Multimedia and Hypermedia.* 12(3), 291–312.

   The value of reading this small study is derived from two sources. First, it is and excellent description of using a multimedia database, a concept not covered in this chapter. Second, it provides further ideas and procedures for working with students and databases. The author reports statistically good learning gains, and also provides the reader with student comments and reflections on the learning process as they used the database.

Jonassen, D. (2006). *Modeling with technology: MindTools for conceptual change.* Upper Saddle River, NJ: Pearson Merrill Prentice Hall, 91–100.

   There are few discussions of the theory and practice of using databases in the classroom. Jonassen's is one of the best. The theory he suggests is very similar to the one proposed in this book. He explains it differently and gives different examples. Reading this chapter will provide you with another good, usable perspective, and more ideas. In fact, the whole book is excellent and covers many of the topics covered in this text. I chose to highlight it here because there is so little information available about databases and classroom use—either theoretical or research-based.

Kaiser, C., & Paul, J. (2005). Do women live longer than men? Using computers to investigate graveyard data. *Micromath.* 21(2), 6–10.

Both mathematics and history teachers can benefit from reading this article. It provides lessons learned as well as advantages and tips for executing a lesson of this kind.

LaBarre, K. M., Klotz, R. L., & Witherow, E. (2000). Using online databases to teach ecological concepts. *The American Biology Teacher.* 62(2), 124–127.

Before the Internet, long-term data was not available to students. Now it is. The authors discuss sources of data and how it can be used to teach ecological concepts. The article emphasizes the way that the database allows learners to visualize their environment.

Companion Web Site www.ablongman.com/thorsen3e

1. Go to Chapters 10–12 of the TechTactics web site. You will see links to many databases. Some of these links provide numbers only, which you must import into a database like Access or a spreadsheet like Excel. Others store their data in an online database, which allows you to do queries online without having to import data into Access or Excel. Two such databases on the web site are Valley of the Shadow 1 and 2 and County and City Data Books.
   - ▨ Browse each database to find out what it is like and how it works.
   - ▨ Write a question that you would like to answer using each database.
   - ▨ Enter your queries and draw your conclusions. List your queries and in a short paragraph explain your conclusions.
   - ▨ Write a short essay (less than 200 words) comparing and contrasting the operation of the two databases.

2. Go to Chapters 10–12 of the TechTactics web site. Go to any of the links that provide data as numbers that must be imported into a database for the creation of queries and sorts (NASA and the U.S. Census Bureau are two examples).
   - ▨ Successfully import the data into the database that you are using.
   - ▨ Write three questions you would like to answer with the data.
   - ▨ Do the appropriate sorts and write related queries. Note these on the paper that you turn in to your instructor.
   - ▨ Write a short essay (less than 200 words) on the conclusions that you drew from your sorts and queries.

CHAPTER 11 APPENDIX: A SPECIAL NOTE ABOUT DATABASES IN MATHMATICS

| Mathematics and databases |

Databases in mathematics are useful for giving students a large view of an entire topic. Although databases are not used in mathematics as frequently as spreadsheets are in science, nevertheless there are some appropriate moments. Databases are useful in mathematics for the same reasons they are useful in other content areas—they provide students another way to study a concept. Here are some mathematical concepts for which useful databases could be built:

Number concepts—lower elementary
Shapes and formulas (geometry)—upper elementary through senior high school
Word problems (middle through high school)

To understand how a database for mathematics might be constructed and used, we will look at word problems in more detail. Mildred Johnson (1992) wrote *How to Solve Word Problems in Algebra: A Solved Problem Approach* (New York: McGraw-Hill), which summarizes different kinds of word problems and how they are solved. The problem is, given all of this information, how would we convert it to a database format that students could use to understand and learn how to work word problems better? The kind of database we will build using this information falls loosely into the category of "describing an unknown."

First, we will construct a table. To make our table clear for students, the kinds of word problems will come first in the table (coins, time, finance, mixtures, levers, age, numbers, work, plane geometric figures, digits, etc.). When we teach students how to do word problems, we associate some fact or formula with the kind of problem that the student is solving. We also teach them how to sketch the problem. Finally, we provide them with examples and explanations of solutions. Given this information, we can construct a table that will be the basis for a database (see Table 11.9).

This database could be made more complex. For example, there are different kinds of time, rate, and distance problems (two trains meeting versus how long it takes to get from one place to another). There may be more than one row for each kind of word problem. Your database may have eight or ten different examples of time, rate, and distance problems. Also note that the complex sorts and queries that are possible with other example databases in this book are not possible for this database. The only column that may be sorted or queried meaningfully is the first one, which holds the names of the different kinds of word problems. Your students could simply use the database as a reference—or you could modify it and leave out information in some cells, asking students to provide it. The construction and use of such a database puts word problems into a larger context and allows students to see that there are patterns for solving word problems in general, as well as patterns for the solution of individual word problems.

TABLE 11.9 Example of Some Fields for a Database on Word Problems

Name	Fact	Solved Example (problem statement)	Sketch of Solved Example	Unsolved Problem 1
Time, rate, and distance	Time × rate = distance Sketches are helpful.	The distance from Boston to Chicago is. . . .	<table><tr><td>Time</td><td>Rate</td><td>Di</td></tr><tr><td>X</td><td>45</td><td>900</td></tr></table>	A train leaves New York going 75. . . .
Mixtures	Amount of the mixture times the percent of pure stuff equals the amount of pure stuff. Sketches are helpful.	You are getting your car ready for winter and discover that you need to add antifreeze to. . . .	6% + 12% + 15%	A cook is making a large batch of soup that requires a mixture of milk and. . . .
Levers	$W_1D_1 = W_2D_2$ Sketches are helpful.	A weight at one end. . . .	60 130 8 ft X	Using a crowbar. . . .
Plane geometric figures	1. The perimeter of a rectangle = its width × 2 + its length × 2 2. The sum of the angles of a triangle = 180° 3. The area of a rectangle. . . . 4. The sides of a square are. . . . 5. Sketches are helpful.	A rectangle is 3 feet less than four times its width. The perimeter. . . .	2x − 3	One angle of a triangle is three times the next angle and. . . .

12

Acquiring Data

OBJECTIVES

- Know where to look for electronic sources of data.
- Know how to transform the data to a usable format.

Acquiring data for a database is one of the biggest challenges for teachers who use database-supported lessons. Classes can construct some databases themselves, but database construction is a time-consuming process and not always the best use of a student's time. During the past several years, the number of datasets available on the Internet has increased significantly. Knowing where to find them is difficult.

Once you do locate a dataset, it is useful if you know how to change the format of the information for use with a database engine. Once you have reformatted data into a comma- or tab-delimited format, you may use it not only for databases but also for spreadsheets, the topic of the next chapter. The skills you should know or learn as you study this chapter include:

- Use an Internet search engine
- Download a file to a floppy drive or hard drive
- Use a word processor to convert data to a comma- or tab-delimited text file
- Use a database

HOW DO TEACHERS ACQUIRE DATASETS?

Teachers and their classes do not always have to make their own databases. More and more often an Internet search will turn up a database that is appropriate for some unit of content. Science and social studies teachers are most fortunate in this area. To the extent that students study the historical context of the works that they read, literature teachers also find databases that are helpful. In the social sciences, the U.S. Census and state and county records are available as databases on the Internet. In the sciences, NASA maintains a large number of databases on astronomical objects, and other branches of the government maintain databases on the weather, ecological studies, health, and nutrition.

Data on the Internet: Examples of Some Good Sites

Internet addresses change often, so there is no point in providing a long list of Internet data resources. However, there is a short list of sources that have had a relatively long life, electronically speaking. Each has its own quirks and peculiarities. Following are comments and Table 12.1, with the name of the site and an accompanying address. What you can take from the sites as much as data is an understanding of the variety and amount of data available to anyone with a computer.

The Data and Story Library (DASL Project, 2004) is an excellent location for finding data related to a large number of content areas. Although this database is meant for students of statistics, the data for the problems is available in tables. The tables cover the following content areas:

Archeology	Education	Finance	Miscellaneous	Social science
Astronomy	Energy	Food	Nature	Sociology
Automotive	Engineering	Geography	Nutrition	Sports
Biology	Environment	Government	Physics	Weather
Consumer	Europe	Health	Psychology	Zoology
Economics	Famous datasets	Medical	Science	

These tables are not supported by a database engine, but can be copied and imported into a database engine as tab-delimited data. What distinguishes this site from the government sites in Table 12.1 is the variety of data not connected to topics that the government wants to know about.

The National Climatic Data Center (2004) has a huge library of up-to-date statistics on local, national, and world climate. However, the site charges for its data. The charges are not high, but if you plan on using the site, you must plan ahead. Some of the data that you can get include the following:

▓ Monthly climatic data for the world
▓ Storm data
▓ Local climatological data, edited
▓ Climatological data
▓ Hourly precipitation data
▓ Climatography of the United States: monthly normals
▓ Heating and cooling degree day data
▓ Climates of the world; wind climatology
▓ Freeze/frost data for the United States

FedStats (2004) is an agency that collects statistics from over seventy government agencies. Not only does this site provide links to the data, it also provides tools

> Data and Story Library

> National Climatic Data Center

> FedStats

TABLE 12.1 Summary of Sample Databases and Their Internet Addresses	
Bureau of Labor Statistics	www.fedstats.gov
U.S. Department of Agriculture (In the "Search Site" box type "data." You will get a listing of the different types of data on the site and how to access them.)	www.ars.usda.gov
Bureau of Alcohol, Tobacco and Firearms	www.atf.treas.gov/stats.htm
Bureau of Transportation Statistics	www.bts.gov/index.html
National Mental Health Information Center	http://mentalhealth.samhsa.gov/cmhs/MentalHealthStatistics/URS2005.asp
Centers for Disease Control and Prevention	www.cdc.gov/DataStatistics
CIA World Factbook	https://www.cia.gov/library/publications/the-world-factbook/index.html
Consumer Product Safety Commission (Check both the "Library" heading "Consumer Product Safety Statistics," and "No Fear ACT Data" on the main menu of the home page.)	https://www.cia.gov/library/publications/the-world-factbook/index.html
DASL Project	www.usgs.gov
Department of Veterans Affairs (See "Veteran Data" on the main menu of the home page.)	www.va.gov
Energy Information Administration	www.eia.doe.gov
Environmental Protection Agency	www.epa.gov/epahome/Data.html
Federal Aviation Administration	www.faa.gov/data_statistics
Federal Bureau of Investigation	www.fbi.gov/research.htm
Federal Deposit Insurance Corporation	www.fdic.gov/quicklinks/analysts.html
Federal Interagency Council on Statistical Policy	www.fedstats.gov
Forest Service (Enter the word "data" into the site search list box.)	www.fs.fed.us
Maritime Administration	http://marad.dot.gov/MARAD_statistics/index.html
Mine Safety and Health Administration	www.msha.gov/drs/drshome.htm
National Aeronautics and Space Administration	http://science.hq.nasa.gov/research/space_science_data.html
National Climatic Data Center	www.ncdc.noaa.gov/oa/mpp/freedata.html
National Center for Education Statistics	http://nces.ed.gov/
National Highway Transportation Safety Administration	www.nhtsa.dot.gov
National Oceanic and Atmospheric Administration	www.education.noaa.gov/teachers1.html
National Science Foundation	www.nsf.gov/statistics
National Resources Conservation Service (See "Plants Database" on the Main Menu.)	www.nrcs.usda.gov
U.S. Census Bureau	www.census.gov/main/www/stat_int.html

TABLE 12.1 Continued	
U.S. Department of Energy (Enter the word "statistics" into the site search list box.)	www.energy.gov
U.S. Department of Health and Human Services (Enter the word "data" into the site search list box.)	www.hhs.gov
U.S. Department of Housing and Urban Development (Be sure to scroll down the page to find the "Data" section.)	www.hud.gov/library/bookshelf03/index.cfm
U.S. Fish and Wildlife Service	www.fws.gov/data/FWSNatlData.htm
U.S. General Services Administration (Although this does not feature databases themselves, it leads to many different sites that have both text and multimedia databases).	www.kids.gov
U.S. Geological Survey (Links lead to data in both text and graphical form—one of the best sites on the list.)	www.usgs.gov

Note: If you do not find what you are looking for, you can "back off" from many of these web addresses to get to the home page. The base address for a site usually ends in .gov.

to access the data. That is, the data are supported by a database engine so that you do not have to download and convert it. Some of the major agencies to which FedStats links include the Bureau of the Census, Bureau of Labor Statistics, Energy Information Administration, Environmental Protection Agency, National Agricultural Statistics Service, National Center for Health Statistics, National Science Foundation, Bureau of Justice Statistics, and the National Center for Education Statistics.

The U.S. Census Bureau (2004) has an enormous site with free data on every question asked by the census and more. From this site you may get national data as well as regional and state data. Buried in the U.S. Census Bureau Site is the Statistical Agencies (International) site, which lists statistics on approximately one hundred countries beginning with Algeria and ending with Yugoslavia. The countries themselves maintain these sites, and often the listings are available in both English and the language of the country listing the statistics. Not only are these sites good places to obtain data for a social studies class, they can also serve as a valuable resource for foreign language classes.

> U.S. Census Bureau

The Journal of Statistics in Education (2004), much like the DASL project, is aimed at providing data and analyses of that data for students studying statistics. However, like DASL, this project provides data on topics about which the government is not typically interested. To give you a flavor for the variety of information on this site, titles of some of the data sets and accompanying articles include: Population at Risk and Death Rates for an Unusual Episode (data on the sinking of the *Titanic*); What Does It Take to Heat a New Room?; Time of Birth, Sex, and Birth Weight of 44 Babies; The Draft Lotteries of 1970, 1971, and 1972; Fitting Percentage of Body Fat to Simple Body Measurements; Sexual Activity and Lifespan of Male Fruit Flies; Galileo Motion Data; U.S. Senate Votes on Clinton Removal; Normal Body Temperature, Gender, and Heart Rate; and The Statistics of Poverty and Inequality.

> Journal of Statistics in Education

FORMATTING DATA FOR USE IN A DATABASE

Making downloaded databases useful is a challenge. Sometimes you can find a great database, but it is in a large table with no database engine to support it. Hence, students are unable to do sorts and queries; all they can do is look at the facts, which is not the point of a database at all. However, in many cases, it is not too difficult to download a table from the Internet and convert it to a format that a database engine can use. The other possibility is finding a database that is supported by a search engine on the Internet. Let us look first at how to make online databases usable.

> Much data on the Internet must be reformatted to work with a database engine

Technique 1: Making Raw Internet Data Usable

Consider, for example, a database found on the NASA web site called the Planetary Factsheet (NASA, 2004). In Figure 12.1 you see the screen as it is displayed on the NASA site. The database is an HTML table with no database engine to support it. What if you want your students to manipulate those numbers and find the largest, smallest, most distant, least distant, fastest, slowest, coldest, and hottest planets and do some comparisons? You need to make this information accessible to a database engine. More recent versions of word processors and database engines make this possible. The examples that you will see are in Microsoft Word and Microsoft Access.

To make the file in Figure 12.1 accessible to Access, you should use the following procedure.

1. Download the HTML file (what you see in Figure 12.1) and save it.

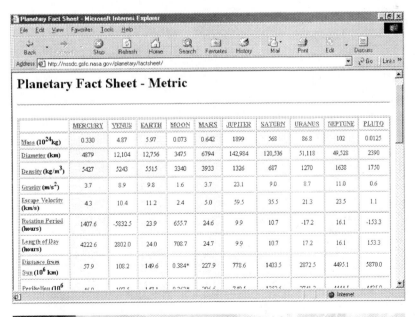

FIGURE 12.1 First Half of Planetary Factsheet from NASA Web Site

2. Open Word.
3. Open the HTML file that you downloaded and save it in Word.
4. Click on the Table menu and click on Convert Table. Choose Table to Text. Then choose either comma-delimited or tab-delimited format. This table will look ugly, like Figure 12.2. But don't worry. Things will get better.

At this point you should be sure that your table displays the correct headings over the correct data. If, for example, your headings and data are reversed as they are in Figure 12.3, you will need to use a spreadsheet to transpose the data before your import it into Access. When you do get it right, your table will look like the one in Figure 12.4.

5. Save the downloaded file as a text file. Save it as "Text with line breaks."
6. Open Access, and open the text file you just saved.
7. Access will ask you whether it is tab- or comma-delimited when you try to open it. Choose the correct option box, and the table will open in Access and look just like Figure 12.3. You are almost there.
8. Now you must format each field (remember that column headers are the field names) so that it reflects the kind of data in the field. In this case, you will want to make sure that the computer sees these fields as "numeric" fields.
9. Now your database is ready for your students to use. Once you have gone through the process a few times, you will find that it takes less than fifteen minutes from the beginning of the download to the appearance of the usable table in the database.

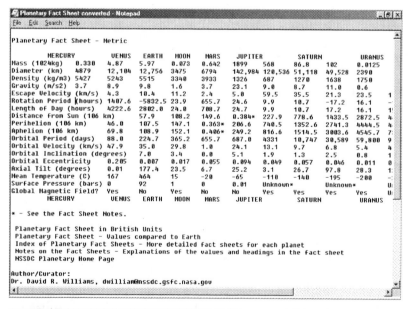

FIGURE 12.2 Internet Planetary Factsheet Converted to a Tab-Delimited Text File

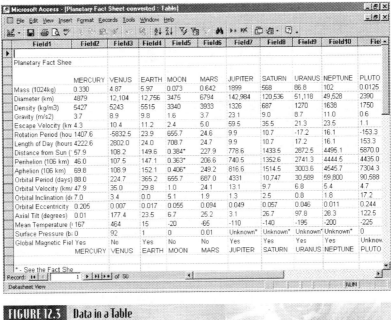

FIGURE 12.3 Data in a Table

Products other than Microsoft Office offer similar features. Every major database and spreadsheet manufactured allows the user to import tab- and/or comma-delimited data. Many, but not all, word processors allow users to convert tables to text. If your school does not use the Office suite or uses an older version, you may need to

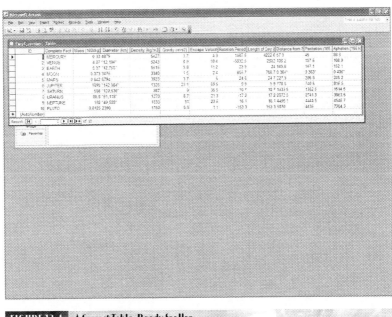

FIGURE 12.4 A Correct Table, Ready for Use

request a copy of either Office or other software that does convert HTML tables to text. This is the critical step in using much of the data that you can retrieve from the Internet.

Technique 2: Internet Databases with Their Own Search Engines

Another fortunate find on the Internet is a database with its own search engine. An example of such a site is the The Valley of the Shadow (Ayers, 1998a), which is dedicated to helping students understand the U.S. Civil War from the perspective of the average citizen of the North and the South. The site provides parallel information about two small towns, one Northern and one Southern. Included are letters between soldiers and their families. There are many graphics, pictures of the people from the two towns, and of the war. In addition, the site has extensive databases (Ayers, 1998b). These databases include U.S. Census records, military records, church records, and local government records. The interface for the search engine that accesses these records looks like Figure 12.5. Notice the fields with the "greater than" (>) sign in front of them. This sign means that all of the comparison operators are available for the search, which allows for much fine-tuning. The Personal Estate Value field shows this drop-down box extended, allowing the user to choose a symbol.

The Valley of the Shadow is an excellent example of a site that includes not only databases but also other material prepared specifically for use in teaching. You will find other databases with their own search engines on the Internet as well, though supporting materials aren't included, and they are not designed for classrooms. Some of the database search engines that you will find have their own quirks and operational

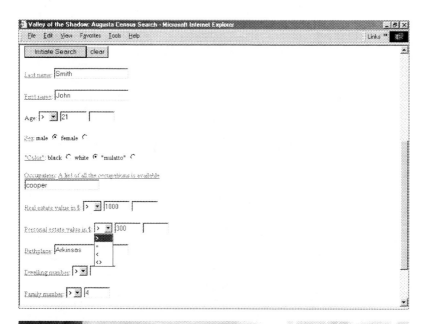

FIGURE 12.5 A Sample Search of The Valley of the Shadow Database

differences that will require you and your students to learn how to use the interface before you can proceed with queries. Usually, figuring out how to use a new search interface takes no longer than ten or fifteen minutes, and often there are instructions. The more search engines you use, the easier it will be to learn new ones.

Technique 3: Building Your Own Database

The lack of a prepared database for a topic that a class is studying should not stop a determined teacher from using databases as a tool for teaching. Students can make their own databases. In making the database themselves, students are looking up facts and working with them. Having students create their own database is no more tedious or meaningless than the practice of having students look up and memorize definitions, do worksheets, and answer questions at the end of the chapter.

> Students use both low- and high-level thinking skills when they build their own databases

In fact, the difference between doing these activities and building a database is significant. When students are building a database, they are doing it with a goal in mind—building a tool that will help them think more clearly. They must think about information and enter it accurately, because their carefulness will affect the usability of the database they create. A second benefit of building a database is that students must design the database themselves. They must decide which fields to include and how to format the information in each field. Before they commit themselves to their design (their decisions about which fields to include), they will run some trial sorts and queries to determine whether the design is adequate. Ultimately they will use the dull, fact-finding work and precise requirements of building a database to formulate creative, thoughtful questions and skillful queries that give them answers to difficult questions with fuzzy edges. Furthermore, building a database gives some purpose to the tedious part of learning that everyone must endure. *In order to reason and think analytically, people must have a base of accurate, available facts.* Building a database is one way of acquiring these facts. A database can be graded for accuracy and completeness just like worksheets, end-of-chapter questions, and pages of terms and definitions.

> Building a database takes time

From a practical standpoint, having students build their own databases means that during the first few years you teach with databases you will be building one almost every time you want to do a database-supported lesson. Therefore, for the first year you may only build one per quarter or even less. Nevertheless, you will start the next year with four ready-made databases and will be able to add to your repertoire. Furthermore, if other teachers in your subject build databases, you will soon have databases for every topic for which they are appropriate. Then, you and your students will simply need to maintain the databases you have.

There is another reason why your students might build a database, other than the fact that a database does not already exist for the topic your class is studying. You may want to have your class build a database as they collect data. For example, a class studying plant growth under various conditions may want to build a database in which they record their observations. Or your class may do a survey and put the data that they collect into a database. In either case, your class would have to design the database and develop a form for entering the information that they collect.

CHECKING YOUR UNDERSTANDING

12.1

1. Using one of the Internet resources listed in this chapter, find and convert an electronic database. Write a topic for research, writing, or discussion for students at a grade level that would use this database. Write ten sample queries that would shed light on this topic.

2. Using The Valley of the Shadow databases, design a lesson. Provide a writing topic for students at your grade level of interest. Write ten sample queries you would do that would shed light on your writing topic.

3. Think of a topic that is appropriate to a grade level that you will teach. Design a database to support that topic. List the fields you will use. Write ten sample queries.

▓ SUMMARY

Acquiring a database is a key part of building a database lesson. There are three different methods for obtaining them:

1. Downloading them from an electronic source and converting them into a format that a database engine can read
2. Finding data on the Internet or on a CD that has its own database engine
3. Having your class build databases based on the information that they are studying

If there is time, your students can learn at several levels by building their own. They must find facts and transfer them accurately to the database. They must understand the structure of the information that they are studying in order to design the database, and they must decide whether they have designed a useful database before they commit themselves to entering all of the data they need.

▓ REFERENCES

Ayers, D. R. (1998a). *The valley of the shadow.* http://jefferson.village.virginia.edu/vshadow2/choosepart.html. Retrieved September 3, 2004.

Ayers, D. R. (1998b). *The valley of the shadow.* http://valley.vcdh.virginia.edu/govdoc/public1.html. Retrieved September 3, 2004.

DASL Project. (2004). Data and Story Library. http://lib.stat.cmu.edu/DASL. Retrieved September 4, 2004.

FedStats. (2004). Federal Interagency Council on Statistical Policy. www.fedstats.gov. Retrieved September 4, 2004.

Journal of Statistics in Education. (2004). JSE Data Archive. www.amstat.org/publications/jse/archive.htm. Retrieved September 4, 2004.

NASA. (2004). Planetary Factsheet. National Aeronautics and Space Administration. http://nssdc.gsfc.nasa.gov/planetary/factsheet. Retrieved September 4, 2004.

National Climatic Data Center. (2004). Publications. www5.ncdc.noaa.gov/pubs/publications.html. Retrieved September 4, 2004.

U.S. Census Bureau. (2004). Statistical Agencies (International). www.census.gov/main/www/stat_int.html. Retrieved September 4, 2004.

▓ ANNOTATED RESOURCES ▓▓▓▓▓▓▓▓▓▓▓▓▓▓▓▓

Collis, B. (1990). The best of research windows: Trends and issues in educational computing. Eugene, OR: International Society for Technology in Education. ERIC ED323993.

This is a summary of six database studies addressing the ability of students to formulate appropriate questions when they query a database.

Ehman, L., Glenn, A., Johnson, V., & White, C. (1992, Spring). Using computer databases in student problem solving: A study of eight social studies teachers' classrooms. *Theory and Research in Social Education.* 20(2), 179–206.

This article has information on problem-solving strategies, constructing fields, learner characteristics that prevent maximum use of a database lesson, appropriate size of a database, evidence of higher-order thinking, the role of the teacher, length of time for teaching a database-supported lesson, structure in a database lesson, and grouping.

Gaffuri, A. (1991). Expanding third graders' vocabulary using a data base, individual thesauri and brainstorming strategies. Ed.D. Practicum I Report, Early and Middle Childhood Program, Nova University, Ft. Lauderdale, FL. ERIC ED331035.

This is a study on using a database to help third-grade students improve their vocabularies.

Kern, J. F. (1990). Using "Readers' Guide to Periodical Literature" on CD-ROM to teach database searching to high school students. Ed.S. Practicum Report, Nova University, Ft. Lauderdale, FL. ERIC ED328291.

This is a comparison of student database searching of both computerized and print databases in an English class.

Lockard, J., & Abrams, P. D. (2001). *Computers for 21st century educators* (5th ed.). New York: Longman.

In Chapter 6 of their book, the authors discuss research on databases. They state that "relatively little research has appeared concerning measurable impacts of learning with databases, and so one must be cautious about generalizations." They have, however, found some older studies (1992, 1991, 1990, 1988) that support some general conclusions. Sources that Lockard and Abrams summarized are included in this annotated resources section.

Maor, D. (1991). Development of student inquiry skills: A constructivist approach in a computerized classroom environment. Paper presented at the Annual Meeting of the National Association for Research in Science Teaching (Lake Geneva, WI, April 7–10, 1991). ERIC ED336261.

This is about inquiry-based science teaching and the use of a computerized database on birds of Antarctica.

Rawitsch, D. (1988, November). The effects of computer use and student work style on database analysis activities in the social studies. In *Improving the use of technology in schools: What are we learning.* Research Bulletin #1. St. Paul, MN: MECC/University of Minnesota Center for the Study of Educational Technology, pp. 1–3.

In this practicum third graders built a database of words which they used as a thesaurus to support writing assignments. The focus of the work is on writing using a self-built database as a tool to encourage vocabulary development. A diagram of the format for the thesaurus/database is included.

White, C. S. (1990, Spring). Access to and use of databases in the social studies. *International Journal of Social Education.* 5(1), 61–73.

These studies yield some empirical evidence that database use improves students' higher-order thinking skills. Other conclusions resulted from this study as well.

Companion Web Site www.ablongman.com/thorsen3e

1. Go to Chapters 10–12 of the TechTactics web site. You will see links to many databases. Some of these links provide numbers only, which you must import into a database like Access or a spreadsheet like Excel. Others store their data in an online database, which allows you to do queries online without having to import data into Access or Excel. Two such databases on the web site are Valley of the Shadow 1 and 2 and County and City Data Books.

   ▓ Browse each database to find out what it is like and how it works.
   ▓ Write a question that you would like to answer using each database.
   ▓ Enter your queries and draw your conclusions. List your queries and in a short paragraph explain your conclusions.
   ▓ Write a short essay (less than 200 words) comparing and contrasting the operation of the two databases.

2. Go to Chapters 10–12 of the TechTactics web site. Go to any of the links that provide data as numbers that must be imported into a database for the creation of queries and sorts (NASA and the U.S. Census Bureau are two examples).

   ▓ Successfully import the data into the database that you are using.
   ▓ Write three questions you would like to answer with the data.
   ▓ Do the appropriate sorts and write related queries. Note these on the paper that you turn in to your instructor.
   ▓ Write a short essay (less than 200 words) on the conclusions that you drew from your sorts and queries.

Using Spreadsheets to Think about Numbers

- Describe when the use of a spreadsheet is appropriate in science, social studies, mathematics, and language arts.
- Be able to explain mean, median, mode, and standard deviation.
- Use descriptive statistics to describe phenomena about which you have found or gathered data.
- Know how to make graphs and charts using computer software.
- Know how to use charts and graphs to visualize information.
- Know how to use pivot tables to tease out patterns in information.
- Design a pivot table.
- Use formulas and "Goal Seek" to ask "what if" questions.

NUMBERS AS TOOLS BEYOND MATH

Numbers are among humankind's oldest friends. Cuneiform tablets in the Middle East, examples of our first writing, were engraved with numbers. These numbers recorded business transactions. Do you recall the reason for the development of the first electrically powered computer? Numbers were, again, at the root of this development. The U.S. military needed to make complex calculations quickly during World War II; it needed to calculate the trajectory of artillery shells.

Although one could not say that we are in love with numbers (in fact, numbers scare many people), numbers and the ability to manipulate them quickly and accurately are the basis for everything that makes modern medicine, science, and business viable. Knowing how to use and think about numbers is one reason for our metamorphosis from hunter-gatherer to information worker.

> Our society is based on our ability to use numbers effectively

A criticism of our educational system is that children learn only the mechanics of working with numbers instead of learning how to apply numbers to practical situations. At some level this may be true in many classrooms, but for a number of reasons other than teacher negligence or district apathy. From the point of view of a classroom teacher, the task of helping children think with numbers is quite daunting.

> Spreadsheets help students think about the concepts behind numbers

For example, one challenge lies in children's skill level in working with numbers compared to the kinds of problems that are interesting and useful for them to solve. It

242

is only interesting to figure out where two cars, boats, or trains that are going different speeds meet between points A and B once or twice. The reason most students learn how to solve this problem is for practice in identifying and practicing the steps leading to its solution. Once students find a solution, they know nothing more about the world than they did before they learned how to solve the problem.

Another challenge lies in our perception of where numbers fit in the curriculum. Many teachers, as students themselves, struggled to understand numbers. Because so many people lack confidence with numbers, they see them as obstacles rather than useful tools that help us think well. Students study history, social studies, and science diligently. They learn the meanings of words. For example, when they study government they learn the definition of an oligarchy. In science, they learn the definition of a mitochondrion. Moreover, they learn to attach words to pictures, such as recognizing the tundra from an unlabeled picture or recognizing countries on a map in geography. They use words and pictures as tools to understand our world.

Numbers are tools too, and like words they have meaning both as text and as pictures. However, we use them less frequently than words or pictures to help students make sense of the world. Very few social studies teachers have had the training and tools to show students how to analyze social and historical problems and trends with numbers. Young science students are limited to using numbers they know how to calculate manually as they study complex problems. They must learn facts and theories on faith from those who do know how to work and think with numbers derived from complex calculations.

> Numbers, like text, are tools that help us understand our world

The goal of this chapter is to raise the level of understanding of the contribution of spreadsheets to the learning process for those who teach science, social studies, and to some extent mathematics. The purpose of this chapter is not to focus on mathematics or tools for mathematics. That is a book of its own, especially for high school-level mathematics. Rather, the aim here is to provide some examples where spreadsheets have helped students explore common science and social studies topics that are taught from elementary school through high school. You must use your imagination as you read about the different possibilities and use your creativity and experience with children to generate lessons that will work in your classroom.

> Teachers in many content areas can use numbers to help students learn concepts

Spreadsheets provide answers to the same kinds of problems as databases: analysis, prediction, and description of an unknown, but they are designed to work with numbers rather than text. They even provide tools for performing sorts and queries. Furthermore, spreadsheets require a very similar instructional model to databases, though there is some variation. First, there must be a problem. Second, the students must choose and/or acquire the data they need to solve the problem. Third, students must figure out how to set up the problem on the spreadsheet and decide which tool(s) to use. Finally, students must analyze and present their results as well as check their results with an outside source.

> Methods for using spreadsheets are similar to those for databases

Managing the classroom using spreadsheets is very similar to managing the classroom using databases. In the one computer classroom, the teacher uses an LCD projector and works through the problem with the whole class, using the spreadsheet to stimulate class discussion. Another approach is to set up the computer as a center and require groups to work through the problem together while other groups work at other centers. For five-computer classrooms, spreadsheets, like databases, are

> It is helpful to have students work in groups when they use spreadsheets

especially suited to group work because of the interactive question-generating process they stimulate. In addition, students working together can generally decide on the keystrokes they need to get their problem solved, while students working alone sometimes are utterly lost. To begin our exploration of spreadsheets, let us look at the kinds of problems that spreadsheets can solve.

Choosing the Problem

At this point in the book, you will know without being told that the first step in using a spreadsheet is choosing and describing the problem. The focus in this chapter is on choosing problems for which the solution involves only simple arithmetic that we have all learned by upper elementary school: using formulas, elementary statistics, and percentages. Table 13.1 is a list of some possible problems and the kind of elementary mathematics that people use to think about them. As an expert in what you teach, you can probably generate more if you think about it.

Table 13.2 lists further topics that you can explore if you wish to read the articles they reference. K–12 teachers wrote all of these articles, and the lessons have been executed in classrooms. Some of the problems described in Table 13.2 involve different mathematical concepts than formulas, statistics, and percentages and are for specific scientific and mathematics topics in high school. If high school mathematics or science is your specialty, these resources will provide you with some valuable insight into uses for spreadsheets in your classroom.

THE VERSATILE SPREADSHEET

"Technology is an essential tool for teaching and learning mathematics effectively; it extends the mathematics that can be taught and enhances students' learning." (National Council of Teachers of Mathematics, 2003)

A spreadsheet is a collection of tools

Spreadsheets are a tool made of many tools. They are like a Swiss Army knife. If you need a screwdriver, it is available. If you need a knife, saw, or bottle opener, those tools are available as well. Some tools are more complex than others.

The remainder of this chapter will be devoted to a study of some simple and intermediate tools available in spreadsheets. Not every tool is appropriate for every age level or every problem. For example, tools used on a regular basis in the ninth grade may be used for enrichment in the fifth or sixth grade. Nor can this chapter capture every possible use for every spreadsheet tool. As you read, you must think about the curriculum you teach or that you will teach someday.

Easy Spreadsheet Tools

A spreadsheet is a grid that consists of cells with columns designated by letters and rows designated by numbers. The spreadsheet at its most simple level allows the user to type numbers into the cells and then add, subtract, multiply, or divide them. Once

TABLE 13.1 Examples of Problems for Which Spreadsheets Are Useful	
Problem	**Spreadsheet Tool**
Use demographic data for populations (human, animal, plant) to track changes in their (numbers, locations, health, wealth) over time. Use the data to explain the changes.	Charts and graphs; elementary statistics
Determine the monthly payment on a loan using different repayment amounts, terms, and interest rates.	Formula
Measure the speed and distance objects move over different lengths and heights of inclined planes.	Formula
If the sun were the size of a basketball, what would be the relative sizes and distances for objects in the rest of the solar system?	Percentages
Given the history of change in my city (country, hemisphere), what will my city be like in fifty years when I am getting ready to retire? In ten years when I will start looking for a job?	Creating a formula; charts, graphs
Given the rate of extinction of plant and animal species over the last fifty years, how many more species will be extinct by the time I am 20? 30? 40?	Creating a formula; charts, graphs
Using the equation $e = mc^2$, how much matter would I need to run my refrigerator (my house, our city) for a year?	Formula
How would a change in the minimum wage affect the businesses in my city? How would it affect me as a young worker?	Percentages
What happens to the number of bacteria in a bean infusion over time? (Cuevas, 1994)	Charts, graphs
Measure the temperature change of water in different-colored containers that are standing in the sun.	Charts, graphs
How are population growth, land area, and irrigated land related to a country's wealth and to each other?	Percentages, charts, graphs
How do prices change when there is a shortage or surplus of a commodity?	Percentages, charts, graphs
Is there a relationship between the accumulation of national debt and national income?	Charts, graphs
Compare the effect of acid rain to ordinary water on sprouting seeds. Compare the sprout rate of weed seeds to food seeds (Cuevas, 1994).	Elementary statistics; charts, graphs
What are the effects of natural disasters and the weather on national economies?	Charts, graphs
Analyze voting patterns to determine how diverse populations affect politics in the United States.	Charts, graphs

a series of numbers has been computed or acquired, the spreadsheet user then builds a chart or graph to visualize this data. The chart is created with a pop-up menu and either displayed on the worksheet with the numbers or on a sheet by itself. Furthermore, the chart and all of the numbers may be cut and pasted into a word-processed document or **dynamically linked** to a presentation. Simple arithmetic problems that

DYNAMICALLY LINKED
If the student changes the chart in the spreadsheet, then the copy of the chart that was put in the presentation will reflect those changes.

TABLE 13.2 Examples of More Problems, Their Content Areas, and Grade Levels		
Topic	**Grade Level**	**Subject**
Understand the stock market (Whitmer, 1992)	7, 8, 9	Math/economics
Set up and solve word problems (Verderber, 1990)	7, 8, 9	Math
Explore the composition and amount of marine debris (Lynch & Walton, 1998)	9–12	Science
Teach area and perimeter (Widmer & Sheffield, 1998)	5–12	Math
Compare average yearly concentration of carbon dioxide to average midtropospheric temperature for a lesson on greenhouse gasses (Slattery, Hundley, Finegan-Stoll, & Becker, 1998)	11–12	Science
Trend analysis of weather (Slater, 1998)	8–10	Science
Model population growth (Slater, 1998)	10–12	Science
Explore the history of convicts in Australia (Lloyd, 1998)	10–12	Social studies
Set up and solve equations (Niess, 1998)	7–9	Math
Calculate ratios and proportions of the human body using their own and classmates' measurements as the data. Compare these calculations to Leonardo da Vinci's calculations based on his drawing "The Proportions of the Human Figure" (1492) (Morgan & Jernigan, 1998)	7–12	Art, science, math
Track expenses on a virtual trip (Bitner, Wadlington, Partridge, & Bitner, 1999)	4–8	Social studies
Understand probability (Pugalee, 1999)	7–9	Math
Understand how batteries work (Albrecht & Firedrake, 1999)	2–12	Science
Teach matrices and geometric transformations (Feicht, 1999)	7–12	Math
Understand exponential population growth and patterns (Drier, 1999)	3–9	Social science, math
Model graphs and functions (Manouchehri & Pagnucco, 2000)	7–11	Math

yield elementary statistics (mean, median, range, mode, and standard deviation) and resulting charts are powerful tools to help children see the relationships numbers have to each other and the real world.

Another mathematical tool that children use at an early age is the formula. Examples of mathematical formulas that children learn early include:

Distance = rate $\times$ time

Interest = rate $\times$ principal

Perimeter = S1 + S2 + S3 . . .

Area of a rectangle = length $\times$ width

Percentage = $N1 / N2$

Spreadsheets are built to allow people to enter a formula and then ask "what if" questions. When you are using a formula in a spreadsheet, it is easy to solve more than one problem. Consequently, students can see what the formula means in many problems rather than looking for an answer to just one problem.

One Cautionary Note

In a study on the effective use of spreadsheets in the classroom (Clarke, Ayres, & Sweller, 2005), the researchers found that if students are being taught a math concept using spreadsheets and are learning to use the spreadsheet simultaneously, they have difficulty with both the spreadsheet and the concept. The research indicates that the spreadsheet manipulations should be taught first and then the math concept. The reverse was found for students already skilled in the use of spreadsheets. These students learned more if both the concept and any minor spreadsheet operation are taught at the same time.

The basis of this research results comes from theories about cognitive load. Remember Miller's 7 ± 2 rule. Only so much can be held in working memory and transferred to long term memory at the same time. The results of this research can be generalized to topics other than mathematics—science and social sciences, for example. Be sure students understand how to operate the tool before they try to use the tool to learn content.

DESCRIPTIVE STATISTICS

Example: Understanding How Soil Affects Plants

We will continue now by looking into two classrooms where the students are studying topics that involve descriptive statistics. These two upper-elementary science classrooms are studying soil composition and plant growth. The reason the students are using a spreadsheet is to help answer the question, "What do these numbers we are collecting mean?" The question the two teachers have given their students is, "Do different soils affect how fast plants grow?" Although the teacher in the first classroom is trying to do a good job with what she has, she could be doing more to help her students realize the potential that numbers have to help us understand our world better.

The Mean Bean

FIELD TRIP
13.1

Picture in your mind Ms. Clayton's fifth-grade students, who are growing twenty bean plants in different kinds of soil–humus, clay, and sand. The beans all received the same sunlight and the same amount of water. The students measured the growth of the beans at the end of three weeks. Then they calculated their averages by hand, and none of the groups' averages matched the others. Ms. Clayton finally told the students that their averages were pretty much "in the same ballpark" and since they were studying science, not math, they didn't have to go back and recalculate one more time to see whose math was wrong. Her real reason for saying this is that she just didn't have time to have the students redo the calculations. Furthermore, she knew that some of her more challenged students would just get frustrated and not redo their averages anyway. The point was that the beans grown in humus were taller according to everyone's calculations, even though the numbers didn't match exactly.

In creating such a lesson, the teacher may *feel* that she or he has encouraged students to use numbers to analyze and solve a problem. She may take some pride in the fact that she didn't let the students get so bogged down in arithmetic problems that they lost sight of the real goal: to study soil types. In fact, however, a lesson conducted this way encouraged the development of some misconceptions on the part of students, all having to do with numbers and how to use them to solve problems.

▨ She ignored "precision of measurement" issues.
▨ She has led the students to believe that because one average is different from another average, the two populations they represent are always different.

In contrast, let us look at Ms. Hull's fifth-grade classroom doing the same experiment but using a spreadsheet. In this classroom, the experiment was the same, but keeping and analyzing records was different. At the end of the experiment, the students measured the beans and entered their measurements into a spreadsheet. Mrs. Hull had students work in groups at the five computers in her classroom. The teacher asked the students which soil grew the tallest beans. The students determined the average height of the beans in each group. There was no need for them to do the calculations by hand when a spreadsheet calculated quickly and accurately. She reminded students of the importance of accuracy as they entered the numbers they had obtained from their measurements. She asked each group to check their work against the work of the other groups. The averages that the different groups calculated didn't match, but not because of inaccurate math. Each group found that its average was slightly different than the average of other groups because the students weren't able to be precise in their measurements. Ms. Hull used this activity to generate a discussion about errors in measurement. After the "error of measurement" discussion was over, each group concluded that the beans grown in humus were the tallest, while beans grown in sand were a very close second. The beans grown in clay were much shorter than the beans grown in either of the other two media.

Ms. Hull's next exercise for the students was to send them back to their five computers to create a chart illustrating the growth rates of beans in the three different kinds of soil. Students took some time getting their chart right. It was not clear to them whether to use the height of the beans or whether they should use three averages that they calculated. They had to argue and experiment before they completed their charts correctly (Figure 13.1).

Then Ms. Hull said, "Our calculations and charts show that the beans grown in humus are, on the average, 1 centimeter taller than beans grown in sand and 4 centimeters taller than beans grown in clay. What would happen if we changed the scale of the charts from 10 centimeters to 64 units?" The children re-created the chart after changing the scale of the chart from 10 to 64 (Figure 13.2). Ms. Hull then asked them why the two charts were so different. She also asked them whether, if they saw only the chart based on 64 units, they would think that the beans grown in clay are very much shorter than the beans grown in humus. As the children worked through this exercise, they learned how people could lie to them using statistics (Huff, 1982). Their teacher concluded this part of the lesson by asking if it is right to try to influence people by changing the units on a chart or graph to make it say what they want it to say. In this way, she was teaching them not only science but also the ethics of science.

Then Ms. Hull made another observation. She said, "Look! Here is a bean growing in sandy soil that is taller than some of the beans growing in humus. How can we really know that beans grown in humus are generally taller than beans that are planted in sandy soil? According to our averages, all beans grown in humus should be taller than beans grown in sand."

The children did not know how to explain this, so Ms. Hull proceeded to introduce standard deviation to her class. She explained that there is a mathematical way of determining how likely it is that beans grow in humus better than they grow in sand. Using an LCD to display the spreadsheet of bean measurements that students have entered, she showed them how to find the standard deviation for each group of beans. First she explained that the term *standard deviation* means "a way of comparing individual scores of measurements to the mean."

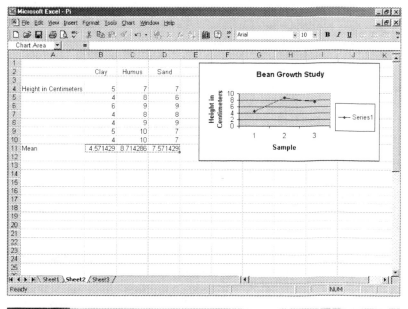

FIGURE 13.1 Bean Problem

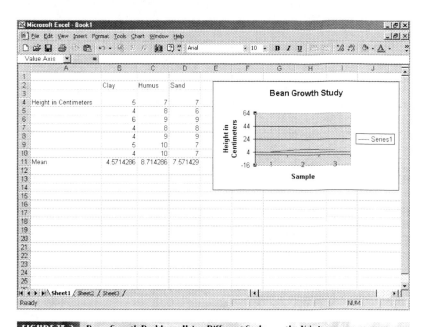

FIGURE 13.2 Bean Growth Problems Using Different Scales on the Y Axis

She went to the Insert menu item and chose Function (Figure 13.3). She said, "This can seem very intimidating because none of the words on the list mean anything to you because you have never studied statistics. Nevertheless, if you just persevere and click on Statistics first and then STDEV, for 'standard deviation' you will get a dialogue box (Figure 13.4). In this dialogue box, enter the range of

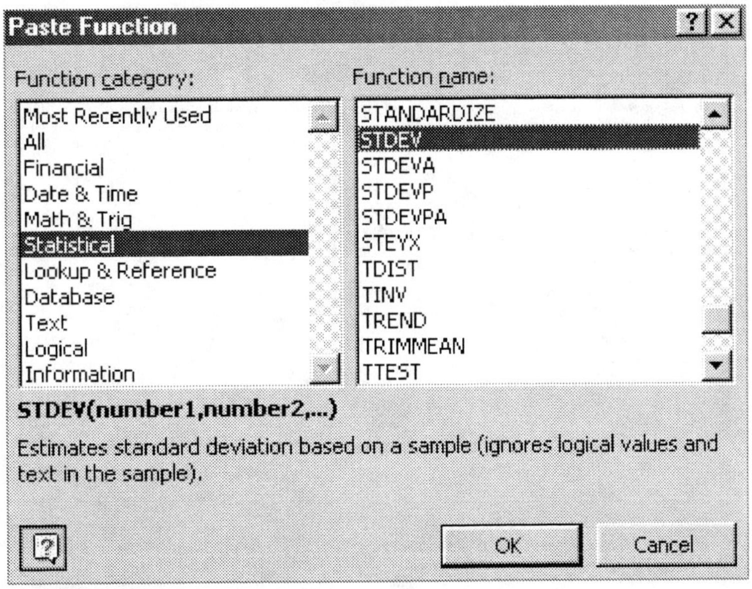

FIGURE 13.3 Choosing to Calculate a Standard Deviation

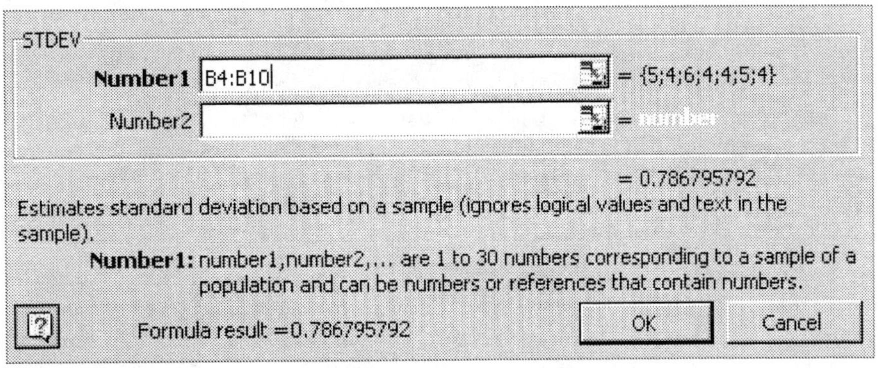

FIGURE 13.4 Calculating a Standard Deviation

cells (in this case B:4 to B:10) for which you want a standard deviation. Click on OK and the standard deviation will appear in the cell where you left your cursor. After doing this, you can repeat the process for the other two columns of bean measurements, or a shortcut is to simply select the cell where you have the completed standard deviation and drag your cursor across the next two rows. When you have finished, the worksheet will look like this." She showed them Figure 13.5.

Because this is a fifth-grade classroom, none of Ms. Hull's students understands the mathematics or mathematical theory behind a standard deviation. Nevertheless, they do understand "average." They can also understand that the "mean" does not describe any

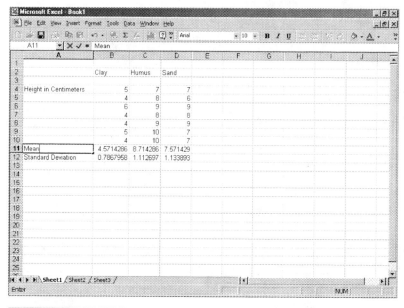

FIGURE 13.5 Standard Deviation of Bean Heights

one bean. Each bean is a little taller or shorter than the "mean bean." What they did not understand until this lesson is that even though one average is higher than another average, the two averages do not necessarily represent statistically different populations.

The spreadsheet helps students understand what the data mean

What does this mean? The standard deviation of clay-grown beans is 0.79 centimeter, for humus-grown, 1 centimeter, and for sand-grown, 1 centimeter (rounded). Now look at the heights of the clay-grown beans: 5, 4, 6, 4, 4, 5, 4 (centimeters). If you added 0.79 centimeter to any of the clay-grown beans, none of them would be as tall as either the humus- or the sand-grown beans. In other words, all the beans grown in clay are truly shorter than the beans grown in sand or humus. Common sense suggests that in another experiment, beans grown in clay are not likely to grow as tall as beans grown in sand or humus. On the other hand, if you look at the heights of the humus- and sand-grown beans and add or subtract 1 centimeter (the standard deviation for each group) to the height of any of the beans, then compare that bean to beans in the other group, you can see that there are many overlaps between the two groups. It could be that in a different test, the mean height of the beans grown in sand might be greater than the beans grown in humus.

Students in this fifth-grade classroom are learning some important lessons:

▓ You can't always believe what you see.
▓ Sometimes charts or graphs help you understand what numbers mean, but you have to be clever about reading them.
▓ There are ways to test numbers that can help you make difficult judgments.

Before going further with Ms. Hull and her students, we must come to an understanding about a philosophical question. The question is, "Should a class of fifth graders

Why should students learn to apply descriptive statistics to the problems they study?

be introduced to a difficult statistical concept such as standard deviation?" These children cannot understand or do the math behind this statistical test. What purpose is there in introducing such an idea? The premise behind many examples in this book is that the teacher is not teaching mathematics but rather science and social science concepts and methods. Advanced math teachers in high school have students use graphing calculators to free students from the tedium, distraction, and possibility of error created by doing pencil-and-paper calculations. Similarly, science and social studies teachers can free students of similar distractions by using spreadsheets. In the example of Mrs. Hull's class, the concept behind the standard deviation is not difficult to grasp. That a student doesn't understand the mathematics behind a standard deviation makes no more difference than the same student not knowing the chemistry behind a pH test strip. Both the standard deviation and the pH test strip are *tools*. When a skilled teacher uses them effectively, they can help students better understand the concepts and events that they study.

We have just looked in on two teachers' classrooms, Ms. Clayton who did not use spreadsheets and Ms. Hull who did. You have a general idea of how a spreadsheet might work in a classroom. You can see how it might change and amplify children's conceptual understanding of the information that they study as well as provide a basis for a constructivist approach to developing a lesson plan. To further whet your appetite for using spreadsheets, we will back up and take a more global view of some spreadsheet-assisted problems involving statistics that other teachers have integrated into the work of their classrooms.

DESCRIPTIVE STATISTICS: WHAT DO THEY MEAN?

We are going to talk about four different statistical terms: mean, median, mode, and standard deviation. Mathematically, they are quite easy to compute. A third grader working at grade level can calculate the first three by hand and the fourth with three clicks of a mouse in a spreadsheet. Meaning is more difficult than computing. There are two stages through which students progress as they learn what these statistics mean. In the first stage, students can understand the implications of a mean or a median for a data set if a teacher or another student explains it. At another level, the student says, "Oh, if I could just compare the mean and the median for this data set, I could understand why *x* happened instead of *y*."

Descriptive statistics are derived from a range of data. Let us return to the bean study. In Figure 13.6, you see the mean, median, and mode for each group of beans. Notice also the formula in the formula bar. The spreadsheet does the math. All you have to do is indicate the range of cells for which you want one of these measures of **central tendency**. While we were on our field trip, we did not look at the medians and means of the three types of beans. However, they are easily calculated. Each of these statistics gives us slightly different information about a data set.

Mode

The mode is the most frequently occurring score in the **distribution** or group. Although mode is the least reliable of the three measures of central tendency, it neverthe-

Understanding the implication of a number

CENTRAL TENDENCY
What the "middle" of the data looks like. The **mean** is the arithmetic average that students are familiar with because grades are often based on students' mean scores. The **mode** is the most frequently occurring number, and the **median** is the middle score.

DISTRIBUTION
The group of scores that you are working with. For example, all of the heights for the beans grown in clay are one distribution.

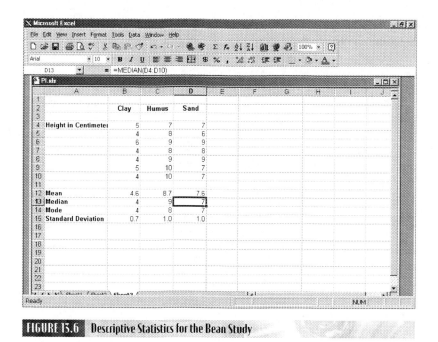

FIGURE 13.6 Descriptive Statistics for the Bean Study

less provides information. For example, if you knew that in Africa the most common (mode) gross national product is $7 billion per year but the average (mean) gross national product for the continent is $32 billion, you might guess that there are many poor countries and a few rich ones. Likewise with the bean study, you know that the mode for beans grown in sand is 7 centimeters and the mean is 7.6 centimeters. There are a few beans that are shorter than the "mean" bean.

> The mode is the most frequently occurring number

Median

The median is the middle score—the point above and below which an equal number of data fall. It is the most stable measure of central tendency. That means that if there are outliers in the data (extremes), these outliers do not influence the median nearly as much as they affect the mean. A classic example is a data set of salaries. In Figure 13.7 you see a list of salaries with both the mean and median salary for the data set. Note that the median reflects the more common salary, not the mean. The outliers are $56,000 and $75,000. These two people may represent management, while the rest of the salaries may represent clerical or professional staff. If someone wanting to get a job with this company had noted only the mean salary in the company, not the median salary, she would be disappointed with the company's offer. Similarly, if the bean study had had outliers, our impression of the "average" height of the beans would be far different if we looked at the mean rather than the median. Looking again at Figure 13.6, you can see that the mean and median are similar because there are no outliers. This is an important concept to teach children. Viewed from one perspective, using a mean when a median is more appropriate is another way that people can lie to them using statistics. From another perspective, understanding the concept of computing a

> The median is the middle number

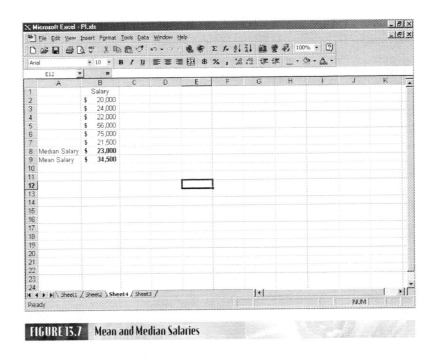

FIGURE 13.7 Mean and Median Salaries

median rather than a mean when there are outliers will give them a better understanding of what a "middle data point" of a data set is.

Mean

The mean is the arithmetic average of a group of numbers

The mean is the measure of central tendency with which most of us are most familiar. For example, when teachers compute student grades, they get a mean by adding each score and dividing by the number of scores. It is most helpful for data sets where the distribution of data points is normal. "Normal" means that they reflect a symmetrical curve—the proverbial "bell-shaped" curve. An example of a set of data points describing a roughly normal curve is 50, 60, 60, 70, 70, 70, 80, 80, 90. It is the same concept as grading on the curve—that is, constructing standards based on the highest and lowest grade. It is reflected in the assumption that on any test the fewest students will get As and Fs while the most will get Cs, with a fewer number of students receiving Bs and Ds. Look back a few lines at the data points describing a normal curve. This could be a set of scores on a test.

The mean, median, and mode give no different information about a range of numbers

The mean is a very useful measure of central tendency, but its flaw is the disruption caused by outliers. For this reason, it is important that students learn to report and reason with not only the mean, but also the median and the mode. You have already read one example in the previous section about how the mean is misleading when there are outliers in a distribution. Just to reinforce that point, let us try another, this one from *How to Lie with Statistics* (Huff, 1982). If the Oklahoma City Chamber of Commerce wanted to attract people to come to Oklahoma to live, they could advertise a comfortable average (mean) temperature of 60.2 degrees between 1890 and 1952.

The temperatures actually ranged between –17 and 113 degrees. We didn't even have to look at the median to catch the flaw in this use of the mean. We simply looked at the *range* of temperatures. You never have the whole picture of what a data set means unless you can see and explain the mean, median, mode, and range of the numbers in a dataset.

Using descriptive statistics to interpret a survey

Mean, Median, and Mode and Scales of Measurement

Not all measurements are the same. If your students do a survey, for example, they could collect information in several different formats. Not all of these formats are appropriate for use with all measures of central tendency (mean, median, and mode).

Suppose you are working as a team with a group of history and English teachers who have assigned their students to do an oral history of your community. Your students visit a retirement home to collect stories from residents, and as a part of the project ask residents a series of demographic questions to provide context for the oral histories. Some of the questions include the following.

1. Sex (1 = male, 2 = female)
2. Year born
3. Age you began your first full-time job
4. Preference on a scale between 1 and 4 for watching television
5. Preference on a scale between 1 and 4 for going on a walk
6. Actual hours spent watching television each week
7. Actual hours spent walking outside each week

The first three questions represent different kinds of numbers (questions 4 through 7 represent the same kind of number). Table 13.3 provides examples for each kind of number. With Table 13.3 in mind, think about the following statements:

1. The mean sex at the retirement home is 1.7.
2. The mode for sex at the retirement home is 2.

TABLE 13.3 Measurement Scales

Scale of Measurement	Example	Appropriate Measure of Central Tendency
Nominal	1 = Male 2 = Female 1 = Yes 2 = No	Mode
Ordinal	1 short 2 medium 3 tall height	Mode
Interval	30 31 32 22 34 35 36 37 degrees Celsius	Mean, median, mode
Ratio	10 20 30 40 50 60 70 80 miles, watts, people, cattle	Mean, median, mode

3. The median age at the retirement home for first full-time job was 15.5 years.
4. The mean age at the retirement home for first full-time job was 13 years.
5. The mean preference for watching television was 1.5; the mean preference for taking a walk was 3.5.
6. The mean hours spent watching television each week was 30; the mean hours spent walking outside each week was 1.

What does this all mean? Before you read the answers below, on a sheet of practice paper write your own interpretation of the survey results.

1. This finding is meaningless unless you believe that the nursing home is full of hermaphrodites in transition. Finding the mean of nominal results is a meaningless conclusion.
2. This finding is quite meaningful. It tells us that more women than men live at the retirement home.
3, 4. Three and four are interesting. If the mean age for first job is 15.5 years and the median age is 13 years, some of those old folks are outliers and must have started working when they were very young.
5, 6. Preferences for walking versus television were revealing and meaningful. The number of hours is interval data and thus meaningful when a mean, median, and mode are computed. Residents would rather be out walking, but instead they are sitting in front of televisions.

Standard Deviation

During our field trip when we observed students growing beans, we learned something about the standard deviation. It is probably the most commonly used measurement of **variability** because it is so stable. It is important to know how variable scores or other values are because it helps you understand whether you are dealing with the difference between two groups or just chance variation. Standard deviation also helps us decide whether two groups of people or objects ("populations") are the same or different. Just to reinforce the concept of standard deviation, let's look at it again in a different context. You just looked at a portion of a survey taken by a group of high school students working on an oral history of elderly residents at a nursing home. One part of the project was to compare their demographics with students' demographics to learn more about what causes the differences of viewpoints and lifestyles that exist between the generations. If, for example, the mean hours spent per week watching television at the retirement home is thirty and among high school students it is twenty-five, are retirement home dwellers and these high school students members of two different populations or members of the same group whose mean hours varied simply by chance? If the standard deviation for retirement home residents were six hours, the difference is most likely chance rather than genuine. If the standard deviation for high school students were six hours, the same would be true.

There are other, more precise methods for determining how likely it is that different means indicate different populations. At a basic level, however, this technique can begin to help students understand how to think about data. It is one more tool to help

> Understanding how to judge whether two groups of data are really different

VARIABILITY
The amount of dispersion of scores about a central value, such as the mean (Borg & Gall, 1989).

move students' interaction with information to the higher levels of Bloom's taxonomy. If this kind of analysis moves from the math teacher's classroom to the classrooms of the history teacher, science teacher, and English teacher, it will become second nature to our children early in their academic careers.

USING SIMPLE ARITHMETIC OUTSIDE THE MATH CLASS

Simple arithmetic means using addition, subtraction, multiplication, division, and percentages to solve problems. One way of using these spreadsheet functions is to allow students to check their math problems with spreadsheets. If they do their problems once by hand, they focus on knowing their math facts, such as what is "5 – 3"? If they use the spreadsheet to check their computational skills, they focus on process—for example, how to set up a subtraction problem.

However, there are many other ways to use simple arithmetic outside of math class. Since we have already looked at a science problem, let us consider a social studies problem and use a spreadsheet to think about it.

Suppose you are studying the Middle East in current affairs and you would really like your students to know more about the demographics of the countries and the relationships of the demographics to the turmoil in that area of the world. You have your students go to the CIA (2000) World Factbook on the Internet and make the worksheet shown in Figure 13.8. Think about how students might work with these

> Using arithmetic in social studies

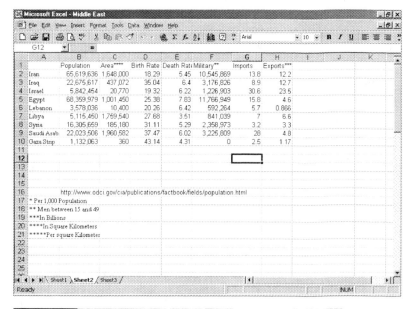

	A	Population	Area****	Birth Rate	Death Rate	Military**	Imports	Exports***
2	Iran	65,619,636	1,648,000	18.29	5.45	10,545,869	13.8	12.2
3	Iraq	22,675,617	437,072	35.04	6.4	3,176,826	8.9	12.7
4	Israel	5,842,454	20,770	19.32	6.22	1,226,903	30.6	23.5
5	Egypt	68,359,979	1,001,450	25.38	7.83	11,766,949	15.8	4.6
6	Lebanon	3,578,036	10,400	20.26	6.42	592,264	5.7	0.866
7	Libya	5,115,450	1,759,540	27.68	3.51	841,039	7	6.6
8	Syria	16,305,659	185,180	31.11	5.29	2,358,973	3.2	3.3
9	Saudi Arab	22,023,506	1,960,582	37.47	6.02	3,225,809	28	4.8
10	Gaza Strip	1,132,063	360	43.14	4.31	0	2.5	1.17

http://www.odci.gov/cia/publications/factbook/fields/population.html
* Per 1,000 Population
** Men between 15 and 49
*** In Billions
**** In Square Kilometers
***** Per square Kilometer

FIGURE 13.8 Middle Eastern Demographics

numbers to learn more. Given the numbers they have, they can ask the following questions:

1. What is the differential between the birth and death rate for each country? What are the implications of this differential? What do the countries with the largest and smallest differentials have in common?
2. How many people are there per square kilometer in each country? What are the implications of these numbers?
3. What is the differential between imports and exports in each country? What are the implications of this differential? What do the countries with the largest and smallest differentials have in common?
4. What percentage of the population of each country are men of military age? Why is it larger in some countries than others? Are countries with more men of military age more aggressive than others?

Students can use the spreadsheet to quickly acquire the answer to these questions. Using their reasoning skills, together with data in their texts and on the Internet, they can synthesize the answers to the other questions listed above as well.

The categories in Figure 13.8 are only a few of the categories the students could be working with. In addition, there are other demographic categories (see Figure 13.5) along with accompanying text information on such topics as religion and kind of government. With some imagination, a student could ask and answer many questions using simple addition, subtraction, division, multiplication, and percentages.

> Different kinds of charts and graphs are useful for different purposes

CHARTS AND GRAPHS

Once you or your class has gathered numbers on a topic, entered them into a spreadsheet, and calculated means, medians, modes, and percentages, there is more that you can do to help your students understand the significance of their findings. They can turn their numbers into pictures with charts and graphs. Not all charts and graphs do the same thing. Spreadsheets typically offer many different kinds of charts. Excel, for example, offers fourteen different kinds of charts and graphs, with subsets for formatting associated with each. The rest of this section will be devoted to explaining the major kinds of charts and the kinds of information for which they are most useful.

Bar Charts and Column Charts

> Bar charts for comparisons

First, let us look at the anatomy of a chart. In Figure 13.9, you see data with labels that indicate how those numbers are represented on a chart. In Figure 13.10, you see a chart representing one data series. In Figure 13.11, you see a chart representing two data series. You can see that this graphic representation brings the numbers to life. The name for what you are looking at is "a bar chart representing two data series." Look again at the data in Figure 13.10. Would it make sense to add a third series to this chart given the data available in Figure 13.9? The answer is "probably not," unless you would

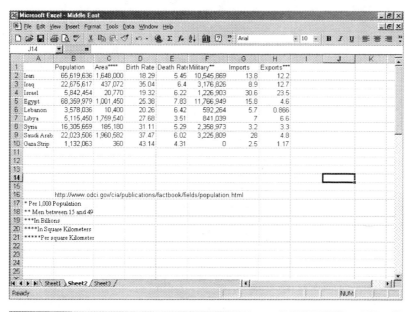

FIGURE 13.9 Anatomy of a Chart

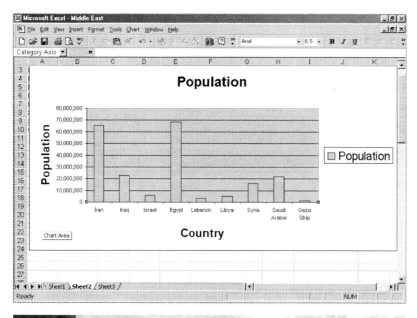

FIGURE 13.10 Chart for One Data Series: Population

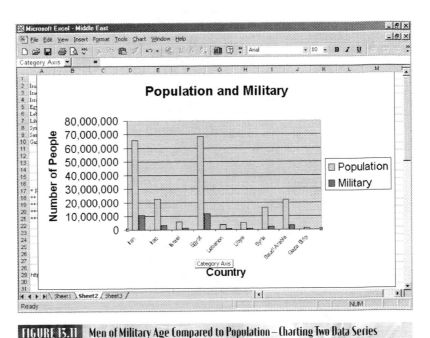

FIGURE 13.11 Men of Military Age Compared to Population – Charting Two Data Series

want to add a series that compares land area for each country. The units for birth rate, death rate, imports, and exports are very different and would not even show up on a chart measuring other series in the millions.

Pie Charts

Use pie charts to see a relationship of the parts to the whole

Pie charts are always used with only one data series. They give the viewer a sense of how the parts relate to the whole. See Figure 13.12.

Area Charts and Bar Charts – Looking at Data over Time

Use area and bar charts to look at trends

One activity that is common in both history and the sciences is looking at data over time ("trends"). Charts are helpful because they make relationships between numbers quite clear. Read the following numbers: income per household in 1990 and 1995 ($29,606 and $32,606) and retail sales per household in 1990 and 1995 ($16,645 and $25,309). Having just glanced at these numbers, what could you say about them? Now read the chart in Figure 13.13 and make a relevant comment about the numbers. Your students will experience similar epiphanies.

Pivot Tables

Pivot tables are one more way to help students summarize information. This time, let's take our example from a biology class. In your biology class you may have had

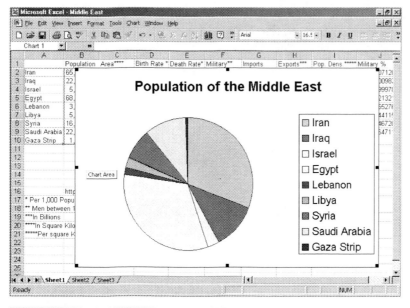

FIGURE 13.12 The Pie Chart — Looking at the Whole

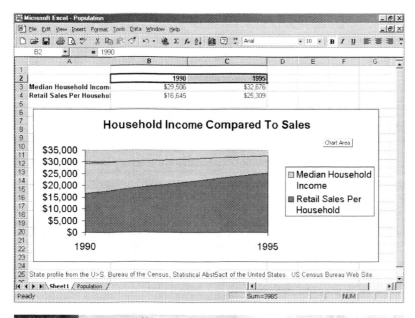

FIGURE 13.13 Comparison of Income and Spending

students count the number of certain kinds of birds that visited the area outside the classroom window at a certain time of day during the months of December and April. At the end of April, your students have a table that looks like Figure 13.14, only much longer. Now they need to summarize and interpret the data that they have collected. This is where the pivot table is quite helpful. Look at Figure 13.15. Even without the help of a chart, patterns emerge when students read the totals columns and rows. For example, it is clear that chickadees are winter birds and goldfinches and meadowlarks are spring birds. Not only can students read this pivot table, they may also turn it into a series of charts and graphs, depending on the questions they are asking.

> Use pivot tables to get different perspectives on data

Formulas

> Use formulas to answer "what if" questions

Finally, we will look at the formula, a way of using the spreadsheet to do "what if" exercises with students. The spreadsheet function that we will use for this exercise is "Goal Seek." First, let us start with a simple problem, understanding the relationships among distance, rate, and time.

Suppose you would like to investigate how long it will take to get between two cities driving a car at different speeds and how that might compare to flying in an airplane. You simply set up the formula on a spreadsheet as you see it in Figure 13.16. Now you want to ask a "what if" question. Simply by changing numbers in the cells D7 and E7, you can get a variety of combination of rates and times. Try it.

The "Goal Seek" dialogue box (Figure 13.17) is another tool for asking "what if" questions. An example of a goal seek question is, "How fast would I have to go

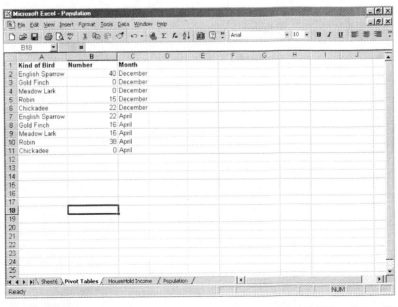

FIGURE 13.14 Data for a Pivot Table

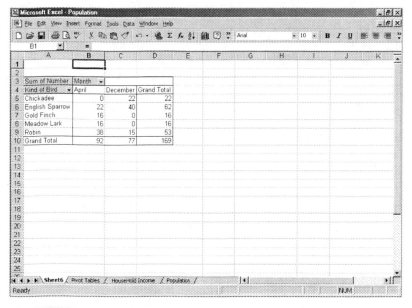

FIGURE 13.15 The Pivot Table

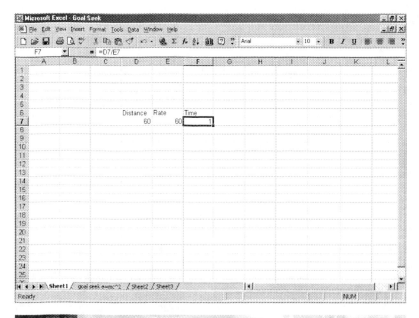

FIGURE 13.16 Distance, Rate, and Time

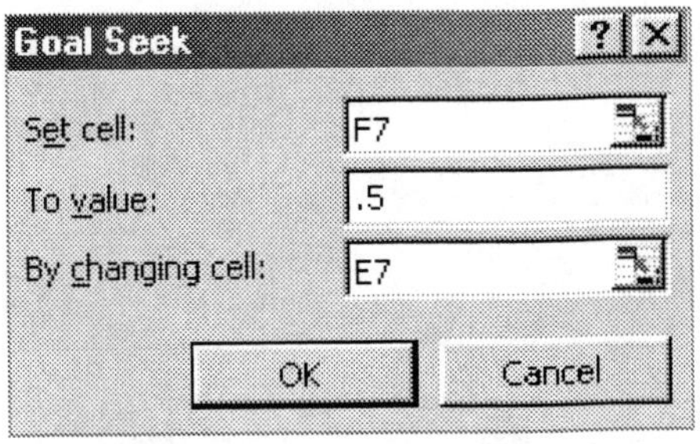

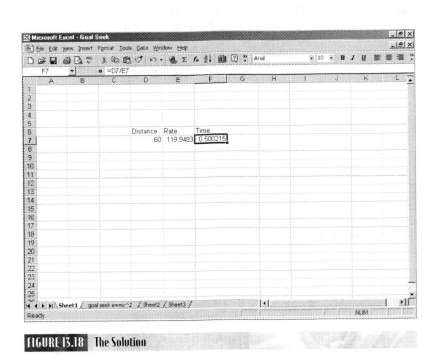

FIGURE 13.17 Looking at Alternatives

if I wanted to go somewhere 60 miles away in a half an hour?" (Figure 13.17). The answer is 119 miles per hour in the Rate cell (Figure 13.18). To change the time to three-quarters of an hour, invoke the goal seek dialogue box and replace ".5" with ".75." You may change the kinds of questions you ask the formula by changing the cell that contains the base formula for the problem. In other words, any time the content you teach contains a formula, you may design problems that encourage students to ask "what if" questions to explore the meaning and implications of the concept they are studying. The trick with this exercise, as it is with all spreadsheet functions, is providing a meaningful scenario or context from which students can work.

FIGURE 13.18 The Solution

A MODEL FOR SPREADSHEET USE

Like databases, spreadsheets are useful for specific problems. Typically, the spreadsheet is not used in isolation, but as a tool in working on a larger problem (see Table 13.4). Use of the spreadsheet is part of a larger picture. The overall model includes several steps:

1. Write a problem scenario or case study. (Teacher)
2. Identify the parts of the problem to which a spreadsheet applies. (Teacher and students)
3. Determine which spreadsheet tools will be useful.
4. Gather the data. (Students)
5. Place the data in a spreadsheet and format it so that it can be used. (Students)
6. Do the analysis, create the charts/graphs, etc. (Students)
7. Explain the analysis—what does it mean? Does it make sense? (Students)
8. Compare the analysis to conclusions made by experts if available. (Students)
9. Write a report or create a presentation to describe and explain the findings. (Students)

BLOOM'S TAXONOMY AND SPREADSHEETS

Spreadsheets are tools that challenge students to work at the middle and higher levels of the taxonomy (Table 13.5). Because spreadsheets encourage students to be thoughtful and to use numbers to solve problems (as opposed to teaching them to manipulate numbers), the levels of the taxonomy that are addressed are different. As you make an effort to teach to all levels of the taxonomy, you will find that spreadsheets assist you in filling in the middle and upper levels with meaningful exercises.

PDAs

A PDA is a personal digital assistant. It is smaller and less expensive than a computer, with prices ranging from $200 to $500. It has an operating system (OS) just like

TABLE 13.4 Summary of Common Spreadsheet Uses

Analyzing information gathered from the school, community, and environment	Descriptive statistics functions; charts and graphs
Comparing numbers: populations, speeds, distances, time	Descriptive statistics functions; charts and graphs
Viewing the same information from different perspectives	Pivot table; charts and graphs
Asking "what if" questions	Formulas

TABLE 13.5 Bloom's Taxonomy for Spreadsheets

The Cognitive Process Dimension	The Knowledge Dimension			
	Factual	Conceptual	Procedural	Meta-Cognitive
Remember	Recognizing information on a chart or graph	Recognizing categories of facts	Knowing how to create a chart, pivot table, or graph; linking pages, using functions, etc.	–
Understand	Knowing how to generate descriptive statistics	Knowing the use of descriptive statistics and formulas	–	–
Apply	Implementing/combining spreadsheet tools and processes to generate solutions	Applying descriptive statistics, pivot tables, or a formula to a problem	–	–
Analyze	Knowing what kind of chart or graph, formula, or pivot table matches the information at hand	Interpreting the results of statistics, formulas, or pivot tables	–	Knowing when a chart or graph is useful; knowing how to relate a finding in a spreadsheet to other knowledge
Evaluate	Checking the accuracy of spreadsheet entries	Looking at spreadsheet results to see that they make sense	Trouble shooting formulas, pivot tables, charts, and graphs when they don't work	–
Create	Creating a spreadsheet	Planning the configuration of information in a spreadsheet	Generating new formulas	Generating the kind of problems that spreadsheets solve

a computer. The two most common operating systems are Palm and Windows CE. These operating systems synchronize with the operating systems of desktop computers to allow for the transfer of files and data among the PDA and as many computers as necessary. Also, PDAs support scaled-back versions of software used on desktop/laptop machines, such as Word, Excel, and Access. Furthermore, there are special applications and hardware for PDAs, such as outlining software, sketching software, calculators, e-books, keyboards, and probes (instruments for the collection of data from events occurring outside the computer—thermometers, movement measurement, etc.). Used for collecting data in the field and uploading it to a spreadsheet on a large computer, PDAs can be a valuable tool for teachers.

FIELD TRIP 13.1

PDAs

Mr. Wang teaches middle school health. Aware of the current trend for young people to eat the wrong foods and eat too much of them, Mr. Wang used PDAs to give what he hopes will be lifelong skills to his students for watching and monitoring their diet. He wrote and received a grant that allowed him to buy one PDA for every five students in his class, along with Excel and Word. He also found a spreadsheet on the web, of calories and portion sizes of most foods available to his students.

At the beginning of the unit, Mr. Wang gave the students basic instruction on how to use the Excel spreadsheet on the PDA—just enough information so that they would know how to enter information. He set up their spreadsheets himself and downloaded the basic spreadsheet with the information he had.

He then divided the students into five groups of six and had the students take the PDAs home and go through their cupboards, entering the names of boxed and packaged foods, portion sizes, and nutrition information that might be missing from the spreadsheet he pre-loaded into the PDAs. At the end of the entry cycle, Mr. Wang collected the PDAs and combined the spreadsheets, making one spreadsheet for the whole class. The culminating activity for the class was a trip to the computer lab, where students worked in pairs with the spreadsheet for which they had collected data, making a two-week menu of meals with correct portion sizes, and listing the amount of proteins, fats, and carbohydrates. Mr. Wang wanted to use the foods students had in their homes for this assignment to be sure that their learning was contextualized—that is, it related to their real lives, not what they dreamed they might eat if they had the money or the access.

In a perfect world, Mr. Wang's lesson plan would have worked just like this, but as any teacher knows, the world is not perfect. Perhaps the most time-consuming glitch in this scheme was combining the spreadsheets. In spite of Mr. Wang's encouragement to be accurate, students misspelled names of the foods they entered (Cherios, Cheerios, Cherrios). Mr. Wang had to sort the spreadsheet and eliminate duplicate entries and change misspelled ones. In the end, he was not entirely sure all of the numbers were correct, so he tried to choose what seemed to be the most sensible.

And then there was the shy, confused little girl who somehow deleted her group's spreadsheet after two of the students in her group had already entered their information. The worst part of that was that Mr. Wang hadn't yet given those students credit for the number of foods they had entered, so not only was their work lost, he didn't know how to score them on their work. In the end, he used the honor system and asked them how many foods they had entered. Privately, he vowed to keep up the next time he did this.

Another problem which Mr. Wang could not control was with a spreadsheet that would not load. No matter what he did, he received nothing but error messages. So in the end, Mr. Wang was able to combine only three and a half spreadsheets for the class to use for their meal planning exercise.

More about PDAs—Thinking about the Field Trip

As you can see, although they were not indispensable in this case, the PDAs were useful timesavers. Having students write their data down on a sheet of paper and bring it to school to enter on a computer would have been logistically difficult and even more prone to error than using the PDAs, since the information would have needed to be entered twice. This example is not the most flashy or cutting edge way a PDA can be used, but it does illustrate how a PDA can enhance a typical kind of lesson by saving time. It also gave the teacher the luxury of being able to contextualize the information students were learning. Any time data must be gathered, a teacher should wonder whether a PDA could save time, simplify logistics, and improve accuracy.

In some cases, PDAs allow for data collection in the field that cannot be performed any other way. Thinking about choices, would a teacher rather have students take a $1,500 portable computer to a stream to collect water quality data or a $200 PDA? Furthermore, a teacher can buy seven PDAs for the price of the portable, and in the same amount of time, seven different areas of the stream can be sampled by seven different groups of students.

There are more mobile devices than PDAs, and there are many highly sophisticated uses for mobile devices in the classroom not covered here because they will not be widely available in the next five years. To read about the possibilities, see an excellent 48-page article listed in the annotated bibliography, by Naismith et al. (2004). This article provides case studies not unlike the field trip above.

Facts about PDAs

Researchers have identified some major categories of use for PDAs (Patten, Sanches, McGreen, Clarke, Brennan, and Tangey, 2006; Swan, van 't Hooft, & Kratcoski, 2005). Some uses listed by these authors include:

- ▓ Administration
- ▓ Reference
- ▓ Interactive activities
- ▓ Data collection (scientific, multimedia, and reflective)
- ▓ Collaborative uses

Administration refers to teacher recordkeeping. Reference uses allow students to access e-books, dictionaries, and works in progress, such as Word documents. A more interesting use of handhelds involves wireless response systems that allow students to type the answer to a question posed in multiple-choice format by the teacher, allowing the teacher to gauge student understanding immediately. Students also may use handheld devices to carry quizzes and other study materials as well.

Data collection is most likely the most common use for handhelds. These devices open up the world of real science to youngsters. Using probes attached to handhelds, students collect real-time data about weather, water, movement, heat, light, and other natural phenomena. Additionally, students can collect survey data such as wildife/plant counts or data from surveys they administer to people. They can then use a spreadsheet on the handheld or upload their data to a computer spreadsheet and analyze it. Unlike the functions listed in the last paragraph, none of these activities are replicable any other way. Additionally, handhelds allow students to take and use digital pictures, as well as provide them with ways of annotating both pictures and data as they work. Collaborative uses include editing during the writing process (Swan et al., 2005).

In a study, Swan and colleagues (2005) asked the question, "Do handhelds support learning processes (in grades 3–7)?" Teachers' comments indicated that students' writing processes were improved. The teachers mentioned mechanics and spelling, especially in the special-needs student population. In science classes, students said that handhelds were useful for "taking notes, test review, and doing calculations while keeping their work on the devices helped them stay more organized." The authors of this study also caution that the study could have been tainted by the novelty effect of the handhelds since they had not previously been used routinely in the population they studied. They also indicated that equipment problems are a genuine concern.

Researchers suggest other uses as well, but they are at this point limited. One important conclusion by the authors is that at this point, no one has found a "killer application" for the handheld (Patten et al., 2006).

Issues with handheld use listed in the literature (Swan et al., 2005) include:

- Inappropriate use
- Management issues
- Usability issues
- Equipment damage
- Theft

The Palm corporation has done extensive research on the use of PDAs in classrooms. This research was implemented by SRI Corporation in order to increase the credibility of the findings. Although there were no statistically based studies, SRI collected a great deal of ethnographic information as well as many ideas for using PDAs across curricula and grade levels. For more information on the research, you can go to www.palmone.com/us/education/programs/pepgrant.

▨ SUMMARY

Spreadsheets are to numbers what databases are to text. Both are collections of tools that help users analyze information. With the spreadsheet the user can do simple calculations, complex calculations, and use spreadsheet functions to do calculations that are either too time consuming or too difficult to do by hand. Although they do not assist students with their knowledge of math facts, they do allow students across disciplines to think about problems and concepts that involve numbers. Using spreadsheets to calculate simple, descriptive statistics, students may analyze their own experiments and surveys. Using charts, they may visualize their data. Using pivot tables, they can organize their data into different formats, which allows them to look for patterns. Using formulas and tools such as the "Goal Seek" function, they can experiment with numbers to look for patterns and ask "what if" questions.

CHECKING YOUR UNDERSTANDING

13.1 Pick one of the following groups of countries:

- The European Union
- South America
- Central America
- Asia

Use your spreadsheet to focus on following problems:

- Will the region be able to feed itself in twenty-five years?

- ▪ Is the region capable of producing its own energy? (Think outside the box—don't just ask if they have to import oil.)
- ▪ What is the quality of healthcare and life in general in this region?
- ▪ How likely is it that this region or countries in this region will go to war in the next twenty-five years?

Write an essay discussing your conclusions and how you arrived at them. Bear in mind that your spreadsheet will only be as smart as the person that designs it. If you leave out key fields of information, the spreadsheet may be of no help to you at all. If you do some statistics on the fields and don't use them correctly, you could come to an incorrect conclusion. If you use a chart or graph to do comparisons, it should be the right kind of chart or graph. Design is the key to a successful project.

13.2 Find a classmate who has focused on a region of the world different from yours. Given the information that you have gathered and combining your spreadsheets, discuss whether these two regions will fight each other in the next twenty-five years, become aligned with each other, or just ignore each other. Justify your conclusions based on data from your spreadsheet.

▪ REFERENCES

Albrecht, B., & Firedrake, G. (1999). Flash enlightenment. *Learning and Leading with Technology.* 26(7), 36–39.

Bitner, N., Wadlington, S., Partridge, E., & Bitner, J. (1999). The virtual trip. *Learning and Leading with Technology.* 26(6), 7–9.

Borg, W., & Gall, M. (1989). *Educational research.* New York: Longman.

CIA. (2000). The World Factbook. https://www.cia.gov/library/publications/the-world-factbook/index.htm. Retrieved July 1, 2007.

Clarke, T., Ayres, P., & Sweller, J. (2005). The impact of sequencing and prior knowledge on learning mathematics through spreadsheet applications. *Educational Technology Research and Development.* 53(3), 15–24.

Cuevas, M. (1994). *Holt physical science.* Austin, TX: Holt, Rinehart and Winston.

Drier, H. (1999). Do vampires exist? *Learning and Leading with Technology.* 27(1), 7–9.

Feicht, L. (1999). Creating a mathematical laboratory. *Learning and Leading with Technology.* 26(7), 46–51.

Huff, D. (1982). *How to lie with statistics.* New York: Norton.

Lloyd, M. (1998). The problem cycle: A model for computer education. *Learning and Leading with Technology.* 26(3), 7–13.

Lynch, M., & Walton, S. (1998). Talking trash on the Internet. *Learning and Leading with Technology.* 25(5), 26–31.

Manouchehri, A., & Pagnucco, L. (2000). Julio's run. *Learning and Leading with Technology.* 27(4), 7–13.

Morgan, B., & Jernigan, J. (1998). A technology update: Leonardo da Vinci and the search for the perfect body. *Learning and Leading with Technology.* 26(4), 22–25.

National Council of Teachers of Mathematics. (2003). The Use of Technology in the Learning and Teaching of Mathematics. www.nctm.org/about/content.aspx?id=6360&itemid=6360&linkidentifier=id. Retrieved July 1, 2007.

Niess, M. (1998). Using computer spreadsheets to solve equations. *Learning and Leading with Technology.* 26(3), 22–27.

Pugalee, D. (1999). Rolling the dice. *Learning and Leading with Technology.* 26(6), 19–21.

Slater, T. (1998). Collecting science in a net. *Learning and Leading with Technology.* 26(2), 28–36.

Slattery, W., Hundley, S., Finegan-Stoll, C., & Becker, M. (1998). Collecting science in a net. *Learning and Leading with Technology.* 26(1), 25–30.

Whitmer, J.C. (1992). *Spreadsheets in mathematics and science teaching.* Bowling Green, OH: School Science and Mathematics Association.

Widmer, C., & Sheffield, L. (1998). Modeling mathematics concepts. *Learning and Leading with Technology.* 25(5), 32–35.

U.S. Census Bureau. (2000). www.census.gov/hhes/poverty/povanim/pvmaptxt .html.

Verderber, N. (1990). Spreadsheets and problem solving with Appleworks in mathematics teaching. *Journal of Computers in Mathematics and Science Teaching.* 9(3), 51.

▪ ANNOTATED RESOURCES ▨▨▨▨▨▨▨▨▨▨▨▨▨▨

Miscellaneous

Albrecht, B., & Davis, P. (2001). Model the movements of the planets. *Leading and Learning with Technology.* 28(8), 33.

Bryan, J. A. (2005). Video analysis: real world explorations for secondary mathematics. *Leading and Learning with Technology.* 32(6), 22–24.

Bryan describes how to use several inexpensive technologies to study the physics of motions, with applications and examples covering middle school physics through high school math or physics. He has used this approach in his own classrooms and recommends the use of these techniques to teach physics and math.

Enderson, M. (2001). Marking time with math. *Leading and Learning with Technology.* 28(5), 28.

One software tool math teachers use is Geometer's SketchPad. This software title is a tool used to build geometric shapes. Once students have defined a shape, the tool allows them to study the many properties (angles, distances) of the shape as well as the theorems associated with the shape. This reference will help you understand how this tool works.

Ezell, B., Johnson, D., and Rice, M. (2006). Creating interactive Excel learning tools. *Learning and Leading with Technology.* December/January, 29–31.

This practical articles demonstrates specific uses for spreadsheets. Concepts covered include:

- ▪ Fractions, decimals, and percentages
- ▪ Multiplication
- ▪ Science and history—general ideas

Additionally, the article lists more resources for math, science, and history lessons at the following locations:

Math lessons with spreadsheets: http://math.about.com/od/excel
Science and history lessons: www.internet4classrooms.com/lesson.htm

Lowery, L. (1998, November). How new science curriculums reflect brain research. *Educational Leadership.* 56(3), 26.

One point made repeatedly in the chapters on data analysis tools is their importance in helping children perceive and understand relationships. This article provides another perspective on this. Even if you do not teach science, you will take much from this article with respect to the importance of helping students construct their own knowledge.

Niess, M. L. (2005). Scaffolding math learning with spreadsheets. *Leading and Learning with Technology.* 32(5), 24–25, 48.

The author demonstrates how to solve five different math problems with spreadsheets. These include:

- ▨ Order of operations: Hit the target number of 13 using each of these numbers only once: 1, 4, 6, 8
- ▨ Patterns: Solve this mystery to find the 100th value in the pattern . . .
- ▨ Entering formulas: Use the spreadsheet to make a multiplication table from 1–6.
- ▨ Entering formulas: Extend the multiplication table for a variety of numbers.
- ▨ Exploring linear functions: Juan and Sylvia each have a cell phone, and they want to see who has the better deal. Juan's company charges 20¢ for making a call and then charges 60¢ for each minute of the call. Sylvia's company charges 30¢ per minute, but charges 80¢ for making the call. How many minutes can they talk on the phone such that the charges are equal?

Paul, J. R. M., & Kaiser, C. (2005). Do women live longer than men? Using computers to investigate graveyard data. *Micromath.* 21(2), 6–10.

This is an interesting and very readable article about how to design and implement a spreadsheet-based lesson for primary school children. The author lists many valuable concepts children acquire when they do this lesson. Among the results you will learn about when you read this article are:

1. "The group graph activity resulted in the discussion of their findings where they made comparisons and tried to work out the reasons for the differences."
2. "Working with primary evidence meant that the pupils could draw their own conclusions for the questions which they had formulated."
3. "Primary level children do not get many chances to work with statistical data and find it difficult to formulate questions based on it. The nature of this data, and especially the fact that it was their own, made it easier for them to pose questions which could be investigated and to make hypotheses that could be proved or rejected."

4. "The interpretation of the data required higher order thinking, linking mathematics and history."

5. "The task resulted in a thirst for further reading and research, particularly where individual graves provided points of interest. A poem and a bird bath on the grave of a young nature conservation officer, the names of various battles in which soldiers had lost their lives, and references to a local train disaster in which several scores of people had lost their lives provided much interest and areas of focus for further reading."

U.S. Census Bureau. (2007). The 2007 statistical abstract. www.census.gov/compendia/statab. Retrieved February 16, 2007.

This is by far the best source of data that I have found for spreadsheets. The data is all in ready to use spreadsheets. It is fast, easy to use and comprehensive. Topics include:

- ▦ Accommodation, Food, and Other Services
- ▦ Agriculture
    - Agricultural Exports and Imports
    - Crops
    - Farm Income and Balance Sheet
    - Farms and Farmland
    - Meat and Livestock
- ▦ Arts, Entertainment, and Recreation
    - Arts Activities
    - Consumer Expenditures
    - Establishments, Revenue, Employees, and Payroll
    - Recreation and Leisure Activities
    - Travel and Tourism
- ▦ Banking, Finance, and Insurance
    - Banks, Savings Institutions, Credit Unions
    - Finance and Insurance Industries
    - Financial Assets and Liabilities
    - Household Financial Assets and Liabilities
    - Insurance
    - Money Stock, Interest Rates, Bond Yields
    - Mutual Funds, Securities Industry
    - Payment Systems, Consumer Credit, Mortgage Debt
    - Real Estate, Rental, and Leasing
    - Stocks and Bonds, Equity Ownership
- ▦ Business Enterprise
    - Economic Indicators
    - Establishments, Employees, Payroll
    - Investment, Capital Expenditures
    - Multinational Companies
    - Patents, Trademarks, Copyrights
    - Profits
    - Sole Proprietorships, Partnerships, Corporations
    - Women and Minority-Owned Businesses

▓ Comparative International Statistics
    Agricultural Production and Trade
    Climate, Environment
    Economy
    Finance
    Foreign Commerce and Aid
    Government Receipts, Expenditures, Debt
    Labor Force
    Natural Resources and Energy
    Population, Households
    Prices
    Telecommunications, Computers
    Vital Statistics, Health, Education
▓ Construction and Housing
    Authorizations, Starts and Completions
    Commercial Offices
    Construction Indices and Value
    Construction Industry
    Homeownership and Housing Costs
    Housing Sales
    Housing Units and Characteristics
    Housing and Neighborhood Quality
▓ Education
    Adult Education
    All Levels of Education
    Educational Attainment
    Elementary and Secondary Education: Completions and Dropouts
    Elementary and Secondary Education: Schools and Enrollment
    Elementary and Secondary Education: Special Topics
    Elementary and Secondary Education: Staff and Finances
    Elementary and Secondary Education: Summary
    Elementary and Secondary Education: Technology, Courses, and Test
        Scores
    Higher Education: Degrees
    Higher Education: Finances, Fees, and Staff
    Higher Education: Institutions and Enrollment
    Higher Education: Summary
▓ Elections
    Campaign Finance
    Congressional
    Elected Public Officials—Characteristics
    Gubernatorial and State Legislatures
    Presidential
    Voting-Age Population and Voter Participation
▓ Energy and Utilities
    Crude Oil, Petroleum

Electricity
Gas Utility
Nuclear
Prices, Expenditures, Sales
Production, Consumption, Trade
Solar and Renewable Energy
Utilities
Water and Sewage Systems
▨ Federal Government Finances and Employment
Federal Budget—Receipts, Outlays, and Debt
Federal Civilian Employment
Federal Individual Income Tax Returns
Federal Land
▨ Foreign Commerce and Aid
Exports and Imports
Foreign Aid
Foreign Investment
International Transactions
▨ Geography and Environment
Air Quality
Environmental Industry; Threatened and Endangered Species
Land and Land Use
Solid Waste, Hazardous Waste, and Superfund
Water, Water Use, and Quality
Weather Events and Climate
▨ Health and Nutrition
Food Consumption and Nutrition
Health Care Resources
Health Care Utilization
Health Conditions, Diseases
Health Expenditures
Health Insurance
Health Risk Factors
Medicare, Medicaid
▨ Income, Expenditures, and Wealth
Consumer Expenditures
Family Income
Gross Domestic Product and Gross State Product
Household Income
Income and Poverty—State and Local Data
Income for Persons
Personal Income
Poverty
Wealth
▨ Information and Communications
Broadcasting

Information Sector Summary
Information Services and Data Processing
Internet Access and Usage
Motion Picture and Sound Recording Industries
Publishing Industries
Telecommunications

▨ Labor Force, Employment, and Earnings
Compensation, Wages, and Earnings
Employed Persons
Employment Benefits
Employment Projections
Employment and Earnings—Establishment Basis
Injuries and Fatalities
Labor Force Status
Productivity
Unemployed Persons
Work Stoppages, Union Membership

▨ Law Enforcement, Courts, and Prisons
Arrests
Correctional Facilities, Prisoners
Courts
Crimes and Crime Rates
Criminal Victimizations
Fire Losses
Juvenile Delinquency, Child Abuse

▨ Manufactures
Aluminum, Steel, Machine Tools
Finances
Manufactures—Establishments, Shipments, Employees,
    Payroll
Nondurable Goods Industries
Semiconductors, Computers, Communications Equipment
Shipments, Orders, Inventories
Transportation Equipment, Appliances

▨ National Security and Veterans Affairs
Defense Outlays
Homeland Security
Military Personnel and Expenditures
Veterans

▨ Natural Resources
Coal
Fisheries, Aquaculture
Mining, Mineral Industries
Natural Resource-Related Industries
Petroleum Industry, Natural Gas
Timber-Based Manufacturing

- Population
    - Ancestry, Language Spoken At Home
    - Elderly, Racial and Hispanic Origin Population Profiles
    - Estimates and Projections by Age, Sex, Race/Ethnicity
    - Estimates and Projections—States, Metropolitan Areas, Cities
    - Households and Families
    - Immigration
    - Marital Status and Living Arrangements
    - Migration
    - National Estimates and Projections
    - Native and Foreign-Born Populations
    - Religion
- Prices
    - Consumer Price Indexes, Cost of Living Index
    - Food Cost and Prices
    - Fuel Prices
    - Price Indexes
    - Producer Price Indexes
- Puerto Rico and the Island Areas
- Science and Technology
    - Employment
    - Expenditures
    - Space
    - Students and Degrees Conferred
- Social Insurance and Human Services
    - Child Support, Head Start, Child Care
    - Food Programs
    - Government Transfer Payments, Social Assistance
    - Philanthropy, Nonprofit Organizations, Volunteering
    - Social Security, Retirement Plans
    - Supplemental Security Income, Temporary Assistance to Needy Families
    - Unemployment, Disability, Workers' Compensation
- State and Local Government Finances and Employment
    - Employment and Payroll
    - Federal Aid to State and Local Governments
    - Governmental Units
    - Local Government Finances
    - Receipts, Expenditures, Investment
    - State Government Finances
    - State and Local Government Finances
- Transportation
    - Air Transportation Fatalities and Complaints
    - Airline Operations and Traffic
    - All Modes of Transportation
    - Highway Financing
    - Highway Infrastructure and Use

Motor Vehicle Accidents and Fatalities
Motor Vehicle Registrations, Alternative Fueled Vehicles
Trucks, Railroads, Pipelines
U.S. Postal Service
Urban Transit
Water Transportation
■ Vital Statistics
Births
Deaths
Family Planning, Abortions
Life Expectancy
Marriages and Divorces
■ Wholesale and Retail Trade
Establishments, Sales, Payroll, and Employees
Motor Vehicle Sales
Online Retail Sales
Retail Sales
Shopping Centers
Wholesale Trade

PDAs

Naismith, L., Lonsdale, P., Vavoula, G., & Sharpless, M. (2004). Report 11: Literature review in mobile technologies and learning. *FutureLab,* 1–48. www.futurelab.org .uk/resources/documents/lit_reviews/Mobile_Review.pdf. Retrieved July 2, 2007.

This review is the most comprehensive of all of the literature presented in the annotated bibliography. Although it presents no lesson plans, it does provide some in-depth case studies. It is scaffolding material, meaning that a student who reads this article will have the fundamental theoretical constructs necessary for knowing when, why, and how a mobile computing device is useful. The review itself proves the best summary of its purpose, quoted below:

■ To identify the different types of mobile technologies that are applicable to learning
■ To explore new and emerging practices relating to the use of mobile technologies for learning
■ To identify the learning theories that are relevant to these new practices
■ To present a set of exemplary case studies demonstrating uses of mobile technologies for learning
■ To present key issues and guidelines to inform current educational practice and policy
■ To encourage educators and technical developers to rethink their roles for the future of learning with mobile technologies

Patten, B., et al. (2006). Designing collaborative, constructionist and contextual applications for handheld devices. *Computers & Education.* 46(3), 294–308.

Penuel, R. (2005). Implementing a handheld program: Lessons from a district-level initiative. *Learning and Leading with Technology.* 32(6), 6–10.

Penuel provides an overview of handheld implementation. Although some of his discussion is common sense, he does contrast the difference between implementing 1:1 computer use to 1:1 handheld use. There are no lesson plans in this article.

Swan, K., van 't Hooft, M., & Kratcoski, A. (2005). Uses and effects of mobile computing devices in K–8 classrooms. *Journal of Research on Technology in Education.* 38(1), 99–112.

Companion Web Site   www.ablongman.com/thorsen3e

1. Go to the TechTactics web site for Chapter 13 and click on the link for the 2007 Statistical Abstract. You will find Excel-based spreadsheets for many categories of information from agriculture and the arts, to science, technology, and business. After finding a spreadsheet that relates to your area of study, make a list of at least two questions each that you could answer using sorts, formulas, and functions.

2. Use the same table that you used in question 1 and turn it into a pivot table. List the additional questions you can answer when you use the pivot table function on the information that you have chosen.

A Your Network

Before you begin learning about how to use the tools we discussed briefly in Chapter 1, you need to know a little bit about the infrastructure that supports those tools. How well your infrastructure works for you will have either an enabling or disabling effect on everything you do. You may design a wonderful lesson based on presentation software and find that the network is down the day you had planned to have your students search the Internet for graphics. Or worse, they may have done their Internet search for graphics and lost them all somewhere on the network. Or worst of all, some child may have finished the assignment and deleted it because she or he did not know how file management works. You expect your students to know how to use a pencil sharpener to keep their pencils sharp and to store their papers in notebooks and folders where they can find them when they need them. Similarly, you will develop a set of expectations for them about their work with computers.

Your Intranet (your school network) is both a giant filing cabinet and your connection to the world beyond your classroom. It provides you with storage space, effortless file transfer among computers, and a pipeline to the Internet. Knowing just a little bit about how it works and its capacity will help you use the computer tools that you have more efficiently. Just what should you know about your Intranet to be an effective advocate for and teacher of your children? Some terms that you should be familiar with are server, router, hub, host, client, bandwidth, and modem. If you know these terms you can talk knowledgably with your technology coordinator or technician. You may be cynical about having to know such technical-sounding terms. To help you understand why you are learning this new vocabulary, I am providing some statements that your technology coordinator might say to you. If you can understand what he or she is saying, you will be able to make an informed decision about how to respond. If you don't understand, you and your students will be at the mercy of someone who does not know you, your students, or your instructional objectives. Now, the statements:

- "Your class can't add any more information to your web site—the server is full."
- "We can't put another computer in your classroom. The hub is full."
- "We don't want you to try using Internet video in your classroom. There just isn't enough bandwidth."
- "No wonder that takes you so long to download at home. You only have a 28K modem."

- ■ "The name of our web server is Plato.K12.edu. You will need to know that name in order to upload the web site you just finished."
- ■ "You need to either archive your e-mail or delete it. You are taking up too much space on the server."
- ■ "No wonder your e-mail isn't working. Your client isn't configured correctly. You have the wrong name for the host."
- ■ "The network is down."

As you can see, the statements that a technician might say to you someday will affect you at a very practical level in your classroom. What if you don't want to delete all of your e-mail? What are the alternatives? What if there isn't room on the hub for another computer—is that the end of the world, or can it be fixed? If the server is full, what are the alternatives for the kids and the web site that they built for their project on Central America? So the client isn't properly loaded—what should be done? How long will it take to fix? When will the class have e-mail again? What do you mean the name of the web server is Riverside? I thought you just put a web site in a directory and everyone sees it. If the network is down, what can't you do and what can you do?

Imagine if your school network administrator said all of these things to you in the same week. If you had made your lesson plans around the belief that all of the bad things listed previously weren't going to happen to you and then they did, your classroom would be chaos. If, on the other hand, you understand what is going on, you can make contingency plans, understand timelines, ask intelligent questions, and even argue a little. So let's go to work figuring out how the computers in your classroom communicate with other computers in the school and ultimately to the outside world.

Figure A.1 is a diagram of some computers that reside at Riverside High School. Although we are looking at a high school, such a configuration would be just as common at an elementary school. We see four classrooms, each with three computers. We see the server room with a variety of different kinds of servers. We can also see downtown Riverside, where the local Internet service provider has offices, and not far from there to the west we see Mr. Tibbs's house. Let us do a tour of the server room first.

A Tour of the Server Room

FIELD TRIP
A.1

Server 1, the district e-mail host, provides e-mail service to all of the students and faculty in the Riverside district. The server has a name, Riverside, and address, Riverside.K12.edu. Mrs. Frederick's e-mail address is, for example, frederik@riverside.K12.edu. Mr. Smith's e-mail address is smith1@riverside.K12.edu. E-mail gets to and from all of the teachers' rooms when their computers send or receive it through the hub in the wiring closet outside of Mr. Jones's room. From there it goes directly to or comes from the server. If the e-mail is being sent out of the district, the server sends it to the server of the school's Internet provider downtown (Server 5), where it is routed on to its destination. If the e-mail is going to remain in the district, then Server 1 deposits it in the box of the recipient named in the address, where it waits until that person decides to open it. There are nearly 10,000 students and teachers in Riverside School district, who each send several messages a day. The district had to make a rule about leaving e-mail on the server. Each person is allowed to accumulate 1 megabyte of information. After that, the person's e-mail account will not receive any more messages. This makes it hard for students and teachers to send attachments, especially graphics files. They had to learn how to use compressed .JPG files to exchange graphics using e-mail.

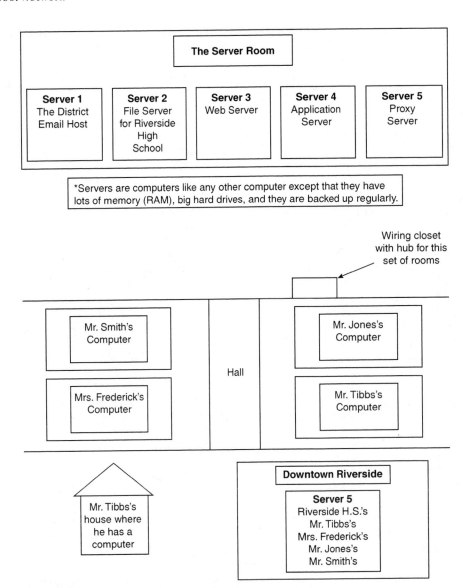

FIGURE A.1 Floor Plan, Center Section, South Wing, Riverside High School

Server 2, the file server, serves only the students and teachers at Riverside High School. This server does many different tasks for students and teachers. One important function of the file server is to provide a place where students and teachers can store their work. The hard drives of the computers in the classroom are not large enough to store all of the text and graphics files that everyone uses for the many ongoing projects in each classroom. Each student and each teacher has a secure folder, which only he or she can access. There they can make their own subdirectories, where they store drafts of documents they are word processing, presentations they are making, graphics files they have downloaded or scanned, and e-mail messages they have had to delete from the mail server. In addition, there are public directories. All of the teachers share a folder where they can exchange files. Mr. Smith, for example, has just downloaded a wonderful series of graphics on cloud formations that he found on the Internet and wants to share it with Mr. Jones, who is just starting his unit on weather. Mr. Smith simply needs to copy these files to Mr. Jones' public folder and Mr. Jones will have them. All of the teachers provide public folders for their students as well, so that they can just drop files into a student's folder. They use this to provide electronic materials and curriculum that are often a part of their assignments. The teachers also provide a special assignments folder for each student. When a student finishes an electronic assignment, she or he may simply drop it into the appropriate folder. Only the teacher and the student have the rights to access this folder. When the teacher has graded the assignment, he or she drops it back into the student's folder where the student may open it, read comments, and see the grade. This is especially helpful for files that are too big to fit on a floppy disk. But even if the files aren't too big, it saves the teachers and students from having to deal with keeping track of a floppy disk while they are keeping track of so many other more important things as well.

All of this activity to and from File Server 2 in the diagram goes through the hub on the other side of the wall of Mr. Jones's classroom. The network administrator named this server Socrates. Since it is not connected to the Internet, it doesn't have an address. Another way of saying that information goes back and forth between classroom computers and the server is, "Information that goes from a client (a computer in one of the classrooms) to the server goes through the hub." The hub is a small box with holes for network cables. When a computer is on a network, it has a network card that has a plug-in for a network cable. That cable goes to a hub that then directs the information to a server through a larger cable. Each of the computers in each of the four classrooms has a network card with one end of the cable plugged into it and into the hub at the other end. Soon each of these classrooms will have five computers instead of three. Before these new computers will be able to communicate with any of the servers, they will have to plug into a hub as well. The hub that the four teachers are using now only has fifteen ports (the holes where the network cable is attached), so when the school ordered the new computers, they ordered a new hub as well. Mr. Tibbs asked the network administrator to order a hub large enough to handle another five computers above the twenty, because he is writing a grant and thinks that he will get an additional five computers for his classroom. His network administrator, a sometimes parsimonious person, told him to write an extra hub into his grant and take care of it himself. Mr. Tibbs is just grateful he knows what a hub is, and he is not so sure he is going to write a hub into his grant. This may be a matter for the principal to decide. It seems to Mr. Tibbs that if he is willing to write a grant for the district, the district should be willing to chip in $200 for a hub to help him with the matching money his grant requires. Technology is such a new item in the district that traditions and procedures regarding who pays for what have not yet been established, and oftentimes getting things done is a matter of negotiation and compromise.

But back to the server room—we are now gazing at the web server, Server 3. Its name is Aristotle, and its address is Aristotle.Riverside.K12.edu. It is a large, sleek machine that hums with the sound of constant activity. Like the other machines, it looks like a wire farm with cables leading to a tape backup drive, the network, and the Internet service provider downtown. On this web server each teacher maintains a home page so that parents, students, and others can see a picture and get some background on that teacher's education, interests, and accomplishments. Each class also maintains a web page. On the web page are assignments for each day as well as pictures of each member of the class. In addition, the teacher has posted the syllabus for the class and the learning objectives for the semester and year.

Server 4, named Dewey and the last machine in the row of servers on our tour, is the application server. This server really just serves one application. It is a large integrated learning system that provides computer-based instruction (CBI) in language arts and mathematics. Teachers use it for kids who have trouble keeping up with the rest of the class or when a particular concept is hard for a whole class. Mr. Tibbs, for example, uses it when he teaches fractions to his general math class. Not only does the machine display the lessons, it also keeps track of each student's score on the exercises and quizzes and the amount of time that the student is logged on. To use this CBI, Mr. Tibbs had to go to a special two-hour workshop and learn how to enter students' names and passwords into the course management system, assign lessons, and get reports on student work.

Server 6, the proxy server, came as the result of much debate and a "precipitating incident." A proxy server filters Internet sites, allowing students only to access sites that do not contain objectionable content. Some companies that provide software for proxy servers provide a basic set of filters and also allow districts to add additional filters. One mechanism for setting up these filters is to type in a list of words that will block a site from being downloaded. There are disadvantages to proxy servers. The primary disadvantage is that they slow down the user's ability to move from page to page. Some even require teachers to bookmark sites ahead of time so that they can be searched. Because of these inconveniences, there was a lively debate among teachers, parents, and administrators in Riverside about whether to install a proxy server. Many did not want the additional baggage of having to deal with a proxy server. Instead, they wanted each student to sign an "Internet Code of Honor," by which they promised not to go to sites with violent or sexual content. Neighboring Arlington School District had implemented such a program successfully. Students in that district all signed the Code of Honor. Of course, within six weeks of school starting, a student was discovered in violation of the code, and his computer privileges were revoked for a semester. After that, things settled down and there were no more violations.

However, the whole situation played out differently at Riverside. Before the issue had been decided, four fifth-grade boys secretly downloaded a bomb-making manual and went to work on a homemade bomb in the basement of one of the boys' houses. Since they were more curious (and dumb) than malicious, their parents discovered the plot, extracted the story about downloading the manual at a school web site, went to the principal, superintendent, and school board about the evils of unprotected web sites, and Riverside School District installed a proxy server the next month. The presence of a proxy server in a district is a reflection of local values and how a community wants to buffer and protect its young people from the dangerous and unsavory side of life. A truly determined and skillful student can find his or her way around anything, and the best protection is the watchful eyes of a caring teacher and parents as well as a lot of discussion and problem solving about right, wrong, and the Internet.

The final stop on our tour of servers is in downtown Riverside, where Speedo Internet Services maintains Server 5, the equipment that Riverside School District uses to connect to the Internet. It is important to understand that in order to be connected to the Internet, anyone—individual or school district—must use an Internet provider (gateway). The quality of the service to the individual or district depends on how much bandwidth the individual or organization buys.

Riverside has one T1 line running from Speedo to the district. Information runs through wires much like water runs through pipes. The amount of information that gets through a wire depends on its size. T1 is a size of cable and is one of the most common kinds of large "pipes" that Internet Service Providers (ISPs) use for school districts and other large customers. In the beginning that was enough, but as more students and teachers began using the web to get information and graphics for assignments, web pages began loading more and more slowly. The district is now trying to figure out where it is going to find another $500 per month to pay for an additional T1 line.

One of the real problems the low bandwidth has created in the district is the inability of teachers to video conference with other schools and experts across the country. Mr. Smith received a grant from the National Science Foundation (NSF) for money to buy a fast computer, a special video card, and a camera so that his AP biology class could consult experts in various biological sciences during the school year. The first time Mr. Smith and his class used the system, traffic on the school network slowed to a crawl. Web sites took minutes to load, and Internet lessons and work in other classes came to a standstill. Mr. Smith was embarrassed, the network administrator was cranky, and the school administrators had to explain to the teachers why they evaluate teachers on their creative and innovative use of technology in their classrooms when the infrastructure does not support it. The short-term solution to the problem came as the result of negotiation and compromise. Mr. Smith and his AP biology class, who had to use the equipment to keep the grant, agreed to do some of the interviews after school. On days when interviews could only be conducted during school hours, the rest of the school was informed and teachers tried to keep Internet usage to a minimum while the biology class conducted an interview. This was a patch. The real answer to the problem was to get more bandwidth from the Internet service provider (Speedo).

Notice that Mr. Tibbs's house is also in the diagram in Figure A.1. He has a computer there that he bought because he found that he really can't keep up with his work at school without having a computer at home. When he is at school he rarely has time to sit at a computer and try things out, and he definitely has no time to look for new and interesting web sites. He hardly ever has access to the computers in his room because the kids are always using them. When he bought his computer, he knew that he wanted access to the Internet. For that, he had to buy a modem along with his computer and contact an Internet service provider to give him a logon to an Internet server. Since he gets his Internet service through his telephone line, Mr. Tibbs knew that his connection would probably be slow. Nevertheless, he bought the fastest modem available and hoped for the best. Although Mr. Tibbs could have chosen a national company like AOL, he chose Speedo instead. Mr. Tibbs was set up with both an e-mail account and Internet access that would allow him to get to any Internet site in the world. Since the server at Riverside High School is a POP3 server, Mr. Tibbs can access his school e-mail account at home along with his e-mail account provided by Speedo. He uses his Speedo account to send and receive personal messages from friends and family and does business on the school account. Nevertheless, he can configure his home e-mail program that he downloaded for free from the Internet to access both accounts. Some e-mail software does not allow e-mail readers POP3 access to their comments. These closed systems can only be read with their proprietary software. If your technology coordinator tells you that your district has a POP3 server, that means that you can use nonproprietary e-mail software, such as Pegasus or Eudora (both are downloadable free on the Internet), to access your school e-mail at home.

If Mr. Tibbs is lucky, he lives in an area where he can subscribe to a broadband service—DSL, cable, or a more expensive satellite service. If this is possible, it is the best alternative, because browsing the web using a telephone line connected to a modem is tedious, at best.

The story you just read is typical of the thousands of schools across the country. If you are a preservice teacher, the classroom technology configuration and the political problems that you step into when you have finished your training will be similar to the ones that you just read about. If you are already teaching, you will recognize both the hardware and the political problems.

To make this information your own, you must now find out (if you do not already know) the specifics of the network and Internet providers where you are. "Checking Your Understanding A.1" will help you find out about your local resources. It will provide you with the right questions to ask and the right words to use when you ask them. Once you open a dialog with a network administrator and Internet provider and try using language that you have just learned, you will be able to use all of the resources that you have more effectively. One of the best ways you can help yourself is to use key words we have learned so far with other people who know more about this than you do. Do not be afraid of using the wrong word. You will only sound silly once (as we all have at one time or another), and then you will gain the power that comes with knowledge.

CHECKING YOUR UNDERSTANDING

1. Survey your network by answering the following questions. Take notes. These questions are just the minimum. As you ask questions, you will generate more questions. As you get answers, you will probably get more information than you asked for.

   a. With your instructor's help, use your computer's file management system to learn the names of the computers on your network.

b. With your instructor's help, use your computer's file management system to learn how the file server in your lab is set up. Which folder on which drive belongs just to you? What is the procedure for getting a folder where you can make subfolders for your whole class? How do you request a folder that you and other teachers can share?

c. What is the name of the Internet provider for your school district or university? How much bandwidth does your school district or university buy every month? Name three local Internet providers and answer the following questions about each.

 i. How many hours of service does the provider give you per month and at what price?
 ii. What is the highest speed modem that the provider will support?
 iii. Name the hours per week that technical support is available.
 iv. How often has the provider's service been down in the last year (they should be able to tell you)?
 v. When they were down, how long were they down on average?
 vi. How much space will the provider give you to store your e-mail?
 vii. Will the provider allow you to put up a web site for free? If they will, how much space will they give you for your site?

d. Find out if there is an application server on your school or university network. Which applications does it serve?

e. Where is the server room in your university or school? Ask your instructor or network administrator for a brief tour.

f. Where is the wiring closet in your school or university for your lab? Ask the network administrator to open the door and let you look at the hub(s) for your floor or wing. Are there extra ports? How many?

g. If there are three extra ports on the hub that serves your wing or your floor, what does this mean?

2. With the information that you have collected from the questions you just answered, complete two of the following three activities and present your work to the class:

a. Write and present a presentation (Hyperstudio, PowerPoint, Web) to your (future) school board outlining why you need more network resources.

b. Write and present a presentation (Hyperstudio, PowerPoint, Web) for the class that you teach on the new file management system that you have set up for them that will allow them to have:

 i. Their own private directories
 ii. Directories where they can share information with other students
 iii. A private directory where each student may hand in electronically generated work

 Note: You should present this to the class that you are in first. You should have screen shots (captured pictures of the screen) of the folders you have created for your students and walk them through the process of submitting, copying, and pasting work to and from those directories.

c. Using a word processor, write a comparison/contrast paper of 300 words, discussing the following topic: Of the three Internet providers that you investigated, which would you choose? Why?

File Management

B

Before each semester starts, you will want to take an inventory of the storage space available for both you and your students. You will want to check out the hard drives of the machines in your classroom and clean off unnecessary folders and files left by last year's students or last semester's students. These hard drives are not good places for students to store everything that they collect electronically, because of space issues. However, local drives are good places for students to back up items they are working on so that they will be available if the network goes down. You should make folders for students ahead of time so that when students first sit down to the computer their space will be ready for them. You should do the same thing on the network. To do this you will work with your network administrator to establish a network drive where you can create folders for your students. You will want to create several different kinds of folders, including:

- A private folder as a workspace for each individual student
- A public folder where students can share files
- An assignments folder that is a private drop box for each student

You should also understand how many megabytes of space the network administrator will allow for your class. If you plan on students creating presentations that will require extensive graphics and audio/video, you should tell the network administrator and negotiate something workable for both of you. To help you understand how much you will need for each student, you should look at the size of electronic presentations that are about the size and complexity that you will expect your students to make. Then double the space because the students will be working on other projects as well—word-processed documents, spreadsheets, and databases. Your class will probably only have enough room to work on one presentation per person at a time. Once the class is finished with their presentations, you might then have to upload them to the web server in order to display to parents and others for a while, and save them on a "zip" disk of some kind or press them to a CD for storage. It is important to understand that since you and your class are sharing computer space with many people, you need a plan to move work through the storage space on the server, so that once an assignment is completed you and your students can clear out the space and begin a new project.

287

From *Tech Tactics: Technology for Teachers*, 3/e. Carolyn Thorsen. Copyright © 2009 by Pearson Education. All rights reserved.

This moving around of information brings us to an important skill that you and your students should acquire early: file management. Understanding where files go when they are saved will save you many hours of either searching for one you have misplaced or redoing lost work. If many of your students are constantly misplacing their files, you will spend countless valuable hours helping them track down their work. One of the first activities you will want to provide for your students is a refresher on how to get around your school network and a tour of the folders you have set up for them. Although some will understand immediately, others will be lost.

An always popular activity that will get your students started is called Fruit Files. To get students used to moving among folders and drives on their local computers' network, create folders and subfolders named for fruit or animals or other groups of objects for easy identification. An example of such a folder with its subfolders appears in Figure B.1. In each of these folders, place a text file with a joke or interesting fact and directions about where to go next. Require students to find and open each of these files in a word processor, saving each file that they find to the next folder they must visit. So, for example, if their first visit is to the Apple directory, they will copy a file and place it in the next directory, which might be the Banana directory. Then they will copy and paste both files to the next directory to which they are instructed to proceed, and so on until they reach their destination. Success on the assignment means having collected all of the files into a single destination folder. A good destination folder is a folder labeled Assignments, to get students used to the idea that they should drop their finished assignments into a folder.

This skill is typically not learned in one sitting but over several different attempts. It is always helpful to provide your students with a physical analogy. Figures B.2 and B.3 are some simple diagrams that you can copy and display as you introduce the concept of folders to your students. For very young students you might actually put files in a real filing cabinet and have them walk through the physical process before they attempt the virtual process. Another way to ease into this process if your students are really new to file management is to put all of the Fruit files on a floppy disk and have students solve the problem in groups. Once the students have solved the problem in groups, give each student a fresh disk and have him or her solve it alone. If the student is still confused, have the student work with a peer or mentor who is good at getting around on the computer. Once you are satisfied that students can find and save files on a floppy disk, you

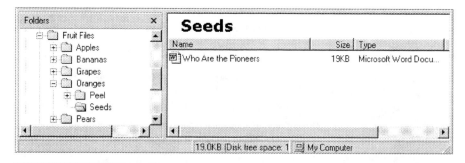

FIGURE B.1   A Simple Fruit File Folder Structure

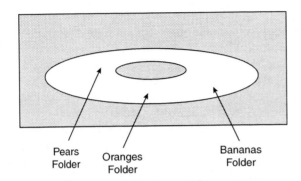

Pears
Folder

Oranges
Folder

Bananas
Folder

Information is stored on discs inside of disk drives that are part of your computer. Some discs are removable, like floppy discs, and others stay inside your computer.

FIGURE B.2   Where Do My Files Go?

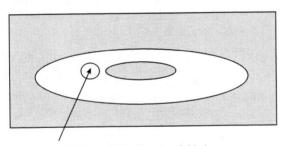

Let's magnify this spot (the Oranges folder) on a disk drive to see what it might look like.

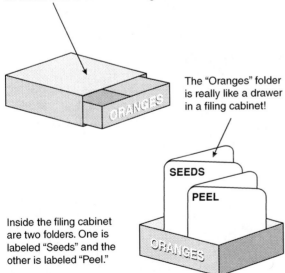

ORANGES

The "Oranges" folder is really like a drawer in a filing cabinet!

SEEDS

PEEL

Inside the filing cabinet are two folders. One is labeled "Seeds" and the other is labeled "Peel."

ORANGES

FIGURE B.3   The Disk Drive as a Filing Cabinet

can then show them the network, explain about different drives and drive letters, show them where their private and public spaces are, and have them complete the next Fruit File assignment. For the final assignment, use the following locations to place your fruit folders and files: the student's directory on a classroom machine, several public directories on the network drive, and the student's assignment folder.

There is one thing that can go wrong with this assignment. When you place a file in a directory where many students can get to it, someone invariably moves it or cuts and pastes it rather than copying it. You will want to point this difference out to your students and also be ready to replace files in public directories at a moment's notice while the exercise is in progress.

Another item that always comes up is the skill differential in the class. By the time the class has finished doing this exercise on the network, some of your students will be experts, many will be OK, some will still be really fuzzy, and others still utterly lost.

As soon as you find two or three students who really understand the process, rather than having them complete this exercise again, have them create more of these exercises for students who are still having a hard time understanding file management on the computer. Although you will not be able to give these students the rights that allow you to access student's private directories, they can still make very good searches using a floppy disk, the hard drive on a class computer, and the public directories on the network drive.

One of the most difficult concepts for some people to understand, young and old, is that of the virtual filing cabinet—the hard drive, floppy drive, and network drive. Without that understanding, working on a computer is extremely frustrating and time consuming for the student and the teacher. You can never be too sure that your students have this fundamental skill. After all of your preparation, explanations, and exercises, you will still often find one or two who still don't understand and frequently misplace their work. With these students you must spend individual one-on-one time until they understand this very basic but essential process.

CHECKING YOUR UNDERSTANDING

 B.1 Build a file search exercise for your students like the Fruit Files exercise discussed above. Design it to work on a floppy disk. When you submit your assignment, be sure that you submit a cover sheet that specifies the grade level for which your exercise is intended and the visuals that you will use to introduce this first lesson in file management.

Chat and Internet Conferencing

As the Internet becomes more available in each classroom, live chat will evolve into another tool that teachers and students will use to communicate with people at a distance. When people engage in chat over the Internet, they type in text that is seen immediately by someone in a remote location. This person may answer immediately, and a conversation ensues. Some chat utilities are very helpful in that they display not only the text, they also tell the participants in the conversation whether the other person is actually typing in an answer at any given moment. NetMeeting, CuSeeMe, and MSN network are examples of applications that enable chat.

On the open Internet there are chat rooms that are, for the most part, dangerous places for children. These are sites where strangers congregate to have virtual discussions, sometimes on a specific topic or maybe just general conversations. Most schools filter these locations. Unless you come upon a chat room built by educators for a specific purpose and monitor student use carefully, you should keep your students away from these sites. Furthermore, you should warn them that some people go to these sites to try to find others who are vulnerable, and warn them to beware of anyone who tries to make live personal contact with them after a visit or series of visits in a chat room.

The dangers of chat aside, there are some uses for chat in the classroom. Speaking with an expert and speaking to children from a different culture are two possible ways to use chat with your students. Figure C.1 is an example of a distance connection to an expert. In this case, a high school math class exploring careers in mathematics is talking to a college student majoring in computer science (CS). The teacher is projecting the chat session with an LCD projection panel and the class is asking questions.

WHITE BOARD

Some chat software not only allows a text conversation but also allows a "white board" in which participants may jointly view and operate a virtual whiteboard on which they may both draw and make notes. Further along in the chat session with the CS student, the student mentioned that he was currently taking a class on parallel computing. The math class asked him to draw a parallel computer, and he sketched a diagram of

291

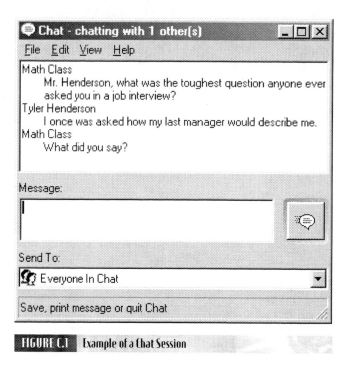

FIGURE C.1 Example of a Chat Session

the CPU arrangement that he was building with a team of computer scientists and students at his university (see Figures C.2 and C.3). Notice the spelling error. This happens during chat sessions. Students should understand that they should try very hard to communicate clearly so that how they write doesn't interfere with communication. However, sometimes in the rush of trying to communicate, mistakes happen. In this case it was the expert who made the mistake.

APPLICATION SHARING

One further useful tool attached to chat applications is application sharing. The tool is activated when one of the conversants starts an application, a database, for example. The chat dialogue box remains visible, but in addition, one or all of the parties in the conversation may control the application. Several users may be discussing "what if" questions, for example. During the chat session, anyone may compose sorts or queries for the database and everyone sees the results. Or, the person who launched the database may not allow others in the chat session, in order to control the database and retain control of the application. You can see an example of a dialogue box that launches an application in Figure C.4. In this case the user is getting ready to share a spreadsheet named Pi with other members of an online discussion.

FIGURE C.2 Asking a Question That Requires a White Board

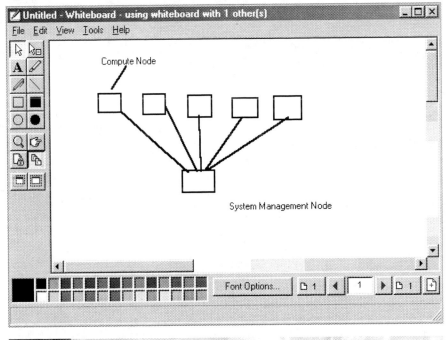

FIGURE C.3 Using the White Board

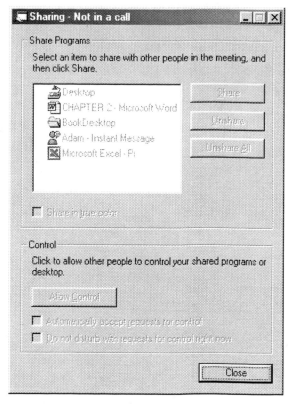

FIGURE C.4 Example of Application Sharing

FILE SHARING

A fourth tool offered by most computer communications interfaces is file sharing. With this tool you may send and receive files from the people with whom you are in communication. This is not an especially remarkable advantage, because people may also send files to each other using e-mail attachments. However, it is sometimes convenient during a conversation to send a file that someone forgot to send or to send a file that becomes important because of the conversation without having to leave the conversation and send an e-mail to do it.

ADVANTAGES AND DISADVANTAGES

Chat requires very little bandwidth. In a classroom with no telephone line, it is the only way to have a conversation with a remote expert or other person of interest. You can be confident that if you decide to use chat, you will not affect your school network significantly, and even on a bad (slow) Internet day, chat will function as quickly and effectively as on a good day.

Some days on the Internet are better than others. Some times of the day are better than others, depending on where you live. If every computer in your school is accessing the Internet simultaneously, it will probably be slower than if just half of them are using the Internet. The effect is the same at each level of the network. If all of the computers using your district's T1 line are on the network, the whole district will be slow. Or, if someone is doing live video over your school's Internet connection and your school doesn't have enough bandwidth to support it, everyone's access will be slower.

As for disadvantages, chat is text based. Consequently, students can huddle around a monitor, five at a time, or the teacher must set up an LCD projector for the whole class to see the conversation. Or, students may engage in their chat sessions one at a time. But then it is difficult to find an expert who is willing to give that kind of time. One-at-a-time chat is more feasible if students are connected with other students for some reason, such as a cultural exchange. One-on-one sessions are successful for foreign language students, for example. Slow readers or slow writers are at a disadvantage. Watching a second grader attempting chat with another second grader is excruciating because of its slowness. One questions the actual instructional benefit of such an exchange.

Application sharing is also slow on the open Internet. The graphic of the complete application is transmitted across the Internet each time the screen is redrawn (for example, moving from one screen to the next with presentation software). On a bad Internet day it is easier for people to bring up their own application and run it locally and then talk about the results. If one of the members of the chat group does not have the specific file that people are working with (e.g., a database, spreadsheet, or word processor file), it may easily be transmitted using the file sharing tool discussed previously.

AUDIO AND VIDEO CONFERENCING

Live video conferencing will soon come of age in the public school classroom. Supported by the same software that enables chat (Windows Live Messenger and CuSeeMe, for example), video conferencing enables the same kinds of interactions that chat does, except the computer provides a video image of the participants with accompanying audio. A small camera typically attaches to the computer's parallel or universal serial bus (USB) port, or, in the case of Macs, is built in. Cameras range widely in quality and price. Modest but usable cameras and supporting software cost under $100, while others with zoom or wide-angle lenses and special microphones cost as much as $800 to $1,000.

When the Internet connection is activated, the user may simply launch the camera's software, enter another user's IP address, and begin the session. An IP address is an Internet facility that allows computers to identify themselves and be found by other computers. Think of it as your computer's "telephone number." You can find your own IP address on a PC by clicking on Run in the Start menu and typing *winipcfg*. Sometimes, computers have "static" IP addresses. That means they stay the same. However, it is more likely that you have a dynamic IP address and will have to look it up every time you log on. When people who have dynamic IP address want to video conference and need each other's IP addresses, they most often contact each other by e-mail first, exchange the IP address of one machine or the other, and then begin the conference.

Video conferencing over the open Internet is not yet very reliable. On a bad Internet day, the video is slow and jerky (even with a T1 connection if people are using it for functions other than video) and the audio breaks up. On a good day, the picture is small, but it works and the audio is tolerable. The size of a typical video image looks like the one in Figure C.5. If you make it larger (which is possible), it becomes quite grainy. Notice that from this box, all four of the tools (chat, application sharing, file transfer, and white board) are available for simultaneous use. Once our local and national infrastructure provides us with the bandwidth that we really need to use these tools in a practical way, they will begin to have an impact on classrooms.

All of this points to one conclusion. Video conferencing is only now coming of age. For now it is an unpredictable adolescent that is sometimes moody and a little uncontrollable. You will want to think very carefully before you invest in the time and effort to use this technology. If, instead of spending all of the time that it would take you to set up and test the video conferencing equipment for one thirty-minute video conference, you use that time to prepare a great e-mail lesson, you may be far ahead in getting content into kids' heads. On the other hand, if you have an opportunity to show your class some historic moment or provide them the opportunity to talk to a world-famous expert, you might want to consider the video conference.

There is another option for video conferencing that might be more useful, and that is the "web cam" observation site. For example, zoos place web cameras in the pens of baby and adult animals, and you simply need to log on to the Internet site to observe them. You do not have to set up a camera of your own. Such a site might be a center in a biology class, for example, if you have found a site that matches your curriculum and you have a specific objective for your students' observations. It is

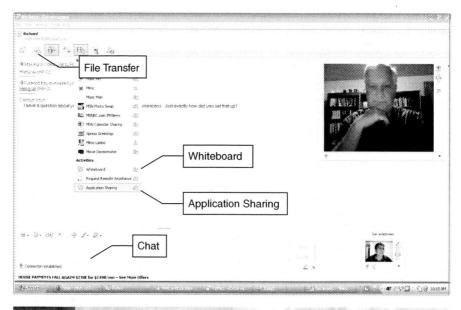

FIGURE C.5 Video Image Size, Transmitting Over the Open Internet

impossible to list sites here, because they come and go on a daily basis. If you visit educational sites regularly (such as The Global School House), you will see addresses of these sites and leads to where you can find more addresses. An example of one site that is a directory for web cameras is www.earthcamforkids.com.

Audio conferencing is a very viable alternative to video conferencing. Although it is sometimes "broken sounding," audio without video usually transmits quite well even through connections with low bandwidth. The same applications that provide for video conferencing include audio-only conferencing. The connection is made the same way, with an IP address. For best quality on both ends of the connection, participants should use headsets, because speakers produce feedback. If, however, your class is consulting an expert, you will want to have the expert's voice come from speakers for the whole class to hear. This means that the expert must put up with the feedback. It is always best to set up the system and do a trial run with the person to whom your class will connect. A speakerphone is a better alternative if your classroom has a telephone line. The drawback to the telephone line is the long-distance charge. With an Internet connection there is no charge. You can talk to anyone in the world for as long as you want.

CHECKING YOUR UNDERSTANDING

C.1 Using chat and audio and video conferencing is notoriously tricky and fails when you least want it to. Chat is the most reliable, audio conferencing is second, and video conferencing comes in as a distant third. Before you attempt to execute a lesson with a class using any of these technologies, you should be very familiar with them. The only way that you will be able to diagnose and fix a problem that occurs while your class is trying to use one of these technologies is to have run into it before. As a part of training yourself, you should set up chat and audio and video conferencing sessions with another person and run through the checklist of items to practice as listed below.

Chat Practice Items

1. Make a connection with another person using an IP address.
2. Conduct a conversation.
3. There is usually an item listed somewhere in the menu structure called Options. Find this in the software you are using. See Figure C.6 for an example. As you conduct your conversation, practice changing the options and observe the effects. For example, if you are projecting a chat session with an expert with an LCD projector for the whole class to see, how would you change the font size of the text to make it more readable for your students?

Audio Conferencing Practice Items

1. Set up an audio conference with a partner using a headset and microphone. Plug in the headset and microphone yourself, so that you know where the plugs go.
2. Use an IP address to connect with your partner.
3. Spend a few minutes conversing to get used to the sound quality as well as the delays that occur after you speak and before your partner hears you.
4. Find the audio options dialogue box and open it. Practice with the settings. Find out what each one does. Be sure that you make note of the default settings, so that you can return your computer to its original state when you have finished practicing or in case you change a setting and the audio stops working.

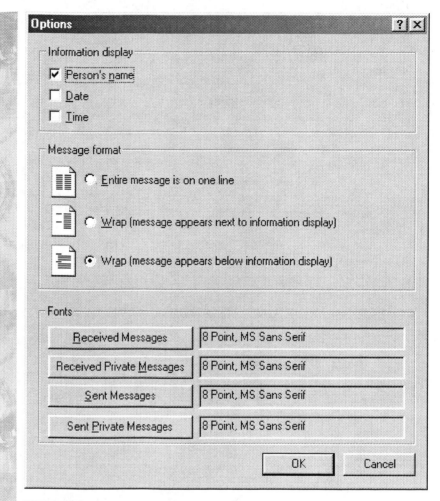

FIGURE C.6 Example of a Chat Options Menu

Video Conferencing Practice Items

1. Set up a video conference with a partner using a headset and microphone. Plug in the headset and microphone yourself, so that you know where the plugs go.
2. Use an IP address to connect with your partner.
3. Spend a few minutes conversing to get used to the sound quality as well as the delays that occur after you speak and before your partner hears you.
4. Practice turning the video off, leaving the audio on. This is sometimes helpful on a bad Internet day. You can see a picture of the person with whom you are conversing for a while, but when the connection is too slow you can turn off the video and talk more comfortably using only audio.
5. Find the video options dialogue box and open it. Practice with the settings. Find out what each one does. Be sure that you make note of the default settings, so that you can return your computer to its original state when you have finished practicing or in case you change

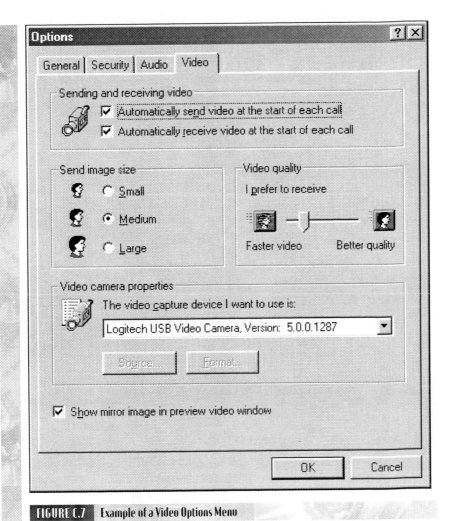

FIGURE C.7 Example of a Video Options Menu

a setting and the audio/video connection stops working. See Figure C.7 for an example of a video settings dialog box.

6. Practice speaking without using earphones. Note the feedback and how it affects your conversation.

C.2 You should complete this exercise at least once each for chat and audio and video conferencing. Have your instructor or your partner disable some element of your conferencing software or hardware without telling you what she or he has done. Using the familiarity with the hardware and software that you acquired in Checking Your Understanding C.1, fix the problem. As you or you and your partner debug the problem, speak out loud, explaining your problem-solving strategies as you proceed. This will help you become more familiar with the language associated with this genre of hardware and software.

D Concept Maps

Different kinds of knowledge are expressed with different kinds of idea maps

There is a variety of different kinds of idea maps for organizing concepts. *Visual Tools for Constructing Knowledge,* by Hyerle (1996), is a well-written, in-depth book on the subject. Because this book is about computer tools, we will not cover idea mapping in the depth that it deserves, but rather encourage you to look at other books and articles to help you develop your skills with these thinking tools. Our goal is to help you understand a few basic mapping techniques very well.

Let's begin with brace and tree maps, ideal tools for knowledge that you want students to classify. If you look carefully at the brace map in Figure 7.2 and the tree map in Figure 7.3 of Chapter 7, you can see that they could show one of the following relationships for any concept:

is part of	is contained in
comprises	includes/is included in
is an example of	

All of the categories in this idea map may contain subcategories. For example, most countries contain states or provinces (which were explored), and states or provinces usually have smaller units, such as counties. It is easy to list all of these levels on a tree or brace map. The following topics yield good tree or brace maps: polygons; plant, animal, or insect classifications; and language groups (for example, Indo-European languages > Romance languages > Spanish).

Brace maps and tree maps are best for classifying examples of concepts, because concepts often exist in hierarchies. However, you cannot completely explain a concept by listing its examples. You must also list its properties or descriptors. *Properties* are qualities that define concepts (categories). Human beings have many properties in common with mammals (i.e., warm blooded, young are born alive, etc.). Properties do not arrange themselves in hierarchies as examples do. They appear in clusters or webs. To compare and contrast the difference between examples and properties, look at Figure D.1. Template idea maps for concepts and their examples are on the left, and maps for concepts and their properties are on the right.

Now look at the properties map in Figure D.2. Notice that there is a central idea (concept), "Plant Organ Systems." It is surrounded by and connected to circles labeled with words that describe it. In the case of "Composition" there are additional

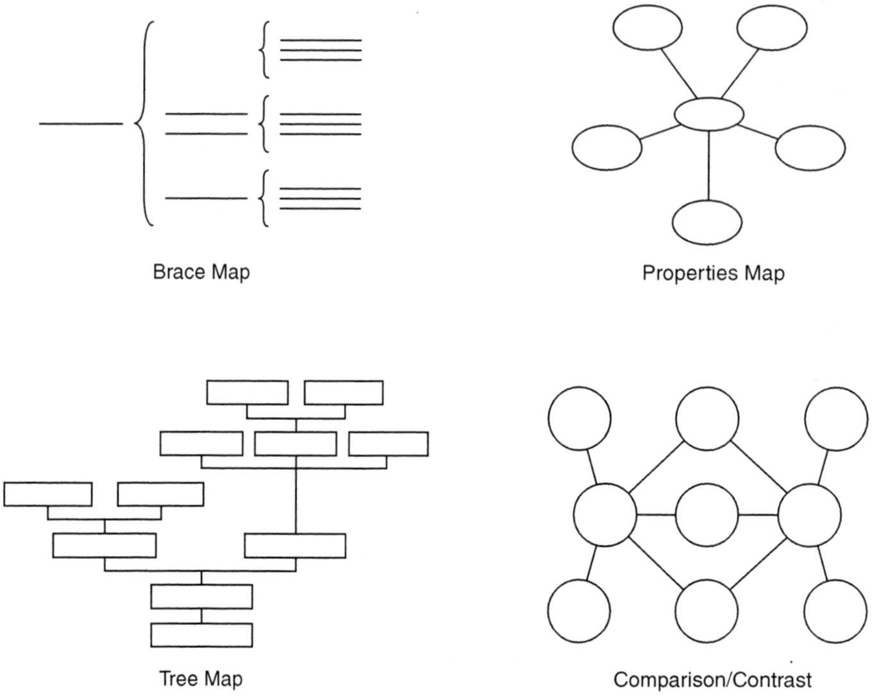

Brace Map

Properties Map

Tree Map

Comparison/Contrast

FIGURE D.1 Some Idea Maps

properties. The map in Figure D.3 is the beginning of a web. Properties maps are concerned with descriptive information rather than levels of detail. They do not have examples. Plant organ systems in this idea map are defined by function, composition, and location. Function would never be below composition or location in a hierarchy. No matter how you think about it, there simply is no hierarchy. Connecting lines and circles to each of the properties (function, composition, location) will add detail to this map. For example, you could draw additional lines out from function that would further explain the function of an organ, such as the chemicals it produces and its relationship to other organs.

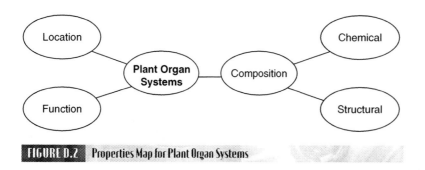

FIGURE D.2 Properties Map for Plant Organ Systems

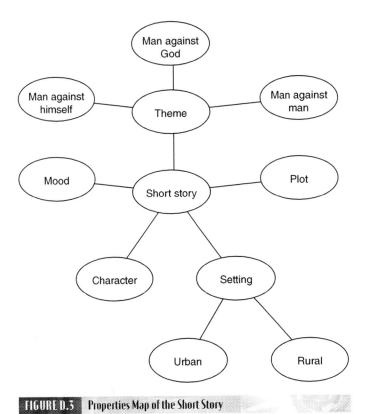

Properties Map of the Short Story

Examples of properties

Thinking of a different example, let us look at a properties map for a short story. Short story is the concept. Theme, setting, character, and mood are its properties. When we look at each of those properties, we find that they themselves have properties. See Figure D.3 for a properties map of the short story. Properties for mood and character are missing, but you get the idea. Using this properties map as a basis for planning, consider how you would develop the navigation for a presentation about a short story based on this map. If the presentation that is a basis for this map were a simple explanation of the short story, then the first ring of ovals around "Short story" would probably represent a menu page. The second set of ovals around each property of short story would represent an information page with explanations and examples of the different ideas that the ovals represent.

As you remember from the preceding paragraphs, you were able to classify examples of concepts using two kinds of idea maps (tree and brace). Properties are no different. There are many ways to draw pictures of properties. Once you start thinking about concepts as either properties problems or classification problems or a combination, you will find that your abilities to express them graphically will become more diverse. For example, one common activity in language arts and social science classes is to compare and contrast. Comparing and contrasting is really a properties problem. You are asking the students to tell you how the properties of some concept are alike and different. This activity can be mapped, and the map can then be

Using properties in language arts and social science

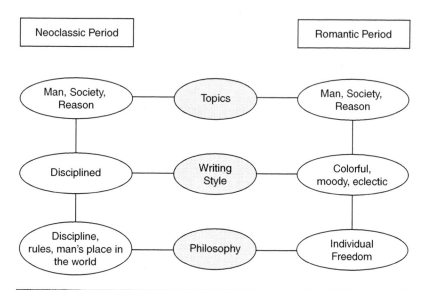

FIGURE D.4 Comparison/Contrast Map of the English Neoclassic and Romantic Periods

used to provide your students with the beginnings of a navigational structure for a presentation.

For an example, let's use a comparison/contrast problem commonly assigned in a senior high English literature class—"Compare and contrast the Neoclassical period in English literature with the Romantic period." Look at Figure D.4, an example of a comparison/contrast map. The gray ovals in the center name the properties that are the basis for the comparison. They are also those ideas that each literary period had in common; each period had a writing style, a set of common topics, and a philosophy. The white circles provide the space where differences (the contrasts) are displayed. Now think about how this map would translate to the design of a presentation. It is clear that the dark gray ovals could represent a menu page, while the light-colored circles would represent the content of the destination pages on the menu.

CHECKING YOUR UNDERSTANDING

D.1 Activity 1

Let's see if you can match an idea with its corresponding kind of idea map. You will be able to choose among the four kinds of idea maps you have just read about. Use a sheet of paper to cover each answer. Write your suggestion before you look at the answer. You will be using the concept map templates in Figure D.1. Which concept map would be most helpful for thinking through the following concepts and the relationships they represent?

Parts of the human body

(*Tree map*)

Similarities and differences between two cultures

(*Compare/contrast map*)

Description of a character in a short story or novel

(*Properties map*)

Illustrating the different levels of government in the United States

(*Tree map*)

Kinds of clouds

(*Properties map*)

The composition of the solar system

(*Tree map*)

Similarities and differences in characters, settings, theme, and mood in short stories, poems, and novels

(*Comparison/contrast map*)

Activity 2

Choose two of the concepts from the list above: one for which you would use a properties map and one for a tree map. Draw the maps.

IDEA MAPS FOR EVENTS

Events are a second kind of knowledge that we have about the world. Unlike concepts, events usually have steps or stages. They are mapped and presented differently than concepts. Events can be chains with a beginning and an end, or they can be cycles with no beginning or end. Figure D.5 is a tree map illustrating how events are classified and Table D.1 provides examples of each of these kinds of events.

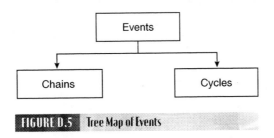

FIGURE D.5 Tree Map of Events

TABLE D.1 Examples of Events Classified by Type

Chain	Cycle
Tornado	Farming
Development of a disease	Maintaining a car
Circulation of blood through the body	Tying a shoelace
The seasons	Working a long division problem

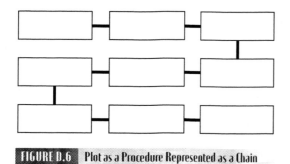

FIGURE D.6 Plot as a Procedure Represented as a Chain

Figure D.6 is an example of how a chain is diagrammed as a map. It could be a description of the steps leading to the birth of a hurricane or the writing of a short story. There is a beginning step and an ending step, and at a low-to-middle level of detail, the steps are quite straightforward. Looking at a chain with content, such as the one in Figure D.7, you would think that building a presentation from a chain diagram would be quite simple. Such a presentation would go from the first page to the last, each page describing each step with some text in a box and perhaps a picture or appropriate audio or video clip.

Such an approach, however, is probably a waste of time and computer resources. As an English teacher, I would rather have the students describe plot with a word processor if this is all they did with the topic when they wrote a presentation. If they wrote a paper with a word processor, at least they would get practice organizing and writing good paragraphs to form a coherent whole. It is important to recognize that a simple event, either chain or cycle, can be made into a richer presentation than a mere recitation of steps. The reason is that within every step there are embedded concepts, each of which has properties and examples. Embedded concepts are the ideas basic to a procedure or process. For example, if you are trying to describe the process that creates a thunderstorm and you don't know what barometric pressure means, then you can't fully understand the process because barometric pressure is an embedded concept in the process of the formation of a thunderstorm.

Idea maps for events

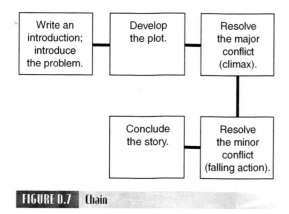

FIGURE D.7 Chain

In the short story example, step one involves introducing a problem or conflict. The student could easily elaborate on this step by linking to a screen that explains that problems are based on themes. This screen could lead to another screen explaining prototypical themes (man against man, man against God, man against society, etc.) that usually form the basis for the problem or conflict. In other words, each step in the chain is really the basis for providing for a rich web of branches to embedded concepts, depending on the students' age and the complexity of the finished product.

Another example of enhancing an explanation of an event by using concepts embedded in each of its steps is provided for you as a map of a hurricane in Figure D.8. Notice that the steps of the event are described in boxes, while the associated concepts appear in ovals. The boxes are connected with arrows to indicate the flow of the event.

The next four figures are examples of how such a chain diagram might develop into a presentation. Spend some time looking at Figure D.8 and then at Figures D.9,

> Adding embedded concepts to a map that describes an event

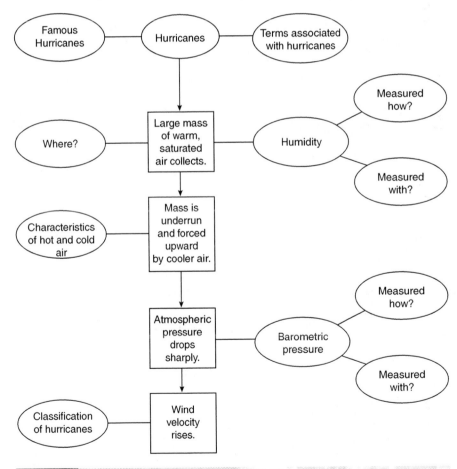

FIGURE D.8 Process in a Chain Diagram Showing Embedded Concepts

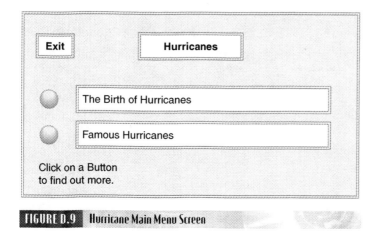

D.10, D.11, and D.12. Associate each screen in these figures with a box or an oval in the chain diagram in Figure D.8.

Now, back to events. The cycle is similar to a chain, in that it is a series of steps or stages. However, there is no beginning or end to the cycle. Now look at Figure D.13, a template for a cycle map, and at Figure D.14, an example of a map of the evaporation cycle. Cycles may be treated very much like chains in a presentation. They, too, have embedded concepts. For example, if you look carefully at Figure D.14, you will see the embedded concepts *vapor* and *precipitation*. These terms are surely worth branches in a presentation. There is an added twist in the evaporation cycle. There are also other events embedded in the Evaporation Cycle map. Note the terms *evaporate* and *condense*. Both are chains that students need to comprehend in order to understand the evaporation cycle.

> Embedded events
> in a cycle

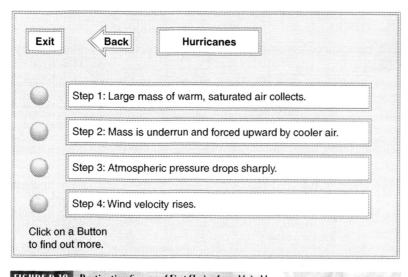

FIGURE D.10 Destination Screen of First Choice from Main Menu

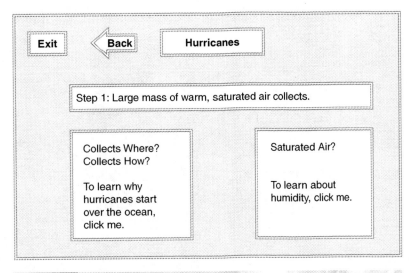

FIGURE D.11 Destination Screen for Step 1

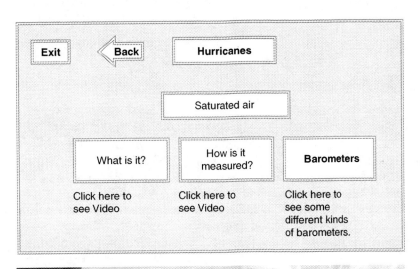

FIGURE D.12 Final Screen Following Step 1 Branch to Humidity

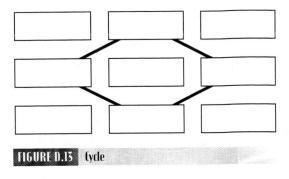

FIGURE D.13 Cycle

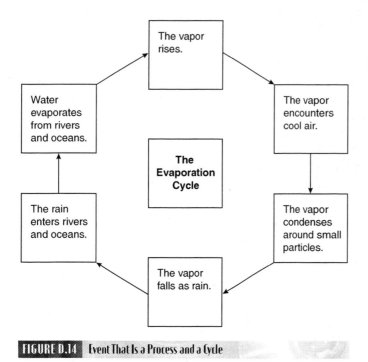

Event That Is a Process and a Cycle

Now think about how students often study these events. They read about the evaporation cycle in their textbooks and learn *vapor, precipitation, condense,* and *evaporate* as vocabulary words. Ideally, the class might do an evaporation/condensation experiment, but most likely, students will learn evaporation or condensation by answering end-of-chapter questions and/or by memorizing definitions.

Students who are practiced at idea mapping and using presentation software, on the other hand, will be compelled to notice embedded concepts in their idea map, make boxes for them, and find out what belongs there. These students may then illustrate them, explain them with text, audio, or even make a narrated video of an evaporation/condensation experiment. Working in this way, students will do the organization and elaboration that they need to attach their new knowledge to old knowledge. This, in turn, will move the evaporation cycle and its embedded concepts and processes to their long-term memory, where these ideas will become part of their permanent store of knowledge.

Summarizing Events   Events are not difficult to recognize, but here are two tips that will help you recognize them.

1. They are composed of segments in which one segment of action must always follow or precede another segment.
2. Certain words are a clue to processes and procedures: "precedes," "follows," "a step in," "is a stage in," "results from," "causes/is caused by," "influences/is influenced

| Why use concept maps? |

by," "enables/originates from," "uses," "exploits/is exploited by," "consumes/is consumed by," "evolves," "provides/is provided by," or "regulates/is regulated by" (Jonassen, 2000).

Remember that events, though seemingly simple and linear on the surface, are often quite complex. Not only do they contain embedded concepts that are prerequisite knowledge for understanding the event, they may also contain embedded events. As students create idea maps, they must be trained to find these ideas and explain them.

LOOKING AT THE BIG PICTURE

You have read a lot about idea maps and seen quite a few examples. You have learned about concepts and events. What you have learned about them is summarized in a short outline below.

1. Concepts are ideas (social class, war, love, kinds of themes in literature) or groups, things, or living creatures (the animal kingdom, kinds of clouds, kinds of rocks) and have
   a. Properties that describe them
   b. Examples
2. Events are either
   a. Chains (beginning and an end)
   b. Cycles (no beginning or end)

Your students should try to diagram these two basic kinds of knowledge in a way that makes sense to them and to you. If people understand the organization of what they are learning, they remember it better (Gagne et al., 1993). You have seen some basic patterns for mapping concepts and events, and there are more. Pause for a moment to study the diagrams in Figures D.15–D.20. Look at how they are alike and different. Think of the topics you teach and how they fit the diagrams.

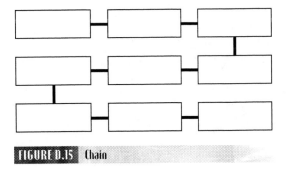

FIGURE D.15 Chain

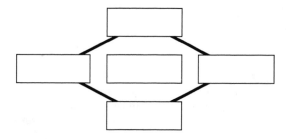

FIGURE D.16 Another Cycle

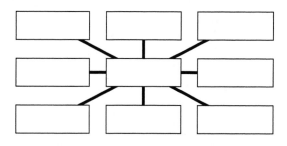

FIGURE D.17 Star (For concepts – comparison/contrast)

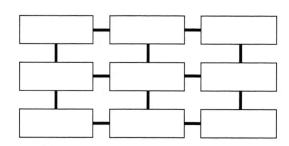

FIGURE D.18 Grid (For concepts – like a table – column headings are properties and rows are examples)

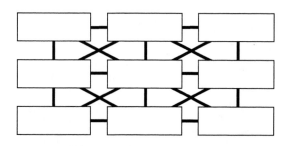

FIGURE D.19 Web (For concepts – shows relationships)

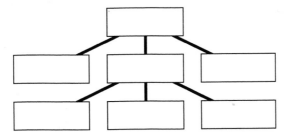

FIGURE D.20 Tree (for concepts – helps with classification)

CHECKING YOUR UNDERSTANDING

D.2 Now we are going to try another exercise. This time, the exercise will provide the topic and you must provide the map. Each topic will fit into one of the six figures (D.15–D.20). Study the shapes carefully. Then take a sheet of paper, and after covering the answers in italics, look at the cue and write the answer to each of these two questions:

1. Is the cue a concept or an event? If it is an event, is it a cycle or a chain?

2. Which map would be most appropriate for describing the cue?

Cover the italicized words below and begin the exercise.

Cue: Mitosis

(Event)

(Cycle)

Cue: Forms of Government

(Concept)

(Tree)

Cue: Plot

(Event)

(Chain)

Cue: Volcanic Eruption

(Event)

(Chain)

Cue: The Four Seasons

(Event)

(Cycle)

Cue: Dinosaurs

(Event)

(Tree or Brace)

Cue: Passing a Bill in Congress

(Event)

(Chain)

Cue: Theme (in a short story or novel)

(*Concept*)

(*Properties diagram*)

Cue: Testing for pH

(*Event*)

(*Chain*)

Cue: Earthquake

(*Concept* [Think about what the characteristics of an earthquake are.])

and/or (could be either)

(*Process* [There is a beginning and an end, and the moments in between are somewhat predictable; i.e., the quake itself and then the aftershocks.])

(*Properties map attached to a chain map*)

▓ REFERENCES

Gagne, E., Yekovich, C. W., & Yekovich, F. R. (1993). *The cognitive psychology of school learning.* Boston: Little Brown & Company.

Hyerle, D. (1996). *Visual tools for constructing knowledge.* Alexandria, VA: Association for Supervision and Curriculum Development.

Jonassen, D. (2000). *Computers as MindTools for schools: Engaging critical thinking.* Upper Saddle River, NJ: Prentice Hall.

Sample Database for an English Class

U.S. SOCIETY REFLECTED IN FICTION

The stories and poems that you have read over the last semester represent different themes, settings, characters, plots, and historical periods. Fiction can tell you a lot about the people and time in which it was written. Your assignment is to write a paper analyzing changes in U.S. society reflected in the stories and poems that you have read this semester.

The way that authors handle theme, plot, character, and setting reflects the conflicts of the society in which they live. If you look for patterns in the key information about each story or novel and then think back to your reading, you will see that American attitudes toward many aspects of life have changed over the last two hundred years. Your database will look something like Table E.1, but it will have many more fields.

Step 1

The first thing you should do is to get to know your database and think about how you might use it. Take a few moments to study the names of the fields below and think about the kind of information they provide for you.

TABLE E.1 Database of U.S. Stories and Poems

Story	Theme	Setting in Time	Gender of Main Character	SES of Main Character
Rip Van Winkle	Man against himself	18th century	m	Lower class
Billy Budd	Man against society	19th century	m	Lower class
The Fall of the House of Usher	Man against himself	19th century	m	Upper class
The Outcasts of Poker Flat	Man against society	19th century	m	Lower class
The Pearl	Man against God	20th century	m	Lower class

1. Conflict (man against himself/other men/God/nature)
2. Setting in time
3. Gender of main character
4. Socioeconomic status (SES) of main character
5. Gender of antagonist
6. SES of antagonist
7. Setting (urban/rural)
8. Setting (name of continent)
9. Mood (tragic/comic/satire)
10. Plot (episodic/linear/*in medias res*)
11. Narrator (first person/third person)
12. Nature (good/bad/no effect)
13. City (good/bad/no effect)
14. Does anyone die violently? (yes/no)
15. If someone dies does the death have meaning? (yes/no)
16. Is there a romantic relationship? (yes/no)
17. If there is a romantic relationship, is it (happy/unhappy)?
18. Does the main character control his or her own destiny? (yes/no)
19. Is there heavy use of symbolism? (yes/no)
20. Date that the story was written
21. Does religion play a role in the story? (yes/no)

Again, your goal is to trace change in American attitudes about life and society over the past two hundred years. To use the database, you will need to think of questions that are related to your goal.

Step 2

Before you actually start asking questions of the database, you must decide what you want to know. List some of the items you think have changed over the past two hundred years. Examples of some are provided below.

1. Role of women
2. An individual sense of who is in control
3. Attitudes toward nature
4. The role of violence in storytelling
5. The kind of people the public is interested in reading about
6. Attitudes toward religion
7. Respect for society and its rules

Step 3

Now that you have thought about some of the ideas that might help you analyze how American attitudes have changed over time, it is time to begin asking questions of the database. Use the hints below to help you work through all of the questions you listed in Step 2. When you key in your questions, remember that sometimes it might take you several tries to translate your question to a format that the computer understands. If the computer gives you an error message or won't give you an answer, try to think of another way to ask the question.

1. Ask a question about one of the ideas you listed in Step 2.

   _____

2. First, you must decide which available fields will give you information about this problem. What are they? _____

3. Next, you must decide how the information in these fields can help you make a comparison. You may only need to ask two questions or you may need to ask four or five to get the information you need to build a query. To help you ask questions, try to divide your thinking into two parts: the facts you need, and the conclusion that the facts point to.

   ◼ Fact (evidence for what I want to know): _____
   ◼ Fact (evidence for what I want to know): _____
   ◼ Fact (evidence for what I want to know): _____
   ◼ Conclusion (What I want to know): _____

Step 4

Now that you have asked questions of the database about all of the items that you listed in Step 2, you should have enough information to begin writing. Use quotes and examples from the stories to support your arguments about how American life and attitudes have changed over the last 150 years. You will present your ideas to the class. After you have listened to your classmates present their findings, answer the questions below.

What changes did you observe that others in the class did not find?

1. _____
2. _____
3. _____
4. _____
5. _____

What changes did others find that you did not find?

1. _____
2. _____
3. _____
4. _____
5. _____

19

Supporting Student Content Learning

My Trip to the Beach

Every summer me and my family and most of my relatives go to the beach in New Jersey. Me and my family and sometimes my aunts and uncles and cousins stay at my uncle's house. I have six uncles but I only see five when I am in New Jersey. One of my uncles on my mom's side, the only one that lives in New Jersey, does not live in Cape May all the time. He owns a lot of houses, about half the time he lives in Cape May County and the other half of the time he lives in New York because he works there.

Case: What Do You Know?

As you read the following scenario, note the different concerns that policymakers, administrators, and other educational stakeholders have about how technology is implemented in schools.

Because of its status as a high-poverty school with students who do not make adequate yearly progress (AYP) on the state's high-stakes test, East Park High School recently received a large federally funded technology grant. The grant requires the school to create a technology plan before receiving funding. The plan must be tied to district goals and national and state standards and must provide a specific action plan that addresses how technology will help meet the content learning achievement of the school's high-needs population. In addition to other information, the plan must include a rationale for the school's proposed computer/student ratio, specific objectives with standards and timelines, and projected yearly improvement in test scores over the next five years. The technology funded by the grant is to be aimed primarily at students who are not performing at grade level or who have not passed the state-mandated exit test after at least one attempt; this includes a large population of English language learners. However, all students at the school are expected to use the technology at some time for content learning.

Mr. Yates, the technology teacher, is the chair of the Technology Committee (TC) at East Park. In addition to Mr. Yates, the TC consists of the vice principal, one teacher from each department at the school, and several staff members. The committee's job is to draft the technology plan. To address the criteria required by the grant, they decide to suggest first how the technology will be assigned, to whom, and in what configurations, what types of hardware and software will be purchased, and how the technology will be accessed equitably and effectively by teachers and students. The TC will also be responsible for creating professional development opportunities for the teachers. The overall focus of its work is to figure out which needs are the most crucial and how technology can help meet those needs.

Answer these questions about the case with your current level of knowledge. Change or add to your answers as needed as you read and understand the issues in this chapter.

1. *What kinds of hardware components should the committee choose? Why?*

    _____

    _____

    _____

2. *What kind of software and/or Internet access should the computers have? Why?*

    _____

    _____

    _____

3. *How can the needs of ELLs and other students with special needs be addressed in the technology plan?*

    _____

    _____

    _____

4. *How should the computers be assigned and laid out?*

    _____

    _____

    _____

5. *Do you see any problems in the way the grant was awarded or how it will be implemented? If so, what are the problems?*

    _____

    _____

    _____

Mr. Yates and the Technology Committee have quite a job ahead of them, but others also have knowledge and experience that can help. Teacher input in particular will be very important to the effective development and implementation of the school's technology plan. All teachers need to understand the implications of the issues that the committee is addressing to help make effective choices for their districts, schools, classrooms, and individual students. To this end, when you finish this chapter, you will be able to:

* Explain how content learning takes place.
* Explain the role of content learning in meeting other instructional goals.
* Discuss guidelines and techniques for using technology in content learning and teaching.
* Analyze technologies that can be used to create opportunities for content learning for all students, including simulations, raw data sites, and even word processing.
* Describe and develop effective technology-enhanced content learning activities.
* Create appropriate assessments for technology-enhanced content learning activities.

Review the NETS for teachers in chapter 1. After mastering the content of this chapter, which of these standards will you be able to meet?

_____

_____

_____

There are many theories about how the learning of "facts" takes place, from behaviorism that emphasizes the importance of practice to constructivism that focuses on the social construction of knowledge. Regardless of which theory seems most believable to individual teachers, all teachers must consider certain principles of learning, particularly when teaching with technology. This chapter will consider many of these principles. To start, see the Meeting the Standards feature for standards that address content learning.

• • • • Meeting the Standards: Content Learning and Technology • • • •

Because content knowledge is seen as fundamental to what schools do, the standards in every subject area list, sometimes explicitly, what content students should grasp to be considered knowledgeable. Words like "understand," "identify," "memorize," and "recognize" are used to describe the content that students should be able to work with. For example, in math, students in grades 6–8 are supposed to "Understand both metric and customary systems of measurement" (NM-MEA.6–8.1) and in health K–4 students should be able to "describe the basic structure and functions of the human body system" (NPH-H.K–4.1). In science,

secondary students need to develop an understanding of the structure of atoms, the cell, energy, and other concepts (NS.9–12.2,3,4) and in social studies to explain how the national government is organized (NSS-C.9–12.3). The national K–12 educational technology standards for students (NETS*S) also address content learning—content in this case includes how to use tools, what responsible use implies, and the "nature and operation of technology systems" (NT.K–12.1). The key to content learning is to understand how content is learned, including what skills are needed and how technology can help.

Find the content-learning standards for your state, grade level, and content area in the Standards section of the Resources Module on the Companion Website. List some of the content that your students will be expected to know.

_____

_____

_____

CW

• • • •

OVERVIEW OF CONTENT LEARNING AND TECHNOLOGY IN K–12 CLASSROOMS

Content knowledge is essential for students in order to meet student learning goals such as problem solving and effective communication. Teachers should first understand the importance of content learning and then how it can be learned and supported by technology while students work toward learning goals.

What Is Content Learning?

There are two parts to the question "What is content knowledge?" The first, what content is, seems rather basic, but the second, what learning is, can be fairly complicated. A look at how content knowledge is acquired can help to answer both parts of the question.

FIGURE 2.1 Creating Connections with Kidspiration

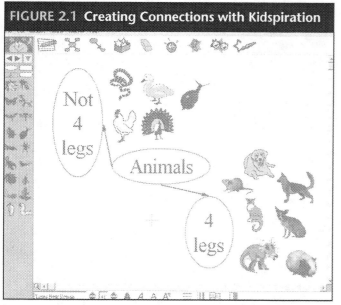

Source: Diagram created in Kidspiration® by Inspiration Software®, Inc.

Researchers and educators typically divide knowledge into three categories: declarative, structural, and procedural. **Declarative knowledge** consists of discrete pieces of information that help us identify things and events (Wignall, 2005). For example, declarative knowledge includes the definition of "democracy" or the names of all the U.S. presidents. Declarative knowledge forms the basis for all other types of knowledge and is essential for students to achieve more complex goals such as creative and critical thinking, communication, production, and inquiry. It is often learned through memorization, drill, and practice, although a variety of scaffolding strategies such as mnemonics, concept mapping, and metaphoric techniques support the acquisition of simple facts. Software packages such as Where in the World Is Carmen SanDiego (Broderbund) and Reader Rabbit (The Learning Company), in which specific facts are the focus, can help students to acquire and practice declarative knowledge. However, students must also have structural and procedural knowledge to carry out the functions in these software packages.

Structural knowledge is an understanding of how pieces of declarative knowledge fit together. When students have pieces of information among which relationships are created in their minds, this information has been *contextualized* and/or *schematized*. Another way to describe structural knowledge is as information that has been developed into a mental model. For example, structural knowledge includes the understanding that a toothbrush is necessary to brush teeth, or that evaporation is related to liquids. Structural knowledge can be represented through, for example, concept maps, categorizations, and classifications, and it is supported by concept-mapping software such as Inspiration or Kidspiration. An example of animal classification using Kidspiration is shown in Figure 2.1. Jonasson and Wang (1992) note that when learners focus on structural relationships among pieces of information, they acquire structural knowledge. This leads to the ability to use higher order thinking skills.

Procedural knowledge is the knowledge of action, or the knowledge of how to do something (Williams, 2000). Examples include how to speak Spanish, how to teach with technology, how to drive a car or use a cell phone. It is based on declarative knowledge but learned through the relationships in structural knowledge. Teachers often access procedural knowledge through student performance, having students construct a technology-enhanced product such as an essay, a presentation, or a graphical representation of a concept.

Figure 2.2 presents a simple model of the relationships among these knowledge types.

Make a short list of ways that students might acquire declarative knowledge. What techniques or strategies can they use? How might this process affect the technology plan under development? Why?

_____

_____

_____

_____

FIGURE 2.2 Simple Model of Knowledge Acquisition

Declarative knowledge
"This is the computer's 'on' switch"

fits into

Structural knowledge

This is the computer's "on" switch

The computer works if you turn it on

Switches can be pressed

This is a computer

Switches often require electricity to work

can lead to

Procedural knowledge
To make this computer work, turn on the computer by pressing the "on" switch.

Traditionally, many educators have thought of declarative knowledge as "content," and some of the standards reinforce this view by listing discrete pieces of information that students should know. However, many standards also list procedures that students should be able to carry out, so simple declarative knowledge is not enough to say that students "know" something. Students must also be able to do something with the knowledge/content to show that they have mastered it.

Educators have mixed views of when students can be deemed knowledgeable about a subject—and legislators and tests often determine the current understanding. For example, some claim it to be when students have memorized the names of the scientific elements and others when they can use the periodic chart to make statements about living things. In other words, while *information-knowing* is the goal set for some students, *knowledge creation* is the goal for others. Teachers who do not go beyond declarative knowledge teaching and testing, however, are doing their students a disservice by ignoring students' needs to be able to make connections and to use knowledge to act.

It seems a rather simple matter for students to learn content, but it is far more complex than most people think. Some content, and the relevant skills needed to learn it, is disciplined-based; for example, science uses a different form of exploration and expression than English literature, and the way that math is presented, used, and produced is different still. This implies that different ways to learn and teach content might be necessary across disciplines.

In addition, although brain science is making great strides in providing information about how and why people learn, the factors that make students learn in different ways are still not entirely clear. It is clear, however, that individual sets of factors such as culture, economic status, first language, educational background, and age can affect learning on a person-by-person and day-by-day basis (Norman, 2004). In addition, brain research has also shown that stress hinders learning and that "emotionally important content learned in school is very likely to be permanently remembered" (Erlauer, 2003, p. 13). That means that content that is tied in some important way to learners' lives will have more impact on their learning. Clearly, both internal (i.e., learner characteristics) and external (i.e., environmental) factors contribute to knowledge acquisition. Teachers can consider all of these ideas as they plan content lessons supported by technology.

Among the external factors that affect learning, the classroom environment, focusing on the arrangement of technology, is important to discuss. Although some external factors are not under the teacher's control, the teacher often has choices in setting up technology in the classroom and school.

Physical Contexts for Technology-Supported Learning

The physical arrangement of the classroom, including placement of desks, whiteboard, and other resources, can affect how students learn because the roles that these resources, including technology, can play vary by how the classroom is designed. Most teacher education programs address the physical environment in their classroom management course, but the importance of the location of technology, particularly computers, is often overlooked. As McKenzie (1998) notes, classroom design can actually work against good teaching by restricting the use of the equipment or creating barriers to good use.

Technology can be configured in many ways. Typical designs are a one-computer classroom, multiple-computer classroom, and lab, and all of these configurations can be used for different activities at different grade levels.

One-computer classroom

Although not typically the optimal situation for all students to receive maximum benefit from the power of computing, a lot can be done with one computer. For example, the teacher can use the computer to provide prereading exercises, focus whole-class discussion, or lead teams through a game or simulation (other examples are provided throughout this book). However, the computer must be accessible to all students; in other words, it should have a high-quality projector or large monitor attached, and there must be room for all students to sit, view, and participate. In addition, students with special needs must have access to tools that help them to participate. These include special keyboards, screen readers, and other tools described later in this chapter.

Excellent content software and resources for K–12 that make effective use of the one-computer classroom are available from Tom Snyder Productions (www.tomsnyder.com) and Sunburst (www.sunburst.com). For example, in Tom Snyder's Decisions, Decisions series, the

Inclusion

FIGURE 2.3 Learning in a One-Computer Classroom

software presents a scenario and then offers students choices of how to proceed. With the teacher facilitating, the students discuss the issues and come to a decision as to which choice is best based on the information they have. The software shows the consequences of that action and presents students with another choice, and the task concludes after several additional decisions. The photo in Figure 2.3 shows teacher Jennifer Robinson leading her students through Tom Snyder's Decisions, Decisions: Prejudice software.

Multiple computers

In a classroom of 25 students, three to five computers do not seem like much help, and they are not if they are relegated to a corner of the room and only used for free time or remediation. However, separated into "activity zones" or "interest centers" (McKenzie, 1998), they can blend into the daily workings of the class and be integrated into classroom goals. For example, in a classroom where students are producing books, one center could be used for research, one for development, and one for printing. Or, where students are studying ancient Egypt, each team of students could work with their topic in a different area of the classroom.

Lab

There are all kinds of designs for computer labs. Unfortunately, the most common is still computers in separate carrels or in rigid rows that create physical barriers between the students and teacher or the students and their peers. This makes it difficult for students to collaborate, use other spaces for learning, and observe modeling by and receive feedback from the teacher. In fact, Theroux (2004) notes that the "most difficult and least effective way to integrate technology is to consistently take all students into the computer lab to work on the same activities at the same time" (p. 1). In part this is because the individual nature of the lab setting is a barrier to working with the teacher or other students, and the activity does not consider differences among students in technology skill or content knowledge.

A variety of effective alternative arrangements can make a lab setting a more flexible and useful space. These arrangements include furniture such as hideaway desks into which the monitor can be completely recessed (shown in Figure 2.4), groupings such as pods of four to six computers, and tables where students can work offline. These arrangements can all contribute to making the computer classroom a place where instructional goals can be met.

FIGURE 2.4 Hideaway Desk

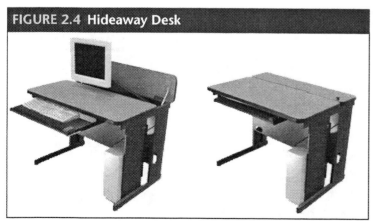

Source: Used with permission of Computer Comforts, Inc.

Flotillas

According to McKenzie, another useful layout for schools that do not have a critical mass of computers is a **flotilla,** or a set of computers that rotate among classrooms. Students use the computers for several weeks to participate in technology-intensive projects, and then the technology moves on to another classroom. Many schools use mobile labs (moveable carts that store 20–30 laptops) to provide computers to classrooms when needed.

Equal access

Whichever layout is chosen, the Americans with Disabilities Act (ADA) and state and local regulations require that all students have equal access to the technology. To make sure that there are as few physical barriers as possible, teachers, students, and school staff can make it a point to make sure that:

- Pathways in classrooms and labs are wheelchair accessible.
- One or more desks allows for wheelchair access.
- The printer and other peripherals are located in easily accessed locations.
- Any tables or other work spaces are at a variety of heights.
- Assistive devices such as screen glare reducers, alternative keyboards, and screen readers that might be used fairly often are immediately available.
- Any important documents are available in a variety of formats and prints so that diverse users can access them.
- Web sites and other technologies are accessible.

The Tool CloseUp: AlphaSmart provides a description of a tool that supports equal access. For more information about equal access, see the Accessibility section of the Resources module for this chapter on the Companion Website (http://www.prenhall.com/egbert).

To determine the technology's layout and design, we must consider what students need to do with the technology and what design allows them to do it. McKenzie (1998) recommends that teachers view other classrooms and expert designs before making decisions about the layout of technology. Some ideas are available in photo shots at www.fno.org.

Other technologies

The availability and accessibility of cameras, handhelds, microphones, tape recorders, overhead projectors, printers, and other hardware tools also need to be considered for effective student learning. How will they be accessed? Where will students need to and be able to use them? Yatvin (2004) points out that printers should be in the workspace with computers so that students do not get frustrated by having to travel or wait to get their printed products. Similarly, tools that are locked in a closet on the other side of the school or can only be checked out on Thursday morning provide little support for content learning.

Other considerations in the physical space

McKenzie and other educators suggest that a computer is needed for every 3–4 students for all students to have the access they need to participate in effective technology-enhanced tasks. Not all the computers need to be the newest; rather, students can draft assignments on lower-end computers and use better ones for more advanced tasks. An important consideration is that students have storage space on the network so that they can move from computer to computer on the network and not be tied to one computer or to an (easily lost) CD or floppy disk.

There is no one right way to design the layout of technology to support student learning. Whichever layout teachers and technology coordinators decide on, they need to understand the implications for learning. This goes for other tools as well; sometimes electronic technologies do not provide authentic information and sometimes the information is not exactly what students need. Therefore the physical space assigned to desktop computers should also provide access to other basic resources such as books, films, and a variety of other tools that might be more reliable, easier to access, and easier to carry.

Which of these designs should Mr. Yates and the TC choose for the high school? Why?

_____

_____

_____

Characteristics of Effective Technology-Supported Content Learning Tasks

Teachers teach from different philosophical standpoints, and students learn based on many different variables—such as the arrangement of the classroom, as noted above—many of which are discussed throughout this text. However, there are basic principles of teaching and learning that

Tool CloseUp: AlphaSmart

A teacher recently introduced the AlphaSmart to her peers in this way:

> An AlphaSmart is a portable word processor. Usually it allows the student to see 2–3 lines of their typing. It is used with a lot of my students on IEPs [individualized education programs, typically written for students in special education] whose handwriting and the motor act of writing keeps them from demonstrating their thinking and writing skills so keyboarding is a better option. It is also used to teach typing. They can then be connected to a computer and the piece can be transferred on the computer for editing or to be saved to the student's folder on the server. The down side to the AlphaSmart is the inability to see the whole essay or story so sometimes it makes for tricky editing and I find it really impacts paragraphing. Some of my students have the newer super version that also has Inspiration loaded on it. With the newer ones there are cords that allow the student to transfer from AlphaSmart to Mac back to AlphaSmart then to home onto PC and then back to AlphaSmart to be used at school and repeat the cycle as needed.

There is even more that the AlphaSmart can do. These portable keyboards can be set up for right-hand only or left-hand only use. In addition, the amount of time that a key must be pressed to make it work can be adjusted so that students who cannot move quickly can type accurately. These relatively inexpensive machines can also be adapted to specific students in other ways; for example, less nimble students can use one-finger (rather than the usual two-finger) capitalization; the font size can be changed easily for those with visual impairments; and the Alpha-Smart DANA model can translate text into speech. Most important for schools that allow students to take Alpha-Smarts home, the AlphaSmart is extremely durable—unlike most PCs, the AlphaSmart can be dropped and even smashed and come out unscathed.

In inclusive classrooms, all students can be equipped with AlphaSmarts for the price of about three new high-end PCs. Giving each student this tool means not singling out certain students and ensuring that students can help each other make use of the technology. For more information and lessons that use AlphaSmarts, see http://www1.alphasmart.com.

The AlphaSmart 3000

Source: Used with permission of AlphaSmart, LLC.

How could an AlphaSmart help to meet the guidelines in this chapter? Should Mr. Yates include it in the technology plan? Why or why not?

_____

_____

_____

_____

Tutorial
CW

To learn more about AlphaSmarts, see the AlphaSmart tutorial in the Tutorial module on the Companion Website (http://www.prehall.com/egbert).

support all of the learning goals. Following these principles in task development can help teachers to support all students, including those who are often underserved, such as ELL, gifted, and students with special needs.

In general, effective content learning tasks

1. *Engage students.* Students are motivated and find the tasks meaningful. Work does not always have to be "fun," but it should be interesting and meaningful and take place in an environment that is emotionally safe (Erlauer, 2003).

2. *Help students become responsible for their own learning, in whole or in part.* If students are engaged, teachers can use a gradual release of responsibility to move students toward independent learning (Pearson & Gallagher, 1983). To do so, tasks must allow students to investigate some of their own questions rather than having them supplied.

3. *Encourage students to be strategic.* During effective tasks, students make systematic, thoughtful choices of how to meet learning challenges. They decide which strategies, resources, and tools will help them complete the task (see New Horizons for Learning, 2002, for strategy descriptions and research support).

4. *Require collaboration.* Effective learning takes place through interaction with others, so tasks must require that students work together, share information, and contribute to the understanding of others (Vygotsky, 1978).

5. *Focus on essential questions.* Rather than just gathering information, students need tasks during which they frame and investigate important questions. Such tasks are more likely to use technology well, engage students, and lead to gains in learner achievement. According to McKenzie (2004a), these questions include:

   • Why do things happen the way they do?
   • How could things be made better?
   • Which do I select?

These questions integrate the need for declarative knowledge, or data, with a requirement to consider, transform, and make decisions that result in insight. Instead of content knowledge being only the forebear of other types of thinking such as problem solving or creativity, gains in content knowledge are also a *result* of those types of thinking. Examples of student research with essential questions can be found at http:// questioning.org/. A more thorough explanation of the research process can be found in Falk & Blumenreich (2005).

In other words, content can be learned before, throughout, and as a result of working toward learning goals such as critical and creative thinking, communication, production, and inquiry. Students who learn content as procedural knowledge can also perform well on tests of declarative knowledge and on performance assessments. On the other hand, learning content solely through information gathering can result in students handing in hundreds of pages of data printed directly from the Internet and not understanding a single page. Figure 2.5 sums up the characteristics of effective content learning tasks.

How do the characteristics of effective content learning tasks affect decisions that Mr. Yates and the TC will make? Remember to consider the structure of high schools and the fact that this high school is in a high-poverty area.

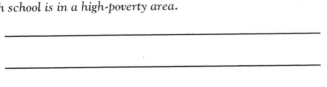

FIGURE 2.5 Characteristics of Effective Technology-Supported Content Learning Tasks	
Characteristic	**Example**
Students are engaged.	Students work on tasks that are important and meaningful to them.
Students are encouraged to become responsible for their own learning.	Students ask and answer their own questions.
Students are strategic.	Students can plan their learning.
The task requires collaboration.	Students must work with each other throughout the task, not just compile individual results at the end.
The task focuses on essential questions.	Why? How? Which?

Student Benefits from Technology-Supported Content Learning

Content learning, if we define it only as the acquisition of declarative knowledge, is important because it forms the basis for gaining other kinds of knowledge. Some educators believe that students only need to know *where* to find and *how* to obtain declarative knowledge rather than controlling or mastering the information itself, and that computer technologies are best suited to this purpose. However, this focus leaves students with researching skills but without content to which to apply these skills. For students to benefit from content study they must build schema and learn how to act in various situations. This will result in both the acquisition of information and the knowledge that can result from interacting with it.

THE TECHNOLOGY-SUPPORTED CONTENT LEARNING PROCESS

Figure 2.2 showed relationships among declarative, structural, and procedural knowledge. Although the exact biological and psychological mechanisms that lead to the acquisition of declarative knowledge, and in turn to the other types of knowledge, are not known, it is fairly clear that new content is attached to old content in the brain in some way (Erlauer, 2003; Johnson, 2004); therefore, for tasks to be meaningful they must activate students' prior knowledge.

Although we do not yet know the specifics of how the brain processes content, teachers can still teach and observe student outcomes to help understand how these links are made in classrooms. Content learning in classrooms occurs through general stages of planning, engaging, and evaluating. During an effective content learning process, students:

1. *Understand where they are supposed to go.* Goals and objectives are clear and accessible to all students, including those who speak different first languages and others who access information in diverse ways.

2. *Assess their current knowledge and skills and the level of each.* Students should reflect on how they can reach the goals and what knowledge and skills they need to get there. Planning is facilitated by the teacher, peers, and others.

3. *Engage in activities that help them to acquire the knowledge and skills they need.* Students must find and be given resources that directly apply.

4. *Evaluate how they did.* Feedback from the teacher and others, self-reflection, standardized tests, comprehension questions, and interviews contribute to an understanding of the extent to which goals were met.

This outline does not really speak to how each step in the process is carried out specifically—teachers have to make that choice knowing their students. For example, in a diverse class of first graders, the teacher may decide that both a teacher-fronted discussion and a cooperative group work will help the students understand their task. After she has worked with her learners for a while, she may skip the teacher-fronted discussion and go right to the cooperative group format for task instruction. In eighth grade, one English teacher may use a spontaneous writing task to evaluate the level of written proficiency for her class; another English teacher may decide to give both a standardized test and interviews because she knows that her students perform differently on different tasks. Figure 2.6 presents an overview of the content learning process.

FIGURE 2.6 Overview of the Technology-Supported Content Learning Process

Student Stage	Ideas for Technology-Supported Implementation
Understand	Make overall learning goals and objectives clear. Present them in many ways—text, audio, graphics—and refer back to them during the process.
Assess	Help with personal goal-setting and current understanding of content knowledge. Use Inspiration and other graphical organizers to describe declarative, structural, and procedural knowledge.
Engage	Provide appropriate resources and make sure that tasks work toward learning objectives. Give students access to Web sites, book lists, content software, and experts.
Evaluate	Provide feedback through test scores, interviews, and other assessments and allow opportunities for self-reflection. Students can use a word processor to create knowledge summaries and digital sound recorders to record observations and ideas.

What does this process imply for the development of the technology plan at East Park High School?

_____

_____

_____

Teachers and Technology-Enhanced Content Learning

In any classroom, the teacher's role in the content learning process may change from task to task, and task-specific challenges may arise for both teachers and students. Understanding both possible roles and potential challenges is crucial for teachers.

The teacher's role in content learning

To help students move from declarative knowledge to structural and procedural knowledge, teachers can guide students to make connections, test hypotheses about how things work, and explore how ideas go together. Realistically, for expediency and to meet some student needs, the teacher's role must sometimes be to model, demonstrate, or lecture to the whole class. At other times, the teacher can facilitate and support as students explore.

Challenges for teachers

Because content teaching often occurs while students work toward the learning goals of critical thinking, problem solving, communicating, and so on, many of the same challenges are present whether electronic technologies are used or not. However, computer use presents some particular challenges. For example, plagiarism (discussed in chapter 6) can be particularly rampant with Web-based research or content-gathering projects. However, by asking students to answer essential questions rather than just having them gather information, plagiarism can be controlled to some extent.

A real challenge for teachers using technology is to first learn the technology; teachers cannot help students with technical issues if they do not understand the software and/or hardware. Tips and guidelines throughout this text suggest ways for teachers to overcome this barrier, and resources are offered in chapter 9.

Time, always an issue for teachers, is an especially relevant challenge in content teaching and learning, especially with pressures to cover the curriculum, having to teach students research skills, and competing with other teachers for resources (Goldman, Cole, & Syer, 1999). The use of expert teacher or student groups that have mastered a concept or technology and can teach it can help with time issues. Additionally, resources such as Kids Click (http://www.kidsclick.org) give teachers a list of Web sites that have already been evaluated for use by students. Another useful resource is the "Kids' Search Engines" section of searchenginewatch.com, which describes search engines such as Ask Jeeves for Kids (http://www.askforkids.com) that are prefiltered or otherwise appropriate for students.

Learning to use and integrate technology with educational goals, especially specific content, does take time and effort. However, it can be made easier. Start with the essentials as presented in this book—an understanding of how students learn, what the goals of education are, what steps can be taken to help students achieve, and how technology can help. Then, by applying strategies mentioned throughout this book, learn more about what technology works in your specific contexts. One very effective and often overlooked resource is the school library media specialist, who is specially educated to support learning with technologies of all kinds.

GUIDELINES FOR SUPPORTING TECHNOLOGY-ENHANCED STUDENT CONTENT LEARNING

Content *teaching* is the focus of many teacher education programs, but more important is to understand how to make content *learning* most effective. The guidelines in this section focus on how to give all students opportunities to learn.

Designing Opportunities to Learn Content

All students can and do learn something, regardless of how they are taught. However, to focus that learning in productive ways and maximize learning gains, teachers can follow these guidelines:

Guideline #1: Incorporate principles of just-in-time learning. **Just-in-time (JIT) learning** is learning that occurs just when it is needed (Riel, 1998), but it is more planned than what educators call a "teachable moment," or a spontaneous opportunity to introduce a new concept or idea. As a complement to an ordered, standardized series of lessons that accomplish the curriculum, JIT learning delivers skills and information when students can best use, learn, and remember them. For example, an ELL who is working on reporting a historical event needs to know how to form and use the past tense of verbs, and JIT presentation of this grammatical concept will occur effectively during the broader task. When the teacher observes that the student needs this information, she can tutor the student, provide resources for the student to check, or assign another student to explain the concept. As another example, during the study of an abstract scientific concept in the textbook, some students might need a JIT lesson in finding the main ideas, particularly if their preferred learning style is visual or kinesthetic. The teacher can meet with the small group and teach a lesson on main ideas, have students use a computer program such as Tom Snyder's *Reading for Meaning* to practice finding main ideas, or assign class "reading experts" to work with those who need help.

Students do not often grasp the utility of a concept or the connection of ideas when they are first presented if there is not a true need to know. JIT learning necessitates careful observation by the teacher so that she can provide help and scaffolds when needed. It also requires teachers to have resources ready, or train students to access them, for potential areas of need, and to guide students in whatever way they need through the information.

Technology can support JIT learning and teaching in many ways; for example, the vast amount of information that is accessible in various formats and languages on the Internet means that ELLs and other students can find help on just about any issue. When the student asks the teacher for help with a grammar topic or needs a more simplified explanation of a science topic, the student can probably find something on the Web to help. However, the teacher's guidance is still central to ensuring that students find the information they need and use it in appropriate ways.

Guideline #2: Differentiate instruction. One of the chapter 5 tips recommends enriching the classroom environment through the use of materials that appeal to students' different senses and intelligences. From that discussion it is clear that students respond to different kinds of enrichment. **Differentiated instruction** is another way to provide enrichment for students' abilities, interests, and learning needs. In differentiated instruction, the goals and concepts are the same for all students, but the challenge varies so "all students are challenged and no students are frustrated" (Theroux, 2004, p. 2). According to Theroux (2004), teachers can differentiate instruction by giving students three to four different options in their work. She notes that some students will take different options at different times, depending on varying interests, subject-area ability or readiness, and learning preferences. Teachers can start out slowly by varying the content, process, product, or tool, or they can provide choices in any or all four at different stages of an activity.

Technology can help differentiate instruction (Tomlinson, 2001; Yatvin, 2004) by providing a variety of tools for different tasks at different times or for the same task by different students. For example, in a unit about bugs, one group of students may access information about how bugs communicate by using the videos and games in the Sidewalk Science program "Bugs" (Scholastic), while more proficient students might use a Web site such as http://insectzoo.msstate.edu/. Less proficient students might use another tool that is suited to their level. For all students, but particularly ELLs and

---

FROM THE CLASSROOM

Differentiation

This year at my school the staff has focused on differentiation of instruction to ensure all students reach the standards. All students are involved in the same goal, but how the teacher helps individual students reach the goal is different. Using differentiation in my class has helped more students master benchmarks versus having modified lessons for different students. My ELL students need to learn to write a persuasive paper—at the computer is a template that "guides" them through the process, prompting them with specific questions to answer in their paper. Other students may be working at their desk brainstorming, drafting, peer sharing [w]hile other students may be using a graphic organizer to organize the content of their writing. When lessons are modified—some students are then not necessarily working at reaching a standard. The technology available in the classroom helps develop differentiated learning opportunities. (Jean, sixth-grade teacher)

students with diverse needs, differentiated instruction can provide opportunities to access the content and language they are learning, an essential component of learning. Read as one teacher describes differentiation at her school in From the Classroom: Differentiation on the previous page.

Guideline #3: Teach in a culturally responsive manner. Research shows that students whose lives are addressed and supported in classrooms learn better and achieve more. Teachers can make sure this happens by teaching in a *culturally responsive* manner. This means using materials that are **culturally relevant,** or that celebrate the lives and heritages of all students and reflect the contributions of all groups. Being culturally responsive empowers learners and makes learning meaningful for them, whether they are from another country, a different religion, or a minority group. For example, many groups throughout history have contributed to our current understandings of math, from the discovery of zero (see an overview at http://www-groups.dcs.st-and.ac.uk/~history/HistTopics/Zero.html) to contributions by women and people of many ethnicities (see http://www.ncrel.org/sdrs/areas/issues/educatrs/presrvce/pe3lk36.htm). Teachers can access culturally relevant information both on the Web and through software such as Culturegrams (http://www.culturegrams.com/). Teachers can also find lessons on the Web that suggest different ways to be more culturally responsive. Additionally, by connecting with families through software such as Parent Organizer (http://www.parentorganizer.com/) or Connect-Ed (Notification Technologies, Inc., http://www.notification.com/), teachers can find help in understanding and integrating learners' cultural resources.

Guideline #4: Adapt materials to be accessible for all students. Teachers can adapt, modify, and enhance materials in many ways to make the content more accessible to students. Adaptations can include:

a. Using graphic depiction
b. Outlining the text
c. Rewriting the text
d. Using audiotapes
e. Providing live demonstrations
f. Using alternate books (Echevarria & Graves, 2002)

However, it is important that adapted materials not sacrifice academic content for simplistic understandings. Adaptations allow ELLs, students with various physical impairments, and students with different learning preferences to have equitable chances to access the materials.

As Egbert (2005) notes, teachers do not have to make all of these changes themselves—they can enlist more proficient students to help, work in teacher groups and share materials, and find these materials on the Web.

Guideline #5: Balance content and tools. As Goldman et al. (1999) and many others have noticed, when computer technologies are adopted, learning the technology tools often takes precedence over learning the content. Teachers can help students find a balance between the two. For example, a student's first PowerPoint presentation does not have to include audio and video. Read as two classroom teachers discuss balance in different ways in From the Classroom: Balance. In addition, make it easy for students to save their work; losing work that then has to be redone not only frustrates students but wastes considerable time and energy. Given the extra learning time that technology use might add to a project, plan more time for projects that involve technology, including technology down times and problems. Teachers can decide not to use electronic technologies in favor of content learning. However, striking a balance between the two often leads to achievement in both.

Figure 2.7 on page 50 lists the guidelines from this chapter.

FROM THE CLASSROOM

Balance

We have all heard the advantages and disadvantages of these tools. The concern I heard most often—how will they ever learn (math facts, spelling), students are too dependent on the tools and don't try on their own first. Teachers need to remember: What is the goal or objective of a lesson, how can the goal be reached—strategies/skills/tools needed to reach the goal, what support does a student need—scaffolding, language, drill. And, remember the assessment must be integrated in the learning. I prefer that my students first try to solve problems using their thinking power—then use the tools available—spell check, calculator, resources, each other, teacher. (Jean, sixth-grade teacher)

In regards to students using IRC [Internet Relay Chat] with friends, has anyone noticed a decline in students' abilities to write correctly with grammar and spelling? IRC has given rise to an entire new subculture language that kids are using for hours on end. I actually had a middle school student turn in homework with IRC lingo. To her, the word "for" is spelled "4," and that's how she turned in her paper. Is anyone else seeing evidence of this in the school setting? (Barbara, third-grade bilingual teacher)

How can the guidelines described here help Mr. Yates and the TC with the technology plan?

_____

_____

_____

FIGURE 2.7 Guidelines for Content Teaching

Suggestion	Ideas for Technology-Supported Implementation
Understand	Make overall learning goals and objectives clear. Present them in many ways——text, audio, graphics——and refer back to them during the process.
Guideline #1: Incorporate just-in-time learning.	Have mini-lessons ready to go on topics relevant to the lesson. Bookmark Web sites ahead of time.
Guideline #2: Differentiate instruction.	Vary content, process, product, and/or technologies to give students a variety of possible challenges.
Guideline #3: Teach in a culturally responsive manner.	Connect with parents to better understand students' home cultures. Send technology and the products of technology home to share with parents.
Guideline #4: Adapt materials.	Find, create, and share materials that have been modified to work with different ability levels but the same content. Set up a database by grade/topic/curricular goal that all teachers can access.
Guideline #5: Balance content and tools.	Use the simplest technology that serves the purpose when starting out. Add features as projects and activities warrant and extensions for those capable.

CONTENT LEARNING TECHNOLOGIES

Most teachers have a pretty good idea of how to teach content, but they may not understand as well how technology can help. Of course students can get facts and information from software and Web sites, but how does technology help content learning result in more than declarative knowledge? For one, it can "offer representations, visualizations, and interactions that really help students negotiate concepts and abstractions" (Goldman et al., 1999, p. 8). For example, students may understand that towns need people and that people need schools and so on. However, until they use the simulation SimTown (Maxis) to create their own towns and watch their towns succeed or fail, they may not understand how a complete town system really works.

In addition, students can obtain all kinds of raw data that do not have meaning until they transform the data in some way. For example, the National Center for Educational Statistics (nces.ed.gov) compiles data on education trends across the nation. Until students transform and apply the statistics to look at how the numbers are affecting their lives and communities, they may not understand the impact of demographics on their lives.

Many Web sites emphasize content learning, such as the Student Page of the global Cable News Network site (www.cnn.com), the U.S. National Aeronautics and Space Administration site (www.nasa.gov), and the Electronic Zoo (http://netvet.wustl.edu/e-zoo.htm; see Figure 2.8). In addition, professional organizations such as the National Council of Teachers of Mathematics, the National Science Teachers Association, and the International Reading Association suggest many useful sites for content learning.

Software programs such as Encarta (Microsoft) and Sammy's Science House (Edmark) can support content-based learning. Students can use office software such as PowerPoint, Excel, FrontPage

(Microsoft) and other multimedia development packages to compile and report their findings. The Tool CloseUp: Microsoft Word on page 53 describes how this common tool can play an important role in content learning.

ELLs can use these tools successfully if their use is *carefully planned* so that the language and content are made accessible to the students. Teachers can add external documents, as described in chapter 4, and provide any necessary organizers, prompts, or adaptations to make the content and language relevant and authentic.

For free office tools with many of the capabilities in the Office Suite, go to http://www.goffice.com or http://www.thinkfree.com.

A variety of bilingual software products may also help teacher confidence when using technology with ELLs. Software packages such as Bilingual Timeliner (Tom Snyder Productions), the I Spy/Veo, Veo Series from Scholastic, Decimal & Fraction Maze (Great Wave Software), MathKeys (The Learning Company), Usborne's Animated First 1,000 Words (Tom

FIGURE 2.8 The Electronic Zoo

Source: Used with permission of Washington University.

Snyder Productions), or Physics at Work (Videodiscovery) aim specifically at bilingual students in their content and skill learning. Other software packages such as Kid Pix (Broderbund) give students the option of using either English or Spanish but keeping icons consistent in both versions. In the classroom, teachers and students can also use native language-specific and bilingual Web sites as interactive tools for content learning. Find a list of additional Web sites in this chapter's Resources module on the Companion Website (http://www.prenhall.com/egbert).

ELL

EVALUATING TOOLS

New and "improved" content-focused tools for ELLs, special needs, and traditional students are introduced in the market all the time. These tools need to be carefully evaluated to justify the cost and to ensure they meet learning goals. Although having one teacher evaluate the tool is better than purchasing it without a review, it is better to use it in a classroom for its intended purpose to see how well it helps meet learning goals.

How should software and other tools be evaluated? Multitudes of Web sites and books suggest evaluation schemes and **usability tests** (an observation of the actual use of the product by a target user). Excellent resources can be obtained from ISTE (http://cnets.iste.org) and on Kathy Schrock's amazing Web site at http://kathyschrock.net/. Most of these resources suggest that tools must be evaluated according to the context in which they will be used. Because schools and programs differ widely, this means that evaluations should be adapted to each situation. In many cases this can work, but in others it is not feasible due to personnel, time, and budgetary constraints. Some software companies such as Tom Snyder Productions will lend software to teachers for a free 30–90-day trial, and time extensions are often granted.

The diversity of context and other situational features means that teachers and IT coordinators often use a general, premade form that has a broad fit with the school's purposes. In addition to the two mentioned above, another useful evaluation is enGauge Resources' *Resource Evaluation Form* provided by NCREL (http://www.ncrel.org; Figure 2.9 on page 52), and a short list of evaluation questions with examples can be found in Egbert (2005, pp. 26–31).

Teachers who need to evaluate software tools can also rely on others who have already done some of the work. Many software review sites exist, and a check of multiple sites might help

FIGURE 2.9 Part of enGauge's Resource Evaluation Form

Please circle the appropriate answer.

8. Are any additional software or plug-ins required for the site?   Yes   No
   Type

9. Does the site appear stable? (does not freeze or crash)   Yes   No

10. The organization that created this site is readily identifiable.   Yes   No

11. Is this resource part of a larger Web site?   Yes   No
    If Yes, what is the URL?

12. Amount of text.   ☐ Not Applicable

   1   2   3   4   5

too little   too much

13. Ease of use.   ☐ Not Applicable

   1   2   3   4   5

too little   too much

14. Which 21st Century Skills are addressed? (Check all that apply.)

Digital-Age Literacy	Inventive Thinking	Effective Communication	High Productivity
☐ Basic, scientific, mathematical, and technological literacies	☐ Adaptability/ability to manage complexity	☐ Teaming, collaboration, and interpersonal skills	☐ Ability to prioritize, plan, and manage for results
☐ Visual and information literacies	☐ Curiosity, creativity, and risk taking	☐ Personal and social responsibility	☐ Effective use of real-world tools.
☐ Cultural literacy and global awareness.	☐ Higher-order thinking and sound reasoning	☐ Interactive communication	☐ Relevant, high-quality products

Source: Excerpted from *enGauge Resources: Resource Evaluation Form,* available online at http://www.ncrel.org/engauge/resource/resource/toolform.htm. Copyright © 2005 Learning Point Associates. Used with permission of the publisher.

teachers eliminate a software package from their list or decide to try it in their own classrooms. Free sites that can save time and money include:

- World Village's Schoolhouse Review (http://www.worldvillage.com/wv/school/html/scholrev.htm)
- California Learning Resource Network's outstanding searchable review database (http://clrn.org/search/)
- Inexpensive subscription sites such as Children's Technology Review (http://www.childrenssoftware.com/)

Some of these sites even suggest software that a school or program might not have considered. Also, to save time and energy, ask colleagues for their thoughts on software they have used. For content-area and technology-specific electronic lists that teachers can join, go to http://www.edwebproject.org/lists.html.

Table 2.1 presents software programs and Web site examples that can be used to teach a variety of content areas. Many more useful sites are listed in the learning activities section of this chapter. Integrated Learning Systems, which isolate and often decontextualize discrete content items to be learned, are not mentioned here because of their extreme expense and lack of flexibility.

TABLE 2.1 Tools for Content Learning

Tool	Location or Publisher	Objectives/Content
History Mystery	http://teacher.scholastic.com/histmyst/index.asp	Leads students through the problem-solving process while learning history content on a variety of topics.
Math Mysteries	Tom Snyder Productions	Students understand mathematical operations; understand the process of solving word problems; have fun doing math.
BER Collecting Data	http://www.edzone.net/%7Emwestern/BER/data.html	Provides links to fun and effective raw data sources; links to forums and activities for exploring raw data.
Multicultural Calendar	http://www.kidlink.org/KIDPROJ/MCC/	Provides data on holidays from all over the world in a searchable database.
Biography Maker	http://fno.org/bio/biomak2.htm	Helps students frame biographical information to create exciting and lively stories.
Musical Plates	http://www.k12science.org	This section of the CIESE Web site provides activities for turning science information into science knowledge.
Project Gutenberg	http://www.gutenberg.org/	Provides access to thousands of primary source texts; also includes audio books for those with visual impairments or who prefer to listen.
Lemonade Stand, Geometric Presupposer, Splish Splash Math	Sunburst	These and many other Sunburst content-based programs provide fun, context-based practice with concepts in basic numeracy, science, text-based literacy, and social studies.
Magic School Bus Series	Microsoft	Each CD provides facts and ideas on a different topic and allows students to practice and drill in fun ways.

Tool CloseUp: Microsoft Word

One advantage to using tools in the Microsoft Office Suite (Excel, PowerPoint, FrontPage, and Word) for content learning is that these tools are widely used in business and education and help is available in many formats. For example, an excellent beginning instructional guide can be found at http://www.utexas.edu/its/training/handouts/UTOPIA_WordGS/. Other resources include the tutorial at http://www.baycongroup.com/wlesson0.htm and Gookin's text *Word 2003 for Dummies* (2003, For Dummies). Another advantage is that Word files cross platforms with ease, making students' letters to the editor or pamphlets on home safety readable whether on a Mac or a PC. In addition, the menus and icons are consistent throughout the Office programs. For example, once a student understands that the icon ☐ indicates "print" in Word, he will also be able to print in the other tools in the suite. (Take the quiz at http://www.sw/avriersb.qc.ca/english/edservices/pedresources/webquest/word_game/index. html to see how many of the icons you know.)

On the other hand, some educators feel that Word has too many options to learn and that students can become lost in the formatting to the detriment of learning goals. They also express concern about how student typing skills affect their work. However, as noted previously in this chapter, teachers and students do not need to use all the features of a program like Word to receive the benefits that it offers. And, with a little creativity, Word can be used for an amazing number of tasks.

Two of the features that make Word a valuable tool in classrooms are its editing and multimedia capabilities. Many research and anecdotal reports tell how students revise more with the computer than they do with paper and pencil. However, there is more to Word's editing capabilities. For example, using the commenting feature, teachers and peers can make comments on a student's paper that do not interfere with the original text. If multiple reviewers make comments, their names will appear with their comments. Mistakes in the text can be highlighted with color or font changes, or voice annotation can be used to make it easier for aural learners to understand.

To some people it may seem odd to call a word processing program multimedia. However, most word processors have gone far beyond this simple typing feature and make it easy to integrate graphics (including pictures, drawings, and charts), color, text, sound, and a variety of formats. (Of course, if the document is printed, the sound will not work.) Teachers can use a word processor to prepare different versions of documents that all students can use, for example, highlighting focal vocabulary for ELLs and others who need it, using sound for students who have hearing impairments, large text for students with visual impairments, and links to more advanced information for students capable of using it. Students can also use these features to make their reports interesting and accessible and to learn how to design appealing documents.

Word processors such as Microsoft Word, if integrated effectively into classroom practice, can help teachers and learners address the needs of diverse students and work toward all the learning goals. Additional examples of activities that are supported by the use of a word processor can be found throughout this book.

How do you use a word processor in your daily life? What additional features should you learn in order to use it in the ways noted in this CloseUp?

_____

_____

_____

Tutorial

CW

To learn more about Microsoft Word, see the Microsoft Word tutorials in the Tutorials module on the Companion Website (http://www.prenhall.com/egbert).

FROM THE CLASSROOM

Content Tools

I'm locating Web sites for students and although it has taken me a long time to find some quality sites, I have finally found some that I can't wait to share . . . I found a cute site called Word Central. It has a lot of fun activities such as a rhyming dictionary, great kids' dictionary, games/activities, and message encoding/decoding. Check it out at http://www.wordcentral.com/. Okay, one more. Kidshealth.com is awesome too. If you ever teach health or the human body, you've got to go here because there are cute videos, songs, and lots of informational articles for kids on all sorts of health-related issues: http://www.kidshealth.com/kid/index.jsp.

(Jennie, first-grade teacher)

Read as one teacher describes her search for exciting content tools in From the Classroom: Content Tools.

In addition to effective content-based classroom learning, students need to participate in activities that help them to understand the foundations of technology use, including concepts of ethics.

What kinds of tools will help East Park High School reach its technology and learning goals? Why do you think so?

_____

_____

_____

LEARNING ACTIVITIES: CONTENT LEARNING

Integrating technology throughout the curriculum, the task that Mr. Yates and the Technology Committee have taken on, may seem like an overwhelming task. As described above, there are many technologies to help teachers present content. The problem is how to get started. McKenzie (2004b) believes that we can "invent curriculum rich lessons that take students half an hour but engage them in powerful thought with considerable skill." He says this can happen through "tight lesson design, no waste, no bother and no wandering about." He calls these short, structured, Web-based lessons "Slam Dunk Digital Lessons." Slam Dunks are tasks that focus on content learning through essential questions and Web-based resources. Teachers can integrate Slam Dunks into larger lessons or units (see http://fno.org/sept02/slamdunk.html for a brief, clear explanation) or use them as a starting point to develop lessons that integrate technology. A sample page of a lesson from Way Elementary is presented in Figure 2.10. The basic format consists of these six parts:

1. *The essential question and learning task:* The important question that students will have to work to answer, along with any other preview of the material and a picture if appropriate/ available.

2. *The information source:* A picture and information about the site(s) appropriate for your students that they will use to answer the essential question.

3. *The student activity:* What students will do with the information, typically completing some kind of graphic organizer using the links provided.

4. *The assessment activity:* The performance or product that will show what students understand.

5. *Enrichment activities:* A brief list of extra sites that have been checked for appropriateness.

6. *Teacher support materials:* Helpful hints, standards, instructions, and objectives.

For more details and examples, go to http://questioning.org/.

McKenzie recommends building the lesson from the foundation of one or more content standards. The learning activities that follow adapt the basic Slam Dunk outline to demonstrate how digital tools can be used in different

FIGURE 2.10 Slam Dunk Lesson from Way Elementary

Animal Adaptations

1. The Question

How does climate and habitat affect an animal's physical and behavioral adaptations?

➡ Next page

Source: Used with permission of Bloomfield Hills Schools.

content areas to meet specific content standards. Each activity can be modified to make it effective for older or younger learners. As you read, think about the kind of content learning (declarative, structural, or procedural) each activity is designed to help students achieve.

Question: Why do we need to understand fractions?

Source(s): Beginning fractions, http://www.aaamath.com/ B/fra16_x2.htm

Activity: List all the ways that you use fractions during your day.

Assessment: Write a summary of your answers and share it with peers.

Enrichment:

- Hungry for Math, http://library.thinkquest.org/ J002328F/default.htm
- Identify with circles, http://www.visualfractions.com/EnterCircle.html
- Fresh Baked Fractions, http://www.funbrain.com/ fract/

Support: Understand commonly used fractions (Standard NM.NUM.PK-2.1).

Question: Which body system is the most important?

Source(s): Human Anatomy Online, http://www. innerbody.com/htm/body.html (Figure 2.11)

Activity: Chart the parts of the main body systems and their roles in the body.

Assessment: Write a brief position statement based on the data that answers the question "Which body system is the most important?"

Enrichment:

- Virtual Body, http://www.medtropolis.com/VBody.asp
- Interactive body, http://www.bbc.co.uk/science/humanbody/
- Atlas of the Body, http://www.ama-assn.org/ama/pub/category/7140.html

Support: Describe the basic structure and functions of the human body systems. Students will learn what the body systems are and the roles they play (Standard NPH-H.K–4.1, 5–8.1).

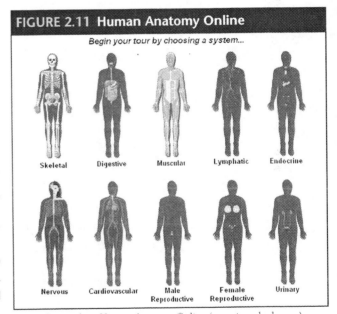

FIGURE 2.11 Human Anatomy Online

Begin your tour by choosing a system...

Skeletal   Digestive   Muscular   Lymphatic   Endocrine

Nervous   Cardiovascular   Male Reproductive   Female Reproductive   Urinary

Source: Images from Human Anatomy Online (www.innerbody.com) provided by INTELLIMED International Corporation.

Question: If you could no longer live on the earth, which planet in the solar system would you most want to live on?

Source(s): The Nine Planets (http://www.nineplanets.org/)

Activity: Complete a planet chart with average temperatures, length of days/years, atmospheric composition, and two other features of your choice.

Assessment: Present your argument to the class about which planet you would most want to live on.

Enrichment:

- Welcome to the Planets!, http://pds.jpl.nasa.gov/planets/welcome.htm
- Zoom Astronomy, http://www.enchantedlearning.com/subjects/astronomy/planets
- Comparing the Planets, http://www.nasm.si.edu/research/ceps/etp/compare/etpcompare.html

Support: Students develop an understanding of objects in the sky. Students have to define what makes living on Earth good and how that definition changes as they look past the earth. They will learn or review the order of the planets in the solar system and some of their features (Standard NS.K–4.4, 5–8.4).

Question: If you had to eliminate one of the rights in the Bill of Rights, which would it be?

Source(s): *The Bill of Rights: Evolution of Personal Liberties* (CD-ROM from socialstudies.com)

Activity: Create a chart with pros and cons for each original amendment.

Assessment: Work in groups to choose one amendment to eliminate and defend your choice.

Enrichment:

- The National Archives, http://www.archives.gov/national_archives_experience/charters/bill_of_rights.html
- ACLU Student Rights, http://www.aclu.org/students/
- The Bill of Rights, http://www.billofrightsinstitute.org/

Support: What is the U.S. Constitution and why is it important (Standard NSS-C.K–4.3, 5–8.2, 9–12.2)?

The approach in this lesson involves the same content as a traditional overview of the Bill of Rights but requires students to understand the issues more deeply and to make an untraditional choice.

Question: Your school has money to purchase one piece of art by an American painter to display in the main hallway. Which piece of art should it be?

Source(s): Inventories of American Painting and Sculpture, http://americanart.si.edu/search/search_data.cfm

Activity: Choose five pieces of art from different genres. Create a table that includes the art's "message," its defining characteristics, and reasons why it should be displayed in the school.

Assessment: Peers from around the school vote on the choices.

Enrichment:

- Whitney Museum of American Art, http://www. whitney.org/
- National Gallery of Art (Figure 2.12), http://www.nga. gov/education/american/aasplash.htm

Support: Students know the differences among visual characteristics and purposes of art; students describe how different expressive features and organizational principles cause different responses (Standard NA-VA.K–4.2, 5–8.1, 9–12.2). As a follow-up, students can make interpretive versions of the artwork chosen.

Tasks like these that provide structure and appropriate resources and clearly meet standards might be the ideal tool for teachers who are just starting to integrate technology into their teaching. The tasks above are also useful to help students understand how to frame essential questions that include *why? how?* and *which?*

What implications does this section on learning activities have for the TC's technology plan?

FIGURE 2.12 American Art at the National Gallery

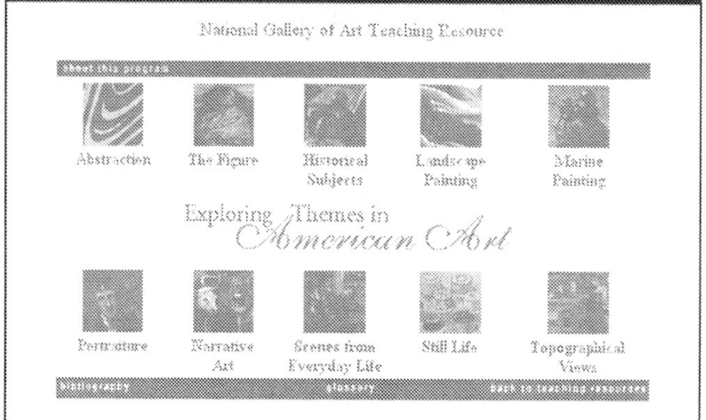

Source: Images © Board of Trustees, National Gallery of Art, Washington.

ASSESSING CONTENT LEARNING: SCORING GUIDES

Because content knowledge plays an important role in meeting other learning goals, teachers must assess content in ways that help them understand what students know and can do. As suggested in this chapter's learning activities section, students can be assessed through technology-supported summaries, retellings, and debates. Content knowledge can also be assessed through rubrics (chapter 3), tests (chapter 4), and a variety of performance assessments (chapter 6). The North Central Regional Educational Laboratory (NCREL) suggests that in addition to assessing students, teachers should evaluate their own instructional design and assessment process. To do so, they can employ scoring guides. **Scoring guides** are like rubrics, but they are used to evaluate learning in a broader sense than more local rubrics. The three functions of scoring guides are:

1. To help teachers and evaluators evaluate student learning in a relatively objective way based on predetermined standards

2. To identify and assess not only student learning but also instructional design

3. To serve as models for teachers in developing their own rubrics for a wide variety of assessment purposes. (NCREL, n.d.(b), p. 1)

NCREL provides a customizable scoring guide for the effective use of technology at http://www.ncrtec.org/tl/sgsp/overview.htm. Teachers can choose among 14 categories of student products and choose items from relevant checklists to construct their scoring guide. Figure 2.13 shows the first three sections of the scoring guide. More information on scoring guides can be found in the Assessment section of the Resources module on this text's Companion Website (http://www.prenhall.com/egbert).

What technologies should Mr. Yates's committee add to the plan to address student assessment? Why?

_____

_____

_____

FIGURE 2.13 Scoring Guide

	5	4	3	2	1	0	Comments
Standards/ Learning Objectives	Curriculum standards and learning objectives are specific and focused, intentionally driving the use of technology.		Curriculum standards and learning objectives are correlated to technology uses.		Curriculum standards and learning objectives are superficial uses of technology.	No demonstration of curriculum standards and learning objectives connected to the use of technology.	
Curriculum Linking with Technology Uses	Curriculum linking creates unique content learning benefits. Content learning experiences/benefits are extended and would be impaired or impossible without the use of technology.		Curriculum linking adapts or varies present student learning or work. Content learning experiences or benefits are enhanced but possible without the use of technology.		Curriculum linking provides topics " for technology skills or uses. Content learning incidental—student uses primarily to learn/practice technology skills.	Curriculum linking is incidental to technology use. Content learning not focused. Technology uses are mostly supplemental, or to provide fun/ motivation activities.	
Cognitive Tasks	Task requires synthesis and evaluation of information. Going beyond existing understanding to create own original position or product. Knowledge creation is expected.		Task requires analysis of information and/or putting together information from several sources to demonstrate an understanding of existing knowledge.		Task requires little analysis and is focused on simplistic tasks or concepts using a single source. Cookie-cutter, look-alike products are likely to develop.	The task has little relevance to content learning.	

Source: Excerpted from *Scoring Guide for Lesson Plans That Use Technology Resources,* available online at http://www.ncrtec.org/tl/sgsp/lpsg.htm. Copyright © 2001 Learning Point Associates and Bernajean Porter Consulting. Used with permission of Learning Point Associates.

SAMPLE LESSON: CONTENT LEARNING

Mr. Yates's committee has successfully completed a technology plan that meets the requirements of the funding. Before submitting the plan for approval, each member of the committee has been assigned a grade and content level for which to find or develop a sample lesson that meets the goals of the plan. These sample lessons are to accompany the technology plan through the approval process.

Mr. Yates must produce a plan for fifth- and sixth-grade science. As a result of a Web search, he finds the lesson "What Color Are Your Skittles?" from the Educators Desk Reference site (http://www.eduref.org/). The lesson is reproduced here.

WHAT COLOR ARE YOUR SKITTLES?

Submitted by: *Ellyn Bewes*

Grade Level: 5, 6

Subject(s):

- Computer Science
- Mathematics/Process Skills

Description: Students enter data into a spreadsheet to create a pie graph showing the percentage of colors found in a bag of Skittles.

Goals: Students will create and manipulate spreadsheets and graphs.

Objectives:

1. Students will create a spreadsheet to chart the different colors found in a package of Skittles.
2. Students will collect data, create appropriate charts, and use percentages to describe quantities.

Materials:

- 1 package of Skittles for each student
- computers with Microsoft Excel/access to the Internet
- floppy disks
- index cards
- What Color Are Your Skittles? Instruction Sheet

Procedure:

(Depending on class size and computer availability, teachers may choose to have students work individually or in pairs.)

Begin the lesson by distributing a bag of Skittles to each student, along with an index card. Have students look at their package of Skittles. Ask students, "How many different colors of Skittles are there? What percentage of each color do you think is in your bag?" Have students write their predictions on their index cards. "Now open your package of Skittles and tally the amounts of the different colors of Skittles." (Students can write the colors and numbers on the back of their index cards.)

After the results have been tallied, hand out an instruction sheet to each student. The instruction sheet provides step-by-step directions for creating a graph using Microsoft Excel. Students should be able to follow the instructions with minimal help, but the teacher should circulate around the room to answer students' questions. (The teacher can also encourage students to ask each other for help if the teacher is busy assisting another student.) When students have completed their graphs, they should print out a copy of their work. Students can compare their results to their earlier predictions.

> *Extension:* Have students go to the Skittles Web site (http://www.skittles.com) to find out what percentage of each color is supposed to be in a package of Skittles—to see if their pie charts and percentages are similar to those advertised on the Web.
>
> **Assessment:**
> Collect students' completed work to check for accuracy.
>
> *Source:* From HotChalk (www.HotChalk.com).

Mr. Yates uses a Lesson Analysis and Adaptation Worksheet (found in chapter 1 on page 33 and in the Lesson Planning Module on the Companion Website) to help him analyze the lesson. He concludes these things about the lesson:

- No standards are mentioned.
- The lesson requires students to use skills of data collection, estimating, counting, and data entry. There could certainly be more originality, a greater variety of language skills, and more integrated interaction. There is some scaffolding through the instruction sheet that gives step-by-step directions for completing the spreadsheet.
- Grouping arrangements could be included to differentiate the process. A clearer connection needs to be made between this lesson and students' lives outside school.
- The technology is used to support student content learning. Allowing for a variety of student products might help this issue and also differentiate by allowing students to show what they know in other ways.
- The variety of materials (Skittles, external document, computer, peers) means that ELLs and other students with diverse needs will likely be able to participate. However, the instruction sheet is only text and might be difficult for students with language barriers to understand and follow.
- The assessment is not sufficiently detailed and does not directly link to the objectives. It uses controlling feedback and does not leave room for students to show what they know in a variety of ways.

Mr. Yates believes that the idea of this technology-supported lesson is good but that it needs to focus more on students using 21st-century skills to learn content. Based on his analysis, he decides to make these changes before submitting the lesson:

1. Note relevant content area, language, and technology standards.
2. Include more skills and content. Students should work in groups so they communicate, and they should record their estimates, their actual count, and their process on a worksheet to include more language. At the end of the activity, students should also make a graph of the numbers from the Skittles Web site and compare their two graphs in text or visuals. This will require them to summarize and synthesize the information. More advanced students can also prepare a professional presentation based on their findings.
3. Hang the resulting graphs on the wall and let students peruse them. They can make notes on a worksheet of which bag of Skittles they would prefer the most, differences between how the graphs were made, and other ways they might present the information.
4. Provide visuals on the instruction sheet that show actual screens from the software so that students who need or prefer more visual orientation can access the information.
5. Provide more specific assessment and formative feedback. Mr. Yates will work with the students to develop a scoring guide that assesses not only student performance but their thoughts about the lesson in general and connections to their lives.

With these changes, Mr. Yates feels, this lesson will reflect the goals of the technology plan and provide evidence that the plan will work.

What other changes, if any, should Mr. Yates make to this lesson? Why?

_____

_____

_____

CHAPTER REVIEW

Key Points

- **Explain how content learning takes place.**

  Learning occurs when new information is attached to other information in the brain. If this information is isolated pieces of data, this process results in declarative knowledge. When declarative knowledge sorts into different webs of meaning, structural knowledge is the result. Procedural knowledge is the result of understanding connections among pieces of data. Procedural knowledge is the knowledge that allows students to take action. Teachers can and should support learners in every aspect of knowledge acquisition. Technology can help, but only if it is used wisely and arranged to fit the goals.

- **Explain the role of content learning in meeting other instructional goals.**

  Problem-solving, creativity, and other instructional goals depend, to an extent, on student mastery of content. However, content can also be learned through the process of reaching these goals.

- **Discuss guidelines and techniques for using technology in content learning and teaching.**

  Teachers must prepare their lessons in culturally responsive ways and use techniques such as differentiation and material adaptation to help all students access the content. They must also be flexible and observant enough to understand when students need a just-in-time lesson.

- **Analyze technologies that can be used to create opportunities for content learning for all students.**

  Teachers and students can employ a variety of electronic tools to support content learning, but they must also be aware of the content, nature, and viability of the tools that they use.

- **Describe and develop effective technology-enhanced content learning activities.**

  Effective content learning activities are those that consider students' backgrounds and needs, are designed on the basis of how students learn, and use technologies that are appropriate, relevant, and necessary.

- **Create appropriate assessments for technology-enhanced content learning activities.**

  In order to create appropriate assessments, teachers can evaluate the design of their instruction and their evaluation measures through the use of scoring guides.

Which information in this chapter is most valuable to you? Why? How will you use it in your teaching?

_____

_____

_____

CASE QUESTIONS REVIEW

Reread the case at the beginning of the chapter and review your answers. In light of what you learned during this chapter, how do your answers change? Note any changes below.

1. *What kind of hardware components should the committee choose? Why?*

_____

_____

_____

2. What kind of software and/or Internet access should the computers have? Why?

_____

_____

_____

3. How can the needs of ELLs and other students with special needs be addressed in the technology plan?

_____

_____

_____

4. How should the computers be assigned and laid out?

_____

_____

_____

5. Do you see any problems in the way the grant was awarded or how it will be implemented? If so, what are the problems?

_____

_____

_____

_____

Chapter Extensions

For more information on school technology plans, see the resources from the Michigan Department of Education at http://www.techplan.org/ and the Tech Plans section of the Resources module on the Companion Website (http://www.prenhall.com/egbert). To answer any of the following questions online, go to the Chapter 2 Extensions module for this text's Companion Website.

Adapt

Choose a lesson for your potential subject area and grade level from the lesson plan archives at Educators Desk Reference (http://www.eduref.org/). Use the Lesson Analysis and Adaptation Worksheet from chapter 1 on page 33 (also available on the Companion Website) to consider the lesson in the context of _content learning_. Use your responses to the worksheet to suggest general changes to the lesson based on your current or future students and context.

Practice

1. _Describe content learning._ Review the lessons in the activities section of this chapter. For each lesson, tell which kind of knowledge each activity is designed to help students achieve (declarative, structural, or procedural).

2. *Evaluate software.* Choose a piece of software or a Web site and evaluate it for cultural responsiveness. Use these basic guidelines adapted from NWREL (2005) or develop a set of your own guidelines based on the literature:

   a. The software supports a climate of caring, respect, and the valuing of students' cultures.

   b. The software helps to build a bridge between academic learning and students' prior understanding, knowledge, native language, and values.

   c. The outcomes of software use help educators learn from and about their students' culture, language, and learning styles to make instruction more meaningful and relevant to their students' lives.

   d. Local knowledge, language, and culture are fully integrated into the software, not added on to it.

   e. Tasks provided or supported by the software are challenging, cooperative, and hands-on, with less emphasis on rote memorization and lecture formats.

3. *Obtain resources.* Search the Web for resources that you could access for JIT lessons that students in your classroom might need. Make a list of your findings to share with peers.

4. *Support strategies with technology.* Choose one or more strategies for content learning learned in your other classes and note how technology might make the process more efficient or effective. For example, you may have studied mnemonic devices. How could technology be used to support mnemonics?

5. *Create balance.* Find or use a technology-enhanced lesson for your grade level and content area. Analyze the lesson and describe how you will balance the need to learn the technology with the requirement to learn the content.

Explore • • •

1. *Adapt a model of knowledge.* Review the model in Figure 2.2. Using your content area, recreate the model with content-based declarative knowledge and a schema into which it could develop.

2. *Practice differentiating.* Choose one of the learning activities from this chapter and differentiate, creating choices for one of these elements: process, product, tool, or assessment. Explain why your change is effective and for what learners.

3. *Adapt an activity.* Choose one of the learning activities in the chapter. Adapt it *as little as possible* to make it work for older or younger learners or those who have different levels of skill or knowledge. Explain your changes.

4. *Reply to a teacher.* Look at the teachers' comments in this chapter's From the Classroom features. Choose one teacher's comment and write a reply.

5. *Create a lesson.* Choose a content area standard and develop a Slam Dunk lesson based on the framework presented in this chapter.

6. *Create a context-based software evaluation.* Explore a classroom or school context that you are familiar with. Develop an evaluation scheme for tools for that context.

7. *Review technology plans.* Find technology plans for other schools and districts on the Web by using one of the links that follow or doing a Web search. Examine the plans. What ideas can you see that you could use? What is missing?

   http://www.bham.wednet.edu/technology/2004-07TechPlan1-24.htm

   http://www.sabine.k12.la.us/mhs1/techplan.htm

   http://www.kent.k12.wa.us/ksd/DE/technology/tech_plan.html

8. *Research implementation.* Interview an IT coordinator for a school or district. Find out how their technology plan was implemented, what the pros and cons were, and what could be done differently.

9. *Adapt materials.* Briefly outline a technology-enhanced activity or lesson that you might use in your classroom. Review materials that you might use during the activity. Adapt the materials to make them accessible to: (a) students with less proficient English, (b) students with more advanced reading skills, and (c) students with a variety of prior knowledge and experience.

REFERENCES

Echevarria, J., & Graves, A. (2002). *Sheltered content instruction: Teaching English language learners with diverse abilities* (3rd ed.). Boston, MA: Allyn & Bacon.

Egbert, J. (2005). *CALL essentials: Principles and practice in CALL classrooms.* Alexandria, VA: TESOL.

Erlauer, L. (2003). *The brain-compatible classroom: Using what we know about learning to improve teaching.* Alexandria, VA: Association for Supervision and Curriculum Development.

Falk, B., & Blumenreich, M. (2005). *The power of questions: A guide to teacher and student research.* Portsmouth, NH: Heinemann.

Goldman, S., Cole, K., & Syer, C. (1999). *The Secretary's conference on educational technology—1999: The technology/content dilemma.* (ERIC Document Reproduction Service No. ED 452821).

Johnson, S. (2004). *Mind wide open: Your brain and the neuroscience of everyday life.* New York: Scribner.

Jonassen, D., & Wang, S. (1992). Acquiring structural knowledge from semantically structured hypertext. Proceedings of selected research and development presentations at the Convention of the Association for Educational Communications and Technology and sponsored by the Research and Theory Division. (ERIC Document Reproduction Service No. ED348000).

McKenzie, J. (1998). Creating technology enhanced student-centered learning environments. *From Now On, 7*(6).

McKenzie, J. (2004a, Summer). Five types of slam dunk lessons. *From Now On, 13*(9).

McKenzie, J. (2004b). Making good lessons quickly. Available: http://questioning.org/module2/quick.html.

NCREL (n.d.b). *Using scoring guides vs. rubrics.* Available: http://www.ncrtec.org/tl/sgsp/rubguide.htm.

New Horizons for Learning (2002). *Teaching and learning strategies.* Available: http://www.newhorizons.org.

Norman, D. (2004). *Emotional design: Why we love (or hate) everyday things.* New York: Basic Books.

NWREL (2005). *Culturally responsive practices for student success: A regional sampler.* Available from: http://www.nwrel.org/request/2005june/what.html.

Pearson, D., & Gallagher, M. (1983, July). The instruction of reading comprehension. *Contemporary Educational Psychology, 8*(3), 317–344.

Riel, M. (1998). *Education in the 21st century: Just-in-time learning or learning communities.* Paper prepared for the Challenges of the Next Millennium: Education and Development of Human Resources, 4th Annual Conference of the Emirates Center for Strategic Studies and Research, 137–160.

Theroux, P. (2004). *Differentiating instruction. Enhance learning with technology.* Available: http://members.shaw.ca/priscillatheroux/differentiating.html.

Tomlinson, C. (2001). *How to differentiate instruction in mixed-ability classrooms.* Alexandria, VA: ASCD.

Vygotsky, L. S. (1978). *Mind in society.* Cambridge, MA: Harvard University Press.

Wignall, E. (2006). *Media, minds, methods: Linking online instruction and media for maximum effect.* Paper presented at the 21st annual conference on Distance Teaching and Learning, May, 2006. Available: www.uwex.edu/disted/conference/Resource_library/proceedings/05-1898.pdf.

Williams, P. J. (2000, Spring). Design: The only methodology of technology? *Journal of Technology Education, 11*(2), 48–60.

Yatvin, J. (2004). *A room with a differentiated view: How to serve ALL children as individual learners.* Portsmouth, NH: Heinemann.

20

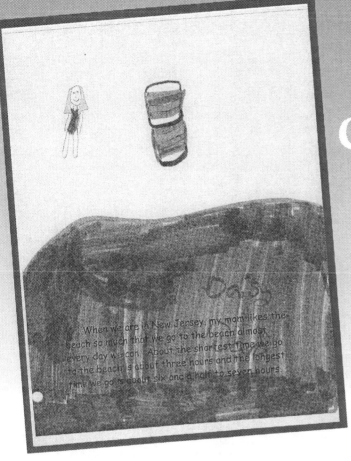

When we are in New Jersey, my mom likes the beach so much that we go to the beach almost every day we can. About the shortest time we go to the beach is about three hours and the longest time we go is about six and a half to seven hours.

Supporting Student Communication

Case: Geography Mystery

As you read the following case, pay attention to how and with whom the teacher plans for the students to communicate during their telecommunications project.

Mr. Finley, a junior high school social studies teacher, is planning a telecommunications project for his seventh-grade students while they study the geography of the United States. His project will employ technology to support interaction among students at a distance from each other. Participating in this project will help students understand the use and importance of latitude and longitude and the role of geographical features in people's lives. It will also help the students to meet other content, language, and technology goals and standards.

During this project, Mr. Finley's class will work on geography mysteries via email with Ms. Stewart's sixth-grade class in a different state. Mr. Finley's students will work in teams of three students. Each team will choose a place somewhere in the United States. Team members will pretend that they were dropped unexpectedly in that particular place and need help figuring out the name of the place where they are located. They may choose a city, a landmark, the top of a mountain, or some other specific point for which they will figure out such details as the latitude, longitude, nearby geographic features, how the people in the area use the land, and mileage to nearby landmarks. They will send clues about their location in email messages to a team in Ms. Stewart's class, who will respond through email to try to discover where Mr. Finley's students are. A message from a team in Mr. Finley's class might look like this:

We are located near the capital of a state whose major industry is farming because of the large amount of volcanic soil. We are at the southern end of the largest wilderness area in the United States.

Ms. Stewart's students will use both online and offline resources to help make guesses and formulate questions to ask. A reply from the partner team in Ms. Stewart's class could be:

Are you in either Idaho or Washington? What is your elevation? Are you above the 45th parallel?

After Ms. Stewart's students guess the location correctly, they will make a map online at M. Weinelt's Online Map Creation site (www.aquarius.geomar.de/omc/), using latitude and longitude to show the location. The classes will then switch roles and Ms. Stewart's students will send clues to Mr. Finley's class.

Mr. Finley expects the project to take six weeks, during which time students in both classes will be studying different aspects of geography that will help them solve the mysteries. In addition, Mr. Finley has developed some scaffolds in the form of handouts to help students think about their group processes and to make good guesses. Mr. Finley also plans lessons on skills needed to communicate effectively, on email etiquette, on group work, and on logic and problem solving. Mr. Finley has done a similar telecommunications project with previous students and expects that his current students will work enthusiastically on this one.

As he makes copies of the starting instructions, which he will also explain orally to the students, Mr. Finley feels excited to begin the project, but he wonders if he has considered everything he needs to make this project a success.

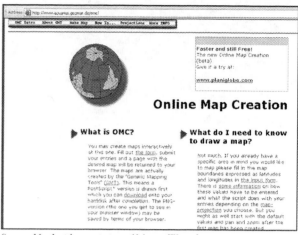

Source: Used with permission of Martin Weinelt.

* *

Answer these questions about the case. There are no right or wrong answers to this chapter preview—the goal is for you to respond before you read the chapter. Then, as you interact with the chapter contents, think about how your answers might change.

1. *What learning benefits might the sixth- and seventh-grade students derive from participating in this telecommunications project?*

———————————————————————————

———————————————————————————

———————————————————————————

2. *How can working with students at another school contribute to Mr. Finley's students' achievement?*

———————————————————————————

———————————————————————————

———————————————————————————

3. *How did Mr. Finley approach the use of technology to meet his goals?*

———————————————————————————

———————————————————————————

———————————————————————————

4. *What other ways can Mr. Finley ensure the success of this telecommunications project?*

_____

_____

_____

Mr. Finley chose to have his students communicate with students in another school by email for the geography mystery project, but he could have chosen a variety of other participants and means of communication. It is important for teachers to understand the implications of the available choices to choose wisely. To this end, when you finish this chapter you will be able to:

- Define communication, collaboration, and related terms.
- Describe the communication process and explain how communication affects learning.
- Discuss guidelines and techniques for creating opportunities for technology-supported communication and collaboration.
- Analyze technologies that can be used to support communication, including MOOs, email, chat, blogs, and wikis.
- Describe and develop effective technology-enhanced communication activities.
- Create appropriate assessments for technology-enhanced communication tasks.

When you have completed this chapter, which NETS*T will you have addressed?

_____

_____

_____

Meeting the Standards: Communication

Guidelines for every content area include communication as an essential component for meeting national standards. For example, the education technology standards (NETS*S) address student mastery of technology communication tools, including being able to "interact, collaborate, and publish with peers, experts, and others," and "communicate information and ideas effectively to multiple audiences using a variety of media and formats." The national math standards have a complete section on math communication that emphasizes students "organizing and consolidating their mathematical thinking through communication" and being able to "communicate their mathematical thinking coherently" (NM–COMM PK–12). Fine arts standards ask students to work together to develop improvisations; English focuses on communication skills, strategies, and applying language skills (4, 5, and 12); the first goal of the foreign language and ESL standards is communication; and even PE standards support the goal of communicating about health (NPH-H.5). In every area, communication is understood to be a foundation of learning, and technology can help students to communicate with a variety of audiences for a variety of purposes by connecting them both online and off. Some of the communication standards are mentioned in this chapter in the activities section.

Review the national or state standards for a content area that you will teach. How many of the standards address communication in some way? What kinds of connections do your students need to make to meet those standards? How do you think technology can help?

_____

_____

_____

As you read the rest of the chapter, look for ways to use technology to help your students communicate and make connections in the ways you outlined above. See national standards and your state standards for communication in the **Standards module** on this text's Companion Website.

Technology-supported communication projects can be fun and effective learning experiences for students and teachers, but, as this chapter will show, preparation is necessary. For standards that guide communication and how technology is used to support them, see the Meeting the Standards feature.

OVERVIEW OF COMMUNICATION AND TECHNOLOGY IN K–12 CLASSROOMS

In keeping with the premise of this text, before discussing how technology supports communication it is important to understand what communication is and why it is an important learning goal.

What Is Communication?

Communication is a general term that implies the conveyance of information either one-way or through an exchange with two or more partners. Shirky (2003) identifies *three basic communication patterns*, also shown in Figure 3.1:

1. Point-to-point two-way (e.g., a two-person Internet chat or a phone conversation)
2. One-to-many outbound (e.g., a static Web site, a lecture, a TV show, a three-way phone conversation)
3. Many-to-many (e.g., a group discussion)

Learning takes place when the communication is based on true **social interaction**. Social interaction means that the communication is two-way, but it does not mean that participants are just giving each other information. Social interaction is communication with an **authentic audience** that shares some of the goals of the communication. It also includes an authentic task in which the answers are generally unknown by one or more (perhaps all!) participants. This kind of

FIGURE 3.1 Basic Communication Patterns

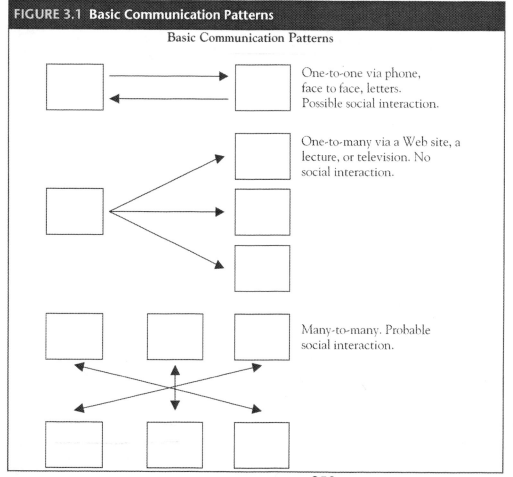

Basic Communication Patterns

One-to-one via phone, face to face, letters. Possible social interaction.

One-to-many via a Web site, a lecture, or television. No social interaction.

Many-to-many. Probable social interaction.

FIGURE 3.2 MSN Messenger

To: David

David says:
  Wanna grab a cup of coffee?
Jeanne says:
  Yup.
Jeanne says:
  You buying?

interaction requires interdependence and **negotiation of meaning**; in other words, during their communication participants ask for clarification, argue, challenge each other, and work toward common understanding. These features of communication can lead to effective learning by assisting students in understanding information and constructing knowledge with the help of others.

In fact, research shows that "social interactions play a fundamental role in knowledge apprehension and in skills acquisition as well as in socio-cognitive development" (Cesar, 1998). In other words, "any communicative act, be it verbal or nonverbal, which is apprehended by another, will alter that individual's perceptions, attitudes, beliefs, and motivations, even if ever so slightly" (Berger & Burgoon, 1995, p. 1).

This implies that, although educational software companies often advertise "interactive software," true social interaction cannot occur with a software program because it cannot offer original, authentic, creative feedback or meet the other requirements for social interaction. Social interaction can, however, occur *through* technology (e.g., directly between two or more people via email, a cell phone, or other communications technology), *around* technology (e.g., students discussing a problem posed by a software program), or *with the support of* technology (e.g., teacher and students interacting about a worksheet printed from a Web site).

Social interaction, in other words, occurs between people. The interaction can be **synchronous** (in real time during which participants take turns, such as during a phone call, face-to-face discussion, or chat) or **asynchronous** (not occurring at the same time, such as in an email conversation or letters—also known as "snail mail"). There are benefits and challenges for both types. For example, during synchronous communication in the popular MSN Messenger (Figure 3.2), learners can receive instant feedback, express themselves as ideas come to mind, and learn turn-taking and other skills.

FIGURE 3.3 Features of Social Interaction

- Is two-way
- Includes an authentic audience
- Can occur through, around, or with the support of technology
- Based on negotiation of meaning
- Offers authentic, creative feedback
- Synchronous or asynchronous
- Forms the basis for cooperation and collaboration

During asynchronous communication, such as an email exchange, learners have more time to think about and format what they want to say and how they want to say it. In addition, they have time to consider ideas from other participants. They also have a record of the communication that they can refer to. For both types of student interaction to be successful, participants must learn and practice skills such as listening, speaking, writing, reading, and communicating nonverbally. A list of features of social interaction is presented in Figure 3.3.

With whom do you interact socially on a daily basis? Why? With whom do K-12 students typically interact?

_____

_____

_____

_____

What Is Collaboration?

One type of communication that involves two-way interaction is collaboration. **Collaboration** is social interaction in which participants must plan and accomplish something specific together. A more specific definition is provided by Coleman (2002), who defines collaboration as when "[m]ultiple interactions occur between two or more people for the transfer of complex information for some common goal over a specified period of time" (n.p.). Collaboration is a discovery process, with students bringing their strengths to bear on reaching an outcome together. According to Hofmann (2003), true collaboration is when "the success of the group is paramount and all individuals must contribute to that success." She adds that "no member of the group can be left behind and everyone within the group will do whatever it takes to reach the common goal" (n.p.). Clearly, good communication based in social interaction is central to collaboration.

What Is Cooperation?

Although both cooperation and collaboration require social interaction—and technology can support both—they are not exactly the same processes (Panitz, 1996). Cooperation generally implies that students have separate roles in a structured task and pool their data to a specific end, whereas collaboration means that students work together in different ways from the planning stage on. Both collaboration and cooperation are beneficial to student learning.

The Role of Technology in Communication

Technology can play a central role in learning through all forms of communication. Shirky (2003) claims that

> what is really revolutionary about the Internet is that it facilitates many-to-many two-way communication patterns. Prior to the Internet, the last technology that had any real effect on the way people sat down and talked together was the table. There was no technological mediation for group conversations. The closest we got was the conference call, which never really worked right—"Hello? Do I push this button now? Oh, shoot, I just hung up." It's not easy to set up a conference call, but it's very easy to email five of your friends and say "Hey, where are we going for pizza?" So ridiculously easy group forming is really news. (n.p.)

In addition, research shows that students are more task-attentive and positively collaborating around the computer than in non-computer-supported tasks (Svensson, 2000). Often, this is because the nature of the collaborative computer-based task is new, exciting, and requires different skills and language than previous tasks. It also might be because students feel that more individualized instruction and help are available. Research in these areas will continue to shed light on how and why collaboration and social communication lead to learning.

In classrooms, teachers and students often participate in a combination of the communication patterns and processes noted in Figure 3.1—most commonly simple one-way outbound communication in the format of a lecture or presentation—but sometimes in variations of cooperative or collaborative tasks. Creating tasks in which students interact socially can be challenging, but teachers need to understand how to promote social interaction through technology-supported communication tasks in order to help students achieve. The discussion of communication tasks in the next section will assist in that challenge. First read what two classroom teachers have to say about classroom interaction in From the Classroom: Classroom Interaction.

Is Mr. Finley's task cooperative or collaborative? Why do you think so? What kinds of interaction patterns does his mystery project support? Give examples.

_____

_____

_____

FROM THE CLASSROOM

Classroom Interaction

Students involved in group projects will have a positive experience with writing, reading, and speaking English when the emphasis is placed on the group versus on the individual. Students practice reading, writing, and speaking English through brainstorming of ideas. Through peer editing and revising students are involved in using/learning language. Using technology to locate information and publish group activities encourages careful use of reading strategies, following directions, creative thinking to solve problems, and respect and constructive behavior to accomplish a task. As the classroom setting becomes a group of students accustomed to sharing common interests and pursuits, mutual respect, trust, acceptance, responsibility, and self-evaluation will be fostered. These are lifelong skills needed to function productively in any society. (Jean, sixth-grade teacher)

While I think that cooperative learning has its place, I am not that enthralled with it. I disagree with always giving kids a specific job to do in a group activity. I think the student learns more from collaborative learning, when he or she is involved with the whole process. I like the idea better of all members sharing ideas to accomplish a task. I don't think all members of a cooperative learning team learn as much as they could because they are limited by their specific tasks. For example, how much learning does the timekeeper really get out of an activity when all he or she is doing is just keeping track of the time? Sure the timekeeper watches, but the timekeeper could be watching a demonstration in the front of the room and learn from observing. I think we want our kids to be actively involved. We want each one of them to be using as many senses as possible when learning. When we purposefully limit them to using only a few senses, I think we are shortchanging them. Collaborative learning, on the other hand, requires all students to be active participants in the learning. Students share in the total experience, and I feel much more learning can take place. I am not saying that cooperative learning does not have any place in the classroom. I think there are times when what we want to teach is accomplishing a task with each member of the group helping with just one role. In those cases I think cooperative learning is great. For the most part, however, my vote would be with collaborative learning. (Susan, fifth-grade teacher)

Characteristics of Effective Technology-Supported Communication Tasks

Like tasks in other chapters of this book, communication tasks span a wide range of structures and content. As noted previously, effective communication is based on social interaction. Other components of effective communication tasks include those summarized in Figure 3.4 and explained here.

Component	Focus
Content	Based on curricular goals and student needs.
Time	Appropriate for all students to finish their task.
Communication technologies	Help all students access the interaction.
Participants	Knowledgeable audience that can work with students at their level.
Roles	Everyone has a part to contribute.
Intentional focus on learning	Task and pacing help students stay on task.

FIGURE 3.4 Components of Technology-Supported Communication Tasks

Content

The content of communication tasks and projects must be based on curricular goals and students' needs.

Time

Time is an important element and is also based on students' needs and on the task. Some classroom communications may take place very quickly, for example, giving instructions. Others, however, take longer, such as creating a joint bill to pass through the multischool student congress. Typically, the more people involved and the more communication required, the more time the task may take. Also, if new technologies must be learned, time must be allotted for students to do so. In addition, students need time to think before responding in order to have the benefits of communication (Kumpulainen & Wray, 2002), and some students may need more time to formulate their communication than others.

Communication technologies

Just as work toward other learning goals can take place without electronic technologies, so can communication. To support social interaction, communications tools should allow for "exploratory and argumentative talk" (Kumpulainen & Wray, 2002, p. 15). However, project participants outside the classroom may not be accessible in a timely manner without the use of electronic tools such as email or the telephone. Additionally, technology can make communication more accessible to learners with different physical abilities. For example, screen readers (discussed further in the Guidelines section of this chapter) that voice the text on a computer page can help students who do not see or read well to understand the content of a communication, and dictation software can help those who cannot type well to speak their messages while the computer translates them into text. Find more information on these assistive tools in the Accessibility and Special Education section of the Resources module of this text's Companion Website (http://www.prenhall.com/egbert).

Communication participants

There are a variety of people who can communicate with students. These include classmates and schoolmates (internal peers), peers from another school or area (external peers), parents, teachers, and content-area specialists (experts), and the general public. Lev Vygotsky (1962, 1978) and other researchers working in the sociocultural tradition show that participants are crucial to student success. These researchers posit that students learn by working through social interaction with the help of others on tasks that are slightly above their current level. Although the tasks could not be performed by the student alone, they are achievable with guidance and collaboration. Research in this area shows that what is learned with peers and others transfers to other situations over the long term, even when students are later working individually (Cesar, 1998). Find more Vygotsky resources in the Learning Theories section of the Resources module of this text's Companion Website (http://www.prenhall.com/egbert).

Participant roles

As noted previously, communication tasks work effectively when everyone has a part to contribute to the whole. Roles can be structured and assigned by the teacher or they can be chosen less formally by students within their groups. Students can each be responsible for a certain part of the content—e.g., a different set of years in the life of a famous person—and/or a specific part of the process, such as typist, illustrator, editor, and so on.

Learning focus

Socializing, although certainly an important part of the communications process, will not help students learn content—students need to communicate about the concepts rather than just make conversation. Task structure and pacing can help students focus on the goals during tasks that require social interaction.

What form do these components of communication tasks take in Mr. Finley's project? Fill in this chart:

Element	Mr. Finley's Plan
Content	
Time	
Technologies	
Participants	
Roles	
Learning focus	

Student Benefits of Technology-Supported Communication

By communicating around or through technology in tasks with the characteristics listed above, students benefit in many ways. For those students who have access to relevant collaborators and technologies, benefits include

- Not being limited by the school day or the school confines
- Participating in individualized instruction
- Feeling more free to exchange ideas openly
- Being motivated to complete tasks (from Eisenberg, 1992)

As they interact and negotiate meaning with others during communication tasks, students gain in language and content by

- Having access to models and scaffolds
- Thinking critically and creatively about language and content
- Constructing meaning from joint experiences
- Solving problems with information from multiple sources
- Working with different points of view and different cultures
- Learning to communicate in new and different ways, including using politeness tactics, appropriate turn-taking, and taking and giving constructive feedback
- Working with an authentic audience
- Expressing thoughts during learning

In addition, students working in teams can receive additional benefits. For example, teams tend to be better at solving problems, have a higher level of commitment, and include more people who can help implement an idea or plan. During collaboration, students learn and use more communicative strategies (Kumpulainen & Wray, 2002). Moreover, teams are able to generate energy and

interest in new projects. Especially important is that groups can be significantly more effective at reaching a goal than individual students would be. Because teamwork can offer students a chance to work toward their strengths supported by these scaffolds, students with all kinds of barriers to learning can benefit. The role of technology is to connect all students with a variety of audiences and interactants so that they receive the maximum benefit from their communication.

Which of the above benefits would you expect Mr. Finley's students to get from his project? Why? Are there additional ways in which they might benefit?

_____

_____

_____

THE TECHNOLOGY-SUPPORTED COMMUNICATION PROCESS

The process of supporting communication with technology, like the content learning process described in chapter 2, includes the basic categories of planning, developing, and analysis/evaluation. Following the steps in Table 3.1 can help teachers plan communication and collaboration activities effectively and efficiently.

Planning

During the *planning* stage, teachers should make sure that the process and outcomes are specific, relevant, and based on goals. Using objectives that state what the student will be able to do, to what extent, and in what way will assist in developing the rest of the lesson plan. For example, an objective that states, "The student will be able to describe five ways in which PCs and Macs differ" would

TABLE 3.1 Steps in Creating Technology-Supported Communication	
Planning	1. Choose the goals for the project.
	2. Choose the structure of the activity and other details.
	3. Review other projects for examples and explanations (e.g., those in the resources section of this chapter).
	4. Compile resources and models, check that the technology is available and works.
	5. Prepare ways to help students communicate by, for example, demonstrating how to use emoticons in email messages and using proper turn-taking manners. (For more on emoticons and the language of email, see the chapter 3 Resources module on the Companion Website.)
Development	1. Have students introduce themselves to their collaborators as necessary.
	2. As the project progresses, get copies of all student work, online and off.
	3. Communicate with teachers and other participants directly.
	4. Prepare updates and summaries as needed.
	5. Provide skills lessons as needed.
Analysis and evaluation	1. Thank audiences and/or participants.
	2. Help students to reflect, remember, and assess both good and bad aspects of the process and outcomes.
	3. Share results with participants and other stakeholders.
	4. Analyze overall project for successes, weaknesses, and changes needed.

Source: Adapted from Harris (1995) and 2Learn.ca Education Society of Canada (2005).

be more effective in helping focus the lesson than a very broad objective that states, "Students should understand computers." In addition to clear outcomes, the plan should include how and with whom students should interact. During the planning stage, teachers and students can decide whether technology is needed and if so, what kind of technology and how the chosen technology can meet the needs of students with different abilities. At this point, a review of other technology-supported communication projects might help teachers and students from forgetting something important that can make or break the activity.

During the planning stage the teacher should also find and evaluate potential participants and prepare them to understand the goals and responsibilities of the project. Many electronic lists and Web sites provide details of projects that teachers can join and allow teachers to post their own projects to find participants. iEARN (www.iearn.org) and Kidlink (www.kidlink.org) are two excellent project sites. Kidlink offers projects in many languages so that beginning English language learners can participate. Before they participate in the tasks, students should understand the writing conventions of their partners, especially if they are using a slightly different form of English (British English, for example). In addition, teachers should help students to figure out the language and content knowledge they need to grasp to communicate clearly and effectively during the project.

ELL

Development

The planning stage is the most crucial for creating a successful project, but the teacher's job does not end there. It is essential during the project *development* and implementation stage that the teacher observes students and makes changes in the project as necessary to meet student needs and curricular goals. Providing just-in-time skills lessons and coaching on team-building are also part of this stage.

Analysis

Analysis of the project should be conducted by all participants so that different perspectives are gained. Participants should also take part in the *evaluation* of the task process and product. Finally, the teacher must provide appropriate closure, such as whole group discussion, a summary, or a debriefing about group process. More information on the assessment of communication projects is included in the assessment section of this chapter.

What other steps in planning could Mr. Finley add to his project? What, if anything, did he neglect to do?

_____

_____

_____

Teachers and Technology-Supported Communication

The communication process, as outlined above, can pose any number of challenges for teachers and students, but teachers can make it easier by assuming different roles and giving their students opportunities to teach themselves and others. Technology-supported communication projects can be effective vehicles for providing such opportunities, as described here.

The teacher's role in communication projects

Teachers can take different roles in communication projects depending on the needs of their students. In some instances, for example, with younger or less-English-proficient students, the teacher may provide more help, resources, and structure and fewer truly collaborative tasks. In other projects the teacher may be more of an active facilitator in that she or he

ELL

- Provides structure through choices and limits
- Scaffolds and models
- Provides ongoing feedback

FIGURE 3.5 Roles for Teachers

1. The teacher encourages students to share and initiate.
2. The teacher scaffolds and strategizes with students.
3. The teacher assists in shaping the rules that help everyone participate and understand different perspectives.
4. The teacher paces the task according to student needs and acts as a member of the learning community.

- Addresses issues that come up with lessons on grammar or other skills
- Helps students to deal with any problems that arise

Some teachers may even act as "co-learners" in the task, collaborating with their students to construct meaning during a reciprocal experience. For example, teachers and students can co-learn while using Web-based resources to answer an essential question, as described in chapter 2. Because there is no "right" answer to the task, the teacher can work with students to decide "which is best" or "how it should be done."

Although teachers can take many roles, research shows that students are more willing to help and collaborate when the teacher is a facilitator rather than a guide or an all-knowing sage (Svensson, 2000). Kumpulainen and Wray (2002) outline four effective roles for the teacher in any project. These are shown in Figure 3.5.

The most important role for teachers in communication projects is to understand what their students need and to help them to meet the challenges of the task.

Which of the roles in Figure 3.5 best describe Mr. Finley's role(s) in the mystery project? Why do you think so?

_____

_____

_____

Challenges for teachers

Potential challenges for Mr. Finley and his students in completing his telecommunications project include:

- Dealing with technical difficulties and nonresponses from participants
- Planning around school breaks
- Making sure the distant partners understand the goals and procedures
- Handling inappropriate message content
- Providing just-in-time feedback and scaffolding

Group dynamics, or how people interact in a group, might also be an issue that Mr. Finley and his students must deal with, regardless of the type of interaction. For example, Kumpulainen and Wray (2002) point out that students' social status and other characteristics of group members might lead to breakdowns in participation and collaboration. The guidelines discussed in the next section suggest ways to overcome these barriers.

The more technology, distance, and participants involved in a communication project, the more challenges participants face in keeping the project going and making it an effective learning experience. That does not mean, however, that it is not worth the effort, but rather that careful planning and flexibility are necessary.

What should Mr. Finley do to avoid or meet some of these challenges?

_____

_____

_____

GUIDELINES FOR SUPPORTING COMMUNICATION WITH TECHNOLOGY

Designing Technology-Supported Communication Opportunities

Planning is crucial for the success of any communication project, regardless of how and whether it uses technology. Mr. Finley has chosen participants carefully, matched his project to standards and curriculum, and developed scaffolds to help his students succeed. Two other useful guidelines for planning include considering the context and making safety a primary focus.

Guideline #1: Consider the context. In the chapter's opening scenario, Mr. Finley has planned his task carefully. Among the many resources he will employ, he has decided to use Gaggle.net email as the most efficient way to give his students time to work on the project without having to learn a new technology. Gaggle.net is a Web-based email program to which teachers can control access and that they can set up to meet the needs of their specific students. Mr. Finley's students are familiar with Gaggle.net, and his classroom has a computer with the program set up for each team. For benefits of computer-based resources for students with special needs, see the Tool CloseUp: Assistive Support in Windows and Apple Operating Systems on page 76.

Mr. Finley did have other choices of tools, but he chose the most efficient for his physical context. In classrooms or schools that do not have reliable Internet access, participants still can access collaborators in other ways, such as through fax, phone, or letters, depending on the project timeline and the suitability of the technology to the project. If a classroom has only one computer, a project that is computer intensive for all students probably would not be efficient or effective.

Guideline #2: Safety first. The email tool that Mr. Finley chose (Gaggle.net) is one device that can help keep students safe in the context of the Geography Mystery project. Having children on the Internet is fraught with possible dangers, from accessing inappropriate Web sites to providing access to themselves; given only a child's name and general location, anyone can search the Web and obtain a map to the child's home. (For current statistics on Internet dangers and ideas about how to avoid them, see the excellent Enough is Enough site at http://enough.org/.) Three aspects of safety must be considered to ensure that students are not harmed during communication and collaboration projects.

1. *Classroom and school safety policy.* Many schools and districts have a safe use policy for the technology in their school. Students and parents must read and understand the issues and deal with them swiftly if the rules are broken. Teachers can model their rules on the "Rules for Online Safety" from the Safekids site (safekids.com). These rules for students include:
   - Never give out personal information or passwords, or send a picture without permission.
   - Tell adults if they come across information that makes them uncomfortable.
   - Do not meet online buddies without permission and a chaperone.
   - Do not respond to mean or uncomfortable messages.
   - Make rules with parents for going online.
   - Do not download anything without permission.
   - Do not hurt others or break the law.
   - Teach parents about the Internet.

   Samples of other acceptable use policies are provided by the Virginia Department of Education at http://www.pen.k12.va.us/VDOE/Technology/AUP/home.shtml#samples.

2. *Safe contexts.* There are two issues in providing a safe context—with whom students interact and about what. This aspect is easier to control in face-to-face communication projects, but even within the classroom students can be subjected to harassment, inappropriate interaction, and other types of harm. Teachers should choose participants with whom they are familiar and whom they have evaluated carefully as being able to carry out the project within the boundaries set.

3. *Safe tools.* The Internet can be a scary place, and open-ended software and access are fraught with financial, privacy, legal, and other potential problems. However, Mr. Finley felt that his project would work best by communicating with another class, so he chose Gaggle.net (see Figure 3.6). Gaggle minimizes risks to students by providing Web-based email access focused on

TOOLS

Tool CloseUp: Assistive Support in Windows and Apple Operating Systems

As technology improves, it becomes more accessible to everyone who needs to access it. Communication becomes possible even for severely challenged students. Formerly most assistive tools were add-ons or special purchases, but now a host of tools can be found on every new computer.

Mr. Finley's project can take advantage of many of these tools. For example, because Gaggle.net is Web based, students with visual impairments and those who learn best orally can use *screen readers* that turn text into speech to read the emails to them. Screen readers are built into most new operating systems. Windows XP includes Narrator, and Apple OS X includes the screen reader VoiceOver. For a list of other screen readers see the "list of screen readers" at wikipedia.org.

In addition, during the computer-supported project students with visual impairments can use the magnifier function built into the computer's accessibility features to make the text large enough for them to read comfortably. The user can choose the level of magnification and how the magnified items will appear. In Windows, the user can choose start>control panels and find the magnifier easily.

Students who have trouble typing can use the sticky keys function, which allows the user to press a keyboard command such as Shift or Control only once and have it stay active until pressing another command key. In addition, an onscreen keyboard can make it easier for some students to type. Other accessibility features contained in the computer's operating system are available as needed. Some of the options in Windows XP are shown here.

Find the accessibility options offered by the operating system on your computer and list them here. Which ones might help you use the computer more effectively?

For more information on Assistive Support in Windows and Apple Operating Systems, see the Assistive Support in Windows and Apple Operating Systems in the Tutorials module on the Companion Website (http://www.prenhall.com/egbert).

classroom use. It filters all messages and provides access to a variety of administrators and other participants, and it includes message boards that are monitored for content and chat rooms just for the school. The teacher can review all messages, and the system sends the teacher messages that might have inappropriate content. In addition, teachers can develop a list of inappropriate words that the software monitors. Teachers have the power to deny student access to their account and can block **spam,** or unsolicited, unwanted, or inappropriate messages, from external domains. Mr. Finley felt that using Gaggle could help keep his students safe during the telecommunication project that he designed. He could also have chosen tools from a wide variety of student-safe offerings, including Kidmail (kidmail.net), www.epals.com, and other emailing options and filtering software such as NetNanny (http://www.netnanny.com/), so he could access and control what comes in and out of students' email boxes.

Read a classroom teacher's comments on the safety procedure at his school in From the Classroom: Safety.

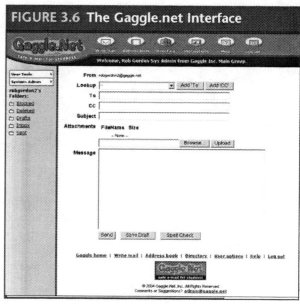

FIGURE 3.6 The Gaggle.net Interface

Source: Used with permission of Gaggle.net, Inc.

Guideline #3: Teach group dynamics and team building skills. When students work face to face around or with the support of the computer they can use *pragmatic cues* such as facial expressions and gestures to help with understanding. It is sometimes difficult for students to work well in teams even when they do have these cues. When students work through the computer, these cues are absent, and therefore meaning has to rely solely on text. Lack of pragmatic cues can lead to miscommunication, misunderstanding, or worse, particularly if students from diverse backgrounds are participating. Therefore, students in all contexts need to develop or reflect on team building and group dynamics skills. In addition to clearly communicating the process and product expectations to students, teachers can help them learn to understand and work within groups by making sure that they can:

- State their views clearly, and provide constructive criticism.
- Listen to others and take criticism, intended or unintended.
- Evaluate information that affects both their individual contribution and the group product.
- Define their roles.
- Deal with dissent; ask about miscommunications or misunderstandings (conflict resolution).
- Use appropriate levels of politeness and language.
- Develop an effective self-evaluation process.

Scenarios, modeling, and role-plays can be effective tools for developing these skills.

Guideline #4: Provide students with a reason to listen. Teaching students to listen actively to each other is no easy task. However, if they do not develop this skill, time on task is lessened and learning is less successful. Often teachers assume that students will listen because they are expected to, but this does not always happen. A great project that does not require students to listen to each other wastes some of the most effective learning opportunities. For example, a group presentation aimed solely at getting a grade from the teacher typically isolates the rest of the class from the knowledge being presented, especially if the topic of the presentation is the same for the group before and the group after. Likewise, chats, online discussions, or even emails that are too long, too unstructured, or in which it is difficult to find the relevant information can also allow students not to listen. Students are more likely to listen actively if they have a good reason to do so, and project structures can give that reason. For example, teachers can provide "listening" handouts on which students have to record some of the information for future use, or assign students the role of presentation evaluator. In addition, authentic tasks in which outcomes are not all the same help students to listen. Figure 3.7 on page 78 presents a summary of these guidelines.

FROM THE CLASSROOM

Safety

Our students have to get a form signed by their parents allowing them to use the Internet. It also acts as a contract stating that the student will follow the school guidelines on Internet use. Furthermore, their core teacher has to sign the form, agreeing with the student and the parent that the student will use the Internet for appropriate, scholastic reasons. So in order for the student to have Internet use, not only does the parent have to sign the form but the student and the teacher as well. (Adrian, sixth-grade teacher)

What did Mr. Finley do to get his students to listen to each other? What other structures can you think of to give students a reason to listen?

_____

_____

_____

FIGURE 3.7 Guidelines for Designing Opportunities for Communication

Guidelines	Explanation
Consider the context.	• Use technologies that work with the students, audience, and task.
Make safety a primary focus.	• Review the classroom and school safety policies. • Choose safe technologies and a safe audience. • Work with parents.
Teach group dynamics and team-building skills.	• Help students understand how to work effectively in groups with people of all kinds.
Provide students with a reason to listen.	• Provide opportunities for students to listen actively for important information. • Make the information crucial to their success.

COMMUNICATION TECHNOLOGIES

Guidelines like those above are useful for developing communication tasks, but the right tool is essential. Egbert (2005) notes, "Many educators believe that technology's capability to support communication and collaboration has changed the classroom more than any of its other capabilities. In fact, it is how educators make *use* of that capability that can change classroom goals, dynamics, turn-taking, interactions, audiences, atmosphere, and feedback and create a host of other learning opportunities" (pp. 53–54). One crucial aspect of effective use is a tool that fits the tasks that they are requiring of their students. There can be many such tools, from MS Word's commenting feature, with which the teacher and peers can communicate about a student's writing (Figure 3.8), to Yahoo! Messenger with Voice (Figure 3.9), through which students can communicate both in text and orally.

FIGURE 3.8 MS Word Commenting

My Family

My family is not *very* big. I have to *bruthers* and a sister and a mom and a dad and a dog. We live in a house. *Sumtims* I *fite* with my *bruthers* but I still like them. My sister is little. We all like to use computers

Comment: Check your spelling here. Sometimes words don't look like they sound, right?

Comment: Can you tell us more about what your family likes to do?

Source: Reproduced with permission of Yahoo! Inc. © 2007 by Yahoo! Inc. Yahoo! and the Yahoo! logo are trademarks of Yahoo! Inc.

FIGURE 3.9 Yahoo! Messenger with Voice

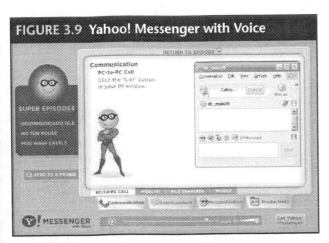

Shirky (2003) states, "The number of people writing tools to support or enhance group collaboration or communication [what he calls social software] is astonishing" (n.p.). This rapid growth attests not only to the value of social connections, but also to the importance of those connections to life and learning. Wikis and weblogs (described in Table 3.2) are some of the more recent developments in social software, but often the older (and sometimes simpler) tools such as tape recorders and basic email can provide what teacher and students need, and these tools can be more accessible to a variety of users.

In addition to telephones and other communication technologies that are fairly ubiquitous, Table 3.2 describes tools that can facilitate communication *through* the computer. It is by no means an exhaustive list, but it includes many tools commonly used in schools. Where the software or Web site lists a specific grade level it has been included, but most of these tools can be adapted for a variety of student skills and levels. For more detailed descriptions of these tools, look them up in online dictionaries at http://webopedia.com and http://dict.die.net/email/.

Two-way interactive video and other communication technologies that are also used frequently for distance education or elearning are described in chapter 8.

TABLE 3.2 Examples of Communication Tools

Tool and Examples	Description	Sample Classroom Uses
MOO • Schmooze schmooze.hunter.cuny.edu (cross-cultural communication) • Digital Space Traveler www.digitalspace.com/traveler (any) • Mundo Hispano www.umsl.edu/moosproj/mundo.html	• Text- or graphics-based virtual worlds • Accessible by a large number of users simultaneously • Users type in words to "talk" to other users • Synchronous • Some have voice capabilities and include 3D and color graphics	*MOO visitors can:* • Converse with people from many different places • Collaborate on building new parts of the MOO • Play interactive games • Find resources and ideas A collaborative MOO treasure hunt can be fun!
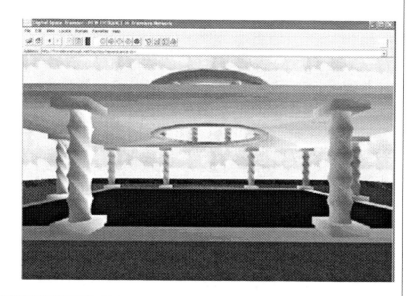 **An Entrance to the Traveler's Network at Digital Space Traveler** *Source:* Used with permission of Bruce Damer.		
Text chat/voice chat/instant messaging (IM) • MSN Messenger messenger.msn.com • Yahoo Messenger Messenger.yahoo.com • ICQ ("I Seek You") http://www.icq.com/	• Synchronous, interactive messaging • Does not typically lend itself well to intensive consideration of an issue or to use by learners who need more time • Available through cell phones, handhelds, and other types of hardware • Usually involves the use of a special "language" built of abbreviations (For more information, see the "text message abbreviations" entry in http://www.webopedia.com)	• Chat is useful when students can type well and the teacher wants everyone to have a chance to participate (and not be outshouted) • Voice chat can be useful for longer discussions of issues with collaborators at a distance • Computer video cameras can also be connected and used with chats for short demonstrations or sharing

370

continued

TOOLS

TABLE 3.2 Continued

Tool and Examples	Description	Sample Classroom Uses

Email (electronic mail)
• Pine
  www.washington.edu/pine
• Eudora
  www.eudora.com
• Gaggle
  www.gaggle.net
• Microsoft Outlook
  office.microsoft.com
	• Sent asynchronously over the Internet
	• Requires the user to have the recipient's email address
	• For a discussion of netiquette, or rules for using email, see the Resources module on this chapter's Companion Website (http://www.prenhall.com/egbert)
		• Email communication is useful for asynchronous conversation during tasks when participants need time to do something between messages
		• Email allows documents to be attached and shared

Electronic Discussion Forum and Courseware
• Blackboard
  www.blackboard.com
• Webworkzone
  Webworkzone.com
• Daedalus Integrated Writing Environment
  www.daedalus.com
• Yahoo groups
  groups.yahoo.com
• Nicenet
  Nicenet.org (free)
	• Asynchronous
	• Threaded so that replies and conversation turns are obvious
	• Discussions are included in most courseware packages
	• Often used in hybrid (face-to-face with distance components) and distance courses (described further in chapter 8)
		• Students can have an ongoing conversation that they can access from any computer that has the software (usually just a Web browser)
		• Team spaces can provide a place for members to post tasks during the process and to discuss their ideas privately
		• The teacher and students can have a permanent record of the discussions

The Interface of Nicenet, a Free Web-Based Forum

Source: Used with permission of Nicenet.

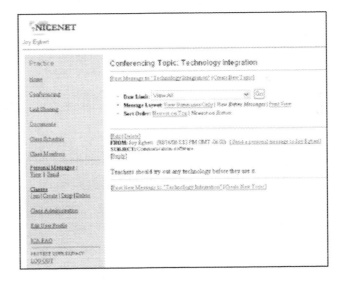

Electronic list See a list of education lists and electronic journals at www.edwebproject.org/lists.html	• Often known as a "listserv" • Messages posted by users through their email arrive in the inbox of all users who subscribe to the list • Asynchronous	• Students can communicate with experts by finding and joining a list to discuss a specific topic such as the Vietnam War, polynomial equations, or the use of technology in education • A list is a good way to disseminate a message to a large group of people

TABLE 3.2 Continued

Tool and Examples	Description	Sample Classroom Uses

Weblog (Blog)
• VisitMyClass
  www.visitmyclass.com
• Blogger
  www.blogger.com
	• Web site where users can add comments to the original content posted by an individual author
	• Only the author can modify or delete messages once they are posted
	• Typically used as an individual's personal journal
	• Asynchronous
	• Covers all range of subjects from the blog author's point of view
		• Students can quickly and easily post messages, photos, and graphics and interact with others
		• Keep a class journal
		• Post handouts
		• Share with external stakeholders
		• Keep parents informed, especially if the blog has tools to "push" the information to subscribers' computers

Opening Screen at Blogger.com *Source:* Blogger logo © Google, Inc. Used with permission.		

Voice email
• Talksender (download free from http://www.tucows.com/preview/164878
• Vemail
  http://www.nch.com.au./vemail/
• MailAmp
  http://www.mailamp.com/
	• Allows the user to send a recorded audio message through the Internet	• Students with physical barriers to typing or who are still developing written skills can use voice email to communicate in the same way that others use email
		• Students can keep audio journals
		• Students can communicate with distant "voice" pals

Wiki
• Wikipedia
  http://www.wikipedia.org/
• EvoWiki
  http://wiki.cotch.net/ (science topics)
	• Asynchronous
	• Collection of work by any number of people, all of whom can modify the content
		• Wikipedia is an Internet encyclopedia being built by users from all over the world
		• Students can add information to any topic
		• Students can understand topic views from many perspectives

Some of the tools listed in Table 3.2 are free (called **freeware**); others are shareware. **Shareware** is software that users can test, and if they decide to keep it they pay a small fee to the developer. Typically, freeware and shareware are created by individuals or small groups of developers. Other tools in the table are commercial products sold by software companies. They vary in how easy they are to use and what they can do. Commercial products are usually more sophisticated and have many more features, but that does not always make them better for classroom

TOOLS

Tool CloseUp: Asia Inspirer

As implied in this chapter, the designation of software as *communication* software characterizes how the software is *used*, not what it *contains*. Asia Inspirer (Tom Snyder Productions) has teams of students (or, alternatively, the whole class or a single team) traveling in contiguous countries throughout Asia to land in countries that have specific demographic, economic, and/or geographic features. The accompanying trip assignment image shows the features that one team must aim for. They are trying to land in countries that have the most tea and lumber and end up in a country with a specific population density on the last of their 10 moves.

Each student on the team has a different map of Asia that shows one or more of the features, and students must pool their information to travel to countries with the highest number of features to earn the most points from their travels. Student interaction is initiated not only by the need to cooperate on the facts but also on the need to figure out how they will cooperate at all. They have to negotiate turn-taking, leadership, and other roles in the group in addition to describing and answering questions about the countries on their maps. The level and amount of interaction is up to the team, and the maps provide scaffolding, so even limited-proficient language learners can join in easily. In addition, the teacher chooses the difficulty level, timer settings, and different configurations (head-to-head competition or team cooperation); this provides slower learners or those who need more time or support with more opportunity to participate.

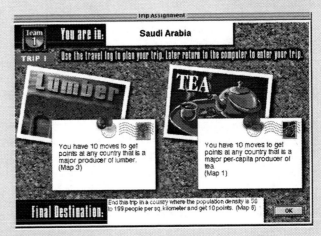

Source: Used with permission of Tom Snyder Productions.

Asia Inspirer is designed for use in the one-computer classroom. Groups take turns inputting their moves while the rest of the groups are plotting their routes at their desks. In this way the objectives of learning Asian geography and economy and of collaborating are central, and the technology is used as support for goals.

Under what circumstances might a teacher choose to use a program with these features with the whole class? With teams? For a single team? Why?

_____

_____

_____

_____

use. As with any tool, teachers should check them carefully for characteristics that support effective and/or efficient learning before adopting them for classroom use.

Most teachers probably think of telecommunication tools as those mentioned in Table 3.2, but software packages can both directly and indirectly support communication. Even common software packages such as word processors can be used for collaboration; as noted in chapter 2 and above, the "comment" function in Microsoft Word allows learners to comment on one another's work in writing inside the document. Voice (oral) annotations are also possible and are a good alternative for students who do not type well, who have physical barriers, or whose written skills are not understandable.

In addition, much of the software from educational software companies such as Tom Snyder Productions (www.tomsnyder.com) is based on student collaboration. Packages such as the Inspirer (geography/social studies), Decisions, Decisions (government/social studies), and Fizz and Martina (math) series are aligned with content-area standards and have built-in mechanisms for collaboration. The teachers' guides that accompany these software packages also include ideas about how to make the collaboration work for all learners, including ELLs. Perhaps essential for some contexts, much of the Tom Snyder software is intended for students to work with as a class in the one-computer classroom. However, more important than *how* the software connects learners is *why* and *with whom* learners connect. Much content-based software guides students into predetermined conclusions, and teachers must take care to make sure that those conclusions are equitable and socially responsible. See the Tool CloseUp: Asia Inspirer on the previous page for more information about students interacting around the computer.

Choose a communication tool to investigate further. What features might be useful for the way you plan to teach? Why? Be creative in your thinking and response.

_____

_____

_____

LEARNING ACTIVITIES: COMMUNICATION TASKS

Communication opportunities are mentioned throughout this book because learning results from the interaction that takes place during these opportunities, regardless of the task goal. Many of the activities in this book have a communication component. Although examples of telecommunications projects like Mr. Finley's abound, there are fewer examples of communication projects in which students work around and with the support of technologies, as in the Asia Inspirer example in the Tool CloseUp. However, in addition to the tools listed previously, Web sites and other Internet tools, such as the free tools on the Intel Education Thinking Tools' Web site (http://www.intel.com), provide an amazing number and variety of opportunities for students to communicate around, with, *and* through technology.

This section presents examples of communication activities. Each of the examples described begins with a content-area standard as its goal. All examples also address the technology standard that students learn to communicate effectively with and to a variety of audiences. Audiences for the examples are included; an internal peer refers to a classmate or schoolmate, and an external peer is someone in another school, district, region, or country. Teachers are not included as participants in these examples because it is a given that much classroom communication will be aimed at or filtered through them.

In the activities, students work around, with the support of, and through the computer. As you read the activities, reflect on how the guidelines from this chapter might be applied in each case and which technologies from Table 3.2 starting on page 79 might be used to support the learning opportunities.

Inclusion
ELL

Inclusion
ELL

LEARNING ACTIVITIES

Participants	Activity
Internal peers	Create and present a multimedia presentation for younger students about some aspect of health and fitness.
External peers	Through email, build an argument that uses online and offline resources to convince peers to try your favorite healthy recipe.
Experts (doctors)	Check WebMD.com or other sites for advice or information about a health issue and then discuss any questions, especially about the answers you found, on Ask a Doctor at http://www.mdadvice.com/ask/ask.htm. Use the findings to create a persuasive essay or letter to the editor.
General public	Develop Web pages that provide feedback about healthy eating, or create a survey that provides results about how healthy a particular diet is.

Standard: Physical Education—Demonstrate the ability to influence and support others in making positive health choices.

Which of these activities involve simple communication? Collaboration?

Participants	Activity
Internal peers	Work together to build an electronic text on animal habitats. Present the text to students in other grade groups to help them prepare for a test.
External peers	Complete a series of science mysteries using the format that Mr. Finley developed. Use mystery animals from another region of the world as the subjects of the project.
Experts	Complete a habitat WebQuest, such as the one at http://questgarden.com/47/03/2/070226113229, and then have the products evaluated by local scientists or zoo personnel.
General public	Prepare the lesson on animal habitats located at http://school.discovery.com/lessonplans/programs/habitats/. Develop the Mystery Animals extension of the lesson and post the mysteries to the Web for others to guess.

Standard: Science—Students develop understanding of organisms and environments.

Science Example: Mad Sci (http://www.madsci.org/)

In addition to features such as links, lessons, "random knowledge," the Visible Human tour, and lots of fun experiments, the Mad Sci site provides Ask-a-Scientist. Be sure that students understand the rules of use, published clearly on the site, before they pose questions to the experts. Students should also learn how to write succinct, pointed questions that experts can answer in a short amount of time. The people who run the site and its policies and procedures are clearly stated, making it easy for teachers to decide whether this is a safe site and how it can best be used. Use the information in "Setting Up an Ask the Expert Service" to create your own expert site.

Review Guideline #4 on page 77. What gives students a reason to listen during these activities? What group skills do they need in order to succeed?

375

Standard: Social studies——Work together to promote the values and principles of American democracy.

Participants	Activity
Internal peers External peers Experts General public	Work with internal peer teams using a worksheet and Web site such as those presented in Figure 3.10 from Education World to find out more about local democracy. Take one political organization or body (who serve as experts) to interview, or each team member can gather information on one aspect of each organization, by email, telephone, or face to face. Then create a report to share with the rest of the class. Build posters to hang in town so that the general public is also informed. Work with external peers to compare and contrast community decision makers across states, regions, and countries.

FIGURE 3.10 Education World Internet Scavenger Hunt Democracy in Your Hometown

Name: _____

Directions: What do you know about people who make big decisions for a community? Explore the Web site provided below. Then read each statement and answer each question based on the information on the Web site. Three possible answers appear below each question. Circle the correct answer.

Web Resource: Hometown U.S.A http://www.pbs.org/democracy/inyourtown/hometown/index.html

1. Commuters are discussing how to spend the local transportation budget. Who will decide whether to spend the money on more buses or on better roads?

   police chief   governor   city council

2. A school is looking for a new principal. Who is responsible for finding and hiring the person who will do the best job?

   PTA   school board   mayor

Source: Reprinted with permission of Education World, Inc.

Social Studies Example: Voices of Youth (http://www.unicef.org/voy/)

Current discussions on this site supported by UNICEF

include "education for all," tsunami bracelets, and "what is your school like?", posted by students from around the world. The site includes Youth Digital Diaries to listen and add to, a one-minute video contest about international issues, and both research data and steps for action by students. Figure 3.11 presents opportunities offered on the Voice of Youth home page.

In what other ways could this social studies standard be met? How can technology help (or hinder) communication or collaboration centered on this standard?

_____

_____

_____

FIGURE 3.11 Voices of Youth

Source: Used with permission of UNICEF.

Standard: Math—Organize and consolidate mathematical thinking through communication. Communicate thinking coherently and clearly to peers, teachers, and others.

Participants	Activity
Internal peers	Collaborate in groups around one computer as the teacher facilitates Fizz and Martina's Math Adventure (Tom Snyder Productions). Communicate answers and understandings as the work progresses.
External peers	Work on a math activity, such as The Cylinder Problem, at http://mathforum.org/brap/wrap/elemlesson.html. Email understandings and questions to peers who are also studying this problem. Together, the groups come to solutions and conclusions.
Experts	Work with family members to perform the same calculations. Use the Family Math Activity provided by Math Forum at http://mathforum.org/brap/wrap/familymath.html.
General public	Write word problems and challenge members of the public to solve them, through email, a Web site, or public mail.

Math Example: The Globe Program Student Investigations (http://www. globe.gov/)

At this site, teachers and their students can join any number of collaborative student investigations with peers from around the world, submit reports and photos of their projects, and discover information from other projects.

What other math activities lend themselves well to collaboration and communication? List three, then add Web sites or other technologies that might enhance these activities for your grade level and curricular goals.

_____

_____

_____

Standard: English—Students adjust their use of spoken, written, and visual language to communicate effectively with a variety of audiences for different purposes.

Participants	Activity
Internal peers External peers Experts General public	Write a persuasive essay collaboratively. Share the essay with internal and external peers for feedback and get help with content from experts during the process. Publish a hard copy of the paper at the school or a digital copy in an electronic forum for public consumption and response.

In what other ways can students communicate or collaborate around writing?

_____

_____

_____

377

Participants	Activity
Internal peers	Work on a project using Tom Snyder Productions' Cultural Reporter books and templates. Conduct interviews, library research, and use other resources to find answers to a question about American culture.
External peers	Use the SchMOOze University MOO (described in Table 3.2) to meet and converse with peers from around the world.
Experts	Go to Dave's ESL Café (http://www.eslcafe.com/) to ask questions about grammar and other language and culture issues.
General public	Create an electronic forum using Blogger or another platform to discuss idioms, jargon, and colloquial speech from all over the United States. Ask follow-up questions to contributors and thank them for their participation.

Standard: ESL—Use English to participate in social interaction.

ELL

What do teachers need to consider before asking ELLs to interact socially? Brainstorm a list of challenges with your peers.

Multidisciplinary Example: iEARN (http://www.iearn.org/)

One of the most popular sites on the Web for "collaborative educational projects that both enhance learning and make a difference in the world," the International Education and Resource Network (I*EARN) provides three different types of opportunities for students and schools—to join an existing project, to develop a project relevant to their curriculum, or to join a learning circle. Projects span content and skill areas and include students from countries around the world. One ongoing project is the Art Miles Mural, in which students are attempting to create three miles of themed murals and capture a record in the *Guinness Book of World Records*. Other projects, on topics from folktales to funny videos and values to sports, incorporate every subject area and result in a product or exhibition that is shared with others. Figure 3.12 shows part of the amazing list of social studies projects underway.

Communicating in Limited Technology Contexts

Benefits of using the kinds of ready-made projects provided by I*EARN, described above, include the support that is available, such as tips for helping participants understand each other, software that is accessible for learners with slow Internet access, and offline work for students in limited technology contexts.

Of course, there are classrooms around the world that do not have access and cannot participate in the electronic portion of these amazing technology-enhanced projects. That does not mean that they are not valuable as interactants. Teachers and students

FIGURE 3.12 iEARN Social Studies Projects

Projects

Main
Creative/Language Arts
Science/Technology/Math
Culture and Society
Learning Circles
Alphabetical Project List
Search Project Database
Forum Tutorial

Social Studies

- **Against Scholar Dropout** - A place for students, parents, teachers and others responsible for education to think about the main problems in education.
- **Ancestor Photographs Project** - Create a world of past times making them as close to the contemporaries as possible.
- **Architecture and Living Spaces** - Student research the architecture and history of the houses, buildings and monuments of their town.
- **Atlas de la Diversidad** - A multi-media database of cultural products, created by the students, as the outcome of their learning.
- **Backtalk Journal: International News Magazine** - Students participate by contributing interviews of people, who play some kind of leadership role in service to sustainable development, for publication
- **Breaking the Silence** - This project serves to raise awareness of issues pertaining to disease prevention in adolescents.
- **Breaking the Silence: The Trans-Atlantic Slave Trade Project** - Joining together in a serious examination of the legacy of the Trans-Atlantic Slave Trade (TST).
- **Bullying Project** - A collaborative attempt to address the issues of bullying, teasing and school violence.
- **Celebrations and Mournings** - A project to collect statements, pictures, poems and stories from children and their teachers about what they do when they are happy or sad
- **Child Labour Project** - Youth collaboration in research and awareness-raising on the issues of child labour and exploitation.
- **Child Soldier Project** - This is a project where youth can bear witness to the issue of the child soldier and how it affects their lives, their families, their communities and their countries.
- **Cities Near the Sea** - Learning and working together by students

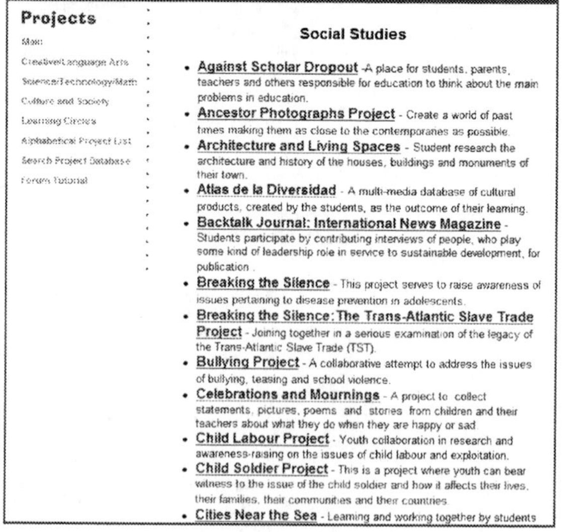

Source: Used with permission of iEARN-USA.

Follow-Along

Last year I participated with my class in a wonderful Web-based project where a group of teachers registered as part of Iditarod. We shared general information about our classes: age, demographic, geographic location, etc. This information was posted in a list-serv. There were suggested activities and opportunities for classes to interact with one another as we researched the history of the Iditarod and followed the race itself in March. Each of my table groups picked a musher to follow through the race. They emailed the musher—all but one group received personal email responses from the musher. There are tons of resources that accompany the project, some submitted by teachers, others by the Web master. It connected the kids with real action following the daily postings of the Iditarod race. (Jennie, first-grade teacher)

need to reflect on how to communicate and collaborate with peers regardless of their access to electronic technologies.

Other Communication Projects

Some particularly powerful learning experiences based on communicating come from follow-alongs, in which classes interact with experts and adventurers around the world as they travel through space, bicycle around the world, compete in the Iditarod, or make discoveries along the Amazon River. For examples of these and other communication projects, teachers can conduct a Web search with the terms "student examples" and "telecommunications projects." This search will provide more responses than it is possible to review. To make the search more useful, add a content area, grade level, and other details to the search. Teachers do not necessarily need to develop projects from the ground up—there are plenty of project frameworks and examples for teachers to join or use in developing their own. Of course, teachers should give credit to the originator of the lesson or project and modify it to fit their specific contexts.

Read as a classroom teacher describes a follow-along in which her class participated in From the Classroom: Follow-Along.

Find a project (either online or one that you created) that fits the grade level and content area in which you will teach. Consider the content and technology standards and technology accessibility. Does this project meet the guidelines and incorporate the tips from this chapter? If not, what changes or additions would you make to have it do so?

_____

_____

_____

ASSESSING COMMUNICATION TASKS: RUBRICS

The wide variety of communication activities noted in the previous section, along with the diversity in student skills, goals, and needs in every classroom, indicate that student achievement during communication tasks should be assessed at different times in different ways. This section describes ways to assess student process and outcomes during communication tasks. Other assessments throughout this text may also be applicable to the assessment of communication tasks—as you read other chapters, keep this in mind.

Planning

In the planning stage, teachers can check on the effectiveness of the project design using the Lesson Analysis and Adaptation Worksheet (found at the end of chapter 1 and in the Lesson Planning module of the Companion Website).

Development

During the project, teachers can use **formative** assessment tools, or tools that help students understand their process and provide feedback to help them work better. Formative assessments include teacher observations. Teachers can make observations using personal digital assistants or other portable technologies in conjunction with checklists like the inclusion checklists from http://www.circleofinclusion.org/ or a teacher-made checklist that notes student progress toward individual goals. Student self-reports—for example, "a list of what I accomplished today" or "a question that came up today"——can also help to make sure that students are on task and that the project is moving toward the goals effectively.

Analysis

To make a **summative** evaluation, in other words, to assess outcomes or products, it is important to strike a balance between team outcome and individual accountability. Peer assessments, based on team participation or progress, are often useful for evaluating individual performance, and if the project consists of online segments, teachers can collect copies of the discussion and other participation examples. Another option for peers is to keep an "I did/he did/she did" list (McNinch, personal communication, 2005). Students list what each team member contributed to the project. The teacher can cross-reference the lists and observations and have a pretty good idea of what was done by whom and perhaps even what affected the group dynamics.

Rubrics are also useful to assess product and process. A rubric provides both criteria for evaluation and the performance levels that should be met. Rubrics also help students to understand what is expected of them throughout the project. Teachers can find many free rubric-makers and sample rubrics on the Web. Some guide the teacher through the whole rubric construction process (e.g., Rubistar, http://rubistar.4teachers.org/), and others supply different rubrics for different types of tasks (e.g., Teach-nology, http://teach-nology.com/web_tools/rubrics/). See Figure 3.13 for rubrics for a cooperative learning project. Even if teachers and students use these technologies, they still need to understand how and why to create assessment rubrics. Prentice Hall School Professional Development's Web site (www.phschool.com/professional_development/assessment/rubrics.html) sums up the following guidelines for rubric development:

1. Specify student behaviors that you will observe and judge in the performance assessment.
2. Identify dimensions of the key behaviors to be assessed. If the assessment tasks are complex, several dimensions of behaviors may have to be assessed.
3. Develop concrete examples of the behaviors that you will assess.
4. Decide what type of rubric will be used: one that evaluates the overall project, one that evaluates each piece of the project separately, a generic rubric that fits with any task, one created specifically for this task, or a combination.
5. Decide what kind of outcomes you will provide to students: checklists, points, comments, or some combination.
6. Develop standards of excellence, or criteria, for specified performance levels.
7. Decide who will score each performance assessment——the teacher, the students (either self-scoring or peer scoring), or an outside expert.
8. Share scoring specifications with other stakeholders in the assessment system—parents, teachers, and students. All stakeholders must understand the behaviors in the same way.

Rubrics are best understood by students when they have a hand in making them. Regardless of who makes the rubric, students must be able to access the criteria and have clear examples of performance levels throughout the project. For example, Mr. Finley provided handouts and mini-lessons during his project. He can use both the completed handouts and his observations to give students feedback on their progress. To measure the outcomes, Mr. Finley will develop a rubric with his students based on the objectives of the project. They will decide together that the important criteria for the project include providing well-written clues based on accurate data, asking good questions, arriving at the correct conclusions, using resources (including technology) appropriately, and making the map correctly. Mr. Finley will then work with the students to clarify each level of performance (excellent, good, fair, poor) and to help them use the rubric to assess their own performance.

Is this evaluation scheme appropriate for Mr. Finley's project? Why do you think so?

FIGURE 3.13 Cooperative Learning Project Rubric

Cooperative Learning Project Rubric A: Process

Name: _____

Date: _____

Class: _____

	Exceptional 4 points	Admirable 3 points	Acceptable 2 points	Amateur 1 point
Group Participation	All students enthusiastically participate	At least 3/4 of students actively participate	At least half the students confer or present ideas	Only one or two persons actively participate
Shared Responsibility	Responsibility for task is shared evenly	Responsibility is shared by most group members	Responsibility is shared by 1/2 the group members	Exclusive reliance on one person
Quality of Interaction	Excellent listening and leadership skills exhibited; students reflect awareness of others' views and opinions in their discussions	Students show adeptness in interacting; lively discussion centers on the task	Some ability to interact; attentive listening; some evidence of discussion or alternatives	Little interaction; very brief conversations; some students were disinterested or distracted
Roles Within Group	Each student assigned a clearly defined role; group members perform roles effectively	Each student assigned a role but roles not clearly defined or consistently adhered to	Students assigned roles but roles were not consistently adhered to	No effort made to assign roles to group members

Cooperative Learning Project Evaluation Form A: Process

Name: _____

Date: _____

Class: _____

	Exceptional 4 points	Admirable 3 points	Acceptable 2 points	Amateur 1 point
Group Participation				
Shared Responsibility				
Quality of Interaction				
Roles Within Group				

COMMENTS:

381

FIGURE 3.13 Continued

Cooperative Learning Project Rubric B: Outcome or Product

Name: _____

Date: _____

Class: _____

	Exceptional 4 points	Admirable 3 points	Acceptable 2 points	Amateur 1 point
Organization	Extremely well organized; logical format that was easy to follow; flowed smoothly from one idea to another and cleverly conveyed; the organization enhanced the effectiveness of the project	Presented in a thoughtful manner; there were signs of organization and most transitions were easy to follow, but at times ideas were unclear	Somewhat organized; ideas were not presented coherently and transitions were not always smooth, which at times distracted the audience	Choppy and confusing; format was difficult to follow; transitions of ideas were abrupt and seriously distracted the audience
Content Accuracy	Completely accurate; all facts were precise and explicit	Mostly accurate; a few inconsistencies or errors in information	Somewhat accurate; more than a few inconsistencies or errors in information	Completely inaccurate; the facts in this project were misleading to the audience
Research	Went above and beyond to research information; solicited material in addition to what was provided; brought in personal ideas and information to enhance project; and utilized more than eight types of resources to make project effective	Did a very good job of researching; utilized materials provided to their full potential; solicited more than six types of research to enhance project; at times took the initiative to find information outside of school	Used the material provided in an acceptable manner, but did not consult any additional resources	Did not utilize resources effectively; did little or no fact gathering on the topic
Creativity	Was extremely clever and presented with originality; a unique approach that truly enhanced the project	Was clever at times; thoughtfully and uniquely presented	Added a few original touches to enhance the project but did not incorporate it throughout	Little creative energy used during this project; was bland, predictable, and lacked "zip"
Presentation Mechanics	Was engaging, provocative, and captured the interest of the audience and maintained this throughout the entire presentation; great variety of visual aids and multimedia; visual aids were colorful and clear	Was well done and interesting to the audience; was presented in a unique manner and was very well organized; some use of visual aids	Was at times interesting and was presented clearly and precisely; was clever at times and was organized in a logical manner; limited variety of visual aids and visual aids were not colorful or clear	Was not organized effectively; was not easy to follow and did not keep the audience interested; no use of visual aids

continued

FIGURE 3.13 Continued

Cooperative Learning Project Evaluation Form B: Product

Name: _____

Date: _____

Class: _____

	Exceptional 4 points	Admirable 3 points	Acceptable 2 points	Amateur 1 point
Organization				
Content Accuracy				
Research				
Creativity				
Presentation Mechanics				

COMMENTS:

Source: © 2005 Pearson Education, Inc., publishing as Pearson Prentice Hall. Used by permission.

SAMPLE LESSON: COMMUNICATION

Mr. Finley's telecommunications project went very well, and he and his students are excited about trying another project. Mr. Finley decides to look at other communication-based lessons to find another project that might be appropriate for his students. The standards addressed by this lesson include math standards such as problem solving, reasoning, connections, and skills (statistics); content reading standards such as variety of sources, information access, and evaluation; and writing content standards.

The lesson Mr. Finley chose from the Educators Reference Desk (http://www.eduref.org/) is presented here.

MINI STUDY OF A STATE

Author: *Unknown*

Grade Level(s): 4, 5, 6, 7

Subject(s):

- Social Studies/State History

Objectives:
The students will learn to do research while comparing their state with one of the states of the U.S. They will be graded on information, drawing and art work, spelling and punctuation, and neatness.

Activities:
The students are given the following questions in a prepared booklet in which they write their answers. There is also room provided for them to draw the state flag, flower, tree, bird, and a map of the state.

1. Name of state:
2. Capital:
3. Is this state larger or smaller than (*******)?
4. Name all of the states, countries, or bodies of water that surround this state.
5. About how many people live in this state? Is that more or less than (*******)?
6. Name two prominent people that are from this state. Why are they famous?
7. What are the chief products of this state?
8. What kind of climate does this state have?
9. Tell about three things in this state that are very different from (*******).
10. Tell about three things in this state that are much the same as we have in (*******).
11. If you were traveling from_____, (******) to the capital of this state, how many miles would you drive?
12. How long would it take you to drive it if you drove 50 miles an hour?
13. These are facts about this state that I think are interesting . . .
14. I would like to live in this state because . . .
15. I would not like to live in this state because . . .
16. Make a pictorial graph of the population of your state and the state of (********).
17. When did it get its statehood?
18. Who is given credit for finding this state?
19. How did the U.S.A. get the land?
20. Tell three other historic things about your state.
21. Draw the state symbol and give an explanation.
22. What is the state motto?
23. What is the state's nickname?
24. Name three places to visit and tell about these places.

Mr. Finley completed a Lesson Analysis and Adaptation Worksheet (found in chapter 1 on page 33 and in the Lesson Planning module of the Companion Website) and concluded these things about the lesson:

- There are no standards mentioned, but learning about the geography of the states is part of the grade 7 standards.
- Some of the questions ask students to do more than memorize, but 21st-century skills and literacies could be incorporated more.
- No explicit resources are mentioned—a variety is needed.
- Links are made between students' home states and the states they are studying, and all students can actively search for information.
- There is no mention of technology use, but there are obvious ways to integrate it.
- A variety of resources, languages, and options is needed to meet the needs of diverse students.
- No assessment is included.

Mr. Finley likes the basic idea of this lesson and the variety of questions asked. However, based on his analysis and his knowledge of his students, he decides to make some small but important changes to the lesson. He wants to especially make sure that all students have access to the information. In addition to adding appropriate standards, he decides to make these changes based on his analysis:

- Provide students with prescreened resources at a variety of levels and in a variety of media to do the initial investigation of their state. In this way, all students will have information that they can access.

- Provide scaffolds such as formulas, worksheets, and experts to support student responses to the questions. In addition, students can choose to work in groups if they have a plan for completing the work.
- Incorporate seventh-grade keypals (electronic penpals) from each of the states under investigation who can verify and/or discuss responses to students. This telecommunications component will allow students to check the verity of their initial resources and gain different perspectives on some of the information they find.
- Vary the product, allowing students to produce a book, make a poster, or prepare a multimedia presentation. Doing so takes into consideration the variety of skills, abilities, and desires of his students.
- Ask the students to help develop process and product rubrics for the project.

With these changes, Mr. Finley feels that this lesson will help all his students meet many learning goals.

What other changes, if any, should Mr. Finley make to this lesson? Why?

_____

_____

_____

If students are safe and well prepared, communication around, through, and about computers can help them to achieve in a variety of ways. It can also support 21st-century skills such as critical thinking, the topic of chapter 4.

CHAPTER REVIEW

Key Points

- **Define communication, collaboration, and related terms.**

  The boundaries between communication, interaction, cooperation, and collaboration can be blurry. In the simplest sense, "communication" can be seen as the umbrella term. Communication can be one-way or two-way. Communication includes interaction, meaning give-and-take between participants. Interaction can be cooperative or collaborative, both of which require negotiation of meaning. Interaction can also be asynchronous or synchronous. Both types of interaction have advantages and disadvantages.

- **Describe the communication process and explain how communication affects learning.**

  The communication process includes planning, developing, and analysis/evaluation. Each step is important for communication tasks to be effective. This chapter has described the importance of social interaction to learning. Social interaction provides scaffolds for language and content, which help move students to new understandings. Benefits include exposure to new cultures, language uses, views of content, and the use of critical thinking skills.

- **Discuss guidelines and techniques for creating opportunities for technology-supported communication and collaboration.**

  Choosing the best technology for the task and making sure that students are safe while using the chosen tools are paramount objectives for successful projects. Most important for such projects is that tools can be used to facilitate the language and content acquisition of all students, from differently abled to differently motivated. In addition, teaching group dynamics and team-building skills and giving students reasons to listen help avoid communication breakdowns during projects that rely on communication. Fair, useful, and ongoing assessment facilitates students' understanding of their roles, their progress, and the effectiveness of the project. Careful planning that includes these strategies can support effective learning experiences.

385

- **Analyze technologies that can be used to support communication, including MOOs, email, chat, blogs, and wikis.**

  People probably think of communication tools as telephones, email, and other technologies that students can use to connect through. However, students can also connect around and with the support of technologies such as stand-alone software and Web sites. The technology must be appropriate for the goal, support the intended communication, and be accessible to all participants.

- **Describe and develop effective technology-enhanced communication activities.**

  Teachers can work with students to provide learning experiences that address the needs of a wide range of learners while addressing standards and curricular requirements by:

  - Using the planning, development, and evaluation processes outlined in the chapter
  - Keeping in mind student needs and the physical context
  - Focusing on crucial language and content goals

  This chapter's activity examples provide only a small sample of a very large set of interesting and fun projects that involve communication around, supported by, and through technology. The true scope of projects that include some kind of communication is beyond the ability of this book to address. Teachers can use existing resources and their own (and their students') knowledge and imagination in developing relevant tasks that achieve learning goals.

- **Create appropriate assessments for technology-enhanced communication tasks.**

  A wide range of tools is available for teachers to use in assessment. One tool that can help in a variety of contexts is a rubric-maker. In addition, ready-made rubrics and checklists are available across the Web. Understanding how to develop and use rubrics is an important step in creating appropriate assessments.

Which information in this chapter is most valuable to you? Why? How will you use it in your teaching?

_____

_____

_____

CASE QUESTIONS REVIEW

Reread the case at the beginning of the chapter and review your answers. In light of what you learned during this chapter, how do your answers change? Note any changes below.

1. *What learning benefits might the sixth- and seventh-grade students derive from participating in this telecommunications project?*

_____

_____

_____

2. *How can working with students at another school contribute to Mr. Finley's students' achievement?*

_____

_____

_____

3. *How did Mr. Finley approach the use of technology to meet his goals?*

_____

_____

_____

4. *Can you think of any other ways that Mr. Finley could ensure the success of this telecom-munications project?*

_____

_____

_____

CHAPTER EXTENSIONS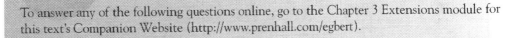

To answer any of the following questions online, go to the Chapter 3 Extensions module for this text's Companion Website (http://www.prenhall.com/egbert).

Adapt • • •

Choose a lesson for your potential subject area and grade level from the lesson plan archives at Educators Desk Reference (http://www.eduref.org/). Use the Lesson Analysis and Adaptation Worksheet from chapter 1 on page 33 (also available in the Lesson Planning module of the Companion Website) to consider the lesson in the context of *communication*. Use your responses to the worksheet to suggest general changes to the lesson based on your current or future students and context.

Practice • • •

1. *Integrate the standards.* Choose one or more of the activities in the chapter and note which technology standard(s) the tasks can help to meet.
2. *Improve an activity.* Choose a technology-supported activity example from the chapter and add details that would help to make it successful. For example, you may need to outline specific roles, choose a specific technology, or note an important safety tip.
3. *Think about learning.* Choose an activity from the chapter and explain how the communication might lead to learning. Say *what* students will learn, both what is obvious and less obvious.
4. *Create a rubric.* Create a rubric to assess both group process and individual participation for any of the example technology-supported tasks. Use one of the rubric generators listed in the assessment section of the chapter or develop your own.
5. *Reflect on language.* Use the chat abbreviations at http://www.webopedia.com/ to send a message to a friend, peer, or the instructor. Describe how this "language" differs from the classroom language that students must learn and use. How can you use this knowledge in your teaching?

Explore • • •

1. *Revise an activity.* Choose one of the learning activities in the chapter and adapt it for your content area and/or grade level. Add or change technology and change the existing audience as necessary. Briefly explain your changes.

2. *Assess.* Review the sample rubric in the assessment section of the chapter. Keeping the general structure and intent, change the question to evaluate a different activity.

3. *Create a project.* Choose a grade level and content area and create a telecommunications project following the guidelines from this chapter. Note what other ideas not mentioned in this chapter should be included, e.g., a different form of assessment or another type of technology.

4. *Explore a tool.* Choose a communication and/or collaboration tool and evaluate it for use by your current or potential students. Make a handout to help students use it effectively or a handout with guidelines for a project using the tool.

5. *Invent a tool.* Be imaginative—invent a tool that would meet the goals for collaboration without any of the challenges we currently experience. What would it look like and do?

REFERENCES

Berger, C., & Burgoon, M. (Eds.). (1995). *Communication and social influence processes.* East Lansing, MI: Michigan State University Press.

Cesar, M. (1998). Social interaction and mathematics learning. Nottingham, England: Centre for the Study of Mathematics Education. Retrieved from the World Wide Web on February 23, 2005: http://www.nottingham.ac.uk/csme/meas/papers/cesar.html.

Coleman, D. (2002, March). Levels of collaboration. *Collaborative strategies.* San Francisco, CA: Collaborative Strategies. Retrieved 4/15/05 from the World Wide Web: http://www.collaborate.com/publication/newsletter/publications_newsletter_march02.html.

Egbert, J. (2005). *CALL Essentials: Principles and practice in CALL classrooms.* Alexandria, VA: TESOL.

Eisenberg, M. (1992). Networking: K-12. *ERIC Digest* ED354903. Retrieved 2/19/05 from http://www.ericdigests.org/1993/k-12.htm.

Harris, J. (1995). Organizing and facilitating telecollaborative projects. *The Computing Teacher,* 22(5), 66–69.

Hofmann, J. (2003). Creating collaboration. *Learning circuits.* Alexandria, VA: American Society for Training and Development. Retrieved February 23, 2005 from the World Wide Web: http://www.learningcircuits.org/2003/sep2003/hofmann.htm.

Kumpulainen, K., & Wray, D. (Eds.). (2002). *Classroom interaction and social learning: From theory to practice.* New York: RoutledgeFalmer.

Panitz, T. (1996). A definition of collaborative vs. cooperative learning. *Deliberations on Learning and Teaching in Higher Education.* London, England: Educational and Development Unit, London Guildhall University. Retrieved 4/13/05 from http://www.city.londonmet.ac.uk/deliberations/collab.learning/panitz2.html.

Shirky, C. (2003, April). *A group is its own worst enemy.* Presented at the O'Reilly Emerging Technology conference in Santa Clara, CA. Retrieved 2/20/05 from the World Wide Web: http://www.shirky.com/writings/group_enemy.html.

Svensson, A. (2000). Computers in school: Socially isolating or a tool to promote collaboration? *Journal of Educational Computing Research,* 22(4), 437–453.

2Learn.ca Education Society. (2005). Explore or join projects@2Learn.ca. Retrieved 2/19/05 from www.2learn.ca/Projects/projectcentre/exjoproj.html.

Vygotsky, L. (1962). *Thought and language.* Cambridge, MA: MIT Press.

Vygotsky, L. (1978). *Mind in society.* Cambridge, MA: Harvard University Press.

21

Supporting Student Critical Thinking

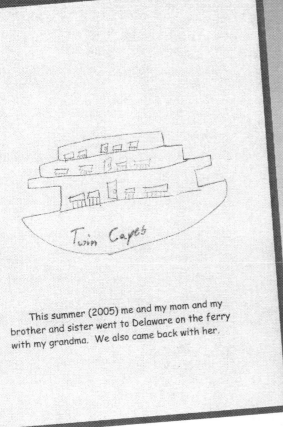

This summer (2005) me and my mom and my brother and sister went to Delaware on the ferry with my grandma. We also came back with her.

Case: Urban Legends

As you read the following scenario, note how the teacher guides the students to think critically about the information that they receive as a result of technology use.

• •

Mr. Andres's fourth-grade class was abuzz. The noise was coming from near one of the room's computers, where the teacher's aide and one of the students, David Perez, were involved in a discussion in front of the computer. Many of the other students in the class were gathered around listening and commenting. Mr. Andres approached the group to see why so many students seemed to be off the task he had assigned.

"What's up?" he asked as he approached the scene. One of the bystanders explained that David had received an email from his penpal in New York that contained some interesting news. Hmmm, thought Mr. Andres, I've read all the emails and didn't read something that I thought would cause such a stir. He asked David and the aide, "What's this all about?"

David exclaimed excitedly, "Janet is afraid to ride the subway to school any more! She says there are alligators in the sewers that could get into the subway! Is that cool or what?!"

"My," responded Mr. Andres. "Alligators in the sewers of New York? That's interesting." He remembered seeing the story in Janet's email. It was an urban legend, or a popularly believed story, that he had heard before. He had thought that Janet mentioned it as a joke to entertain David.

"Oh, yeah, well, it's true," replied David. "Janet read about it on the Internet. The story said that they were flushed down the toilet as babies by people who didn't want them as pets and now there's lots of them!"

"Ah," said Mr. Andres. "She saw it on the Internet."

Anna, another student, said, "It's not true, is it, Mr. Andres? Tell us!"

Other students chimed in. "Yah, tell us!" "What's up with that?!" "Is that for real?!" they exclaimed.

Then the teacher's aide broke in and said to Mr. Andres, "I've been trying to tell them it isn't true, but they won't listen!"

"Well," said Mr. Andres, "Maybe they need to find out for themselves whether there are alligators in New York's sewers. Sounds like a great project to me. Let's finish up what we're doing and then we'll talk about how we'll discover the truth."

At the end of the class, Mr. Andres had David explain the situation to the rest of the students. Mr. Andres asked how many students thought that there might be alligators under New York City, how many believed that there could not be, and how many weren't sure. Most of the students were not sure.

"How can we find out?" Mr. Andres asked the class.

The students brainstormed how they might find out whether there really were alligators in the sewers of New York City. After brainstorming, the students decided that they needed to read the original story on the Internet that Janet had written about, do some Internet and library research about alligators, discover online and offline resources for information about sewers, and find email contact information for some New York City officials to gather more data. When they had enough useful information from reliable sources, they would decide whether Janet really had a reason to fear.

Mr. Andres thought that this was a great opportunity for his students to develop critical thinking skills such as analysis, evaluation, interpretation, and explanation. At the same time, students would also enhance their technology skills by using a variety of tools; discover more about government agencies, reptiles, and big city life; and practice reading, writing, and other skills that were part of the fourth-grade curriculum.

* *

Answer these questions about the case. There are no right or wrong answers to this chapter preview—the goal is for you to respond before you read the chapter. Then, as you interact with the chapter contents, think about how your answers might change.

1. *What kinds of skills do David and his peers need to use to discover the answer to their question?*

_____

_____

_____

2. *What support should Mr. Andres give to facilitate the students' critical thinking?*

_____

_____

_____

3. *What should Mr. Andres's role be in teaching critical thinking skills?*

_____

_____

_____

4. *What role will technology play in helping the students to think critically?*

_____

_____

_____

Mr. Andres recognized an immediate opportunity to help his students learn and practice critical thinking skills. He made the choice knowing that he was deviating from his original unit plan, but he understands the importance of teachable moments, particularly when they focus on essential skills such as critical thinking. The goal of this chapter is to help you to understand the roles that teachers and technology can play in developing student critical thinking skills. After reading this chapter, you will be able to

- Define critical thinking.
- Understand the role of critical thinking in meeting other learning goals such as creativity and production.
- Discuss guidelines for using technology to encourage student critical thinking.
- Analyze technologies that can be used to support critical thinking, including strategy software to help students organize their thoughts, Web-based tools that both encourage and evaluate critical thinking, content software from companies such as Tom Snyder Productions, and content-free programs such as spreadsheets.
- Create effective technology-enhanced tasks to support critical thinking.
- Employ technology to assess student critical thinking.

When you have completed this chapter, which NETS*T will you have addressed?

_____

_____

_____

The ideas, sample activities, and technology descriptions provided throughout this chapter will help you understand how to create and take advantage of opportunities to support student critical thinking with technology. To begin, see this chapter's Meeting the Standards for a discussion of critical thinking across the curriculum.

• • • • Meeting the Standards: Critical Thinking • • • •

Critical thinking is fundamental to learner achievement in all subject areas. The following standards represent only a part of the great number and variety of standards that students are expected to meet using critical thinking skills such as analyzing, evaluating, and assessing.

- *Music:* Listen to, analyze, and describe music (NA-M.9–12.6).
- *Visual Arts:* Reflect on and assess the characteristics and merits of their work and the work of others (NA-VA.K–4.5).
- *Dance:* Identify possible aesthetic criteria for evaluating dance (NA-D.5–8.4).
- *Math:* Analyze change in various contexts (NM-ALG.6–8.4).
- *English:* Evaluate and synthesize data from a variety of sources. Participate as critical members of a variety of literacy communities (NL-English K–12.7/.11).

- *Health/PE:* Analyze the influence of culture, media and technology, and other factors on health (NPH.K–4.4).
- *Science:* Develop abilities necessary to do scientific inquiry (NS.5–8.1).
- *Social Studies:* Evaluate rules and laws (NSS-C.K–4.1).
- *Technology:* Evaluate and select new information resources and technological innovations based on the appropriateness for specific tasks (NETS*S).

Critical thinking is essential for students to lead productive lives. Facione (1990) argues that it is also necessary for societies to hang together, stating, "Being a free, responsible person means being able to make rational, unconstrained choices. A person who cannot think critically, cannot make rational choices. And, those without the ability to make rational choices should not be allowed to run free, for being irresponsible, they could easily be a danger to themselves and to the rest of us" (p. 13).

Do you agree with Facione's statement? Why or why not? Write your own statement about the importance of critical thinking.

_____

_____

_____

 Now read the rest of the chapter, starting with the overview of critical thinking, and see if any of your ideas change as you read. Explore the above standards in more detail in the Standards module on this text's Companion Website.

OVERVIEW OF CRITICAL THINKING AND TECHNOLOGY IN K–12 CLASSROOMS

In order to implement technology use with a learning focus, teachers need to understand critical thinking before attempting to support it with technology.

What Is Critical Thinking?

Critical thinking skills refer to abilities to analyze, evaluate, infer, interpret, explain, and self-regulate (Facione, 1990; vanGelder, 2005). A simple way to define critical thinking is the ability to make good decisions and to clearly explain the foundation for those decisions. When using technology, being able to think critically allows one to:

- Judge the credibility of sources.
- Identify conclusions, reasons, and assumptions.
- Judge the quality of an argument, including the acceptability of its reasons, assumptions, and evidence.
- Develop and defend a position on an issue.
- Ask appropriate clarifying questions.
- Plan experiments and judge experimental designs.
- Define terms in a way appropriate for the context.
- Be open-minded.
- Try to be well-informed.
- Draw conclusions when warranted, but with caution. (Ennis, 1993, p. 180)

To some extent all humans, even very young children, continually think critically to analyze their world and to make sense of it. However, most people's skills are not as well developed as they could or should be. Sarason (2004) adds that schools are not the most productive learning environments for critical thinking, and that schools need to take a stronger focus on critical thinking.

Critical thinking is part of a group of cognitive abilities and personal characteristics called **higher order thinking skills** (HOTS). These skills also include creative thinking (chapter 5) and problem solving (chapter 6). This list of cognitive skills is based on the well-known *Bloom's Taxonomy of Educational Goals* (Bloom, 1956). Bloom's first three competencies—knowledge, comprehension, and application—are generally equated with the acquisition of declarative knowledge (discussed in chapter 2). The second three competencies—analysis, synthesis, and evaluation—are generally considered critical thinking or higher order skills. Figure 4.1 on page 102 presents an example of critical thinking skills from Bloom's taxonomy and the types of technology-enhanced tasks that might support them during Mr. Andres's class project. Anderson and Krathwohl (2001) recently revised Bloom's taxonomy to add a "metacognitive knowledge" category and to make it easier for teachers to design instruction that requires critical thinking. Excellent resources for using the revised taxonomy are available from Kurwongbah State School in Australia at http://www.kurwongbss.eq.edu.au/thinking/Bloom/blooms.htm. See the Learning Theories section of the Resources module of the Companion Website (http://www.prenhall.com/egbert) for more resources on Bloom's taxonomy and critical thinking.

Critical thinking has been central to education since the time of Socrates (469–399 B.C.E.). The focus of the Socratic method is to question students so that they come to justify their arguments; this teaching strategy is still used in many classrooms to foster critical thinking. One software program, Reason!Able (see this chapter's Tool CloseUp: Reason!Able), even has Socrates asking questions so that students can reflect on their work. Other critical thinking software provides tasks that require critical thinking and includes prompts to help students understand how to come to effective decisions. Regardless of the tool that students use to support their critical thinking, it is important to note the crucial role of critical thinking skills both in school and out. In fact, since Socrates, philosophers throughout history such as Plato, Francis Bacon, Rene

FIGURE 4.1 Higher Order Thinking Skills from Bloom's Taxonomy

Competence	Skills Demonstrated	Sample Technology-Enhanced Tasks
Analysis	• Seeing patterns. • Organize parts. • Recognize hidden meanings. • Identify components.	• Students brainstorm about the information they need and the questions they need to ask and make a chart using Inspiration software.
Synthesis	• Use old ideas to create new ones. • Generalize from given facts. • Relate knowledge from several areas. • Predict, draw conclusions.	• Students gather facts from electronic and paper resources about alligators, sewers, and New York and input them into a database. They arrange and study the data to suggest conclusions.
Evaluation	• Compare and discriminate between ideas. • Assess value of theories, presentations. • Make choices based on reasoned argument. • Verify value of evidence. • Recognize subjectivity.	• Students use the Reason!Able software described in the Tools CloseUp in this chapter to evaluate their argument and conclusions about alligators in the sewers before they present their argument to the class.

Source: From Benjamin S. Bloom, *Taxonomy of educational objectives.* Published by Allyn & Bacon, Boston, MA. Copyright © 1984 by Pearson Education. Adapted by permission of the publisher.

Descartes, William Graham Sumner, and John Dewey have emphasized the need for students to think critically about their world.

More specifically, Ellis (2002) notes that critical thinking is one foundation for learning, in part because all of the learning skills are interdependent and, as Paul (2004a) points out, "everything essential to education supports everything else essential to education" (p. 3). For example, as Mr. Andres's students consider how to decide whether they can believe everything they read on the Internet, they use a variety of skills to

- Understand basic content.
- Communicate among themselves and with others.
- Think creatively about resources.
- Assess the veracity of the information they come in contact with.
- Produce a well-supported conclusion.

In other words, they must think critically throughout the process as they develop other learning skills.

It is also clear that critical thinking "has applications in all areas of life and learning" (Facione, 1990, p. 4). Making a good decision about whether to buy a laptop or an iPod, and then which model, requires research, assessment, evaluation, and careful planning, just as deciding what to eat for dinner or how to spend free time does.

Although there may be discipline-specific skills, general critical thinking skills may apply across disciplines and content areas (Ennis, 1992; McPeck, 1992). For example, Facione (1990) notes that critical thinking skills test scores correlate positively with college GPA. Although this is not a *causal* relationship (in other words, the research does not show that effective critical thinking *causes* a high GPA), there appears to be something about students who can think critically that helps them succeed in college. In addition, the processes that students use to think critically appear to transfer or assist not only in the reading process but in general decision making. However, experts disagree to what extent this happens. Some researchers believe that much critical thinking is subject- or genre-specific (Moore, 2004). Nonetheless, all agree that it is crucial to help students hone their critical thinking abilities, and many believe that technology can help by providing support in ways outlined throughout this chapter (Jonassen, 2000).

In addition to the lessons presented in this chapter based on these ideas, other chapters of this book present ideas and activities that involve critical thinking either implicitly or explicitly. As you read through the text, see if you can find those examples. Now read what one classroom teacher says about the relationship between technology and higher order thinking in From the Classroom: Thinking Skills.

Critical Thinking and Media Literacy

Critical thinking, as defined in the previous section, is especially important because media, particularly television and computers, is increasingly prevalent in the lives of K–12 students. Students have always needed to have general **information literacy**, or "knowing when and why you need information, where to find it, and how to evaluate, use, and communicate it in an ethical manner" (CILIP, 2007). However, students who are faced with a bombardment of images, sounds, and text need to go beyond information literacy to interpret and assess (in other words, think critically about) information in new ways. In other words, they must be media literate.

In general **media literacy** means that students are able not only to comprehend what they read, hear, and see but also to evaluate and make good decisions about what media presents. There are many variations on how to support students in becoming media literate (Schwarz & Brown, 2005). For example, the Center for Media Literacy, the world's largest distributor of media education materials, recommends activities such as tracing racial images in the media throughout history, exploring how maps are constructed (and asking "Why does 'north' mean 'up'?"), and challenging gender stereotypes in TV comedies. These activities are crucial because learners of all ages watch TV, and even kindergartners use the computer and may have access to the Internet. Much of what learners read, see, and hear they believe verbatim and share as truth with others, as in this chapter's opening case. This occurs whether the message is intended as fact or not. To become more media literate, teachers and students need to learn and practice critical thinking skills that are directed at the ideologies, purveyors, and purposes behind their data sources. Most important, students must use the Internet responsibly and with the necessary skepticism; in particular, this includes investigative skills and the ability to judge the validity of information from Web sites.

Read what a classroom teacher has to say about getting started with media literacy in From the Classroom: Media Literacy.

There are many resources to help teachers and students to become media literate. One of the best is the Center for Media Literacy's free MediaLit Kit for K–12 Media Literacy (available from http://www.medialit.org/). The kit includes a clear, theory-based definition and outstanding lessons based on the five core concepts of media literacy. The lessons and handouts focus on students learning to ask these five "key questions":

1. Who created this message?
2. What creative techniques are used to attract my attention?
3. How might different people understand the message differently from me?
4. What values, lifestyles, and points of view are represented in, or omitted from, this message?
5. Why is this message being sent?

Another focus of the MediaLit Kit is the "Essential Questions for Teachers" that teachers should ask themselves:

1. Am I trying to tell the students what the message is? Or am I giving them the skills to determine what THEY think the message(s) might be?

FROM THE CLASSROOM

Thinking Skills

There are many activities young children need to be involved in before learning the ins and outs of working a computer. A good book on this topic is *Failure to Connect: How Computers Affect Our Children's Minds and What We Can Do About It*, by Jane M. Healy. All that said, computers can be extremely motivating and engaging. They can enhance our students' use of collaborative skills and problem-solving skills. These things are very powerful in helping people learn. So while the activities you are thinking of using don't directly match up to whatever test your students need to take, there are many computer activities that will involve many higher level thinking skills that will help our students learn, not only for THE TEST, but for life in general. (Susan, fifth-grade teacher)

FROM THE CLASSROOM

Media Literacy

Learning to recognize bias in any form of media is important, especially on the Internet where anyone can publish. When are students developmentally ready to recognize bias? This is a tough question and will vary for individual students. I think that [the] use of preselected Web sites for fifth and sixth graders is a logical step. This is a good age to point out why you, as the teacher, have selected certain sites for their validity and reliability. This can be contrasted with sites that don't meet the criteria. (Sally, fifth- and sixth-grade teacher)

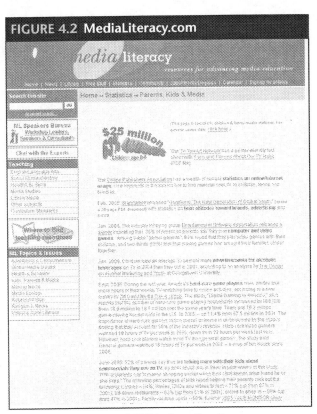

FIGURE 4.2 MediaLiteracy.com

Source: MediaLiteracy.com © 2007 by Susan Freas Rogers.

2. Have I let students know that I am open to accepting their interpretation, as long as it is well substantiated, or have I conveyed the message that my interpretation is the only correct view?

3. At the end of the lesson, are students likely to be more analytical? Or more cynical? (p. 11)

During the MediaLit lessons, students use technology to construct their own critically evaluated multimedia messages. The MediaLit Kit is an excellent resource both for teachers just beginning to explore media literacy and for those looking for additional pedagogically sound ideas and activities.

Another outstanding source of lessons, articles, and activities for K–12 is the Critical Evaluation Tools section of Kathy Schrock's Web site (http://school.discovery.com/ schrockguide/), as is the useful medialiteracy.com Web site (see Figure 4.2).

Characteristics of Effective Critical Thinking Tasks

There are many ways to help students become media-literate critical thinkers. In general, effective critical thinking tasks:

1. Take place in an environment that supports objection, questioning, and reasoning.
2. Address issues that are ill-structured and may not have a simple answer.
3. Do not involve rote learning.
4. Provide alternatives in product and solution.
5. Allow students to make decisions and see consequences.
6. Are supported by tools and resources from many perspectives.
7. Help students examine their reasoning processes.

Teachers who want to promote critical thinking can employ the terms in Figure 4.3 in their student objectives and assignments. For example, if the objective is for students to analyze their use of technology, the teacher can ask students to contrast, categorize, and/or compare. If the objective is for students to evaluate technology use in schools, the teacher might ask students to defend, justify, or predict.

Write three objectives for Mr. Andres's project that focus on the thinking skills that he might expect students to learn or practice while they research the alligator question. Use terms from the list in Figure 4.3.

_____

_____

_____

Student benefits of critical thinking

It should be clear from the previous discussion that good critical thinking skills affect students in many ways. Additional benefits that accrue to good critical thinkers include:

- Better grades (Facione, 1990)
- Independence
- Good decision making
- The ability to effect social change
- Becoming better readers, writers, speakers, and listeners

> **FIGURE 4.3 Critical Thinking Objectives**
>
> - *Application:* apply, choose, construct, classify, demonstrate, dramatize, employ, illustrate, interpret, manipulate, modify, operate, practice, schedule, sketch, show, solve, use, write
> - *Analysis:* analyze, appraise, calculate, categorize, compare, contrast, criticize, differentiate, discriminate, distinguish, examine, experiment, investigate, question, separate, test
> - *Synthesis:* arrange, assemble, collect, compose, construct, create, design, develop, devise, formulate, imagine, invent, manage, organize, plan, prepare, propose, set up, write
> - *Evaluation:* appraise, argue, assess, attach, choose, compare, debate, decide, defend, estimate, evaluate, judge, justify, predict, rate, select, support, value, verify

Source: Adapted from Clark, 1999; Dalton and Smith, 1986; and Office Port, 2002.

- The ability to uncover bias and prejudice (Fowler, 1996)
- Willingness to stick with a task

Because critical thinking skills can be learned, all students, including those with different language and physical abilities and capabilities, have the potential to reap these benefits.

THE CRITICAL THINKING PROCESS

Although all students can benefit from critical thinking, no two people use the exact same skills or processes to think critically. However, teachers can present students with a general set of steps synthesized from the research literature that can serve as a basis for critical thinking. These steps are:

1. *Review* your content understanding/*clarify* the problem. Compile everything you know about the topic that you are working on. Try to include even small details. Figure out what other content knowledge you need to know to help examine all sides of the question and how to get that information.
2. *Analyze* the material. Organize the material into categories or groupings by finding relationships among the pieces. Decide which aspects are the most important. Weigh all sides.
3. *Synthesize* your answers about the material. Decide why it is significant, how it can be applied, what the implications are, which ideas do not seem to fit well into the explanation that you decided on.
4. *Evaluate* your decision-making process.

Students can use this process as a foundation for discovering what works best for them to come to rational decisions. As outlined in the following section, teachers play a central role in supporting students in this process.

Teachers and Critical Thinking

To support the critical thinking process with technology, teachers must first understand their roles and the challenges of working with learners who are developing their critical thinking skills. These issues are discussed here.

The teacher's role in critical thinking opportunities

Facione (1990) and other experts see the teacher's role in critical thinking as being a model, helping students to see the need for and excitement of being able to think critically. In modeling critical thinking, teachers should:

- Overtly and explicitly explain what they do and why.
- Encourage students to think for themselves.

- Be willing to admit and correct their own mistakes.
- Be sensitive to students' feelings, abilities, and goals and to what motivates them.
- Allow students to participate in democratic processes in the classroom.

By modeling self-questioning and other strategies, teachers can help students to understand what critical thinkers do.

Teachers can also decide to teach critical thinking skills directly and/or through content—both are appropriate in specific contexts. Techniques that teachers can use to support critical thinking are presented in Figure 4.4. Additional ideas are listed in the Guidelines section of this chapter.

FIGURE 4.4 Common Techniques to Support Critical Thinking

- Encourage students to find and use information from a variety of sources both online and offline.
- Provide support for information structuring (modeling with graphical organizers, for example).
- Assist students to compare information from different types of sources.
- Develop student debates.
- Allow students to reflect in different modes (e.g., writing, speaking, drawing).
- Help students make assumptions and values explicit.
- Use real experiences and materials.
- Involve students in creating and questioning assessments.

As Weiler (2004) notes, often students who are in a dualistic stage of intellectual development, in which they see everything as either right or wrong, will need a gradual introduction to the idea that not everything is so clear-cut. Rather than direct teaching of critical thinking, students can be led to understand this idea by encountering inexplicable or not easily answerable examples over time. For example, Mr. Andres in the chapter's opening case might ask his students to suggest what the sewers of New York might be like, and then to compare that to what they know about alligators' natural habitats. This might lead to a thoughtful consideration of whether alligators could really survive in New York sewers. The teacher's role in this case is to ask questions to support student movement toward more complex reasoning.

Challenges for teachers

As the process above implies, learning to think critically takes time, and it requires many examples and practice across a variety of contexts. The school library media specialist is an excellent source for resources and ideas for teaching all aspects of critical thinking.

ELL

However, teaching students to think critically is not always an easy task, and it may be made more difficult by having students from cultures that do not value or promote displays of critical thinking in children in the same way as schools in the United States do or believe that it is the role of the school to do so. As Ennis (1998) points out, critical thinking in itself is probably not culturally biased, but the instruction of critical thinking can be. Teachers need to understand their students' approaches to reasoning and objection and to teach critical thinking supported by technology in culturally responsive ways (as mentioned in chapter 2) by:

- Understanding and exploring what critical thinking means in other cultures
- Avoiding "invisibility, stereotyping, selectivity and imbalance, unreality, fragmentation and isolation, and language bias" (Abdal-Haqq, 1994) during the process, particularly in the tools used
- Taking into consideration the strengths and differences of students

What challenges might Mr. Andres face in supporting his students to think about alligators in New York sewers? How might he address these challenges?

_____

_____

_____

GUIDELINES FOR SUPPORTING STUDENT CRITICAL THINKING WITH TECHNOLOGY

Mr. Andres is on the right track by having his students think about how they can find the answers to their questions. There are other techniques that he can use to support their critical thinking; these are discussed in this section. As with all the goals outlined in this text, there are many things for teachers to think about when deciding how to support critical thinking. Many of the guidelines in other chapters also apply. The guidelines here are not specific only to critical thinking.

Designing Critical Thinking Opportunities

Guideline #1: Ask the right questions. Research in classrooms shows that teachers ask mostly display questions to discover whether students can repeat the information from the lesson and can explain it in their own words. However, to promote critical thinking and reasoning, students need to think about and answer "essential" questions that help them to meet universal standards for critical thinking such as *clarity, accuracy, precision, relevance, depth, breadth,* and *logic* (Paul, 2004a; Wiggins & McTighe, 1998). These standards are directly related to analysis, synthesis, and evaluation (and sometimes to application), discussed above as characteristics of effective critical thinking tasks. For example, questions about clarity (Can you give me an example of . . . ? What do you mean by . . . ?) ask students to apply their learning to their experience, and vice versa. Questions that focus on precision or specificity (Exactly how much . . . ? On what day and at what time did . . . ?) ask students to analyze the data more deeply. A question about breadth (How might _____ answer this question? What do you think _____ would say about this issue?) might also challenge students to synthesize.

Whichever set of standards or objectives teachers decide to use, it is important that the teacher support the critical thinking process by providing **scaffolds**, or structures and reinforcements that help guide learners toward independent critical thinking. Critical thinking does not mean negative thinking; therefore, questions should be "direct, clear, relevant, concrete, as unbiased as possible, specific, asked in a civil tone" (Petress, 2004, p. 462). Question formats and strategies for creating effective questions are provided by Kentucky Prism at http://www.kyprism.org, and see Cotton (2001) for both the research on questioning and strategies to make it work in classrooms. On the Web, find lists of questions that can lead to critical thinking by conducting a search on the term "critical thinking questions." Find more information in the 21st Century Literacies section of the Resources module of the Companion Website for this text (http://www.prenhall.com/egbert).

Guideline #2: Use tasks with appropriate levels of challenge. Mihalyi Csikszentmihalyi (1997) and other researchers have found that the relationship between skills that students possess and the challenge that a task presents is important to learning. For example, they discovered that students of high ability were often bored with their lessons and that the balance of challenge and skills could be used to predict students' attitudes toward their lessons. Their findings indicate that activities should be neither too challenging nor too easy for the student. Teachers can use observation, interview, and other assessments to determine the level of readiness for each student on specific tasks and with different content. Teachers can then use student readiness to change the challenge that students face in a task by:

- Changing the way students are grouped
- Introducing new technologies
- Changing the types of thinking tasks
- Varying the questions they ask
- Altering expectations of goals that can be met

Differentiation, a strategy for designing instruction that meets diverse students' needs (discussed in chapter 2), can help teachers to provide tasks with appropriate levels of challenge for students.

Guideline #3: Teach strategies. Supporting critical thinking by modeling and asking questions is useful but not enough for all students. Good critical thinkers use **metacognitive** skills—in other words, they think about the process of their decision making. The actual teaching of metacognitive strategies can have an impact on when and if students use them. To help students think about their thinking, teachers can prompt the students to ask themselves:

- Did I have enough resources?
- Were the resources sufficiently varied and from authorities I can trust?
- Did I consider issues fairly?
- Do all the data support my decision?

For English language learners, this might mean teaching *how* to formulate and ask questions for clarity and specific information and to use relevant vocabulary words. One way this could happen is to have ELLs create interview questions and interact with an external audience via email. Through the interaction and feedback from their email partners, the students could learn whether their questions were clear and specific and the vocabulary appropriate.

FIGURE 4.5 Guidelines for Critical Thinking

Guideline	Example
Ask the right questions.	Can you give me an example of . . . ? What do you mean by . . . ? What do you think _____ would say about this issue?
Use tasks with appropriate levels of challenge.	Differentiate for different levels of students (see chapter 2 for more about differentiation). Give choices of tool, task, group.
Teach strategies.	Help students ask themselves questions about their learning processes.
Encourage curiosity.	Address and ask curious questions.

Guideline #4: Encourage curiosity. Why is the grass green? Why do I have to do geometry? Why are we at war? What are clouds made of? How do people choose what they will be when they grow up? Children ask these questions all the time, and these questions can lead to thinking critically about the world. However, in classroom settings they are often ignored, whether due to curricular, time, or other constraints. The Internet as a problem-solving and research tool (chapter 6) can contribute to teachers and learners finding answers together and evaluating those answers. However, if teachers stop learners from being curious, avoid their questions, or answer them unsatisfactorily, teachers can shut down the first step toward critical thinking.

A summary of these guidelines is presented in Figure 4.5.

Which of these guidelines is Mr. Andres following? How can he incorporate the others as he and his students develop their project?

_____

_____

_____

THE CRITICAL THINKING TECHNOLOGIES

What Are Critical Thinking Tools?

Critical thinking tools are those that support the critical thinking process. Critical thinking instruction does not *require* the use of electronic tools. However, many of the tools mentioned throughout this book can be used to support critical thinking, depending on the specific activity. For example, word processing can help students lay out their thoughts before a debate, and concept mapping software such as Inspiration (described in the chapter 7 Tool CloseUp) can help students to brainstorm and plan their ideas. Likewise, the Internet can supply information, and databases and spreadsheets can help students organize data for more critical review (see the Tool CloseUp: Microsoft Excel for examples).

This chapter presents tools that are specifically focused on building critical thinking skills. The following examples are categorized into:

- *Strategy software*—content-free and structured to support critical thinking skills with student-generated content.

Tool CloseUp: Microsoft Excel

Many content-free tools can be used effectively as part of critical thinking tasks. Tools in the Microsoft Office Suite can be considered "content-free." In other words, although they contain specific structures, the content that is entered into those structures is up to the user. Teachers are sometimes reluctant to introduce spreadsheets like Microsoft Excel to students because they perceive them as difficult to understand and use and because they think of them as tools for specific purposes. However, as with all powerful tools, students do not need to understand every feature or capability to use a spreadsheet effectively for a variety of tasks.

Students (and teachers) first need to understand what a spreadsheet is and what it can be used for. A **spreadsheet** is a table that consists of cells. Each cell contains a value, usually (but not always) in number form. After users input data into the cells, they can generate relationships between cells, called *formulas*. The formula is typed in the formula bar and indicates the values in the cells that are part of the formula and also the operations (e.g., addition, division) that will be performed using those values. Making a formula is most like using a calculator.

As a simple example, look at the accompanying screen. I want to add 2 (the value I enter in cell A1) and 2 (the value in B1). I click on the cell where I want the answer (C1). Then, I enter the formula "=Sum(A1:B1)" and when I press Enter, the answer, 4, appears in cell C1.

In spreadsheet software, several pages or sheets can be linked together, and the results of calculations can be made into graphs and charts with one click. Spreadsheets can be used to make all kinds of calculations, from the monthly payment on a car to converting Fahrenheit to Celsius temperatures. More important, spreadsheets help students turn data into information that can be used as the basis of critically made decisions. For example, i4c (www.internet4 classrooms.com/) shows teachers and students not only the basics of using Excel but also how to calculate the price of pizza per square inch and so decide if the snack is worth the money. Other tasks presented on this through Web site include calculating the cost of a trip by car (the same can be done for air travel and the results compared) and figuring out how much a student would weigh on another planet. With the additional training provided in tutorials across the Web, Excel and other spreadsheets can be used in an uncountable number of ways to support critical thinking. Another example of spreadsheet use in a critical thinking activity is provided in the lesson at the end of this chapter. While the tools presented in the Critical Thinking Technologies section of this chapter may be developed expressly for critical-thinking tasks, it is important for teachers to note ways that they can support critical thinking with software like Excel, which may already be available in their classrooms.

A note of caution: Younger students or students with motor disabilities may have difficulty using Excel or another spreadsheet program if their fine motor skills are not developed enough to designate the appropriate cells using the mouse. This can lead to frustration with the software. There are many possible solutions. For example, a larger mouse can be used, the zoom feature can make the cells appear larger, or the students can provide the contents and a more expert computer user can input the data.

For free spreadsheet software that works in the same manner as Excel, go to http://www.goffice.com or http://www.thinkfree.com.

How could Mr. Andres's students use a spreadsheet for their project? How do you use spreadsheets?

_____

_____

_____

_____

Tutorial

CW

Find more resources and links for spreadsheets in the Technology Tools module of the Companion Website (http://www.prenhall.com/egbert).

FROM THE CLASSROOM

Critical Thinking and Word Processing

[An article I read said that] one computer tool [that encourages students to think critically] is the word processor, because as students type, typographical, grammar or misspelled words are highlighted. Students should try to correct it themselves before looking at the suggestions by the computer. . . . this helps students become aware of their mistakes and make a conscious effort to avoid them in the future . . . I think that a conscious effort to avoid mistakes is probably going to take more than just seeing it highlighted as wrong on the computer. I think that some direct instruction or work related to those mistakes might be necessary to really help students critically think about what they did and why it wasn't right . . . because in my experience, the computer's tips aren't always all that helpful. Sometimes I even wonder if spell check helps me to be a critical thinker or a carefree writer who is reliant on the computer to make corrections for me. I'm certainly not dedicated enough to try and correct my mistakes before doing a spelling and grammar check. Can we expect our students to do this? (Jennie, first-grade teacher)

- *Content software*—content is predetermined and strategy use is emphasized. Students typically read the software content and work out answers to questions.

Many other tools in these categories exist; those described here are some of the most popular, inexpensive, and useful. First, read about what one teacher has to say about critical thinking and word processing in From the Classroom: Critical Thinking and Word Processing.

Strategy Software

CMap v.3.8 (IHMC, 2005)

This software is easy to learn and use for third grade and up. The user double-clicks on the screen and inputs text into the shape that appears. Users can change the colors of the graphics and text to show different categories of reasoning such as objections, reasons, and claims. A very useful feature allows users to put text on the connecting lines to show the reasoning behind the connections they made. Figure 4.6 is an example map of the argument for and against alligators in the New York City sewer system. Download this software free from http://cmap.ihmc.us/.

First Step KidSkills (Kid Tools Support System, 2003)

KidSkills is a free software package intended for students ages 7–13. Of the four sections, titled Getting Organized, Learning New Stuff, Doing Homework, and Doing Projects, the last has the greatest focus on critical thinking. This section has five activities: Project Planner, Getting Information, Big Picture Card, Working Together, and Project Evaluation. Each of the activities focuses on students combining information and printing or saving it in the form of a "card" or page. In the Project Planner exercise, students make a card that lists their question, topics for them to investigate, possible resources, and an evaluation of the resources (authority, fact, opinion, or don't know). There is also a Second Step available, and resources and tips for use are provided on the Kid Tools Web site. Although intended for use with learners with learning disabilities or emotional/ behavioral problems, it is useful for all children and simple enough for students with limited English proficiency to understand and use, particularly because all instructions are presented in text and audio.

Inclusion
ELL

Some teachers may find it too simple, but its simplicity is also part of its effectiveness. See Figure 4.7 on the next page for a resource plan for Mr. Andres's project in KidSkills Project Planner.

Athena 2.4 (Wright State University)

Another free tool, Athena is powerful reasoning and argument mapping software intended for students in higher education but accessible to students in upper secondary. It is more difficult to learn and use than the other programs mentioned here, but it also has more capabilities. It does use the standard Microsoft icons, so many of the workings will be familiar to students who already use programs in the Office Suite. Available through http://www.athenasoft.org/.

The Argument Clinic (University of Northern Colorado)

This Web tool allows students to type in their argument, have it examined by experts, and receive a reply about the strength of the argument. UNC requests an email address and name to send their reply, so the teacher might want to be the "front man" for this activity. Available through http:// www.univnorthco.edu/philosophy/clinic.html.

FIGURE 4.6 CMap Example

Source: Used with permission of Institute for Human & Machine Cognition.

Content Software

BrainCogs (Fablevision, 2002)

A CD-based strategy program, BrainCogs helps students to learn, reflect on, and use specific strategies across a variety of contexts. The software employs an imaginary rock band, the Rotten Green Peppers, to demonstrate the importance of and techniques for remembering, organizing information, prioritizing, shifting perspectives, and checking for mistakes. Although the focus is more on strategies to help students pass tests, the general strategy knowledge gained can transfer across subjects and tasks because it is not embedded in any specific content area (Bransford, Brown, & Cocking, 2000). The software is accompanied by a video, posters, and other resources that function as scaffolds for diverse learners. The exercises, in addition to being entertaining and fun, employ multimedia (sound, text, and graphics) in ways that make the content accessible to English language learners and native English speakers with diverse learning styles. Available through http://www.fablevision.com/.

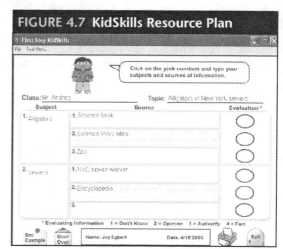

FIGURE 4.7 KidSkills Resource Plan

Source: Fitzgerald G., Koury, K., Peng, H., & Cepel, C. (2003). First Step KidSkills [Computer Software and CD]. Columbia, MO; University of Missouri. Funded in part of U.S. Department of Education Grant #H033271. Available: http://kidtools.missouri.edu.

Mission Critical (San Jose State University)

This Web tool provides information and quizzes on critical thinking. Although intended for college students, the quizzes are simple and well explained and could be used at a number of different grade levels with support from the teacher. The site addresses arguments, persuasion, fallacies, and many other aspects of logic and critical thinking. The site begins at http://www2.sjsu.edu/depts/itl/graphics/claims/claims.html.

WebLemur (LeBlanc, 2004)

Intended for college-level students, this site can also be useful for upper secondary, although it requires advanced reading skills. The program asks users to identify an argument, an explanation, or neither, to logically conclude a statement or paragraph, and to evaluate language used in arguments, the use of analogy, and causal arguments. It works in a simple multiple choice format, but it also provides review to support student choices. Teachers can pick and choose which parts are useful. The site is located at http://www.humanities.mcmaster.ca/~leblancj/weblemur/contents.html.

Choices, Choices: Taking Responsibility (Tom Snyder Productions)

Taking Responsibility helps students in grades K–4 work through a five-step critical thinking process:

1. Understand your situation.
2. Set goals.
3. Talk about your options.
4. Make a choice.
5. Think about the consequences.

Used on a single computer and facilitated by the teacher, the simulation in this software title provides a scenario in which two students have broken one of the teacher's possessions; however, no one else saw them. The class acts as the two students in the scenario. Through a series of decisions, the class must decide which actions to take and face the consequences of their decisions. There are 300 different ways that students can get through this software, so the consequences are not always clearcut until they are presented to students. Figure 4.8 presents the Taking Responsibility goal-setting screen.

The software comes with many resources to help students think critically about the situations and their decisions and to assist the teacher in integrating literature, role-play, and other activities into the lesson. Each step of the simulation is presented in pictures, audio, and text, which helps ELLs and other students to access the information.

The Choices, Choices series includes a number of other titles. Tom Snyder Productions also provides a similar Decisions, Decisions series for older students.

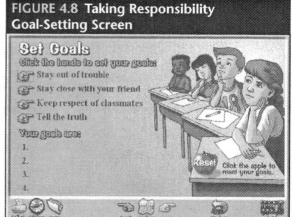

FIGURE 4.8 Taking Responsibility Goal-Setting Screen

Source: Used with permission of Tom Snyder Productions.

Tool CloseUp: Reason!Able

The Reason!Able software package provides scaffolds for students who are trying to answer a question or prove a claim. A screen shot for Mr. Andres's project using this software is shown here. On the left of the screen is Socrates, who asks questions about the claims, reasons, and objections that students input (he can be turned off). The user starts with a central claim—in this case, that there are alligators in New York City sewers. The user is then prompted to add one or more reasons and to include evidence that supports those reasons. The user is also prompted to add objections to the claim and to the reasons, and then to add any reasons to the objections. The interface is simple, clear, and easy to use. After all reasons and objections have been made, Socrates prompts the user to evaluate the reasons and objections. The user can see how the logic is working and where the weaknesses in the argument are. The evaluation prompting box is shown on the left of the screen.

This software would be great for whole class, small groups, and individual work in creating a reasonable argument. It is fun, colorful and icon-based, making it useful for ELLs and students with visually based learning needs.

A newer and a bit different version of the software, called Rationale, is now available from Austhink. Download a free preview version at http://www.austhink.com.

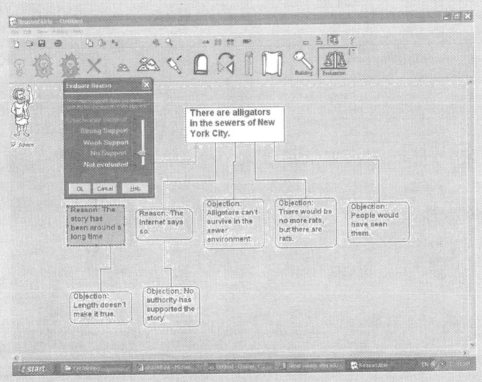

Source: Used with permission of Tim vanGelder.

In what other ways could Mr. Andres use this software for the project? What questions could he ask to help students look for more reasons and objections?

_____

_____

_____

Teachers who want to use this type of software should be aware that the choices that students are allowed to make within the software are preset and represent the views of the software author. Teachers and students must understand the limitations and biases of this software to use it in ways that demonstrate true critical thinking.

Tom Snyder Productions is located on the Web at http://www.tomsnyder.com/.

Other Options

There are a variety of other tool options for teachers and students to support critical thinking. Brainstorming and decision-tree software, strengths/weaknesses/opportunities/threats (SWOT) analysis packages, and Web-based content and question tools are available. Some of the best tools are free: these include Seeing Reason and Showing Evidence in Intel Education's suite of "Teaching Thinking Tools." In this chapter, the logic tool Reason!Able is highlighted in the Tool CloseUp: Reason!Able.

Whichever tools teachers decide to use, they need to remember that the tool should not create a barrier to students reaching the goal of effective critical thinking.

Read as one classroom teacher talks about the role of the Internet in critical thinking in From the Classroom: Critical Thinking and the Internet.

Which of the tools mentioned above might the students in Mr. Andres's class benefit from as they build their arguments about alligators in the sewers?

_____

_____

_____

FROM THE CLASSROOM

Critical Thinking and the Internet

I appreciate the fact that using the Internet can promote critical thinking because the students move from being passive learners to participants and collaborators in the creation of knowledge and meaning (Berge & Collins, 1995). The technology is empowering for students. . . . They seem to feel more control over what they are able to learn and this seems to be motivating! I wish I could figure out how to transfer that feeling to activities that are not suited for technology! (April, sixth-grade teacher)

TECHNOLOGY-SUPPORTED LEARNING ACTIVITIES: CRITICAL THINKING

As noted previously, instruction in critical thinking can be direct through the use of explicit instruction or indirect through modeling, describing, and explaining. The goal is to help learners understand clearly why they need to think critically and to give them feedback on how they do and how they can improve. Unfortunately, few software packages and Web sites, let alone textbooks, require critical thinking skills of students. Software that does support critical thinking, such as those packages and Web sites listed in the Tools section of this chapter, often require supplementing to help students understand and use them. Teachers can supplement these resources and facilitate critical thinking during activities by developing external documents. An **external document** is a kind of worksheet that can involve students in, for example, taking notes, outlining, highlighting, picking out critical information, summarizing, or practicing any of the skills that support critical thinking. An external document can also enhance students' access to critical thinking software or Web sites by providing language or content help. All kinds of external documents exist across the Internet in lesson plan databases, teacher's guides, and other educational sites to be shared and added to.

The goal for an external document is to overcome the weaknesses of the software. An external document should:

- Be based on current knowledge in the content area.
- Enhance interpersonal interaction.
- Provide higher order thinking tasks.
- Provide different ways for students to understand and respond.
- Enhance the learning that the software facilitates.
- Be an integral part of the activity.

- Make the information more authentic to students.
- Expose students to information in a different form.
- Give students more control.

Teachers can use the terms from Figure 4.3 on page 105 to help plan and create external documents. Like any other tool, external documents need to be clearly explained and modeled before students use them. To make documents more accessible to students with learning challenges and/or diverse learning styles, teachers can:

Inclusion

- Print instructions in a color different from the rest of the text.
- Provide oral instructions along with the written document.
- Provide visual aids when possible.
- Provide slightly different documents for students at different reading or content levels.
- Use large, clear print.

In this section, technology-enhanced lessons in critical thinking are supplemented by external documents to demonstrate how teachers can make do with the tools they have and also make the tools more effective. Each example provides an overview of the lesson procedure and the tools used and a sample external document that supports student critical thinking during the lesson. Specific grade levels are not mentioned, because the focus is on the principles behind the activities, and the tasks can be easily adapted for a variety of students. As you read, think about how each external document supports critical thinking and what additional documents might encourage student critical thinking in other ways.

Science Example: Shooting for the Moon

Procedure:

1. The class reads *Space Day—Inventors Wanted* at the about.com site (http://childparenting. about.com/). The site gives students guidelines for designing and creating an item for astronauts to take into space.

2. The class uses a planning tool to decide how to address this task and to make a timeline for completion.

3. Students make teams and brainstorm their ideas in a word processing or graphics program. They list their resources and reasons for using each resource in the external document, a resource handout (Figure 4.9).

4. After they make a preliminary decision about their invention, they use the Space Day Invention external document handout (Figure 4.10) to analyze their choices.

5. Students complete a model of their invention, then use the Invention Justification external document (Figure 4.11) to plan the written explanation that will accompany their model.

The simple external documents in this case give students a foundation for

FIGURE 4.9 Space Day Invention Resources

	Source 1	Source 2	Source 3
Complete citation			
Type of source			
Authors authority			
Author's purpose			
Contribution of this resource			

FIGURE 4.10 Space Day Invention Design Requirements

Requirement	Results	Meets guidelines? (Yes/no)	Evidence	Changes needed
Weight				
Capacity				
Power				
Gravity				
Health and Safety				

thinking, a permanent record of their thinking, and assistance for thinking, speaking, and writing about their invention. The range of documents that can be created to facilitate this activity is large; the documents can also be adapted for different students. For example, documents intended for ELLs can include graphics and vocabulary explanations, and those for students with reading barriers can be set up online and read by an electronic text reader. When students finish their project, they can be asked to review their documents to reflect on their thinking processes.

What other documents might help students think critically during this task? Describe one or more.

FIGURE 4.11 Invention Justification Handout

INVENTION JUSTIFICATION

Instructions: Answer the questions below. When you are finished create a summary of your answers that addresses all the questions.

1. In what ways is your invention compact and lightweight? Use examples and information to give evidence that it is. You might compare it to something that we use on earth.

2. What makes your invention easy for astronauts to use? Describe every way that it is easy to use. For examples, you might estimate how long it would take them to learn to use it or how much time and energy it might take.

3. How does your invention improve the astronauts' working or living conditions? Imagine that you are an astronaut being asked to use this item. Describe how it helps you.

Social Studies Example: Election Year Politics Debate

Procedure:

1. The class reads a variety of Internet sources, popular press, and opinion pieces to gather information to complete the Election Year Issues chart external document in Figure 4.12.

2. Students choose the issue they decide is most important according to the criteria given and use the Debate Planning document in Figure 4.13 on page 116 to organize their position.

FIGURE 4.12 Election Year Issues Chart

Which social problem is the most important?			
	Number and People Affected	Financial Cost	Other Costs
Racism			
Pollution			
Drugs			
Religion in Schools			
(write in your issue)			

FIGURE 4.13 Debate Planning Handout

Debate Planning

Claim	Evidence	Possible counter-claims

3. During the debate, students keep track of and summarize the arguments on a computer screen using Reason!Able software (described in this chapter's Tool CloseUp: Reason!Able).

4. After the debate, students try to come to a consensus using all their documentation for support.

The Issues chart helps students to focus on crucial aspects of the topic that they are thinking about. This type of grid can be used for almost any topic area. The debate planning handout is also a multiuse external document that can be employed in debate planning or discussion throughout the year in almost any subject area.

What issues might be more suitable for students at your grade level and content area to think about? Why?

_____

_____

_____

English Example: Critical Reading

Procedure:

1. After appropriate introduction by the teacher, students in groups of three read one of the three stories about the death of Malcolm X from Dan Kurland's Web site (http://criticalreading.com/ malcolm.htm).

2. Student groups complete the Reading Analysis external document (Figure 4.14), which they would have used previously for other readings.

3. Student groups reconfigure, with one student from each of the initial three reading groups in a new group (known as **jigsaw learning**). In their new groups students compare the reports and understandings from their first group and summarize their analysis of all the readings.

4. Students go online to discover other discussions and reports on the death of Malcolm X and to make conclusions about the events and the sources that reported them.

FIGURE 4.14 Reading Analysis Worksheet

Instructions: Read the selection carefully. With your group, write answers to the questions. Use examples from the reading and other evidence to support your answers.

1. Choose the purpose of this selection from these three choices:

    a. To relate facts
    b. To persuade with appeal to reason or emotions
    c. To entertain (to affect peoples emotions)

2. Explain why you think this is the purpose. Use examples from the selection to support your idea.

3. Why did the author write this selection?

4. Where and by whom was it published?

5. List all the main ideas in this selection.

6. List any words that you do not know, and add a definition in your own words.

7. Write a short summary of the selection. Limit your summary to five sentences.

8. Decide if the information in this selection is well written. What makes you think so?

9. What are the selection's strengths and weaknesses?

10. What is your group's opinion about this selection? Does it seem fair, logical, true, effective, something else? Explain clearly why you think so and give evidence to support your ideas.

Reading is not only covered in English or language arts areas. Teachers in all subject areas need to help students evaluate sources and become more media literate, and external documents that help them to do so can be used across the curriculum.

What other kinds of documents or support might students need to help them think critically about what they read?

_____

_____

_____

Math Example: Write to Dr. Math

Procedure:

1. Throughout the semester, students choose a math problem that is giving them trouble. They complete the Dr. Math Questions worksheet (Figure 4.15, page 118) about that problem. The teacher helps students post their questions to the Write to Dr. Math Web site (http://mathforum.org/dr.math/).

2. Students use the answer from the experts to analyze their approach to the problem and to answer a similar problem.

Presenting a problem and their thought processes to an external audience helps students clarify, detail, and explain—supporting the development of critical thinking.

What other questions could help students work through the critical thinking process during this task?

_____

_____

_____

LEARNING ACTIVITIES

FIGURE 4.15 Dr. Math Questions

Write to Dr. Math

Instructions: Answer all of these questions as completely as possible to prepare to ask Dr. Math your question.

1. What is your question about?

   (Please be as specific as you can. Writing something too general, like *math* or *word problem* or *I need help* makes it likely that your question will be **ignored**.)

2. Write your question, with one specific example.

3. Tell us what you find most difficult or confusing about it.

4. Show us your work or thoughts on this question.

Source: Reproduced with permission from Drexel University. Copyright 2005 by The Math Forum @ Drexel. All rights reserved.

Art Example: Pictures in the Media

Procedure:

1. Students look at the use of art in advertisements on the Web. Students choose an advertisement about a familiar product.
2. Examining the art that accompanies the ad, students complete the Advertising Art document (Figure 4.16).
3. Students choose or create new art for the advertisement based on their answers.

Look back at the section earlier in the chapter about media literacy. What other questions might you ask students about advertising to help them think critically about it?

_____

_____

_____

External documents help make the technology resources more useful, more focused, and more thought-provoking. The combination of technology tools and external documents can lead to many opportunities for critical thinking.

> **FIGURE 4.16 Advertising Art**
>
> *Instructions:* Look at the art in your advertisement. Carefully consider your answers to these questions. Answer as completely as possible.
>
> 1. Describe the art objectively, including color selection, line direction, use of shadow and light, and other features. In other words, try not to use any opinion in your description.
>
> 2. In words, what do you think this picture is saying? Why do you think so? Give evidence and examples as support.
>
> 3. Is it an accurate representation of the product? How is it related to the product? Explain your answers clearly.
>
> 4. How do you think someone else would respond to the art in this ad? Think of several different people you know and project what effect the art might have on them.
>
> 5. What is the purpose of this art? What do the publishers of this ad hope to accomplish? Why do you think so?
>
> 6. What are the consequences of not knowing the influences that art can have on people?

ASSESSING CRITICAL THINKING WITH AND THROUGH TECHNOLOGY

Evaluating student work on external documents like those described in the previous section is one way to evaluate student progress in critical thinking. Student use of strategy and other critical thinking software tools can also aid in assessment. Many of the assessment means and tools mentioned throughout this text can assist teachers in evaluating the process and outcomes of student critical thinking.

Ennis (1993) provides several purposes for assessing critical thinking:

- Diagnosing students' level of critical thinking
- Giving students feedback about their skills
- Motivating students to improve their skills
- Informing teachers about the success of their instruction

Although critical thinking tests do exist, Ennis recommends that teachers make their own tests because the teacher-made tests will be a better fit for students and can be more open-ended (and thereby more comprehensive). He makes a logical argument that the use of multiple-choice tests that ask students for a brief written defense of their answers might be effective and efficient.

In addition, both content and thinking skills can be tested simultaneously. For example, asking students about the resources they used, Mr. Andres might ask:

> *Which is more believable? Circle one:*
>   a. The sewer worker investigates the alligators and says, "I've never seen one, so they don't exist."
>   b. The mayor says, "Of course there are no alligators. I would know if there were."
>   c. A and B are equally believable.
>
> *EXPLAIN YOUR REASON:* _____
>
> _____
>
> _____

This format gives students who have credible interpretations for their answers credit for answering based on evidence. It can also eliminate some of the cultural and language differences that might otherwise interfere with a good assessment. For example, although the student might mark the multiple-choice part of the question incorrectly due to language misunderstandings or a slip of the hand, the teacher will be able to tell from the written explanation whether the student understands the question and is able to use thinking skills to think through and defend the answer. Students can complete this kind of test on the computer, avoiding problems with handwriting legibility.

Technology can aid teachers in developing tests of this sort. Test-making software abounds both from commercial publishers and nonprofit Web sites; however, few of the multiple-choice test creators also allow for short answers. An effective choice is to use a word processor to develop the test. The test can then be easily revised for future administrations. Teachers who have technical support and/or are proficient in Web page creation can also use an html editor such as Microsoft's FrontPage or Macromedia's Dream Weaver to create a Web-based test.

Facione (1990) adds that teachers should measure students' proficiency in using critical thinking skills for relevant activities. Measuring these skills is not easy, but observation over time, a criterion-referenced task, and/or talk-alouds by students during activities are some ways to do so. Self-assessments can also encourage student reflection on how well they have done. Teachers can use a personal digital assistant (PDA) such as a Palm Pilot or BlackBerry to quickly note and store observations and, if necessary, later transfer the notes into a desktop computer for editing and sharing.

Most important is to assess many situations using different methods to get the best idea of which critical-thinking skills students understand and to what degree they use them. For additional examples of measures, see the Critical Thinking assessments in the Assessment Library at Intel Education (http://www.intel.com/education).

SAMPLE LESSON: CRITICAL THINKING

After completing the Urban Legends project with his class, Mr. Andres realizes that his students need more instruction in and practice with critical thinking. He decides to create a project that will help his students gain these skills while addressing curricular goals related to nutrition and basic economics. He chooses a promising lesson from the Internet4Classrooms Technology Integrated Lesson Plans page (http://www.internet4classrooms.com/). The lesson is presented here.

FAST FOOD FUN

[Sample Spreadsheet] [Rubric]

Objective:
   Use the Internet and spreadsheets to find calories and fat in a typical fast food meal.

Project Rubric:

Information on how this project will be graded.

Procedure:

Step One:

Decide which fast food restaurant you would like to visit. Click on that restaurant's Web site below.

McDonald's: http://www.mcdonalds.com/app_controller.nutrition.index1.html

Burger King: http://www.bk.com/

Wendy's: http://www.wendys.com/the_menu/nut_frame.html

Other Restaurants: http://www.nutritiondata.com/ (This site allows you to search many fast food restaurant sites.)

Once there, plan a meal with a sandwich, salad or other main dish, a side dish (french fries, etc.), a drink, and a dessert. For each item on your menu, record the total calories and the calories from fat.

Step Two:

Enter your data in an Excel spreadsheet. Click here to see a sample and directions for completing the spreadsheet. When you have finished your spreadsheet and charts, complete the handout and return here for the rest of the project directions. Compare your answers to at least one other student. In your notebook, record information about which restaurant they visited, what food they ate, and the nutritional content of that food.

Step Three:

Visit the United States Department of Agriculture to find out more about healthy eating guidelines: http://www.nal.usda.gov/fnic/dga/dguide95.html. Browse through this site and answer the questions on your handout.

Step Four:

Using Microsoft Word, type a three-paragraph report about your findings. Use the format for a one-page report.

Paragraph #1: Introduction including which restaurant you chose and the items on your menu.

Paragraph #2: Summarize your findings about your meal, including number of calories, percentage of fat, etc. Copy and paste one of your charts into your document as supporting evidence.

Paragraph #3: Compare and contrast your meal with another student. Use the information you recorded in step 2.

Paragraph #4: Use the information from the Department of Agriculture to evaluate your meal. How does your percentage of fat compare to the percentage recommended? What about other guidelines like eating fruits and vegetables? Have you planned a healthy meal? What changes might you make in your meal to make it healthier?

Source: Web Weavers Education Page. Copyright © 2000. Karen Work Richardson.

Mr. Andres read the lesson and the links to the lesson supplements carefully to make sure that students would meet the goals he requires. He completed a Lesson Analysis and Adaptation Worksheet (found in chapter 1 on page 33 and in the Lesson Planning module of the Companion Website) and concluded these things about the lesson:

- No standards are mentioned, but Mr. Andres can easily align the lesson with state and national standards.
- Students are asked to use some higher order thinking skills such as summarizing, but adding some essential questions might help focus even more on critical thinking. Students are also asked to work on communication and technology skills.

- Students have a choice of fast-food companies to focus on, but the materials are mostly online and text-based.

ELL

- Students have their own authentic task to accomplish. ELLs can choose the level of reading that works for them in the fast-food sites, but they may also need more scaffolding to collect the initial data.
- The technology supports access to a variety of resources and focal calculations that students must do to complete the task.
- The lesson includes an appropriate rubric, samples and scaffolds to help students use the spreadsheet, and both reading and writing components. However, all students are required to complete an essay, and no accommodations are made in the product requirement for students who reflect their learning better in other ways.

This lesson has many outstanding aspects. However, based on his analysis and his knowledge of his students, Mr. Andres decides to make some small but important changes to the lesson. He especially wants to make sure that the ELLs in his class will be able to participate fully. He decides to make these changes based on his analysis:

ELL

- Spell out the appropriate standards and curricular goals.
- Add additional resources such as charts, pamphlets, and other sources of information about fast food. Some of these will be in the first language of his ELLs.
- Include additional questions to help students think critically. For example, ask them to think about the resources they are using—would any bias be expected? Why or why not? What other resources would help them determine if they have factual information? Also ask them to take a position and argue whether people should eat fast food based on its nutritional value alone.
- Give students a choice of products. They may produce the essay or a poster, a multimedia presentation, a letter to a fast-food company, or an oral argument.

Mr. Andres thinks that this lesson supports critical thinking and other skills with technology well and will help his students be better consumers both of fast food and information.

What else would you add to this lesson to make it effective for your current or future students? What would you delete? Why?

_____

_____

_____

CHAPTER REVIEW

Key Points

- **Define critical thinking.**

  There are many different lists of the specific components of critical thinking, but in general experts agree that critical thinking is the process of providing clear, effective support for decisions.

- **Understand the role of critical thinking in meeting other learning goals such as creativity and production.**

  Teachers cannot teach their students all the content that they will use in their lives. They can, however, help them to become aware of and develop tools to deal with the decisions they will have to make in school and after. Learning to think critically will help students to become better communicators, problem solvers, producers, and creators and to use information wisely.

- **Discuss guidelines for using technology to encourage student critical thinking.**

  Techniques such as asking the right questions, using tasks with appropriate challenges, teaching thinking strategies, and encouraging curiosity facilitate more than critical thinking; they are good pedagogy across subjects and activities. Teachers do not need to search for tools to support critical thinking. There are plenty of free tools on the Web, and critical thinking can be supported by common tools such as word processors.

- **Analyze technologies that can be used to support critical thinking.**

  People do not often think of a word processor or spreadsheet as a critical-thinking tool, but when their use is focused on aspects of thinking, they can certainly support the process. Many electronic tools can be used to support critical thinking, but teachers must ensure that the tools do not create a barrier to students reaching the goal of effective critical thinking.

- **Create effective technology-enhanced tasks to support critical thinking.**

  Any task can have a critical thinking component if it is built into the task. Understanding how to promote critical thinking and doing so with external documents can turn ordinary technology-enhanced tasks into extraordinary student successes.

- **Employ technology to assess student critical thinking.**

  Multiple-choice tests in which students are asked to explain their reasons for their answers seem to be a logical and effective way to test not only content but thinking processes. However, this is only one way to assess critical thinking. Teachers need to employ observation, student self-reflection, and other assessments over time to gain a clear understanding of what students can do and how they can improve. Technology can help teachers prepare for and perform assessments.

Which information in this chapter is most valuable to you? Why? How will you use it in your teaching?

_____

_____

_____

CASE QUESTIONS REVIEW

Reread the case at the beginning of the chapter and review your answers. In light of what you learned during this chapter, how do your answers change? Note any changes below.

1. *What kinds of skills do David and his peers need to use to discover the answer to their question?*

_____

_____

_____

2. *What support should Mr. Andres give to facilitate the students' critical thinking?*

_____

_____

_____

3. *What should Mr. Andres's role be in teaching critical thinking skills?*

_____

_____

_____

4. *What role will technology play in helping the students to think critically?*

_____

_____

_____

CHAPTER EXTENSIONS • • • • • • • • • •

To answer any of the following questions online, go to the Chapter 4 Extensions module of this text's Companion Website (http://www.prenhall.com/egbert).

Adapt • • •

Choose a lesson for your potential subject area and grade level from the Internet4Classrooms page of Integrated Technology Lesson Plans (http://www.internet4classrooms.com/integ_tech_lessons.htm). Use the Lesson Analysis and Adaptation Worksheet from chapter 1 on page 33 (also available in the Lesson Planning module of the Companion Website) to consider the lesson in the context of *critical thinking*. Use your responses to the worksheet to suggest general changes to the lesson based on your current or future students and context.

Practice • • •

1. *Find out more.* Complete this WebQuest for teachers about Essential Questions: http://www.k12.hi.us/~dtisdell/webquest/ssessques.htm. What did you find out?
2. *Integrate the standards.* Choose one or more of the activities in the chapter and note which content and technology standard(s) the lesson can help to meet.
3. *Write a test question.* Review any of the tasks or activities in the chapter. Choose one, and write one test question that can assess students' critical thinking. Explain how your question assesses student thinking about content or language.
4. *Revise an external document.* Review the external documents presented in the chapter. Make improvements by editing or revising according to the goals for external documents. Justify your changes in writing.
5. *Review a tool.* Obtain one of the critical thinking tools discussed in this chapter and learn more about it. List 5 ways that you could use this tool effectively in your future classroom.

Explore • • •

1. *Revise an activity.* Choose one of the learning activities in the chapter and adapt it for your content area and/or grade level. Add or change technology. Change the existing document or create a new external document as necessary. Briefly explain your changes.
2. *Assess.* Review the sample test question in the assessment section of the chapter. Keeping the general structure and intent, change the question to evaluate the activity that you adapted for the previous question.
3. *Think about challenges.* Revisit a lesson that you have created. Think about and describe the challenges that students face during the lesson. Who might be bored? Who might feel too challenged? How can you adjust the lesson so that everyone feels the appropriate amount of challenge? How can technology help?
4. *Create a document.* Choose or create a technology-enhanced task or activity. Develop an external document that supports the use of critical thinking skills to accompany your activity. Justify your choices.

5. *Create questions.* Look at a reading, online or off, that you might use in your classroom. Discuss how the use of this reading might be improved by asking the right questions (what would they be?) and/or using critical thinking technologies.

6. *Develop a lesson on critical thinking.* Create a task or lesson to help students learn about the critical thinking process. Explain how your lesson meets this goal. Describe how your lesson could effectively use technology.

REFERENCES

Abdal-Haqq, I. (1994). *Culturally responsive curriculum.* ERIC Clearinghouse on Teaching and Teacher Education, Washington, D.C. ED370936. Available: http://www.ericdigests.org/1995-1/curriculum.htm.

Anderson, L. W., & Krathwohl, D. R. (Eds.). (2001). *A taxonomy for learning, teaching, and assessing: A revision of Bloom's taxonomy of educational objectives.* New York: Longman.

Bloom, B. S. (Ed.). (1956). *Taxonomy of educational objectives: The classification of educational goals: Handbook I, cognitive domain.* New York: Longmans, Green.

Bransford, J., Brown, A., & Cocking, R. (Eds.). (2000). *How people learn: Brain, mind, experience, and school.* Washington, D.C: National Academies Press.

CILIP (2007). *Information literacy: Definition.* www.cilip.org.uk/

Clark, D. (1999). *Learning domains or Bloom's taxonomy.* http://www.nwlink.com/~donclark/hrd/bloom.html.

Cotton, K. (2001). *Classroom questioning.* NWREL School Improvement Research Series, Close-Up #5. Available online: http://www.nwrel.org/scpd/sirs/3/cu5.html.

Csikszentmihalyi, M. (1997). Flow and education. *NAMTA Journal, 22*(2), 2–35.

Dalton, J., & Smith, D. (1986). Extending children's special abilities: Strategies for primary classrooms, pp. 36–37. Available: www.teachers.ash.org.au/researchskills/dalton.htm.

Ellis, D. (2002). *Becoming a master student* (10th ed.). Boston, MA: Houghton Mifflin.

Ennis, R. (1993). Critical thinking assessment. *Theory into Practice, 32*(3), 179–186.

Ennis, R. (1998, March). Is critical thinking culturally biased? *Teaching Philosophy, 21*(1), 15–33.

Ennis, R. (2002). *An outline of goals for a critical thinking curriculum and its assessment.* Available: http://faculty.ed.uiuc.edu/rhennis/outlinegoalsctcurassess3.html.

Ennis, R. H. (1992). The degree to which critical thinking is subject specific: Clarification and needed research. In S. Norris (Ed.), *The generalizability of critical thinking: Multiple perspectives on an educational ideal* (pp. 21–27). New York: Teachers College Press.

Facione, P. (1990). *Critical thinking: A statement of expert consensus for purposes of educational assessment and instruction: "The Delphi report."* Millbrae, CA: The California Academic Press. ED 315 423.

Fowler, B. (1996). *Critical thinking definitions.* Critical Thinking Across the Curriculum Project. Available: http://www.kcmetro.cc.mo.us/longview/ctac/definitions.htm.

Jonassen, D. (2000). *Computers as mindtools for school: Engaging critical thinking.* Upper Saddle River, NJ: Merrill/Prentice Hall.

McPeck, J. (1992). Thoughts on subject specificity. In S. Norris (Ed.), *The generalizability of critical thinking: Multiple perspectives on an educational ideal* (pp. 198–205). New York: Teachers College Press.

Moore, T. (2004). The critical thinking debate: How general are general thinking skills? *Higher Education Research and Development, 23*(1), 3–18.

Office Port (2002). Bloom's taxonomy. http://www.officeport.com/edu/blooms.htm.

Paul, R. (2004a). Critical thinking: Basic questions and answers. The critical thinking community. Dillon Beach, CA: Foundation for Critical Thinking. http://www.criticalthinking.org/aboutCT/CTquestionsAnswers.shtml.

Paul, R. (2004b). A draft statement of principles. The critical thinking community. Dillon Beach, CA: Foundation for Critical Thinking. Available: www.criticalthinking.org/about/nationalCouncil.shtml.

Petress, K. (2004). Critical thinking: An extended definition. *Education, 124*(3), 461–466.

Sarason, S. (2004). *And what do YOU mean by learning?* Portsmouth, NH: Heinemann.

Schwarz, G., & Brown, P. (Eds.). (2005). Media literacy: Transforming curriculum and teaching. *The 104th yearbook of the National Society for the Study of Education, Part 1.* Malden, MA: Blackwell.

vanGelder, T. (2005). Teaching critical thinking: Some lessons from cognitive science. *College Teaching 45*(1), 1–6.

Weiler, A. (2004). Information-seeking behavior in Generation Y students: Motivation, critical thinking, and learning theory. *The Journal of Academic Leadership, 31*(1), 46–53.

Wiggins, G., & McTighe, J. (1998). *Understanding by design.* Alexandria, VA: ASCD.

22

Supporting Student Creativity

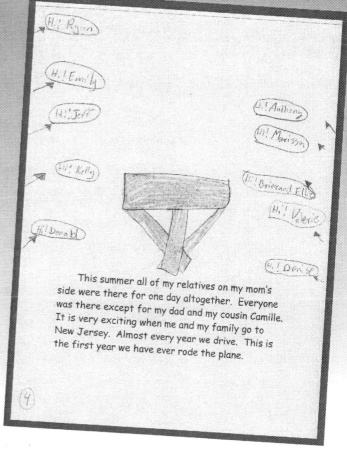

This summer all of my relatives on my mom's side were there for one day altogether. Everyone was there except for my dad and my cousin Camille. It is very exciting when me and my family go to New Jersey. Almost every year we drive. This is the first year we have ever rode the plane.

Case: Circus Train

As you read the following scenario, think about how teachers and technology can support student creativity.

· ·

The students in Pam Groves's first-grade class were excited about their circus project. Not only did they get to draw their own circus train cars on the computer, but also the completed train with all the students' pictures would be displayed for the whole school. Jamie Johnson had worked hard sketching her animal car on paper using crayons and a ruler as the teacher required. She had also learned how to use KidPix software from the student technology leader in her group. Earlier in the week she had started the computer rendering of her circus car. Now it was her group's computer center time again, and they were to finish drawing their train cars in KidPix following their sketches as carefully as they could.

Jamie had drawn a rectangle for the outside of her car and circles for the wheels. She had colored the car bright pink, her favorite color, and the wheels light blue. Now, looking at her sketch, she decided that the bars on the car looked much too zoo-like and that she would use windows and curtains instead in her KidPix version to make her animals feel more comfortable. She carefully drew squares for the windows and used the KidPix paintbrush tool to add colorful striped curtains. She was pleased with the result and was working on drawing a lion in one of the windows when Ms. Groves came by to check on the team's progress.

Ms. Groves looked at Jamie's sketch and then at the computer where her drawing was almost finished.

"What are these, Jamie?" asked Ms. Groves.

"Windows," said Jamie.

"But why are there windows? There are no windows in your sketch. And why are your wheels blue instead of black like they should be?" the teacher questioned.

"I wanted the animals to be comfortable. And they look better this way," Jamie explained.

"Yes, but it's not real," said Ms. Groves as she reached over and deleted the picture. "Now start again and do it right. You'll have to hurry if you're going to have your car displayed with all the rest."

· ·

Answer these questions about the case. There are no right or wrong answers to this chapter preview—the goal is for you to respond before you read the chapter. Then, as you interact with the chapter contents, think about how your answers might change.

1. *What should Ms. Groves have done when she saw Jamie's colorful circus train car with windows? Why?*

   She should have praised her, noting that Jamie's got a very creative picture. In this way she would have motivated her to develop

2. *What role did Ms. Groves take in this project? What should the teacher's role be in enhancing student creativity?*

   She should be a facilitator and guide. She shouldn't impose her own preferences

3. *What roles can technology play in enhancing and supporting student creativity?*

   It can help to change & improve their product. As a result, develop their creative thinking

4. *What are some benefits that students might derive from using technology to support creativity? Are there any potential disadvantages?*

   multiple trials, experimenting;

Ms. Groves missed an opportunity to support Jamie's creativity and to reinforce her creative thinking skills. Because she had a specific idea of how she wanted the finished product to look, Ms. Groves expected all the students to do it the "right way." The goal of this chapter is to help you understand that often there is no "right way," and that student creativity should be nurtured and encouraged. Technology can be used in many ways to meet this goal, particularly because it gives teachers and students options. This chapter addresses some of the ways that technology can help. After reading this chapter, you will be able to

- Define creativity.
- Understand the importance and benefits of creativity to life and learning.
- Discuss guidelines and technological tools for encouraging student creativity.
- Create effective technology-enhanced tasks to support creativity.
- Assess creativity and technology-enhanced creative tasks.

When you have completed this chapter, which NETS*T will you have addressed?

The chapter extensions at the end of the chapter will help you to practice and reflect on providing opportunities for student creativity. For standards that guide creativity and therefore the content of this chapter, see the Meeting the Standards feature.

• • • • Meeting the Standards: Creativity • • • •

It is curious how often people assume that creativity is relegated to subjects such as art and drama and overlook its importance in areas such as science, math, and social studies. People often ignore the fact that creative thinkers have established essential breakthroughs in knowledge in all areas—although their ideas may have been considered crazy at first. Of course, K–12 students are not expected to discover a new virus or found a new school of art, but they should be able to think creatively and to understand why it is important to do so.

Naturally, the standards for the fine arts mention creativity very clearly and often. For example:

NA-D.K.4.4 Applying and demonstrating critical and creative thinking skills in dance.

NA.VA.9–12.1 Students conceive of and create works of visual art.

In English students are also expected to create texts of different kinds. But how can math be creative? As explained in this chapter, creativity can be characterized as involving the ability to think

- *Flexibly*, or able to use many points of view
- *Fluently*, or able to generate many ideas
- *Originally*, or able to generate new ideas
- *Elaboratively*, or able to add details (Guilford, 1986; Torrance, 1974)

These abilities come into play in many ways in the subject areas. For example, in math, NM-NUM.6–8.1 says that students should be able to "work flexibly with fractions, decimals, and percents to solve problems." In NM.ALG.PK 2.2, meeting the standard to "use concrete, pictorial, and verbal representations to develop an understanding of invented and conventional symbolic notations" also takes creative thinking. Even NPH.K–12.7 requires that "a physically educated student understands that physical activity provides opportunities for enjoyment, challenge, self-expression, and social interaction."

In addition, deciding how citizens can take part in civic life (NSS-C.9–12.5), using technology tools to promote creativity (NT.K–12.3), and understanding science as a human endeavor (NS.K–4.7) all require creative thinking. In this age of high-stakes testing, creativity is often seen as a curricular "extra," but there are many compelling reasons, noted throughout this chapter, why it should be central. Clearly, thinking creatively is an important goal for teachers and students.

Explore the state standards for your content area and/or grade level. Which address creativity? How important do those standards make it seem? Why do you think so?

_____

_____

 See and explore your standards for creativity in the Standards module on this text's Companion Website.

OVERVIEW OF CREATIVITY AND TECHNOLOGY IN K–12 CLASSROOMS

Employing a learning focus to support creativity means that before decisions are made about technology use, the whys and hows of creativity are understood.

What Is Creativity?

There are many definitions of creativity. Which one is relevant depends on whether you are looking at the process, the outcome, or the goal, and which cultural and philosophic views you

FROM THE CLASSROOM:

Technology and Creativity

I try to look at my goals for using the computer. What am I trying to accomplish by using the computer? If it is just to give the students something fun to do, then I ask, can I stimulate their creativity and intellect in some other way? I read an article in the *New York Times* about a year or two ago by one of their technology writers who was all excited about teaching his 3-year-old to use the computer to work some kitchen software where they simulated making a cake. I personally thought this was a horrible use of the computer. His time would have been much better spent taking his 3-year-old into the REAL kitchen, putting the toddler on a stool, and making a REAL cake together. I think we need to look carefully at how and why we are using technology in our classrooms. While I feel that technology is great, and my students use it regularly, I think we want to make sure we are not using technology just to use technology. In addition to all the great things that technology can do, it can also limit creativity and learning. Kids will learn things much better if they can actually experience it through all their senses, rather than the limited number of senses that can be used when using the computer. So I think that we should make sure we have a valid reason for choosing the computer over real-life experiences. I think there are more and more kids nowadays that haven't had as many real-life experiences as kids from 20 years ago. They aren't out playing in the mud and making dams, or forts or whatever, because a lot of their time is spent on TV and video games. (Susan, fifth-grade teacher)

are taking. Generally, creativity can be defined as the creation of original ideas, processes, experiences, or objects. For example, inventions such as the computer and the printing press and paintings such as the *Mona Lisa* are creative endeavors. Creativity can also be described as the ability to see ordinary things differently. An often-cited example of this kind of creative thinking is the creation of Velcro, which arose from the observation of cockleburs clinging to clothes. The inventor, George deMestral, clearly was able to see a common item in a different and original way and was able to generate a clear, detailed idea that resulted in his million-dollar product. The developers of the iPod, the cell phone, and the YouTube Web site all employed creative thinking in the creation of their products.

Read what one teacher says about technology and creativity in From the Classroom: Technology and Creativity.

Creativity, or creative thinking differs from critical thinking (chapter 4) in that critical thinking involves the *evaluation* of whatever is created through the creative thinking process. In real life it is often difficult to separate creative thinking from critical thinking because they are closely related. For example, Rusbult (n.d.) suggests that putting a creative idea into practice without first evaluating it (i.e., thinking critically about it) could result in new problems, and therefore these two processes must go hand in hand. However, it is clear that critical and creative thinking should not happen at the exact *same* time for most people because criticism can create a barrier to creativity.

Research on creativity goes back a long way—the first formal study was conducted in 1869—and creativity was a topic of discussion and interest long before. In different cultures and disciplines creativity is described and investigated somewhat differently. However, many of the same findings hold true. Paul Torrance, considered a pioneer in creativity research, in his seminal book on creativity (published in 1962) noted as most important that stifling creativity (as the teacher in the opening scenario did) is dangerous both to the mental health and the educational and vocational achievement of children. Other researchers have found that teachers do tend to stifle creativity and focus more on solving close-ended problems that have only one correct answer. However, when teacher involvement in creativity is high, the creative achievement of students is also greater (Craft, 2001; Fasko 2000–2001). Research also shows that when appropriate creativity-enhancing processes are valued and supported by a "mentor," the results are markedly greater. This process can be supported beneficially by technology in ways outlined later in this chapter.

Fasko (2000–2001) reports the following findings in his review of the creativity research that teachers might consider:

- Some students are *assimilators*, or those who prefer to use known understandings to solve problems, and others are *explorers*, who like to find new solutions. A match between cognitive type and task leads to good problem solving. The variety of resources that the Internet provides can help teachers to create different types of tasks for different types of learners.

- Students find tasks more meaningful and so are more motivated when they choose their own tasks. This also applies to the products or outcomes of the tasks. For example, the teacher can provide a variety of WebQuests on the same topic from the WebQuest matrix at webquest .sdsu.edu and allow students to choose their specific topic, task, and creative outcome.

- A focus on *problem finding,* or being able to discern what a real problem is, is as important as one on creative problem solving. Technology can support problem finding in many ways, including by being used as a resource for world news and views, as an instrument to record survey information, or as a communication tool for brainstorming about problems.

Research also shows that creativity skills do not always transfer from one subject to another. This is because creativity can take on different looks in different subject areas, depending on the goals and values of that discipline. Therefore creative thinking needs to be taught across disciplinary genres. In other words, creativity is not just a set of technical skills, but rather involves feelings, beliefs, knowledge, motivations, and disciplinary understanding. In addition, a creative idea can arrive in a "Eureka!" moment or be developed over time. It can be completely innovative, or it can be an incremental, original change to something that exists. In the accompanying photograph, Kirk works on developing an original piece of art in a paint program.

Russell Robinson

Creating using a paint program.

Although most creativity researchers believe that all humans have natural creative abilities, they also note that these abilities are rarely fully developed. This could be, as Plsek (1997) notes, because people have certain patterns in their minds that help them to recognize how certain problems can be solved. For example, if a person knows that electric devices do not work unless they are plugged in, when confronted with a device that is not working the person will probably first check whether the device is, in fact, plugged in. This use of previous knowledge will work until the person confronts a situation in which plugging in the device, or seeing that the device is already plugged in but does not work, does not lead to the desired outcome. Plsek suggests that people must break free from the habits of mind that are stored in memory in order to establish new (creative) patterns. Teaching creativity can help this to happen.

What habits of mind might Ms. Groves possess that led to her reaction to Jamie's creative drawing?

personal understang and view of the established notion

Characteristics of effective creativity tasks

Figure 5.1 presents characteristics of an effective creativity task. There is no specific checklist for what a creativity task should contain. More important is what the task *does*. It should:

1. *Focus on content.* Although creative thinking can be taught and supported *through* lesson content or *as* lesson content, effective creative tasks are based on students' understanding of subject-area concepts. Like critical thinking and problem solving, creative thinking *cannot* occur without some content knowledge (Csikszentmihalyi, 1996). Therefore, a clear focus on content is the most important characteristic of effective tasks. Technology can support content learning in ways described in chapter 2, including supporting endless practice and helping students to connect ideas.

2. *Emphasize divergent thinking.* The task should encourage thinking that is out of the norm and goes in many different ways, rather than the typical *convergent thinking*, which emphasizes working quickly to get to *the* right answer and is typically used for information learning. In other words, tasks that encourage creativity are open-ended and have many possible solutions or outcomes. Four features of creativity, described in Meeting the Standards in this chapter, are often used to teach and

FIGURE 5.1 Characteristics of Effective Creativity Tasks	
Effective creativity tasks. . .	For example. . .
• Focus on content.	• Work from what students know.
• Emphasize divergent thinking.	• Let students hypothesize, experiment, suggest.
• Incorporate strategies.	• Make students aware of how creativity happens.
• Engage students.	• Use authentic content.
• Provide informational feedback.	• Help students understand their strengths and weaknesses.

measure divergent thinking: flexibility, fluency, originality, and elaboration. Ms. Groves in the opening case wanted Jamie to converge and did not support Jamie's divergent thinking. The result could be that Jamie would be careful not to diverge in the future.

3. *Incorporate creativity strategies.* Although first published in 1953, the book *Applied Imagination*, by Alex Osborn (1963), is still one of the most useful books for understanding what creativity is, why it is important, and how it can be nurtured. Osborn's list of more than 70 strategies to promote creative (divergent) thinking has been simplified throughout the creativity literature into eight categories. Tasks that ask students to be creative can include one or more of these strategies:

   - *Combine.* Blend two things that do not usually go together.
   - *Rearrange.* Try different sequences or layouts. Change parts with other things. Sort it differently.
   - *Adapt.* Look at other ways this can be used.
   - *Reverse.* Turn it upside down, inside out, front-side back. Change black to white and white to black. Choose the opposite.
   - *Substitute.* Find something else that could be a part of this or could do what this does.
   - *Modify.* Change the meaning, purpose, color, movement, sound, smell, form, or shape.
   - *Magnify.* Enlarge the size, the duration, the frequency; make smaller pieces into bigger segments.
   - *Minimize.* Decrease the size or strength; break it down into smaller pieces.

   These strategies can be used individually or with each other; they form the basis of the creative thinking techniques mentioned later in this chapter.

4. *Engage students.* Student engagement is also essential for tasks in which students are expected to think creatively. Typically, teachers can facilitate student engagement by using authentic content that students understand applies to their lives. The Internet is full of authentic content posted by and for students of the same age and with similar interests as yours. Check Egan's (2005) suggestions in the References module of the Companion Website for interesting ways to engage students' imaginations in content (http://www. prenhall.com/egbert).

5. *Employ informational rather than controlling feedback.* **Informational feedback** helps students to understand how their audience understands their work and what the strengths and weaknesses of their work are so that they can continue to assess themselves. **Controlling feedback,** which evaluates only how well students did compared to other students or to their previous work, can be threatening and disengaging for students (Starko, 1995). Jamie's reaction to Ms. Groves's controlling feedback might be to not try again.

Should Ms. Groves have incorporated more opportunities for creativity into the circus train project? Why or why not?

> Yes, she should have. It would help to develop creativity

Student benefits from creativity

Students who can think creatively can determine alternatives, solve problems (see chapter 6 for more information on problem solving), and avoid being what Lutus (2005) calls "lifelong idea consumers" who must consult others rather than working out problems themselves. Creative thinkers can also learn to make "original contributions to the store of human knowledge" (Lutus, 2005, p. 2) and can propose innovations that change their world. Creative students also tend to stay on task longer and therefore achieve more. In addition, creative thinkers can participate in mature risk taking, be flexible and adaptable, and read with greater engagement. Most important, students who can think creatively can have richer and more fulfilled lives (NCREL, 2004).

These benefits might seem abstract, and therefore not useful, to many students. How would you help your students understand the practical importance of creativity?

to provide some real-life cause - effect situations

THE CREATIVE THINKING PROCESS

Although the creativity literature focuses more on creative thinking strategies than on a specific process, there is some general agreement on the processes that help students become better creative thinkers. Keller-Mathers and Murdock (2002) suggest the following three-stage process for teachers to use in presenting lessons, based on Torrance's (1962) and other approaches:

Stage 1: Warm up. The purpose is to help students get excited about the activity, access prior knowledge, and understand what to expect. This stage is based on what students already know so that they can generate ideas rather than search for knowledge upon which to base ideas. This is particularly important for ELLs and other students who will be better prepared with the appropriate vocabulary and expectations when these connections are made.

Stage 2: Deepen expectations. During this stage, teachers lead students to become more aware of the challenge that they are facing and apply skills and strategies to deal with the challenge.

Stage 3: Extend the learning. Teachers help students to connect information to their lives, to experiment, and to diverge.

ELL

During the three lesson stages, students might employ some variation of the following steps, adapted from Plsek (1997):

- *Clarify* the focus, concept, or problem that requires new ways of thinking.
- *Review* the facts. Student prior knowledge is activated as they lay out the problem or idea in detail.
- *Identify* elements that could be modified. Content knowledge is called on as students apply new ideas to old.
- *Restate* the focus by suggesting modifications. Osborn's strategies (listed previously) are useful here, as are creativity techniques that fit the context.
- *Develop* the idea further to meet practical constraints; this requires critical thinking skills.
- *Test it.* Say it, create it, try it, and look at the results.

Figure 5.2 demonstrates the integration of the lesson stages and student creative thinking processes.

Black (1990a) provides a fun example using the idea that 1 + 1 does not always equal 2. He shows how, through the creative thinking process, students can come to understand that two insects of different genders, left alone, may come to equal many more than two; one dollop of blue paint added to one dollop of yellow will equal a new color entirely; one person's ideas added to another person's ideas can equal many new ideas; and one computer and one person together can equal all kinds of things. This example also demonstrates clear divergent thinking. Keller-Mathers and Murdock (2002) provide useful lessons that apply the stages of the creative thinking process. One of these lessons is reproduced in Figure 5.3 on page 134.

FIGURE 5.2 The Creative Thinking Process

Lesson stage	Student processes
Stage 1: Warm up	• Clarify • Review
Stage 2: Deepen expectations	• Identify • Restate
Stage 3: Extend the learning	• Develop • Test

FIGURE 5.3 Creative Thinking Process Lesson Example

Look At It Another Way Lesson

Content AND Creativity Objective

1. to identify and practice the key characteristics of Look At It Another Way by examining different perspectives
2. to promote incubation through the deliberate use of the three stages and strategies of the TIM.

Materials: kaleidoscopes, multiple examples of half of eight, pictures that can be viewed in more than one way (e.g., two faces/vase, old woman/young woman).

Warming Up

To get attention and heighten anticipation, have the room arranged in a different way before students come in (e.g., reverse back to front). To arouse curiosity about what is going to happen, have small kaleidoscopes out on every desk.

To provide focus and motivation, use the kaleidoscopes to encourage playfulness, and then begin a discussion about the characteristics and results of looking at things differently. Have students view the room through a kaleidoscope and describe what they see. Ask them *How do things look different? What do you notice that you didn't see before?* Discuss how familiar things begin to look different through the kaleidoscope.

Continue the warming up practice by showing a picture that can be viewed in more than one way (for example, the old woman/young woman perception drawing). Ask students: *What do you see? What else do you see? Who sees something different? How were you able to switch from one view to another? Was it easy or hard?*

Deepening Expectations

To make the transition into deepening expectations while sustaining motivation, begin a discussion on the various responses that are common when asked *What is half of eight?* Then ask students to dig deeper into this question and consider answers that require a different perspective. If you were playing a game of pool, for example, half of eight might represent half of the number eight ball. If you considered fractions, you might answer 4/8th. If you examined the question from the perspectives of the months of the year, the answer might be April. Have students draw, write, or state many perspectives to answer this question. Encourage surprising angles and uncommon views. Discuss how in viewing this differently you've taken something that's familiar (half of eight is four) and made it strange by considering the various ways one might answer this question.

Extending the Learning

To facilitate incubation and continued thinking, encourage students to keep their kaleidoscopes with them for the rest of the day and to take them out at least three times to look around and remind themselves to look at things differently. Ask students to stop and consider a different perspective to situations or concerns that arise throughout the day. Continue students' thinking through a journaling activity where they observe, discuss, or reflect on looking at things differently by "making the strange familiar and making the familiar strange."

Source: Used with permission of Susan Keller-Mathers and Mary Murdock, Buffalo State.

How could technology be used to support this lesson?

_____

_____

_____

Teachers and Creativity

The teacher's role

Teachers may inadvertently stifle creativity in the push to complete the assigned curriculum (as seen in the opening case with Ms. Groves), but there is no reason why creativity cannot be an integral part of the curriculum. As with the other instructional goals and strategies described in this text, to truly support student creativity the teacher should structure activities according to curricular goals, standards, and students' knowledge and needs, and then provide relevant support as students work toward their own understandings.

In structuring creative activities, teachers can follow some general guidelines that apply to developing technology-supported critical and creative capacities in students of all ages. These include:

- Choose real objects and experiences over workbooks and textbooks in developing understanding whenever possible. For example, instead of a drawing of the inside of a frog, use a Web site that shows actual dissection photos, such as NetFrog (http://frog.edschool .virginia.edu//). Or, rather than using templates, used open-ended software such as a word processor for presentations, brochures, cards, and other products.

- Consistently allow for students' input into establishing the criteria for the evaluation of classroom activities, assignments, and behaviors. Let students describe the ways in which they should be evaluated, whether by computer-based test or multimedia-supported presentation.

- Choose to display students' work over commercially prepared displays. Allow students to decorate the classroom with important concepts and information presented in creative ways through the use of computer technologies.

- Consistently offer and encourage students to seek alternative ways of responding to structured art activities, fulfilling learning requirements, or completing a craft, project, or assignment. Make all kinds of technologies available so that students have choices in their responses. (Adapted from Saskatchewan Education, n.d., n.p.)

Creativity tasks are great for avoiding plagiarism (described in chapter 6) because individual responses are expected to be original and there is not one "right" way to complete such a task.

In addition, teachers need to ask good questions, as they do to reach many instructional goals. For creative thinking, teachers need to ask students questions that encourage them to be flexible, to think of more ideas, to expand on their ideas, and to think "out of the box."

Another role for teachers is to model creative thinking. To do so, teachers should:

- Be open-minded, encouraging students to follow their own thinking and not simply repeat what the teacher has said.

- Change their own position when the evidence warrants, being willing to admit a mistake.

- Consistently provide opportunities for students to select activities and assignments from a range of appropriate choices.

- Exhibit genuine interest, curiosity, and commitment to learning.

- Undertake the organization and preparation required to achieve learning goals.

- Seek imaginative, appropriate, and ethical solutions to problems.

- Be sensitive to others' feelings, level of knowledge, and degree of sophistication.

- Show sensitivity to the physical elements that contribute to a stimulating learning environment through the physical arrangements and displays they provide or facilitate.

- Allow for student participation in rule setting and decision making related to all aspects of learning, including assessment and evaluation. (Saskatchewan Education, n.d., p. 5)

Most important is that teachers learn how to teach playfully, which, as Renzulli and Callahan (1981) suggest, means working on creativity tasks right along with the students, suggesting "crazy" ideas, taking risks, using humor, and modeling their own creative thinking process. This helps all students to understand both the process and the outcomes of creativity.

What does Ms. Groves need to do to meet these guidelines?

to change her thinking and perception!

Challenges for Teachers in Creating Technology-Supported Opportunities for Creativity

Teachers can be challenged by any part of the creative thinking process, whether in developing their own abilities or working with students. However, two central barriers exist. First, as seen in the chapter case, school is often a place where creativity is not supported, having an individual thought is not encouraged by peers, and conformity is expected. It would be difficult to teach in a classroom without any rules or norms, but there can be different ways to conform that also allow creativity to flourish. The challenge for teachers is to find these ways.

A second challenge, mentioned at the end of the previous section, is for teachers to model creativity. This includes learning and using strategies and techniques, developing and using tasks that call for creative thinking, and exhibiting enjoyment and achievement in creativity. All teachers are creative in some ways; teachers need to discover these ways and build on them. The guidelines in the next section of this chapter provide some basic suggestions for how teachers might address both challenges.

GUIDELINES FOR SUPPORTING STUDENT CREATIVITY WITH TECHNOLOGY

The description of the teacher's role, task characteristics, and benefits of creative thinking presented in this chapter help teachers to understand the basics of creativity in classrooms. The following guidelines, while more practical, also present more in-depth information.

Designing Creativity Opportunities

Many classrooms are physically sterile, with commercially made visuals posted just so, rows of desks that do not move, and everything in its "correct" place. Such classrooms are often also psychologically sterile, with rules about cleanliness, orderliness, and what *must* get done rather than what *can be* done. According to Black (1990b) and to those who study brain-based theory (Clemons, 2005), positive psychological factors in the environment are most important in encouraging creativity. Black notes that people need their environments to be fun, honest, caring, sincere, flexible, supportive, encouraging, challenging, growth-oriented, free of politics, focused on learning, open to nonsuccess, free of manipulation, and free of "backstabbing" (1990b, p. 2). Ai-girl and Lai-chong (2004) and Craft (2001) agree, noting that learners need to be in an environment where they feel free to take risks; have opportunities to play with materials, information, and ideas; and have the time and feedback they need, whether individually or in groups. The following guidelines suggest ways to deal with these issues.

Guideline #1: Create an enriched environment. Features of the environment that can smother creativity include rewards, time pressures, overmonitoring, competition, restricted choice, and high-stakes evaluation. Environments that support creativity are those that create alternatives to these features and allow students to explore, cooperate, and pace themselves. An environment that supports creativity is also one that is rich with examples and opportunities; technology is particularly useful for providing a wide range of resources and choices. Moving desks around, taking a playful attitude, having students share their work with local and online peers, providing both quiet and group areas, and posting new ideas are some ways to enrich both the physical and psychological spaces in the classroom.

In addition, a creative environment must "feed the senses" by including visual, aural, kinesthetic, and other stimulation. Students can decorate, bring in something that smells different, play a variety of music, and use different group and physical arrangements to incite creativity. An environment that supports creativity in these ways also allows students with diverse abilities, language and cultural backgrounds, and content and language skills not only to access more easily what is happening in the classroom but perhaps also to participate more in creative tasks.

Inclusion

ELL

Guideline #2: Teach techniques. During the creative thinking process, an amazing number of specific techniques can be taught and used, many of which are based on Osborn's strategies discussed in the process section of this chapter. More than 200 techniques are described at www.mycoted.com/creativity/techniques/index.php (Mycoted, 2004), and another useful list can be found at members. optus-net.com.au/%7Echarles57/Creative/ Techniques/index.html. Figure 5.4 presents just the "B" portion of the creativity techniques from mycoted.com. Most teachers will be familiar with brainstorming and browsing, but may be surprised to read about all of the other possible ways to teach creative thinking techniques. For example, "bug listing" is described as:

> *simply a list of things that bug you! It should be personal and illuminate specific areas of need. Adams recommends keeping it fluent and flexible, remembering humorous and far-out bugs as well as common ones. He suggests that if you run out of bugs in under ten minutes, you are either suffering from a perceptual or emotional block or have life unusually under control! It may well be the most specific thinking you have ever done about precisely what small details in life bother you; if properly done, your bug list should spark ideas in your mind for inventions, ideas, possible changes, etc. (http://www.mycoted.com/Bug_Listing)*

FIGURE 5.4 Creativity Techniques Starting with "B" from mycoted.com

B
- Backwards Forwards Planning
- Boundary Examination
- Boundary Relaxation
- BrainSketching
- Brainstorming
- Brainwriting
- Browsing
- Brutethink
- Bug Listing
- BulletProofing
- Bunches of Bananas

Source: Used with permission of Mycoted Ltd.

If students feel comfortable sharing, they could word-process and share their lists with peers, possibly sparking ideas in *their* minds, too.

Brainstorming is without doubt the most important technique for encouraging creative thinking, but it has to be done correctly in order to maximize its benefits. Rules for classic brainstorming include:

- Do not criticize any ideas during the brainstorming process. There will be time for this later.
- Generate as many ideas as possible. Do not worry whether they are practical or possible at this point.
- Do not stop to discuss the ideas—keep generating them for as long as possible.
- Try to piggyback on other ideas, generating still more ideas. Do not worry if they are only incrementally different.

Research has shown repeatedly that the more ideas a person generates, the better the chance that one of them will be new and useful (Renzulli & Callahan, 1981).

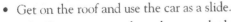

Fogler and LeBlanc (2005) provide a funny and useful list that shows the results of brainstorming. Some of their "suggested uses of old cars as equipment for a children's playground" include:

- Get on the roof and use the car as a slide.
- Take the seats out and use them as a bed to rest between activities.
- Teenagers could take the engine apart and try to put it back together.
- Make a garden by planting flowers inside.
- Use the tires to crawl through as an obstacle course.
- Take off the doors and use as a goal for hockey. (n.p)

Guideline #3: *Let students show what they can do, rather than what they cannot.* The high-stakes testing that is prevalent nationwide lets teachers know what their students cannot do; standardized tests cannot easily do more. Although tests can provide teachers with important information, they do not provide a whole picture of students' abilities. Allowing students to produce creatively builds on student successes and helps students to understand that they can think differently and still "pass." This idea is discussed further in the assessment section later in this chapter.

Guideline #4: *Teach respect for ideas and people.* When students fear criticism or are worried about competition, they may find it difficult to take risks and to be creative. This does not mean that classroom activities always have to be cooperative or that students should be taught to always agree with others, but teachers and their students can reflect on the reasons for treating people and ideas with respect and how this can be done. Working on respect also supports the team-building skills mentioned in other chapters in this book.

Figure 5.5 on page 138 presents the guidelines from this chapter.

FIGURE 5.5 Guidelines for Supporting Student Creativity

Suggestion	Example
Guideline #1: Create an enriched environment.	Set up desks in new arrangements; share student work on walls and other spaces.
Guideline #2: Teach creative thinking techniques.	%Teach students the "rules" for effective brainstorming and check that they abide by them.
Guideline #3: Let learners show ✓ what they can do.	Use assessments in addition to tests that allow students to show their creativity.
Guideline #4: Teach respect for ideas and people.	Make respect an overt part of every lesson; bring it to the forefront by addressing it directly.

Which of these guidelines did Ms. Groves meet? Which does she still need to work on?

_____

_____

_____

_____

_____

CREATIVITY TOOLS

Criticism can have a negative effect on creativity. Do computer tools also suppress creativity? Lutus (2005) suggests that they may when the user is "reduced to following a single behavioral pattern built into the program by its designers" (p. 3). Microsoft PowerPoint, in particular, has been criticized fairly often for allowing users to apply only prespecified formats (however, see the Tool CloseUp: PowerPoint for benefits of using this software).

Cameron (2000) suggests that computers are taking away creativity in music and art, just as calculators might de-skill students in math, because they take away opportunities for students to work with other tools. However, creative learners and teachers can use these tools in ways that support and inspire creativity if they understand the options that the tools afford. That tools *might* work against creativity—for example, by providing preset formats and inserts that students cannot change or limiting what can be included on a page—means that teachers must ensure that the tools used enable students to do what they need to and want to do. It also calls attention to the idea that students need to develop skills and *then* use technology, not use technology as a replacement or shortcut. Cameron (2000) explains,

> in those fields where creativity is to be fostered, we must teach students that the ideas and content of their work must precede and supercede the implementation of the work. Technology helps them implement. Only their own creativity and thoughts can make their work original and worthwhile. (p. 6)

There are electronic tools that can support different strategies and parts of the creativity process. For example, videos that stretch the boundaries of what can happen can provide fodder for imagination. In addition, communication tools such as those described in chapter 3 allow students to exchange ideas and build on each other's creativity. Productivity tools (chapter 7) allow learners to put their ideas into practice and explain them to others. Critical thinking tools (chapter 4) help students to evaluate their creative process and products. Most important for the use of technology to support creativity is that teachers and students choose the one(s) that best help them express themselves. However, teachers who are daunted by the range of tools that can support creative thinking can invest in learning about one or two tools (for example, Inspiration and a good word processor) that can facilitate a large range of ideas and products.

Of course, as Cameron notes, being creative does not require electronic technologies. However, if technology can stir creative ideas, support their expression, facilitate and/or provide opportunities for creativity, and encourage the use of strategies and techniques, it can benefit the creative thinking process. The following creativity tools can be used effectively during one or more parts of the creative process. They are listed by type of tool and include a brief description of what it does followed by some possible classroom uses and specific examples.

TOOLS

Tool CloseUp: PowerPoint

Microsoft's PowerPoint presentation software allows teachers and students to create interactive, multimedia presentations containing text, graphics and photos, animation, audio, and video. PowerPoint is one of the most widely used software packages in the world not only because it often comes bundled with new computers but because it is easy to learn. It allows creative users to use it creatively and is limited in application only by the users' imaginations.

PowerPoint consists of a number of screens, or "slides," to which the user adds content and then links to other slides in a "slide show." The software includes templates for slide layouts and designs for students who need such scaffolding, but students can also work from scratch. Other tools in PowerPoint include online collaboration and broadcast, diagrams and charts, drawing tools, and notes pages.

In addition to presenting information to the class, the software can support teachers and diverse students in creative pursuits. For example, students or the teacher can use PowerPoint to create an action maze. In an action maze, the user receives information on the first screen and has to choose a response among several. The chosen response leads to more information and more choices, and so on.

Students can also use PowerPoint to make multimedia books for younger children, providing the story in a variety of modes (audio, text, and pictures) so that ELLs and other students with special needs can access the content.

ELL

In fact, PowerPoint is being used even with elementary students like those in Cara Bafile's project in which students created an oral history of their town (http://www.educationworld.com/a_curr/curr202.shtml). Second graders are using it to create "Me Collages" that are literature related (http://iisme.org/etp/Elementary% 20Language%20 Art-Me%20Collage.pdf). At upper levels students are using PowerPoint for everything from science fair projects to public policy presentations (http://www.big6.com/showenewsarticle.php?id=253).

However, a look across the Web shows that often the projects that students are asked to do with PowerPoint are very prescriptive, from font size to exact number of graphics. Having some guidelines does help many students to be on task and work with the content, but without room for creativity there will not be any.

What other ways can you think of to use PowerPoint to support creativity? Brainstorm and list as many as you can.

_____

_____

_____

Tutorial

CW

_____

gOffice (www.goffice.com), OpenOffice (http://www.openoffice.org/), and Thinkfree (www.thinkfree.com) include free alternatives for PowerPoint, and other presentation packages such as Hyperstudio have many of the same features as PowerPoint. Find tutorials for these and other tools that can support creativity in the Tutorials module of the Companion Website (http://www.prenhall.com/egbert).

Puzzles/Puzzlemakers

Description and uses

There are many kinds of puzzles, from jigsaws to math equations, and most require creative thinking to put together or solve. Jigsaw puzzles with content arranged in specific ways can be used as a fun warm-up activity or as a visual to assess student understanding. Puzzles are useful to promote interaction during group work, and creativity is definitely required to develop puzzles for others.

Examples:

- Creative Java Puzzles, http://www.enchantedmind.com/
- Jigsaw maker at http://www.shockwave.com/
- Content/jigsaw maker or bigjig, http://www.lenagames.com/bigjig.htm
- Primary Power Pack (Puzzle Power, Jigsaw Power) from Centron Software

There are also many crossword puzzle makers that encourage students to work creatively with language.

What else would you add to this list of puzzles that support creativity?

_____

_____

_____

Authoring Environments

Description and uses

These tools allow users to design and create software, Web sites, documents, and other products such as book reports and projects that include sound, graphics, animation, and video. A wide variety of classroom uses is possible, from designing a classroom Web site for parents to access to developing a system for interacting with peers around the world.

Examples:

- PowerPoint (www.microsoft.com) or other presentation software (www.goffice.com, www. thinkfree.com)
- Hyperstudio, for any multimedia project, www.hyperstudio.com
- Moodle, a course development tool, http://moodle.org/
- Arachnophilia, a Web development tool, http://www.arachnoid.com/arachnophilia/index.html
- Macromedia Director, multimedia authoring software, http://www.macromedia.com/software/director/?promoid=BIHT

There are many more tools for course, Web, multimedia, and MOO development, some of which are aimed at K–12 classrooms, and some of which require more technical skills. However, they all require creativity and allow users to determine the look and feel of their electronic environment.

What other resources would you add to this list?

_____

_____

_____

Video Editing Software

Description and uses

Video editing software can allow students the freedom to create amazing products. For example, students can create their own brief videos from photos or graphics, interpret a story or poem that they have written, or edit a performance.

Examples:

- iMovie, bundled with the Mac operating system and also available through http://www.apple.com
- MovieMaker, bundled with some of the Microsoft operating systems and available free elsewhere on the Web, www.microsoft.com
- CyberLink PowerDirector 4, http://www.cyberlink.com
- Adobe Premier Elements, http://www.adobe.com

Software is available for novice users who want to make videos for MP3 players or to post to Web logs (blogs).

What other resources would you add to this list?

_____

_____

_____

Thought Exercises

Description and uses

Thought exercises are problems from any field that usually require minimal content knowledge. They can be used to show transfer of creative thinking from one domain to another, as warm-up exercises, as free-time tasks, or to apply newly learned creative thinking techniques. Students could also use them as models to build their own exercises.

Examples:

- Robert Black's creativity challenges, www.cre8ng. com/CC/index.shtml
- Creative Mindxercises, http://www.mindbloom.net/

Figure 5.6a presents a list of some of Robert Black's creativity challenges, and Figure 5.6b shows the details of one of them.

FIGURE 5.6a Robert Black's Creativity Challenges

Contents

1 - RAINBOW BY ANOTHER NAME
2 - No Matter How Often You Look
3 - Stories, stories, stories...tools for creativity
4 - What if-ing?
5 - Else-ing?
6 - From Smiles to Smirks to Laughs to Creativity
7 - It Won't Work!!!
8 - It Will Work if You Work It!!!
9 - Emotions Can Yield Creativity!!!
10 - Creativity and Creative Thinking Smell
11 - Creative Thinking Tastes Goooooooooood!!!????
12 - Creative Thinking Feeeeels Gooooooooood!!!????
13 - Creative Thinking Sounds Soooo Gooooooooood!!!????
14 - Creative Thinking Looks Soooo Gooooooooood!!!????
15 - Create With Just a Few Words
16 - 1,000 or More Words from Each Image
17 - Each Image Can Produce a 1.000 Words
18 - Combing Headlines for Fun
19 - Add Movement to Your Life and Challenges
20 - I'm Possible Not Impossible
21 - Think About Thinking
22 - Add Richness to Your Life Through More Color
23 - Collect Creative People and Learn from Them
24 - READ BACKWARDS . . . SDRAWKCAB DAER
25 - Make Your Own Stories
26 - Collecting Helps Us Be More Creative
27 - Switching Professions
28 - To Be More Creative Choose to Act More Creative
29 - Honoring Dr. E. Paul Torrance

Source: Used with permission of Robert Alan Black, alan@cre8ng.com, http://www.cre8ng.com.

FIGURE 5.6b Each Image Can Produce 1,000 Words from Robert Black's Creativity Challenges

MONDAY

Pick up a newspaper photograph and write at least 1,000 words about it. Just write. Your writing does not need to be grammatical or end up a gradable piece of writing. Simply write.

TUESDAY

Pick out a scene involving 2 or more people around you and write at least 1,000 words about it. Just write. Your writing does not need to be grammatical or end up a gradable piece of writing. Simply write.

WEDNESDAY

Pick up a magazine and randomly select a photograph or two and write at least 1,000 words about it or them. Just write. Your writing does not need to be grammatical or end up a gradable piece of writing. Simply write.

THURSDAY

Look through a children's picture book and write at least 1,000 words about any one or combination of the pictures or drawings. Just write. Your writing does not need to be grammatical or end up a gradable piece of writing. Simply write.

FRIDAY

Let your mind wander visually into your past. Once you see a scene or image that is powerful write at least 1,000 words about it. Just write. Your writing does not need to be grammatical or end up a gradable piece of writing.

Simply write.

The goal is to practice your abilities to communicate through words about images and to be creative in writing. If you are visually challenged use your 3rd eye to experience images of various types for each of the assignments.

Source: Used with permission of Robert Alan Black, alan@cre8ng.com, http://www.cre8ng.com.

Collaborative Idea Databases

Description and uses

A creativity pool is a database that gathers innovative ideas. Students can search for an idea under a specific topic or they can contribute their own.

> **Example:** The Creativity Pool, http://www.creativitypool.com/

Idea/Object Generators

Description and uses

A generator, typically, randomly generates an idea or an object in some topic area. Using a generator can help students get an idea going, figure out what questions to ask, get their mind off a problem for a while, or relate to content in some creative way.

> **Examples:**
>
> There is a fairly comprehensive list of generators at http://generatorblog.blogspot.com/, but many of the generators are not appropriate for K–12 classrooms. Some of the more fun or interesting generators that may be used with K–12 students include:
>
> - Generate your own painting, http://artpad.art.com/artpad/painter/
> - Make-a-Flake (make your own snowflake), http://snowflakes.barkleyus.com/
> - What animal are you? http://www.2on.com/
> - The What-if inator by seventh sanctum generates all kinds of interesting and often wacky ideas, at http://www.seventhsanctum.com/generate.php?Genname=whatif
> - Good Idea Generator software by managing-creativity.com

Another fun generator site is Ben and Jerry's, http://www.benjerry.com/fun_stuff/. Located at this site, "Ice Box Poetry" has magnetic words that students can arrange into poetry, and students can dress the "Virtual Snowman" in hundreds of ways.

What other creativity resources would you add to these lists?

_____

_____

_____

Graphics/Concept Mapping

Description and uses

Graphic organizer software is useful for all the goals mentioned in this book. During the creativity process, students can use it to generate and connect ideas, design, plan, and even evaluate.

> **Examples:**
> - The most popular are Inspiration and Kidspiration (http://www.inspiration.com/; see the Tool CloseUp in chapter 7 for more information).

Painting/Drawing

Description and uses

Most computers come preloaded with some type of paint program (on your PC, look under Programs—Accessories), and other more powerful programs are available commercially. Still others can be downloaded free from the Web (search, for example, http://www.freedownloads center.com/). Students can use paint software to create original art or to reconfigure photos and other graphics files.

Examples:

- Microsoft Paint, bundled with the Microsoft operating system
- MacPaint, bundled with older Macintoshes
- Paint Shop Pro, a professional paint package, http://www.corel.com
- Adobe Illustrator/Adobe Photoshop, http://www.adobe.com

Other software packages such as KidPix (see the Tool CloseUp later in this section) and Microsoft Word include painting and drawing tools.

Story Starters/Bookmaking/Publishing Software

Description and uses

These software types allow students to create stories and books, produce pamphlets and posters, and develop cards for all occasions. Although structured in some ways, most of these software packages are content free. They include audio, choices of graphics, and even a variety of languages, so English language learners can use them effectively, too. Students can create new holidays and cards to go with them, develop an ad campaign for a new invention, or write a book that presents history in a new way.

ELL

Examples:

- Storybook Weaver Deluxe 2004 (Riverdeep)
- Hollywood High and Hollywood (Grolier Interactive/Tom Snyder Productions)
- Publisher (Microsoft)
- Imagination Express (Edmark/Riverdeep)
- The PrintShop 22 (Broderbund)
- Any word processor

Inclusion

ELL

The teachers' guides for these software packages include ideas for assisting ELLs, students with physical disabilities, and other students with special needs to use them effectively.

Brainstorming Software

Description and uses

There are many brainstorming tools, most made for business, that support user idea generation. Students can use them to generate story starters, gather ideas to solve problems, discover names for the class pet, or any number of other tasks.

Examples:

- Brainstorming Toolbox, Infinite Innovations Ltd., http://www. brainstorming.co.uk
- Kidspiration/Inspiration, versatile software that can be used in many of these categories, http://www.inspiration.com

Figure 5.7 shows the Challenge Facts technique from Brainstorming Toolbox.

What other resources would you add to this section on creativity tools?

_____

_____

_____

FIGURE 5.7 Brainstorming Toolbox Challenge Facts Screen

Source: Used with permission of Infinite Innovations Ltd.

Tools CloseUp: KidPix

TOOLS

KidPix Deluxe, by Broderbund, is a versatile tool that children (and adults!) of all ages can learn to use quickly and easily. The software allows the user to draw using a variety of electronic tools, including a paintbrush, pencil, crayon, and spray paint can. Features include more than 600 stamps that students can include in their creations; categories include animals, events, backgrounds, and many more. Students can add audio and text to their pictures and make a slide show or movie by adding their drawings to the slide show maker. Users can choose how unwanted items are deleted and a special sound for each type (e.g., dynamite blows up the item with a booming sound). This can sometimes make the destruction more fun than the creation, so teachers need to watch the use of this feature. Figure 5.8 shows the KidPix Deluxe interface and a partial drawing of a circus train car like the one Jamie was working on in the opening case.

Students can use KidPix to construct content-based slide shows and presentations, to illustrate a piece of music, to write books for younger students, and to experiment with color, sound, pattern, photos, and text. Examples and a list of great ideas to help students in grades K–6 be creative with KidPix across the content areas are provided by teacher Joyce Morris (2000) at http://www.uvm.edu/~jmorris/kidpix.html.

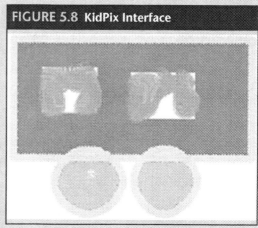

FIGURE 5.8 KidPix Interface

Source: Used with permission of Alpha Smart, LLC.

What other tools could enhance students' access to and expression of creative thinking skills? What assistive tools might be helpful for students with special needs?

_____

_____

_____

_____

Tutorial

CW

Find KidPix tutorials and other information in the Tutorials module of the Companion Website (http://www.prenhall.com/egbert).

Students can use many of these tools merely by clicking, but there are also assistive tools for students who cannot type on a regular keyboard or who need graphics to understand key functions. **Overlay keyboards,** also known as concept keyboards, are flat input devices connected to a computer. An overlay is laid on the board to show what will happen when parts of the board are pressed (or, for students who cannot press, when they are touched lightly). Overlay keyboards can be used for foreign languages, for simple keyboard layouts, for larger keys, for graphical representations of the input, and for tactile or other assistance for students with visual impairments. See Figure 5.9 for an example of an overlay.

It is how the tool is used, not necessarily what it contains, that makes it a creativity tool. Paton (2002), among other ideas, recommends that students build Lego robots as a creativity exercise. In this chapter's opening case, Ms. Groves had her students use KidPix to draw their circus train cars. For more information on this tool, see this chapter's Tool CloseUp. Other creativity tools are listed in the learning activities section.

FIGURE 5.9 IntelliKeys USB with Overlays

Source: Image used courtesy of IntelliTools, Inc..

LEARNING ACTIVITIES: CREATIVITY

Many of the learning activities described in other chapters of this book require students to think in creative ways, but they do not have a specific focus on creativity. For example, the activity in chapter 4 during which students develop an invention combines production, communication, and creativity. However, no specific creative strategies or techniques were mentioned. The activities in this section are examples of different ways to model, practice, and/or use creative thinking during technology-enhanced tasks. Each content area example includes a goal and describes a specific creative thinking strategy or technique (although others may be included) and an appropriate tool. These examples can be modified for a variety of classrooms.

Math Example: What Would Pythagoras Say?

Goal: To show flexibility in mathematical understanding.

Technique: Analogical thinking. This technique asks students to transfer an idea from one context to another. For example, in learning addition, students might make an analogy such as, "It's like when you have a cookie and you really, really want two, and since you already have one you need to ask your mom for another one. You are adding one and one to have two cookies."

Activity and Tool: Students come up with analogies that Pythagoras might have used to explain his theory. They then use Crazy Talk software to animate Pythagoras' photo and make him explain the analogy. This activity also can be done in most other content areas. Figure 5.10 shows the Crazy Talk interface with Pythagoras chosen in the top right corner.

FIGURE 5.10 Making Pythagoras Talk with Crazy Talk

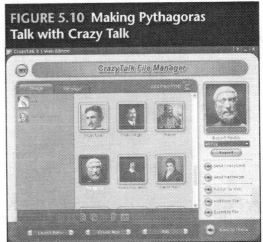

Source: Used with permission of Reallusion, Inc.

Vocational/Life Skills Example: Who Will You Be?

Goal: Use humor to understand college and career possibilities and to think about these options in different ways.

Technique: Rearrange/combine. Students use these strategies, described previously in the process section, to come up with innovative college programs.

Activity and Tool: Students use online college catalogs and put together courses that could lead to a degree in a profession not generally taught. For example, a job as a mermaid might require courses in oceanography, physical education (diving), botany, veterinary medicine, and organic nutrition, among others. Students can use tools such as Washington State University's online catalog at http://catalog.wsu.edu/. They can produce pamphlets for their programs using desktop publishing software.

English Example: Everything Old Is New Again

Goal: Conceptualize a modern version of a classic novel.

Technique: Storyboarding. This technique requires students to post their ideas in text or other visuals so that they can clearly reflect on what they have said and add to the ideas.

Activity and Tool: Students study a piece of classic literature and specify its attributes (plot, characters, etc.). They use a variety of strategies while brainstorming to change/adapt the attributes and write a modern version of the story. Students can brainstorm using a text chat program (see chapter 3 for more information on chatting) or Wimba Voice Board (http://www.horizonwimba.com/products/voicetools/) and use digital corkboard software to post and consider ideas (e.g., Corkboard from www.mycorkboard.com).

Social Studies Example: Alternative Pasts

Goal: To understand how events interact and how history is made.

Technique: Assumption dropping. Students list the assumptions associated with the events, and then explore what happens as they delete each of these assumptions individually or in combination. They would ask, for example, what if Paul Revere *couldnt* ride his horse? What if Japan *hadn't* bombed Pearl Harbor?

Activity and Tool: Students must come up with a plausible series of past events that would have changed history in some way and then carry forward the historical stream to the present. As they create their alternative history, they document and compare it to the actual events using Tom Snyder Production's Timeliner software (http://www.tomsnyder.com). This software is bilingual (English/Spanish) and comes with graphics and other visuals to make it accessible to diverse learners. The teacher's guide and Web site also provide scaffolds and ideas for using Timeliner across the curriculum.

Language Arts Example: Break the Code

FIGURE 5.11 Can You Break This Code?

Χαν ψου βρεακ τηισ χοδε?

Goal: Help students to understand patterns in language.

Technique: Modify. As mentioned previously, students use this strategy to change an item or idea by modifying the meaning, purpose, color, movement, sound, smell, form, or shape.

Activity and Tool: Students type a message using a word processor and then change it to a symbol font and see if others can "break" their code (adapted from James & Kerr, 1997, p. 28). Figure 5.11 has a sample coded message.

Music Example: What Is Music?

Goal: Demonstrate understanding of characteristics of musical genres by creating a parody.

Technique: Exploratory browsing. Students look through a series or collection of ideas or things looking for inspiration.

Activity and Tool: Students search one of the many online lyric databases (e.g., A-Z Lyrics Universe [azlyrics.com] or SoundTrack Lyrics [stlyrics.com]) to analyze songs from one or more musical genres. They define the attributes of that genre and then create their own parody using a popular song from the chosen genre. Different kinds of song parodies can be found in many places on the Web, including http://www.amiright.com/. Students must be aware, however, that parodies are satire, not fact.

Science Example: Home Sweet Home

Goal: Recognize the contributions to physical, social, and cultural environments made by residential buildings and work to enhance beneficial aspects.

Technique: Attribute listing. This technique requires students to identify the key features of something and then think of modifications.

Activity and Tool: Students create an ideal community based on balancing the needs of the environment with residents' social and cultural needs. They can use Community Construction Kit (Tom Snyder; http://www.tomsnyder.com) or SimTown (Maxis; http://www. maxis.com) to demonstrate their plans. The SimTown simulation will also provide feedback on whether the plan is viable or not.

Physical Education Example: Let's Pretend

Goal: To invent a new game.

Technique: Random input. Among a list of words, choose one randomly and try to use it.

Activity and Tool: Students write random words on index cards and mix them into a pile. Students take one (or more) card(s) from the pile and use the word(s) as a basis for developing a new game. They must lay out the rules in a word processor clearly enough so that other students can actually play the game. Students try it, then the creators revise it and submit it to the Physical Education Lesson Plan Page at http://members.tripod.com/~pazz/lesson.html.

There is really no end to the ways that creative thinking can be supported in classrooms and in the ways that technology can support and enhance creativity.

Based on your chapter reading, how do you think Ms. Groves could have made better use of the KidPix program with her class?

_____

_____

_____

ASSESSING LEARNER CREATIVITY

More than 200 standardized instruments exist that measure creativity, but most are not useful for everyday assessment. This is because they often need to be evaluated by experts, there is some cost attached, and they can require expertise to administer. However, there are ways for teachers to assess creativity. Most of the literature on assessing creativity suggests three types of assessment: (1) tests of knowledge and skills, (2) performance assessments to evaluate the process, and (3) personal communication and observation to understand both process and product.

First, because content knowledge is essential for creativity, assessing students' knowledge base is crucial for understanding why and how they use creative thinking skills. Content assessments are discussed in chapter 2.

Second, in order to use performance assessments that are authentic tasks, Mau (1997) notes that clear assessment criteria are necessary. Guilford (1986) and Torrance (1974) propose as criteria the four aspects of divergent thinking mentioned several times in this chapter:

- Fluency (number of ideas)
- Flexibility (variety of ideas)
- Originality (new or unusual ideas)
- Elaboration (adding detail to ideas)

Renzulli & Callahan (1981) support the idea that students should be assessed on these aspects during an authentic task, adding that "unless we reward [students] for the sheer quantity of ideas that they produce, they may never get beyond the ordinary and the obvious."

These aspects of creativity can form the basis of a rating scale. Teachers can, for example, provide a rubric that asks students to generate a certain number of ideas, explain how they came to their ideas, and provide a rationale for their final choices. Students can respond in reflective journals. Another option for an elementary rubric is presented in Figure 5.12 on page 148.

Checklists, in which teachers or students check off criteria when they are met, can also help students to move through the process. Students can self-evaluate according to their performance on the checklist items. Figure 5.13 on page 148 presents a middle school creativity checklist from Intel Education.

FIGURE 5.12 Elementary Creativity Fluency Rubric from Intel Education

Elementary Creativity Fluency Rubric

Use this rubric to assess students' ability to generate numerous possible ideas and solutions to problems.

4	3	2	1
I can think of lots of different ideas.	I can think of some ideas.	With help, I can think of some ideas.	I have a hard time coming up with ideas.
I can look at things from several different points of view.	I can look at things from more than one point of view.	I need help to see things from different points of view.	I usually can only see things from one point of view.
When I see a problem, I can think of several different solutions.	When I see a problem, I can think of more than one solution.	With help, I can think of more than one solution to a problem.	I can usually only think of one solution to a problem.
I can think of many ways to reach a goal.	I can think of more than one way to reach a goal.	With help, I can think of more than one way to reach a goal.	I can usually only think of one way to reach a goal.

Source: Used with permission of Intel Corporation.

FIGURE 5.13 Creativity Checklist from Intel Education

Middle School Creativity Evaluation Checklist

Use the following checklist when observing and assessing students' ability to evaluate the value and quality of their ideas.

Choosing Projects

☐ Considers resources when choosing projects
☐ Considers time when choosing projects
☐ Considers available support when choosing projects
☐ Considers skills when choosing projects
☐ Chooses challenging projects

Determining Quality

☐ Uses rubrics, scoring guides, and checklists to guide work
☐ Creates rubrics, scoring guides, and checklists to guide work
☐ Compares work with exemplars to judge quality
☐ Solicits feedback from peers and experts on quality of work

Communication

☐ Gives good reasons why a particular project was selected
☐ Clearly and thoroughly describes why features of project are examples of excellent work

Source: Used with permission of Intel Corporation.

Craft (2001) notes that assessment of creativity should be left to teachers rather than to a set of predetermined criteria, because teachers can use observation and data records to determine what is creative for each child. Personal communication between students can also be valuable for assessment and for creativity; students who assess another's creative process and product may benefit from looking at the ideas of their peers. Electronic portfolios, discussed in chapter 8, may also be an effective way of assessing creativity because they allow students to store and reflect on a variety of artifacts and show progress and change over time.

However teachers choose to assess creativity and creative tasks, the assessment needs to take place across disciplines to account for the disciplinary bases of creativity that may not transfer across subject areas. Now read as one teacher questions the use of technology in assessment in From the Classroom: Technology and Assessment on page 150.

SAMPLE LESSON: CREATIVITY

A teacher at the high school in Ms. Groves's district, Ms. Farelli, supports her students in thinking out of the box, imagining, and developing their creativity in many different activities throughout the day. She often adapts lesson plans found on the about.com site, particularly their inventors site, to take her students through the stages of the creativity process and to practice a variety of strategies. One of her (and the students') favorite lessons helps students find and create solutions to classroom problems.

ACTIVITY: PRACTICING INVENTIVE THINKING WITH THE CLASS

Mary Bellis, 2007

http://inventors.about.com/od/lessonplans/a/creativity_3.htm

Before your students begin to find their own problems and create unique inventions or innovations to solve them, you can assist them by taking them through some of the steps as a group.

Finding the Problem

Let the class list problems in their own classroom that need solving. Use the "brainstorming" technique. Perhaps your students never have a pencil ready, as it is either missing or broken when it is time to do an assignment (a great brainstorming project would be to solve that problem). Select one problem for the class to solve using the following steps:

- Find several problems.
- Select one to work on.
- Analyze the situation.
- Think of many, varied, and unusual ways of solving the problem.

List the possibilities. Be sure to allow even the silliest possible solution, as creative thinking must have a positive, accepting environment in order to flourish.

Finding a Solution

- Select one or more possible solutions to work on. You may want to divide into groups if the class elects to work on several of the ideas.
- Improve and refine the idea(s).
- Share the class or individual solution(s)/invention(s) for solving the class problem.

Ms. Farelli has used the Lesson Analysis and Adaptation Worksheet to help her explore the lesson. She concluded that these changes make this lesson more effective:

- Although standards for the lesson are not mentioned, she focuses on general creativity standards across content areas.
- Some of her students are more hesitant to participate than others, so she gives students the choice to brainstorm in small groups, either face to face or anonymously on the computer. This provides a scaffold for students who need it and gives all students more chances to participate. This also allows students more chances to communicate and use other skills.

SAMPLE LESSON

FROM THE CLASSROOM

Technology and Assessment

I also can see the benefit of using the computer to support assessment, as well as to prepare it. Performing assessment is a bit troublesome for me as well. I think that for certain things, such as the state driver's license exam, the computer tests are probably a lot more efficient because they get so many more people tested in the same amount of time, with little preparation for the people administering the test . . . I do question the ability of the computer to accurately assess or measure, as it can only do what it is programmed to do. Students and kids are way more creative and spontaneous than any software program! Also, we have to ask the question if using the computer to perform the assessment would be an authentic measurement. Was instruction and content similar to the form of the assessment? I'm also concerned that some teachers might use computers to perform assessments without taking into consideration the importance to adapt or accommodate the diverse needs of their students. Perhaps some students are ELLs, or others have a learning disability. How will the computer treat them? (Jennie, first-grade teacher)

The use of the computer as an assessment tool has revealed many limitations so far. But the major benefit of a computer assessment tool might be that it can provide students expanded opportunities to represent their abilities. For example, students can freely express their abilities by using audio/video tools if they are well trained in the use of technology. In addition, once a certain assessment tool is made, it can be semi-permanently used. And the performance information of students can be easily stored. (Keun, teacher educator)

- Ms. Farelli provides a handout with instructions for students to follow as she explains the task, and she will have students model so that everyone understands. This supports ELLs and other students with special needs in accessing the instructions and participating.

- Student groups are asked to support their solutions with a PowerPoint presentation, a poster, or another product that clearly explains their solution.

- For those students who need help finding resources to support their solutions, she provides some general resources.

- No assessment is mentioned in the lesson, but Ms. Farelli observes and questions as the groups work. She notes who is participating and who is not, how the groups interact, and what roles students take in the process. She intervenes where necessary, so that each student has input. Finally, she will listen to the culminating discussions and wrap up with a give-and-take about creativity with the students.

Ms. Farelli does not give grades for this lesson, but she does provide each student with comments about both their process and outcomes. She believes that the changes she will make to this lesson will make students more active, support their learning more clearly, and make the lesson memorable so that students will use what they learn.

In what other ways could Ms. Farelli change this lesson to make it even more effective for her students?

_____

_____

_____

Like the other learning goals addressed in this text, creativity is important to the lives of teachers and students. Although creativity cannot be taught per se, its development can be supported in an enriched, respectful environment that values creative thought. Creativity, as you will see in chapters 6 and 7, is an especially crucial attribute for students to become effective critical thinkers and problem solvers.

CHAPTER REVIEW

Key Points

- **Define creativity.**
  This chapter defined creativity as the creation of original ideas, processes, experiences, or objects, or the ability to see ordinary things differently. However, these are relatively simplistic explanations of a complex phenomenon. Researchers are just beginning to understand the biological, social, cultural, and environmental foundations of creativity.

- **Understand the importance and benefits of creativity to life and learning.**
  There are both psychological and more practical reasons for students to be creative thinkers. From helping students to find meaning in their learning to meeting standards to making students highly employable, creative thinking skills are in demand in almost every arena. More important, they are needed for quality of life before, during, and outside of school.

- **Discuss guidelines and technological tools for encouraging student creativity.**

  Although humans may be biologically predisposed to creativity, most people have not developed their creative potential. Teachers can help their students in this process by creating an enriched environment, direct teaching of creative thinking techniques, letting learners show what they can do, and teaching students respect for ideas and people. Tools that can enhance creative thinking and the development of creative thinking skills range from the word processor to brainstorming programs. Most important is that teachers use tools that are appropriate for what students are expected to do. Teachers also can be creative in the selection of such tools.

- **Create effective technology-enhanced tasks to support creativity.**

  Effective creativity tasks consider students' content knowledge, use convergent but emphasize divergent thinking, incorporate creative thinking strategies, engage students in tasks that have meaning for them, and provide informational feedback so that students understand their progress.

- **Assess creativity and technology-enhanced creative tasks.**

  Creativity and creative tasks should be assessed in at least three ways—through content testing, performance assessment, and personal communication. The format of these assessments can vary, but specific criteria should be used and formative feedback should be one outcome.

Which information in this chapter is most valuable to you? Why? How will you use it in your teaching?

_____

_____

_____

CASE QUESTIONS REVIEW

Reread the case at the beginning of the chapter and review your answers. In light of what you learned during this chapter, how do your answers change? Note any changes below.

1. *What should Ms. Groves have done when she saw Jamie's colorful circus train car with windows? Why?*

_____

_____

_____

2. *What role did Ms. Groves take in this project? What should the teacher's role be in enhancing student creativity?*

_____

_____

_____

3. *What roles can technology play in enhancing and supporting student creativity?*

_____

_____

_____

4. *What are some benefits that students might derive from using technology to support creativity? Are there any potential disadvantages?*

_____

_____

_____

CHAPTER EXTENSIONS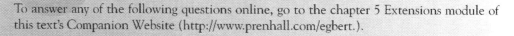

To answer any of the following questions online, go to the chapter 5 Extensions module of this text's Companion Website (http://www.prenhall.com/egbert.).

Adapt

Choose a technology-enhanced lesson for any subject area and grade level from the lesson plans at Teachers.Net lessons (http://www.teachers.net/cgi-bin/lessons/sort.cgi?searchterm=Computer). Use the Lesson Analysis and Adaptation Worksheet from chapter 1 on page 33 (also available in the Lesson Planning module of the Companion Website) to consider the lesson in the context of *creativity*. Use your responses to the worksheet to suggest general changes to the lesson based on your current or future students and context.

Practice

1. *Test a tool.* Choose one of the tools mentioned in this chapter. Try it out, and then describe how you might use it to support creativity for a diverse student population.
2. *Brainstorm ideas.* Write down as many ways as you can think of how to help students develop an ongoing respect for people and ideas in your classroom.
3. *Create an assessment.* Develop a rubric with specific criteria that address creativity for one of the activity examples in this chapter.

Explore

1. *Integrate creativity in a lesson.* Review a lesson that you have written recently. Describe opportunities for creativity that are included in the lesson. If there are none, describe how you might include such opportunities and how you might support them with technology.
2. *Think about creative teaching.* Pick a content area and theme (e.g., science and the water cycle), and brainstorm as many innovative ways to present it as you can. Then, brainstorm ways that technology can help you present your theme.
3. *Match techniques and tools.* Look at some of the creative thinking techniques from the technique Web sites mentioned in the chapter. Choose 5 techniques that sound useful for your current or future students and your teaching context. Make a T-chart, listing on one side a brief description of the technique, and on the other side an electronic tool that might help you and/or your students to learn and practice that technique. An example is shown here.

Technique	Tool
Example: Brainstorming	Text chat

REFERENCES

Ai-girl, T., & Lai-chong, L. (2004). *Creativity for teachers.* New York: Marshall Cavendish Academic.

Black, R. (1990a). But we can't allow 25 different answers to the same question in our classrooms! *Cre8v Thoughts Newsletter #12.* Available: http://www.cre8ng.com/newsletter/news12.shtml.

Black, R. (1990b). Establishing environments for creativity. *Cre8v Thoughts Newsletter #14.* Available: http://www.cre8ng.com/newsletter/news14.shtml.

Cameron, S. (2000). *Technology in the creative classroom.* ED441260.

Clemons, S. (2005, January). Encouraging creativity in online courses. *International Journal of Instructional Technology and Distance Learning, 2*(1). http://www.itdl.org/Journal/Jan_05/article05.htm.

Craft, A. (2001). *An analysis of research and literature on creativity and education.* Report prepared for the Qualifications and Curriculum Authority, UK. Available: http://www.ncaction.org.uk/creativity/creativity_report.pdf.

Csikszentmihalyi, M. (1996). *Creativity: Flow and the psychology of discovery and invention.* New York: HarperCollins.

Egan, K. (2005). *An imaginative approach to teaching.* San Francisco, CA: Jossey-Bass.

Fasko, D. (2000–2001). Education and creativity. *Creativity Research Journal, 13*(3–4), 317–327.

Fogler, H., & LeBlanc, S. (2005). Suggested uses of old cars as equipment for a children's playground. Available: http://www.engin.umich.edu/~cre/probsolv/strategy/mag-minify.htm.

Guilford, J. (1986). *Creative talents: Their nature, use and development.* Buffalo, NY: Bearly.

James, F., & Kerr, A. (1997). *Creative computing: Essential and imaginative activities using information technology with children from five to eleven years.* Dunstable, UK: Belair.

Keller-Mathers, S., & Murdock, M. (2002). Teaching the content of creativity using the Torrance Incubation Model: Eyes wide open to the possibilities of learning. *Celebrating Creativity Newsletter* (National Association for Gifted Children), *13*(2), 3–4, 7–9 (electronic version: www.buffalostate.edu/orgs/cbir/readingroom/html/TIMc-02.html.

Lutus, P. (2005). Creative problem solving. Available: http://www.arachnoid.com/lutusp/crashcourse.html.

Mau, R. (1997, December). The role of assessment in developing creativity. *REACT, 2*(7). Available from http://eduweb.nie.edu.sg/REACTOld/1997/2.7.html.

Morris, J. (2000). *KidPix Resources.* Available: http://www.uvm.edu/~jmorris/kidpix.html.

Mycoted. (2004). Classic brainstorming. Available: http://www.mycoted.com/creativity/techniques/classic.php.

North Central Regional Educational Laboratory (NCREL). (2004). 21st century skills: Creativity. Available: http://www.ncrel.org/engauge/skills/invent4.htm.

Osborn, A. (1963). *Applied imagination: Principles and procedures of creative problem-solving* (3rd ed.). New York: Charles Scribner's Sons.

Paton, B. (2002). Children and creativity resources. Available: members.optusnet.com.au/%7Echarles57/Creative/Children/index.html.

Plsek, P. (1997). *Creativity, innovation, and quality.* Chicago: Irwin.

Renzulli, J., & Callahan, C. (1981). Developing creativity training exercises. In J. Gowan, J. Khatena, & E. P. Torrance (Eds.), *Creativity: Its educational implications* (2nd ed.). Dubuque, IA: Kendall/Hunt.

Rusbult, C. (n.d.). Creating thinking. ASA Science Education. Available: www.asa3.org/ASA/education/think/creative.htm.

Saskatchewan Education. (n.d). *Understanding the common essential learnings.* Regina, SK: Author.

Starko, A. (1995). *Creativity in the classroom: Schools of curious delight.* White Plains, NY: Longman.

Torrance, E. P. (1962). *Guiding creative talent.* Englewood Cliffs, NJ: Prentice-Hall.

Torrance, E. P. (1974). *Torrance tests of creative thinking.* Lexington, MA: Ginn.

23

Supporting Student eLearning

Almost every day at lunch my Uncle Shawn's kids, Anthony, Jarrod, and Marissa, come to my uncle's house where we stay for the summer. Every year they come. My other aunt, Denise, comes every year, but not her kids, Ryan and Emily. My mom's other sister is Valerie. Her kids are Camille, Liam, and Donald. My youngest Uncle is Micheal. His kids are Brier and Ellie. Jeff, my uncle who owns the house we stay in does not have any kids. Almost everyone goes to the beach together almost every day except for my aunt Gina and my grandparents.

Case: Long Way to Go

As you read the following scenario, note potential benefits and drawbacks of using technology to help students learn when they are physically separated from the teacher.

Jim Sanderson, the science teacher at Wedmore High School, is concerned that his four advanced students are not getting the courses that they need for college preparation. He wants to offer Advanced Placement (AP) courses, but because of the school's rural location, small student body, and lack of resources, offering such courses is not feasible. Jim recently came across an article in a teaching journal about electronic learning (eLearning), instruction that uses technology to enhance learning, often when the teacher and students are not in the same location. The article noted districts that are partnering via video conferencing and other technologies to make it possible for students in schools like his to get the courses they need. Jim is excited about the idea of joining with other schools to offer AP science courses, and he has decided to learn more about it.

Jim discovers through his research that his district is part of the statewide K–12 telecommunications system that connects all of the districts in the state. He also learns that the technology class at his school is already using video conferencing technologies to meet with students in different locations. He sends a message out on an electronic discussion list for science teachers and receives replies from other teachers in rural districts around his state who are interested in collaborating on AP courses. Jim decides to develop a proposal to create at least one online shared AP course and present it to the principal as soon as possible.

Answer these questions about the case. There are no right or wrong answers to this chapter preview—the goal is for you to respond before you read the chapter. Then, as you interact with the chapter contents, think about how your answers might change.

1. *What other information does Jim need before he writes his proposal?*

   _____

   _____

   _____

2. *What are some potential benefits of eLearning?*

   _____

   _____

   _____

3. *What are some potential disadvantages of eLearning?*

   _____

   _____

   _____

4. *How could Jim most easily teach and assess students who are at a distance from him?*

   _____

   _____

   _____

5. *If you were Jim's principal, how would you react to this proposal? Why?*

   _____

   _____

   _____

Like many other teachers wanting to serve their students better, Jim is excited about the prospects that eLearning can offer his students, but he has just begun to understand what it involves. eLearning, particularly learning that takes place completely online, often requires students and teachers to have different skills and understandings than face-to-face classroom learning does. In addition, student needs are different in some ways, and to be effective, the techniques, approaches, and technologies used might also have to change. Teachers who may want to use aspects of eLearning need to be aware of the essentials before they get started. To this end, when you finish this chapter, you will be able to:

- Explain eLearning and how it can help meet learning goals.
- Discuss guidelines for creating eLearning opportunities.
- Describe eLearning tools.
- Develop and evaluate effective technology-enhanced eLearning activities.
- Create appropriate assessments for technology-enhanced eLearning activities.

When you have completed this chapter, which NETS*T will you have addressed?

_____

_____

_____

Although the process may be somewhat different, the standards that address eLearning are not different from those that guide all student learning. For more on these standards, see Meeting the Standards: eLearning.

• • • • Meeting the Standards: eLearning • • • •

Although many states and organizations are developing standards for distance education, a widely accepted set does not yet exist. Rather, distance educators agree that eLearning should support content standards and state learning goals in the same ways that traditional classroom learning does. In addition, participating in distance learning can help students meet many of the NETS-S standards such as using technology tools to collaborate, communicate, solve problems, and inquire. The National Education Association (NEA, 2006) has put together some guidelines for eLearning that, used along with standards and other curricular guidelines, can help focus the design of eLearning opportunities. These guidelines include:

1. **Curriculum**—Online curricular offerings should be challenging, relevant, and aligned with appropriate national, state, and/or district standards for student learning.

2. **Instructional Design**—Online courses should be informed by and reflect the most current research on learning theory. They should be designed to take advantage of the special circumstances, requirements, and opportunities of the online learning environment and support the development of 21st-century learning skills.

3. **Teacher Quality**—Teachers should be skilled in the subject matter, learning theory, technologies, and teaching pedagogies appropriate for the content area and the online environment.

4. **Student Roles**—Students should be actively engaged in the learning process and interact on a regular basis with the teacher and online classmates in the course.

5. **Assessment**—Assessment should be authentic, formative, and regular, providing opportunities for students to reflect on their own learning and work quality during the course. End-of-course assessments should give students the opportunity to demonstrate appropriate skills and understandings that reflect mastery of the course content.

6. **Management and Support Systems**—The course should be managed to ensure effective student and school participation. Support systems should provide resources to teachers, students, and parents comparable to those provided by face-to-face courses, as well as special support necessitated by the unique circumstances of the online environment.

7. **Technological Infrastructure**—Finally, the technical infrastructure supporting the online course should provide the necessary tools for instruction and interactivity. The technology behind the course should work reliably, simply, and economically. Technical assistance should be available whenever needed by students or teachers.

Source: Used with permission of NEA.

More specific guidelines are being developed, but for now teachers can think about how eLearning might better help them meet curricular goals and student needs. If eLearning cannot meet these goals and needs, then a different instructional strategy should be used.

In what situations might eLearning not be the best solution? Why do you think so?

_____

_____

CW♪　See your state standards for eLearning in the Standards section of the Resources module of this text's Companion Website (http://www.prenhall.com/egbert).

• • • •

OVERVIEW OF eLEARNING IN K–12 CLASSROOMS

What Is eLearning?

Because learning through or with the aid of technology like the Internet is a relatively new phenomenon, there are many terms to describe it and few consistent understandings of what these terms mean. For example, common terms to describe some or all aspects of learning through technology include *distance education, distributed learning, open learning, online education, virtual classrooms,* and *eLearning.* Clearly, eLearning is not a learning goal per se but rather a structure or context for technology-supported learning through which content, communication, critical thinking, creativity, problem solving, and production can all take place. For this book, the term **eLearning** (short for electronic learning) means that the learning environment:

- Is enhanced with digital technologies, particularly but not necessarily computer-mediated communication software (CMC, described in chapter 3)
- Involves learning situations where interaction between the student and instructor is **mediated,** or bridged by technology, in some way
- Uses technology in an ongoing and consistent way, not in isolated events
- Is learner-centered
- Focuses on students with instructor and student with student interaction
- Uses a wide variety of resources

According to this definition, eLearning can occur in contexts such as

- A face-to-face (f2f) classroom in an online chat
- Video conferencing
- A virtual school that is completely online (for examples, see the Idaho Virtual Academy, www.idahova.org/—a lesson provided by K–12, Inc. is shown in Figure 8.1; Florida Virtual School, www.flvs.net/; or www.class.com)
- Situations that combine these options (see the U.S. government's Star Schools at www.ed.gov/)

All of these examples fit the definition of eLearning in this chapter.

A combination of face-to-face and electronic learning can be referred to as **blended, hybrid,** or **mixed-mode** environments. Generally, in blended contexts f2f time is partly given over to eLearning experiences. These optimal environments allow teachers to blend the best of f2f and online learning. Abate (2004) explains, "The traditional face-to-face elementary classroom imparts the social contact that children need to guide their learning while the online, or Web-based, learning environment offers flexibility and opportunities not possible in a traditional classroom. To create a learning environment using both modes to enhance the learning experiences of the students would provide the greatest benefit" (p. 1). Cavanaugh, Gillan, Kromrey, Hess, and Blomeyer (2004) note that blending f2f and eLearning results in higher quality achievement and a higher number of students who complete the course successfully. Figure 8.2 on page 210 presents online projects that could be integrated into a blended learning environment.

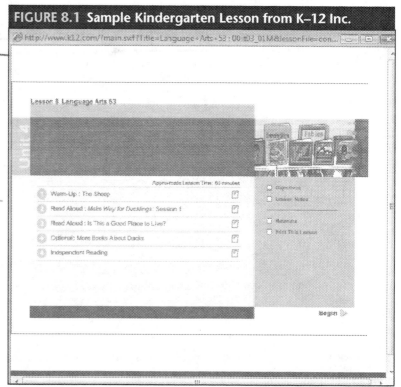

FIGURE 8.1 Sample Kindergarten Lesson from K–12 Inc.

Source: Used with permission of K–12, Inc.

FIGURE 8.2 Online Projects

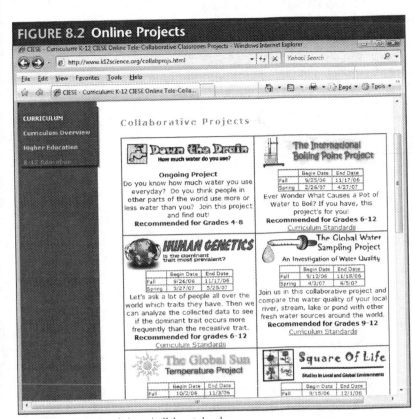

Source: http://stevens.edu/ciese/collabprojs.html

As in most instructional contexts, three general components interact to comprise eLearning:

1. *Instructional and learning strategies,* such as collaboration, reflection, problem solving, communication
2. *Pedagogical models or constructs,* which indicate how learning takes place
3. *Learning technologies,* including everything from Web sites to communication software and digital cameras (Dabbagh & Bannan-Ritland, 2005)

However, there can also be crucial differences between traditional learning in f2f classrooms and eLearning; for example, Dabbagh and Bannan-Ritland (2005) contrast the characteristics of traditional and Web-based learning as outlined in Table 8.1.

Have you ever participated in eLearning? Of what kind? Why do you think eLearning was used? How effective was it? Why?

_____

_____

_____

TABLE 8.1 Characteristics of the Web as a Learning Environment versus Those of Traditional Learning Environments

Traditional Learning Environments	Web-Based Learning Environment
Bounded	Unbounded
Real time	Time shifts: asynchronous communications and accelerated cycles
Instructor controlled	Decentralized control
Linear	Hypermedia: multidimensional space, linked navigation, multimedia
Juried, edited sources	Unfiltered searchability
Stable information sources	Dynamic, real-time information
Familiar technology	Continuously evolving technology

Note: Data from *Why the Web? Linkages,* by M. Chambers, 1997. Paper presented at The Potential of the Web, Institute for Distance Education, University of Maryland University College, Adelphi, MD.
Source: Dabbagh & Bannan-Ritland (2005).

Who Are eLearners?

Today, students of all kinds are participating in distance learning through a variety of eLearning opportunities. According to the U.S. Department of Education, 36% of school districts and 9% of all public schools have 328,000 students enrolled in some kind of eLearning. High-poverty districts are among the most ardent supporters of using eLearning to provide services that the district cannot otherwise afford to provide to students, as in the opening scenario (Setzer & Greene, 2005).

Most K–12 eLearners access their online courses from their schools, which often provide onsite help for eLearners. However, home learners, homebound learners, juvenile detainees, alternative school attendees, and school dropouts also use eLearning resources. eLearning is flexible enough to meet their needs for easy access and alternative curricula. Although the majority of eLearners are in high schools, even younger children are taking part in eLearning tasks in their classrooms. Schools generally provide eLearning for advanced study and remediation, but many schools and districts are also making a systematic effort to use eLearning in reforming what they do across their classrooms. For example, second graders are communicating regularly through email with experts about class content, and ninth graders are working with students in other countries through the Internet to understand culture.

Because distance education at the K–12 level is just developing, the full results of these changes will not be available for some time. However, preliminary research shows that, done well, eLearning environments can be effective for K–12 learners (see, for example, Moore & Koble, 1997; Zucker & Kozma, 2003). Because eLearning concepts and understandings change rapidly and the research cannot keep up, Conceicao and Drummond (2005) suggest that the best place to find out about eLearning in K–12 contexts is to look at Web sites that provide examples of how eLearning is taking place.

Contexts for eLearning

Many eLearning tasks and courses are interactive multimedia explorations among a variety of participants. However, some eLearning formats still replicate the isolating, one-way correspondence course. There is no one set format or way to conduct eLearning, but what it should not (and usually cannot) be is traditional teaching moved to a new medium. For example, in a text-based electronic forum, if the teacher monopolizes the discussion (the equivalent of offline lecture), it is easy enough for students to ignore her postings.

The use of technology for eLearning makes it imperative that teachers rethink how they teach and investigate what the new mediums afford (Tallent-Runnels et al., 2006). Such reassessment is necessary because during eLearning, communication can take place synchronously (at the same time) or asynchronously (at different times), and participants can be in a variety of spaces and places. The variety in these instructional features calls for a variety of approaches, as seen in the three scenarios that follow.

Scenario One—Videoconferencing

The teacher and students at four different sites videoconference twice per week for an hour each session. Students find materials on the course Web site, use online chat to work in teams to collaborate on assignments, and receive help from teachers at their local school site when they have questions and concerns. They fax their assignments or post them to their Web site for evaluation, and they each have an office visit with the teacher by phone once per month.

Scenario Two—Online Course

In a completely Web-based course, students who never meet their instructor f2f go into their course space in an online learning environment such as WebCT (WebCT.com) and find instructions for the current assignment. As they proceed through the assignment, they interact with other students and the teacher asynchronously through the discussion forum. They can ask for help and feedback, post comments and Web site URLs, and participate in an analysis of the topic at hand. They also send and receive emails with the teacher and consult the online resources available in the course space, including rubrics for the activities. After they turn in (fax, email, or post) the final draft of their assignments, they receive comments and a grade in a virtual space online that is only seen by them. Figure 8.3 on page 212 shows the interface of one electronic forum where an ELL student and teacher are discussing weather as part of a unit on creativity. In the threaded discussion shown, the comments are inset to show the order in which the comments were input and whether they are new messages or replies to a previous message.

ELL

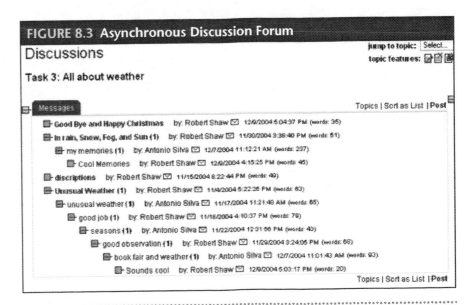

FIGURE 8.3 Asynchronous Discussion Forum

Scenario Three—Blended Learning

In an example of a hybrid or blended course, students in advanced high school science are released from two class periods each week to work on individual projects. They keep in touch with the other students and the teacher about their projects using an electronic forum where they post information about their progress.

As discussed in chapter 3, students could participate in other eLearning activities including communicating with external experts, accessing remote resources, mentoring and tutoring students at other sites, and working in projects where students collaborate with external peers or other audiences. There are many variations on eLearning, but all must comply with standards and guidelines for effective teaching. Blomeyer (2002) notes that the most important understanding that teachers and administrators must have about eLearning is:

> In the final analysis, eLearning isn't about digital technologies any more than classroom teaching is about chalkboards. eLearning is about people and about using technology systems to support constructive social interactions, including human learning. (p. 5)

Which eLearning context might best suit Jim's students' needs? Why?

_____

_____

_____

Characteristics of effective eLearning tasks

Small but critical differences exist between tasks in face-to-face classrooms and in online contexts. For example, Jackson (2004) contrasts content-high and process-high tasks that occur during eLearning. Content-high tasks, the most common in face-to-face instruction, are one-way resource dumps from instructor to student with little interaction. If this occurs during eLearning, students may drop the task or not do well because of the lack of support. Process-high tasks, on the other hand, acknowledge the importance of interaction and communication among students and instructors before, during, and after the task. Employing process-high tasks is a principle emphasized throughout this text to support all learning goals and is especially important for online learning experiences (Tallent-Runnels et al., 2006). However, even process-high online activities lack the kind of student gestures, facial expressions, and other feedback that allow teachers to "read" how their students are doing. Teachers in f2f contexts find this type of feedback essential during process-high tasks and must learn either to do without it or obtain it in another manner during online courses. To address this potential problem, effective eLearning tasks must have carefully designed opportunities for interaction. In addition, teachers can help students learn to convey their intentions through the use of text color and size (e.g., ALL CAPS MEANS SHOUTING), format (e.g., use italics for emphasis), and emoticons, or text-based emotion icons (find a complete definition and a list of emoticons at the What is . . . site at http://whatis.techtarget.com/).

In addition, effective eLearning tasks employ multimedia rather than one medium. If the interaction during eLearning is solely in writing it can pose a barrier to language learners and other students with different reading and writing abilities. To overcome this barrier, accompany instructions sent in an email message with a recording of the message and/or attach a handout with graphics.

ELL

To be effective, tasks must also be diverse and have clear instructions so that students are not bored or confused before they begin. To avoid confusion, effective eLearning tasks should include ways for students to:

- Receive reinforcement.
- Review or repeat any part of the task.
- Ask for help or remediation for parts of the task that are not clear or are too challenging.

This is relatively easier to do in blended contexts because the teacher can interact f2f with students and understand their needs more readily.

Finally, because students typically work more independently when involved in eLearning tasks, extra time may be needed to complete tasks. Therefore, build flexibility into the assignment ahead of time. Characteristics of effective eLearning tasks are summarized in Figure 8.4.

> **FIGURE 8.4 Characteristics of Effective eLearning Tasks**
>
> Effective eLearning tasks:
> - Are process-high rather than content-high.
> - Include carefully designed opportunities for interaction.
> - Offer help and instructions in a variety of media.
> - Include diverse tasks and clear instructions.
> - Are flexible.

Student benefits from eLearning

Students can derive a number of benefits from participating in effective eLearning tasks. *A Teacher's Guide to Distance Learning*, published online by the Florida Center for Instructional Technology (http://fcit.coedu.usf.edu/distance), suggests that eLearning can have the following benefits for students:

- *Flexibility/control.* When students participate in true eLearning, they have more control over their learning. They can choose the pace, site, and format of their learning. Students in many eLearning situations can also choose what they wear to learn.
- *Responsibility.* During eLearning, students are required to become active, responsible learners. To be successful, students must develop skills in working independently, in asking for help, and in interacting with fewer nonverbal cues from other participants.
- *Exposure.* Often, eLearning exposes students to resources, people, and interactions that may not occur in traditional f2f tasks or environments. This idea was outlined in chapter 3 and throughout this book.
- *Interaction.* During eLearning, students learn technology and have more opportunities to interact with teachers than in traditional classrooms. Shy students, those with limited language skills, and those with physical limitations can often have more time and more access to the interactions because they can read and respond at their own pace.
- *Anonymity/equity.* When students are online, cultural, physical, and other personal attributes are not focal and are often invisible during interaction. The online format can be more equitable for students with noticeable speaking differences, physical disabilities, and other characteristics that might present barriers in f2f interactions.
- *Convenience.* eLearning opportunities come in all shapes and sizes. While some require attendance or a starting date at specific times, others allow teachers and students to set their own schedules.

Inclusion

ELL

Overall, research shows no significant difference in student achievement between good f2f instruction and eLearning. In other words, if done well, both can work toward student achievement. However, in a way the comparison is a false one—students do different kinds of tasks during eLearning and they learn in different ways, and therefore it is important to offer a variety of options for learning, including face-to-face time. Researchers are looking into these outcomes more closely to see which factors promote what kind of achievement for which students. For example, according to an analysis of the research on distance learning, Cavanaugh et al. (2004) concluded that:

> Students in virtual schools showed greater improvement than their conventional school counterparts in critical thinking, researching, using computers, learning independently, problem-solving, creative thinking, decision-making and time management. (p. 5)

School and district eLearning benefits

In addition to student benefits, eLearning also has benefits for schools and districts. According to the National Education Technology Plan (Office of Educational Technology, 2004),

> A perennial problem for schools, teachers and students is that textbooks are increasingly expensive, quickly outdated and physically cumbersome. A move away from reliance on textbooks to the use of multimedia or online information (digital content) offers many advantages, including cost savings, increased efficiency, improved accessibility, and enhancing learning opportunities in a format that engages today's web-savvy students. (n.p.)

These are benefits that cannot be overlooked in this age of shrinking funding, teacher shortages, and increased accountability. Of course, there are also disadvantages to eLearning.

Disadvantages of eLearning

The disadvantages of eLearning, like the benefits, vary by context. These include, for example:

- Teachers might find it difficult to meet all learners' needs in a completely online course since some need more structure or f2f interaction than exists in eLearning contexts.
- Learners at a distance from the teacher might not have support for technical problems.
- Students who do not have access to technology outside of school may not have the option to participate.
- Teamwork is more complicated in online contexts because the typical classroom immediacy of contact is mediated by access to and use of the technology.
- If information and resources are not carefully chosen, the learner can be overwhelmed with the amount of information available online.
- The often huge number of discussion postings and assignments for teachers to check in completely online classes might prevent students from getting the direct, immediate feedback that they need.

Figure 8.5 summarizes some of the benefits and disadvantages of eLearning.

In spite of these difficulties, adding eLearning to f2f courses, such as integrating a discussion board or class blog, for example, can enhance effective learning. As Cavanaugh et al. (2004) note, "the importance of knowledge about effective virtual schooling cannot be overstated" (p. 22). They include knowledge by teachers and students but also by the "broader educational community" who can contribute to the experiences.

Read two teachers' description of their thoughts about eLearning in From the Classroom: eLearning on the next page.

Review Figure 8.5. In your opinion, do the benefits of eLearning outweigh the disadvantages? Why or why not?

_____

_____

_____

FIGURE 8.5 Benefits and Disadvantages of eLearning

Benefits	Disadvantages
Provides students with flexibility/control	Might be harder for teachers to meet student needs at a distance.
Builds responsibility	Technology glitches must be solved by students.
Exposes students to new resources, people, and interactions	Some students do not have access outside of school.
Provides equity through anonymity	Teamwork is more complicated online.
Is convenient	Students may have to wait for feedback.
Cost savings, efficiency, and improved accessibility in schools and districts	The amount of written data can be overwhelming for students.
Engages students	The amount of written work to evaluate and respond to may be overwhelming for teachers.

eLEARNING PROCESSES

The benefits from eLearning will accrue if participants pay careful attention to the processes involved. These include:

- The teacher's (or instructional designer's) process of creating eLearning opportunities
- The student's process in taking those opportunities

According to Bowman (1999), teachers and instructional designers generally use the following process to create and implement successful eLearning experiences:

- *Plan*—assess the learners and the technology.
- *Design*—develop learning objectives that advance content to [achieve] desired learning outcomes.
- *Develop*—match learning objectives to media using multiple strategies to engage creativity (e.g., lecture, text, audio, video, case study, team projects, practical exercises and individual assignments, interactive problem solving, student-to-student interaction).
- *Implement and evaluate*—use iterative (repeating) design so activities can be improved and updated easily. (n.p.)

During eLearning tasks, students must:

- Understand the assignment.
- Learn the technology to a level sufficient to complete the task(s).
- Interact with the online community to build understandings.
- Complete the assignments and related assessments.

Depending on the goals of the eLearning course, students will also use processes to solve problems, communicate, produce, and meet other learning goals.

Teachers and eLearning

Teachers must often learn new skills and take on new responsibilities in eLearning environments. Davis and Roblyer (2005) note that online instructors, while sharing the need for good communication and organization skills with f2f teachers, also require a different set of skills. These include:

- Planning for asynchronous or other distant interaction
- Organizing detailed tasks and instructions
- Using presentation skills specific to eLearning environments
- Using questioning strategies for different (often unseen) students
- Involving students across different sites

These needs might require that the instructor learn new technologies and teaching strategies, as described in the following section.

The teacher's role

There are cases where electronic instruction consists of lectures posted online, but these are not *good* examples of eLearning. The teacher's role in eLearning is to be a *facilitator*, making sure that students are engaged in working toward learning goals. In this role, teachers can:

- Build rapport with students by meeting with them f2f or working on a personal basis at the start.
- Encourage eLearners by addressing feedback to them by name, and guide them in finding their own answers.
- Make sure students are spending their time effectively, not spending a disproportionate amount of time on assignments but working efficiently toward the course or task objectives.

FROM THE CLASSROOM

eLearning

Technology and machines have become such an integral part of our lives. There are certainly consequences—both good and bad—that are a result of this. You are probably all familiar with the many online educational classrooms/schools there are now. It just fascinates me when I go to some of their Web sites and browse through what a typical "school day" is for elementary and high school students who stay at home and learn via the computer/online courses. I think a balance is best. I can't imagine how those student graduates of Internet schools negotiate people and peer skills. (Jennie, first-grade teacher).

It's easier to see another angle or point of view when you don't have those emotional cues in your face! (April, middle school teacher)

- Divide classes into discussion groups. More than six members in a group tends to isolate at least one member. Fewer tends to shut down the group in the event two members become unavailable (Jackson, 2004).
- Require individuals to identify their discussion posts clearly. Also require groups to summarize their group discussions so that students do not need to read every posting.
- Create a presence in the course or task. Let students know that the teacher is observing and is available.

Above all, teachers must be able to promote successful interaction during eLearning.

Challenges for teachers in creating eLearning opportunities

There are barriers that teachers may face when first using eLearning. For example, the technology chosen for the course can get in the way of instruction because it mediates in ways that prevent teachers from receiving and providing visual cues or instant feedback. Therefore, teachers and course designers must make instruction direct and concise. They must also take into consideration:

- The difficulty for students of reading extensive text on a monitor
- The time it takes students to type their responses
- The pace and amount of information such as video clips, discussion postings, and Web-based data

To work around these challenges, during course design teachers can work with an instructional designer, a technology specialist, the library media specialist, and even students.

Once the course or task is designed, teachers can and should partner with the students' on-site teachers and counselors. To see an example of teachers partnering with others, take the online tour of Virtual High School at www.govhs.org/website.nsf.

What can Jim suggest that will help teachers of the proposed AP classes overcome barriers to effective eLearning?

_____

_____

_____

GUIDELINES FOR SUPPORTING STUDENT ELEARNING

This chapter has shown that eLearning is not entirely different from f2f learning, nor does it require completely different teaching skills. Likewise, the guidelines in this section apply to all learning contexts, but take on particular importance in eLearning contexts, whether hybrid or fully online.

Guidelines for Designing eLearning Opportunities

Four guidelines for building effective, interactive eLearning opportunities are presented here.

Guideline #1: Build community. Whether participating in a Web-based course or a technology-enhanced homework assignment, students need to know that they are not alone and that others are working toward the same goals. It is important that students identify themselves as members of the learning community whether they are face-to-face with other students or in a virtual online classroom. Strategies for building community include encouraging all students to participate, providing support for group work, connecting learning to students' lives as a group, and incorporating team-building exercises into tasks. Community can also be built using strategies such as all participants using others' names when they are interacting online, posting profiles (and possibly photos) that help learners choose group members and get to know more about each other, and having online chats to give learners a chance to work together in real time.

Guideline #2: Consider the hidden curriculum. In any curriculum, there are elements that are not explicitly taught (i.e., they are "hidden"). These include values, relationships, societal norms, and expectations. These are essential elements that students are expected to learn. eLearning also has its hidden curriculum, such as the cultural and social impacts of eLearning. Questions for teachers to answer that address this **hidden curriculum** include:

- Who benefits from the way information is being presented?
- What dominant ideology, explicit or implicit, is being espoused?
- What is credit being given for in the course? Participation? Writing well? Citing the course texts?
- What kind of student will succeed or fail in this context?
- How is technology valued?
- Who should be allowed to participate in this eLearning experience?

This last question arises from the economic impact of courses that are offered for a fee. Find more information about the hidden curriculum of 21st-century schools by playing the simulation Hyddyn at www.people.coe.ilstu.edu/rpriegle/mysted/.

What aspects of the hidden curriculum might Jim need to be aware of as he creates his AP science course?

_____

_____

_____

Guideline #3: *Organize ahead of time.* Bowman (1999) notes that a Web site that accompanies eLearning opportunities and provides the following can help students and teachers work more efficiently and effectively. This site should include:

- One-stop location for up-to-the-minute course announcements, materials, assignments, etc. Digitized information is also easily modified and maintained.
- Resource and access capabilities for all students.
- A way to display and receive resources which may otherwise be difficult to assemble or locate, such as samples of assignments (good and bad with reasons why), or hot links to Web sites used for course assignments (for example, analyses of corporate annual reports).
- Online archive of course slides, graphics, digitized video, for student retrieval and study on their own time.
- Digitized multimedia that illustrate course concepts, especially those that are interactive. (n.p.)

By organizing ahead of time and creating a Web site with all the essential information and tools, teachers will have more time to dedicate to the important interactions necessary to the success of eLearning.

Guideline #4: *Give clear instructions.* Part of organizing eLearning is clarifying what students need to do and how they should do it. Because students are generally not in the same room as the teacher and typically cannot ask questions on the spot, the instructions for eLearning tasks need to be very explicit and models, if available, should be accessible to students. This seems easier than it really is—classroom teachers usually rely on being able to "read" their students to clarify and add to instructions, and it takes practice to write good instructions that do not need further explanation.

Table 8.2 on page 218 presents general guidelines for writing clear instructions.

Figure 8.6 on page 218 summarizes the guidelines for eLearning.

How can Jim make sure that the course he is proposing follows these guidelines?

_____

_____

_____

TOOLS

TABLE 8.2 Guidelines for Writing Instructions
• Use titles and subtitles for each section of the instructions (e.g., "Instructions for posting to the discussion," "Posting a new message," "Posting a reply."
• If students have different roles or tasks, write separate, well-labeled instructions for each.
• Start each instruction with a command word (also known as an imperative verb). For example: "*List* three alternatives," "*Click* on this link," "*Summarize* the comments."
• Try not to combine instructional steps. For example, the instruction "Write a 50-word description using your personal vocabulary words and post it to the discussion in the task 1 thread" should be broken into two steps—one to write and one to post.
• Write for the reading and skill level of your audience. Provide examples and models where appropriate.
• Avoid long lists of instructions. Break lists of more than 10 steps into two or more sets of instructions.
• Clearly instruct the student what to do when the task is complete. Note what the next task is and where to find the instructions.

FIGURE 8.6 Guidelines for eLearning	
Guideline #1: Build community.	Help students find common interests and goals and interact in productive ways.
Guideline #2: Consider hidden curriculum.	Reflect on the impacts of what is taught and how.
Guideline #3: Organize ahead of time.	Lay out the documents and information that students will need.
Guideline #4: Give clear instructions.	Put everything in writing and/or graphics that you might say or show to embellish the same instructions in a f2f context.

eLEARNING TOOLS

Because eLearning occurs in so many configurations and contexts, many different tools, alone or in combination, are used. Electronic tools for eLearning can include any of the tools mentioned throughout this text (CD-ROMs, videos, and so on). From printed materials such as textbooks and handouts to simple audio material such as audiocassettes to the latest computer technologies, almost any tool can be integrated into eLearning. However, most eLearning contexts currently include interactive technologies such as the World Wide Web, email, and video technologies. It is not within the scope of this text to discuss how to use all the tools that are used for eLearning, but the annotated collection presented in this section can help teachers begin an investigation of common eLearning tools. Most of the tool Web sites include tutorials and other support for new users.

In addition to an Internet connection, a Web browser (e.g., Netscape, Internet Explorer, Mozilla, Safari) with add-ons (i.e., mini-applications or **plug-ins**) will help students listen to audio, see video, and compose and send email. Other tools that can be used during hybrid and online classes include the following.

1. Learning environments

Learning environments provide online or "virtual" places to interact and post course content. Some environments are commercially produced, others are free. Some are **authorable**, or able to be changed by users, while others cannot be changed. Many commercial environments come with preset content; others allow the use of **homegrown** (locally produced) content. Each tool has specific strengths and weaknesses that can best be found by using it in context (most offer a demonstration version and technical assistance for evaluation purposes).

Some popular learning environments are listed here. They typically include some preset features such as asynchronous threaded discussion, internal email, document and link posting, and synchronous chat capabilities. For less structured environments, see authorable platforms later in this section.

Commercial environments
- Blackboard and WebCT (www.webct.com)
- eClassroom (www.eclassroom.com)

- Idaho Virtual Campus (http://ivccourses .ed.uidaho.edu)
- Sitescape/Webworkzone (www.sitescape.com)
- Nicenet (www.nicenet.org; free for teachers)

For an overview of one of these tools, see the Tool CloseUp: Internet Classroom Assistant on page 220.

MOOs and other free virtual spaces

MOOs can also function as learning environments where students can go to practice what they learned face to face, interact with other students in different locations, or hold class meetings. For more information on MOOs visit Rachel's Super MOO list of educational MOOs at http://moolist.yeehaw .net/edu.html. Some of the more popular MOOs used for online learning include:

- Tapped In (tappedin.org; see Figure 8.7 for the campus map that shows some of the places users can go). Teachers can use classrooms here for group meetings.
- Diversity University (www.marshall.edu/commdis/moo)
- Digital Space Traveler (www.digitalspace.com/traveler/). Users of this space can discuss with others who appear as graphical characters on their computer screens.

Authoring platforms

These eLearning environments can be integrated into a second-grade class to allow students to post their electronic work or a tenth-grade math class that is completely online. Some of the most popular authorable eLearning environments, or those that can be changed by teachers and/or students, include:

- Macromedia Breeze/eLearning Studio (www.macromedia.com)
- Moodle (www.moodle.org; free of charge)
- Mambo (www.mamboserver.com; free of charge)
- Sakai (http://sakaiproject.org/; free of charge)

Figure 8.8 shows the Moodle interface developed for a high school history course. Because Moodle is authorable, the look and content can change from course to course.

To compare many of these eLearning platforms and environments, go to edutools at www.edutools.info/course/index.jsp. A more complete list of environments can be found at www.ncsa.uiuc.edu/~jfile/learnenv/.

2. Quiz and assessment tools

Many online assessment tools are listed throughout this book and on the Companion Website (http://www.prenhall.com/egbert). A large number of quiz and survey tools are available to conduct pre- and postassessments with students both online and off. For example:

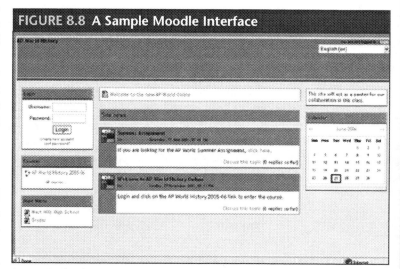

FIGURE 8.7 The Campus Map from Tapped In

Source: Copyright SRI International. Tapped In is a registered trademark of SRI International.

FIGURE 8.8 A Sample Moodle Interface

Source: Used with permission of Moodle.

Nicenet.org, part of the California Community Colocation Project, provides a free learning environment called the Internet Classroom Assistant (ICA) to members of non-profit organizations. Teachers can use the features of the ICA to support both online and hybrid courses.

The ICA is easy for teachers and students to learn and use. It has a simple interface and includes many of the features mentioned previously: conferencing (discussion), email, link sharing, and space for teachers to post assignments and documents. The screen shot here shows the ICA interface. The accompanying main menu appears on each page of a course and allows teachers and students to navigate through sections of the course easily. The "class administration" link is only for teachers.

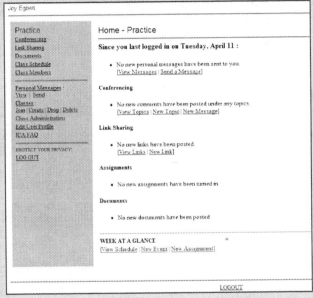

Source: Used with permission of Nicenet.

Teachers have a variety of choices in administering a course within this environment.

A search for "nicenet" in a Web browser brings up a large number of Web sites with suggestions and instructions that can assist teachers and learners in using ICA. For example, teacher Peggy Maslow's page on www.teachersnetwork.org provides instructional ideas and some cautions. In

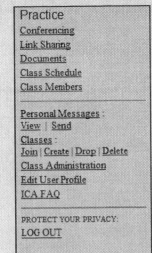

Source: Used with permission of Nicenet.

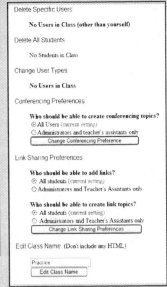

Source: Used with permission of Nicenet.

addition, many examples of teacher uses of ICA are described in detail. McKeand (www2.selu.edu/) even provides sample student comments about ICA use:

> Using www.nicenet.org is very easy for me to check my homework and also to receive my teacher's comments about my homework. Another is that if I am in home doing my homework and if I am concerned about something I just write to my teacher asking about it, and she right away can advise me.
>
> —FA

> One of the best things is that I can read my classmates work. I don't need to print it. Also, I can give opinions. It is a good way to learn. . . . Schedule in Nicenet is clear. We know when we must do something. . . . It is a good way to save paper.
>
> —CV

Teachers can begin to use this simple but powerful tool by signing up for an account and exploring its features one at a time.

What are the benefits for Jim of proposing that his course use the ICA? What might be some disadvantages, evidenced in the student excerpts above?

_____

_____

_____

_____

Link to a tutorial from the Tutorials module of the Companion Website (http://www.prenhall.com/egbert).

- QuestionMark (www.questionmark.com). QuestionMark can be integrated into some commercial learning environments and provides quizzes, surveys, and tests.
- QuizRocket (www.learningware.com/quizrocket/). A free trial allows teacher to create multiple choice, sequencing, matching, true or false, short answer, and branching surveys and quizzes.
- Quizstar and Rubistar (www.4teachers. org). Create quizzes and rubrics easily with these free tools.
- Advanced Surveys (www.advancedsurvey.com/surveys/). After creating an account, surveys can be published to the Web for all kinds of data-gathering purposes.

3. Video and audio conferencing tools and resources

Not typically as comprehensive as learning environments, conferencing tools allow students to meet and discuss as part of hybrid and completely online classes. For example, third graders learning about space can call a scientist at NASA for free, or middle school students in an online course can hold a videoconference with peers in Germany to compare ideas about important world problems. Usually these resources provide some combination of video, audio, and/or text capabilities, and many are free. Telephony software, or software that allows the user to make telephone calls over the Internet, is currently becoming very popular. Examples of free conferencing and telephony software include:

- Netmeeting 3 (www.microsoft.com/windows/NetMeeting/Features/default.ASP)
- CUSeeMe (www.cuworld.com)
- MSN Messenger with Video and/or Voice (imagine-msn.com)
- Yahoo Messenger (http://messenger.yahoo.com)
- iChat (www.apple.com)
- Skype (www.skype.com)

To get started with videoconferencing, check out the PacBell videoconferencing guide at www.kn.pacbell.com/.

4. Digital libraries

Students and teachers can take advantage of digital libraries in hybrid and online courses. These libraries contain everything from raw data to online texts. Examples include:

- Digital Video Library from United Streaming (www.unitedstreaming.com/)
- Library of Congress (www.loc.gov/index.html)
- NASA Astrophysics Data System(http://adswww.harvard.edu/)
- Project Gutenberg (www.gutenberg.org/)
- Visible Human Project (www.nlm.nih.gov/research/visible/visible_human.html)

Find more resources for both teacher and student use in the digital libraries section of www.itcnetwork.org/.

5. Web page hosts

All of the following Web sites host personal Web space for free, although some do require registration. Instructors and students in eLearning courses can create Web pages to share their ideas and work, whether they are in different locations or in the same classroom. There are many more providers across the Web than are listed here.

- Geocities (www.geocities.com)
- Quia (www.quia.com/)
- FreeSite.com (www.thefreesite.com/Free_Web_Space/)
- Bravenet.com (www.bravenet.com)
- Blogger (www.blogger.com)
- TeacherWeb (http://teacherweb.com)
- SchoolNotes (www.schoolnotes.com/)
- Tripod (www.tripod.lycos.com)

Tool CloseUp: iPods and Handhelds

Handheld electronic devices of all kinds are beginning to find a place in eLearning. In fact, the term "M-learning" (mobile learning) has been coined to describe learning with portable hardware and software (Clyde, 2004). From cell phones that take pictures and allow Web surfing to Palm handheld computers, the use of small handheld devices is taking off in K–12 classrooms as teachers begin to realize their potential.

Podcasting

According to Lucas (2005), creative teachers are using iPods (Apple), or small digital MP3 players, in a variety of situations to engage students. One use is for podcasts, or online radio shows. Students can record the show on a computer, convert it to the appropriate format (called MP3) and upload it to the Web. Other users can download and listen to the shows on their iPods or other devices that use the MP3 format. Using detachable microphones and other iPod add-ons, students can record interviews and other audio information, from history lessons to explanations of mathematical functions. Lucas claims that even third graders are easily integrating iPods into their daily schoolwork. One school in Washington State is using MP3 players to send assignments home so that parents of English language learners can listen and respond with their children. The accompanying figure presents another blended class that is using podcasts to learn about history in effective and innovative ways.

ELL

Approximately 10,000 podcasts are posted around the world (Tumulty & Locke, 2005). Many of them can be found listed at www.ipodder.org/. For those interested in podcasting, a good entry site is http://learninginhand.com/podcasting/. For educational uses and how-tos, check the site's find.html and links.html.

Handhelds

Whereas an iPod is really a listening device, handheld computers can do much more. The K12 Handhelds Web site (www.k12handhelds.com/101list.php) lists 101 educational uses for a handheld computer. Some of them are shown in the screen shot here.

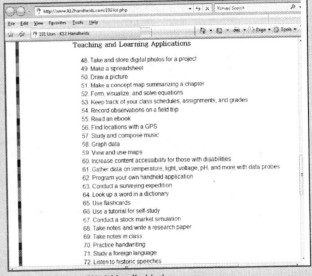

Source: Courtesy of K12 Handhelds, Inc.

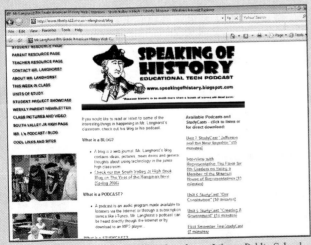

Source: Used with permission of Eric Langhorst, Liberty Public Schools.

Research shows that when students take handhelds home, they experience achievement gains. They not only learn the technology better, but the use of handheld computers also allows students to discover the content material at their own pace and ability level (see http://kathyschrock.net/power/ for research).

Kathy Schrock's Power in the Palm of Your Hand Web site is one among many that provides ideas, resources, and research on handhelds and demonstrates their growing use. For example, teachers can send programs and information to students, and students can use the handheld to organize

continued

Tool CloseUp: Continued

and transform the data in many of the same ways they might use a desktop computer. However, a handheld is portable, underscoring the goal of eLearning anytime, anywhere. The student in the accompanying photo is working on a writing assignment on his handheld computer.

A concern with the growing use of handheld computers is how the use connects to learning standards and goals. To enhance learning, schools must provide teachers and students with the technical and curricular support to use the tools well. In addition, educational stakeholders must understand, value, and support the use of technology. For information about funding, using handheld devices in classrooms, classroom management with handhelds, and many other "tips and tricks," visit the thorough and useful page by Midge Frazel at www.midgefrazel.net/pda.html.

Russell Robinson

How could Jim use podcasting or handheld activities to enhance the eLearning courses that he is proposing?

_____

_____

_____   **Tutorial**

_____   **CW**

Find podcasting tutorials in the Tutorials module of the Companion Website (http://www.prenhall.com/egbert).

6. Content-based learning sites

Content-based Web sites, along with content-based stand-alone software packages, are mentioned throughout this text and can be integrated into both hybrid and online classes at all grade levels. Here are some useful sites:

- National Geographic Kids' Network (www.nationalgeographic.com/education/)
- i*earn Learning Circles (www.iearn.org/circles/ lcguide/)
- WebCurrents from Learners online (www.learnersonline.com/weekly/index.htm)
- Library of Congress learning page (http://lcweb2. loc.gov/ammem/ndlpedu/)

7. Software archives

These online storage places for software offer free or very cheap downloads for education software that can be integrated into eLearning contexts. Not all of it is the best, and teachers need to review their selections carefully.

- Tucows (www.tucows.com)
- WinSite (www.winsite.com)
- download.com (home and education; www.download.com/)
- ZDNet (teaching tools; http://downloads-zdnet.com)

FIGURE 8.9 eLearning Tools

Tool	Examples
Learning environments	MOOs, commercial environments, authorable platforms
Quiz and assessment tools	Surveys, rubric makers, quiz makers
Video and audio	Conferencing and telephony software
Digital libraries	Video and text compilations
Content-based learning resources	Lesson archives, activity sites, resource pages, software packages
Software archives	Shareware and freeware

One of the best sources on the Internet for online learning resources is e-Learning Centre's School e-Learning Showcase at www.e-learningcentre.co.uk/. Figure 8.9 summarizes some of the tools available for eLearning. Other tools are gaining popularity as eLearning flourishes. See the Tool CloseUp: iPods and Handhelds for more information.

How can Jim choose the most effective tools for his AP science class among all of the tools that exist? What features should he look for in the tools that he proposes?

_____

_____

_____

LEARNING ACTIVITIES: ELEARNING

As noted throughout this book, it is not the tool that makes the difference, but how it is used. This is also true for eLearning. Throughout this text, eLearning activities such as epals, virtual field trips, ask the expert, and technology-supported communications have already been mentioned. Like other parts of this chapter, this section looks at the differences between hypothetical face-to-face (f2f) contexts and eLearning opportunities. It describes what an instructional feature or task might look like as part of an eLearning context. The features and tasks described here could be part of a hybrid or an online course. The green text signals adaptations for eLearning. All of the links can be found in the Web Links module of this chapter's Companion Website (http:// www.prenhall.com/egbert).

Feature: Instructions

F2f: The teacher says, "Do exercise 5 on page 6. Ask me if you have any questions."

eLearning: Written instructions say,

Step 1. Read the instructions for exercise 5 on page 6.

Step 2. Answer the question in no more than a paragraph using complete sentences.

Step 3. Post your answer in the Unit 1 discussion thread in the class discussion forum.

If you have questions, email your online buddy for help. This assignment is due by 3 pm on Thursday.

For eLearning, the instructions must not only be more precise, but in writing them the teacher must also try to predict what questions students might ask.

Feature: Lesson presentation

F2f: The teacher gives a lecture about creating how-to (process) essays and points out the important features.

eLearning: The instructor has students read examples from the course Web site and How Stuff Works (www.howstuffworks.com). Students then go to the online forum and discuss

Learning Activities

the important characteristics they see in process essays. Together they create a features checklist for process essays they will write.

In the online environment, this task becomes much more learner-centered.

Feature: Lesson presentation

F2f: The teacher leads a discussion based on drawings of how the Internet works from the textbook's technology section.

eLearning: Students work in teams to complete one or more of the Peter Packet missions in Cisco's Packetville at www.cisco.com/. (See Figure 8.10 for the introduction screen.) Using external documents such as questionnaires and graphic organizers posted to their course site by the teacher, students record important information as they discover it. They post their findings to the discussion area of the course site for other students to review.

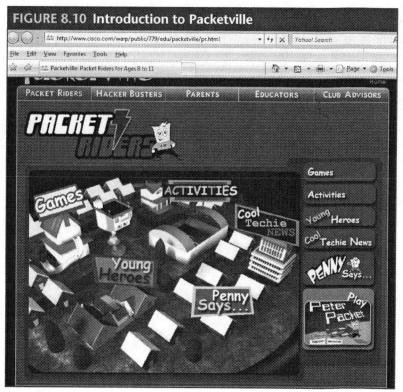

FIGURE 8.10 Introduction to Packetville

Source: These materials have been reproduced by Prentice Hall Inc. with the permission of Cisco Systems, Inc. Copyright © 2005 Cisco Systems, Inc. All rights reserved.

The addition of online resources not only pushes students to be more independent learners but also addresses the needs of students with different learning preferences.

Task: Propose solutions for how to end world poverty

F2f: Students read texts about world poverty and discuss solutions with classmates.

eLearning: Through the United Nation's Millenium Development site (www.un.org/), students work with information and people from all over the world to investigate, understand, and work toward solutions for world poverty.

With eLearning integrated into the course, students can receive information directly from those involved in the issue, which broadens not only their audience but also their potential understanding.

Task: Prepare to study sharks

F2f: Teacher asks students to look at pictures of sharks in their text and brainstorm a list of what they understand about sharks from the photos.

eLearning: Students watch the shark videos from Nova Online at www.pbs.org/ and brainstorm a list of what they understand about sharks from the videos.

The online videos provide a more authentic glimpse of sharks and allow students to produce more language and content than the still photos from the book.

Students can learn without participating in eLearning. However, it is clear from these simple examples that, although eLearning might require more advanced planning and reassessment of important teaching skills, electronic resources and technologies can help teachers to change, in powerful ways, the focus of learning from teachers to students.

What changes do you see when eLearning is added in the examples above? Are there any changes that are not beneficial? If so, explain.

_____

_____

_____

_____

ASSESSING eLEARNING

eLearning requires different options for assessment because, particularly in Web-based courses, the instructor cannot always observe students. Tests, quizzes, surveys, and other standard evaluations can be constructed and implemented with the tools noted above and in other chapters. However, as in traditional classrooms, these assessment tools do not provide the whole picture of student progress and achievement. Portfolios are one solution to this problem.

Overview of Portfolios

A **portfolio** is a purposeful, reflective collection of student work. *Purposeful* means that it is not a folder that contains everything students have done, but rather it is a focused compilation of student work that is developed with guidelines from both the teacher and the student. Traditional portfolios help students set learning goals, encourage students to reflect on their growth and achievement, serve as a basis for communication with parents and other stakeholders, and allow teachers to see how students are performing and plan to address gaps. There are many types of portfolios. Two common types are:

- Showcase—Students display only their best work.
- Developmental—Students show their progress over time.

In each case, the binding element is student reflection. Many excellent texts describe the use of portfolios to assess student progress and achievement; see the Assessment section on the Resources module of the Companion Website for suggestions (http://www.prenhall.com/egbert).

ePortfolios

ePortfolios are portfolios that are kept in an electronic format (video, audio, computer-based). There are many reasons to use ePortfolios. In addition to the benefits mentioned above, ePortfolios are easy to store and access. They require students to develop multimedia skills that support the NETS standards. In addition, they can include sound, video, graphics, and photos, allowing students to demonstrate their learning in multiple ways.

The steps for developing ePortfolios are the same as for paper-based portfolios, except that ePortfolios require a technological aspect. The general steps that teachers and students can take are outlined below (adapted from Barrett, 2000a, 2000b; Chamberlain, 2001; Niguidula, 2002):

1. *Identify the purpose of the portfolio.* Is it to showcase students' outstanding work, to show progress, to share with stakeholders, to demonstrate mastery, or something else?

2. *Identify the desired learner outcomes.* These should be based on national, state, or local standards and curricular requirements and include learner goals.

3. *Identify the hardware and software resources available and the technology skills of the students and teachers.* Barrett (2005) provides examples of commercial portfolio software and other tools such as PowerPoint (Microsoft) that can be used in ePortfolio development.

4. *Identify the primary audience for the portfolio.* The audience could include a college registrar, a future employer, a parent, or peers, for example. Choose a format—Web-based, CD-ROM, video—that the audience will most likely have access to. Chamberlain (2001) notes that teachers are required to obtain permission from students' legal guardians before posting student work online. She provides sample permission letters at www.electricteacher.com.

5. *Determine content*. Teachers and students can develop a checklist of required content, including the sequencing of the information.

6. *Gather, organize, and format the materials*. Students should be required to include reflections on each piece and on the entire portfolio. Figure 8.11 shows a page from a sixth-grade social studies ePortfolio.

7. *Evaluate and update as necessary*. Software such as SuperSchool Portfolio Assessment Kit (SuperSchool Software), Hyperstudio (Roger Wagner), Grady Profile (Aurbach), and even Microsoft Word can be used to provide templates for students to enter work samples and other relevant material. ePortfolios can be evaluated by rubrics that assess each step of the process (see chapter 3 for a discussion of rubrics) and that focus on meeting the standards or on other qualities deemed important, such as collaboration and participation. A sample rubric is shown in Figure 8.12.

Other examples using a variety of tools can be found in the electronic portfolio samples section of www.forsyth.k12.ga.us/ and http://dragonnet.hkis.edu.hk/. More links can be found in the Resources module of the Companion Website for this chapter (http://www.prenhall.com/egbert).

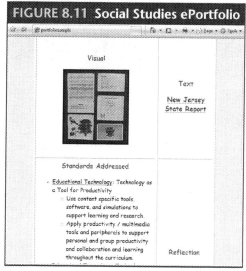

FIGURE 8.11 Social Studies ePortfolio

Source: Used with permission of Maunawili Elementary, Kailua, Hawaii.

Should Jim plan to use ePortfolios in his AP science class? What would the advantages be? The disadvantages?

_____

_____

_____

FIGURE 8.12 ePortfolio Rubric Sample

Electronic Portfolio Scoring Rubric

	Missed the Mark! 5 pts.	Getting Close! 10 pts.	Right On Target! 15 pts.	Bulls Eye!!! 1˜ pts.
Title Card:	Design is inappropriate	Design could be neater or might be inappropriate	Design is attractive and colorful	Design is attractive, colorful, and shows creativity.
Mechanics:	Spelling and punctuation errors are distracting.	Spelling and punctuation errors are evident.	Errors in spelling and punctuation are minor and few.	There are NO errors in spelling or punctuation.
Buttons:	The student project card contains 4 or less buttons that link to projects.	The student project card contains 5 or 6 buttons that link to projects.	The student project card contains 7 buttons that link to projects.	The student project card contains 8 buttons that link to projects.
Sounds:	Many sounds are inappropriate and/or distract from the stack.	Some sounds are inappropriate and/or distract from the stack.	Sounds are of high quality and are appropriate.	The sounds enhance the quality of the stack.
Content of project reflections:	Few reflections include the program used and the main skills learned	Some reflections include the program used and the main skills learned	All reflections include the program used and the main skills learned	All reflections include the program used and a detailed account of all skills learned
Personal reactions to projects:	Few reflections include personal reactions. Reactions are vague or repetitive.	Some reflections include personal reactions. Reactions may be vague or repetitive.	Reflections include personal reaction that clearly reflect the student's feelings.	All reflections include personal reactions that are descriptive and insightful.

Source: www.essdack.org/port/rubric.html

SAMPLE LESSON: eLEARNING

The principal asked Jim to submit a sample lesson plan with his proposal for distance AP science courses. The lesson is to be an example of what might be posted to the electronic forum used for the distance courses. Because the students will see the lessons and use them to direct their learning, Jim needs to ensure the lesson is student-friendly. Jim understands that other teachers have created wonderful lessons for online learning and, after searching the Web, he selects a ninth/tenth-grade lesson in the form of a WebQuest created by K. Nuthall, a science teacher in Poway, California (www. powayschools.com/projects/elnino/ default.htm). The stated standards addressed by this lesson include math standards such as problem solving, reasoning, connections, and skills (statistics); content reading standards such as variety of sources, information access, and evaluation; and writing content standards such as modes.

Following is the lesson Jim chose.

EL NIÑO OR EL NO-NO

Have you ever watched the evening news with your folks and wondered how the weather person could have been so wrong? You wore shorts to school that day only to find yourself freezing during lunch. Predicting the weather is a very difficult task. The many factors which impact your daily local weather can be thousands of miles away, so Meteorologists use a variety of different remote tools including satellites and buoys to help them make predictions. These experts make their predictions by building models using historical and current data.

El Niño and La Niña cycles are examples of these complex patterns. In this investigation, you will learn more about El Niño and La Niña cycles, and how they impact the weather in your area. To accomplish this task, you will be logging into one of same ocean buoys that scientists use to develop their models.

Your Task

You will be part of an expert team. Your team will be responsible for collecting data, organizing it in an appropriate graphic form, and analyzing it for the purpose of making weather predictions in your community. After making your prediction, you will write a speculation paper that details how you reached your conclusion. Your last task will be to share your findings with the scientific community.

As winter approaches, you will be on the hot seat, and you'll get a taste of what it's like to be a weather person. To be successful, you need to ask great questions, seek out the answers, develop new relationships, and take a stand.

The Process

Your team will be taking a seven-step approach to accomplishing the project. You will begin by learning more about El Niño and La Niña. After gaining a solid understand of these cycles, you will log into an ocean buoy and begin gathering your data and building a model. Your final task will be to craft an effective speculation paper about the coming winter, and share your findings with the scientific world.

Step 1: In the news

El Niño and La Niña cycles have a tremendous impact on the world's weather. It is hard to believe that ocean water temperatures in the Pacific Ocean can impact mid-America states, but the national news organizations have reported on the extensive impact of the cycle. Read the two articles below, and write a short summary of each one.

- La Niña leaves states high and dry - CNN News
- Flotilla of sensors to monitor world's oceans - CNN News

Step 2: Background information

Split up and assign each member of your group one of the Web pages listed below. After exploring the Web pages individually, get back together in your group and answer the following questions.

1. What is the difference between El Niño and La Niña?
2. Why is predicting these cycles important?
3. What are the possible impacts on weather due to a La Niña cycle?

4. What are the possible impacts on weather due to an El Niño cycle?

5. Is the earth always in either an El Niño or La Niña cycle?

6. Write and answer four additional questions that you believe would help people understand the El Niño and La Niña Cycles.

Resources

- About La Niña and El Niño - Climate Prediction Center
- Global La Niña Impacts - Climate Prediction Center
- El Niño Impacts - Climate Prediction Center
- El Niño Basics - Climate Prediction Center

Step 3: Real-time data

It's time to start gathering sea surface temperatures (SST), so your team can begin to build a useful model. You will be using a buoy located at 110 degrees West and 0 degrees North. You will begin by gathering today's real-time data, and then adding that value to the temperatures for the last 14-days.

Current Real-Time Data
Java Applet #1
Java Applet #2
Last 14-days
(Make sure you use the data from the buoy at 110 W)

1. Use the link above to collect the today's daily (SST) for the 110 W 0 N buoy.
(Note: When you place the mouse on the correct buoy, the window below will show the real-time information.)

2. Access and print the data for the last 14-days.

3. Calculate anomaly for each day. (Mean SST Values)

4. Place the data and calculations in a well-constructed table. Be sure to include a table title, column headings, and units.

5. Create a line graph for both the SST data and your calculated anomalies. (Example anomaly graph I Example SST graph)

Step 4: Historical model

Scientists have been tracking SST for many years, and it has allowed them to create a historical model that helps them predict El Niño and La Niña cycles. Use the link below to answer the following questions:

- Which two years show the greatest "positive" anomalies?
- Which two years show the greatest "negative" anomalies?
- Compare the anomaly graph you created in step 5 with the historical anomaly graph. Does it look like the current year is either an El Niño or La Niña cycle?
- How could you make your model a better predictor of the cycle?

Historical Anomaly Graph - TOA/TRITON

Step 5: Temperatures and participation

The buoy we have been tracking is several thousand miles away, so it is hard to believe that sea surface temperatures can have an impact on your local weather. Use the links below to investigate how the El Niño and La Niña cycles impact your local weather. You may want to split up the links between each of your team members, and allow each individual to become a site expert. Be prepared to use this information when you write your final speculation paper.

- La Niña Seasonal U.S. Temperature & Precipitation - Climate Prediction Center
- Seasonal Mean Temperatures and Precipitation for the United States during Strong El Niños - Climate Prediction Center

(continued)

- <u>Words of CAUTION</u> - by William S. Kessler NOAA / Pacific Marine Environmental Laboratory
- <u>Cold and Warm Episodes by Season</u> - Climate Prediction Center

Step 6: Speculation

It's time for you to take a stand. The model you developed in step 5 was only for a 15-day period, so you may also want to extend your graph to include a longer period of time. You can access additional SST by visiting the <u>TOA / TRITON Data Delivery System</u>. (Note: Make sure you are gathering data from the correct buoy.)

Is the world currently in an El Niño or La Niña cycle? What are your predictions for temperature and precipitation in your local area? You will be required to provide solid support when making your case. Your group needs to work together to reach consensus. After your group has reached consensus, your task is to construct a solid speculation essay, so you may want to read a few <u>Tips on Writing Speculation Papers</u>. You may also want to view a possible grading rubric before beginning.

Step 7: Share your prediction

Your last step is to share your speculation with the world. Access the <u>Climate Prediction Center Feedback Form</u>, and cut and paste your paper into the form. Maybe you'll hear back.

Conclusion

Good Luck! Remember, luck only occurs where opportunity and preparation meet. Read, write, gather data and create your model with care. This winter you may actually live out your speculation.

Source: Project Design Team: Keith Nuthall, Cindy DeClercq, and John Windbury. Poway Unified School District, Poway, California.

Jim read the lesson carefully to analyze its appropriateness for the ninth/tenth-grade AP course he is envisioning and to adapt it to his teaching context. He completed a Lesson Analysis and Adaptation Worksheet (found in chapter 1 on page 33 and on the Lesson Planning module of the Companion Website, http://www.prenhall.com/egbert) and concluded these things about the lesson:

- The standards, objectives, and task are aligned.
- The standards and objectives are appropriate for ninth/tenth graders. The NETS*S could be mentioned, but technology is also mentioned in the content standards.
- In each of the steps students are asked to search for and analyze data. The overall project goal is to create an informed speculation, an important skill.
- Graphs and data charts address visual literacy; students use technology in new ways; students use a variety of media—a real strength of this lesson.
- This lesson addresses all the learning goals through its emphasis on working in teams, coming to consensus, developing summaries and tables, searching for data to answer the question, and delivering a product to an authentic audience.
- The Web materials/resources in the lesson are not marked for reading level or content. There is limited variety in materials since almost all of them are other Web sites. This needs to be expanded so that all students can access them at an appropriate level.
- Roles are not outlined specifically—the students need more guidance here. A good connection is made to real life in both the introduction and the conclusion. "How does weather work?" is an essential question.
- The raw data sources are completely authentic, as are the news articles. The communication supported by the technology makes the task easier for most students, but ELLs may need other types of input. It is unknown whether the students will learn faster, but they will probably be very engaged, so they may. The goal of understanding is foremost.

ELL

S A M P L E   L E S S O N

- The vocabulary and instructions are repeated, which helps with comprehensibility. However, some instructions need more explanation. There need to be more offline resources and models of finished products. Choices of resources would help students work in different ways, but more choice in other areas would also help.

- The rubric is too simple and does not explain clearly what is required. It seems to focus as much on writing as content—maybe these should be separate rubrics so that the focus is on the thought process first. It would be useful for students to help with the rubric creation, but that might be difficult from a distance. Maybe they can write a reflection based on what they see as the main points of their work.

This lesson has many outstanding aspects. However, based on his analysis and his knowledge of his students, Jim decides to make some small but important changes to the lesson. He especially wants to make sure that his adaptations meet the needs of the ELLs and other students with challenges who will take the course. He decides to make these changes based on his analysis:

ELL

- Link content words that some students might need to have explained (such as "remote," "cycle," and "historical") to an online dictionary.
- Boldface important words such as "buoy" so that students will notice them.
- Bullet the content of the Task section to separate the goals and make it easier to read.
- Create a link to simple instructions for summary writing.
- Add models of the assignments.
- Annotate the Web links for reading level and content.
- Add additional resources such as books, magazine articles, and links to scientists.
- Include more graphics that help explain the goals and content of the lesson.
- Provide detailed suggestions for assigning roles within teams.
- Create a new rubric that includes more specific guidelines for each part of the task, and include guiding questions for students to reflect on their learning. Also include a rubric for discussions, such as:

  Quality (Do you show reflection in your posting? Do you integrate readings, resources, and activities? Do you refer to your experiences and others' ideas? Do your comments add something to the discussion?)

  Support (Do you provide evidence for your assertions?)

  Professionalism (Do you get to the point? Do you use strategies to enhance others' understanding [e.g., give examples]? Are you a positive and supportive participant? Do you welcome different opinions and perspectives? Do you show respect to others in the discussion?)

Jim also decides to note places where the teacher will provide direct facilitation; how chat, video, and other tools of the learning environment will be integrated into the assignment; and how course management issues will be addressed. With these changes, Jim feels that this lesson will work well not only for his students but for students from other classrooms participating in the online ninth/tenth-grade AP course.

What other changes, if any, should Jim make to this lesson? Why?

_____

_____

_____

Conclusion

Bailey (2001) sums up the focus and importance of eLearning:

1. We need to move beyond the notion that education is about school buildings, school days, and classrooms. For us to move forward with not just eLearning, but learning in general, we

must accept the reality that education can now be delivered to students wherever they are located.

2. Schools need to become education centers. With distance education, schools become access points to a whole range of educational opportunities. Until schools recognize that their mission is fundamentally changing as a result of eLearning, we're only going to make incremental progress toward this important objective.

3. Every educational program is a technology opportunity and every technology program is an educational opportunity. While our investment in technology does help schools purchase computers and networks, it is also fundamentally about purchasing math courses and additional online resources and distance education classes for their students. It isn't about the boxes and the wires. It is about teaching and learning. It is the instructional content and its applications that should drive technology, not the other way around.

4. Online assessment, particularly online assessment with eLearning technologies, is one of the next generation "killer applications" that is waiting for us out there. When online assessment results are tied into eLearning systems, the potential benefits become very significant. The result should be more effective use of class time and a system of education that isn't based on mass production, but is instead based on mass customization.

5. Finally, together as industry and as government, we need to be relentless in measuring and assessing the impact that technology has on education and on academic achievement. We need evidence that teaching and learning are improved as the result of technology. Using technology to teach using traditional methods will only lead to traditional results.

As better, faster, cheaper, and more accessible technologies are developed and classrooms move more toward online learning, these issues will be crucial to understand and implement. However, we must also remember the face-to-face interactions that students need and value.

Which information in this chapter is most valuable to you? Why? How will you use it in your teaching?

_____

_____

_____

CHAPTER REVIEW

Key Points

- **Explain eLearning and how it can help meet learning goals.**

  eLearning consists of three basic components: (1) instructional and learning strategies, (2) pedagogical models or constructs, and (3) learning technologies. eLearning contexts range from hybrid classes to those completely online and at a distance from the teacher. eLearning can help schools meet the needs of a variety of students.

- **Discuss guidelines for creating eLearning opportunities.**

  Although guidelines and tips for eLearning can also apply to f2f classrooms, they are especially crucial to follow in eLearning contexts. Teachers must work toward building a community of learners and consider what the hidden curriculum means for the students in the class. To facilitate online learning, teachers can organize ahead of time and work toward giving clear instructions.

- **Describe eLearning tools.**

  Almost any electronic tool, and many other types of tools, can be and are used as part of eLearning. The tools must, however, support and enhance student learning and not impede it.

- **Develop and evaluate effective technology-enhanced eLearning activities.**

  Features of effective eLearning activities are much the same as for those in f2f contexts, but with the added elements of technology and differences in how time is used. Activities that follow guidelines for good teaching will be effective both online and off, as long as the medium in which they are employed is considered.

- **Create appropriate assessments for technology-enhanced eLearning activities.**

  Although this book outlines many kinds of assessment that are available for eLearning, ePortfolios have many benefits for teachers, students, and other educational stakeholders.

CASE QUESTIONS REVIEW

Reread the case at the beginning of the chapter and review your answers. In light of what you learned during this chapter, how do your answers change? Note any changes here.

1. *What other information does Jim need before he writes his proposal?*

   _____

   _____

   _____

2. *What are some potential benefits of eLearning?*

   _____

   _____

   _____

3. *What are some potential disadvantages of eLearning?*

   _____

   _____

   _____

4. *How could Jim most easily teach and assess students who are at a distance from him?*

   _____

   _____

   _____

5. *If you were Jim's principal, how would you react to this proposal? Why?*

   _____

   _____

   _____

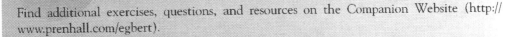

CHAPTER EXTENSIONS

Find additional exercises, questions, and resources on the Companion Website (http://www.prenhall.com/egbert).

Adapt

Choose a lesson for your potential subject area and grade level from the Lesson Plan Library at Discovery Schools (http://school.discovery.com/lessonplans/). Use the Lesson Analysis and Adaptation Worksheet from chapter 1 on page 33 (also available on the Companion Website), to consider the lesson in the context of *blended* or *completely online eLearning*. Use your responses to the worksheet to suggest general changes to the lesson based on your future students and context.

Practice

1. *Give online instructions.* Using a classroom document in which you have outlined instructions for students or a lesson that you have created, write specific instructions that students could follow in a setting *without* immediate access to a teacher. Use the examples in the Guidelines section of this chapter. Check to see if a classmate can follow the instructions exactly as you intended without your help, and if not, revise them.

2. *Review an eLearning tool.* Choose an eLearning tool mentioned in this chapter. Go to the ISTE Web site and follow the instructions to choose an appropriate evaluation form for the tool you choose (http://cnets.iste.org/teachers/web/t_form_software-eval.html). Use the form to review the features and uses of the tool. Write a short reflection about your findings.

3. *Interview a teacher.* After reading this chapter, what questions do you have? List them. Now, interview a teacher who you think has the experience or understanding to answer your questions. Report your answers to the class.

4. *Develop an ePortfolio rubric.* First, list a goal for the portfolio and create a brief table of contents. Then use one of the tools mentioned in this text to develop a rubric to assess the expected contents.

Explore

1. *Avoid plagiarism.* Brainstorm with your classmates how teachers might ensure that the assignments turned in have actually been completed by the student rather than someone else. Check online for solutions that other teachers have found and share them with your class.

2. *Reconstruct an activity.* Choose a lesson you have developed or one that you find for your content and grade level on the Web (see the Lesson Planning module of the Companion Website, http://www.prenhall.com/egbert, for lesson plan sites). Using information from this chapter, examine the activity. Are there parts of it that are too high in content and not high enough in process? If so, revise the activity. If not, explain why the level of process in the activity would be appropriate for eLearning.

3. *Explore resources.* Find a technology not listed in this book that could be used for eLearning. How can this tool support eLearning? Your answer should contain an explanation of the instructional and learning strategies, pedagogical models or constructs, and other learning technologies that could support eLearning with this tool.

4. *Create an ePortfolio assignment.* Revisit the standards for your grade level and content area(s). Outline requirements for an ePortfolio that would help your future students show how they have met the standards.

REFERENCES

Abate, L. (2004, September 1). Blended model in the elementary classroom. *tech*learning*. Available: http://www.techlearning.com/story/showArticle.php?articleID=45200032.

Bailey, J. (2001, October). Keynote address presented at the Center for Internet Technology in Education (CiTE) Virtual High School Symposium, Chicago, IL.

Barrett, H. (2000a). *Electronic portfolios = Multimedia development + Portfolio development: The electronic portfolio development process.* Available: http://electronicportfolios.com/portfolios/EPDevProcess.html.

Barrett, H. (2000b). *How to create your own electronic portfolio.* Available: http://electronicportfolios.com/portfolios/howto/index.html.

Barrett, H. (2005). *Alternative assessment and electronic portfolios.* Available: http://electronicportfolios.com/portfolios/bookmarks.html.

Blomeyer, R. (2002). E-learning policy implications for K–12 educators and decision makers. NCREL/Learning Point Associates. Available: http://www.ncrel.org/policy/pubs/html/pivol11/apr2002d.htm.

Bowman, M. (1999). What is distributed learning? Tech Sheet 2.1. Available: http://techcollab.csumb.edu/techsheet2.1/distributed.html.

Cavanaugh, C., Gillan, K., Kromrey, J., Hess, M., & Blomeyer, R. (2004). *The effects of distance education on K–12 student outcomes: A meta-analysis.* Naperville, IL: Learning Point Associates.

Chamberlain, C. (2001). *Creating online portfolios.* Available: http://www.electricteacher.com/onlineportfolio/presteps.htm.

Clyde, L. (2004). M-learning. *Teacher Librarian, 32*(1), 45–46.

Conceicao, S., & Drummond, S. (2005, Fall). Online learning in secondary education: A new frontier. *Educational Considerations, 33*(1), 31–37.

Dabbagh, N., & Bannan-Ritland, B. (2005). *Online learning: Concepts, strategies, and application.* Upper Saddle River, NJ: Prentice Hall.

Davis, N., & Robyler, M. (2005). Preparing teachers for the "schools that technology built": Evaluation of a program to train teachers for virtual schooling. *Journal of Research on Technology in Education, 37*(4), 399–409.

Jackson, R. (2004). Web learning resources, page 1 of 3. Available: http://www.knowledgeability.biz/weblearning/#CoursewareandContentPublishers.

Lucas, C. (2005, July). Pod people. *Edutopia, 1*(5), 12.

Moore, M., & Koble, M. (1997). *K–12 distance education: Learning, instruction, and teacher training.* American Center for the Study of Distance Education: The Pennsylvania State University.

NEA. (2006). Guide to online high school courses. http://www.nea.org/technology/onlinecourseguide.html.

Niguidula, D. (2002). *Getting started with digital portfolios.* Available: http://www.essentialschools.org/lpt/ces_docs/224.

Office of Education Technology. (2004). *National education technology plan Web site.* Available: http://nationaledtechplan.org/.

Setzer, J., & Greene, B. (2005, March). *Distance education courses for public elementary and secondary school students: 2002–2003 (NCES 2005-010).* Washington, DC: National Center for Education Statistics, U.S. Department of Education.

Tallent-Runnels, J., Thomas, J., Lan, W., Cooper, S., Ahern, T., Shaw, S., et al. (2006, Spring). Teaching courses online: A review of the research. *Review of Educational Research, 76*(1), 93–135.

Tumulty, K., and Locke, L. (2005, August 8). Al Gore, businessman. *TIME*, pp. 32–34.

Zucker, A., & Kozma, R. (2003). *The virtual high school: Teaching generation V.* New York: Teachers College Press.

24

Supporting Student Production

This year for the first time I got to go crabbing. It is very fun! Every year I go to the beach a lot, but this year was different because we couldn't go to the beach until about the first week and a half we were there. We were there for five weeks.

Case: See You on TV!

As you read the following scenario, note both the processes in which students are involved and the products that they generate.

Students in Ms. Farber's fifth-grade class are working on a media literacy unit that will help them to become more critical consumers of media. Ms. Farber has incorporated standards-based content and language goals across the unit and has planned carefully so that all students are active participants in their learning.

Part of the unit is a five-stage project focusing on one area of media—television advertising—with the goal of producing infomercials, or long commercials. In order to focus their infomercials, students first researched and then designed new products that they believe they can sell to other fifth graders (an authentic audience) using persuasive techniques (Stage 1). With the use of graphics software and copyright-free clip art from the Internet, student teams have developed a three-dimensional model and a one-paragraph description of their products for use in their 5-minute commercials (Stage 2). Teams are currently in the process of writing scripts using both print and electronic resources (Stage 3). Each team must spell-check its script and check it against both the project grading rubric and an "infomercial checklist" before asking another team and then Ms. Farber to evaluate it. As the unit progresses, readings, class discussions, skills-based lessons, and other exercises and activities inform the students' understanding of media literacy and the development of student products.

During script development, Ms. Farber observes one team reviewing sample infomercials using the VCR, members of different teams using two of the three class computers to do research, and most of the students working with great animation on their scripts around their desks. Because each team is required to gather feedback from at least one other team about their script, she also sees a lot of intergroup interaction.

In future classes, when the scripts are drafted and have passed evaluation by another team and Ms. Farber, they will go into production (Stage 4). This stage requires the most advanced technology use. Students will prepare whatever scenery and props they need and use one of the school's digital cameras to film their segment. Students will then use either iMovie (Apple) or Avid Free DV (Avid) video editing software to edit their infomercial, add any text, and burn it (save it) to a digital video disk (DVD) (Stage 5).

Final versions of the infomercials will be shown to the other fifth-grade classes, who will provide feedback on which products they would buy and why. After the project teams debrief, students will turn in an explanation of the assignment and a reflection on the different processes they experienced and ideas and skills they learned. They will include any questions they still have about any aspect of the project or unit.

* *

Answer these questions about the case. There are no right or wrong answers—the goal is for you to respond before you read the chapter. Then, as you interact with the chapter contents, think about how your answers might change.

1. *What are some learning benefits that students might derive from creating this product?*

   _____

   _____

   _____

2. *What aspects of the process seem to be most important to student achievement toward the goals? Why do you think so?*

   _____

   _____

   _____

3. *What is the teacher's role in this project?*

   _____

   _____

   _____

4. *What role does the technology play?*

   _____

   _____

   _____

Ms. Farber has chosen a specific process and product for the student media literacy project, but there are many other choices that she might have made. The goal of this chapter is to help you to understand the range of choices for student production by exploring why production is important to student learning and the many ways in which production can be supported effectively with technology. After reading this chapter you will be able to

- Define production.
- Describe the benefits of student production for learning.
- Explain the role of process in production.
- Discuss guidelines for supporting student technology-enhanced production.

- Describe technologies for supporting student production.
- Evaluate and develop pedagogically sound technology-enhanced production activities.
- Design appropriate assessments for technology-enhanced process and product.

When you have completed this chapter, which NETS*T will you have addressed?

_____

_____

_____

The sample activities, tools, and student products presented in this chapter will help you understand how to apply the standards described in this chapter and address the learning goals for student production. For standards that guide production and therefore the content of this chapter, see the Meeting the Standards feature.

• • • Meeting the Standards: Standards That Guide Production • • •

Production is mentioned in the standards in every content area and also in the national standards for English language learners (Goal 2.2). The words "compose" (NA-M.5–8.4, NA-M.9–12.4), "design" (NA-M.9–12.3), "create" (NA-M.PK–12.1, NA-D.K–4.7, NL-ENG.K–12.6, NM-GEO.PK–2.3), "model" (NM-ALG.PK–2.3), "develop" (NPH-H.5–8.6), and "report" (NSS-G.K–12.1) are used to indicate that an important aspect of student learning across the content areas involves student products such as musical scores, written descriptions, models, multimedia presentations, posters, and role-plays. In science and social studies, as in math, music, and English, teachers and students are expected to use the production process to learn. In addition, the third goal of the National Educational Technology Foundation Standards for All Students (NETS*S) requires that "Students use technology tools to enhance learning, increase productivity, and promote creativity" (National Academies of Science, NT.K–13.3). It also states that "Students use productivity tools to collaborate in constructing technology-enhanced models, prepare publications, and produce other creative works." Production projects also meet many of the other standards because they involve understanding, communicating, collaborating, and other learning goals.

How do your state standards address student production? Find terms that your standards use that indicate production as a goal.

_____

_____

_____

 See your state standards for production in the Standards module of this text's Companion Website (http://www.prenhall.com/egbert).

• • • •

OVERVIEW OF TECHNOLOGY-SUPPORTED PRODUCTION IN K–12 CLASSROOMS

In order to support production effectively, teachers must understand why production is important and how it occurs.

What Is Production?

Production is a form of learning whereby students create a **product,** or a concrete artifact that is the focus of learning. Production is one kind of project-based learning; production can be seen as the process, and the product is typically the end result. There are many kinds of tasks used in classrooms, but not all of them result in a tangible product. For example, some tasks lead to new understandings, a discussion, or an action. In production projects, both the impetus and outcome of learning are a material object. In other words, a tangible, manipulable outcome is the driving force behind the development of each stage of the production project.

Products can take many forms, for example, a slide show, photographs, three-dimensional objects, or a portfolio (discussed further in chapter 8). They can range from essays to multimedia presentations to more elaborate productions like the infomercials that Ms. Farber's students are creating. Good products are the result of communication, collaboration, creativity, and other student goals discussed in this book. Production is also a valuable activity in itself, particularly if the products are based in curriculum standards and support language and content learning. Read as a teacher describes projects in her classroom in From the Classroom: Projects.

Because it is a relatively new teaching strategy for many classrooms and contains many elements of other strategies, and because it is hard to measure, there is not yet a great deal of research on project-based learning or production per se. However, the theoretical support for project-based learning goes back to Dewey's idea (1938) of learning by doing, and the components of production have received a great deal of attention in the literature. Learning goals that can be included in the production process are widely supported in the literature as leading to gains in student achievement; for example, *collaboration* (discussed in chapter 3), *problem solving* (chapter 6), and *critical thinking* (chapter 4). In addition, **active learning**, or learning activities in which students do and think about what they do, has been found to be more useful for students than inert knowledge transfer (i.e., lecture). Active learning is more likely to be remembered and applied (Thomas, 2000). In addition, as noted in several other chapters in this text, the literature shows that "learning is maximized if the context for learning resembles the real-life context in which the to-be-learned material will be used" (Thomas, 2000, p. 7). This means that authentic activities that are meaningful in students' lives support student achievement. For one tool that can support student production, see the Tool CloseUp: Quandary on page 184.

Overall, research exploring the use of project-based learning shows that students gain in subject matter, in skills and strategies worked on as part of the project, in problem solving with groups and other work behaviors, and in attendance and attitude (George Lucas Foundation, 2005; San Mateo County Office of Education, 2001; Thomas, 2000). More important for some stakeholders in the educational process, some evaluations of project-based learning show student gains of more than 10% on statewide skills assessments (San Mateo County Office of Education, 2001).

Characteristics of effective production tasks

There is no one accepted model of project-based learning. In fact, it is implemented in so many different ways in classrooms that the distinctions between it and other learning activities are often blurred. The results of production activities can span the range from highly structured and prescribed outcomes, such as a written dialog with five lines that must contain certain vocabulary and grammatical items, to a very loosely controlled outcome, such as some type of new invention. During highly structured projects, students are provided with a clearly defined outcome, which they attempt to reproduce to the teacher's specifications; in loosely controlled projects, students are given a general area in which to produce and have many choices in the forms and features of their products.

Review the project in the opening scenario. On the continuum from highly structured and prescribed to loosely controlled, where do you think it lies? Why do you think so?

_____

_____

_____

FROM THE CLASSROOM

Projects

I use a lot of projects as a means to teach concepts. This approach works for me, because I can have the same basic thing that all kids are doing, but adjust expectations or requirements depending on students' various abilities. I feel that the projects give the kids problems to solve and help encourage critical thinking. I also think projects on the computer that require students to make an end product really encourage this as well. The computer projects have been great for my ELLs. (Susan, fifth-grade teacher)

T O O L S

Tool CloseUp: Quandary

TCU Quandary 1

Henry II and Thomas Becket

| SchoolHistory.co.uk | Restart game | What really happened? |

Theobald's recommendation

The year is 1154, Theobald, your Archbishop of Canterbury, recommends a young agreeable gentleman as Chancellor.

Do you:

⇒ Agree to see him

⇒ Ignore the recommendation

⇒ Jump to a later stage in events

Source: Used with permission of Half-Baked Software, Inc.

The figure above shows a Web-based action maze. It was made with Quandary, a software package from Half-Baked Software that helps users create action mazes, surveys, and other branching learning exercises. The authors describe Quandary in this way:

> A Quandary exercise consists of a large number of *Decision Points*. These are like nodes in a tree. Each decision point represents a situation in the "adventure," or a position in the maze. The user reads the information at the decision point and then chooses from a range of alternative courses of action by clicking on a link.
>
> Each time the user makes a choice, he or she moves to another decision point and is faced with a new situation. In this way, the user moves through the adventure, or maze, and may eventually find a solution or reach a dead end. As the author, your job is to create the series of decision points and link them together. Quandary should make this process easy for you. (http://www.halfbakedsoftware.com/quandary/version_2/tutorial/tutorial.htm)

Other tools, for example, PowerPoint and Hyperstudio, can support learners in making action mazes. However, Quandary provides more focused and powerful tools in a clear framework for students who need more structure and scaffolding. The Quandary interface shows exactly where to place the elements on each page of the maze. Producing action mazes with Quandary allows students to learn actively, to focus on the content rather than the technology, and to develop products that can be used by authentic audiences around the world. Working in teams, students can learn and practice communication, collaboration, and creativity skills and provide a learning tool for other students.

Quandary is shareware, so teachers can download and test its basic features before deciding to buy a license. To

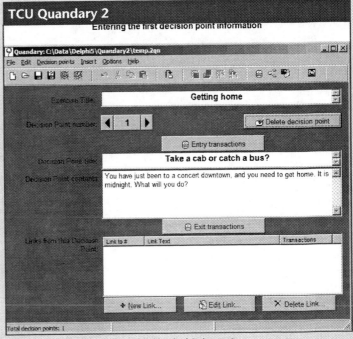

Source: Used with permission of Half-Baked Software, Inc.

help make that decision, view examples of a range of Quandary uses at http://www.halfbakedsoftware.com/quandary/version_2/examples/.

Try out one of the action maze examples linked to the Quandary home page. What ideas do you have for using it to support production and other learning goals with your current or future students?

_____

_____

_____

_____

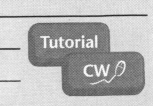

Find tutorials for Quandary in the Tutorials module of the Companion Website (http://www.prenhall.com/egbert).

The flexibility involved in creating production tasks means that teachers with different philosophies of teaching and learning can take advantage of production as a strategy. In the educational literature on production, characteristics of an effective production task generally include those in Figure 7.1

How well does Ms. Farber's infomercial project display the characteristics noted in Figure 7.1? Explain why you think so.

_____

_____

_____

FIGURE 7.1 Production Task Characteristics

1. It is developed over time.
2. It involves more than one discipline.
3. It includes student choices.
4. It deals with authentic (real-world) issues.
5. Students receive help and scaffolding (support) from a variety of sources.
6. Assessment is ongoing from many sources, including the students themselves.

Source: Adapted from Bazeli, 1997; Blumenfeld et al., 1991; San Mateo County Office of Education, 2001.

Student benefits of production

Production can serve as a motivator by engaging students in the process of their learning. Production also allows students some leeway to work in ways that they prefer, helps them to develop real-world skills, and develops their abilities to communicate and collaborate with others. Most important for production projects, students are motivated by producing a tangible outcome. Like other types of group projects, well-planned production projects can result in the following student gains:

- Individual and group/social responsibility
- Planning, critical thinking, reasoning, and creativity
- Strong communication skills, both for interpersonal and presentation needs
- Cross-cultural understanding
- Visualizing and decision making
- Knowing how and when to use technology and choosing the most appropriate tool for the task (George Lucas Foundation, 2005)

Production projects can also benefit a wide range of students. For example, these projects can support the skills and abilities of English language learners. Production offers all students opportunities to communicate in a variety of modes (e.g., speaking, drawing, gesturing), to receive language and content input in a variety of modes (e.g., graphics, video, listening), and to use different learning styles (e.g., hands-on, visual, aural) during the production process. This helps ELLs to receive input in English that is comprehensible, to work in ways that they understand, and to play a role in the project regardless of their language fluency. Project-based learning also helps less-motivated students to "engage in and persist at" learning activities (Blumenfeld et al., 1991).

ELL

In addition, the variety of tasks that are part of the production process, described in the following section, makes it easier to integrate students with different physical, social, and psychological abilities. Students can play roles that most suit their needs and aptitudes.

Inclusion

Which of the benefits listed above would you expect Ms. Farber's students to gain from the project? Why?

_____

_____

_____

THE PRODUCTION PROCESS

What Is the Production Process?

Producing facilitates learning in many ways, but creating a product is not enough to promote effective learning. The **production process** is crucial to learning as students work to understand

and make decisions about the product. During a production project, students may go through a process like the one presented in Table 7.1. The three main stages are *planning, development,* and *evaluation.* These stages are similar to those used in other learning activities, but the focus here is on a product.

Stage	Focus	Steps and Activities
TABLE 7.1 The Student Production Process		
Planning	*Preproduction*	1. Understand the project goals, objectives, and evaluation criteria. 2. Understand the overall project plan stages. 3. Research the product. 4. Understand the audience. 5. Outline ideas for the product and a plan for getting there.
Development	*Production*	6. Students create their product.
Evaluation	*Postproduction*	7. Students and other stakeholders assess the product and process.

The preproduction stage

In the preproduction or planning stage, students may help the teacher to uncover the features of a good product and develop rubrics and other evaluations to guide both process and product. Students construct a schematic that lays out in different ways the various steps in the project. They then conduct initial research, include finding information from print and electronic sources and evaluating existing products (if any). Students can also conduct interviews and plan other interactions with their intended audience. Students brainstorm, draw, discuss, demonstrate, and create a draft plan that includes roles for team members, tools needed, and a plausible timeline for each step. They use feedback from the teacher and other stakeholders to revise their plans as necessary.

The production stage

During the production or development stage, students engage in direct creation, including designing, making models of their products, and performing the other tasks outlined in their plan. Teams use feedback from audience members and other stakeholders and the rubric criteria to form their product.

The postproduction stage

During postproduction, or the evaluation stage, students reflect on feedback from their audience and on the process and product. They debrief, or discuss and reflect, individually, in teams, or as a class.

The production process is not linear; rather, it is iterative in that students can repeat previous stages at any time as needed. In other words, if they find that they need to do additional planning or replanning during the production stage, they can do so.

What other steps or activities could be included in this process? How do these additions make the process more effective?

_____

_____

_____

Teachers and Production

The teacher's role in production projects

The teacher plays a crucial role in the success of production projects. It takes skill to plan well and keep the process running smoothly. The teacher's role in projects can range from a very directive to a more facilitative role, depending on student level and abilities and the project goals. Teachers need to provide guidelines and models for what the product should be, not necessarily so that students can copy them exactly, but so that they realize what is expected and why. To keep students most active, teacher planning should include ways to have students make their own decisions and work closely with each other. The teacher can help students to identify roles and/or to disseminate them, provide clear goals and benchmarks, model both the language and content needed for the project, and provide ongoing feedback and skills lessons as students require them. However, not all students can work so autonomously and it is often difficult for teachers to loosen control; in these cases, a more structured project with a very specific product can be used.

What role(s) does Ms. Farber play in the infomercial project? What makes you think so? Is this effective? Why or why not?

_____

_____

_____

Challenges for teachers

In addition to the challenges of developing good projects, teachers may face school, community, and classroom obstacles to developing production projects. For example, projects often take time that standardized testing schedules or a rigid curriculum do not permit. Some teachers (or administrators) cannot abide noisy classrooms or relinquishing control to students. Another challenge for teachers is to understand how to provide enough scaffolding, or assistance, as students need it without interfering too much; they might also have to learn new technologies and learn how to assess the process and the product. All these challenges can be overcome with time and practice. The guidelines, tools, and resources mentioned in the next section can help teachers understand how to avoid or work through these challenges.

Which of these obstacles seems the most likely to challenge you in your future or current teaching? Why do you think so? What ideas do you have for overcoming these challenges?

_____

_____

_____

GUIDELINES FOR SUPPORTING STUDENT PRODUCTION

Guidelines for Designing Production Opportunities

In the chapter's opening scenario, Ms. Farber has carefully planned the project so that students understand the process and understand that the technology is secondary in importance to the content and goals of the project. Students are active learners; they make decisions, ask questions, write dialog, draw, direct, suggest, critique, and disagree. Students have the opportunity to play many different roles. Students who are not as competent in one area, for example, students whose language proficiency is not at grade level or those who have difficulty performing certain tasks, have the opportunity to work in other areas. However, the work of all students is valued and none of the students is exempt from working toward the final goal. By requiring that learners ask each other for help and evaluate one another's work, Ms. Farber is providing frameworks of support (scaffolding) and guiding learners to use valuable resources (their peers). Read as another teacher describes using roles in her classroom in From the Classroom: Roles.

FROM THE CLASSROOM

Roles

I have used the strategy of assigning roles to students for group work. I've used it in the middle school and with adults. You may choose to play a smaller part in this and list the different roles on the board: time keeper, recorder, etc., and have students decide who will do what in their group. Assigning roles also eliminates the possibility of hitch-hikers, students who just go along with everything and don't contribute. For younger students I would have jobs assigned at random or make smaller groups with fewer roles. Just simplify it and it will still be successful. Rotating also helps everyone participate in the different types of roles available, which you can alter according to your lesson plans and expected outcomes. (Gabriela, second-grade teacher)

Ms. Farber has clearly put a lot of thought into how the media project should be accomplished. She has planned carefully to give students opportunities not only to produce but to get the most out of the process. Some of the guidelines for designing effective production projects that she followed are discussed here.

Guideline #1: Focus on process. Ms. Farber has put a clear focus on process. This is important because often while creating projects, learners may get caught up in the graphics and other "fun" parts of production and lose some of the project's opportunities for learning. Teachers must ensure that the task is devised so that students focus on the use of the language and content that are to be learned and used. Like Ms. Farber in the opening scenario, designing opportunities means:

- Establishing both language and content goals that students understand
- Involving students in the evaluation of content and process
- Helping all students be actively involved in every aspect of the project

To help students get the most out of the process, Ms. Farber has assigned the teams roles for each stage of the infomercial project. Her students are familiar with these roles because they have used them before. Each stage has a Technology Operator, an Editor, a Team Liaison, and an Idea Generator. Team members redistribute the roles for each stage of the project so that all students have a chance to work to their strengths and also improve on their weaknesses. At each stage, Ms. Farber, the school technology coordinator, and the library media specialist work with an expert group (one member of each team) in a form of "cascade learning" to train students who are playing the role of Technology Operator. In different stages, for example, the Technology Operator is responsible for Internet searching, the digital camera, the editing software, and word processing. In each stage a different student is the Editor, who is responsible for both editing text documents and completing project paperwork. A third team member, who serves as the Team Liaison, works with other students and the teacher as a representative of the team, and an Idea Generator leads the development of the different stages of the project.

By focusing on all students being actively involved with content and language, Ms. Farber can assist learners in completing a process that will meet their goals and result in a useful product. Ms. Farber has found that her ELL students, although not at grade level in reading and writing, are very successful at learning and teaching the technologies, generating ideas, and working as Liaison. She encourages them to take on the role of Editor in the last stage of the project when they are familiar with the vocabulary, ideas, and tasks involved in the project. In this way, she is helping them work from their strengths to developing their weaknesses while still holding them accountable for each part of the task.

ELL

What other roles could students in this project play? What would be an appropriate role for a monolingual Spanish-speaking student? What about a student with dyslexia?

_____

_____

_____

Guideline #2: Use an authentic audience. Research on student production shows that students work harder when their work will be viewed by others. However, publishing student products for only the teacher to view generally is not enough to support this kind of motivation and effort. Instead, learners need an audience that is external to the immediate classroom and that cares about and has knowledge of the product, because such an audience will provide useful, authentic, and effective feedback. The audience should also be able to engage in interaction around both the process and the product and should clearly understand their roles in the project. Finding such an audience can be a difficult task, but it is one that students and teacher can share. For example, students might suggest that their reports on the first Gulf War be read by veterans of that conflict. The teacher can ask for volunteers from a veterans' electronic list or a local veterans organization. Remember that providing student products to an authentic audience in the public sector, for example, on a Web site that has open access, means that safety and other issues must be considered (these issues are discussed in chapter 3).

What additional authentic audiences could Ms. Farber use for the infomercial project? How could these audiences be contacted? What guidelines would you give the audience members?

_____

_____

_____

Guideline #3: Teach the tools. It is important that students understand how to use the computer tools that might help them in their production process (see Table 7.2 in the next section for tools). Students do not need to understand every component of the program, but the salient features that support their current process should be clear. This information, like all important content, should be presented in a variety of ways for all learners to access the instructions: graphically, orally, and in written form, at a minimum. ELLs and other students who may need extra help to understand have more chance to comprehend when the information is presented in many ways. Multimodal presentation also addresses the different student learning preferences present in every classroom.

Ms. Farber decided to use expert groups to teach the technologies that her students need for their projects, such as video editing, word processing, disk burning, graphics, and downloading or copying clip art from the Internet. She teaches a subset of the students and they, as experts, teach other students in the class. Because each stage of the project requires different skills and tools, all students have a chance both to be the expert and to learn about different technologies from their peers. Students might see this as just another part of the project, but Ms. Farber knows the power that students feel when they are allowed to be experts and how teaching others leads to greater learning.

To deal with her challenge to learn the technologies for each stage of the infomercial project, Ms. Farber has called on part of her support network in the school, the information technology coordinator and library media specialist, to teach her and each group's current Technology Operator. This way, she learns as the students learn rather than trying to figure out multiple tools herself before the project begins.

Guideline #4: Understand the tools. It is important that students know not only how to use the tools but also that they understand the opportunities that each tool affords. To this end, teachers and learners can brainstorm the kinds of tasks that can be accomplished with tools such as a database program, a word processor, or a graphical organizer. For example, if students were to produce a newspaper, they would need to understand that graphical organizer software could help them brainstorm and lay out a process, but it could not help to format the newspaper in the way that a word processing or desktop publishing program could. Teachers and their students can consider how the use of the tools limits or structures what they can produce, and they can continue to add to the list over time so that students use tools that provide them the most effective opportunities for producing content and language.

Think of a computer tool that you use frequently. In what ways does the tool help you to be more productive? How does it limit what you can produce?

_____

_____

_____

Guideline #5: Scaffold experiences for all learners. Some students, such as ELLs and students with disabilities, may need extra time, help, and modeling while working on projects. To facilitate their understanding, teachers can present information about project instructions, goals, and outcomes in a variety of modes (written, oral, visual), as described previously. Presenting guidelines and tasks in multiple modes provides opportunities for English language learners and those with special needs to receive content and language input in a variety of ways and helps to support comprehension; it also addresses the needs of students who prefer to learn in diverse ways.

In addition, as in any effective learning experience, projects should start with learners' knowledge in content, language, and technology and build from there. Ms. Farber provided

TOOLS

scaffolds by breaking up the task into logical stages; encouraging students to use a variety of resources in different modes such as writing, graphics, and oral language; and providing examples and models during the process.

In what other ways could Ms. Farber provide scaffolds for her students during this project?

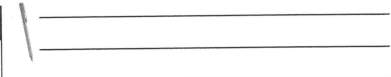

FIGURE 7.2 Guidelines for Designing Production Opportunities

1. Focus on process.
2. Use an authentic audience.
3. Teach the tools.
4. Understand the tools.
5. Scaffold experiences for all learners.

_____

_____

_____

Figure 7.2 presents a summary of the guidelines for designing production opportunities.

TECHNOLOGIES FOR SUPPORTING PRODUCTION

What Are Productivity Tools?

Ms. Farber's students used a variety of tools in creating their media projects, all of which were suited to a particular stage or process. **Productivity tools** are those that maximize or extend students' ability to create products and to solve problems. They also "expand opportunities for expression" (Male, 1997, p. viii), which is an important principle for learning. With productivity tools, students can construct models, publish, plan and organize, map concepts, generate materials, collect data, and develop and present their work. Electronic productivity tools include hardware such as digital cameras and video recorders and many different kinds of software. Many teachers are familiar with at least some of the commonly used productivity software packages in Table 7.2.

It is important to note that the production process does not inherently require the use of technology. Rather, technology is used as it fits into the plan and makes the process more effective and/or more efficient. In developing activities that result in a student product, teachers and students should reflect on *why* they might use technology during the process. As discussed earlier in this book, if the technology does not make the teaching and learning more effective or more efficient, other tools should be considered.

There are many more examples in each category of production tools, including some that are made specifically for different student grade and ability levels. Different schools and classrooms may have entirely different sets of these tools, but they work in similar ways. The tools presented in Table 7.2 do not *necessarily* make learner products better or more creative, but they can be more professional and easier to share with others. Some research shows that learners are encouraged to produce more while using such tools. The more output students produce, the more opportunities they have to learn both content and language.

Student examples

Student iMovie products in a number of content areas can be found on the Springfield, Illinois, school district Web site at http://www.springfield.k12.il.us/movie/. Art, English, math, science, music, and social studies projects are represented. The site also includes tips from teachers, including using iMovie in the science classroom and making commercials with iMovie.

Some interesting high school projects using PowerPoint in a variety of content areas, along with hints and tips on using PowerPoint in the classroom, are found on Jerry Taylor's PowerPoint Projects (2000) page. Others from the same Greece, New York, school district can be found at http://www.greece.k12.ny.us/webworld2000/projects.htm.

Tools for teachers

Productivity tools also provide opportunities for teachers. All of the technologies mentioned in Table 7.2, along with grading programs and worksheet and puzzle-making software, assist teachers in creating products to use in their classes and in being more effective in their instruction (see chapter 9 for more on teacher tools).

TABLE 7.2 Examples of Productivity Software

Tool and Examples	Description	Sample Classroom Uses
Word processor: Microsoft Word, Word Perfect, Appleworks, Text Edit, OpenOffice Write	Used to create, edit, format, and print documents, most commonly text documents.	Students produce letters, essays, reports, and reflections. Can be used to format newsletters, create simple stories, and format handouts.
Database: Access, OpenOffice Base	Stores and organizes information; an electronic filing system in which users can search for and report on specific aspects of the information.	Students can use a database to input information collected from surveys, to make phone lists of class members, to make schedules, or to save data over time.
Spreadsheet: Excel, OpenOffice Calc	Organizes and relates information based on mathematical formulas; used in grade books and other applications where calculations are needed. Users can also make graphs and charts from the data.	Students can produce graphs and charts to support their presentations, make mathematical calculations on data, and keep records of their grades during the semester.
Desktop publisher: Printshop 22, Microsoft Publisher	Like a word processor but typically includes more templates, more powerful graphics capabilities, and greater freedom of layout.	Students can produce pamphlets, newspapers with photos, posters, bumper stickers, and almost anything that uses graphics and text.
Authoring software: Hot Potatoes (Half-Baked Software), Hyperstudio (Roger Wagner), Quandary	Also called authorware, these programs are typically more open-ended and more powerful than presentation software. They allow users to create software applications.	Students can produce action mazes, electronic quizzes, and multimedia presentations in addition to talking books, electronic portfolios, and interactive games.
Presentation packages: PowerPoint, KidPix, OpenOffice Impress	Allows the user to create slide shows that include sound, graphics, and text. These can range from simple to highly choreographed.	Students can produce narrated stories, multimedia presentations, action mazes, and simple slides.
HTML editors or Web page makers: Composer, FrontPage, Nvu	These programs allow the user to make documents for the World Wide Web.	Students can produce WebQuests, school information pages, electronic resumes.
Bookmaking software: Storybook Weaver Deluxe 2004 (Riverdeep) or the Edmark/Riverdeep Imagination Express series	These software programs are preformatted as books to which students can add graphics, text, and sound. The format provides scaffolds for students.	Students produce electronic books of any length and can include narrative text and sound, music, and even moving elements.
Video and video editing: iMovie, Avid, Microsoft Movie Maker, Visual Communicator	Video editing software allows the user to manipulate video images, including editing and moving frames and adding text and other special effects.	Students can produce short or long music videos or commercials, document some aspect of school life, support a presentation, or tell a video story.
Graphical organizer software: Kidspiration, Inspiration (See the Tool CloseUp feature for more information on this software program)	These programs support users in constructing concept maps and organizers of all kinds.	Among many other uses, students can use this software to brainstorm before reading a text, to plan or outline a task, and to categorize sets of items.

Tutorial
CW

Overcoming challenges

With all the guidelines to follow and possible challenges to face, teachers might find creating and using production projects supported by technology overwhelming at this point. However, if teachers build on standards for content and language learning, focus on the process, provide effective scaffolds, and encourage the *principled use of technology* (in other words, grounded in research, standards, and effective practice), they can create an almost limitless number of possibilities for projects that can be effective learning experiences. In addition to those presented in the following section, activities in other chapters throughout this text also support production.

LEARNING ACTIVITIES: PRODUCTION PROJECTS

The production projects described here are not addressed to specific grade or language levels—those for which they are appropriate is a choice that the teacher, knowing her students well, can make. Instead, the multidisciplinary activities are grouped initially by the content area that is most central to the project. Sample emphases for goals in both content and language are provided for each project; these are the focus of task development and tool use. After the product is presented, the examples in each content area are divided into one of three technology categories. Examples in each content area include

- One that employs *basic technologies* (those that involve simple or few features that are generic across many tools)
- One that uses relatively *more sophisticated technologies* (those that require additional features or multiple tools or are relatively new)
- One that could use *advanced technologies* (those that require more in-depth knowledge of the tool or tools that are more complicated)

This format demonstrates that production is not a result of the technology used, but that the technology use is based on the task goals and structure.

The project descriptions do not state the teacher's role, the challenges that teachers may face, how scaffolding should be done, or specific name brands for each project. Think about these aspects as you read the project descriptions, and be prepared to answer the question at the end of this section.

··

English

1. Content and language goals: *Culture, media, adjective use, descriptive writing*
Product: Movie flyer
Basic technologies: Word processor or simple graphics program

Students complete the following process:

- Review movie flyers and advertisements.
- Choose a theme for a movie that they would like to see.
- Develop text about their movie that fits with the genre.
- Use a word processor to type their text and use appropriate fonts and styles, leaving room for any photos or graphics.
- Add fonts/graphics.
- Work with other students to review and revise their poster.

Students can produce very inventive products in this project. Follow up by posting the flyers around the room and letting students comment on which movies they might like to see and why.

2. Content and language goals: *Genres, elements of story, peer editing*
Product: Digital montage

Sophisticated technologies: Word processor, simple authoring program, presentation program, digital camera (optional)

Students work in cooperative groups to:

- Develop themes or stories in a chosen genre.

489

- Develop auto-play presentations with graphics, sound, and text.
- Edit with peers.
- Share with the intended audience.

These tools permit a fairly basic montage, typically slide by slide. Classes of younger children often make a very authentic audience for this activity.

3. Content and language goals: Summary, dialog, culture, text comprehension

Product: Five-minute movie trailer

Advanced technologies: Word processor, digital editor, CD burner and software, digital cameras/ video recorders

Students work together to:

- Create the script for a five-minute movie based on a book they have read.
- Develop costumes and scenery as needed.
- Film the movie.
- Edit the movie and burn it to a CD or DVD.
- Share the movie with the intended audience.

The moviemaking/video editing software seems to be a sophisticated technology, but it is actually easy to use—it can be expensive, however, and many people tend to associate expensive technologies with higher levels of technical skill. Avid DV, mentioned in the opening case, is free video editing software for the PC, as is iMovie for Macintosh computers. This activity is an excellent assessment and provides a different take on postreading activities.

Social studies

1. Content and language goals: Idioms, slang, humor, current events/politics

Product: Magnets and bumper stickers

Basic technologies: Word processing software with magnet or bumper sticker paper

After researching and discussing a current event and related language, students:

- Develop a slogan or saying, explain the meaning and purpose of the slogan.
- Revise based on classmates' or others' comments.
- Type their sayings into a word processor and print.
- Display for an appropriate audience.

Even students with less advanced English proficiency can come up with some witty and thoughtful sayings for this activity. Other content areas can also make use of this kind of task. See Figure 7.3 for an example of a bumper sticker that questions the "top-down" view of maps and globes.

2. Content and language goals: Reporting, five W's (who, what, where, when, and why), historical facts, extrapolation

Product: Simple newsletter for a historical organization

Sophisticated technologies: Desktop publishing software, Web search engines, scanner

Creating a newsletter is a common activity in many classes in which students:

FIGURE 7.3 Sample Bumper Sticker

Why is *North* "up"?

Let's look at the world in new ways.

- Collect historical information from both electronic and print resources.
- Type their articles using a word processor.
- Include whatever graphics are necessary, using a scanner if available.
- Edit, headline, and lay out the articles.
- Print, copy, and deliver the newsletter to relevant readers.

Simple newsletters are often the most interesting. This activity includes many different roles that can assist ELLs and other students who need extra time or feedback to complete their tasks.

ELL

3. Content and language goals: Reported speech and other genres, current events, humor, titles

Product: A newspaper, complete with political commentary, cartoons, features, and ads

FIGURE 7.4 Student Product

Peru

By: Johanna

Read and learn about Peru by using the links.

You can find interesting facts about the country and it's people.

- *Learn about Peru's government. How is it the same?*
- *Read about the people. What do they do for work?*
- *See a physical and political map.*
- *What does Peru sell? Look at it's economy.*
- *Read about a famous person in Peru.*
- *Learn about Peru's history.*
- *Back to Latin America home page.*

Source: Used with permission of Kent School District.

Advanced technologies: Depends on content, but a desktop publishing package, graphics package, word processor, digital image editing software, and others could be used

Students

- Create and assign job responsibilities.
- Collect historical information from print, electronic, and human resources.
- Create their part of the newspaper using appropriate technology.
- Work with team members to revise and improve their work.
- Edit; write headlines, captions, bylines; and design the layout.
- Print, copy, and deliver; solicit feedback.

Students can publish more than one issue during a semester, or use the one issue as a springboard for additional projects and discussion. Roles can change during the additional issues as students learn and become more comfortable with different language and tasks.

Social Studies Sample: Latin America Projects

Sixth-grade students in Washington State's Kent School District present their Latin American projects at http://www.kent .k12.wa.us/. The products are simply designed examples of research that the students did to explore countries in Latin America. Figure 7.4 presents an example of one student's product.

Science

1. Content and language goals: Descriptive language, inventions
Product: New invention
Basic technologies: Word processing, paint program (optional)

During a unit on inventors, learners:

- Design a new invention that they would like to use.
- Type a clear and complete description of the invention.
- Have another student try to draw their invention from the description.
- Revise.
- Post so that other students can try to draw it.
- Compile the drawings and descriptions into a catalog.

This activity allows learners to write as much or as little as they can and practice process writing while focusing on science content. The catalog can be used for a variety of follow-up activities, such as writing stories about the new inventions, calculating costs of making the product, and so on.

2. Content and language goals: Patents, inventions, persuasive language, descriptive language
Product: Patent application
Sophisticated technologies: Desktop publishing software, graphics software, scanner

In teams, students:

- Explain their inventions clearly in text, comparing them to existing inventions as necessary.
- Draw their inventions, scan, and import their pictures to their application document.
- Complete a patent application form.

- Receive feedback from evaluators (e.g., local experts, the teacher, other students) who decide which should be awarded patents and which need more work and why.
- Revise.

Students can have roles that help them to perform their project tasks.

3. Content and language goals: Instructions, imperatives, inventions, and inventors

Product: A WebQuest

Advanced technologies: An electronic encyclopedia, word processing and graphics software, HTML editor, or Web page creation software

After working with WebQuests, student teams:

- Review criteria for WebQuests.
- Download appropriate templates from Bernie Dodge's WebQuest site at http://webquest.sdsu.edu (see Figure 7.5).
- Develop a plan for creating a science WebQuest.
- Design each section, using and including appropriate resources.
- Complete and post their WebQuests for evaluation.

Student teams can also choose one segment of a whole-class WebQuest project to work on, or they can improve a WebQuest that they have participated in.

FIGURE 7.5 Part of a Generic WebQuest Template

Put the Title of the Lesson Here

A WebQuest for _____th Grade
(Put Subject Here)

Put some interesting graphic
representing the content here

Designed by Put Your Name Here

Put Your E-mail Address Here

Introduction | Task | Process | Evaluation | Conclusion |
Credits | Teacher Page

Introduction

This document should be written with the student as the intended audience. Write a short paragraph here to introduce the activity or lesson to the students. If there is a role or scenario involved (e.g., "You are a detective trying to identify the mysterious poet.") then here is where you'll set the stage. If there's no motivational intro like that, use this section to provide a short advance organizer or overview.

Remember that the purpose of this section is to both prepare and hook the reader. It is also in this section that you'll communicate the Big Question (Essential Question, Guiding Question) that the whole WebQuest is centered around.

Task

Describe crisply and clearly what the end result of the learners' activities will be. The task could be a:

- problem or mystery to be solved;
- position to be formulated and defended;
- product to be designed;
- complexity to be analyzed;
- personal insight to be articulated;
- summary to be created;
- persuasive message or journalistic account to be crafted;
- a creative work, or
- anything that requires the learners to process and transform the information they've gathered.

If the final product involves using some tool (e.g., HyperStudio, the Web, video), mention it here.

Source: Used with permission of Bernie Dodge, San Diego State University.

FIGURE 7.6 Examples from the Clean Communities Project

Examples of Student Projects

Source: Used with permission of iEARN-USA.

Science Sample: International Clean Communities Project

In one science-based project, secondary students in Belarus and the United States worked together online and traveled to work face to face to understand waste management around the world and increase communication between these countries about environmental issues. One outcome from their project was student-made posters addressing their concerns. Figure 7.6 presents examples of the posters produced by the students.

Math

1. Content and language goals: Connectors, story writing, discussion, word problems

Product: Action mazes

Basic technologies: Presentation software or a word processor (can also be done in HTML or with an authoring program)

In an action maze, students must solve math puzzles and choose the correct answer to follow a story line. To make their own action mazes, in collaborative groups, students:

- Decide on a math focus, content topic, and layout for their maze.
- Write the text and decide how it will branch at decision points.
- Find or create necessary graphics.
- Create the maze in an authoring program (refer to Table 7.2 on page 191 for suggestions).
- Share it with peers.

Producing and using action mazes (Egbert, 1995; Healey, 2002; Holmes, 2002) can facilitate discussion, collaboration, and creativity in both the creators and the users.

2. Content and language goals: Question formation, percentage, graphs, reporting

Product: Peer survey

Sophisticated technologies: Spreadsheet

Students choose an issue that is important to them and:

- Design a survey to gather student opinions.
- Interview peers or other target audience.
- Use a spreadsheet to calculate results and make graphs.
- Present the results to the administration or other authentic audience.

Students can propose a new traffic light in front of the school, additions to the cafeteria offerings, or new books for the school library while working on math content and language.

3. Content and language goals: Area, house vocabulary, measurement

Product: House design

Advanced technologies: A computer-aided design program

The teacher assigns a specific total house area, and students:

- Brainstorm and/or research the kinds of rooms and their relative sizes that people might want in a home.
- Work with the CAD program to create their house to the specifications.
- Revise to meet the total house area given.
- Present the house plan to an authentic audience.

By creating and producing with other students who have different backgrounds and ideas, learners improve their content knowledge and language abilities while also increasing their cultural capital.

Student Sample: Math Tessellations

Teachers and elementary school students in grades 4 and 5 at Fairland Elementary in Maryland present examples of student products across content areas at http://www.towson.edu/csme/mctp/StudentProjects/FairlandHomePage.html. From tessellations to tall tales, this site has a great variety of interesting products. The site also provides project outlines for teachers to use in developing similar projects. Figure 7.7 presents one of the student tessellations.

Production projects can also be designed to address specific topics and language areas. Following are examples of language skills and vocational skills learning.

FIGURE 7.7 Tweety on Parade

Source: Used with permission of the Center for Science & Mathematics Education, Towson University.

Language skills

1. Content and language goals: Vocabulary, definitions, spelling

Product: Puzzle

Basic technologies: A puzzlemaker program

Students use the vocabulary under study and:

- Choose a puzzle type.
- Create the puzzle text (typically clues or definitions for each word).
- Create the puzzle.
- Share it with peers.

Students are active when the teacher allows them to take responsibility for their learning, including creating opportunities for practice and assessment.

2. Content and language goals: Story elements, sentence formation, cohesive devices

Product: A book

Sophisticated technologies: A book publishing program

Students work with a given topic or develop one of their own into a book. Students:

- Complete a storyboard with text and possible graphics (a sample storyboard is shown in Figure 7.8).
- Revise for grammar and surface features.
- Create the title, text, and graphics in the software.
- Edit as necessary.

Students can share their books with parents or students in another class or grade level. Using software available for different technical levels and language abilities can make this project easy and structured.

3. Content and language goals: Question and statement formation, explaining

Product: Interactive quizzes

Advanced technologies: A Web page composer program or another authoring/authorable software package

Working alone or in groups, students:

- Choose the format, questions, and answers for their quiz and decide on the type of feedback to be provided.
- Create their quiz.
- Give their quiz and take those that other students have made to study for the teacher's version.

Like the simpler puzzlemaker, the products in this project help students study, practice, and review. They can also reinforce correct answers and help learners to understand plausible mistakes.

FIGURE 7.8 A Sample Storyboard

Visual:	Visual:	Visual:
Text:	Text:	Text:
Visual:	Visual:	Visual:
Text:	Text:	Text:

FIGURE 7.9 A Sample Student Business Card

Jicela Cortez, Lawyer
Civil Rights and Immigration
Cortez Law Firm
Los Angeles, CA

"Bilingual and Honest"

Vocational skills (community/business)

1. Content and language goals: Occupations, small talk, future verb tense
Product: Business cards
Basic technologies: Simple word processor

Students prepare for their possible futures and:

- Think about what they might like to be when they are older.
- Decide on the company and location where they want to work (authentic or fictitious).
- Design a business card with their name and work information and print on precut business card stock (see an example in Figure 7.9).
- Role-play their business selves and hand out business cards to their peers.

This project is great for English language learners because it does not require much text and it provides practice in small talk.

2. Content and language goals: Résumé content, book characters, business language, past tense, formatting
Product: Résumé
Sophisticated technologies: Advanced word processing features or desktop publishing program

In this multidisciplinary project, students:

- Answer questions on a character or author's life. The questions require them to discover information typically required for résumés.
- Create their character's résumé using a word processor.
- Compare to the work of others who have chosen the same character, or check with someone who knows the character.
- Revise the résumé.
- Present their character to the class.

This activity facilitates extensive interaction among students and helps students to understand elements of resumes and of literature.

3. Content and language goals: Question formation, business register, surveying, calculating
Product: A business (bake sale), including business cards, a survey, a schedule, advertisements
Advanced technologies: Spreadsheet, advanced word processing features, graphics package

Students, with members of the school parent or student organization:

- Decide on business type and create and distribute roles to each student.
- Make business cards.
- Create a survey asking students at the school their preferences (for favorite bake-sale cookie types or whatever the business will be).
- Enter the numbers into a spreadsheet and calculate percentages.
- Decide on what will be sold and when, how advertising will be done, and other issues.
- Create the advertising and the product.
- Sell it.
- Measure their success by comparing survey results to actual sales.

As long as schools have bake sales, they can be used for learning purposes. In this activity, all students have many choices of how to work, which supports diverse abilities and skills.

Adapting Activities

The steps presented in each project are suggestions and can be adapted in many ways. Some of these activities can also be done using nonelectronic technologies such as pencil and paper. However, in most cases the use of technology adds to the process by giving the products a professional appearance and giving students more time and more resources for creating and learning. For a closer look at one of these tools, see Tool CloseUp: Inspiration. In addition, teaching learners through and about technologies can help them accomplish many language and content goals while also learning valuable technology skills.

ELL

Tool CloseUp: Inspiration

One tool that teachers and students commonly use during the planning process, whether the product is an essay or a five-story architectural wonder, is Inspiration (Inspiration Software). This tool provides a very visual way to create graphic organizers with text, symbols, and graphics. This tool is effective for many ELLs because even the toolbars are visual (iconic). In addition, the text in the graphic organizers that students develop can be converted to outline form, helping students understand the relationship between text and graphic, providing the information in an alternative format for students who prefer it, and supporting their writing. There is also a version of Inspiration developed for younger children called Kidspiration that is widely used to support all the learning goals in this text. The accompanying figure shows an organizer for part of Ms. Farber's infomercial project.

Download a free 30-day trial of this software at www.inspiration.com.

Team 4's Plan for Stage 3 of the Infomercial Project in Inspiration

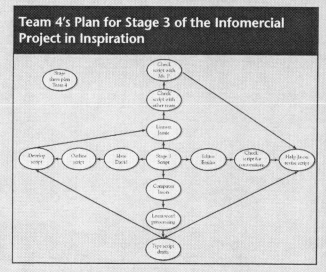

Source: Diagram created in Inspiration® by Inspiration Software®, Inc.

Inspiration has been mentioned throughout this text as a tool to support all the learning goals. What are the advantages to having such a tool? The disadvantages?

_____

_____

_____

_____

Tutorial

CW

Find Inspiration and Kidspiration examples and tutorials in the Tutorials module of the Companion Website (http://www.prenhall.com/egbert).

The examples above are only a few of the activities that facilitate production, and thereby content and language learning. There are others throughout this text and more examples can be found all over the Web. Teachers who want to design their own effective production activities should keep in mind the principles and standards from chapter 1 and also reflect on the process that students will use as they produce. All of the projects can be adapted to use different technologies and to work in different contexts. Even the most sophisticated products can often be completed with basic technologies, although the products will be different in some ways. These examples also illustrate what great products can come from simple technologies and how goals can be met effectively through production.

Choose one or more of the examples above and describe what you think would be the appropriate role for the teacher, the challenges that teachers may face, how scaffolding should be done, and specific technologies that might be useful in developing the product.

_____

_____

_____

ASSESSING PRODUCTION PROJECTS

Evaluating production projects can be different from evaluating other kinds of projects in that one major outcome is tangible; however, it is similar in that both process and product must be evaluated to provide a true understanding of the learning that has occurred. Evaluating the process and product means that teacher and students must be involved in ongoing assessment throughout the project. During the infomercial project in the opening case, Ms. Farber uses observation of student teams as a crucial part of assessment. She has also included assessment by student peers in the other fifth-grade classes. In addition, student explanations and reflections on their learning provide information necessary to assess both the process and the product. Ms. Farber will use the rubric that the class constructed to evaluate the final products.

Teachers and students can use one, more than one, or all of these assessments for project-based learning, and include any of the following:

FIGURE 7.10 Infomercial Checklist

Infomercial Checklist

We have completed these tasks for our infomercial:

____ Made a plan

____ Considered our audience

____ Reviewed models

____ Wrote the script

____ Checked our sources

____ Edited the script

____ Checked the script with another team

____ Filmed our infomercial

____ Edited our infomercial

Our infomercial:

____ Is about 5 minutes long

____ Shows the product

____ Uses advertising language

____ Uses good grammar

____ Is exciting

- *Team activity reports*—These can be written or oral, individual or group, and explain what the group and/or individual has been doing and what help they need to continue. One team activity report for Ms. Farber's project was the infomercial checklist, as seen in Figure 7.10. Notice that this assessment helps students to practice language, in this case past and present tense. ELLs and others who need to work on basic language skills are supported by the simple language used in this assessment.

- *Peer teamwork reports*—Students report on how the collaborative process is working, where it breaks down, and what they are learning by working with their team. These reports can take any number of forms; Figure 7.11 shows one possibility for Ms. Farber's project. Other sample group rubrics can be found on the NALD Web site at http://www.nald.ca/ CLR/btg/ed/evaluation/ groupwork.htm.

- *Self-assessment*—Students can be asked to describe their progress and outcomes according to the rubric criteria, or they can be asked to reflect on how well and in what ways they participated in their group. For Ms. Farber's project, students could be asked in which role they performed the best, in which they achieved the most, which role was most difficult and why, and which they preferred. This information will help students assess their strengths and weaknesses and Ms. Farber to plan future projects.

- *Teams assess each other*—This can be formal or more informal and based on general criteria or on whatever teams find to comment on. During the infomercial project, the teams assessed each other informally based on what they saw as strengths and weaknesses in the scripts. Some teams commented on the interest that the script generated, others how well written it was, and yet others how clearly the product was described.
- *Outside stakeholders*—External reviewers can create their own criteria for the product or use criteria provided by the teacher. For example, the other fifth-grade students who watched Ms. Farber's class projects commented on whether or not they would use the product promoted in the infomercial and why.

These assessments can take place orally, in written form, or both. Students, such as some ELLs who are unable to respond in these formats, can draw pictures or present their information in other ways.

FIGURE 7.11 Teamwork Report for Infomercial Project

Teamwork Report—Stage 2

In my group I:

1. Listened actively	Usually	Sometimes	Never
2. Asked questions	Usually	Sometimes	Never
3. Gave ideas	Usually	Sometimes	Never
4. Agreed or disagreed	Usually	Sometimes	Never

By working with my group, I can do something that I could not do before:

In group work I still need to improve on this:

Do a Web search for sample student projects/products in your content area and/or grade level. What interesting products did you find? Note the product(s) and location(s) here for further reference.

_____

_____

_____

SAMPLE LESSON: PRODUCTION

With sufficient scaffolding, time, and feedback, Ms. Farber's students were able to produce infomercials that demonstrated their understanding of persuasive techniques used in the media. During the project Ms. Farber's students were enthusiastically engaged. Ms. Farber wants to try another project with a relevant product. This time, she wants to focus on some of her curricular math goals. She searches the Web for good ideas and comes up with an idea by teachers Tom Scavo and Byron Petraroja from LessonPlanZ.com. Their detailed description made this math lesson sound like an effective and fun way to meet the standards (http://mathforum.org/trscavo/statistics.html). She copies down the plan's outline:

ADVENTURES IN STATISTICS

Problem: Are the areas of classrooms in the sixth grade larger, on the average, than the areas of the fifth-grade classrooms?

Procedure:

- Students hypothesize what they think the answer to this question might be and document their responses.
- Discuss the practical applications of the ultimate findings.

- Talk about the length and width of the classroom and how to go about measuring it. Estimate these measures by sight and write down the estimates for future reference. Discuss what is meant by the area of the room and then compute using the above length and width estimates.
- Working in pairs, all students measure the length and width of the classroom. First one student from each team measures while the other records, and then they switch roles, measuring again. Record the two sets of measurements on data sheets. When all the teams have completed the measurement task, write the data on the blackboard and compare. Note discrepancies between the measurement pairs. Take again those that cannot be attributed to measurement or round-off error.
- Arrange for the students to measure each of the fifth- and sixth-grade classrooms in the school with the same procedure followed earlier.
- Convert the data to common units and then use calculators to compute the area. Make sure students accompany all answers with appropriate units.
- Examine the data.
- Line graph the data. Then change the line graphs to bar graphs. Examine the graph data.
- Repeat the above lessons for number of students and compare the area to the number of students.
- Compute the average area of fifth- and sixth-grade classrooms and the average number of students, showing student work. Then compute average area per student.
- Prepare a presentation of the data (they invited the principal), each student team taking a different part.

Source: Reproduced with permission from Drexel University, Copyright 2005 by The Math Forum @ Drexel. All rights reserved.

Ms. Farber can instantly see that students will be active and focused on an authentic task, and she likes that many scaffolds are provided in the form of teacher mini-lessons and worksheets. She decides to analyze the lesson with the Lesson Analysis and Adaptation Worksheet (found in chapter 1 on page 33 and in the Lesson Planning module of the Companion Website) to see ways in which the lesson might be improved. As a result of her analysis she decides to use this lesson, but to change it in the following ways:

1. Add the standards and curricular goals that apply. She sees that, in addition to math content standards, the lesson can help students meet goals for communication, problem solving, critical thinking, and even creativity in their final product. In addition, the lesson addresses a variety of literacies (technological, mathematical, visual) and student learning preferences.

2. Add additional resources. Instead of just their meter sticks, students can use a pedometer, a measuring tape, or another rule of their choice to measure. Ms. Farber will also make the computers available for students who want or need to use a spreadsheet to calculate, a word processor or drawing program to make their charts and diagrams, and presentation or other software to produce their final product. These choices help address the needs of a variety of students, from those who need more structure and support to more independent, gifted students.

3. Add more choices for the final product. Students can use the data to argue for or against any of the reasons they gave at the start of the lesson for the practical application of the lesson. For example, one group might create an action maze to help future students carry out the same calculations, while another might write a letter to the school board about overcrowding at their school.

4. Spell out specific assessments. Ms. Farber will observe her students, check their written work, and use a rubric to evaluate their final product. She will also ask the students to write a self-reflection of their process and product, and determine whether their final products should become part of their grade-level portfolios.

Ms. Farber believes that, with these changes, this lesson will be accessible to all of her students and that all of her students will have the opportunity to achieve the intended goals.

499

What else would you add to this lesson to make it effective for your current or future students? What would you delete? Why?

_____

_____

_____

_____

CHAPTER REVIEW

Key Points

- **Define production.**

  Production is the development, through a process, of a tangible, manipulable outcome (a product). The product is the impetus behind the development of each stage of the production project.

- **Describe the benefits of student production for learning.**

  The benefits of student production for learning include student gains not only in language and content but also in social skills, critical thinking and planning, communication, cultural knowledge, and evaluation.

- **Explain the role of process in production.**

  The production process is a carefully designed process and crucial for the success of the project. Planning, development, and evaluation are three general stages in the production process.

- **Discuss guidelines for supporting student technology-enhanced production.**

  Teachers need to focus on the process, provide authentic audiences to view student work, understand and teach the tools, and provide scaffolds for students. In addition, the teacher's role varies from project director to project guide depending on the structure and goals of the project. Research supports the use of production for student learning, although there are challenges for teachers, students, and administrators in designing and carrying out production projects.

- **Describe technologies for supporting student production.**

  Tools such as word processors, spreadsheets, draw programs, and presentation software can support production. The use of production tools alone, however, does not result in learning. As noted above, production projects must be carefully planned so that they meet both content and language objectives and support other learning goals.

- **Evaluate and develop pedagogically sound technology-enhanced production activities.**

  A wide range of products can fit a variety of goals; the role of technology is to support the goals, not to determine them. Teachers and students have a range of choices in meeting production goals. Most important, production can facilitate the achievement of all students, regardless of language background, learning preference, or physical ability. Examples of both teacher and student products and the results of their creative processes are easily accessible on the World Wide Web. A review of some of these Web sites can inspire teachers and learners to integrate and use production tools in their teaching and learning and serve as models for product development.

- **Design appropriate assessments for technology-enhanced process and product.**

  Just as there is a huge range of production projects, there is a great variety of assessments that teachers and students can use to assess them. Most important is that both process and product are evaluated, and that students are involved in the assessments.

Which information in this chapter is most valuable to you? Why? How will you use it in your teaching?

_____

_____

_____

CASE QUESTIONS REVIEW

Reread the case at the beginning of the chapter and review your answers. In light of what you learned during this chapter, how do your answers change? Note any changes below.

1. *What are some learning benefits that students might derive from creating this product?*

    _____

    _____

    _____

2. *What aspects of the process seem to be most important to student achievement toward the goals? Why do you think so?*

    _____

    _____

    _____

3. *What is the teacher's role in this project?*

    _____

    _____

    _____

4. *What role does the technology play?*

    _____

    _____

    _____

CHAPTER EXTENSIONS • • • • • • • • • •

To answer these questions online, go to the chapter 7 section of the Extensions module of this text's Companion Website (http://www.prenhall.com/egbert).

Adapt • • • •

Choose a lesson for your potential subject area and grade level from the technology-enhanced lesson plan archive at KidzOnline (http://www.kidzonline.org/LessonPlans/). Use the Lesson Analysis and Adaptation Worksheet from chapter 1 on page 33 (also available on the Lesson Planning module of the Companion Website) to consider the lesson in the context of *production*. Use your responses to the worksheet to suggest general changes to the lesson based on your current or future students and context.

Practice • • •

1. *Write objectives for a technology-enhanced project.* Write specific content and language objectives for Ms. Farber's project. Share them with a peer and revise them as necessary. Use the "objectives" table from chapter 1 as needed.

2. *Create student roles.* Review the learning activity examples in this chapter. Choose three of the projects and suggest what roles you might create for students and who an authentic audience could be for each of the three projects.

3. *Assess technology-enhanced learning.* Choose one or more of the learning activity examples from the chapter and develop an assessment plan. Address who will be assessed, when, in what categories, based on what criteria. Also suggest how you would generate an overall assessment for the project.

Explore • • •

1. *Create a production handout for students.* On paper, use graphics, text, and any other modes you can to outline for your students a production project that you might use in your class. Include information that explains to students the content and process of the task. Add a brief description of how the task process will be accessible to all students, regardless of language proficiency, content knowledge, or physical abilities.

2. *Create a quick reference for production software or hardware.* One way to learn a piece of software or a technology is to make a reference to help someone else. Choose a piece of software or hardware that you might use in the production process in your classroom (see Table 7.2 for tool ideas). Explore your choice, examining the features and learning about the opportunities that it offers. Then create an explanation for students on how to use it. Be sure to make your reference appropriate for diverse learners.

3. *Examine a production project.* Choose a production project from a text, Web site, or other resource that is relevant to your current or future teaching context. Explain how the project you choose meets the guidelines and provides the opportunities mentioned throughout this chapter. Describe how it might be adapted to better meet the needs of all students and to use technology more effectively.

4. *Create a production project.* Review your content area standards and any other relevant standards. Choose a topic that works within these standards and other curricular requirements for your state or region and develop a technology-enhanced project around it.

REFERENCES

Bazeli, M. (1997). Visual productions and student learning. ERIC 408969

Blumenfeld, P., Soloway, E., Marx, R., Krajcik, J., Guzdial, M., & Palincsar, A. (1991). Motivating project-based learning: Sustaining the doing, supporting the learning. *Educational Psychologist,* 26(3/4), 369–398.

Dewey, J. (1938). *Experience and education.* New York: Collier Books.

Egbert, J. (1995). Electronic action mazes: Tools for language learning. *CAELL Journal,* 6(3), 9–12.

George Lucas Foundation. (2005). *Instructional module: Project-based learning.* Retrieved June 30, 2007, from the World Wide Web: http://www.edutopia.org/projectbasedlearning.

Healey, D. (2002). *Teaching and learning in the digital world: Interactive Web pages: Action Mazes.* Retrieved February 11, 2005, from the World Wide Web: http://oregonstate.edu/~healeyd/ups/actionmaze.html.

Holmes, M. (2002). *Action mazes.* Retrieved from the World Wide Web, February 11, 2005: http://www.englishlearner.com/llady/actmaze1.htm.

Male, M. (1997). *Technology for inclusion* (3rd ed.). Boston, MA: Allyn & Bacon.

San Mateo County Office of Education. (2001). The multimedia project: Project-based learning with Multimedia. Retrieved February 11, 2005, from the World Wide Web: http://pblmm.k12.ca.us.

Thomas, J. (2000). *A review of research on project-based learning.* San Rafael, CA: Autodesk Foundation.

25

Supporting Student Problem Solving

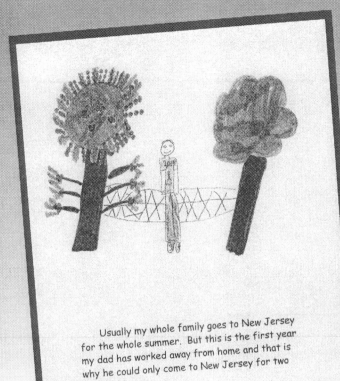

Usually my whole family goes to New Jersey for the whole summer. But this is the first year my dad has worked away from home and that is why he could only come to New Jersey for two weeks this year.

Case: The Big Question

As you read the following scenario, note how the teacher guides the students during the inquiry process.

• •

A major discount retailer wants to build a giant new superstore in the small rural town where Ms. Lee teaches eighth-grade social studies. Ms. Lee's students have been exposed to picketers, mailers, publicly posted flyers, and letters in the local newspaper both supporting and opposing the superstore. On one side, some local small businesspeople are worried that they will be put out of business by the giant, and other town citizens are concerned that their way of life will be ruined by extra traffic, noise, pollution, and low-paying jobs. Others who oppose the superstore complain that the low wages that the store pays will mean fewer good jobs in town. On the other side, the Chamber of Commerce, some educators, and other citizens anticipate more revenue to pay for schools and roads, and some people are looking forward to having a nearby place to shop and save money.

Ms. Lee's students are also divided on the issue, echoing the partisan arguments of their parents and friends. Her students tell her that they would like to know the "real story." Ms. Lee decides that this is an excellent opportunity for students to study a large range of economic, political, and social issues that directly impact them and their families. Ms. Lee agrees to plan a project for the students to help the town solve the dilemma over whether the superstore is in the best interests of the town. During the project she will focus on problem solving and inquiry and use technology to support both.

• •

Answer these questions about the case. There are no right or wrong answers—the goal is for you to respond before you read the chapter. Then, as you interact with the chapter contents, think about how your answers might change.

1. *What prior content and language knowledge do the students need to solve this problem?*

_____

_____

_____

2. *What process should the students follow to find a solution to the problem?*

_____

_____

_____

3. *What should Ms. Lee's role in the project be?*

_____

_____

_____

4. *What role can technology play in helping the students to solve their problem?*

_____

_____

_____

Ms. Lee understands that this issue is important for her students to understand, and that it also presents a learning experience that will help them gain in content knowledge, language, and skills. The goal of this chapter is to help you to understand how teachers and technology can support student problem solving. After reading this chapter, you will be able to

- Define problem solving and inquiry.
- Understand the interaction between problem solving and other instructional goals.
- Discuss guidelines and technologies for encouraging effective student problem solving.
- Create and adapt effective technology-enhanced tasks to support problem solving.
- Assess student technology-supported problem solving.

*When you have completed this chapter, which NETS*T will you have addressed?*

_____

_____

_____

Like critical and creative thinking, problem solving is not an easy thing to teach. However, educators believe it is crucially important that students gain these skills. The standards that support this goal in every content area demonstrate the significance of problem solving. See the Meeting the Standards feature on the next page for an overview of these standards.

• • • • **Meeting the Standards:** Problem Solving • • • •

Across content areas, the standards address problem solving in the form of being able to improvise, decide, inquire, and research. For example:

- NA.T.K–12.2 Acting by assuming roles and interacting in improvisations.
- NL-Eng.K–12.7 Students conduct research on issues and interests by generating ideas and questions and by posing problems.
- NM-NUM.6–8.3 Develop, analyze, and explain methods for solving problems involving proportions, such as scaling and finding equivalent ratios.
- NPH.H.K–4.6 Demonstrate the ability to apply a decision-making process to health issues and problems.
- NS.K–4.1 As a result of activities, students should develop abilities necessary to do scientific inquiry.

- NT.K–12.6
  a. Students use technology resources for solving problems and making informed decisions.
  b. Students employ technology in the development of strategies for solving problems in the real world.

These are only samples; there are many more standards in each area that emphasize inquiry and problem solving. In fact, the national math standards and the national science standards are premised almost completely on problem solving and inquiry. According to the literature, however, these areas are often overlooked or addressed superficially in classrooms, and in some subject areas, are not attended to at all.

Check your state standards in the Standards section of the Resources module of the Companion Website. How do they address problem solving?

_____

_____

_____

CW

• • • •

OVERVIEW OF PROBLEM SOLVING AND INQUIRY IN K–12 CLASSROOMS

In keeping with a learning focus, this chapter first discusses problem solving and inquiry to provide a basis from which teachers can provide support for these goals with technology.

What Is Problem Solving?

Whereas production is a process that focuses on an end-product, **problem solving** is a process that centers on a *problem*. Students apply critical and creative thinking skills to prior knowledge during the problem solving process. The end result of problem solving is typically some kind of decision, in other words, choosing a solution and then evaluating it.

There are two general kinds of problems. **Close-ended** problems are those with known solutions to which students can apply a process similar to one that they have already used. For example, if a student understands the single-digit process in adding 2 plus 2 to make 4, she most likely will be able to solve a problem that asks her to add 1 plus 1. **Open-ended** or **loosely structured** problems, on the other hand, are those with many or unknown solutions rather than one correct answer. These types of problems require the ability to apply a variety of strategies and knowledge to finding a solution. For example, an open-ended problem statement might read:

• •

A politician has just discovered information showing that a statement he made to the public earlier in the week was incorrect. If he corrects himself he will look like a fool, but if he doesn't and someone finds out the truth, he will be in trouble. What should he do or say about this?

Obviously, there is no simple answer to this question, and there is a lot of information to consider.

Many textbooks, teachers, and tests present or ask for only the *results* of problem solving and not the whole *process* that students must go through in thinking about how to arrive at a viable solution. As a result, according to the literature, most people use their personal understandings to try to solve open-ended problems, but the bias of limited experience makes it hard for people to understand the trade-offs or contradictions that these problems present. To solve such problems, students need to be able to use both problem-solving skills and an effective inquiry process.

What Is Inquiry?

Inquiry in education is also sometimes called *research, investigation,* or *guided discovery*. During inquiry, students ask questions and then search for answers to those questions. In doing so, they come to new understandings in content and language. Although inquiry is an instructional strategy in itself, it is also a central component of problem solving when students apply their new understandings to the problem at hand. Each question that the problem raises must be addressed by thorough and systematic investigation to arrive at a well-grounded solution. Therefore, the term "problem solving" can be considered to include inquiry.

Mansilla and Gardner (1997) note that inquiry must occur through "multiple domains and symbol systems" (p. 1). This means that, for students to understand both the question and ways of looking at the answer(s), resources such as historical accounts, literature, art, and eyewitness experiences must be used. In addition, each resource must be examined in light of what each different type of material contributes to the solution. **Critical literacy**, or reading beyond the text, then, is a fundamental aspect of inquiry and so of problem solving. For critical literacy resources, see the 21st Century Literacies section in the Resources module of the Companion Website (http://www.prenhall.com/egbert).

What Is Problem-Based Learning?

Problem-based learning (PBL) is a teaching approach that combines critical thinking, problem-solving skills, and inquiry as students explore real-world problems. It is based on unstructured, complex, and authentic problems that are often presented as part of a project. PBL addresses many of the learning goals, including communication, creativity, and often production.

Research is being conducted in every area from business to education to see how we solve problems, what guides us, what information we have and use during problem solving, and how we can become more efficient problem solvers. There are competing theories of how people learn to and do solve problems, and much more research needs to be done. However, we do know several things. First, problem solving can depend on the context, the participants, and the stakeholders. In addition, studies show that content appears to be *covered* better by "traditional" instruction, but students *retain* better after problem solving. PBL has been found effective at teaching content *and* problem solving, and the use of technology makes those gains even higher (Stites, 1998). Research clearly shows that the more parts of a problem there are, the less successful students will be at solving it. However, effective scaffolding can help to reduce student cognitive overload (Blosser, 1988). Discover technology that can provide scaffolds in Tool CloseUp: Microsoft Student on page 158.

The PBL literature points out that both content knowledge and problem-solving skills are necessary to arrive at solutions, but individual differences among students affect their success, too. For example, field-independent students in general do better than field-dependent students in tasks. In addition, students from some cultures will not be familiar with this kind of learning, and others may not have the language to work with it. Teachers must consider all of these ideas and challenges in supporting student problem solving.

Is the problem that Ms. Lee's students want to solve an open-ended or close-ended problem? Why do you think so? What difference does it make?

_____

_____

_____

Tool CloseUp: Microsoft Student

There are many tools that can support parts of the problem-solving process if the teacher has the time and desire to find and evaluate them. Many of these are described in the Tools section of this chapter. Microsoft Student provides many of these supports in one software package, saving teachers time and effort (but not money—the package costs about $70).

Student features four main tools that serve a variety of purposes. These include:

- *Encarta Premium.* Much more than an electronic encyclopedia, this tool contains 300 video clips, 66,000 articles, over 25,000 photos, an atlas, thesaurus, dictionary, and sound and music clips. It also includes Encarta Kids with content for younger learners. This is a very thorough resource for inquiry about thousands of topics and a good place to start gathering information on a project.

- *Math tools.* The math tools include an online graphing calculator, an equation library, and homework help. Students can use these tools not only for solving math problems but for graphing information to support problems in other areas.

- *Learning essentials.* This section includes tutorials for the Microsoft Office Suite, writing tutorials, and templates for writing in different genres. Students

can get support for presenting their inquiry and problem-solving projects.

Student has additional features such as foreign language tools, but more important than what it has is what it can do. First, Student can help support students during inquiry by providing resources in a variety of modes. By providing information in formats from audio to video, Student makes it possible for ELLs and students with different learning preferences to access the content.

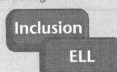

Second, tutorials such as that showing how to make diagrams in Microsoft Word can help students to organize, synthesize, and present information during PBL. In the same way, templates can assist students in preparing and presenting their problem solutions. Other tools scaffold student learning during PBL and make it possible for students with different language backgrounds to communicate. Another benefit is that, because the tools are bundled, students know where to go to find what they need.

There are problems with the software. For example, it runs only on the Microsoft operating system, and teachers need to spend time learning the tools to understand how best to use them with students. In spite of this, Student is a powerful software package that can support effective problem solving and inquiry in K-12 classrooms.

Based on the description of Student, what other characteristics of PBL does it support? Would you try this software? Why or why not?

_____

_____

_____

_____

Find tutorials for Microsoft Student in the Tutorials module of the Companion Website (http://www.prenhall.com/egbert).

Characteristics of effective technology-enhanced problem-based learning tasks

PBL tasks share many of the same characteristics of other tasks in this book, but some are specific to PBL. Generally, PBL tasks:

- Involve learners in gaining and organizing knowledge of content. Inspiration and other concept-mapping software is useful for this.
- Help learners link school activities to life, providing the "why" for doing the activity.
- Give students control of their learning.
- Have built-in and just-in-time scaffolding to help students. Tutorials are available all over the Web for content, language, and technology help.
- Are fun and interesting.
- Contain specific objectives for students to meet along the way to a larger goal.
- Have guidance for the use of tools, especially computer technologies.
- Include communication and collaboration (tools described in chapter 3).
- Emphasize the process and the content.
- Are central to the curriculum, not peripheral or time fillers.
- Lead to additional content learning.
- Have a measurable, although not necessarily *correct*, outcome.

More specifically, PBL tasks:

- Use a problem that "appeals to human desire for resolution/stasis/harmony" and "sets up need for and context of learning which follows" (IMSA, 2005, p. 2).
- Help students understand the range of problem-solving mechanisms available.
- Focus on the merits of the question, the concepts involved, and student research plans.
- Provide opportunities for students to examine the *process* of getting the answer (for example, looking back at the arguments).
- Lead to additional "transfer" problems that use the knowledge gained in a different context.

Not every task necessarily exhibits all of these characteristics completely, but these lists can serve as guidelines for creating and evaluating tasks. Figure 6.1 shows an Educator's Desk Reference Lesson plan that includes many of these features that can be supported by technology. Can you pick them out? Can you see where technology might best fit in this lesson?

FIGURE 6.1 Justice Lesson Plan

Justice

Melanie McCool

Grade Level(s): 7, 8, 9, 10, 11, 12

Subject(s): Social Studies/U.S. Government

Overview: This lesson will allow students to experience brainstorming and open-ended questioning strategies and research to develop a better understanding of the justice system.

Purpose: To provide an opportunity for students to discuss both strengths and weaknesses of the court system in providing equal justice for all and to identify factors that cause these weaknesses and recommend solutions.

Objectives: As a result of this activity:

1. The student will investigate the criminal justice system.
2. The student will analyze the 7 Articles to the Constitution.
3. The student will develop problem-solving and critical-thinking skills.

Activities and Procedures:

1. Students take attitudinal survey.

continued

FIGURE 6.1 Continued

2. Brainstorm "Equal Justice for All" motto on Supreme Court Building. Students write their opinions of what the motto means:
   a. Show picture of symbol of justice.
   b. Ask: What is the meaning of the symbol?
   c. Why is the woman blindfolded?
   d. What does the scale stand for?
3. Constitution Search: Point out "establish justice" as purpose outlined in Preamble. Have students search the Constitution to find ways this purpose is carried out. (Use only the 7 Articles to the Constitution.)
4. Guest: Invite a local trial court judge to discuss the organization of the court system.
5. Guest: Invite an attorney to visit. Raise questions about appeal, time involved in ajudication, and fairness of the system.

Tying It All Together:

1. Students complete attitudinal survey and discuss.
2. After the visit from a local trial court judge have students construct a diagram of the applicable federal and state courts for their jurisdiction. Debrief: Does the flow chart indicate an effort to provide "equal justice?" Ask for suggestions to improve the system.
3. Encourage all students to share the results of this activity with their parents/guardians.
4. Use this activity to introduce the first unit or lesson.

Attitudinal Survey

Instructions: For each of the following statements, circle the one that corresponds most closely with your opinion.

Key: SA=Strongly Agree / A=Agree / U=Undecided/ D=Disagree / SD=Strongly Disagree

1. In a court of law, the defendant is always treated justly. SA A U D SD
2. Trial by jury should be abolished. SA A U D SD
3. A person is always considered innocent until proven guilty. SA A U D SD
4. The more money you have, the more likely you are to be proven innocent. SA A U D SD
5. Everyone should be required to serve on a jury at least once in his life. SA A U D SD
6. Courts are too lenient with criminals. SA A U D SD
7. People who have low IQ's should not be allowed to serve on juries. SA A U D SD
8. In the United States, every defendant who requests a jury trial is actually tried by his peers. SA A U D SD
9. All judges should be elected by the people they serve. SA A U D SD
10. People who do not agree with the outcome of their trial should only be allowed to appeal their case one time. SA A U D SD
11. The news media should be allowed to cover all trials without restriction because the Constitution guarantees the right of freedom of the press. SA A U D SD
12. Courts usually see that justice is served. SA A U D SD
13. People charged with serious crimes should not be allowed out on bail. SA A U D SD
14. Most trials should take place without a judge since his role is only to umpire the proceedings. SA A U D SD
15. The judicial system in the United States is probably the best system which has ever been developed. SA A U D SD

Source: http://www.eduref.org/cgi-bin/printlessons.cgi/Virtual/Lessons/Social_Studies/US_Government/ GOV0022.html

How can Ms. Lee create her project to include these important elements? Where should she start? How can technology help in her planning?

_____

_____

_____

Student benefits of problem solving

There are many potential benefits of using PBL in classrooms at all levels; however, the bene-fits depend on how well this strategy is employed. With effective PBL, students can become more engaged in their learning and empowered to become more autonomous in classroom work. This, in turn, may lead to improved attitudes about the classroom and thus to other gains such as increased abilities for social-problem solving (Elias & Tobias, 1996). Students can gain a deeper understanding of concepts, acquire skills necessary in the real world, and transfer skills to become independent and self-directed learners and thinkers outside of school. For example, when students are encouraged to practice using problem-solving skills across a variety of situa-tions they gain experience in discovering not only different methods but which method to ap-ply to what kind of problem. Furthermore, students can become more confident when their self-esteem and grade does not depend only on the specific answer that the teacher wants. In ad-dition, during the problem-solving process students can develop better critical and creative thinking skills.

Students can also develop better language skills (both knowledge and communication) through problems that require a high level of interaction with others (Dooly, 2005). This is im-portant for all learners, but especially for ELLs and others who do not have grade-level lan-guage skills. For students who may not understand the language or content or a specific question, the fo-cus on process gives them more opportunities to access information and express their knowledge.

ELL

The problem-solving process

The use of PBL requires different processes for students and teachers. The teacher's process in-volves careful planning. There are many ways for this to happen, but a general outline that can be adapted includes the following steps:

1. After students bring up a question, put it in the greater context of a problem to solve (using the format of an essential question; see chapter 4) and decide what the outcome should be—a recommendation, a summary, a process?

2. Develop objectives that represent both the goal and the specific content, language, and skills toward which students will work.

3. List background information and possible materials and content that will need to be addressed. Get access to materials and tools and prepare resource lists if necessary.

4. Write the specific problem. Make sure students know what their role is and what they are expected to do. Then go back and check that the problem and task meet the objectives and characteristics of effective PBL. Reevaluate materials and tools.

5. Develop scaffolds that will be needed.

6. Evaluate and prepare to meet individual students' needs for language, assistive tools, content review, and thinking skills and strategies.

7. Present the problem to students, assess their under-standing, and provide appropriate feedback as they plan and carry out their process.

These steps are summarized in Figure 6.2.

The student process focuses more on the specific problem-solving task. PBL sources list different terms to de-scribe each step, but the process is more or less the same. Students:

1. *Define and frame the problem*: Describe it, recognize what is being asked for, look at it from all sides, and say why they need to solve it.

2. *Plan*: Present prior knowledge that affects the problem, decide what further information and concepts are needed, and map what resources will be consulted and why.

3. *Inquire*: Gather and analyze the data, build and test hypotheses.

FIGURE 6.2 Steps in Planning a PBL Task

Step	Example
1. Contextualize the question.	Ask, "What is the question here? What should we do about it?"
2. Develop objectives.	Figure out the goal and the skills the task will meet.
3. Review background.	Explore materials and tools that focus on the problem.
4. Write the problem.	Be specific about student roles and responsibilities.
5. Develop scaffolds.	Create documents, mini-lessons, and other helps.
6. Evaluate student needs.	Review students' current level of knowledge and skills.
7. Implement.	Provide clear instructions and ongoing observation and feedback.

FIGURE 6.3 Student Problem-Solving Process

Step	Example
1. Define and frame the problem.	Determine what the problem is and why it is important to address.
2. Plan.	Decide how to address the problem.
3. Inquire.	Gather data and come to some conclusions.
4. Look back.	Review and evaluate the conclusions.

4. *Look back:* Review and evaluate the process and content. Ask "What do I understand from this result? What does it tell me?"

These steps are summarized in Figure 6.3.

Problem-solving strategies that teachers can demonstrate, model, and teach directly include trial and error, process of elimination, making a model, using a formula, acting out the problem, using graphics or drawing the problem, discovering patterns, and simplifying the problem (e.g., rewording, changing the setting, dividing it into simpler tasks). Even the popular KWL (Know, Want to Know, Learned) chart can help students frame questions. A KWL for Ms. Lee's superstore project might look like the one in Figure 6.4. Find out more about these strategies at http://literacy.kent.edu/eureka/strategies/discuss-prob.html.

Wilson, Fernandez, and Hadaway (1993) recommend a procedure for teaching problem solving in groups that involves the use of a Planning Board, a Representation Board, and a Doing Board. Using these tools, students post, discuss, and reflect on their joint problem-solving process using visual cues that they create. This helps students focus on both their process and the content.

Throughout the teacher and student processes, participants should continue to examine cultural, emotional, intellectual, and other possible barriers to problem solving.

FIGURE 6.4 KWL Chart

Topic	What I Know	What I Want to Know	What I Learned
The economy of our town			
The political process for new businesses			
How other towns like ours have been affected by superstores			
The impact of many low-paying jobs			
Noise, pollution, and traffic caused by superstores			
Benefits of having local shopping alternatives			

Teachers and Problem Solving

The teacher's role in PBL

During the teacher's process of creating the problem context, the teacher must consider what levels of authenticity, complexity, uncertainty, and self-direction students can access and work within. Gordon (1998) breaks loosely structured problems into three general types with increasing levels of these aspects. He explains:

1. *Academic challenges.* An academic challenge is student work structured as a problem arising directly from an area of study. It is used primarily to promote greater understanding of selected subject matter. The academic challenge is crafted by transforming existing curricular material into a problem format.

2. *Scenario challenges.* These challenges cast students in real-life roles and ask them to perform these roles in the context of a reality-based or fictional scenario.

3. *Real-life problems.* These are actual problems in need of real solutions by real people or organizations. They involve students directly and deeply in the exploration of an area of study. And the solutions have the potential for actual implementation at the classroom, school, community, regional, national, or global level. (p. 3)

To demonstrate the application of this simple categorization, the learning activities presented later in this chapter follow this outline.

As discussed in other chapters in this book, during student work the teacher's role can vary from director to shepherd, but when the teacher is a co-learner rather than a taskmaster, learners become experts. An often-used term for the teacher's role in the literature about problem solving is "coach." As a coach, the teacher works to facilitate thinking skills and process, including working out group dynamics, keeping students on task and making sure they are participating, assessing their progress and process, and adjusting levels of challenge as students need change. Teachers can provide hints and resources and work on a gradual release of responsibility to learners.

What level of inquiry/problem solving might be most effective for Ms. Lee's class? Why do you think so?

_____

_____

_____

Challenges for teachers

For many teachers, the roles suggested above are easier said than done. To use a PBL approach, teachers must break out of the content-dissemination mode and help their students to do the same. Even when this happens, in many classrooms students have been trained to think that problem solving is getting the one right answer (Wilson et al., 1993), and it takes time, practice, and patience for them to understand otherwise. Some teachers feel that they are obligated to cover too much in the curriculum to spend time on PBL or that using real-world problems does not mesh well with the content, materials, and context of the classroom. However, as Gordon (1998) notes, "whether it's a relatively simple matter of deciding what to eat for breakfast or a more complex one such as figuring out how to reduce pollution in one's community, in life we make decisions and do things that have concrete results. Very few of us do worksheets" (p. 2). He adds that not every aspect of students' schoolwork needs to be real, but that connections should be made from the classroom to the real world.

In addition, many standardized district and statewide tests do not measure process, so students do not want to spend time on it. However, we can overcome this thinking by demonstrating to students the ways in which they need to solve problems every day and how these strategies may transfer to testing situations. Furthermore, PBL tasks and projects may take longer to develop and assess than traditional instruction. However, teachers can start slowly by helping students practice PBL in controlled environments with structure, then gradually release them to working independently. Gordon's framework presented above can assist teachers in this effort, and the guidelines in this chapter also address some of these challenges.

GUIDELINES FOR TECHNOLOGY-SUPPORTED PROBLEM SOLVING

Obviously, PBL is more than simply giving students a problem and asking them to solve it. The following guidelines describe other issues in PBL.

Designing Problem-Solving Opportunities

In the opening scenario, Ms. Lee has chosen to address a problem that has no simple correct answer, in which people are very partisan, and in which a variety of resources, not all reliable, are addressed. To help her students work through some of the challenges of solving this problem, she will review and list resources, create scaffolds, and gather appropriate materials and tools. The guidelines described here will assist her in developing the PBL opportunity.

Guideline #1: Integrate reading and writing. Although an important part of solving problems, discussion alone is not enough for students to develop and practice problem-solving skills. Effective problem solving and inquiry require students to think clearly and deeply about content, language, and process. Reading and writing tasks can encourage students to take time to think about these issues and to contextualize their thinking practice. They can also provide vehicles for teachers to understand student progress and to provide concrete feedback. Students who have strengths in these areas will be encouraged and those who need help can learn from their stronger partners, just as those who have strengths in speaking can model for and assist their peers during discussion. Even in courses that do not stress reading and writing, integrating these skills into tasks and projects can promote successful learning.

How can Ms. Lee integrate reading and writing into the superstore project?

_____

_____

_____

Guideline #2: Avoid plagiarism. The Internet is a great resource for student inquiry and problem solving. However, when students read and write using Internet resources, they often cut and paste directly from the source. Sometimes this is an innocent mistake; students may be uneducated about the use of resources, perhaps they come from a culture where the concept of ownership is completely different than in the United States, or maybe their language skills are weak and they want to be able to express themselves better. In either case, two strategies can help avoid plagiarism:

- The teacher must teach directly about plagiarism and copyright issues. Strategies including helping students learn how to cite sources, paraphrase, summarize, and restate.
- The teacher must be as familiar as possible with the resources that students will use and check for plagiarism when it is suspected.

To do so, the teacher can enter a sentence or phrase into any Web browser with quote marks around it and if the entry is exact, the original source will come up in the browser window. Essay checkers such as Turnitin (http://turnitin.com/) are also available online that will check a passage or an entire essay. See the Technology Tools module of the Companion Website (http://www.prenhall.com/egbert) for more information on copyright and plagiarism, and read From the Classroom: Research and Plagiarism, in which one teacher describes how she uses elements of Microsoft Researcher.

Guideline #3: Do not do what students can do. Teaching, and particularly teaching with technology, is often a difficult job, due in part to the time it takes teachers to prepare effective learning experiences. Planning, developing, directing, and assessing do not have to be solely the teacher's domain, however. Students should take on many of these responsibilities, and at the same time gain in problem-solving, language, content, critical thinking, creativity, and other crucial skills. Teachers do not always need to click the mouse, write on the whiteboard, decide criteria for a rubric, develop questions, decorate the classroom, or perform many classroom and learning tasks. Students can take ownership and feel responsibility. Although it is often difficult for teachers to give up some of their power, the benefits of having more time and shared responsibility can be transformational. Teachers can train themselves to ask, "Is this something students can do?"

What responsibilities for planning the superstore project can Ms. Lee give her students?

_____

_____

_____

Guideline #4: Make mistakes okay. Problem solving often involves coming to dead ends, having to revisit data and reformulate ideas, and working with uncertainty. For students used to striving for correct answers and looking to the teacher as a final authority, the messiness of problem solving can be disconcerting, frustrating, and even scary. Teachers need to create environments of acceptance where reasoned, even if wrong, answers are recognized, acknowledged, and given appropriate feedback by the teacher and peers. In this chapter's superstore case, Ms. Lee already knows that her students come to the task with a variety of beliefs and information. In working with students' prior knowledge, she can model how to be supportive of students' faulty ideas and suggestions. She can also ask positive questions to get the students thinking about what they still need to know and how they can come to know it. She can both encourage and directly teach her students to be supportive of mistakes and trials as part of their team-building and leadership skills.

In addition, teachers need to help students to understand that even a well-reasoned argument or answer can meet with opposition. Students must not feel that they have made a bad decision just because everyone else, particularly the teacher, does not agree. Teachers should model for students that they are part of the learning process and they are impartial as to the outcome when the student's position has been well defended.

A summary of these guidelines is presented in Figure 6.5.

FROM THE CLASSROOM

Research and Plagiarism

We've been working on summaries all year and the idea that copying word for word is plagiarism. When they come to me (sixth grade) they continue to struggle with putting things in their own words so (Encarta) Researcher not only provides a visual (a reference in APA format) that this is someone else's work, but allows me to see the information they used to create their report as Researcher is an electronic filing system. It's as if students were printing out the information and keeping it in a file that they will use to create their report. But instead of having them print everything as they go to each individual site they can copy and paste until later. When they finish their research they come back to their file, decide what information they want to use, and can print it out all at once. This has made it easier for me because the students turn this in with their report. So I would say it not only allows students to learn goals of summarizing, interpreting, or synthesizing, it helps me to address them in greater depth and it's easier on me! (April, middle school teacher)

FIGURE 6.5 Guidelines for Problem Solving

Suggestion	Example
Guideline #1: Integrate reading and writing.	Add content-based literature and a text-based product.
Guideline #2: Avoid plagiarism.	Teach explicitly about plagiarism and copyright.
Guideline #3: Do not do what students can do.	Let students develop the problem, search for resources, and design assessments.
Guideline #4: Make mistakes okay.	Teach students how to accept mistakes and use formative (constructive) criticism.

PROBLEM-SOLVING AND INQUIRY TECHNOLOGIES

As with all the goals in this book, the focus of technology in problem solving is not on the technology itself but on the learning experiences that the technology affords. Different tools exist to support different parts of the process. Some are as simple as handouts that students can print and complete, others as complex as modeling and visualization software. Many software tools that support problem solving are made for experts in the field and are very difficult to learn and use. Examples of these more complicated programs include many types of computer-aided design software, advanced authoring tools, and complex expert systems. There are few software tools for K–12 students that address the problem-solving process directly and completely, but the The Factory and other inexpensive programs from Sunburst Technologies, one-computer classroom packages by Tom Snyder Productions, Where in the World? series by Broderbund, and the Jumpstart series by Knowledge Adventure provide examples of software that comes close.

Simple inquiry tools that help students perform their investigations during PBL are much more prevalent. The standard word processor, database, concept mapping/graphics and spreadsheet software can all assist students in answering questions and organizing and presenting data, but there are other tools more specifically designed to support inquiry. The Microsoft Encarta suite (which includes Encarta Researcher and other software) is commonly used to support inquiry. Additional software programs that can be used within the PBL framework are mentioned in other chapters in this text. These programs, such as the Tom Snyder Productions programs mentioned above and in chapter 2, address the overlapping goals of collaboration, production, critical thinking, creativity, and problem solving. Interestingly, even video games might be used as problem-solving tools. Many of these games require users to puzzle out directions, to find missing artifacts, or to follow clues that are increasingly difficult to find and understand. A great place for teachers to start understanding how to support problem solving with technology is Intel Education's "It's a Wild Ride" and other free thinking tools and resources on the http://www.intel.com/education/ Web site.

The following section presents brief descriptions of tools that can support the PBL process. The examples are divided into stand-alone tools that can be used on one or more desktops and Web-based tools.

Stand-Alone Tools

Example 1: Fizz and Martina (Tom Snyder Productions)

Students help Fizz and Martina, animated characters in this software, to solve problems by figuring out which data is relevant, performing appropriate calculations, and presenting their solutions. The five titles in this series are perfect for a one-computer classroom. Each software package combines computer-based video, easy navigation, and handouts and other resources as scaffolds. This software is useful in classrooms with ELLs because of the combination of visual, audio, and text-based reinforcement of input. It is also accessible to students with physical disabilities because it can run on one computer; students do not have to actually perform the mouse clicks to run the software themselves.

This software is much more than math. It includes a lot of language, focuses on cooperation and collaboration in teams, and promotes critical thinking as part of problem solving. Equally important, it helps students to communicate mathematical ideas orally and in writing. See Figure 6.6 for the "getting started" screen from Fizz and Martina to view some of the choices that teachers and students have in using this package.

Example 2: I Spy Treasure Hunt, I Spy School Days, I Spy Spooky Mansion (Scholastic)

The language in these fun simulations consists of isolated, discrete words and phrases, making these programs useful for word study but not for overall concept learning. School Days, for example, focuses on both objects and words related to school. However, students work on extrapolation, trial and error, process of elimination, and other problem-solving strategies. It is difficult to get students away from the computer once they start working on any of the simulations in this series. Each software package has several separate hunts with a large number of riddles that, when solved, allow the user to put together a map or other clues to find the surprise at the end. Some of the riddles involve simply finding an item on the screen, but others require more thought such as figuring out an alternative representation for

---

FIGURE 6.6 Getting Started with FIZZ AND MARTINA

Getting Started

Volume

Materials

1. Make sure you have all the materials you need. Click Materials for a list.

2. Divide students into teams of four or so. Choose a color below for each team by clicking the color.

   Red   Yellow   Blue   Green
   Purple   Orange   Silver   Brown

   Number of teams selected 0

3. Select how you want to view the video:

   Classroom Size   Regular Size

Quit

Contents >

Source: Used with permission of Tom Snyder Productions.

the item sought or using a process of elimination to figure out where to find it. All of the riddles are presented in both text and audio and can be repeated as many times as the student requires, making it easier for language learners, less literate students, and students with varied learning preferences to access the information. Younger students can also work with older students or an aide for close support so that students are focused.

There are many more software packages like these that can be part of a PBL task. See the Technology Tools module of the Companion Website for titles and publishers (http://www .prenhall.com/egbert).

I Spy used alone does not fit all the characteristics of problem-based learning. What can teachers do to make sure that software such as I Spy includes more of the characteristics of PBL?

Inclusion
ELL

CW

_____

_____

_____

Example 3: Science Court (Tom Snyder Productions)

Twelve different titles in this series present humorous court cases that students must help to resolve. Whether the focus is on the water cycle, soil, or gravity, students use animated computer-based video, hands-on science activities, and group work to learn and practice science and the inquiry process. As students work toward solving the case, they examine not only the facts but also their reasoning processes. Like Fizz and Martina and much of TSP's software, Science Court uses multimedia and can be used in the one-computer classroom (as described in chapter 2), making it accessible to diverse students. Figure 6.7 presents a team question from Science Court's "Living Things" title to demonstrate some of the scaffolding available in the program.

Inclusion
ELL

Example 4: Geographic Information Systems (GIS)

The use of GIS to track threatened species, map hazardous waste or wetlands in the community, or propose solutions for other environmental problems supports student "spatial literacy and geographic competence" (Baker, 2005, n.p.), in addition to experimental and inquiry techniques, understanding of scale and resolution, and verification skills. Popular desktop-based GIS that students can access include Geodesy and ArcVoyager; many Web-based versions also exist, including the Student Data Mapper at http://kangis.org/ mapping/sdm/. GIS is not necessarily an easy tool to learn or use, but it can lead to real-world involvement and language, concept, and thinking skills development.

Example 5: The Adventures of Jasper Woodbury (Vanderbilt University)

The Jasper series is actually video-disc–based rather than CD-based and consists of a series of 12 adventures. Each adventure presents a challenge that students must solve using math, science, social studies, literature, and history. It presents the data in natural settings and presents authentic, collaborative problems to be solved.

Web-Based Tools

Many technology-enhanced lessons and tools on the Web come premade. In other words, they were created for someone else's students and context. Teachers must adapt these tools to fit their own teaching styles,

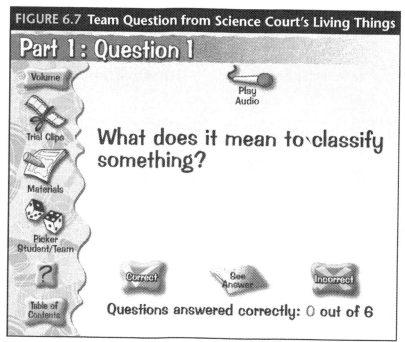

FIGURE 6.7 Team Question from Science Court's Living Things

Part 1: Question 1

Volume

Play Audio

Trial Clips

What does it mean to classify something?

Materials

Picker Student/Team

?

Correct   See Answer   Incorrect

Table of Contents

Questions answered correctly: 0 out of 6

Source: Used with permission of Tom Snyder Productions.

TOOLS

student needs, goals, resources, and contextual variables. Teachers must learn to modify these resources to make them their own and help them to work effectively in their unique teaching situation. With this in mind, teachers can take advantages of the great ideas in the Web-based tools described below.

Example 1: WebQuest

A WebQuest is a Web-based inquiry activity that is highly structured in a preset format. Most teachers are aware of WebQuests—a Web search finds them mentioned in every state, subject area, and grade level, and they are popular topics at conferences and workshops. Created by Bernie Dodge and Tom March in 1995 (see http://webquest.sdsu.edu/), this activity has proliferated wildly.

Each WebQuest has six parts. The Quest starts with an introduction to excite student interest. The task description then explains to students the purpose of the Quest and what the outcome will be. Next, the process includes clear steps and the scaffolds, including resources, that students will need to accomplish the steps. The evaluation section provides rubrics and assessment guidelines, and the conclusion section provides closure. Finally, the teacher section includes hints and tips for other teachers to use the WebQuest.

Advantages to using WebQuests as inquiry and problem-solving tools include:

- Students are focused on a specific topic and content and have a great deal of scaffolding.
- Students focus on using information rather than looking for it, because resources are preselected.
- Students use collaboration, critical thinking, and other important skills to complete their Quest.

FROM THE CLASSROOM

WebQuests

I evaluated a WebQuest for middle elementary (third–fourth grades), although it seems a little complicated for that age group. The quest divides students into groups and each person in the group is given a role to play (a botanist, museum curator, ethnobotanist, etc.). The task is for students to find out how plants were used for medicinal purposes in the Southwest many years ago. Students then present their findings, in a format that they can give to a national museum. Weird. It was a little complicated and not well done. I liked the topic and thought it was interesting, but a lot of work would need to be done to modify it so that all students could participate. (Jennie, first-grade teacher)

Teachers across the United States have reported significant successes for students participating in Quests. However, because Quests can be created and posted by anyone, many found on the Web do not meet standards for inquiry and do not allow students autonomy to work in authentic settings and to solve problems. Teachers who want to use a WebQuest to meet specific goals should examine carefully both the content and the process of the Quest to make sure that they offer real problems as discussed in this chapter. A matrix of wonderful Quests that have been evaluated as outstanding by experts is available at http://Webquest.sdsu.edu/matrix.html. Read what two teachers have to say about WebQuests in From the Classroom: WebQuests.

Although very popular, WebQuests are also very structured. This is fine for students who have not moved to more open-ended problems, but to support a higher level of student thinking, independence, and concept learning, teachers can have students work in teams to build a ThinkQuest (http://www.thinkquest.org/) or employ Web Inquiry Projects, the topic of this chapter's Tool CloseUp.

Example 2: Virtual Field Trips

Virtual field trips are great for concept learning, especially for students who need extra support from photos, text, animation, video, and audio. Content for field trips includes virtual walks through museums, underwater explorations, house tours, and much more. However, the format of virtual field trips ranges from simple postcard-like displays to interactive video simulations, and teachers must review the sites before using them to make sure that they meet needs and goals. Many field trips are available from Tramline Virtual Field Trips at http://www.field-trips.org/trips.htm. Other virtual trips can be found by searching "virtual field trips" on the Web. Tramline has also developed field trip generator software called TourMaker that is inexpensive and helps the user create fun trips, which is a problem-solving/creativity/critical thinking exercise in itself.

Example 3: Raw Data Sites

Raw data sites abound on the Web, from the U.S. Census to the National Climatic Data Center, from databases full of language data to the Library of Congress. These sites can be used for content learning and other learning goals. Some amazing sites can be found where students can collect their own data. These include sites like John Walker's (2003) Your Sky (www.fourmilab.to/yoursky) and Water on the Web (2005, waterontheweb.org). When working with raw data students have to draw their own conclusions based on evidence. This is another important problem-solving skill. Note that teachers must supervise and verify that data being entered for students across the world is accurate or the usefulness of these sites is diminished.

Tool CloseUp: Web Inquiry Projects

Web Inquiry Project (WIP) scaffolds were created to support guided and open inquiry, rather than the very structured inquiry included in WebQuests. WIPs consider that each discipline may have its own understanding and specific processes for inquiry, and so WIPs provide authentic, real-world problems in a discipline; examples are available at http://edweb.sdsu.edu/wip/examples.htm. WIPs require students to make use of uninterpreted data in their area available from a variety of online resources.

Like Gordon (1998), mentioned previously, Molebash and Dodge (2003) and others discuss WIPs by looking at their level of inquiry based on how much students are scaffolded during the task. In other words, they determine the level of the WIP by looking at how students are provided with the problem, procedure, and/or solution. For example, at the "lowest" level of inquiry are close-ended problems to which there is a known and specific answer. At the highest level, students pose the questions and design and select the procedures through which to examine them. WIPs are aimed at the higher levels of inquiry.

The WIP framework provides teachers with six stages through which to lead students in developing their projects: hook, focus, methodology, resources, tools, and defend. Definitions of the stages and WIPs templates can be found at http://edweb.sdsu.edu/wip/. An example is presented in Figure 6.8 to show the focus and presentation of the WIP.

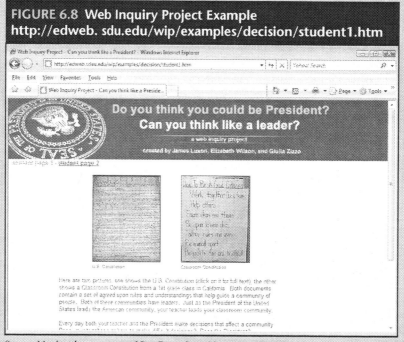

FIGURE 6.8 Web Inquiry Project Example
http://edweb. sdu.edu/wip/examples/decision/student1.htm

Source: Used with permission of San Diego State University.

How could Ms. Lee use WIP to help her students with their project?

_____

_____

_____

_____

Find tutorials for WIP in the Tutorials module of the Companion Website (http://www.prenhall.com/egbert).

TOOLS

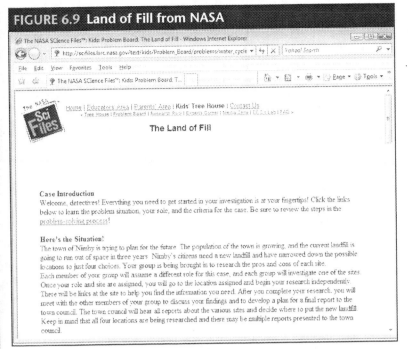

FIGURE 6.9 Land of Fill from NASA

Source: Used with permission of NASA.

Example 4: Filamentality

Filamentality (http://www.kn.pacbell.com/wired/fil/index.html) presents an open-ended problem with a lot of scaffolding. Students and/or teachers start with a goal and then create a Web site in one of five formats that range in level of inquiry and problem solving from treasure hunts to WebQuests. The site provides lots of help and hints for those who need it, including "Mentality Tips" to help accomplish goals. It is free and easy to use, making it accessible to any teacher (or student) with an Internet connection.

Example 5: Problem Sites

Many education sites offer opportunities for students to solve problems. Some focus on language (e.g., why do we say "when pigs fly"?) or global history (e.g., what's the real story behind Tut's tomb?). "Someone in Time" allows students to guess the identity of different people in history. These problems range in level from very structured, academic problems to real-world unsolved mysteries.

The NASA SciFiles present problems in a format similar to WebQuests at http://whyfiles.larc.nasa.gov/. In other parts of the Web site there are video cases, quizzes, and tools for problem solving. See Figure 6.9 for the introduction to The Land of Fill problem from the Why? Files.

One of the most fun and effective problem-solving sites is Verizon's Superthinkers at http://www.superpages.com/ enlightenme/superthinkers/pages/. In addition to the Internet Learning Tutor, Mental Market, Kids' Camp, lesson plans and other resources, the site hosts the Peetnik Mysteries. These problem-solving cases feature a narrative story line about a mystery in town that Penelope Peetnik, of the Problem-Solvers Agency, needs help to solve. A variety of resources that students must consult are included on the site.

There is an amazing number of tools, both stand-alone and Web-based, to support problem solving and inquiry, but no tool can provide all the features that meet the needs of all students. Most important in tool choice is that it meets the language, content, and skills goals of the project and students and that there is a caring and supportive teacher guiding the students in their choice and use of the tool.

Teacher Tools

There are many Web sites addressed specifically to teachers who are concerned that they are not familiar enough with PBL or that they do not have the tools to implement this instructional strategy. The Cycle of Inquiry by the Bay Area School Reform Collaborative is one such site. It provides documents, ideas, and how-to video at http://www.springboardschools.org/tools_resources/coi.html. Another great help is From Now On at http://www.fno.org/toolbox.html, which provides specific suggestions for how to integrate technology and inquiry. Perhaps the most thorough site is University of Illinois' Inquiry Page (http://inquiry.uiuc.edu/). It contains inquiry plans with examples, definitions and articles, and even a mailing list. Any of these resources would be a good place to start for teachers interested in PBL and inquiry.

Inclusion

For teachers developing their own tools, Learning in Motion provides free software that allows teachers to add sign language support at www.learn.motion.com/deaf/ index.html.

Which of these tools, if any, could Ms. Lee use in the superstore project? How could she use them?

LEARNING ACTIVITIES: PROBLEM SOLVING AND INQUIRY

In addition to using the tools described in the previous section to teach problem solving and inquiry, teachers can develop their own problems according to the guidelines throughout this chapter. Gordon's (1998) scheme of problem-solving levels—academic, scenario, and real life—is a simple and useful one. Teachers can refer to it to make sure that they are providing appropriate structure and guidance and helping students become independent thinkers and learners. This section uses Gordon's levels to demonstrate the variety of problem-solving and inquiry activities in which students can participate. Each example is presented with the question/problem to be answered or solved, a suggestion of a process that students might follow, and some of the possible electronic tools that might help students to solve the problem.

Academic problems

Example 1: What Will Harry Do?

Problem: At the end of the chapter, Harry Potter is faced with a decision to make. What will he do?

Process: Discuss the choices and consequences. Choose the most likely, based on past experience and an understanding of the story line. Make a short video to present the solution. Test it against Harry's decision and evaluate both the proposed solution and the real one.

Tools: Video camera and video editing software.

Example 2: Treasure Hunt

Problem: Students need resources to learn about the Civil War.

Process: Teacher provides a set of 10 questions to find specific resources online.

Tools: Web browser.

Example 3: Problem of the Week

Problem: Students should solve the math problem of the week.

Process: Students simplify the problem, write out their solution, post it to the site for feedback, then revise as necessary.

Tools: Current problems from the Math Forum@Drexel, http://mathforum.org/pow/ (see Figure 6.10 for an example).

Scenarios

Example 1: World's Best Problem Solver

Problem: You are a member of a committee that is going to give a prestigious international award for the world's best problem solver. You must nominate someone and defend your position to the committee, as the other committee members must do.

Process: Consult and list possible nominees. Use the process of elimination to determine possible nominees. Research the nominees using several different resources. Weigh the evidence and make a choice. Prepare a statement and support.

Tools: Biography.com has over 25,000 biographies, and Infoplease (infoplease.com) and the Biographical Dictionary (http://www.s9.com/) provide biographies divided into categories for easy searching.

FIGURE 6.10 Problem of the Week

math fundamentals
problem of the week

Print This Problem

Zelma's ZIP Code* - posted May 9, 2005

(Mentor group at work!)

Zelma noticed something unusual about her ZIP Code: each consecutive pair of digits is the product of two one-digit numbers.

For example, look at this four-digit number: 1564

$$15 = 5 * 3$$
$$56 = 7 * 8$$
$$64 = 8 * 8$$

Zelma's ZIP Code contains the digits 2, 3, 4, 6, and 7, exactly once each.

What is Zelma's 5-digit ZIP Code?

Be sure to explain your strategy and show how you know you are right. Include any observations about products or digits that helped you solve the problem.

Just for fun, do you know where Zelma lives?

Extra: Arrange all the digits 1 through 9 similarly, so that each consecutive pair of digits is the product of two one-digit numbers. Include any observations that helped you solve the problem.

Learn About Our Scoring System

Meet the mentors of this puzzle.
Western Oregon University Spring 2005

Source: Reproduced with permission from Drexel University, Copyright 2005 by The Math Forum @ Drexel. All rights reserved.

Example 2: Curator

Problem: Students are a committee of curators deciding what to hang in a new community art center. They have access to any painting in the world but can only hang 15 pieces in their preset space. Their goals are to enrich art appreciation in the community, make a name for their museum, and make money.

Process: Students frame the problem, research and review art from around the world, consider characteristics of the community and other relevant factors, choose their pieces, and lay them out for presentation to the community.

Tools: Art museum Web sites, books, and field trips for research and painting clips; computer-aided design, graphics, or word processing software to lay out the gallery for viewing.

Example 3: A New National Anthem

Problem: Congress has decided that the national anthem is too difficult to remember and sing and wants to adopt a new, easier song before the next Congress convenes. They want input from musicians across the United States. Students play the roles of musicians of all types.

Process: Students define the problem (e.g., is it that "The Star-Spangled Banner" is too difficult or that Congress needs to be convinced that it is not?). They either research and choose new songs or research and defend the current national anthem. They prepare presentations for members of Congress.

Tools: Music sites and software, information sites on the national anthem.

Real-life problems

Example 1: Racism in School

Problem: There have been several incidents in our school recently that seem to have been racially motivated. The principal is asking students to consider how to make our school a safe learning environment for all students.

Process: Determine what is being asked—the principal wants help. Explore the incidents and related issues. Weigh the pros and cons of different solutions. Prepare solutions to present to the principal.

Tools: Web sites and other resources about racism and solutions, graphic organizers to organize the information, word processor or presentation software for results. Find excellent free tools for teachers and students at the Southern Poverty Law Center's Teaching Tolerance Web site at www.tolerance.org.

Example 2: Homelessness vs. Education

Problem: The state legislature is asking for public input on the next budget. Because of a projected deficit, political leaders are deciding which social programs, including education and funding for the homeless, should be cut and to what extent. They are interested in hearing about the effects of these programs on participants and on where cuts could most effectively be made.

Process: Decide what the question is (e.g., how to deal with the deficit? How to cut education or funding for the homeless? Which programs are more important? Something else?). Perform a cost-benefit analysis using state data. Collect other data by interviewing and researching. Propose and weigh different solution schemes and propose a suggestion. Use feedback to improve or revise.

Tools: Spreadsheet for calculations, word processor for written solution, various Web sites and databases for costs, electronic discussion list or email for interviews.

Example 3: Cleaning Up

Problem: Visitors and residents in our town have been complaining about the smell from the university's experimental cattle farms drifting across the highway to restaurants and stores in the shopping center across the street. They claim that it makes both eating and shopping unpleasant and that something must be done.

Process: Conduct onsite interviews and investigation. Determine the source of the odor. Measure times and places where the odor is discernible. Test a variety of solutions. Choose the most effective solution and write a proposal supported by a poster for evidence.

Tools: Encarta and other oneline and offline sources of information on cows, farming, odor; database to organize and record data; word processing and presentation software for describing the solution.

These activities can all be adapted and different tools and processes used. As stated previously, the focus must be both on the content to be learned and the skills to be practiced and acquired. More problem-solving activity suggestions and examples can be found at Judy Harris's site at http://www.2learn.ca/Projects/Together/Structures.html.

ASSESSING LEARNER PROBLEM SOLVING AND INQUIRY

Many of the assessments described in other chapters of this text, for example, rubrics, performance assessments, observation, and student self-reflection, can also be employed to assess problem solving and inquiry. However, Gordon (1998) says that problem-solving tasks also should be judged against "real-world standards of quality" (p. 2). Most experts on problem solving and inquiry agree that schools need to get away from testing that does not involve showing process or allowing students to problem solve; rather, teachers should evaluate problem-solving tasks as if they were someone in the real-world context of the problem. For example, if students are studying an environmental issue, teachers can evaluate their work throughout the project from the standpoint of someone in the field, being careful that their own biases do not cloud their judgment on controversial issues. Rubrics, multiple-choice tests, and other assessment tools mentioned in other chapters of this text should account for the multiple outcomes that are possible in content, language, and skills learning. Figure 6.11 shows a high school rubric for problem solving that can be used to assess students' current levels or be used as an evaluation of progress over time. Figure 6.12 on page 174 presents one for elementary classrooms. These resources can be used as models for assessing problem-solving skills in a variety of tasks.

FIGURE 6.11 High School Problem-Solving Assessment from Intel Education

High School Reasoning Checklist

This checklist can be used by students or teachers to assess reasoning skills.

Forming and Supporting Opinions
- ☐ Values well-reasoned opinions
- ☐ Puts forth effort necessary to form good opinions
- ☐ Focuses on validity of argument rather than personal feelings
- ☐ Recognizes subtle manipulations of facts used to persuade
- ☐ Identifies own assumptions
- ☐ Identifies assumptions of others

Drawing Conclusions
- ☐ Uses personal experiences and knowledge to make inferences and draw conclusions
- ☐ Uses thorough understanding of systems within topic to make inferences and draw conclusions
- ☐ Draws conclusions that add meaning and insight

Logical Thinking
- ☐ Uses deductive reasoning to make generalizations
- ☐ Uses inductive reasoning to understand unfamiliar concepts
- ☐ Uses "If . . . then . . ." statements to draw conclusions about relationships

Determining Cause and Effect
- ☐ Describes multiple cause-and-effect relationships in a system
- ☐ Differentiates between causation and correlation
- ☐ Creates detailed visual representations of inter-related systems that show causes and effects

Communication
- ☐ Uses appropriate subject-area language to explain conclusions and reasoning
- ☐ Uses language of logical thinking to explain conclusions and reasoning

Source: Used with permission of Intel Corporation.

FIGURE 6.12 Elementary Problem-Solving Assessment

Elementary Identifying and Describing Problems Rubric

	4	3	2	1
Anticipating Problems	I think ahead and guess what problems might be coming in a project in time to prevent them.	Sometimes I can think ahead and guess what problems I might have in time to avoid them.	With help, I can tell what problems there might be.	I have a hard time knowing when there is going to be a problem.
Monitoring Processes	When things are not going well on a project, I pay attention to what's happening and figure out where the problem is.	When things aren't going well, I figure out what the problem is.	I need help to figure out what a problem is.	I do not try to figure out what is going wrong.
	I am always looking at how things are going on a project and thinking of ways to make things go better.	I pay attention to how things are going so I can fix problems as they happen.	I usually expect others to notice problems while I'm working and help me fix them.	I do not notice problems while I am working unless someone points them out to me.
Choosing Solutions	I take a lot of time to think about a problem before I try to solve it.	I think about a problem before I start solving it.	If someone reminds me, I think about a problem before I solve it.	I usually just start right in solving a problem without thinking about it.
	I think of as many solutions as I can before I choose one.	I think of more than one solution before I choose one.	With help, I think of more than one solution.	I usually try the first solution I think of.

Source: Used with permission of Intel Corporation.

In addition to the techniques mentioned above, Wilson et al. (1993) suggest keeping a weekly problem-solving notebook, in which students record problem solutions, strategies they used, similarities with other problems, extensions of the problem, and an investigation of one or more of the extensions. Although the authors' focus is on math, using this notebook to assess students' location and progress in problem solving could be very effective.

What are some specific ways that Ms. Lee should plan to assess the process and progress of her students during the superstore project?

_____

_____

_____

SAMPLE LESSON: PROBLEM SOLVING

After they complete their research on the topic, Ms. Lee's students will create a Web site focusing on the superstore issue. They will use the site to collect additional information and opinions. However, before they start Ms. Lee wants to reinforce concepts about fair use and copyright. She finds a lesson that might work at PBS's Teacher Source (www.pbs.org).

INTELLECTUAL PROPERTY IN THE DIGITAL AGE

Grade Level: 4–8, 9–12

Subject: Technology, Arts, Current Events

Introduction: Many people share the misconception that information found on the Internet is free and for all to use without permission. However, by collecting many images, sounds, and readings when creating a Web site you may be violating a person's intellectual property (IP) or copyright.

1. Begin this lesson by introducing your students to the concepts of intellectual property and copyright to your students.

Definitions:

- *Intellectual property* represents the property of your mind or intellect. Types of intellectual property include patents, trademarks, designs, confidential information/trade secrets, copyright, circuit layout rights, plant breeder's rights, etc.

- *Copyright* protects the original expression of ideas, not the ideas themselves. It is free and automatically safeguards your original works of art, literature, music, films, broadcasts and computer programs from copying and certain other uses.

2. Explore these questions with your students: How are the two concepts similar and different? What are the various types of intellectual property? Why do laws protecting IP exist? How has the revolution in communications technology over the past decade complicated issues surrounding IP?

   You and your students may want to use these resources for more information:

- NewsHour Online: Copyrighting in the Digital Age
  http://www.pbs.org/newshour/media/digital_copyright/cases.html
- Crash Course in Copyright
  http://www.utsystem.edu/OGC/IntellectualProperty/ cprtindx.htm
- Intellectual Property on the Web
  http://digitalenterprise.org/ip/ip.html
- *Web and Software Development: A Legal Guide* by Stephen Fishman; *Digital Copyright: Protecting Intellectual Property on the Internet* by Jessica Litman

Source: © 2007 Public Broadcasting Service. Used with permission.

Ms. Lee likes to see that the lesson provides a guideline but is not too prescriptive of what students should do. She uses the Lesson Analysis and Adaptation Worksheet (found in chapter 1 on page 33 and in the Lesson Planning module of the Companion Website) to figure out what she needs to do to make this lesson work for her students. She decides to make these adaptations based on her analysis:

- Because there are no standards or objectives, she will add these. She particularly wants to focus on the NETS*S that recommend that students understand and practice responsible uses of technology and that they use technology resources for solving problems.

- Rather than just answer questions, Ms. Lee will ask her students to research some answers and compare them with what classmates found. Then she will ask them to develop a set of guidelines, in their choice of medium, for the class to refer to when they are using online resources. This addition will support student inquiry, communication, critical thinking, production, and creativity along with content learning and problem solving.

- Ms. Lee will brainstorm with students the possible subquestions that will help them answer the questions in the lesson. She will assign each student dyad to find information on one subquestion, keeping the students active and each making a contribution.

- Technology is used as a tool in this lesson and helps students discover a variety of viewpoints and resources. However, to make sure that all students can access the resources, she will add both print and electronic references at a variety of levels for students to choose from.

- Ms. Lee will use the guidelines that students create as part of her assessment, and she will continue to observe how well her students follow the guidelines as they create their Web pages for the superstore project.

Ms. Lee believes that, with the additions she will make, this lesson will support the objectives and provide her students with practice in many skill areas.

What else would you add to this lesson to make it effective for your current or future students? What would you delete? Why?

_____

_____

_____

CHAPTER REVIEW

Key Points

- **Define problem solving and inquiry.**

  The element that distinguishes problem-solving or problem-based learning from other strategies is that the focal point is a problem that students must work toward solving. A proposed solution is typically the outcome of problem solving. During the inquiry part of the process, students ask questions and then search for answers to those questions.

- **Understand the interaction between problem solving and other instructional goals.**

  Although inquiry is also an important instructional strategy and can stand alone, it is also a central component of problem solving because students must ask questions and investigate the answers to solve the problem. In addition, students apply critical and creative thinking skills to prior knowledge during the problem-solving process, and they communicate, collaborate, and often produce some kind of concrete artifact.

- **Discuss guidelines and tools for encouraging effective student problem solving.**

  It is often difficult for teachers to not do what students can do, but empowering students in this way can lead to a string of benefits. Other guidelines, such as avoiding plagiarism, integrating reading and writing, and making it okay for students to make mistakes, keep the problem-solving process on track. Tools to assist in this process range from word processing to specially designed inquiry tools.

- **Create and adapt effective technology-enhanced tasks to support problem solving.**

  Teachers can design their own tasks following guidelines from any number of sources, but they can also find ready-made problems in books, on the Web, and in some software packages. Teachers who do design their own have plenty of resources available to help. A key to task development is connecting classroom learning to the world outside of the classroom.

- **Assess student technology-supported problem solving.**

  In many ways the assessment of problem-solving and inquiry tasks is similar to the assessment of other goals in this text. Matching goals and objectives to assessment and ensuring that students receive formative feedback throughout the process will make success more likely.

What information in this chapter is most useful to you? Why? How will you use it in your teaching?

_____

_____

_____

CASE QUESTIONS REVIEW

Reread the case at the beginning of the chapter and review your answers. In light of what you learned during this chapter, how do your answers change? Note any changes here.

1. What prior content and language knowledge do the students need to solve this problem?

_____

_____

_____

2. What process should the students follow to find a solution to the problem?

_____

_____

_____

3. What should Ms. Lee's role in the project be?

_____

_____

_____

4. What role can technology play in helping the students to solve their problem?

_____

_____

_____

CHAPTER EXTENSIONS • • • • • • • • • • • • • •

To answer any of the following questions online, go to the Chapter 6 Extensions module of this text's Companion Website (http://www.prenhall.com/egbert).

Adapt • • •

Choose a lesson for your potential subject area and grade level from the Internet4Classrooms page of Integrated Technology Lesson Plans (http://www.internet4classrooms.com/integ_tech_lessons.htm). Use the Lesson Analysis and Adaptation Worksheet from chapter 1 on page 33 (also available on the Lesson Planning module of the Companion Website) to consider the lesson in the context of problem solving. Use your responses to the worksheet to suggest general changes to the lesson based on your current or future students and context.

Practice • • •

1. *Determine tool levels.* Apply Gordon's three-level scheme to the tools listed in this chapter. Which level would each tool be appropriate for? Why?

2. *Review a tool.* Review one of the tools described in the chapter, including tools to spot plagiarism. Explain how it addresses problem solving and inquiry and how you might integrate it into your current or future classroom.

3. *Practice planning.* Review the sample activities in this chapter. Choose three, and describe how you could integrate reading and writing into the activities to promote effective problem solving.

Explore • · · ·

1. *Create an activity.* Outline a WebQuest, ThinkQuest, WIP, or other inquiry or problem-solving activity. Describe each stage briefly but clearly.

2. *Create a standards-based task.* Choose a national or state standard for your subject area and grade level. Write a problem based on that standard following the characteristics described in the chapter, and then evaluate the problem using the characteristics of effective tasks.

3. *Turn theory into practice.* Use the adapted Figure 6.2 on page 161 to develop a classroom lesson based on the PBL process. On the chart below, fill in the "Lesson" column with ideas for each step.

Step	Example	Lesson
1. Contextualize the question.	Ask, "What is the question here? What should we do about it?"	
2. Develop objectives.	Figure out the goal and the skills the task will meet.	
3. Review background.	Explore materials and tools that focus on the problem.	
4. Write the problem.	Be specific about student roles and responsibilities.	
5. Develop scaffolds.	Create documents, mini-lessons, and other helps.	
6. Evaluate student needs.	Review students' current level of knowledge and skills.	
7. Implement.	Provide clear instructions and ongoing observation and feedback.	

REFERENCES

Baker, T. (2005). *The history and application of GIS in education.* KANGIS: K12 GIS Community. Available from http://kangis.org/learning/ed_docs/gisNed1.cfm.

Blosser, P. (1988). *Teaching problem solving—secondary school science.* ERIC/SMEAC Science Education Digest No. 2.

Dooly, M. (2005, March/April). The Internet and language teaching: A sure way to interculturality? *ESL Magazine, 44,* 8–10.

Elias, M., & Tobias, S. (1996). *Social problem solving: Interventions in the schools.* New York: Guilford Press.

Gordon, R. (1998, January). Balancing real-world problems with real-world results. *Phi Delta Kappan, 79*(5), 390–393. [electronic version]

IMSA (2005). *How does PBL compare with other instructional approaches?* Available: http://www2.imsa.edu/programs/pbln/tutorials/intro/intro7.php.

Mansilla, V., & Gardner, H. (1997, January). Of disciplines and kinds of understanding. *Phi Delta Kappan, 78*(5), 381–386. [electronic version]

Molebash, P., & Dodge, B. (2003). Kickstarting inquiry with WebQuests and web inquiry projects. *Social Education, 671*(3), 158–162.

Stites, R. (1998). What does research say about outcomes from project-based learning? Evaluation of project-based learning: The Multimedia project. Available: http://pblmm.k12.ca.us/PBLGuide/pblresch.htm.

Wilson, J., Fernandez, M., & Hadaway, N. (1993). Mathematical problem solving. In P. Wilson (Ed.), *Research ideas for the classroom: High school mathematics.* New York: Macmillan.

Index